1987
SEASON

THE COMPLETE HANDBOOK OF BASEBALL

1987
SEASON

THE COMPLETE HANDBOOK OF BASEBALL

EDITED BY ZANDER HOLLANDER

A SIGNET BOOK
NEW AMERICAN LIBRARY

ACKNOWLEDGMENTS

Fittingly, 40-year-old Reggie Jackson returns to Oakland for what are presumed his last swings. But the independent slugger leaves the door open for 1988, perhaps with an eye on overtaking Harmon Killebrew. In sixth-place on the all-time home-run list with 548, Reggie needs 26 to pass the fifth-place Killebrew's 573. Reggie hit 15 as a DH last year. At the same pace, he could do it in his 20th year in the bigs.

We acknowledge the many hands who contributed to this 17th edition of *The Complete Handbook of Baseball*: contributing editor and purist Howard Blatt, the writers listed on the contents page, Lee Stowbridge, Richard Rossiter, Steve Wisniewski, Fred Cantey, Seymour Siwoff, Bob Rosen, Phyllis Merhige, Blake Cullen, Katy Feeney, the publicity directors of the major-league teams, Dot Gordineer of Libra Graphics and the staff at Westchester Book Composition.

Zander Hollander

PHOTO CREDITS: Cover—Mickey Palmer/Focus on Sport; back cover—Mitch Reibel/Sportschrome. Inside photos—Ira Golden, George Gojkovich, Vic Milton, AP/Wide World and the team photographers.

SIGNET TRADEMARK REG. U.S. PAT. OFF. AND FOREIGN COUNTRIES
REGISTERED TRADEMARK—MARCA REGISTRADA
HECHO EN CHICAGO, U.S.A.

SIGNET, SIGNET CLASSICS, MENTOR, PLUME, MERIDIAN AND NAL BOOKS are published by New American Library, 1633 Broadway
New York, New York 10019

First Printing, March 1987

1 2 3 4 5 6 7 8 9

PRINTED IN THE UNITED STATES OF AMERICA

CONTENTS

Editors Note: The material herein includes trades and rosters up to final printing deadline.

GREAT SCOTT & THE SPLIT-FINGER FASTBALL

By GEORGE WHITE

There is nothing about the man to suggest that he has perfected baseball's deadliest weapon. The face is so soft and kindly that he looks a little like a soft-spoken uncle. Glasses perch on his nose the four days he isn't pitching. He is a voracious reader, loves a quiet game of golf and would much rather the harsh spotlight of sudden fame shift its beam somewhere else.

But, just as the development of the atomic bomb thrust a rather reluctant Dr. Robert Oppenheimer into instant-celebrity status, "The Pitch" has rudely shoved the Astros' Michael Warren Scott onto a publicity plateau that's a little discomforting to him.

"The Pitch" is a split-finger fastball. NL batters speak of it as though it should be immediately quarantined. Mike Scott isn't the only pitcher who throws it, but it is his split finger that is most dreaded for its precipitous, late-breaking action.

After Philadelphia's Mike Schmidt, the NL MVP, flailed in futility at one for a third strike in July, he pronounced, "That was the best pitch I've ever seen."

"He's the toughest pitcher I've ever seen," said San Francisco's Will Clark.

San Diego's Tony Gwynn, one of the top hitters in the game, frets about what might happen if this pitch were mastered by large numbers of pitchers.

"If more pitchers had that pitch," Gwynn warned, "there wouldn't be any hitters in the league—just pitchers and catchers playing catch."

Keith Hernandez of the world champion Mets contemplated

George White, a sports feature writer for the Houston Chronicle, *has had more success following the split-finger fastball than NL batters.*

Mike Scott split-fingered Mets for two wins in NLCS.

the alarming state of affairs after Scott had allowed the Mets only one run in 18 innings in the National League Championship Series.

"He paints," said Hernandez of the man who was named NLCS MVP. "He's a Rembrandt. If everybody threw like that all the time, this game would never make it, because it would just be too bleeping boring."

Scott's catcher, Alan Ashby, has the best seat in the house as the split finger dipsy-doodles its way past impotent bats. "Heaven forbid that the other pitchers perfect the thing," he said. "If they do, the batting title is going to be won by a bunch of guys who hit .210."

Who is this man, who has suddenly sprung up to dominate baseball like some sort of creature from a Transylvanian laboratory?

"He's the nicest, kindest, most polite, most thoughtful human being I've been around in my 35 years in baseball," said Astros' trainer Jim Ewell. "Today he's the best pitcher in baseball, but, until he puts on that uniform and walks out there between those white lines, there isn't one thing about him that says 'Big Shot.'"

Scott is a native Californian, raised around the beaches of Santa Monica. From a distance, he looks like the quintessential beach boy, even at age 31. He's 6-3, slender, with a shock of blond hair.

He moves with the fluidity and grace of a man who has been involved in athletics all his life. Volleyball games on California beaches are saturated with Mike Scotts.

Scott has everything but the beach-boy personality. "He is California laid-back, but he doesn't have anything in his makeup that says he's handsome or great or anything extra special," says Scott's teammate, Phil Garner. "He's one person who is exactly the same off the field as he is on it—dedicated, sincere, determined, serious.

"He does have a funny side to him. If someone in the clubhouse suggests a good practical joke, he definitely wants to be in on it. But basically, Mike Scott is just as genuine a common person as any man on earth."

Scott could have gotten way too big for his cap long ago. He was a star athlete as a teenager at Hawthorne High School, going 9-1 with a 0.67 ERA as a senior. He spent three years in college up the California coastline at Malibu, where he pitched for Pepperdine and was a three-time All-West Coast Athletic Conference pick from 1974-1976.

He was a strong kid with a buggy-whip for an arm and an accomplished fastball that stamped him as a big-league prospect. The Mets made him their second pick in the June 1976 draft and Scott packed up his college dorm furnishings, left Malibu and settled in for instant culture shock in Jackson, Miss.

He did a two-year minor-league tour of duty with the Mets' farm team there, spent a couple of years at Tidewater and finally got a peek at the big club in 1979. He got his first major-league start against Vida Blue and the San Francisco Giants and won it, 10-3.

Not until 1981, though, did Scott stick an entire season with the big club. When he finally arrived to stay, he found himself on a last-place team with a roster full of great prospects.

Scott was not yet a possessor of "The Pitch." He had a fastball, he had a slider and he had an aching arm. The slider puts an enormous amount of strain on a young arm and Scott spent most of his career in New York paying the price of trying to perfect that effective second pitch.

The Mets, recognizing a great arm, tried everything to salvage his future. They tried him as a starter, then tinkered around with him as a long reliever. After he had completed seven erratic years in the organization, the Mets finally gave up, trading Scott to the Astros for Danny Heep in December 1982.

At first, the same pattern followed him to Houston—a mishmash of injuries, inconsistent outings and unsuccessful efforts at establishing himself as a starter.

Scott's futility culminated in 1984, when he slogged through a 5-11 season with a bloated 4.68 ERA. The Astros had run out of patience. Al Rosen, who was then the general manager, was being roasted for having gambled on Scott. It didn't help that Heep had turned into a fairly productive utility man for the Mets.

People pointed to an observation about Scott voiced by George Bamberger, who had managed the pitcher during his days with the Mets. "When Mike gets in trouble," said Bamberger, "he throws his fastball. And when he gets in deeper trouble, he throws a harder fastball."

Scott has come to realize that was a depressingly accurate analysis.

"I realize now that he was exactly correct," said Scott. "The harder you throw it, the harder they'll hit it back—if that's what they're looking for. And that's what they were looking for, because I had lost my slider around the same time (in 1984). It just wasn't breaking. It was four or five miles an hour slower than my fastball and going straight. That kind of told me I'd better find a new pitch."

What he found wasn't just a new pitch, it's something that soon may be discussed over a conference table at Geneva.

Out on the West Coast, Roger Craig had just left his position as pitching coach of the Detroit Tigers. He had been the Astros' pitching coach previously and Rosen knew him as an exceptional teacher. Rosen phoned him to ask him to take on Scott as a project and, since Craig was unemployed at the time, he invited Scott to come out to his laboratory.

That was in February 1985, less than a month before spring training. They worked out on a San Diego high-school field. Craig was impressed from Day 1.

"The first thing he [Scott] told me was, 'I'll stay here as long as it takes,'" remembers Craig. "I knew he had an outstanding fastball, a good body for a pitcher and good mechanics. He looked like a guy with an outstanding arm who needed a breaking pitch.

"They say hitters are born, but a guy who throws 92, 93 miles an hour and has some guts, I'll make a pitcher out of him. We threw every other day, about seven times. He didn't pick it up at first, but by the time he left, I knew he'd have a good one."

The split-finger fastball looked and felt like it might work, but Scott still hadn't thrown it to a major-league hitter. It wasn't long after he arrived in Florida that he realized he had discovered something very special.

"I could tell from the second day of spring training that I was going to use that pitch quite a bit," he said. "I was throwing it and guys were suddenly swinging at balls that were bouncing in the dirt. That's when I said to myself, 'This could work out.'"

He was on the way to perfecting the split-finger fastball. "It was real easy to pick up," said Scott, who went from 5-11, 4.68 in 1984 to 18-8, 3.29 in 1985. "But you have to have the right-sized hands and throw it over the top."

The pitch is thrown with the forefinger and middle finger stretched, placed on top of the wide seams. It is thrown directly overhand with as little wrist action as possible, greatly reducing the stress on the arm. When the ball comes off the fingers, it has very little rotation. That has two beneficial effects—it fools the hitter into thinking the pitch might be a changeup and the lack of rotation causes the ball to dive just as it reaches the plate.

"I aim it right for the middle of the plate, because I know it will never end up there," Scott said. "It's going to drop, and it's going to break as it drops. I never know for sure which way it will break as it's crossing the plate, so it's important that I throw it at the middle.

"Actually, though, that makes the pitch much more dependable. You don't have to worry about trying to bite at the paint. You have that great big target to aim at and then you just let the ball do its thing."

"There isn't any rotation on the ball," said Met catcher Gary Carter. "It's like a dry spitter. It starts out on the plate and it ends up out of the strike zone."

"It looks like a fastball," said Dodger infielder Enos Cabell, "but it isn't. A fastball rises. This pitch drops."

"It's like a fastball with a bomb attached to it," says veteran NL umpire Doug Harvey.

It moves somewhat like a good knuckleball. Ashby, who spent a number of years trying to flag down Joe Niekro's knuckler, insisted this pitch is considerably more comfortable to handle.

"Joe Niekro's knuckleball left my hands in a shambles," he said. "The split-finger pitch has given me no problems. Actually, it's very predictable. Mike is a pleasure to catch."

Not coincidentally, Scott hasn't had any recurrence of his old arm problems, either. "There is absolutely no stress on the elbow or the shoulder with it," Scott said. "I feel like I could throw it for a hundred years."

Heaven forbid, say NL batters. Especially Craig's Giants, who had to look at him at his absolute best on Sept. 25. On that day, Scott not only clinched the NL West title for the Astros, he threw one of the most dominating no-hitters in baseball history.

Craig could see it coming all the way. "I told my coaches in the fifth inning there was no way we were going to get a hit," he said.

Thirty years earlier, Craig had witnessed perhaps the most famous pitching gem of all time—Don Larson's World Series perfect game. "I was on the other side of that one, too," said Craig, who watched from the Brooklyn Dodger bench. "But this was more dominating. Larson didn't have as many strikeouts (Scott had 13). Larson wasn't as overpowering."

Giants' catcher Bob Brenly said he felt ridiculous walking up to the plate with a weapon as puny as a baseball bat.

"I didn't feel helpless—I felt hopeless," he said. "I tried to spread my stance and shorten my swing, but nothing worked. I've never had a game when I didn't even make contact. I struck out three times and I never once touched the ball."

Brenly was not alone. Scott posted an 18-10 record, including five shutouts, a 2.22 ERA and a league-leading 306 strikeouts in 1986, earning him designation as the NL Cy Young Award winner. At the Astrodome, fans began waving bright "K" signs on days Scott pitched, a compliment that caused him no small amount of embarrassment.

"That isn't what Mike Scott is all about," said trainer Ewell. "I know for a fact that it was very embarrassing to him, because he told me on several occasions that that was an honor which should be solely Nolan Ryan's. That was something that was started here on days Nolan pitched and Mike feels that should continue to be Nolan's exclusively."

Scott, in fact, certainly doesn't think he is the best pitcher in baseball today. If he were a manager and had to give the ball to one man to win one big game, Scott would give it to Nolan Ryan.

"He's the best big-game pitcher I've ever seen," said Scott. "You give him a big game and he'll give you a great game. Nobody comes close to him."

Bullfeathers, said Ryan. "Mike's the best pitcher in the league, the best pitcher in baseball," he said with finality.

Scott also said he thinks Dwight Gooden has earned the label of "Doctor K."

"I think Doctor K is a perfect nickname for him. He had a fantastic season in 1985 [when Gooden was the Cy Young winner with 268 strikeouts]. And he was great again this year. He's earned the right to be Doctor K."

Scott suggested that an ideal nickname for him might be "Doctor Daddy." That's because the love of his life isn't the split-finger fastball. It's wife Vicki and his other women, daughters Kimmie and Kelsey.

"They are really my only hobbies," he said, "except for golf. I guess I'm really a pretty boring guy, to people who think I should be out around town being seen here or there. When I'm not at the ballpark, I'm home. I love it there. I don't want to be anywhere else."

Home in the offseason is Hawthorne, Cal., where he grew up. He just moved back there last fall, after spending several years in Chandler, Ariz. At home is his biggest fan, six-year-old Kimmie.

She was watching intently on the afternoon Scott no-hit the Giants. "When I talked to her after the game, she said, 'Daddy, I didn't know you could jump that high,'" said Mike.

Not everyone, though, is a Scott fan. The other side of this story is that some baseball people are convinced that Craig taught him more than just a great pitch. They are convinced Craig taught him an illegal one. Scott's wonder weapon dips and twist, they assert, because he scuffs the ball, causing aerodynamics that make the ball react in a crazy manner.

"He's a cheater," said an angry Blue late in the season, after Scott came within nine outs of throwing a second consecutive no-hitter against Blue and Craig's Giants. "Sure he scuffs it up and it isn't fair. He's a great pitcher when he throws normal stuff. When he scuffs it, no one is going to touch him."

It made great theater in the playoffs, when the Mets constantly complained to the media that they were being strangled by scuff-balls and not split-finger fastballs. Scott's old Tidewater teammate, Met second baseman Wally Backman, was the most vociferous in his accusations.

After Scott won Game 4, 3-1, the Mets claimed they had a bag full of balls that Scott had defaced.

"There were 30 or 40 of them, every foul ball that came to the dugout," said Backman. "We brought about 15 into the clubhouse. Some of them were scuffed twice, he's a master of it. All these balls were scuffed in the same spot, away from the seams."

After that game, home-plate umpire Dutch Rennert said Scott was as innocent as a parson. "There wasn't one batter who asked a ball to be checked that hadn't been hit on the ground," said Rennert. "That's amazing they said they found 30 scuffed, because I didn't see one ball with a mark and I checked the ball at least once every inning. His pitch has an extraordinary way of moving, but it was as clean as a baby's bottom."

The umpires, in fact, have been Scott's most vocal defenders. Harvey is a 25-year veteran umpire who worked the opening play-off game when Scott shut out the Mets and he gave Scott as ringing an endorsement as Rennert.

"On my mother's honor, Mike Scott has come up with a pitch with the movement of a Sandy Koufax curve and with the velocity of a Sandy Koufax fastball," Harvey began.

"I believe the pitches Mike Scott are throwing are legal, and

I believe it with all my heart. During the season I must have checked 65-70 balls that Mike Scott threw, and not one showed any sign of scuff marks. On the 17 balls they showed me from Sunday, at least 16 were probably picked up by the ball boy after they had already been in play. It's easy for those balls to pick up marks out there.

"In Game 1, Mike Scott pitched the damndest game I've ever seen. It's as close to being an unhittable pitch as I've ever seen. He's come up with one hell of a pitch—it just explodes in there.

"For two years, managers have been complaining to me about Mike Scott. In one game this year, Roger Craig told me to check a baseball. When I told him I didn't find anything, he said, 'I know, Doug. I taught him the pitch and I'm just trying to play with his mind.'"

Actually, it was Craig who warned Scott that the pitch would cause him a lot of problems with people who wouldn't believe it was possible to do legally.

"He said, 'You've got to watch out. The ball is going to be doing things that people haven't seen it do before,'" reported Scott. "And he said, 'You'll probably have people screaming at you. But that's good.'"

Craig repeatedly asked to have Scott checked in games this year. He confessed, though, that he never had a concrete reason for doing so.

"One of the reasons I went out, I said to myself, 'How can a pitcher be this good? Nobody can be this good,'" said the Giant manager.

For the record, Scott said he doesn't do anything illegal to the ball. "I am not a cheater," he said emphatically.

He did have a lot of fun joking about the scuffball rap, however. "I do everything to the ball—sandpaper, glue, vaseline, everything," he said sarcastically late in the season. "I hope that's what they think. If they have that on their minds, it's just one more thing for them to worry about."

At Ryan's charity golf tournament the week after the Astros were eliminated, Scott showed up with a bag full of defaced golf balls. Garner opened the golf bag and recoiled in mock disgust when he looked inside. "Look at this—every single one of them scuffed up," said Garner.

"That must be the reason I can't hit them, either," joked Scott.

Now that the offseason had arrived, Scott had big plans for all that leftover sandpaper that he supposedly used to customize his baseballs.

"I'll probably do a lot of furniture refinishing," he said.

Somebody remind the hitters to laugh.

MIKE SCHMIDT BATS DOWN HIS CRITICS

By PETER PASCARELLI

It didn't matter that he had played the game, perhaps better than anyone else, for more than a dozen superb years. Nor did it matter that his off-the-field persona was spotless in an era when urine tests and police blotters had become a fact of baseball life.

No matter how much Mike Schmidt accomplished, it seemed as if he would never be embraced in Philadelphia as a beloved baseball hero. Never mind all the home runs, the Most Valuable Player awards, the Gold Gloves and the All-Star berths.

No, what it came down to was a matter of style. Schmidt was never one to show emotion on the field. He always has appeared too cool, almost casual, as if even he found the apparent ease with which he performed boring.

Then, there was that cerebral side that tended to turn people off. Schmidt's often byzantine explanations and analysis were too lofty for the average fan to comprehend. Even people in the game—including some of his Phillies' teammates and coaches—had the feeling that if "Schmitty didn't think so much, he'd be even better than he is already."

It was as if Schmidt sat on an unreachable pedestal, remote from close scrutiny and above displaying the usual emotions and animation shown by most players.

So, when Schmidt played with something less than perfection, the upper-deck zealots at Veterans Stadium usually let him know about it.

The treatment just didn't figure. Here was one of our generation's greatest players, someone who was a key part of the greatest

---

Peter Pascarelli grew up in Boston, where one of high-school jobs was selling hot dogs in Fenway Park. He has spent the last five years chronicling the career of Mike Schmidt as a baseball writer for the Philadelphia Inquirer.

Mike Schmidt is one of three players to win three MVPs.

years in the Phillies' history, someone whose career will ultimately earn permanent recognition in the Hall of Fame, enduring a stand-offish relationship with the long-suffering Phillies' fans whom he had helped rescue from a legacy of defeat.

But, a funny thing happened during a 1986 season that might have been Schmidt's finest ever. As he turned 37 years old and began to make sounds about retiring soon, the sullen reception turned warm. It was as if the Phils' fans had finally discovered the gem in their midst. Schmidt began to be treated with the reverence a city reserves for its most priceless heirlooms.

On the way to hitting 37 home runs, driving in 119 runs, batting .290 and making a career-low eight errors, the third baseman rode a new wave of respect that peaked on the season's final day, when, in a pinch-hit appearance, he popped out on the first pitch and was accorded a long standing ovation as he trotted back to the dugout.

The change actually began the previous season, when, ironically, Schmidt's rapport with the surly Phillies fans was seemingly at its ebb.

Schmidt was mired in an awful early-season slump, batting around .180 in late May 1985, and the Phils were buried in the standings en route to their first losing season in 11 years. Not surprisingly, the mood in the Vet had turned ugly. And much of the most vicious noise was directed at Schmidt.

Finally, Schmidt unloaded. He gave an interview while the Phils were in Montreal in which he called the Veterans Stadium fans "an uncontrollable mob," among other uncomplimentary things.

Naturally, the interview became big news in Philadelphia. So big, in fact, that when the Phillies returned home, it was feared that Schmidt would be greeted with his worst reception yet. Said one teammate, "No one on this team will be within 20 feet of him when he walks on the field."

But, Schmidt defused the situation with an uncharacteristic gesture. When he took his position that first night back home, he was wearing a long wig and dark glasses. The fans who were ready to boo their lungs out were instantly won over, first laughing and then cheering Schmidt's acknowledgement that bygones should be bygones.

Coincidentally, Schmidt started hitting soon thereafter, launching into a long hot streak that carried through the second half of 1985 and all of 1986. It was as if a cloud had lifted, as if Philadelphia had decided to finally appreciate what kind of player Schmidt has been.

Perhaps, Phillies' fans suddenly realized a special player has been performing in their city for more than a decade. Perhaps, it was Schmidt's approach to the magic 500-home-run plateau, because he finished the '86 season with 495 homers. Perhaps, it was the jarring thought that Schmidt would be retiring in the near future.

Probably, it was a combination of those things and more. But Schmidt noticed the change right away. And he had his own theories.

"I think they've always accepted that I'm a good ballplayer," said Schmidt near the end of last season. "But I think the fact that I'm close to that 500-home-run plateau has made them reconsider things a little.

"I think that when you tell Phillies' fans that one of their guys, one of the people they've lived and died with, is doing something like that, and people start comparing that player to names like Ruth and Aaron and Mays . . . Well, I think the people maybe sit back and take a second look. Maybe they'll say, 'Hey, I didn't know that, I was too busy booing him.'

"And don't forget that the team did a lot better in 1986. That always helps how you're received. Plus, I had very consistent season in which I really didn't have any prolonged periods when I wasn't productive."

How much Schmidt was scarred by the years of tough treatment won't ever be known. At times, he tossed out hints about how much easier life would have been had he played his career somewhere else. It was Schmidt who years ago came up with the classic line: "Philadelphia is the only place where you can experience the thrill of victory and the agony of reading about it."

But, in the last few years, Schmidt has made no bones about his intention to make his lifelong home in a beautiful French-style chateau on three acres in the Philadelphia suburb of Media. He and his wife, Donna, and their children, eight-year-old Jessica and six-year-old Jonathan, are happily settled in. Schmidt, after years of living an almost reclusive existence, is becoming more and more a visible part of the Philadelphia community. For two years, he has had an active association with the Greater Philadelphia United Way campaign. He has made commercial endorsements in the area for the first time. And, with the help of a recently hired public-relations specialist, he has begun the process of structuring a post-retirement image.

He conceivably could begin employing that new image after the upcoming season. Schmidt's $2-million-a-year contract expires after the 1987 campaign. And he declared late last season that he would likely not pursue a new contract.

That feeling stems from fears for his battered knees. "I've been fortunate enough to have been paid a lot of money to play this game," said Schmidt. "I'm not in a position where I have to keep playing for the money. I can afford to walk away from the game without having to try and hang on for another paycheck.

"I want to be able to end my playing career and be able to walk through 18 holes of golf without limping. I want to be able to go out on the driveway and play basketball with my kids. And one more major injury to my knees could jeopardize that. I know

All in the family: Mike, Donna, Jessica and Jonathan.

I couldn't stand another operation. If I had my knee somehow blow out tomorrow, that would be it. I'd quit right away.

"I still have the desire to excel. I would say that, with most players, the desire to excel mentally leaves before their physical skills start leaving. But I know that I will lose it physically before I lose it mentally."

Schmidt will often arrive for games three or four hours early, so he can ice his aching knees. After games, he usually has bags wrapped on the knees and thighs. Years of playing most of his games on artificial turf have taken their toll—not to mention the four operations he has been forced to undergo since high school.

No wonder that Schmidt talks about 1987 being his last season. "I don't know if I want to take the grind anymore," he said. "That's why right now, I don't see myself signing another contract when this one expires after 1987. And really, it comes down to where I'm in a position where I'll go as far as God wants me to go."

Schmidt's faith is a major reason for his growing comfort with himself, a comfort that can have him talk about leaving baseball although he is coming off a season in which he won the NL MVP award for the third time in his career.

He is not a vocal convert, not a Bible waver. He still drives a

Mercedes. He still lives in the beautiful home. One of his passions remains clothes shopping, which he does to fill empty time on the road. He plays golf whenever he gets the chance, whether it's with teammates on an off day or in his own charity tournament, held every fall in Hilton Head, S.C.

But over the last several years, Schmidt professes to have recognized why he was put on this earth and to have acquired an understanding of himself.

"Right now, I consider myself one of His many useful people," said Schmidt.

"I am a thoroughly happy man and only a small amount of that has to do with the good season I had.

"When I get up in the morning and my two kids come in and give me a kiss before they go to school, that's a home-run feeling. When I tee off in the Crosby tournament in January, that's like hitting a home run.

"And giving my testimony about my relationship with God, that's a better feeling than hitting any home run. Sure, it feels good for six months to hit home runs. But in terms of feelings, I get just as much excitement now out of other things."

However, as much as Schmidt talks about how baseball has been de-emphasized in his thinking, no one thinks the game through more than he does. And, though he might retire after the 1987 season, countering that intention is the reality that he is coming off a 1986 season in which he never played better and never was more consistent. It was largely the product of his oft-discussed mental approach. Schmidt drastically altered his batting style last season and it produced a MVP campaign.

"If I just went out there and let it happen, I'd be a mediocre major-league player," said Schmidt. "I've heard so many times about what a great player I would be if I just went out there and didn't think too much and didn't play so cool.

"But maybe people are finally realizing that my approach has been pretty successful. And there's no better example of that than this past year. I probably wouldn't hit .200 if I tried to keep hitting the same way I hit five or six years ago."

Schmidt said the reason for the change was the proliferation of hard throwers in the NL these days.

"A few years ago, everyone was one of those sinker/slider pitchers who tried to keep the ball down in the strike zone," he said. "Now, there are too many Dwight Goodens and Floyd Youmans around. It seems like every team in the league has a couple of guys who can throw 95 miles per hour, guys who throw gas high in the strike zone. And I had to adjust to that to keep from becoming a mediocre hitter.

"I tossed it around in my head for I don't know how long. I thought and I thought about what was wrong with how I was approaching things and what I could correct. I was having a lot of trouble making my approach to hitting work and I knew I had to change my thinking processes at the plate."

Several years ago, Schmidt had adopted a style in which he moved off the plate and concentrated on taking an easy, slightly upper-cut swing. But, in the 1983 World Series, the Baltimore Orioles showed the world you could get Schmidt out by pounding him up and in with fastballs. And the National League took note.

Schmidt's numbers remained decent, but his next couple of seasons were characterized by spurts of production followed by long droughts. He began his transformation during the early part of the 1985 season, when he was struggling to stay at .200. The results came slowly, but Schmidt said the turning point came in an August 1985 game against the Mets.

"I remember, we were facing Dwight Gooden that day and, in batting practice, I just made up my mind that I would try to drive every ball into the ground with every swing I took," he said.

"And on my first at-bat, I got my hands to a point where I knew that no one could get a ball under my bat. Keeping my hands there meant I wasn't going to get tied up by pitches and I wasn't going to swing under all those fastballs and foul 'em back. I ended up singling and homering in that game and I've basically carried those at-bats through the rest of '85 and all of '86."

In the end, Schmidt discarded his distinctive wiggle in the batter's box. He also dropped his uppercut and instead adopted a style in which he concentrated on hitting down on the ball.

"With the way I'm doing things now, more of my swings result in hitting the ball fair," said Schmidt. "More of my swings hit the ball hard. More of my swings create contact, instead of foul balls. I might not walk 120 times anymore [he walked 89 times in 1986, the second-highest total in the league]. But now I hit the ball more, because I don't strike out as much [he fanned only 84 times last season, the first time he has been under 100 whiffs, except for the strike-shortened 1981 season].

"And because I hit the ball more, I don't have long slumps and I have more RBI."

Schmidt's consistency during the '86 season was impressive. "He was amazing," said his manager, John Felske. "Mike came to me during spring training and told me he was going to have a great year and he sure was good to his word.

"I don't think he had a real stretch of any length all season in which he didn't produce. He was as consistent as anyone I've ever seen."

Along with his renewed offense, Schmidt had his best defensive season ever. He made only six errors at third base—his other two were at first—after returning to his natural position and won his 10th Gold Glove. In 1985, he had spent most of his time at first base, amid whispers that he had lost his range and ability to play third.

"I did go through a period of time when I lost confidence at third and the time spent at first might have ended up helping me," he said. "I was worried at the time about how I was hitting and I took those worries out onto the field, where I started pressing.

"But when I moved to first, the focus became whether I could play that position. And that took pressure off me. I ended up playing well at first and then I came into 1986 feeling good at the plate and feeling good in the field and my confidence was restored. I ended up showing people I can be as good as third baseman as I ever was."

And if he's as good as he ever was, how can Schmidt just walk away from the game?

It's a question Phils' president Bill Giles will ask Schmidt in the coming months.

"I think it's a decision he will make during the course of this coming season," said Giles. "Despite what he has said, I don't think his mind is completely set yet.

"Personally, I'd like to see him play through 1989. That could mean he might reach 600 home runs and he would establish himself as the player of the decade.

"But I have to also admire him for wanting to make sure he goes out on top. I think he wants to go out with all the good things on his mind and not like Pete Rose or Steve Carlton. And I've heard a lot of reasonable reasons why he will quit. So I would think it will be difficult to persuade him to change his mind."

And what's next for Schmidt if he indeed does decide to retire? Well, he would make a perfect broadcaster, both articulate and insightful. He also has set the stage for possible film work as evidenced by his impressive public-service ads—one for major-league baseball and another for an anti-drug message.

Another possibility could be managing. "To me that would be the ultimate, in a way," said Schmidt. "To be able to come out to the park early, to lean on a fungo bat and talk about the game with writers and players, to have a say about that night's game. To wear the uniform, to travel and all the rest and not have all those knots in your stomach from trying to perform at the level you want to perform. That might be really something."

But Schmidt has at least one more season to play—and the Phils' fans have another year to say thanks.

BOSTON'S ROGER CLEMENS: "THE FRANCHISE"

By MIKE SHALIN

As Roger Clemens went to the mound to start the ninth inning, the words of teammate Al Nipper were fresh in his mind. "He said, 'Rocket, you have a chance for the all-time strikeout record. Go for it with gusto.'"

The Fenway crowd of 13,414 on April 29 was fully aware of the significance of the moment, aware that Clemens had struck out 18 Seattle Mariners, aware that they might be witnessing a pitching feat never accomplished in 111 major-league seasons. Eight innings of three-hit pitching had taken a toll on the stamina of the 24-year-old righthander, but this challenge was too irresistible to go unanswered.

Mariners' shortstop Spike Owen, who later in the season became one of Clemens' teammates, was the leadoff hitter. With the crowd screaming its support, Clemens fired a 1-2 fastball—a 96-mph dart—past the overmatched Owen for strikeout No. 19.

Clemens had joined Nolan Ryan (Angels, 1974), Tom Seaver (Mets, 1970), Steve Carlton (Cardinals, 1969) and Charles Sweeney (Providence, 1884) in the record books, matching their mark for strikeouts in a nine-inning game. And Clemens was not done. The next hitter was Phil Bradley, whom Clemens had already fanned three times. The Red Sox ace worked the count to 2-2 and threw a lightning bolt that Bradley watched sail into the mitt of catcher Rich Gedman. Umpire Vic Voltaggio signaled strike three. No. 20.

"I watched perfect games by Catfish Hunter and Mike Witt,

Mike Shalin got to the big leagues when he covered the New York Yankees for the New York Post *in the early 1980s. He says life was more serene after he shifted to the* Boston Herald *in 1983—until the dramatic 1986 season of Roger Clemens and the team that came within an out of the World Championship.*

Roger fires rocket to open ALCS Game 7 clincher.

but this was the most awesome pitching performance I've ever seen," said Boston manager John McNamara.

"Rocket was unhittable," said Gedman. "The thing that amazed me the most was that they had so many swings and weren't even able to foul the ball. It wasn't like he was trying to paint the corners or anything. He was challenging them and they weren't able to get a bat on the ball."

Clemens' masterpiece that day, in a 3-1 victory also featuring *zero* walks, served as the symbol of his 1986 emergence from troubled prospect into The Franchise who pitched the Red Sox to within one strike of their first World Championship since 1918. His domination was extraordinary: 14 straight victories from the start of the season, a 24-4 record, a league-leading 2.48 ERA and 238 strikeouts in 254 innings. His selection as a unanimous winner of the Cy Young Award—the first Boston pitcher to win the honor since Jim Lonborg in 1967—was followed by his selection as AL MVP, a rare double for a starting pitcher last achieved by Oakland's Vida Blue in 1971.

However, to fully appreciate the magnitude of Clemens' accomplishment, one must remember that this gifted 6-4, 215-pound youngster began spring training in 1986 as nothing more than a rehab project whose recent arm problems had called both his durability and mental toughness into question.

After a tear in his right forearm had cut short his 9-4 debut with the Red Sox in 1984, Clemens fell victim to a mysterious shoulder ailment in 1985. When doctors couldn't pinpoint the reason he was experiencing weakness in his shoulder, Clemens continued to pitch, insisting, "I can finesse hitters and get by without my good fastball."

Clemens struggled to a 7-5 record before hitting the bottom on July 7, when the ache in his shoulder forced him to stop warming up in the bullpen at Anaheim Stadium. His 1985 season was over and Clemens was frightened. "It was scary. I'm used to throwing 90-mile-per-hour fastballs and then, all of a sudden, I couldn't break a pane of glass. I didn't have any fastball. And it was killing me," he said.

"He just kept saying, 'Why me? Why me? Why, after all the work I've done to get here?'" said Nipper, one of his closest friends. "We sat in the runway for about an hour. He didn't know what was going to happen to his career."

In August, he was sent to the Hughston Clinic in Columbus, Ga., where Dr. James Andrews restored the arm that had pitched the University of Texas to the College World Series title and the New Britain Red Sox to the Eastern League crown in 1983. Andrews removed a fragment of cartilage from the rotator cuff. "He

[Andrews] went in there with that Pac-Man tool and told us it wasn't as bad as anticipated," said Randy Clemens, Roger's brother. "Everyone kind of looked at each other with a sigh of relief."

The mystery behind Clemens' tendency to run out of gas after overpowering hitters for a few innings had been solved and the questions that had been raised by the media concerning his willingness to pitch in discomfort could be dismissed. But another question remained: would the post-operative Clemens still be capable of the greatness that had been predicted for him?

To begin his rehabilitation, Clemens went home to Katy, Tex., a suburb of Houston. Clemens was born in Dayton, Ohio, on Aug. 4, 1962, but the family had moved to Texas a few years after his father died.

Tireless and determined, Roger worked out with friends and relatives, hitting, shagging flies and throwing batting practice.

"You could say the work ethic comes from our family background," said brother Randy. "We were without our father from early on. We had to scrap for everything we got, whether it was on the baseball field or on a job."

Clemens no longer feared for his career. In fact, he spoke with friends about how much fun it would be to pitch in the 1986 All-Star Game, which would be played in Houston. And why not? Getting people out had never been a problem for Clemens.

Even in his schoolboy days at Spring Woods High in Houston, when his fastball was clocked in the low 80s, Clemens had such excellent command of its location that he was drafted by the Twins in the 22nd round of his senior year. By the time he left Jacinto JC and began throwing that heater with more velocity for the University of Texas, there was a new cause of skepticism about his future. The rap on him in the minds of some scouts was that he lacked the heart to finish games. But the Red Sox drafted Clemens, who had turned down a $40,000 offer from the Mets in favor of the scholarship to Texas, as the 19th overall pick in June 1983. He quickly rewarded their faith by posting a sub-2.00 ERA in each of his three minor-league stops before arriving in Boston on May 11, 1984.

Early in spring training of 1986, Clemens bore little resemblance to the pitcher who had excited the imagination during his ascent to the parent club. Relying on an unusual number of breaking pitches, Clemens was hit hard and then deluged with annoying questions concerning his health. It was only after pitching coach Bill Fischer urged him to once again rely on his fastball, the pitch that set him apart from other pitchers, that Clemens found his old form.

Flashing the control he says he developed while competing

Clemens hugs Calvin Schiraldi after ALCS Game 5.

against older kids in Little League ball and throwing with the velocity of Nolan Ryan, his childhood idol, Clemens made it increasingly clear with every start in 1986 that he—and the Red Sox—had arrived.

With Clemens winning every fifth day like clockwork, the rest of the Red Sox staff fell into line behind him. Bruce Hurst, Oil Can Boyd and Nipper filled out the best starting rotation for a Boston team in quite some time. As the indispensable anchor of a club that historically has been known for its sluggers rather than its pitchers, Clemens was the essence of a stopper. Fourteen of his victories followed Red Sox defeats.

"He turned things around for that team time and time again," said Toronto manager Jimy Williams. "He gave them momentum. You could tell that if the team was on a bad streak, the players looked forward to having him come to the mound. It seemed to create a good feeling on the team from what I could see. Roger responded well to that situation all season. Over the course of a 162-game season, a pitcher like him creates a kind of positive feeling."

Building on his nine-strikeout performance in his final spring start, Clemens went from question mark to exclamation point right out of the gate. He beat the White Sox in Chicago, 7-2, on April 11 and came within an out of notching a complete game. Then he disposed of Kansas City and Detroit, running his record to 3-0, slashing his ERA to 1.85 and boosting his strikeout total to 19 in 24⅓ innings. Then came that 20-K gem against the Mariners in which the radar gun clocked him in the high 90s in the late innings.

He carried a no-hitter into the eighth inning of a game in Texas May 25, but Oddibe McDowell singled with two out and Clemens had to settle for a 7-1 victory and the first of his three two-hitters. The victory streak hit 14 before coming to an end in a somewhat controversial fashion on July 2 in Boston. Clemens was removed from the game by McNamara with the score tied at 2-2 and a couple of men on base in the eighth inning. Toronto pushed home the runners against reliever Bob Stanley and Clemens was the pitcher of record on the short end of a 4-2 count. After getting hit hard in a 6-4 loss to Oakland in his next start, Clemens beat California to take a 15-2 record into his All-Star Game start in Houston. He retired nine straight NL All-Stars, was the winning pitcher and was named MVP of the American League victory—a triumphant homecoming if there ever was one.

After suffering back-to-back defeats at the hands of the White Sox and Jose DeLeon—the second a 1-0 heartbreaker—Clemens finished his season with a run of seven straight victories sprinkled with four no-decisions. The final no-decision was a painful one as Clemens was forced to leave his last regular-season start with a bad bruise on his pitching elbow, inflicted by a liner off the bat of Baltimore catcher John Stefaro in the second inning. Clemens vowed that the injury wouldn't keep him from pitching in the postseason, but he was not the same overpowering presence he had been during the year, when opposition hitters hit only .195 against him.

The California Angels routed Clemens in Game 1 of the AL Championship Series. Then, working on three days' rest, he pitched well in Game 4 only to wind up with a no-decision when the bullpen failed Boston in the late innings. In Game 7, however, Clemens capped the Red Sox' remarkable comeback from the brink of Game 5 elimination by beating the Angels at Fenway and giving Boston its first pennant since 1975. As it turned out, the victory was the last 1986 triumph by the pitcher who posted more wins than any Red Sox hurler since Mel Parnell went 25-7 in 1949.

Clemens was a poor imitation of himself in his first World Series start. Showing ill effects from working on three days' rest, he was unable to last the five innings required for him to pick up a victory, despite a 6-3 Boston lead. Faced with the chance to pitch yet another title-clinching victory in Game 6, Clemens bounced back with a strong performance, allowing only one earned run in seven innings. But again, the Boston bullpen was exploited by the Mets in a dramatic 6-5, 10-inning conquest that set the stage for another come-from-behind Met victory in Game 7. Clemens' disappointment made it difficult for him to fully enjoy all the accolades of the offseason.

"In a heartbeat, I'd trade away the (Cy Young) award if I could wear a championship ring," he said. "That's what we started out to accomplish as a team, but we didn't quite finish it."

The Red Sox didn't get the job done, but it wasn't because of The Franchise. Forget the Cy Young jinx and his checkered medical history. The future couldn't look brighter for the man they call "Rocket" in Boston.

The offseason figured to be a busy one for Clemens as he and his wife, Debbie, celebrated the birth of their first child, Koby Aaron, and Roger and his agent, Alan Hendricks, sorted out various endorsement proposals. After the 20-K performance, Clements had done a Zest soap commercial, singing in the shower. And he has signed to do his autobiography.

Is a repeat performance too much to expect?

"I don't know if you can look at a guy and tell whether he is going to be able to come back and have another year like he had," said Yankee manager Lou Piniella. "But he's strong, he's young, he has a good head on his shoulders and he's in great shape. He throws strikes, too, so I don't see any reason why he shouldn't come back and have more great seasons."

And continue being The Franchise in Boston.

The Franchise had feared for career before surgery.

Dykstra & Backman: The Mets' Dead-End Kids

By MARTY NOBLE

With devilish delight, Wally Backman passed the note before the pained eyes of Charlie Samuels, the Mets' equipment manager. The note, delivered to Backman's locker in the Mets' spring training clubhouse, had come from the director of a television camera crew. Backman was invited to attend a team promotional shoot and was requested to wear his "home whites." So Samuels winced. Another day, another dirty uniform.

Samuels was certain the director had no intention of producing footage of Backman fielding a ground ball—nothing so mundane—or Backman trotting around the bases—nothing so uncharacteristic. "They'll have him sliding or something," Samuels said. "Playing in the dirt."

Backman smiled. "It's what I do best," he said.

In the aftermath of the Mets' rousing 6-5 victory over Houston in Game 3 of the National League Championship Series last October, a visitor to the Mets' clubhouse located Lenny Dykstra and introduced himself to the player who had won the game with a two-run, ninth-inning home run. Charlie Fine of Hogan's Cleaners in Bellmore, N.Y., had sought out Dykstra to tell the center fielder of a distinction he had earned. "We clean the uniforms," Fine said. "Yours is always the dirtiest."

"Thanks," Dykstra responded.

Marty Noble of Newsday *has followed Len Dykstra and Wally Backman from their beginnings with the Mets on through that championship season of 1986. He's writing a book with Dykstra on the year that was.*

Mets' mighty mites: Len Dykstra and Wally Backman.

Wally Backman and Lenny Dykstra, Backman and Dykstra or, as they often were deployed in the Mets' batting order last season, Dykstra and Backman. Some people see them as one. Try Wanny Backstra.

Call them whatever you like, but acknowledge them as the Mets' grittiest players and recognize them as integral factors in the Mets' extraordinary success in 1986. "If you put the two of them into one body," Cubs' manager Gene Michael said, "together, they could be the MVP."

Operating as two separate but related entities, the two certainly were among the Mets' most valuable assets. Their impact was as undeniable as the stains on their uniforms were abundant. The World Series champions were a polished act, with Keith Hernandez, Gary Carter, Darryl Strawberry, Dwight Gooden, Ron Darling, Bob Ojeda, et al. But grit is a critical ingredient in any polish and Backman and Dykstra were the grit in the Mets' polish.

The condition of their uniforms attests to their aggressive style of play. "The only guy who wears out more uniforms is Straw," Samuels said, "because of the way he slides. But Lenny and Wally are murder on uniforms. They come in after one inning and each of them has a pound of the infield on his uniform. They attract dirt."

Each harbors a healthy dislike for an unsoiled uniform. To the Mets' "Partners in Grime," *clean* is a four-letter word. "If I come out of a game with a clean uniform," Backman said, "it probably means I didn't do enough."

"Get down and get dirty," Dykstra said. "It's the way we play."

The two have chosen the style of play out of necessity. Each is a product of the same assembly line that produced the Mets' first gritty player, Ron Hunt. Backman's nickname even rhymes with Hunt—"Runt." In more ways than one, they are twin sons of different mothers.

Neither is gifted with the obvious talents of Strawberry, the sweet swing of Hernandez or the power of Carter. Neither is gifted with size. Backman, the 27-year-old Oregonian, stands 5-9 in high-heel spikes and batting helmet. Dykstra, the 24-year-old Californian, measures up to his announced 5-10 only if he stands on the pitching runner. And baseball, though it remains a game for all sizes, frowns on small players. Size and bulk guarantee nothing, but the big guy has to prove he can't; the little guy has to prove he can.

Their size makes them the butt of lots of intramural jockeying. Gooden made an appearance at a Knicks' game last fall and served as the official for the ceremonial opening tap. Standing between 7-0 Patrick Ewing and 7-1 Phoenix center James Edwards, the 6-3 Gooden was dwarfed. "Now," he said, "I know how Lenny and Wally feel."

The similarities of these dead-end kids transcend their physical stature and style of play, however. They often sound alike and sometimes they even think alike at the same moment. Each is brash and each regularly contributes to the aura of arrogance than surrounds the Mets. Opponents often are offended by Backman's candid remarks. Dykstra says less, but is not given to sugar-coating his thoughts, either. Beyond that, Dykstra's on-field demeanor infuriates opponents who warn that a man of his size should stay in his place.

The two shared something of an ESP experience during the introductions prior to Game 3 of the playoffs. Neither was included in the starting lineup against Bob Knepper, the Astros' left-handed starting pitcher. As they took their places on the foul line with the other extras, each turned to the other and said simultaneously, "God, I wish I were playing." It was a chorus of lament.

Before the day was over, however, each would play a significant role in what became a 6-5 Met victory. With Houston leading, 5-4, Backman, who had replaced Tim Teufel at second base in the top of the ninth inning, led off the bottom of the inning with a bunt single that was disputed by the Astros.

Dykstra began World Series Game 3 with HR off Oil Can.

They claimed Backman had run outside the baseline. The Mets and the umpires saw it another way. In characteristically direct words, Backman later wondered why the Astros hadn't been better prepared for a bunt in the first place. "Anyone who saw Met games this year knew I was going to bunt," he said. "Didn't they scout us? Maybe they thought we weren't going to win the division and they scouted the Phillies."

"I knew he was going to bunt," Dykstra said. "He didn't tell me. I just knew."

A passed ball allowed Backman to advance to second base and scoring position. That advance became moot when, one out later, Dykstra hit a Dave Smith forkball that didn't fork over the right-field wall and ushered his compatriot around the bases.

"The most important hit of my career," said reserve catcher Ed Hearn. "And I didn't even hit it."

For Dykstra, the hit launched a brilliant postseason performance that raised the nation's Dykstra-consciousness level. His vital triple in the ninth inning of Game 6 of the playoffs and leadoff home run in Game 3 of the World Series added distinction to his fall work. But the game-winning home run in Game 3 of the playoffs was his finest moment.

Of course, Dykstra credited his "little brother" with having delivered the most important hit. "Once he bunted, I knew we were going to win and I think they did, too," he said. "They

Backman worked hard to make it as a second baseman.

probably started thinking, 'Oh no, here they come.' Wally's bunt made them nervous. Then we get a passed ball. They know we're at least going to tie it up. Then boom. It's over."

Backman returned the compliment with playful sarcasm. "Our hits were equally important. Just because mine went 40 feet and his went 400, what difference does that make?"

Whatever, Wanny Backstra had struck again. And the Mets had won again. "Without one of them, we would have been in trouble all year," Gary Carter said that day. "If we didn't have either of them, it would have been tough winning the division. They just go out and create two runs to win a playoff game. They've done that so many times this year. What else can you ask for?"

* * *

As their husbands manufactured the decisive runs, Margie Backman and Terri Dykstra sat together—of course—in the Shea Stadium stands behind home plate. The couples live a few blocks apart on Long Island during the season. The players car-pool to Shea. The wives do, too. The four often dine together on those rare occasions when the baseball schedule allows for socializing.

"Sometimes, it's like looking in a mirror," Backman said. "The Backmans and the Dykstras, Lenny and I are a lot alike and our wives are together a lot . . . They could exchange clothes. And they do."

"Wally makes a lot more money than I do," Dykstra said. "His wife gives mine a lot of things. She buys expensive clothes, wears them once and gives them to us. My wife goes out and says she's going shopping. I say, 'Where?' She says, 'The Backmans.'"

* * *

"They're like two peas in a pod," Hernandez said. "A lot alike, but Wally will fight you on that."

"Yeah," Backman said facetiously. "There's only one person in the world like Lenny. It's Lenny. He's one of a kind, thank God. Don't get us mixed up. I'm the bigger one."

"Right," Dykstra said. "He'd get lost in my clothes. They'd be too big for him."

"I wouldn't wear your clothes if they did fit," Backman said. "No one would. You shouldn't wear them. They're weak . . . I'm not the best-dressed guy here, but Lenny is no stylemaster. He has to buy his clothes in the boys' department."

And so goes the clubhouse banter. "We talk about other things in the car," Backman said. "That's if I'm not afraid to talk. Did you ever ride with Lenny driving? I put my life in his hands every time he drives. He doesn't let anybody push him around on the expressway."

Or anywhere else.

Actually, those words apply to both men. Each has learned not to back down from the tests often faced by small athletes. "I learned early," Backman said. "When you're my size, guys try to intimidate you. It happens when you're real young. If you let them, you're never going to be as good as you can be. So I learned to fight. Now I don't back down—not from anyone. The next day I might wish that I hadn't, but when it's going on, you know you have to stand up."

"They're two tough guys," said Ray Knight, a former Golden Gloves boxer. "They don't take anything. I just hope they don't fight each other. Neither one would quit."

But who would win? "I don't know," Backman said. "I know it would be fierce. I know I'd bite if I had to. He probably would too, though."

Some of the ferocity they share apparently is inherited. Backman's father, Sam, a onetime Pirate farmhand, was a longshoreman. His father's influence and a childhood spent in Oregon contribute to Backman's ruggedness, his appreciation of the outdoors and his love for hunting.

Backman's ruggedness was reinforced by an older brother who was an All-American scholastic wrestler. Backman, too, became an accomplished scholastic wrestler with abilities he used to pin Dave Kingman in an informal, semi-serious bout in the outfield one day.

"I learned from my family," Backman said. "My brother and I would put the gloves on once in a while. He'd let me get a couple of shots in and get cocky. Then he'd smoke me. That happened a few times. Then I learned. I don't think he was trying to intimidate me. He was trying to toughen me up, so no one could pick on me. I think it worked."

But baseball was his first love, following a successful career at Aloha High School in Oregon. Backman signed with the Mets in the summer of 1977. They had made him their first selection in the June draft.

Backman reached the majors rather quickly—by the end of the 1980 season. He played parts of the 1981 and 1982 seasons with the Mets, appearing in 96 games in 1982. But he spent most of 1983 with the Mets' Triple-A Tidewater affiliate. There, he served as second baseman and leadoff hitter for Dave Johnson's International League champions.

When Johnson was named Mets' manager, Backman's promotion to the majors was almost a foregone conclusion. All Backman needed to do to win the regular second-base assignment was to overcome the challenge of quasi-incumbent Brian Giles. Giles' "too-cool" attitude hardly delighted Johnson, who already admired the resolve of Backman.

The spring-training competition was competitive in name only. Backman emerged as the winner, though it was a partial victory. A switch-hitter, Backman is not nearly as effective from the right-hand side, so he shared second base with right-handed-hitting Kelvin Chapman in 1984 and 1985 and with Tim Teufel last season.

"I want to play regularly," Backman says, "but I don't mind fighting for the job every spring. It makes me better. I've never turned away from a challenge, even as a kid."

Dykstra's toughness can be traced to his uncle, "Tough Tony" Leswick, who came out of Saskatoon, Saskatchewan, to play 12 seasons in the National Hockey League, and to his grandfather, Pete Leswick, who also played professional hockey. Toughness is in his blood and that has been obvious since Lenny's days as an all-league and all-county football player at Garden Grove High School in southern California.

Dykstra was the Mets' 12th selection in the 1981 free-agent draft and he got his first major-league chance in 1985, when a shoulder injury incapacitated center fielder Mookie Wilson.

Dykstra distinguished himself, creating what the Mets considered a positive problem—too much talent at one position. Another injury slowed Wilson's return in spring training last year, so Dykstra owned center field and the leadoff assignment outright until mid-May, when Wilson returned. Wilson mounted a strong challenge and Johnson still regarded Wilson as the regular. But, by late July, Johnson became convinced the Mets were a better team with Dykstra in the lineup.

Dykstra's production slackened somewhat when he began playing regularly, particularly when he faced left-handed pitching, and Wilson eventually gained a share of the center-field responsibilities. But, after Dykstra's outstanding performance in the playoffs, Johnson made Dykstra the regular center fielder in the World Series.

"He gave us something special," Johnson said. "We seemed to play better with the little tough guy in there."

"Nails" doesn't walk away from fights or shy away from outfield walls or angry Reds' pitchers.

When the Mets brawled with the Reds in Cincinnati July 22—one of the Mets' four brawls last season—Reds pitcher Tom Browning was heard by players on each side to be calling for Dykstra. Browning used his favorite term for Dykstra—"That little SOB."

"What am I supposed to be, scared of Tom Browning?" Dykstra said with disdain the following day. "We're out there going against a team with Dave Parker. And I'm supposed to worry about Browning?"

* * *

It was that "the-hell-with-you" attitude of the Nos. 1 and 2 batters that often fueled the Mets' offense. The term table-setters was applied to each of them, but that's applied to any batter at the top of the order. But Dykstra and Backman were tone-setters as well.

"You watch Lenny diving into second with a double in the first inning and it sets a tone for the game right away," Howard Johnson said. "He plays like a man possessed. He's crazy. People tell me I drink too much iced tea . . . that all the caffeine's no good for me. I tell them, 'I drink decaf. With all that I drink, if I drank regular, the caffeine would make me like Lenny.'

"Now you've got Lenny on second and Wally bunts and beats one out. Now you've got runners on first and third, and everyone in the ballpark is standing up screaming. That gets us into the game in a hurry."

No less seasoned an observer than former Met Rusty Staub noted the importance of the two last summer as the Mets were disassociating themselves from their supposed peers in the National League East. "This team sees a lot of left-handed pitching," said Staub, a Met broadcastor. "No other team wants Keith and Darryl facing right-handed pitching if it can be helped. But the table-setters are just as much a reason for all the lefties. Other manager's know if they throw a lefty out there, they might not see either Lenny or Wally. It's a lot easier to face the Mets if those two guys aren't in the lineup."

Hernandez, who batted behind Lou Brock and Garry Templeton as the Cards' No. 3 hitter, said Dykstra and Backman are comparable to that St. Louis tandem. "They get on as much," Hernandez said. "Lou and Tempy were faster, but that's the kind of team we had in St. Louis. Our guys can upset a pitcher as well as any guys. With Lenny and Wally, it's like having two leadoff guys."

The statistics compiled by Dykstra and Backman support Hernandez's words. Dykstra compiled a .377 on-base percentage, one point higher than Backman's. Had they amassed sufficient plate appearances, they would have placed seventh and eighth, respectively, in the National League.

Their other statistics weren't shabby, either. In 431 at-bats, Dykstra batted .295 with 31 stolen bases, 77 runs, 45 RBI, eight home runs and a .445 slugging percentage, excellent for a leadoff batter. His slugging percentage was higher than Carter's .439 and one point lower than Hernandez's.

Backman batted .320 with 67 runs, 27 RBI in 387 at-bats.

Dykstra started 97 games—each as a center fielder and all but two as the leadoff batter for the team that led the NL in scoring. Backman started 92, playing second base and batting second in each. They appeared as an entry—Dykstra leading off and Backman following—in 73 games, and the Mets won 51 of those. The team winning percentage of .699 in those games compares favorably to the rather remarkable .667 overall winning percentage the Mets compiled.

"I'm not surprised," said manager Dave Johnson. "We were a much more dangerous team when I could use them in my lineup. Because they're both on base so much, we had more chances to

Dykstra slides home safely in World Series Game 3.

score, and because they run well, we had more ways to score. I don't think it's a secret that right-handed pitching didn't have much success against us. They were a big part of it. If one wasn't on base, the other one was." And sometimes both were.

Dykstra and Backman were not so highly thought of by opponents, of course. They were regarded as pests, the highest form of flattery afforded a batter at the top of the order. "You get by one pest and there's another pest in your face," said San Francisco lefty Vida Blue. "I didn't have to go against them. And I'm glad. They can be a problem for a lefty, too. I know their kind—pests. Pesky little pests. They annoy you. They foul off your good pitches. They don't swing at your others. They don't get themselves out. And they don't make it easy for anyone else to get them out."

"You can't expect much more from the top of the order," Dave Johnson says. "Lenny gets on base as well as anyone—especially in tough situations. He'll swing the bat with men on base and drive in more runs than most leadoff men.

"Wally's always in the other team's face. He's always doing something to annoy them. They probably hate playing against us because of those two guys. But I'm sure they respect them. How could you not, the way they play?"

INSIDE THE
NATIONAL LEAGUE

By NICK PETERS
Oakland Tribune

PREDICTED ORDER OF FINISH	*East*	*West*
	New York Mets	Houston Astros
	Philadelphia Phillies	Cincinnati Reds
	St. Louis Cardinals	San Francisco Giants
	Pittsburgh Pirates	Los Angeles Dodgers
	Chicago Cubs	Atlanta Braves
	Montreal Expos	San Diego Padres

Playoff winner: Houston

EAST DIVISION		Owner		Morning Line Manager
1	**METS** Orange, white & blue Class of the field	N. Doubleday/F. Wilpon	1986 W 108 L 54	1-1 Dave Johnson
2	**PHILLIES** Crimson & white Moving up fast	Bill Giles	1986 W 86 L 75	5-1 John Felske
3	**CARDINALS** Red & white Speed but no strength	August A. Busch Jr.	1986 W 79 L 82	10-1 Whitey Herzog
4	**PIRATES** Old gold, white & black Young and frisky	Malcolm Prine	1986 W 64 L 98	50-1 Jim Leyland
5	**CUBS** Royal blue & white Tired old horse	Tribune Co.	1986 W 70 L 90	70-1 Gene Michael
6	**EXPOS** Scarlet, white & royal blue Mass confusion at gate	Charles Bronfman	1986 W 78 L 83	100-1 Bob Rodgers

Champion **METS** too strong for a weak field, but **PHILLIES** and **CARDINALS** confident following strong finish in last race. **PIRATES** young and eager to move past stumbling **CUBS** and **EXPOS,** who barely make it to the gate.

ASTRO DERBY

111th Running. National League Race. Distance: 162 games plus playoff. Payoff (based on '86): $86,254 per winning player, World Series: $74,985 per losing player, World Series. A field of 12 entered in two divisions.

Track Record: 116 wins—Chicago, 1906

WEST DIVISION		Owner		Morning Line Manager
1	**ASTROS** Orange & white Solid down the stretch	John McMullen	1986 W 96 L 66	2-1 Hal Lanier
2	**REDS** Red & white A rosy future	Marge Schott	1986 W 86 L 76	3-1 Pete Rose
3	**GIANTS** White, orange & black Highly-rated jockey	Bob Lurie	1986 W 83 L 79	5-1 Roger Craig
4	**DODGERS** Royal blue & white Lost some of old zip	Peter O'Malley	1986 W 73 L 89	10-1 Tom Lasorda
5	**BRAVES** Royal blue & white Same face, same race	Ted Turner	1986 W 72 L 89	25-1 Chuck Tanner
6	**PADRES** Brown, gold & white Too young to go steady	Joan Kroc	1986 W 74 L 88	50-1 Larry Bowa

A much tougher race has **ASTROS** showing too much stamina down the stretch in two-way battle with **REDS.** The **GIANTS** fizzle at the finish and **DODGERS** display improved power to leave aging **BRAVES** and too-green **PADRES** in the rear.

CHICAGO CUBS

TEAM DIRECTORY: Pres.-GM: Dallas Green; Dir. Minor Leagues/ Scouting: Gordon Goldsberry; VP-Adm.: E.R. Saltwell; Dir. Med. Rel.: Ned Colletti; Trav. Sec.: Peter Durso; Mgr.: Gene Michael. Home: Wrigley Field (38,040). Field distances: 335, l.f. line; 400, c.f.; 353, r.f. line. Spring training: Mesa, Ariz.

SCOUTING REPORT

HITTING: The Cubs were third in the league with a .256 average and their 155 home runs topped the NL last year, but the offensive picture isn't as rosy as it might seem because age is catching up to this club. For instance, what can Chicago realistically expect from Gary Matthews and Ron Cey in 1987?

Matthews, 36, provided pop with a surprising 21 home runs, but generated only 46 RBI last year. Cey, 39, overcame a slow start to bat .273, but can the Cubs afford to keep "The Penguin" in the lineup considering he produced only 36 RBI? Keith Moreland (.271, 12 homers, 79 RBI), Jody Davis (.250, 21, 74) and Shawon Dunston (.250, 17, 68) are productive hitters, but it's apparent Leon Durham (.262, 20, 65) will never reach predicted stardom and that Ryne Sandberg (.284, 14, 76) is the only sure thing in the lineup.

PITCHING: This was the worst staff in the NL last year, as evidenced by a 4.49 ERA and 721 earned runs, at least 81 more than any other team allowed. Things don't figure to get much better, either, unless Rick Sutcliffe (5-14, 4.64), Dennis Eckersley (6-11, 4.57), Scott Sanderson (9-11, 4.19) and Steve Trout (15-7, 4.75) can revive the miracle of 1984.

Unless youngsters Jamie Moyer and Greg Maddux come through to support the sagging veteran rotation, it looks like another long year for a tattered staff. The pitching strength continues to be the bullpen. More specifically, that means Lee Smith, who managed 31 saves and nine victories with a club that won only 70 games in 1986.

FIELDING: Only the Cardinals posted a higher fielding percentage than the Cubs' .980 last season. Sandberg is the finest fielding second baseman in the league, making only five errors in 806 chances. Davis has shown dramatic improvement behind the plate and now ranks among the league's best defensively.

There's concern over Dunston's league-leading 32 errors at

Gifted Shawon Dunston is state-of-the-art shortstop.

shortstop, but this strong-armed youngster also handled more chances than anyone and tied the Cards' Ozzie Smith for DP honors. Bob Dernier can play center with the best of them and he has to do just that because of the limited range of Matthews and Moreland.

OUTLOOK: The Cubs won a division flag in 1984, but Dallas Green's quick fix overloaded the club with veterans who now are past their prime. If some newcomers don't knock the oldtimers out of jobs, the future looks bleak for the Wrigley Field faithful.

It also would help if Dernier returns to the form which made him such a valuable table-setter in 1984. Anything from Cey and Matthews would be a bonus. But it would take another MVP year from Sandberg and a rejuvenated Sutcliffe to lift Gene Michael's Cubs from last year's 70-90 finish into the first division in 1987

CHICAGO CUBS 1987 ROSTER

MANAGER Gene Michael
COACHES—Johnny Oates, Jim Snyder, Herm Starrette, John Vukovich, Billy Williams

PITCHERS

No.	Name	1986 Club	W-L	IP	SO	ERA	B-T	Ht.	Wt.	Born
48	Baller, Jay	Chicago (NL)	2-4	54	42	5.37	R-R	6-7	225	10/6/60 Stayton, OR
		Iowa	3-7	59	51	4.40				
38	Davidson, Jackie	Pittsfield	8-3	78	47	3.24	R-R	6-0	175	9/20/64 Ft. Worth, TX
		Iowa	4-5	92	48	4.87				
39	Davis, Ron	Minnesota	2-6	39	30	9.08	R-R	6-4	205	8/6/55 Houston, TX
		Chicago (NL)	0-2	20	10	7.65				
33	DiPino, Frank	Hou.-Chi. (NL)	3-7	80	70	4.37	L-L	6-0	180	10/22/56 Syracuse, NY
43	Eckersley, Dennis	Chicago (NL)	6-11	201	137	4.57	R-R	6-2	195	10/3/54 Oakland, CA
45	Gumpert, Dave	Iowa	2-1	44	33	2.23	R-R	6-1	190	5/5/58 South Haven, MI
44	Hall, Drew	Pittsfield	8-11	158	115	3.58	L-L	6-4	205	3/27/63 Louisville, KY
		Chicago (NL)	1-2	24	21	4.56				
51	Hamilton, Carlton	Pittsfield	10-10	155	92	4.17	L-L	6-2	185	11/4/64 Gary, IN
50	Hoffman, Guy	Iowa	4-0	59	48	2.12	L-L	5-9	175	7/9/56 Ottawa, IL
		Chicago (NL)	6-2	84	47	3.86				
37	Lynch, Ed	Tidewater	1-0	18	7	5.00	R-R	6-5	207	2/25/56 Brooklyn, NY
		NY (NL)-Chi. (NL)	7-5	101	58	3.73				
31	Maddux, Greg	Pittsfield	4-3	64	35	2.69	R-R	6-0	150	4/14/66 San Angelo, TX
		Iowa	10-1	128	65	3.02				
		Chicago (NL)	2-4	31	20	5.52				
49	Moyer, Jamie	Pittsfield	3-1	41	42	0.88	L-L	6-1	170	11/18/62 Sellersville, PA
		Iowa	3-2	42	25	2.55				
		Chicago (NL)	7-4	87	45	5.05				
21	Sanderson, Scott	Chicago (NL)	9-11	170	124	4.19	R-R	6-5	200	7/22/56 Dearborn, MI
46	Smith, Lee	Chicago (NL)	9-9	90	93	3.09	R-R	6-6	225	12/4/56 Jamestown, LA
40	Sutcliffe, Rick	Chicago (NL)	5-14	177	122	4.64	L-R	6-7	215	6/21/56 Independence, MO
34	Trout, Steve	Chicago (NL)	5-7	161	69	4.75	L-L	6-4	190	7/30/57 Detroit, MI

CATCHERS

No.	Name	1986 Club	H	HR	RBI	Pct.	B-T	Ht.	Wt.	Born
8	Berryhill, Damon	Pittsfield	71	6	35	.206	B-R	6-0	210	12/3/63 South Laguna, CA
7	Davis, Jody	Chicago (NL)	132	21	74	.250	R-R	6-3	210	11/12/56 Gainesville, GA
41	Martin, Mike	Pittsfield	28	1	13	.194	R-R	6-2	193	12/3/58 Portland, OR

INFIELDERS

No.	Name	1986 Club	H	HR	RBI	Pct.	B-T	Ht.	Wt.	Born
17	Brumley, Mike	Iowa	103	10	44	.255	B-R	5-10	165	4/9/63 Oklahoma City, OK
11	Cey, Ron	Chicago (NL)	70	13	36	.273	R-R	5-9	185	2/15/48 Tacoma, WA
12	Dunston, Shawon	Chicago (NL)	145	17	68	.250	R-R	6-1	175	3/21/63 Brooklyn, NY
10	Durham, Leon	Chicago (NL)	127	20	65	.262	L-L	6-2	210	7/31/57 Cincinnati, OH
23	Sandberg, Ryne	Chicago (NL)	178	14	76	.284	R-R	6-2	180	9/18/59 Spokane, WA
19	Trillo, Manny	Chicago (NL)	45	1	19	.296	R-R	6-1	164	12/25/50 Venezuela

OUTFIELDERS

No.	Name	1986 Club	H	HR	RBI	Pct.	B-T	Ht.	Wt.	Born
27	Bosley, Thad	Chicago (NL)	33	1	9	.275	L-L	6-3	175	9/17/56 Oceanside, CA
24	Dayett, Brian	Iowa	115	19	87	.281	R-R	5-10	185	1/22/57 New London, CT
		Chicago (NL)	18	4	11	.269				
20	Dernier, Bob	Chicago (NL)	73	4	18	.225	R-R	6-0	165	1/5/57 Kansas City, MO
30	Jackson, Darrin	Pittsfield	139	15	64	.267	R-R	6-1	170	8/22/63 Los Angeles, CA
1	Martinez, Dave	Iowa	92	5	32	.289	L-L	5-10	150	9/26/64 New York, NY
		Chicago (NL)	15	1	7	.139				
36	Matthews, Gary	Chicago (NL)	96	21	46	.259	R-R	6-3	205	7/5/50 San Fernando, CA
6	Moreland, Keith	Chicago (NL)	159	12	79	.271	R-R	6-0	200	5/2/54 Dallas, TX
22	Mumphrey, Jerry	Chicago (NL)	94	5	32	.304	B-R	6-2	200	9/9/52 Tyler, TX
25	Palmeiro, Rafael	Pittsfield	156	12	95	.306	R-R	6-0	180	9/24/64 Cuba
		Chicago (NL)	18	3	12	.247				
18	Roomes, Rolando	Winston-Salem	15	6	14	.238	R-R	6-3	180	2/15/62 Jamaica
		Pittsfield	52	7	42	.272				
15	Smith, Dwight	Peoria	146	11	57	.310	L-R	5-11	175	11/8/63 Tallahassee, FL
29	Walker, Chico	Iowa	158	16	65	.298	B-R	5-9	179	11/25/57 Jackson, MS
		Chicago (NL)	28	1	7	.277				

CUB PROFILES

RYNE SANDBERG 27 6-2 180 **Bats R Throws R**

Tailed off following a spectacular 1985 and an MVP year in 1984 . . . Still was good enough to land a berth in the All-Star Game . . . After he set such high standards the previous two years, perhaps too much was expected of the star second baseman whose .284 BA was his lowest since 1983 . . . "Ryno" was consistent, but not at his accustomed high level and he simply didn't have a banner month to get him over the hump . . . His 34 stolen bases were also a sharp drop from his 54 in 1985 that were the most by a Cub since 1906 . . . Won fourth straight Gold Glove in 1986 . . . Acquired from Phillies prior to 1982 season with Larry Bowa in swap for Ivan DeJesus . . . Born Sept. 18, 1959, in Spokane, Wash.

Year	Club	Pos.	G	AB	R	H	2B	3B	HR	RBI	SB	Avg.
1981	Philadelphia	SS-2B	13	6	2	1	0	0	0	0	0	.167
1982	Chicago (NL)	3B-2B	156	635	103	172	33	5	7	54	32	.271
1983	Chicago (NL)	2B-SS	158	633	94	165	25	4	8	48	37	.261
1984	Chicago (NL)	2B	156	636	114	200	36	19	19	84	32	.314
1985	Chicago (NL)	2B-SS	153	609	113	186	31	6	26	83	54	.305
1986	Chicago (NL)	2B	154	627	68	178	28	5	14	76	34	.284
	Totals		790	3146	494	902	153	39	74	345	189	.287

KEITH MORELAND 32 6-0 200 **Bats R Throws**

Club RBI leader turned a solid start into a decent season, but one which paled in comparison to a career-best campaign in 1985 . . . Picked up where he left off with a .324 April last year and also enjoyed a .322 July, but the other months were sub-par for a player who has worked hard to overcome deficiencies in his game . . . Born May 2, 1954, in Dallas . . . Brutal defensively when he switched from catcher to right field, he now is at least adequate afield . . . A solid clutch hitter . . . Starting defensive back at Texas his sophomore season and broke his wrist on the opening kickoff of the Oklahoma game as a senior . . . An All-American third baseman for the Longhorns and was drafted by the Phillies . . . Came to Cubs with Dickie Noles and Dan Larson in deal for Mike Krukow prior to 1982 season . . . Batted .333 in 1984 NL Championship Series.

Year	Club	Pos.	G	AB	R	H	2B	3B	HR	RBI	SB	Avg.
1978	Philadelphia . . .	C	1	2	0	0	0	0	0	0	0	.000
1979	Philadelphia . . .	C	14	48	3	18	3	2	0	8	0	.375
1980	Philadelphia . . .	C-3B-OF	62	159	13	50	8	0	4	29	3	.314
1981	Philadelphia . . .	C-3B-1B-OF	61	196	16	50	7	0	6	37	1	.255
1982	Chicago (NL) . .	C-OF-3B	138	476	50	124	17	2	15	68	0	.261
1983	Chicago (NL) . .	OF-C	154	533	76	161	30	3	16	70	0	.302
1984	Chicago (NL) . .	OF-1B-3B-C	140	495	59	138	17	3	16	80	1	.279
1985	Chicago (NL) . .	OF-1B-3B-C	161	587	74	180	30	3	14	106	12	.307
1986	Chicago (NL) . .	OF-3B-1B-C	156	586	72	159	30	0	12	79	3	.271
	Totals		887	3082	363	880	142	13	83	477	20	.286

LEON DURHAM 29 6-2 210 **Bats L Throws L**

Something missing from what was supposed to be a superstar career . . . Injuries perhaps have deprived "Bull" of greatness, leaving this first baseman merely a good ballplayer . . . In hibernation, along with most teammates, last year until a September surge (.326, seven homers) boosted stats to respectability . . . Ranked among league triples leaders . . . Born July 31, 1957, in Cincinnati . . . Has donated nearly $50,000 to the Chicago high schools based on payoffs for each Wrigley Field home run . . . Cards dealt him, Ken Reitz and Ty Waller for Bruce Sutter prior to 1981 season . . . Batted .312 in 1982, but hasn't come close to that since . . . That year, he became first Cub with 20 homers and 20 steals since Frank Schulte in 1911.

Year	Club	Pos.	G	AB	R	H	2B	3B	HR	RBI	SB	Avg.
1980	St. Louis	OF-1B	96	303	42	82	15	4	8	42	8	.271
1981	Chicago (NL)	OF-1B	87	328	42	95	14	6	10	35	25	.290
1982	Chicago (NL)	OF-1B	148	539	84	168	33	7	22	90	28	.312
1983	Chicago (NL)	OF-1B	100	337	58	87	18	8	12	55	12	.258
1984	Chicago (NL)	1B	137	473	86	132	30	4	23	96	16	.279
1985	Chicago (NL)	1B	153	542	58	153	32	2	21	75	7	.282
1986	Chicago (NL)	1B	141	484	66	127	18	7	20	65	8	.262
	Totals		862	3006	436	844	160	38	116	458	104	.281

GARY MATTHEWS 36 6-3 205 **Bats R Throws R**

"Sarge" was supposed to be washed up when he batted .236 over the first half last year, but he was almost a .300 hitter the rest of the way to finish with respectable figures . . . Despite his 21 homers, however, RBI production was way off, suggesting he's lost something in the clutch . . . Decline began when injuries limited left fielder to 97 games in 1985 after he'd helped

Cubs win the division with a league-leading 19 game-winning RBI in 1984 . . . Born July 5, 1950, in San Fernando, Cal. . . . He never has been a polished outfielder, but it's not from a lack of hustle . . . A popular player who has found success with four different teams . . . Rookie of the Year for the Giants in 1973 . . . Phillies dealt him to Cubs with Bob Dernier and Porfi Altamirano for Bill Campbell and Mike Diaz prior to 1984 season.

Year	Club	Pos.	G	AB	R	H	2B	3B	HR	RBI	SB	Avg.
1972	San Francisco	OF	20	62	11	18	1	1	4	14	0	.290
1973	San Francisco	OF	148	540	74	162	22	10	12	58	17	.300
1974	San Francisco	OF	154	561	87	161	27	6	16	82	11	.287
1975	San Francisco	OF	116	425	67	119	22	3	12	58	13	.280
1976	San Francisco	OF	156	587	79	164	28	4	20	84	12	.279
1977	Atlanta	OF	148	555	89	157	25	5	17	64	22	.283
1978	Atlanta	OF	129	474	75	135	20	5	18	62	8	.285
1979	Atlanta	OF	156	631	97	192	34	5	27	90	18	.304
1980	Atlanta	OF	155	571	79	159	17	3	19	75	11	.278
1981	Philadelphia	OF	101	359	62	108	21	3	9	67	15	.301
1982	Philadelphia	OF	162	616	89	173	31	1	19	83	21	.281
1983	Philadelphia	OF	132	446	66	115	18	2	10	50	13	.258
1984	Chicago (NL).	OF	147	491	101	143	21	2	14	82	17	.291
1985	Chicago (NL).	OF	97	298	45	70	12	0	13	40	2	.235
1986	Chicago (NL).	OF	123	370	49	96	16	1	21	46	3	.259
	Totals.		1944	6986	1070	1972	315	51	231	955	183	.282

JODY DAVIS 30 6-3 210 **Bats R Throws R**

Continued his batting average decline last year, but kept power figures at normal levels . . . Hasn't hit well since 1985 All-Star break . . . A gastrointestinal infection contributed to his decline in the summer of 1985 . . . An ulcer problem that required surgery in 1980 threatened his career . . . Born Nov. 12, 1956, in Gainesville, Ga. . . . Has gradually improved catching skills after being primarily an offensive player . . . Originally drafted by Mets and traded to Cardinals prior to being plucked by Cubs in minor-league draft of 1981 . . . Became first Cubs' catcher in 40 years to hit more than 20 homers in 1983 . . . Batted .389 with six RBI in 1984 NL Championship Series.

Year	Club	Pos.	G	AB	R	H	2B	3B	HR	RBI	SB	Avg.
1981	Chicago (NL)	C	56	180	14	46	5	1	4	21	0	.256
1982	Chicago (NL)	C	130	418	41	109	20	2	12	52	0	.261
1983	Chicago (NL)	C	151	510	56	138	31	2	24	84	0	.271
1984	Chicago (NL)	C	150	523	55	134	24	2	19	94	5	.256
1985	Chicago (NL)	C	142	482	47	112	30	0	17	58	1	.232
1986	Chicago (NL)	C	148	528	61	132	27	2	21	74	0	.250
	Totals		777	2641	274	671	137	9	97	383	6	.254

SHAWON DUNSTON 24 6-1 175 Bats R Throws R

Nation's No. 1 draft pick in 1982 has been brought along slowly by the Cubs, and it began paying off last year . . . Shawon was drafted ahead of Dwight Gooden, which isn't surprising, since he has the better arm . . . Can throw with any shortstop in the game and has the tools to be the greatest all-around player at his position . . . Will pop the ball without many strikeouts for a young hitter . . . Born March 21, 1963, in Brooklyn, N.Y. . . . Nicknamed "Thunder Pup" . . . Earned No. 1 draft distinction after batting .790 and going 37-for-37 in stolen bases as a high-school senior . . . Batted above .300 first three minor-league seasons . . . Joined Cubs to stay in 1985 and enjoyed solid full season last year . . . Topped club in doubles and was impressive afield with a howitzer arm . . . Ozzie, look out!

Year	Club	Pos.	G	AB	R	H	2B	3B	HR	RBI	SB	Avg.
1985	Chicago (NL)	SS	74	250	40	65	12	4	4	18	11	.260
1986	Chicago (NL)	SS	150	581	66	145	36	3	17	68	13	.250
	Totals		224	831	106	210	48	7	21	86	24	.253

RICK SUTCLIFFE 30 6-7 215 Bats L Throws R

A nightmarish 1986 probably made Cubs regret they signed the free agent to a five-year, $9.5-million contract following a Cy Young Award season in 1984 . . . The fact remains everything went right for Rick in 1984 and little has gone his way since . . . Without him, though, the Cubs wouldn't have won the division that year, so it was fun while it lasted . . . His 1985 problems can be attributed to injuries, but it was more than that during a woeful 1986 . . . Born June 21, 1956, in Independence, Mo. . . . Cubs gave up outfielders Joe Carter and Mel Hall and pitchers Don Schulze and Darryl Banks to get Sutcliffe, Ron Hassey, George Frazier and Pookie Bernstine from Cleveland in June 1984 . . . It looked like a steal when he went 16-1 during the title drive, but Carter led the American League in RBI last year . . . Rookie of the Year with Dodgers in 1979.

Year	Club	G	IP	W	L	Pct.	SO	BB	H	ERA
1976	Los Angeles.	1	5	0	0	.000	3	1	2	0.00
1978	Los Angeles.	2	2	0	0	.000	0	1	2	0.00
1979	Los Angeles.	39	242	17	10	.630	117	97	217	3.46
1980	Los Angeles.	42	110	3	9	.250	59	55	122	5.56
1981	Los Angeles.	14	47	2	2	.500	16	20	41	4.02
1982	Cleveland	34	216	14	8	.636	142	98	174	2.96
1983	Cleveland	36	243⅓	17	11	.607	160	102	251	4.29
1984	Cleveland	15	94⅓	4	5	.444	58	46	111	5.15
1984	Chicago (NL)	20	150⅓	16	1	.941	155	39	123	2.69
1985	Chicago (NL)	20	130	8	8	.500	102	44	119	3.18
1986	Chicago (NL)	28	176⅔	5	14	.263	122	96	166	4.64
	Totals	251	1416⅔	86	68	.558	934	599	1328	3.84

LEE SMITH 29 6-6 225 **Bats R Throws R**

Shattered Bruce Sutter's club career saves record last year during fourth consecutive banner season in bullpen . . . His high heat and size make him an intimidator on the mound . . . Majors' outstanding reliever last July with a 2-1 record and eight saves . . . Finished strong with 11 total saves in August and September to soar past Sutter . . . Born Dec. 4, 1957, in Jamestown, La. . . . He was unspectacular in the minors, but was switched to the bullpen and blossomed down the stretch with the 1982 Cubs, yielding one earned run in his final 22 relief appearances . . . One year later, he registered 29 saves in 32 opportunities and made fans forget Sutter . . . Registered 31 saves in 1986, giving him career total of 144 . . . Cubs' second-round pick in 1975.

Year	Club	G	IP	W	L	Pct.	SO	BB	H	ERA
1980	Chicago (NL)	18	22	2	0	1.000	17	14	21	2.86
1981	Chicago (NL)	40	67	3	6	.333	50	31	57	3.49
1982	Chicago (NL)	72	117	2	5	.286	99	37	105	2.69
1983	Chicago (NL)	66	103⅓	4	10	.286	91	41	70	1.65
1984	Chicago (NL)	69	101	9	7	.563	86	35	98	3.65
1985	Chicago (NL)	65	97⅔	7	4	.636	112	32	87	3.04
1986	Chicago (NL)	66	90⅓	9	9	.500	93	42	69	3.09
	Totals	396	598⅓	36	41	.468	548	232	507	2.89

SCOTT SANDERSON 30 6-5 200 **Bats R Throws R**

Injuries have retarded a promising career, but he showed flashes of brilliance last year . . . Was relatively injury-free following two seasons of problems . . . Overcame back spasms in 1984 to pitch well down the stretch and help the club win a division crown . . . Born July 22, 1956, in Dearborn, Mich. . . . Attended Vanderbilt and starred on 1976 U.S. Pan American Games squad . . . Flourished with Expos in 1980, but hasn't matched that 16-win season . . . Joined Cubs in three-way deal with Expos and Padres, the latter acquiring Carmelo Martinez, Fritz Connally and Craig Lefferts from Chicago . . . Victim of tough luck and injury in 1985, but has the potential for great success if he ever puts it all together.

Year	Club	G	IP	W	L	Pct.	SO	BB	H	ERA
1978	Montreal	10	61	4	2	.667	50	21	52	2.51
1979	Montreal	34	168	9	8	.529	138	54	148	3.43
1980	Montreal	33	211	16	11	.593	125	56	206	3.11
1981	Montreal	22	137	9	7	.563	77	31	122	2.96
1982	Montreal	32	224	12	12	.500	158	58	212	3.46
1983	Montreal	18	81⅓	6	7	.462	55	20	98	4.65
1984	Chicago (NL)	24	140⅔	8	5	.615	76	24	140	3.14
1985	Chicago (NL)	19	121	5	6	.455	80	27	100	3.12
1986	Chicago (NL)	37	169⅔	9	11	.450	124	37	165	4.19
	Totals	229	1313⅔	78	69	.531	883	328	1243	3.40

DENNIS ECKERSLEY 32 6-2 195 Bats R Throws R

Like Scott Sanderson, his contribution to the 1984 title was significant, yet overshadowed by Rick Sutcliffe's . . . Joined Cubs with Mike Brumley in May 1984 swap with Boston for Bill Buckner and was 10-8 with 3.03 ERA rest of the way for champs . . . His best month last year was July, when he went 3-2 with a 2.57 ERA, but his season results matched the club's mediocrity . . . Born Oct. 3, 1954, in Oakland . . . For only the third time in 13 major-league seasons, he wasn't a winner in 1986 . . . Went 8-3 down the stretch for the Cubs in 1984 . . . Became Boston's first 20-game winner in seven years in 1978 . . . Fired a 1-0 no-hitter over the Angels for the Indians in 1977 . . . In 1975, he didn't yield an earned run in his first 28⅔ innings, a major-league rookie record.

Year	Club	G	IP	W	L	Pct.	SO	BB	H	ERA
1975	Cleveland	34	187	13	7	.650	152	90	147	2.60
1976	Cleveland	36	199	13	12	.520	200	78	155	3.44
1977	Cleveland	33	247	14	13	.519	191	54	214	3.53
1978	Boston	35	268	20	8	.714	162	71	258	2.99
1979	Boston	33	247	17	10	.630	150	59	234	2.99
1980	Boston	30	198	12	14	.462	121	44	188	4.27
1981	Boston	23	154	9	8	.529	79	35	160	4.27
1982	Boston	33	224⅓	13	13	.500	127	43	228	3.73
1983	Boston	28	176⅓	9	13	.409	77	39	223	5.61
1984	Boston	9	64⅔	4	4	.500	33	13	71	5.01
1984	Chicago (NL)	24	160⅓	10	8	.556	81	36	152	3.03
1985	Chicago (NL)	25	169⅓	11	7	.611	117	19	145	3.08
1986	Chicago (NL)	33	201	6	11	.353	137	43	226	4.57
	Totals	376	2496	151	128	.541	1627	624	2401	3.67

TOP PROSPECTS

GREG MADDUX 20 6-0 150 Bats R Throws R

Was sharp in Triple-A, but went 2-4 with 5.52 ERA for Cubs in September . . . Regarded as a great competitor, he was 10-1 with a 3.02 ERA for Iowa (AAA) after going 4-3 with a 2.69 ERA for Pittsfield (AA) . . . On Sept. 29, he had the distinction of beating older brother Mike of the Phillies, 8-3, in the first matchup of brothers since the Niekros clashed in 1982 . . . Went 13-9 with a 3.19 ERA at Peoria (A) in 1985 . . . Born April 14, 1966, in San Angelo, Tex.

RAFAEL PALMEIRO 22 6-0 180 **Bats L Throws R**
Groomed as Gary Matthews' successor in left field, this power-hitting youngster may be ready to make the jump from Double-A to the parent club . . . An All-American at Mississippi State, where he was overshadowed by Will Clark . . . First-round pick (No. 22 overall) of Cubs in 1985 . . . Blossomed last year at Pittsfield, leading league in hits (156), RBI (95) and total bases (225) while batting .306 . . . Earned Eastern League MVP honors . . . Showed promise with three homers and 12 RBI in 22 games with Cubs . . . Born Sept. 24, 1964, in Havana, Cuba.

MANAGER GENE MICHAEL: Replaced Jim Frey on June 13 and guided club to 46-56 record the rest of the way . . . Left Yankees for contract to manage Cubs through 1987 . . . Served Yankees as third-base coach after managing them in 1981 and 1982 . . . Also served as Yankee general manager prior to becoming club's field boss . . . Won first-half title in strike-shortened 1981 season, but never managed in playoffs because Bob Lemon replaced him on Sept. 6 . . . Born June 2, 1938, in Kent, Ohio . . . Attended Kent State and signed with Pirates as an infielder . . . Traded to Dodgers with Bob Bailey for Maury Wills prior to 1967 season . . . One year later, he was sold to Yankees . . . Regular shortstop for Pinstripers from 1969-73 and he was among the most popular players on club . . . Concluded major-league career with Tigers in 1975, posting .229 lifetime average in 973 games . . . Won 1979 International League pennant with Columbus (AAA) in only season as minor-league manager . . . Has record of 185-187 in the majors.

GREATEST ALL-TIME ROOKIE

Despite a lengthy tradition and an abundance of stars, the Cubs haven't boasted many knockout rookies. The overwhelming choice as top rookie is Billy Williams, who broke in big in 1961.

Sweet-swinging Billy earned Rookie-of-the-Year distinction that season by belting 20 doubles, seven triples and 25 homers. He batted .278 with 86 RBI.

In 1935, a 19-year-old youngster off the Chicago sandlots broke in and quickly became a favorite of the fans. Phil Cavarretta had 28 doubles, 12 triples, 82 RBI and hit .275.

Gene Baker played all 154 games at shortstop in 1954, contributing 19 homers, 79 RBI and a .275 average. Second baseman Ken Hubbs batted .260 and was Rookie of the Year in 1962.

The most significant pitching performance by a Northside rookie was registered in 1906 by Jack Pfiester, who was 19-9 with a 1.56 ERA and four shutouts.

ALL-TIME CUB SEASON RECORDS

BATTING: Rogers Hornsby, .380, 1929
HRs: Hack Wilson, 56, 1930
RBIs: Hack Wilson, 190, 1930
STEALS: Frank Chance, 67, 1903
WINS: Mordecai Brown, 29, 1908
STRIKEOUTS: Ferguson Jenkins, 274, 1970

MONTREAL EXPOS

TEAM DIRECTORY: Chairman: Charles Bronfman; Pres.-Vice Chairman-Chief Exec. Off.: John McHale; Pres.-Chief Oper. Off.: Claude Brochu; VP-GM: Murray Cook; VP-Baseball Adm.: Bill Stoneman; Group VP: Pierre Gauvreau; Dirs. Pub. Rel.: Monique Giroux, Richard Griffin; Mgr.: Bob (Buck) Rodgers. Home: Olympic Stadium (59,149). Field distances: 325, l.f. line; 375, l.c.; 404, c.f.; 375, r.c.; 325, r.f. line. Spring training: West Palm Beach, Fla.

SCOUTING REPORT

HITTING: The uncertain status of Tim Raines, Andre Dawson and Tim Wallach during the winter months created a lot of concern

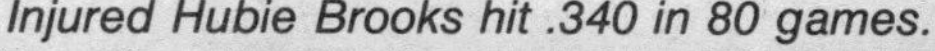

Injured Hubie Brooks hit .340 in 80 games.

about the Expos' offense, which ranked 10th in the NL in runs (637) last year. Obviously, the makeup of the attack will be altered drastically if Raines and Dawson, ineligible to re-sign with the Expos until May 1, take their licks elsewhere.

Raines, the cornerstone of the Expos' offense because of his ability to reach base (.413 on-base percentage) and steal bases (70), will be replaced by Dave Collins. With the loss of Raines and Dawson, a return to top form by Hubie Brooks becomes even more vital. Last season, Brooks was batting .340 after 80 games before a thumb injury shelved him. Also, Mike Fitzgerald was enjoying his best major-league season before breaking his finger.

Tim Wallach (.233, 18 homers, 71 RBI) was on the trading block, but his pop might be needed. Mitch Webster (.290, 8, 49) is solidly entrenched in center and Andres Galarraga (.271, 10, 42) is a comer at first base.

PITCHING: This staff simply isn't as formidable as it was when Charlie Lea, Joe Hesketh and Bryn Smith were in good health. Whatever they might be able to contribute in 1987 would be a bonus for a rebuilt rotation that includes starters Floyd Youmans (13-12, 3.53), Andy McGaffigan (10-5, 2.65), Bob Sebra (5-5, 3.55) and Jay Tibbs (7-9, 3.97).

The strength of this staff is the bullpen, where Jeff Reardon (7-9, 3.94, 35 saves) continues as one of the premier relievers in the game and Tim Burke (9-7, 2.93, 4 saves) is outstanding in a set-up role.

FIELDING: The club's .979 fielding percentage tied for third in the league last year, so defense isn't an area of primary concern. Vance Law made only three errors in 94 games at second base and Galarraga performed well as a rookie at first base, so the right side is solid. Dawson long has been among the premier outfielders in the game, so his absence could affect the outer defense.

OUTLOOK: This is a team in a state of flux. It didn't win big when it had superstars like Gary Carter, Steve Rogers, Raines and Dawson and now it may have to learn to win without them.

It all seemed to fall apart at midseason last year, when injuries turned Montreal from a contender into a pretender. The Expos were 46-38 and chasing the Mets at the All-Star break, but slumped to 32-45 thereafter. The dive coincided with Brooks' injury, but it remains to be seen if he'd be as productive at the plate without Dawson and Raines. Buck Rodgers' Expos look like they'll finish a lot closer to last than first.

MONTREAL EXPOS 1987 ROSTER

MANAGER Buck Rodgers
Coaches—Larry Bearnarth, Ron Hansen, Ken Macha, Jackie Moore, Bobby Winkles

PITCHERS

No.	Name	1986 Club	W-L	IP	SO	ERA	B-T	Ht.	Wt.	Born
52	Brown, Curt	Indianapolis	11-3	95	51	3.21	R-R	6-2	175	1/15/60 Ft. Lauderdale, FL
		Montreal	0-1	12	4	3.00				
44	Burke, Tim	Montreal	9-7	101	82	2.93	R-R	6-3	200	2/19/59 Omaha, NE
57	Cole, Rodger	Indianapolis	12-4	159	75	3.29	R-R	5-7	175	3/21/61 Ann Arbor, MI
38	Hesketh, Joe	Montreal	6-5	83	67	5.01	L-L	6-2	170	2/15/59 Lackawanna, NY
59	Holman, Brian	Jacksonville	11-9	158	118	5.14	R-R	6-4	185	1/25/65 Denver, CO
—	*Lea, Charlie	Montreal	Disabled List				R-R	6-4	205	12/25/56 France
22	McClure, Bob	Milwaukee	2-1	16	11	3.86	R-L	5-11	180	4/29/53 Oakland, CA
		Montreal	2-5	63	42	3.02				
27	McGaffigan, Andy	Montreal	10-5	143	104	2.65	R-R	6-3	195	10/25/56 W. Palm Beach, FL
49	Parrett, Jeff	Indianapolis	2-5	69	76	4.96	R-R	6-3	200	8/26/61 Indianapolis, IN
		Montreal	0-1	20	21	4.87				
41	Reardon, Jeff	Montreal	7-9	89	67	3.94	R-R	6-0	200	10/1/55 Dalton, MA
51	St. Claire, Randy	Indianapolis	5-7	99	72	3.99	R-R	6-2	190	8/23/60 Glens Falls, NY
		Montreal	2-0	19	21	2.37				
48	Sebra, Bob	Indianapolis	9-2	126	91	3.43	R-R	6-2	185	12/11/61 Ridgewood, NJ
		Montreal	5-5	91	66	3.55				
28	Smith, Bryn	Montreal	10-8	187	105	3.94	R-R	6-2	205	8/11/55 Marietta, GA
—	Smith, Mike	Den.-Ind.	6-3	77	50	5.40	R-R	6-1	200	2/23/61 Jackson, MS
		Cincinnati	0-0	3	1	13.50				
50	Tibbs, Jay	Montreal	7-9	190	117	3.97	R-R	6-1	180	1/4/62 Birmingham, AL
46	Valdez, Sergio	W. Palm Beach	16-6	146	107	2.47	R-R	6-1	180	9/7/64 Dominican Republic
		Montreal	0-4	25	20	6.84				
17	Youmans, Floyd	Montreal	13-12	219	202	3.53	R-R	6-0	190	5/11/64 Tampa, FL

CATCHERS

No.	Name	1986 Club	H	HR	RBI	Pct.	B-T	Ht.	Wt.	Born
21	Bilardello, Dann	Indianapolis	3	0	0	.600	R-R	6-0	195	5/26/59 Santa Cruz, CA
		Montreal	37	4	17	.194				
20	Fitzgerald, Mike	Indianapolis	11	0	4	.344	R-R	6-0	190	7/13/60 Long Beach, CA
		Montreal	59	6	37	.282				
—	Stefaro, John	Baltimore	28	2	13	.233	L-R	5-8	184	9/22/59 Sumter, SC
		Rochester	16	2	7	.258				
11	Tejada, Wilfredo	Jacksonville	104	13	46	.272	R-R	6-0	180	11/12/62 Dom. Republic
		Montreal	6	0	2	.240				

INFIELDERS

No.	Name	1986 Club	H	HR	RBI	Pct.	B-T	Ht.	Wt.	Born
56	Beltre, Esteban	W. Palm Beach	69	1	20	.242	R-R	5-10	155	12/26/67 Dom. Republic
7	Brooks, Hubie	Montreal	104	14	58	.340	R-R	6-0	190	9/24/56 Los Angeles, CA
9	Candaele, Casey	Indianapolis	145	2	43	.302	B-R	5-9	160	1/12/61 Lompoc, CA
		Montreal	24	0	6	.231				
16	Foley, Tom	Phi.-Mon.	70	1	23	.266	L-R	6-1	175	9/9/59 Columbus, GA
14	Galarraga, Andres	Montreal	87	10	42	.271	R-R	6-3	230	6/18/61 Venezuela
6	Johnson, Wallace	Indianapolis	58	0	26	.258	B-R	5-11	180	12/25/56 Gary, IN
		Montreal	36	1	10	.283				
2	Law, Vance	Montreal	81	5	44	.225	R-R	6-1	190	10/1/56 Boise, ID
54	Reynolds, Jeff	Jacksonville	149	29	113	.268	R-R	6-1	194	1/27/60 Charleston, WV
12	Rivera, Luis	Indianapolis	100	7	43	.246	R-R	5-9	165	1/3/64 Puerto Rico
		Montreal	34	0	13	.205				
29	Wallach, Tim	Montreal	112	18	71	.233	R-R	6-3	200	9/14/57 Huntington Park, CA

OUTFIELDERS

No.	Name	1986 Club	H	HR	RBI	Pct.	B-T	Ht.	Wt.	Born
—	Collins, Dave	Detroit	113	1	27	.270	B-L	5-10	175	10/20/52 Rapid City, SD
—	Moore, Bill	Indianapolis	104	23	82	.256	R-L	6-1	190	10/10/60 Los Angeles, CA
		Montreal	2	0	0	.167				
55	Powell, Alonzo	W. Palm Beach	25	4	18	.329	R-R	6-2	190	12/12/64 San Francisco, CA
		Jacksonville	121	15	80	.329				
—	Simonson, Bob	Beloit	145	27	96	.277	R-R	6-2	226	5/30/64 Grand Rapids, MI
23	Webster, Mitch	Montreal	167	8	49	.290	B-L	6-1	185	5/16/59 Larned, KS
3	Winningham, Herm	Indianapolis	54	4	24	.269	L-R	5-11	180	12/1/61 Orangeburg, SC
		Monteal	40	4	11	.216				
25	Wright, George	Texas	23	2	7	.217	B-R	6-0	190	12/22/58 Oklahoma City, OK
		Montreal	22	0	5	.188				
		Indianapolis	17	5	21	.327				

*Free agent at press time listed with 1986 team

EXPO PROFILES

HUBIE BROOKS 30 6-0 190 Bats R Throws R

Shortstop was heading for finest season before a damaged left thumb placed a damper on his and Expos' year . . . At the All-Star break, Hubie was in contention for the batting title, had 58 RBI and led the league with a .569 slugging percentage . . . Enjoyed a solid April and took off with a .341 May, earning NL Player-of-the-Month honors with seven homers and 24 RBI . . . Batting .333 at All-Star break . . . Had surgery to repair torn ligaments in thumb on Aug. 3 . . . Born Sept. 24, 1956, in Los Angeles . . . Teamed with Bob Horner at Arizona State, where he was an All-American shortstop . . . Mets' first-round pick in 1978 enjoyed excellent rookie season as third baseman in 1981 . . . Joined Expos with Mike Fitzgerald, Herm Winningham and Floyd Youmans in Gary Carter trade of December 1984.

Year	Club	Pos.	G	AB	R	H	2B	3B	HR	RBI	SB	Avg.
1980	New York (NL)	3B	24	81	8	25	2	1	1	10	1	.309
1981	New York (NL)	3B-OF-SS	98	358	34	110	21	2	4	38	9	.307
1982	New York (NL)	3B	126	457	40	114	21	2	2	40	6	.249
1983	New York (NL)	3B-2B	150	586	53	147	18	4	5	58	6	.251
1984	New York (NL)	3B-SS	153	561	61	159	23	2	16	73	6	.283
1985	Montreal	SS	156	605	67	163	34	7	13	100	6	.269
1986	Montreal	SS	80	306	50	104	18	5	14	58	4	.340
	Totals		787	2954	313	822	137	23	55	377	38	.278

TIM WALLACH 29 6-3 200 Bats R Throws R

A productive major-league player, but has yet to put it all together after showing signs in 1982 . . . Expos moved Larry Parrish to make room for this slugging third baseman, but Parrish has been the more productive player in recent years . . . Rarely missed a game last year despite assorted injuries . . . Has hit poorly two of the last three seasons after being in .260s . . . Born Sept. 14, 1957, in Huntington Park, Cal. . . . College Player of the Year in 1979, leading Cal State-Fullerton to national title and batting .398 with 23 homers and 102 RBI . . . Expos' No. 1 draft pick that year made it to bigs one season later after 36-homer, 124-RBI outburst at Denver (AAA) . . . A streaky hitter who has yet to develop consistency.

Year	Club	Pos.	G	AB	R	H	2B	3B	HR	RBI	SB	Avg.
1980	Montreal	OF-1B	5	11	1	2	0	0	1	2	0	.182
1981	Montreal	OF-1B-3B	71	212	19	50	9	1	4	13	0	.236
1982	Montreal	3B-OF-1B	158	596	89	160	31	3	28	97	6	.268
1983	Montreal	3B	156	581	54	156	33	3	19	70	0	.269
1984	Montreal	3B-SS	160	582	55	143	25	4	18	72	3	.246
1985	Montreal	3B	155	569	70	148	36	3	22	81	9	.260
1986	Montreal	3B	134	480	50	112	22	1	18	71	8	.233
	Totals		839	3031	338	771	156	15	110	406	26	.254

MIKE FITZGERALD 26 6-0 198 Bats R Throws R

Was enjoying his finest season when a fractured right index finger sidelined him the final two months . . . Had a .360 June and was on a 75-RBI pace when injury sidelined him . . . It marked second straight year with Expos that Fitz started fast only to have physical problems ruin things . . . Born July 13, 1960, in Long Beach, Cal. . . . Under considerable pressure when he replaced All-Star Gary Carter as club's catcher in 1985 following winter swap with Mets . . . Through May 10, he'd started all 25 games and was batting .303 before nagging injuries took toll . . . Knee surgery knocked him out in September . . . Club would like to see what he'd do if healthy a full year . . . Had a .995 fielding percentage as a Met rookie in 1984.

Year	Club	Pos.	G	AB	R	H	2B	3B	HR	RBI	SB	Avg.
1983	New York (NL)	C	8	20	1	2	0	0	1	2	0	.200
1984	New York (NL)	C	112	360	20	87	15	1	2	33	1	.242
1985	Montreal	C	108	295	25	61	7	1	5	34	5	.207
1986	Montreal	C	73	209	20	59	13	1	6	37	3	.282
	Totals		301	884	66	209	35	3	14	106	9	.236

MITCH WEBSTER 27 6-1 185 Bats S Throws L

A tremendous finish last year justified club's faith in staying with him through a ragged start . . . Batting .258 at midseason, he was ignited by a .353 July, including five hits at Atlanta on July 6 . . . Center fielder followed with a .330 August and soon ranked among the league leaders, flirting with .300 . . . Also roared past Juan Samuel and Tim Raines to take NL lead in triples . . . The only thing he didn't do was hit home runs . . . Born May 16, 1959, in Larned, Kan. . . . Drafted by Dodgers in 1977 and went to Blue Jays in 1979 minor-league draft . . . Acquired by Expos from Syracuse (AAA) in 1985 and has been a pleasant surprise.

Year	Club	Pos.	G	AB	R	H	2B	3B	HR	RBI	SB	Avg.
1983	Toronto	OF	11	11	2	2	0	0	0	0	0	.182
1984	Toronto	OF-1B	26	22	9	5	2	1	0	4	0	.227
1985	Toronto	OF	4	1	0	0	0	0	0	0	0	.000
1985	Montreal	OF	74	212	32	58	8	2	11	30	15	.274
1986	Montreal	OF	151	576	89	167	31	13	8	49	36	.290
	Totals		266	822	132	232	41	16	19	83	51	.282

ANDRES GALARRAGA 25 6-3 230 — Bats R Throws R

Promising start to rookie season was halted by injuries, but Expos harbor high hopes for this blossoming slugger . . . Had eight homers and was leading all NL rookies in RBI with 25 when he suffered knee injury that required arthroscopic surgery July 10 . . . Was activated Aug. 19, only to be re-disabled the following day after pulling muscles in his rib cage . . . Returned to action Sept. 4 . . . Despite his size, he's a solid defensive first baseman who possesses excellent quickness, earning him the nickname "Gran Gato" or "Big Cat" in Venezuela . . . Born June 18, 1961, in Caracas, Venezuela . . . Signed by Expos as free agent in 1979, on recommendation of Felipe Alou . . . Had 27 homers and 87 RBI for Jacksonville (AA) in 1984 and 25 homers and 87 RBI for Indianapolis (AAA) in 1985, so Expos are looking for those kind of numbers from him in 1987.

Year	Club	Pos.	G	AB	R	H	2B	3B	HR	RBI	SB	Avg.
1985	Montreal	1B	24	75	9	14	1	0	2	4	1	.187
1986	Montreal	1B	105	321	39	87	13	0	10	42	6	.271
	Totals		129	396	48	101	14	0	12	46	7	.255

DAVE COLLINS 34 5-10 175 — Bats S Throws L

Expos signed speedy veteran as free agent Nov. 10 as insurance against loss of Andre Dawson and Tim Raines . . . Playing for eighth major-league club and fourth in the last four seasons . . . Looms as starter in left for Expos . . . Saw limited action with Tigers in 1986, but did steal 27 bases . . . Has always thrived on Astroturf surfaces, so he should enjoy playing at Olympic Stadium . . . Hit .308 with league-leading 15 triples and 60 stolen bases for Blue Jays in 1984, then was dealt to Oakland that winter . . . Born Oct. 20, 1952, in Rapid City, S.D. . . . Attended Mesa (Ariz.) Community College . . . Angels picked him in first round of Secondary phase of 1972 draft. . . . A journeyman who can't possibly fill shoes of Raines, the NL's batting champion and top table-setter.

Year	Club	Pos.	G	AB	R	H	2B	3B	HR	RBI	SB	Avg.
1975	California	OF	93	319	41	85	13	4	3	29	24	.266
1976	California	OF	99	365	45	96	12	1	4	28	32	.263
1977	Seattle	OF	120	402	46	96	9	3	5	28	25	.239
1978	Cincinnati	OF	102	102	13	22	1	0	0	7	7	.216
1979	Cincinnati	OF-1B	122	396	59	126	16	4	3	35	16	.318
1980	Cincinnati	OF	144	551	94	167	20	4	3	35	79	.303
1981	Cincinnati	OF	95	360	63	98	18	6	3	23	26	.272
1982	New York (AL)	OF-1B	111	348	41	88	12	3	3	25	13	.253
1983	Toronto	OF-1B	118	402	55	109	12	4	1	34	31	.271
1984	Toronto	OF-1B	128	441	59	136	24	15	2	44	60	.308
1985	Oakland	OF	112	379	52	95	16	4	4	29	29	.251
1986	Detroit	OF	124	419	44	113	18	2	1	27	27	.270
	Totals		1368	4484	612	1231	171	50	32	344	369	.275

FLOYD YOUMANS 22 6-0 190 — Bats R Throws R

Pitched well enough last year to win a ton of games, but was victimized by poor support . . . Great hits-to-innings ratio and a good strikeout pitcher . . . Won once from July 17 to Sept. 2, receiving one run of support in three losses . . . Had 1.99 ERA in September, but only a 2-2 record to show for it . . . Best month was July, when he went 3-1 with a 2.08 ERA . . . Pitched a one-hitter, a two-hitter and a pair of three-hitters . . . Born May 11, 1964, in Tampa . . . A boyhood chum of Dwight Gooden until family moved to California . . . Drafted No. 2 behind Gooden by Mets in 1982 . . . Swapped to Expos in Gary Carter deal . . . Struck out 404 batters in 422 minor-league innings.

Year	Club	G	IP	W	L	Pct.	SO	BB	H	ERA
1985	Montreal	14	77	4	3	.571	54	49	57	2.45
1986	Montreal	33	219	13	12	.520	202	118	145	3.53
	Totals	47	296	17	15	.531	256	167	202	3.25

TIM BURKE 28 6-3 200 — Bats R Throws R

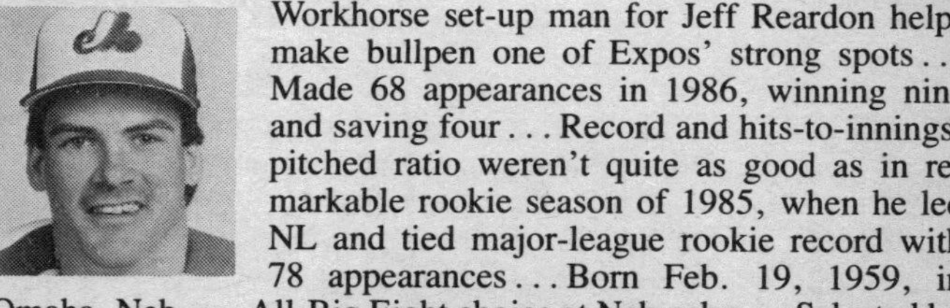

Workhorse set-up man for Jeff Reardon helps make bullpen one of Expos' strong spots . . . Made 68 appearances in 1986, winning nine and saving four . . . Record and hits-to-innings-pitched ratio weren't quite as good as in remarkable rookie season of 1985, when he led NL and tied major-league rookie record with 78 appearances . . . Born Feb. 19, 1959, in Omaha, Neb. . . . All-Big Eight choice at Nebraska . . . Selected by Pirates in second round of 1980 draft . . . Traded to Yankees along with three other minor-leaguers in Lee Mazzilli deal prior to 1983 season . . . Came to Expos' organization in steal of a minor-league deal that sent Pat Rooney to Yanks one year later . . . Went 11-8 with 3.49 ERA for Indianapolis (AAA) in 1984, then surprised everybody when he earned spot with parent club as non-roster invitee the following spring . . . Valuable, durable pitcher on a staff with more than its share of injury problems.

Year	Club	G	IP	W	L	Pct.	SO	BB	H	ERA
1985	Montreal	78	120⅓	9	4	.692	87	44	86	2.39
1986	Montreal	68	101⅓	9	7	.562	82	46	103	2.93
	Totals	146	221⅔	18	11	.620	169	90	189	2.64

JEFF REARDON 31 6-0 200 **Bats R Throws R**

A consistently outstanding fireman . . . Only he and Goose Gossage have registered at least 20 saves each of the last five years . . . NL Pitcher of the Month for May with a 3-0 record, 10 saves and a 1.25 ERA in 13 games . . . Notched seven saves in September to battle Cards' Todd Worrell for league title down to the wire . . . Finished with 35 last season . . . Rolaids NL Reliever of the Year in 1985 with a career-high 41 saves . . . Born Oct. 1, 1955, in Dalton, Mass. . . . Club's all-time saves leader and 10th on all-time list with 162 . . . Boyhood idol was Tom Seaver, who was traded by Mets one day after Jeff signed with New York out of the U. of Massachusetts . . . Went 94 games without a loss for Mets during 1980 and 1981, winning seven and saving 24 . . . Traded to Expos with Dan Norman for Ellis Valentine in May 1981.

Year	Club	G	IP	W	L	Pct.	SO	BB	H	ERA
1979	New York (NL)	18	21	1	2	.333	10	9	12	1.71
1980	New York (NL)	61	110	8	7	.533	101	47	96	2.62
1981	N.Y. (NL)-Mont.	43	70	3	0	1.000	49	21	48	2.19
1982	Montreal	75	109	7	4	.636	86	36	87	2.06
1983	Montreal	66	92	7	9	.438	78	44	87	3.03
1984	Montreal	68	87	7	7	.500	79	37	70	2.90
1985	Montreal	63	87⅔	2	8	.200	67	26	68	3.18
1986	Montreal	62	89	7	9	.438	67	26	83	3.94
	Totals	456	665⅔	42	46	.477	537	246	551	2.80

JAY TIBBS 25 6-1 180 **Bats R Throws R**

Began the season with 3-0 record and 1.25 ERA in April, but then faltered . . . After 20 starts, he had 2-7 record and 11 no-decisions, sealing a mediocre campaign for a promising pitcher . . . Briefly demoted to bullpen before rejoining rotation on July 8 . . . Non-support established prior to last year . . . In 16 losses for Reds in 1985, he received 32 runs . . . Born Jan. 4, 1962, in Birmingham, Ala. . . . Drafted by Mets in second round of June 1980 talent pool . . . Combined with Dwight Gooden to lead Lynchburg (A) to Carolina crown in 1983, going 14-8 with a 2.82 ERA . . . Traded to Reds in 1984 and joined Expos with John Stuper, Andy McGaffigan and Dann Bilardello in deal that sent Bill Gullickson and Sal Butera to Reds prior to last season.

Year	Club	G	IP	W	L	Pct.	SO	BB	H	ERA
1984	Cincinnati	14	100⅔	6	2	.750	40	33	87	2.86
1985	Cincinnati	35	218	10	16	.385	98	83	216	3.92
1986	Montreal	35	190⅓	7	9	.438	117	70	181	3.97
	Totals	84	509	23	27	.460	255	186	484	3.73

TOP PROSPECT

BOB SEBRA 25 6-2 195 **Bats R Throws R**

When Pete Incaviglia refused to sign with the Expos out of college, this guy was one of the two players sent by Texas to Montreal for signing rights to the slugger . . . The Expos can't feel too badly after watching him dominate the Mets in two starts last September . . . The first was a shutout until Darryl Strawberry connected in the ninth, the second a two-hit shutout . . . Born Dec. 11, 1961, in Ridgewood, N.J. . . . Was 10-6 at Oklahoma City before earning a trial with the Rangers in 1985 . . . At Indianapolis (AAA) last year, he went 9-2 with a 3.43 ERA prior to his recall . . . A collegiate standout at Nebraska . . . Was 5-5 with a 3.55 ERA for Expos last season.

MANAGER BUCK RODGERS: His contract was extended through 1987 following a solid rookie season with Montreal in 1985 . . . Despite a rash of injuries and 91 different starting lineups, Expos were 84-77 that year . . . But injuries took much bigger toll in 1986 . . . Expos in second place until Hubie Brooks and Mike Fitzgerald were shelved, accounting for a horrible second half . . . Had a 46-38 record at the All-Star break . . . Signed with Expos after being Minor League Manager of the Year with Indianapolis in 1984 . . . Previously guided Brewers, taking them to a second-half title in strike-marred 1981 . . . Replaced by Harvey Kuenn following a 23-24 start in 1982 and Milwaukee won the pennant . . . Born Aug. 16, 1938, in Delaware, Ohio . . . Played in the majors for nine years, all with the Angels,

as a catcher . . . Lifetime average of .232 . . . Has 286-282 record as major-league manager.

GREATEST ALL-TIME ROOKIE

Expos' all-time rookie honors go to Tim Raines, whose remarkable debut was denied its due by the strike of 1981 and Fernando Valenzuela's shadow. As a rookie that year, Raines batted .304 with a league-leading 71 steals in 88 games.

Gary Carter broke in with a .270 average, 17 homers and 68 RBI in 1975. Two years later, Andre Dawson made an instant impression with 19 homers, 65 RBI, a .282 average and 21 thefts.

Among the Expos' pitchers, Carl Morton had an outstanding season in 1979, the club's second year of operation. He won Rookie-of-the-Year honors in workhorse fashion, toiling 284⅔ innings and going 18-11 with a 3.60 ERA and 10 complete games.

ALL-TIME EXPO SEASON RECORDS

BATTING: Tim Raines, .334, 1986
HRs: Andre Dawson, 32, 1983
RBIs: Andre Dawson, 113, 1983
STEALS: Ron LeFlore, 97, 1980
WINS: Ross Grimsley, 20, 1978
STRIKEOUTS: Bill Stoneman, 251, 1971

NEW YORK METS

TEAM DIRECTORY: Chairman: Nelson Doubleday; Pres.: Fred Wilpon; Exec. VP-GM: Frank Cashen; VP-Baseball Oper.: Joe McIlvaine; Sr. VP-Adm.: Al Harazin; Dir. Scounting: Roland Johnson; Dir. Minor Leagues: Steve Schryver; Dir. Pub. Rel.: Jay Horwitz; Asst. GM-Trav. Sec.: Arthur Richman; Mgr.: Davey Johnson. Home: Shea Stadium (55,300). Field distances: 338, l.f. line; 371, l.c.; 410, c.f.; 371, r.c.; 338, r.f. line. Spring training: St. Petersburg, Fla.

SCOUTING REPORT

HITTING: Everything fell into place for the Mets' offense last season and there's no reason to expect a decline. World Series MVP and free-agent defector Ray Knight's clutch bat will be missed, but there's compensation in the form of newly acquired left fielder Kevin McReynolds (.288, 26 homers, 96 RBI), who ranked among the NL's power leaders with San Diego last season.

The Mets topped the National League with a .263 average and scored more runs (783) than any other NL club en route to a runaway in the NL East in 1986. This happened because Len

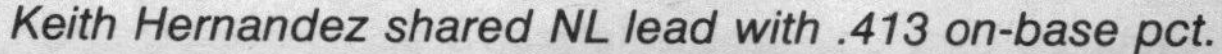

Keith Hernandez shared NL lead with .413 on-base pct.

Dykstra (.295, 8 homers, 45 RBI) and Wally Backman (.320, 1, 27) excelled at setting the table for the heart of the lineup—Keith Hernandez (.310, 13, 83), Gary Carter (.255, 24, 105) and Darryl Strawberry (.259, 27, 93).

PITCHING: Though the club's hitting was the best in the league, it was overshadowed by a pitching staff that was second to none. The Mets edged Houston for the league ERA crown at 3.11, so this young and deep staff should continue its success, despite concerns over Dwight Gooden's diminished fastball.

Gooden (17-6, 2.84), Bob Ojeda (18-5, 2.57), Ron Darling (15-6, 2.81) and Sid Fernandez (16-6, 3.52) made it virtually impossible for the world champs to suffer a lengthy losing streak. With Jesse Orosco (8-6, 2.33, 21 saves) and Roger McDowell (14-9, 3.02, 27 saves) forming a potent one-two bullpen punch, there simply isn't a weakness on the best staff in baseball.

Gooden bombed in the World Series, giving the skeptics fodder, but the bottom line is that he still topped the staff in complete games (12) and innings pitched (250) and tied Fernandez for the strikeout lead with 200. A lot of pitchers would love to have Gooden's problems and a lot of teams would love to have him pitching.

FIELDING: If there's anything average about the Mets, it's their fielding. Their .978 percentage tied five other clubs for fifth in the league and six clubs made fewer errors. However, with all that hitting and pitching, the Mets don't need a premier defense. Still, first baseman Hernandez is a vacuum cleaner at his position, Dykstra is solid in center and shortstop Rafael Santana made only one more error (16) than the Cards' Ozzie Smith, the league's defensive pacesetter.

OUTLOOK: It probably won't be as easy this time, but there's absolutely no reason to believe Davey Johnson's Mets won't break tradition and win back-to-back titles. This club made a shambles of the 1986 race en route to a 108-54 finish, then tight competition in the NL Championship Series and the World Series brought out the Mets' character and added to their confidence.

The Mets probably gave up too much raw talent for McReynolds, whose knees always will be a concern, yet he undoubtedly makes the club stronger in the heart of the batting order, filling a gap left by George Foster and Knight.

Only third base remains a question mark. If a deal isn't made, Howard Johnson, Tim Teufel and rookie Dave Magadan may share the position. Oh, well, nobody's perfect.

NEW YORK METS 1987 ROSTER

MANAGER Davey Johnson

Coaches—Bud Harrelson, Vern Hoscheit, Sam Perlozzo, Bill Robinson, Mel Stottlemyre

PITCHERS

No.	Name	1986 Club	W-L	IP	SO	ERA	B-T	Ht.	Wt.	Born
32	Anderson, Rick	Tidewater	7-2	84	56	2.68	R-R	6-0	175	12/29/56 Everett, WA
		New York (NL)	2-1	50	21	2.72				
15	Aguilera, Rick	New York (NL)	10-7	142	104	3.88	R-R	6-5	193	12/31/61 San Gabriel, CA
49	Bautista, Jose	Jackson	0-1	22	13	8.31	R-R	6-1	177	7/25/64 Dominican Republic
		Lynchburg	8-8	119	62	3.94				
38	Corbell, Charlie	Shreveport	11-6	177	69	2.95	R-R	6-1	180	11/30/60 Baytown, TX
12	Darling, Ron	New York (NL)	15-6	237	184	2.81	R-R	6-3	195	8/19/60 Honolulu, HI
45	Dobie, Reggie	Jackson	13-7	155	123	3.66	R-R	6-1	174	8/17/64 Rosedale, MS
10	Fernandez, Sid	New York (NL)	16-6	204	200	3.5	L-L	6-1	205	10/12/62 Honolulu, HI
61	Givens, Brian	Columbia	8-7	172	189	3.77	R-L	6-5	195	11/6/65 Lompoc, CA
16	Gooden, Dwight	New York (NL)	17-6	250	200	2.84	R-R	6-3	198	11/16/84 Tampa, FL
43	Mitchell, John	Tidewater	12-9	172	83	3.39	R-R	6-2	165	8/11/65 Dickson, TN
		New York (NL)	0-1	10	2	3.60				
48	Myers, Randy	Tidewater	6-7	65	79	2.35	L-L	6-1	190	9/19/62 Vancouver, WA
		New York (NL)	0-0	11	13	4.22				
42	McDowell, Roger	New York (NL)	14-9	128	65	3.02	R-R	6-1	175	12/21/60 Cincinnati, OH
19	Ojeda, Bobby	New York (NL)	18-5	217	148	2.57	L-L	6-1	190	12/17/57 Los Angeles, CA
47	Orosco, Jesse	New York (NL)	8-6	81	62	2.33	R-L	6-2	185	4/21/57 Santa Barbara, CA
39	Sisk, Doug	Tidewater	2-3	30	19	4.20	R-R	6-2	210	9/26/57 Renton, WA
		New York (NL)	4-2	71	31	3.06				
—	Walter, Gene	San Diego	2-2	98	84	3.86	L-L	6-4	201	11/22/60 Chicago, IL
46	West, Dave	Lynchburg	1-6	75	70	5.16	L-L	6-6	207	9/1/64 Memphis, TN
		Columbia	10-3	93	101	2.91				

CATCHERS

No.	Name	1986 Club	H	HR	RBI	Pct.	B-T	Ht.	Wt.	Born
8	Carter, Gary	New York (NL)	125	24	105	.255	R-R	6-2	210	4/8/54 Culver City, CA
35	Gibbons, John	Tidewater	78	3	27	.246	R-R	5-11	187	6/8/62 Great Falls, MT
		New York (NL)	9	1	1	.474				
9	Hearn, Ed	Tidewater	22	1	12	.265	R-R	6-3	215	8/23/60 Stuart, FL
		New York (NL)	36	4	10	.265				
33	Lyons, Barry	New York (NL)	0	0	2	.000	R-R	6-1	205	6/30/60 Biloxi, MS
		Tidewater	69	4	46	.295				

INFIELDERS

No.	Name	1986 Club	H	HR	RBI	Pct.	B-T	Ht.	Wt.	Born
6	Backman, Wally	New York (NL)	124	1	27	.320	B-R	5-9	160	9/22/59 Hillsboro, OR
21	Elster, Kevin	Jackson	117	2	51	.269	R-R	6-2	180	8/3/64 San Pedro, CA
		New York (NL)	5	0	0	.167				
17	Hernandez, Keith	New York (NL)	171	13	83	.310	L-L	6-0	195	10/20/53 San Francisco, CA
20	Johnson, Howard	New York (NL)	54	10	39	.245	B-R	5-10	175	11/29/60 Clearwater, FL
29	Magadan, Dave	Tidewater	147	1	64	.311	L-R	6-3	190	9/30/62 Tampa, FL
		New York (NL)	8	0	3	.444				
62	Miller, Keith	Jackson	116	5	36	.329	R-R	5-11	175	6/12/63 Midland, MI
60	Sanchez, Zoilo	Lynchburg	136	14	85	.296	R-R	6-1	175	8/27/64 Dominican Republic
3	Santana, Rafael	New York (NL)	86	1	28	.218	R-R	6-1	160	1/31/58 Dominican Republic
11	Teufel, Tim	New York (NL)	69	4	31	.247	R-R	6-0	175	7/7/58 Greenwich, CT

OUTFIELDERS

No.	Name	1986 Club	H	HR	RBI	Pct.	B-T	Ht.	Wt.	Born
35	Blocker, Terry	Tidewater	125	9	48	.288	L-L	6-2	195	8/18/59 Columbia, SC
63	Carreon, Mark	Tidewater	123	10	62	.289	R-L	6-0	170	7/19/63 Chicago, IL
4	Dykstra, Lenny	New York (NL)	127	8	45	.295	L-L	5-10	160	2/10/63 Santa Ana, CA
2	Lawton, Marcus	Lynchburg	158	4	66	.279	B-R	6-1	159	8/18/65 Gulfport, MS
13	Mazzilli, Lee	Tidewater	6	1	1	.300	B-R	6-1	185	3/25/55 New York, NY
		Pit.-NY (NL)	37	3	15	.245				
--	McReynolds, Kevin	San Diego	161	26	96	.288	R-R	6-1	207	10/16/59 Little Rock, AK
18	Strawberry, Darryl	New York (NL)	123	27	93	.259	L-L	6-6	190	3/12/62 Los Angeles, CA
1	Wilson, Mookie	Tidewater	8	0	4	.258	B-R	5-10	168	2/9/56 Bamberg, SC
		New York (NL)	110	9	45	.289				

MET PROFILES

GARY CARTER 32 6-2 210 Bats R Throws R

Extended reputation as clutch performer in 1986 by tying Astros' Glenn Davis for NL lead with 16 game-winning RBI, then continued heroics in postseason . . . Had only two hits in first 22 NL Championship Series at-bats, yet each was a game-winner . . . Had a two-homer game and a team-high nine RBI in World Series . . . Crowned a 19-RBI April with his 250th homer, tops among active catchers . . . Named as All-Star starter for sixth straight season . . . Belted 10th grand slam on July 11, making him active NL leader . . . Had 39 RBI in 36-game stretch and finished third in NL race while becoming first Met to notch two 100-RBI seasons . . . Born April 8, 1954, in Culver City, Cal. . . . Tied career high with season-ending, 13-game hitting streak . . . Tied Rusty Staub's club RBI record with 105 . . . Was about to play quarterback for UCLA when Expos drafted him in third round in 1982 . . . Joined Mets after 1984 season in trade for Hubie Brooks, Floyd Youmans, Mike Fitzgerald and Herm Winningham.

Year	Club	Pos.	G	AB	R	H	2B	3B	HR	RBI	SB	Avg.
1974	Montreal	C-OF	9	27	5	11	0	1	1	6	2	.407
1975	Montreal	OF-C-3B	144	503	58	136	20	1	17	68	5	.270
1976	Montreal	C-OF	91	311	31	68	8	1	6	38	0	.219
1977	Montreal	C-OF	154	522	86	148	29	2	31	84	5	.284
1978	Montreal	C-1B	157	533	76	136	27	1	20	72	10	.255
1979	Montreal	C	141	505	74	143	26	5	22	75	3	.283
1980	Montreal	C	154	549	76	145	25	5	29	101	3	.264
1981	Montreal	C-1B	100	374	48	94	20	2	16	68	1	.251
1982	Montreal	C	154	557	91	163	32	1	29	97	2	.293
1983	Montreal	C-1B	145	541	63	146	37	3	17	79	1	.270
1984	Montreal	C-1B	159	596	75	175	32	1	27	106	2	.294
1985	New York (NL)	C-1B-OF	149	555	83	156	17	1	32	100	1	.281
1986	New York (NL)	C-1B-3B-OF	132	490	81	125	14	2	24	105	1	.255
	Totals		1689	6063	847	1646	287	26	271	999	36	.271

LENNY DYKSTRA 24 5-10 160 Bats L Throws L

Earned big chance when Mookie Wilson was injured during the spring and made the most of it . . . His performance in first full major-league season hastened George Foster's departure and knocked Mookie out of center field . . . Topped Mets with a .304 average in NL Championship Series and won Game 3 with a ninth-inning homer . . . Continued to flourish in World Series with two more homers and a .296 mark . . . Batted .327 in April and .357 in July, lifting average to .332 by July 29 . . . An

0-for-21 slump in mid-August cost him a .300 finish... Born Feb. 10, 1963, in Santa Ana, Cal.... Mets' 12th-round selection in 1981 draft... Batted .358 with 132 runs and 105 steals for Lynchburg (A) in 1983, sharing club MVP honors with Dwight Gooden.

Year	Club	Pos.	G	AB	R	H	2B	3B	HR	RBI	SB	Avg.
1985	New York (NL)	OF	83	236	40	60	9	3	1	19	15	.254
1986	New York (NL)	OF	147	431	77	127	27	7	8	45	31	.295
	Totals		230	667	117	187	36	10	9	64	46	.280

DARRYL STRAWBERRY 25 6-6 190 Bats L Throws L

Mets are waiting patiently for "Straw" to put it all together... Getting closer to fulfilling potential in every area other than batting average ... Remarkably consistent, he has belted between 26 and 29 homers in each of first four years... His 15 game-winning RBI were second only to 16 of Gary Carter and Glenn Davis ... Only Mike Schmidt had a higher slugging percentage than his .507... He and Kirk Gibson are only players who have hit 20 homers and stolen 20 bases the last three seasons ... Born March 12, 1962, in Los Angeles... Batting .235 on May 24 before a .352 June got him going... Took .298 average into All-Star Game... Top All-Star Game vote collector, he expressed thanks with prodigious home-run exhibition... No. 1 pick in nation by Mets in 1980.

Year	Club	Pos.	G	AB	R	H	2B	3B	HR	RBI	SB	Avg.
1983	New York (NL)	OF	122	420	63	108	15	7	26	74	19	.257
1984	New York (NL)	OF	147	522	75	131	27	4	26	97	27	.251
1985	New York (NL)	OF	111	393	78	109	15	4	29	79	26	.277
1986	New York (NL)	OF	136	475	76	123	27	5	27	93	28	.259
	Totals		516	1810	292	471	84	20	108	343	100	.260

KEITH HERNANDEZ 33 6-0 195 Bats L Throws L

Peerless first baseman didn't hit for average in the postseason, but made his few hits count... In Game 7 of the World Series, his two-run single triggered a comeback from a 3-0 deficit ... Voted an All-Star Game starter despite mediocre first half... Batting .284 at the break, he went on a .343 binge thereafter to finish among leaders in several departments... Tied Tim Raines for NL on-base percentage lead at .413... Batted .368 with 26 RBI in August to spark runaway... Set club record with at least one RBI in eight straight games during August burst... Born Oct. 20, 1953, in San Francisco... Reached base in 127 of 147 games... Cardinals' 40th-round draft pick in 1971... Shared

NL MVP trophy with Willie Stargell in 1979 . . . Traded to Mets in June 1983 for Neil Allen and Rick Ownbey.

Year	Club	Pos.	G	AB	R	H	2B	3B	HR	RBI	SB	Avg.
1974	St. Louis	1B	14	34	3	10	1	2	0	2	0	.294
1975	St. Louis	1B	64	188	20	47	8	2	3	20	0	.250
1976	St. Louis	1B	129	374	54	108	21	5	7	46	4	.289
1977	St. Louis	1B	161	560	90	163	41	4	15	91	7	.291
1978	St. Louis	1B	159	542	90	138	32	4	11	64	13	.255
1979	St. Louis	1B	161	610	116	210	48	11	11	105	11	.344
1980	St. Louis	1B	159	595	111	191	39	8	16	99	14	.321
1981	St. Louis	1B-OF	103	376	65	115	27	4	8	48	12	.306
1982	St. Louis	1B-OF	160	579	79	173	33	6	7	94	19	.299
1983	St.L.-NY (NL).	1B	150	538	77	160	23	7	12	63	9	.297
1984	New York (NL)	1B	154	550	83	171	31	0	15	94	2	.311
1985	New York (NL)	1B	158	593	87	183	34	4	10	91	3	.309
1986	New York (NL)	1B	149	551	94	171	34	1	13	83	2	.310
	Totals		1721	6090	969	1840	372	58	128	900	96	.302

RON DARLING 26 6-3 195 **Bats R Throws R**

Compensated for poor NL Championship Series start with a 1-1 record and 1.53 ERA in World Series . . . Got off to a great start last season, going 6-0 in first nine outings before tasting defeat June 1 . . . Was 3-1 with 1.47 ERA and two shutouts in July . . . Posted 2.37 ERA in final 23 starts, but twice was a shutout loser . . . Involved in well-publicized scrape with Houston police, but it obviously didn't affect his work . . . Born Aug. 19, 1960, in Honolulu, Hawaii . . . Outstanding career at Yale included two years on football squad as a defensive back . . . Rangers' No. 1 pick in 1981 draft . . . Traded to Mets with Walt Terrell for Lee Mazzilli on April 1, 1982 . . . April Fool's joke was on Rangers . . . His record is gaudy 22 games above .500 after three years as full-time starter.

Year	Club	G	IP	W	L	Pct.	SO	BB	H	ERA
1983	New York (NL)	5	35⅓	1	3	.250	23	17	31	2.80
1984	New York (NL)	33	205⅔	12	9	.571	136	104	179	3.81
1985	New York (NL)	36	248	16	6	.727	167	114	214	2.90
1986	New York (NL)	34	237	15	6	.714	184	81	203	2.81
	Totals	108	726	44	24	.647	510	316	627	3.12

KEVIN McREYNOLDS 27 6-1 207 **Bats R Throws R**

Padres parted with this budding star in eight-player deal that cost Mets blue-chip outfield prospects Stanley Jefferson and Shawn Abner in December . . . Mets filled need for right-handed power hitter to protect Darryl Strawberry in lineup . . . Will move from center to left . . . Former resident in Dick Williams' doghouse flourished last season, turning a hot second half into his most productive major-league season . . . Accumulated 11 home runs and 43 RBI in August and September to vault among leaders . . . Grand slam on final weekend left him just shy of 100 RBI . . . His .504 slugging percentage ranked third in NL, behind Mike Schmidt and Strawberry . . . Born Oct. 16, 1959, in Little Rock, Ark. . . . Starred at Arkansas and Padres wisely overlooked his knee problems to draft him No. 1 in 1981 . . . Posted .376, .352 and .377 averages to prove he was too tough for minor-league pitching . . . Powerful rookie year helped San Diego win pennant in 1984 . . . Batted .300 in NL Championship Series before fractured left hand kept him out of World Series.

Year	Club	Pos.	G	AB	R	H	2B	3B	HR	RBI	SB	Avg.
1983	San Diego	OF	39	140	15	31	3	1	4	14	2	.221
1984	San Diego	OF	147	525	68	146	26	6	20	75	3	.278
1985	San Diego	OF	152	564	61	132	24	4	15	75	4	.234
1986	San Diego	OF	158	560	89	161	31	6	26	96	8	.288
	Totals		496	1789	233	470	84	17	65	260	17	.263

DWIGHT GOODEN 22 6-3 198 Bats R Throws R

Allegations that "Doctor K" lost some of his heat were rampant during 1986 season and seemed justified during woeful World Series, during which he went 0-2 with 8.00 ERA . . . Until then, however, he was solid, including a 1.06 ERA in NL Championship Series . . . Suffered by comparison to his phenomenal 1985 . . . Simply isn't judged by normal standards, so people always expect too much . . . NL Pitcher of the Month in April with 4-0 record and 1.26 ERA . . . Entered All-Star Game with 10-4 record and was 7-2 in second half, including a 3-0 August . . . Nine-game winning streak over two seasons snapped by Reds on May 11 . . . Hurled division-clinching victory over Cubs Sept. 17 . . . Became first pitcher in majors to fan 200 batters in his first three seasons . . . Born Nov. 16, 1964, in Tampa . . . Mets' first-round pick (fifth overall) in 1982 draft . . . Made jump to bigs following 19-4 season with Lynchburg (A) in 1983 . . . Faced charges of assaulting a police officer in Tampa during off-season.

Year	Club	G	IP	W	L	Pct.	SO	BB	H	ERA
1984	New York (NL)	31	218	17	9	.654	276	73	161	2.60
1985	New York (NL)	35	276⅔	24	4	.857	268	69	198	1.53
1986	New York (NL)	33	250	17	6	.739	200	80	197	2.84
	Totals	99	744⅔	58	19	.753	744	222	556	2.28

ROGER McDOWELL 26 6-1 175  **Bats R Throws R**

Enjoyed tremendous success after supplanting Jesse Orosco as top gun out of bullpen . . . Posted 14th victory on Sept. 25 and set a club record for a reliever . . . Went 4-0 with 0.69 ERA and two saves in June, becoming first Met pitcher to go 7-0 . . . Established a club record with four wins and eight saves in August . . . Yielded one hit and no runs in two NL Championship Series performances before proving human in World Series . . . Set club record with 75 appearances . . . Born Dec. 21, 1960, in Cincinnati . . . Became only third NL pitcher since 1969 to post as many as 13 wins and 20 saves in one season . . . Attended Bowling Green and was Mets' third pick in 1982 draft . . . Saved 22 games in 1986, giving him two-year total of 39.

Year	Club	G	IP	W	L	Pct.	SO	BB	H	ERA
1985	New York (NL)	62	127⅓	6	5	.545	70	37	108	2.83
1986	New York (NL)	75	128	14	9	.609	65	42	107	3.02
	Totals	137	255⅓	20	14	.588	135	79	215	2.93

BOB OJEDA 29 6-1 190 **Bats L Throws L**

Regarded by many observers as Mets' most effective and consistent starter in 1986 . . . Went 1-0 in the NL Championship Series and 1-0 in the World Series to crown storybook season . . . Became winningest Met lefty since Jerry Koosman in 1976 . . . Adjustment to NL no problem . . . His ERA never climbed above 3.00 all season . . . Was 5-0 with 1.49 ERA after first six NL games . . . Went 6-0 between June 5 and Aug. 8 . . . Runnerup to Astros' Mike Scott for league ERA title . . . Born Dec. 17, 1957, in Los Angeles . . . Signed as free agent by Red Sox in 1978 . . . Went 44-39 with Red Sox before being sent to Mets with Tom McCarthy, John Mitchell and Chris Bayer for Calvin Schiraldi, Wes Gardner, John Christensen and LaSchelle Tarver prior to last season . . . Gaining Ojeda and having Schiraldi in Boston bullpen probably won World Series for Mets . . . Out pitch is changeup.

Year	Club	G	IP	W	L	Pct.	SO	BB	H	ERA
1980	Boston	7	26	1	1	.500	12	14	39	6.92
1981	Boston	10	66	6	2	.750	28	25	50	3.14
1982	Boston	22	78⅓	4	6	.400	52	29	95	5.63
1983	Boston	29	173⅔	12	7	.632	94	73	173	4.04
1984	Boston	33	216⅔	12	12	.500	137	96	211	3.99
1985	Boston	39	157⅔	9	11	.450	102	48	166	4.00
1986	New York (NL)	32	217⅓	18	5	.783	148	52	185	2.57
	Totals	172	935⅔	62	44	.585	573	337	919	3.83

JESSE OROSCO 29 6-2 185 **Bats R Throws L**

Became first pitcher to go 3-0 in a Championship Series . . . For an encore, he didn't allow Red Sox a run in four World Series outings to regain eminence as a stopper . . . Didn't allow a run and posted three saves in April, but took a back seat to Roger McDowell until postseason . . . Had 21 saves last season and boosted club record total to 91 . . . Unscored upon in first 12 games and 18⅓ innings last year . . . Born April 21, 1957, in Santa Barbara, Cal. . . . Posted four wins and nine saves in final 27 outings . . . Twins' second choice in January 1978 draft . . . Traded to Mets with Greg Field for Jerry Koosman prior to 1979 season . . . Set club saves record of 31 in 1984.

Year	Club	G	IP	W	L	Pct.	SO	BB	H	ERA
1979	New York (NL)	18	35	1	2	.333	22	22	33	4.89
1981	New York (NL)	8	17	0	1	.000	18	6	13	1.59
1982	New York (NL)	54	109⅓	4	10	.286	89	40	92	2.72
1983	New York (NL)	62	110	13	7	.650	84	38	76	1.47
1984	New York (NL)	60	87	10	6	.625	85	34	58	2.59
1985	New York (NL)	54	79	8	6	.571	68	34	66	2.73
1986	New York (NL)	58	81	8	6	.571	62	35	64	2.33
	Totals	314	518⅓	44	38	.537	428	209	402	2.48

TOP PROSPECT

RANDY MYERS 24 6-1 190 **Bats L Throws L**

Converted from a starter into a reliever last year, he progressed to the point where he was regarded as the finest prospect in the International League (AAA) . . . Posted 6-7 record, 2.35 ERA and a dozen saves while yielding only 44 hits and fanning 79 in 65 innings at Tidewater . . . Born Sept. 19, 1962, in Vancouver, Wash. . . . Mets' first pick in June 1982 secondary phase . . . Clocked at 95 mph . . . Had no record and 4.22 ERA in 10 games as a Met last season.

MANAGER DAVEY JOHNSON: Guided a runaway division winner and established a club record with 108 victories in third year as Met manager . . . Team has shown gradual improvement every year, winning 90, 98 and 108 games . . . The 296 victories and 190 losses over last three years represent the best record in the majors over that span . . . Mets were blessed with good fortune in postseason play, but also showed charac-

ter with comeback after comeback . . . It's a tribute to him that club didn't let down after coasting most of the season . . . Born Jan. 30, 1943, in Orlando, Fla. . . . Attended Trinity and Texas A&M before launching playing career as an infielder in Orioles' system in 1962 . . . Reached bigs to stay in 1966 and was the second baseman on champion Baltimore clubs . . . Had the distinction of playing with all-time home-run greats Hank Aaron and Sadaharu Oh with Braves and Tokyo Giants . . . Belted 43 home runs for Atlanta in NL debut in 1973 . . . Won two minor-league managerial titles before taking Mets' job . . . Runnerup to Astros' Hal Lanier for NL Manager of the Year.

GREATEST ALL-TIME ROOKIE

Right-hander Tom Seaver was the Mets' top rookie, with a 16-13 record and a 2.76 ERA in 1967. Then Dwight Gooden came along with trumpets blaring in 1984, and the rest is history.

Seaver turned the Mets around and made them winners and Gooden had a similar impact on the present staff with his sensational debut, which belied his inexperience.

In 1984, Doctor K was 17-9 with a 2.60 ERA and a staggering 276 strikeouts, setting standards by which future rookie hurlers will be measured. And he did it after making the big leap from Class A to the majors.

Among the Mets' hitters, Darryl Strawberry broke in with a bang in 1983 and, like Gooden, Seaver and Jon Matlack, he was awarded Rookie-of-the-Year honors. The Straw had 26 homers, 74 RBI and 19 steals in 122 games.

ALL-TIME MET SEASON RECORDS

BATTING: Cleon Jones, .340, 1969
HRs: Dave Kingman, 37, 1976, 1982
RBIs: Rusty Staub, 105, 1975
Gary Carter, 105, 1986
STEALS: Mookie Wilson, 58, 1982
WINS: Tom Seaver, 25, 1969
STRIKEOUTS: Tom Seaver, 289, 1971

PHILADELPHIA PHILLIES

TEAM DIRECTORY: Pres.: William Y. Giles; Exec. VP: David Montgomery; VP: Paul Owens; VP-Baseball: Tony Siegle; VP-Pub. Rel.: Larry Shenk; VP-Dir. Play. Dev./Scouting: Jim Baumer; Trav. Sec.: Eddie Ferenz; Mgr.: John Felske. Home: Veterans Stadium (64,538). Field Distances: 330, l.f. line; 408, c.f.; 330, r.f. line. Spring training: Clearwater, Fla.

SCOUTING REPORT

HITTING: Philadelphia's .253 average ranked seventh in the NL last season, but it was a deceptive statistic. Only the Mets scored more runs than the Phils' 739, so offense isn't a major concern. How can it be when 1986 NL MVP Mike Schmidt (.290, 37 homers, 119 RBI) is around? And this year he'll have help from newly

Juan Samuel swiped his Phil with 42 stolen bases.

acquired Mike Easler (.302, 14, 78), the ex-Yankee who can do nothing but hit with authority.

Von Hayes (.305, 19, 98) is becoming a superstar, Juan Samuel (.266, 16, 78) can do it all on offense and Glenn Wilson (.271, 15, 84) is a vastly underrated clutch hitter, so the heart of the batting order is solid and dangerous. Imagine what this lineup could do if the shortstop could hit and if the Phils' problems in center field and behind the plate are ironed out?

PITCHING: It's much better than last year's 3.85 ERA would suggest. An injury to Shane Rawley (11-7, 3.54) contributed to the Phils' sluggish start in 1986, but may have been a blessing in disguise because it prompted the development of Don Carman (10-5, 3.22) and Bruce Ruffin (9-4, 2.46) as starters to complement Kevin Gross (12-12, 4.02). Marvin Freeman (2-0, 2.25) may be ready to make an impact in 1987.

The club left its catching shaky by swapping Ozzie Virgil to the Braves prior to last season, but it proved to be a good move because of Steve Bedrosian's stout relief (8-6, 3.39, 29 saves). There's also tireless Kent Tekulve and a rejuvenated Tom Hume in a solid bullpen.

FIELDING: The Phils were among six teams in a .978 rut last year and definitely have defensive problems. The combination of Samuel at second and Steve Jeltz at short combined for 47 errors—the most in the league—and only one first baseman made more errors than Hayes. Schmidt, who won another Gold Glove, is a pillar at third base.

Since the club has elected to place the immobile former DH Easler in left, the center fielder likely will have his tongue wagging. Milt Thompson plays center well, but can he hit enough to stay in the lineup? Wilson is solid in right and his 20 assists led the league's outfielders.

OUTLOOK: If John Felske's Phillies can put two good halves together, they might make things interesting for the Mets. Following a 42-43 first half in 1986, the Phils soared to 44-32 the rest of the way. It also would help if the Phils could play better on the road. They were 49-31 at home and 37-44 away last year.

For the Phils to become a serious contender, the starting pitchers must remain healthy, Easler must hit enough to compensate for his poor fielding, Schmidt will have to maintain his level of excellence and the club must solidify its shortstop, center field and catching positions. Asking Philadelphia to overtake the near-flawless Mets is asking too much.

PHILADELPHIA PHILLIES 1987 ROSTER

MANAGER John Felske

Coaches—Jim Davenport, Lee Elia, Claude Osteen, Mike Ryan, Del Unser

PITCHERS

No.	Name	1986 Club	W-L	IP	SO	ERA	B-T	Ht.	Wt.	Born
40	Bedrosian, Steve	Philadelphia	8-6	90	82	3.39	R-R	6-3	200	12/6/57 Methuen, MA
34	Bittiger, Jeff	Portland	13-8	171	101	4.15	R-R	5-10	175	4/13/62 Jersey City, NJ
		Philadelphia	1-1	15	8	5.52				
42	Carman, Don	Philadelphia	10-5	134	98	3.22	L-L	6-3	190	8/14/59 Oklahoma City, OK
48	Freeman, Marvin	Reading	13-6	163	113	4.03	R-R	6-6	182	4/10/63 Chicago, IL
		Philadelphia	2-0	16	8	2.25				
—	Frohwirth, Todd	Clearwater	3-3	52	39	3.98	R-R	6-4	190	9/28/62 Milwaukee, WI
		Reading	0-4	42	23	3.21				
46	Gross, Kevin	Philadelphia	12-12	242	154	4.02	R-R	6-5	203	6/8/61 Downey, CA
41	Hume, Tom	Philadelphia	4-1	94	51	2.77	R-R	6-1	185	3/29/53 Cincinnati, OH
33	Jackson, Mike	Reading	2-3	43	42	1.66	R-R	6-0	185	12/22/64 Houston, TX
		Portland	3-1	23	23	3.18				
		Philadelphia	0-0	13	3	3.38				
44	Maddux, Mike	Portland	5-2	84	65	2.36	R-R	6-2	180	8/27/61 Dayton, OH
		Philadelphia	3-7	78	44	5.42				
—	Newell, Tom	Clearwater	5-3	85	64	2.85	R-R	6-1	185	5/17/63 Covina, CA
		Portland	2-2	33	25	3.03				
28	Rawley, Shane	Philadelphia	11-7	158	73	3.54	R-L	6-0	180	7/27/55 Racine, WI
47	Ruffin, Bruce	Reading	8-4	90	68	3.29	R-L	6-2	205	10/4/63 Lubbock, TX
		Philadelphia	9-4	146	70	2.46				
—	Scanlan, Bob	Clearwater	8-12	126	51	4.15	R-R	6-7	200	8/9/66 Los Angeles, CA
35	Schatzeder, Dan	Mon.-Phi.	6-5	88	47	3.26	L-L	5-11	204	12/1/54 Elmhurst, IL
27	Tekulve, Kent	Philadelphia	11-5	110	57	2.54	R-R	6-4	190	3/5/47 Cincinnati, OH
43	Toliver, Fred	Portland	1-3	27	15	3.43	R-R	6-1	170	2/3/61 Natchez, MS
		Philadelphia	0-2	26	20	3.51				
—	Watts, Len	Reading	9-3	115	86	3.61	L-L	6-0	159	7/21/65 Galveston, TX

CATCHERS

No.	Name	1986 Club	H	HR	RBI	Pct.	B-T	Ht.	Wt.	Born
45	Cipolloni, Joe	Portland	7	1	2	.241	R-R	5-8	180	8/12/60 Philadelphia, PA
10	Daulton, Darren	Philadelphia	31	8	21	.225	L-R	6-2	190	1/3/62 Arkansas City, KS
29	Reynolds, Ronn	Portland	38	2	22	.230	R-R	6-0	205	9/28/58 Wichita, KS
		Philadelphia	27	3	10	.214				
6	Russell, John	Philadelphia	76	13	60	.241	R-R	6-0	195	1/5/61 Oklahoma City, OK

INFIELDERS

No.	Name	1986 Club	H	HR	RBI	Pct.	B-T	Ht.	Wt.	Born
16	Aguayo, Luis	Philadelphia	28	4	13	.211	R-R	5-9	195	3/13/59 Puerto Rico
—	Dowell, Ken	Portland	133	1	44	.298	R-R	5-9	160	1/19/61 Sacramento, CA
9	Hayes, Von	Philadelphia	186	19	98	.305	L-R	6-5	180	8/31/58 Stockton, CA
—	Jackson, Ken	Reading	93	4	33	.229	R-R	5-9	162	5/27/61 Shreveport, LA
—	Jelks, Greg	Portland	54	8	28	.262	R-R	6-2	188	11/16/61 Cherokee, AL
30	Jeltz, Steve	Philadelphia	96	0	36	.219	B-R	5-11	180	5/28/59 France
11	Legg, Greg	Portland	149	6	66	.323	R-R	6-1	185	4/21/60 San Jose, CA
		Philadelphia	9	0	1	.450				
18	Melendez, Francisco	Portland	113	4	57	.317	L-L	6-0	185	1/25/64 Puerto Rico
		Philadelphia	2	0	0	.250				
8	Samuel, Juan	Philadelphia	157	16	78	.266	R-R	5-11	168	12/9/60 Dominican Republic
20	Schmidt, Mike	Philadelphia	160	37	119	.290	R-R	6-2	203	9/27/49 Dayton, OH
15	Schu, Rick	Philadelphia	57	8	25	.274	R-R	6-0	185	1/26/62 Philadelphia, PA

OUTFIELDERS

No.	Name	1986 Club	H	HR	RBI	Pct.	B-T	Ht.	Wt.	Born
—	Easler, Mike	New York (AL)	148	14	78	.302	L-R	6-1	196	11/29/50 Cleveland, OH
21	Gross, Greg	Philadelphia	25	0	8	.248	L-L	5-11	180	8/1/52 York, PA
26	James, Chris	Portland	64	12	41	.241	R-R	6-1	190	10/4/62 Rusk, TX
		Philadelphia	13	0	5	.283				
—	Olander, Jim	Reading	151	8	67	.325	R-R	6-2	175	2/21/63 Tucson, AZ
22	Redus, Gary	Reading	6	0	0	.250	R-R	6-1	185	11/1/56 Limestone Co., AL
		Philadelphia	84	11	33	.247				
17	Roenicke, Ron	Tacoma	16	0	7	.222	B-L	6-0	180	8/19/56 Covina, CA
		Philadelphia	68	5	42	.247				
14	Stone, Jeff	Portland	40	2	9	.339	L-R	6-0	180	12/26/60 Kennett, MO
		Philadelphia	69	6	19	.277				
24	Thompson, Milt	Portland	56	1	16	.348	L-R	5-11	170	1/5/59 Washington, DC
		Philadelphia	75	6	23	.251				
12	Wilson, Glenn	Philadelphia	158	15	84	.271	R-R	6-1	190	12/22/58 Baytown, TX

PHILLIE PROFILES

MIKE SCHMIDT 37 6-2 203 **Bats R Throws R**

Earned third MVP prize with banner season . . . Powered club's strong second half with 21 homers . . . Surpassed 30 homers for 12th time—only Babe Ruth and Hank Aaron have done it more . . . Topped NL in homers eighth time, a league record . . . Fourth-best home-run ratio in history for veteran third baseman . . . Notched 1,288th RBI in April, a club record . . . Hot in July and September with eight homers and 24 RBI each month . . . Born Sept. 27, 1949, in Dayton, Ohio . . . Attended Ohio U. and was the club's second-round draft pick in 1971 . . . Struggled as a Phillies' rookie in 1973 before winning three straight home-run titles . . . Nobody in his era has done it better at the plate or afield . . . A model citizen and a great athlete.

Year	Club	Pos.	G	AB	R	H	2B	3B	HR	RBI	SB	Avg.
1972	Philadelphia	3B-2B	13	34	2	7	0	0	1	3	0	.206
1973	Philadelphia	3B-2B-1B-SS	132	367	43	72	11	0	18	52	8	.196
1974	Philadelphia	3B	162	568	108	160	28	7	36	116	23	.282
1975	Philadelphia	3B-SS	158	562	93	140	34	3	38	95	29	.249
1976	Philadelphia	3B	160	584	112	153	31	4	38	107	14	.262
1977	Philadelphia	3B-SS-2B	154	544	114	149	27	11	38	101	15	.274
1978	Philadelphia	3B-SS	145	513	93	129	27	2	21	78	19	.251
1979	Philadelphia	3B-SS	160	541	109	137	25	4	45	114	9	.253
1980	Philadelphia	3B	150	548	104	157	25	8	48	121	12	.286
1981	Philadelphia	3B	102	354	78	112	19	2	31	91	12	.316
1982	Philadelphia	3B	148	514	108	144	26	3	35	87	14	.280
1983	Philadelphia	3B-SS	154	534	104	136	16	4	40	109	7	.255
1984	Philadelphia	3B-1B-SS	151	528	93	146	23	3	36	106	5	.277
1985	Philadelphia	1B-3B-SS	158	549	89	152	31	5	33	93	1	.277
1986	Philadelphia	3B-1B	160	552	97	160	29	1	37	119	1	.290
	Totals		2107	7292	1347	1954	352	57	495	1392	169	.268

JUAN SAMUEL 26 5-11 168 **Bats R Throws R**

Became first NL player to reach double figures in doubles, triples and homers in first three seasons . . . Disabled two weeks with muscle strain, costing him shot at third straight 100-run season . . . Second baseman gifted with speed and power . . . If he could hit for a higher average, he'd be a bonafide superstar . . . Defense isn't of star caliber . . . Born Dec. 9, 1960, in San Pedro de Macoris, Dominican Republic . . . Signed as a free agent in 1980 and reached bigs in 1983 after .330 success at Portland (AAA) . . . Sensational rookie season of 1984 produced all-time NL record of 701 at-bats, club stolen-base mark and club rookie record for triples . . . Became first Phils' rookie to make All-Star team since Ray Culp in 1963.

Year	Club	Pos.	G	AB	R	H	2B	3B	HR	RBI	SB	Avg.
1983	Philadelphia	2B	18	65	14	18	1	2	2	5	3	.277
1984	Philadelphia	2B	160	701	105	191	36	19	15	69	72	.272
1985	Philadelphia	2B	161	663	101	175	31	13	19	74	53	.264
1986	Philadelphia	2B	145	591	90	157	36	12	16	78	42	.266
	Totals		484	2020	310	541	104	46	52	226	170	.268

VON HAYES 28 6-5 180 **Bats L Throws R**

An awesome second half placed him among league leaders in most offensive categories . . . Topped NL in doubles and tied Tony Gwynn for most runs . . . Came closer to fulfilling superstar potential than ever before after a slow start . . . First baseman took off in September with a .336 average, eight homers and 19 RBI . . . Born Aug. 31, 1958, in Stockton, Cal. . . . Attended St. Mary's (Cal.) and was MVP of USA-Japan World Series in 1979 . . . Indians' seventh-round draft choice in 1979 . . . As a rookie at Waterloo, he earned batting title (.329) and was Midwest League MVP in 1980 . . . Played third base then, but was switched to outfield and now first base . . . Cleveland traded him to Phillies after 1982 season for Julio Franco, Manny Trillo, George Vuckovich, Jay Baller and Jerry Willard . . . It was a gamble that began paying big dividends last year.

Year	Club	Pos.	G	AB	R	H	2B	3B	HR	RBI	SB	Avg.
1981	Cleveland.	OF-3B	43	109	21	28	8	2	1	17	8	.257
1982	Cleveland.	OF-3B-1B	150	527	65	132	25	3	14	82	32	.250
1983	Philadelphia	OF	124	351	45	93	9	5	6	32	20	.265
1984	Philadelphia	OF	152	561	85	164	27	6	16	67	48	.292
1985	Philadelphia	OF	152	570	76	150	30	4	13	70	21	.263
1986	Philadelphia	1B-OF	158	610	107	186	46	2	19	98	24	.305
	Totals		779	2728	399	753	145	22	69	366	153	.276

GLENN WILSON 28 6-1 190 **Bats R Throws R**

Others get more attention, but this guy is one of the most efficient players in the NL . . . Right fielder is a run producer without the benefit of many homers, as evidenced by 186 RBI the last two years despite only 29 pumps . . . Batted .191 after first two months, but raged down the stretch, hitting .316 with 20 RBI in August and .330 with 16 RBI in September . . . Born Dec. 22, 1958, in Baytown, Tex. . . . Attended Sam Houston State, where he was all-conference in football . . . Tigers' first-round pick in 1980 . . . Set Detroit rookie hitting streak at 19 games in

1982 . . . Sent to Phils with John Wockenfuss for Willie Hernandez and Dave Bergman prior to 1984 season . . . Deal gave Tigers a pennant, but Phils will get better long-term gains . . . Has a great arm, leading NL outfielders in assists last year.

Year	Club	Pos.	G	AB	R	H	2B	3B	HR	RBI	SB	Avg.
1982	Detroit	OF	84	322	39	94	15	1	12	34	2	.292
1983	Detroit	OF	144	503	55	135	25	6	11	65	1	.268
1984	Philadelphia	OF-3B	132	341	28	82	21	3	6	31	7	.240
1985	Philadelphia	OF	161	608	73	167	39	5	14	102	7	.275
1986	Philadelphia	OF	155	584	70	158	30	4	15	84	5	.271
	Totals		676	2358	265	636	130	19	58	316	22	.270

GARY REDUS 30 6-1 185 **Bats R Throws R**

Surgery for the removal of bone chips in his right elbow on May 5 cost him 59 games in his Phillies' debut, but a strong finish suggests a bright future . . . Left fielder had solid extra-base figures despite limited action, including a career high in doubles . . . This could be a make-or-break year as he faces job challenge from Mike Easler . . . Needs a breakthrough to establish himself after flubbing chances with Reds . . . Born Nov. 1, 1956, in Limestone County, Ala. . . . Attended Athens State and was 15th-round draft choice of Reds in 1978 . . . Broke in with one of finest seasons in minor-league history . . . At Billings (A) in 1978, he batted .462 with 100 runs and 42 steals in 68 games . . . Acquired from Reds with Tom Hume for John Denny and Jeff Gray prior to last season.

Year	Club	Pos.	G	AB	R	H	2B	3B	HR	RBI	SB	Avg.
1982	Cincinnati	OF	20	83	12	18	3	2	1	7	11	.217
1983	Cincinnati	OF	125	453	90	112	20	9	17	51	39	.247
1984	Cincinnati	OF	123	394	69	100	21	3	7	22	48	.254
1985	Cincinnati	OF	101	246	51	62	14	4	6	28	48	.252
1986	Philadelphia	OF	90	340	62	84	22	4	11	33	25	.247
	Totals		459	1516	284	376	80	22	42	141	171	.248

SHANE RAWLEY 31 6-0 180 **Bats R Throws L**

Missed the final two months with a broken bone in left shoulder . . . Otherwise, he could have been club's biggest winner . . . He was pitching well when the club was struggling early on . . . Started the season with a 3-1 record and a 2.41 ERA in April . . . Went to 4-0 and 1.76 in June . . . Carried an 11-5 record and a 2.96 ERA into the All-Star Game, but failed to win thereafter . . . Born July 27, 1955, in Racine, Wisc. . . . Has a pilot's license . . . Drafted by Expos in 1974 and reached bigs with

Seattle, but first success came with Yankees . . . Acquired by Phils in June 1984 for Marty Bystrom and Keith Hughes and has posted 34-21 record with Phils.

Year	Club	G	IP	W	L	Pct.	SO	BB	H	ERA
1978	Seattle	52	111	4	9	.308	66	51	114	4.14
1979	Seattle	48	84	5	9	357	48	40	88	3.86
1980	Seattle	59	114	7	7	.500	68	63	103	3.32
1981	Seattle	46	68	4	6	.400	35	38	64	3.97
1982	New York (AL)	47	164	11	10	524	111	54	165	4.06
1983	New York (AL)	34	238⅓	14	14	.500	124	79	246	3.78
1984	New York (AL)	11	42	2	3	.400	2	227	46	6.21
1984	Philadelphia	18	120⅓	10	6	.625	58	27	117	3.81
1985	Philadelphia	36	198⅔	13	8	.619	106	81	188	3.31
1986	Philadelphia	23	157⅔	11	7	.611	73	50	166	3.54
	Totals	374	1298	81	79	.506	713	510	1297	3.80

STEVE BEDROSIAN 29 6-3 200 — Bats R Throws R

Tied Al Holland's club record of 29 saves and shattered Jim Konstanty's mark for right-handers in a dazzling Philly debut . . . Took off in August with a 1-0 record, nine saves and a 2.53 ERA . . . Went back to bullpen last year after starting experiment at Atlanta in 1985 failed because of wildness . . . Control problems cured in new surroundings . . . Born Dec. 6, 1957, in Methuen, Mass. . . . Rabid Celtics' fan . . . Attended U. of New Haven and was third-round pick of Braves in 1978 . . . Exclusively a starter in minors, but switched to bullpen at Atlanta and enjoyed early success . . . "Bedrock" and Gene Garber formed league's top bullpen in 1982 and he posted a 1.71 ERA out of the bullpen in 1984 . . . Acquired with Milt Thompson for Ozzie Virgil and Peter Smith prior to last season.

Year	Club	G	IP	W	L	Pct.	SO	BB	H	ERA
1981	Atlanta	15	24	1	2	.333	9	15	15	4.50
1982	Atlanta	64	137⅔	8	6	.571	123	57	102	2.42
1983	Atlanta	70	120	9	10	.474	114	51	100	3.60
1984	Atlanta	40	83⅔	9	6	.600	81	33	65	2.37
1985	Atlanta	37	206⅔	7	15	.318	134	111	198	3.83
1986	Philadelphia	68	90⅓	8	6	.571	82	34	79	3.39
	Totals	294	662⅓	42	45	.483	543	301	559	3.27

DON CARMAN 27 6-3 190 — Bats L Throws L

Steve Carlton's departure and Shane Rawley's injury forced Phils to pull him out of the bullpen, and he responded marvelously . . . Went 7-3 as a starter, receiving six runs of support in the three losses . . . On Aug. 20 at San Francisco, he took a perfect game into the ninth before Bob Brenly belted a leadoff double . . . In first 30 career innings against Giants, he yielded one earned run . . . Capped great sophomore season with a 3-0 record and 1.73 ERA in September . . . Born Aug. 14, 1959, in Oklahoma City, Okla. . . . Attended Oklahoma . . . Signed as a free agent in 1978 . . . Solid rookie season with Phils in 1985 stamped him for future stardom and the future is now.

Year	Club	G	IP	W	L	Pct.	SO	BB	H	ERA
1983	Philadelphia	1	1	0	0	.000	0	0	0	0.00
1984	Philadelphia	11	13⅓	0	1	.000	16	6	14	5.40
1985	Philadelphia	71	86⅓	9	4	.692	87	38	52	2.08
1986	Philadelphia	50	134⅓	10	5	.667	98	52	113	3.22
	Totals	133	235	19	10	.655	201	96	179	2.91

KEVIN GROSS 25 6-5 203 — Bats R Throws R

A so-so season for the ace of the staff, a distinction which changed when others pitched much better down the stretch . . . An 0-3 July placed him in a hole, but he was 6-4 the rest of the way to salvage a .500 finish . . . Workhorse topped club in most pitching categories in 1985 and 1986 . . . Born June 8, 1961, in Downey, Cal. . . . An accomplished artist . . . Attended Cal Lutheran and selected by Phillies in secondary phase of 1981 draft . . . A starter until he made 30 relief appearances for Phils in 1984 . . . Broke up a Nolan Ryan no-hit bid with sixth-inning double in 1985.

Year	Club	G	IP	W	L	Pct.	SO	BB	H	ERA
1983	Philadelphia	17	96	4	6	.400	66	35	100	3.56
1984	Philadelphia	44	129	8	5	.615	84	44	140	4.12
1985	Philadelphia	38	205⅔	15	13	.536	151	81	194	3.41
1986	Philadelphia	37	241⅔	12	12	.500	154	94	240	4.02
	Totals	136	672⅓	39	36	.520	455	254	674	3.79

BRUCE RUFFIN 23 6-2 205 — Bats R Throws L

Took Steve Carlton's spot in the rotation and found immediate success after making leap from Reading (AA) in June . . . Went 4-1 with 1.45 ERA in August . . . Missed a 10-win season because of no-decision in final game of year, despite yielding no earned runs in nine innings against Expos . . . Born Oct. 4, 1963, in Lubbock, Tex. . . . Attended U. of Texas, going 19-4 in three years and being overshadowed by Roger Clemens, Calvin Schiraldi and Greg Swindell . . . Second-round pick in 1985 as Phils' compensation for Pirates' signing of Sixto Lezcano . . . Started season at Reading, learned sinker from George Culver and went 8-4 with a 3.29 ERA prior to promotion.

Year	Club	G	IP	W	L	Pct.	SO	BB	H	ERA
1986	Philadelphia	21	146⅓	9	4	.692	70	44	138	2.46

TOP PROSPECT

MARVIN FREEMAN 21 6-6 182 Bats R Throws R
Made jump from Reading (AA) in September and provided pleasant surprise with his stout pitching . . . Was 2-0 with 2.25 ERA, including one-hit performance over seven innings against Mets . . . Was 1-7 for Reading in 1985, but improved his control and record to 13-6 with 4.03 ERA last season . . . Nicknamed "Starvin'" . . . Drafted out of Jackson State in second round in 1984 . . . Control problems often overcome by great stuff . . . Walked 111 and struck out 113 in 163 innings at Reading . . . Born April 10, 1963, in Chicago.

MANAGER JOHN FELSKE: Rewarded with a contract extension following solid second half . . . Phils went 44-32 down the stretch after being below .500 at the All-Star break . . . Posted an 11-game improvement over rookie season, but it wasn't a year without conflict . . . Running feud with local media created some unpleasantness . . . Also speculation about rift with some veteran players, but those rumors ebbed as club continued improvement . . . Born May 30, 1942, in Chicago . . . Attended Illinois . . . An excellent defensive catcher, he played 54 games with Cubs and Brewers, but didn't hit his weight, which is 225 . . . Managed six years in Milwaukee system and joined Phillies as Reading (AA) skipper in 1982 . . . Led Portland (AAA) to Little World Series in 1983 and served Phils as coach in 1984 . . . Contract extended through 1988 on final day of 1986 season . . . Managerial record is 161-162.

GREATEST ALL-TIME ROOKIE

Few rookies in the history of the game had the type of season enjoyed by Richie Allen in 1964. The controversial third baseman played in all 162 games that season and placed some big numbers into the books.

Allen's 352 total bases that year are the most ever accumulated by a first-year player. He batted .318 with 201 hits, 38 doubles,

29 home runs and 91 RBI. Allen also led the league with 125 runs and 13 triples.

Grover Cleveland Alexander also had a spectacular beginning when he went 28-13 with a 2.57 ERA and seven shutouts in 1911. Chuck Klein batted .360 in 1928. George McQuillan was 23-17 with a 1.53 ERA and seven shutouts in 1908.

More recently, Richie Ashburn began an illustrious career in 1948 with a .333 average and a league-leading 32 steals.

In 1957, two Phillies' pitchers had tremendous success as rookies. Jack Sanford, a late bloomer, was 19-8 with a 3.08 ERA and a league-leading 188 strikeouts, while reliever Turk Farrell had a 10-2 record, a 2.38 ERA and 10 saves.

ALL-TIME PHILLIE SEASON RECORDS

BATTING: Frank O'Doul, .398, 1929
HRs: Mike Schmidt, 48, 1980
RBIs: Chuck Klein, 170, 1930
STEALS: Juan Samuel, 72, 1984
WINS: Grover Alexander, 33, 1916
STRIKEOUTS: Steve Carlton, 310, 1972

PITTSBURGH PIRATES

TEAM DIRECTORY: President: Malcolm Prine; VP-Finance: Ken Curcio; VP-GM Baseball Oper.: Syd Thrift; Trav. Sec.: Charles Muse; Mgr.: Jim Leyland. Home: Three Rivers Stadium (58,437). Field distances: 335, l.f. line; 375, l.c.; 400, c.f.; 375, r.c.; 335, r.f. line. Spring training: Bradenton, Fla.

SCOUTING REPORT

HITTING: The Bucs are a club on the way up offensively. An influx of new talent created some growing pains last year, but

Barry Bonds looks like chip off the old Bobby.

there's potential for a breakthrough once youngsters like Barry Bonds (.223, 16 homers, 48 RBI, 36 stolen bases), R.J. Reynolds (.269, 9, 48) and Sid Bream (.268, 16, 77) get comfortable and develop continuity.

Johnny Ray (.301) is as productive at the plate as any second baseman in the NL and Jim Morrison provided a bonus when given a chance to play regularly last year, leading the club in homers (23) and RBI (88). Tony Pena (.288) and Junior Ortiz (.336) are the best-hitting combo among the league's catchers.

PITCHING: The staff ranked eighth in the league with a 3.90 ERA last year, but that figure may suffer without Rick Rhoden, who was swapped to the Yankees in December. The Bucs will have difficulty replacing Rhoden's 15 victories, but the ace right-hander wanted out, so the Pirates had to settle for less in return.

With Rhoden gone, Rick Reuschel (9-16, 3.96) becomes the bellcow of the staff, which isn't saying much. It hardly seems possible that ex-Yanks Doug Drabek (7-8, 4.10) and Brian Fisher (9-5, 4.93, 6 saves) can compensate for the loss of Rhoden, Cecilio Guante and Pat Clements, so it may take a minor miracle for the club to come up with a 10-game winner in 1987.

FIELDING: With the exception of the DP combo of shortstop Rafael Belliard and Ray, the Bucs are mediocre defensively. Ray ranked right behind the Cubs' Ryne Sandberg by making only five errors in 764 chances last year. Bream had difficulty at first base (17 errors) and if Morrison were a deft third baseman, he wouldn't have been a reserve so long. Pena has lost some of his prowess behind the plate, making 18 errors last year. His snap throws, however, rank with the best.

OUTLOOK: The disparity between the Bucs and the Mets was evident last year, when the champs won 17 of 18 meetings. That gives you a clue how far away from contending status the Pirates are, but there's hope because of the aforementioned new talent. Bonds has the potential for stardom, Bream has long-ball ability and Reynolds has speed and power.

Jim Leyland's Bucs aren't strong enough to escape the second division this year, but they have enough talented youth to improve on a 64-98 record and perhaps sneak past the Cubs and the Expos. Improvement must begin at home, where the Pirates went 31-50 last year, the worst mark in the NL.

PITTSBURGH PIRATES 1987 ROSTER

MANAGER Jim Leyland
Coaches—Rich Donnelly, Gene Lamont, Milt May, Ray Miller, Tommy Sandt

PITCHERS

No.	Name	1986 Club	W-L	IP	SO	ERA	B-T	Ht.	Wt.	Born
34	Bielecki, Mike	Pittsburgh	6-11	149	83	4.66	R-R	6-3	200	7/31/59 Baltimore, MD
15	Drabek, Doug	New York (AL)	7-8	132	76	4.10	R-R	6-1	185	7/25/62 Victoria, TX
56	Drummond, Tim	Prince William	6-4	74	55	3.79	R-R	6-3	170	12/24/64 La Plata, MD
54	Fansler, Stan	Hawaii	8-9	156	77	3.63	R-R	5-11	188	2/12/65 Elkins, WV
		Pittsburgh	0-3	24	13	3.75				
29	Fisher, Brian	New York (AL)	9-5	97	67	4.93	R-R	6-4	210	3/18/62 Honolulu, HI
60	Hernandez, Martin	Nashua	1-1	7	8	4.91	R-R	6-2	175	1/30/65 Mexico
		Prince William	6-11	112	65	4.51				
50	Jones, Barry	Hawaii	3-6	48	28	3.56	R-R	6-4	225	2/15/63 Centerville, IN
		Pittsburgh	3-4	37	29	2.89				
51	Kipper, Bob	Pittsburgh	6-8	114	81	4.03	R-L	6-2	175	7/8/64 Aurora, IL
		Nashua	0-1	18	19	3.44				
55	Lind, Orlando	Nashua	4-3	53	35	3.59	R-R	6-1	205	1/30/65 Puerto Rico
49	McWilliams, Larry	Pittsburgh	3-11	122	80	5.15	L-L	6-5	185	2/10/54 Wichita, KS
30	Patterson, Bob	Hawaii	9-6	156	137	3.40	R-L	6-2	195	5/16/59 Jacksonville, FL
		Pittsburgh	2-3	36	20	4.95				
16	Pena, Hipolito	Nashua	7-4	99	76	3.55	L-L	6-3	165	1/30/64 Dominican Republic
		Pittsburgh	0-3	8	6	8.64				
48	Reuschel, Rick	Pittsburgh	9-16	216	125	3.96	R-R	6-3	240	5/16/49 Quincy, IL
43	Robinson, Don	Prince William	1-1	13	13	0.71	R-R	6-4	245	6/8/57 Ashland, KY
		Pittsburgh	3-4	69	53	3.38				
57	Smiley, John	Prince William	2-4	90	93	3.10	L-L	6-4	195	3/17/65 Phoenixville, PA
		Pittsburgh	1-0	12	9	3.86				
52	Taylor, Dorn	Nashua	2-2	63	57	1.58	R-R	6-2	180	8/11/58 Abington, PA
		Hawaii	3-1	31	29	2.01				
17	Walk, Bob	Pittsburgh	7-8	142	78	3.75	R-R	6-4	217	11/26/56 Van Nuys, CA
41	Winn, Jim	Pittsburgh	3-5	88	70	3.58	R-R	6-3	215	9/23/59 Stockton, CA

CATCHERS

No.	Name	1986 Club	H	HR	RBI	Pct.	B-T	Ht.	Wt.	Born
26	Ortiz, Junior	Pittsburgh	37	0	14	.336	R-R	5-11	176	10/24/59 Puerto Rico
6	Pena, Tony	Pittsburgh	147	10	52	.288	R-R	6-0	184	6/4/57 Dominican Republic
44	Prince, Tom	Prince William	100	10	47	.253	R-R	5-11	185	8/13/64 Kankakee, IL
7	Rodriguez, Ruben	Nashua	31	0	12	.183	R-R	6-0	175	8/4/64 Dominican Republic
		Hawaii	28	0	15	.259				
		Pittsburgh	0	0	0	.000				

INFIELDERS

No.	Name	1986 Club	H	HR	RBI	Pct.	B-T	Ht.	Wt.	Born
12	Almon, Bill	Pittsburgh	43	7	27	.219	R-R	6-3	191	11/21/52 Providence, RI
19	Belliard, Rafael	Pittsburgh	72	0	31	.233	R-R	5-6	150	10/24/61 Dom. Republic
5	Bream, Sid	Pittsburgh	140	16	77	.268	L-L	6-4	218	8/3/60 Carlisle, PA
28	Gonzalez, Denny	Hawaii	84	10	45	.222	R-R	5-11	185	7/22/63 Dominican Republic
2	Morrison, Jim	Pittsburgh	147	23	88	.274	R-R	5-11	186	9/23/52 Pensacola, FL
3	Ray, Johnny	Pittsburgh	174	7	78	.301	B-R	5-11	185	3/1/57 Chouteau, OK

OUTFIELDERS

No.	Name	1986 Club	H	HR	RBI	Pct.	B-T	Ht.	Wt.	Born
24	Bonds, Barry	Hawaii	46	7	37	.311	L-L	6-1	185	7/24/64 Riverside, CA
		Pittsburgh	92	16	48	.223				
25	Bonilla, Bobby	Chicago (AL)	63	2	26	.269	B-R	6-3	230	2/23/63 New York, NY
		Pittsburgh	46	1	17	.240				
4	Brown, Mike	Pittsburgh	53	4	26	.218	R-R	6-2	205	12/29/59 San Francisco, CA
		Hawaii	33	1	12	.379				
14	Diaz, Mike	Pittsburgh	56	12	36	.268	R-R	6-2	205	4/15/60 San Francisco, CA
11	Orsulak, Joe	Pittsburgh	100	2	19	.249	L-L	6-1	186	5/31/62 Glen Ridge, NJ
23	Reynolds, R. J.	Pittsburgh	108	9	48	.269	B-R	6-0	183	4/19/60 Sacramento, CA

PIRATE PROFILES

TONY PENA 29 6-0 184 Bats R Throws R

Made the All-Star squad despite a relatively poor (.241) first half, but justified the selection by batting above .300 the rest of the way to finish among the league leaders . . . Took off with a .356 August and improved to .360 in September . . . Won a third straight Gold Glove in 1985 and also is regarded as fastest runner among catchers . . . Born June 4, 1957, in Monte Cristi, Dominican Republic . . . His mother, a softball standout, got him started . . . An All-Star for Portland (AAA) in 1980, he joined the Pirates to stay that season . . . Batted .300 in first full season with Bucs and ranked among league leaders in 1982 and 1983 . . . In 1985, he became only the fourth major-league catcher in 40 years to notch 100 assists . . . A veritable cat behind the plate . . . Signed by Bucs as free agent in 1977.

Year	Club	Pos.	G	AB	R	H	2B	3B	HR	RBI	SB	Avg.
1980	Pittsburgh	C	8	21	1	9	1	1	0	1	0	.429
1981	Pittsburgh	C	66	210	16	63	9	1	2	17	1	.300
1982	Pittsburgh	C	138	497	53	147	28	4	11	63	2	.296
1983	Pittsburgh	C	151	542	51	163	22	3	15	70	6	.301
1984	Pittsburgh	C	147	546	77	156	27	2	15	78	12	.286
1985	Pittsburgh	C-1B	147	546	53	136	27	2	10	59	12	.249
1986	Pittsburgh	C	144	510	56	147	26	2	10	52	9	.288
	Totals		801	2872	307	821	140	15	63	340	42	.286

JOHNNY RAY 30 5-11 185 Bats S Throws R

Enjoyed a fifth consecutive solid season in 1986 . . . Remarkably consistent, he overcomes Pirates' up-and-down performances to perform at star level . . . After finishing strong in 1985, second baseman batted .529 the first week of 1986 and earned Player-of-the-Month honors for April with a .380 average and 18 RBI . . . Overlooked for the All-Star Game, but didn't allow it to affect his performance, batting .353 with 16 RBI in August . . . Born March 1, 1957, in Chouteau, Okla. . . . A better hitter from the left side . . . Among the toughest players to strike out . . . A collegiate star at Arkansas before being drafted by the

Astros . . . Joined Bucs with Randy Niemann in August 1981 swap with Houston for Phil Garner and Kevin Houston.

Year	Club	Pos.	G	AB	R	H	2B	3B	HR	RBI	SB	Avg.
1981	Pittsburgh	2B	31	102	10	25	11	0	0	6	0	.245
1982	Pittsburgh	2B	162	647	79	182	30	7	7	63	16	.281
1983	Pittsburgh	2B	151	576	68	163	38	7	5	53	18	.283
1984	Pittsburgh	2B	155	555	75	173	38	6	6	67	11	.312
1985	Pittsburgh	2B	154	594	67	163	33	3	7	70	13	.274
1986	Pittsburgh	2B	155	579	67	174	33	0	7	78	6	.301
	Totals		808	3053	366	880	183	23	32	337	64	.288

MIKE DIAZ 26 6-2 205 — Bats R Throws R

Came to camp as a catcher last year, but found a home in the outfield and showed bursts of power . . . Right at home on a team desperately searching for power, but overshadowed by fellow rookie Barry Bonds . . . Born April 15, 1960, in San Francisco . . . Came to Bucs in 1985 swap with Phillies for catcher Steve Herz . . . Hawaii (AAA) teammates nicknamed him "Rambo" during 1985 season in which he belted 22 homers and batted .312 in the Pacific Coast League . . . Was an All-American schoolboy quarterback and fired a no-hitter in a game in which he had five RBI, with a homer, triple and single . . . A 30th-round draft pick by the Cubs in 1978.

Year	Club	Pos.	G	AB	R	H	2B	3B	HR	RBI	SB	Avg.
1983	Chicago (NL)	C	6	7	2	2	1	0	0	1	0	.286
1986	Pittsburgh	OF-1B-3B-C	97	209	22	56	9	0	12	36	0	.268
	Totals		103	216	24	58	10	0	12	37	0	.269

SID BREAM 26 6-4 218 — Bats L Throws L

The man who ran Jason Thompson out of town came through with a solid season, ranking among the league leaders in doubles . . . The Dodgers' castoff has a solid future with the club if his first full season is indicative . . . Played under former reliever Al Worthington at Liberty Baptist College (Va.), where he led team to NAIA World Series and had a four-homer game . . . Born Aug. 3, 1960, in Carlisle, Pa. . . . A lifetime .329 minor-league hitter, "El Sid" was trapped among the first-base crowd at Los Angeles . . . Got a big break when he was traded along with R.J. Reynolds and Cecil Espy for Bill Madlock in September 1985

... Hit safely in 16 of his last 20 games with Bucs in 1985, batting .284 with new club following a .370 burst at Albuquerque (AAA).

Year	Club	Pos.	G	AB	R	H	2B	3B	HR	RBI	SB	Avg.
1983	Los Angeles	1B	15	11	0	2	0	0	0	2	0	.182
1984	Los Angeles	1B	27	49	2	9	3	0	0	6	1	.184
1985	L.A.-Pitt.	1B	50	148	18	34	7	0	6	21	0	.230
1986	Pittsburgh	1B	154	522	73	140	37	5	16	77	13	.268
	Totals		246	730	93	185	47	5	22	106	14	.253

JIM MORRISON 34 5-11 186 Bats R Throws R

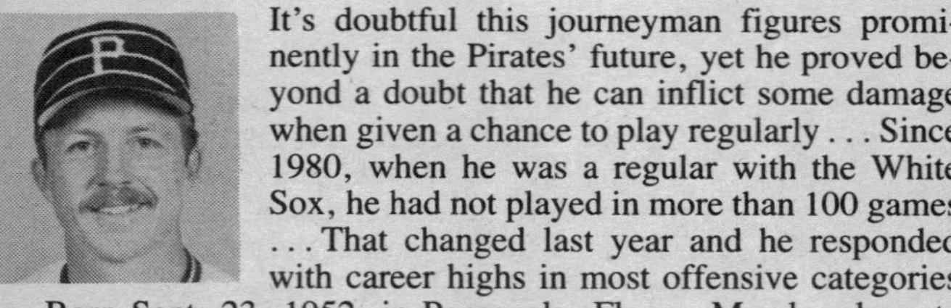

It's doubtful this journeyman figures prominently in the Pirates' future, yet he proved beyond a doubt that he can inflict some damage when given a chance to play regularly ... Since 1980, when he was a regular with the White Sox, he had not played in more than 100 games ... That changed last year and he responded with career highs in most offensive categories ... Born Sept. 23, 1952, in Pensacola, Fla. ... Merely adequate defense has kept him out of the lineup in the past, but the third baseman compensated with a booming bat in 1986 ... He batted .298 in July and improved to .343 with six homers in September ... Popular "Mo" is the club's player rep ... Attended Georgia Southern and was drafted by the Phillies ... Joined Bucs in June 1982 swap with Chisox for Eddie Solomon.

Year	Club	Pos.	G	AB	R	H	2B	3B	HR	RBI	SB	Avg.
1977	Philadelphia	3B	5	7	3	3	0	0	0	1	0	.429
1978	Philadelphia	2B-3B-OF	53	108	12	17	1	1	3	10	1	.157
1979	Chicago (AL)	2B-3B	67	240	38	66	14	0	14	36	11	.275
1980	Chicago (AL)	2B-SS	162	604	66	171	40	0	15	57	9	.283
1981	Chicago (AL)	3B-2B	90	290	27	68	8	1	10	34	3	.234
1982	Chicago (AL)	3B	51	166	17	37	7	3	7	19	0	.223
1982	Pittsburgh	3B-2B-OF-SS	44	86	10	24	4	1	4	15	2	.279
1983	Pittsburgh	2B-3B-SS	66	158	16	48	7	2	6	25	2	.304
1984	Pittsburgh	3B-2B-SS-1B	!00	304	38	87	14	2	11	45	0	.286
1985	Pittsburgh	3B-2B-OF	92	244	17	62	10	0	4	22	3	.254
1986	Pittsburgh	3B-2B-SS	154	537	58	147	35	4	23	88	9	.274
	Totals		884	2744	302	730	140	14	97	351	40	.266

BARRY BONDS 22 6-1 185 Bats L Throws L

A non-roster player last spring, center fielder reached the bigs to stay in only his second pro season ... Made a big impression with his power and speed, reminiscent of his father, Bobby, but also showed pop's strikeout penchant ... His stolen bases and a barrage of extra-base hits, however, make him an outstanding prospect ... Born July 24, 1964, in Riverside, Cal. ... Was drafted by the Giants out of high school, but didn't sign because the club wouldn't throw in an extra $5,000 . . . Attended Arizona State, where he hit .347 with 45 homers and 175 RBI . . . Belted seven straight hits in College World Series as a soph . . . Bucs' first-round pick in 1985 batted .299 at Prince William (A) in first year.

Year	Club	Pos.	G	AB	R	H	2B	3B	HR	RBI	SB	Avg.
1986	Pittsburgh	OF	113	413	72	92	26	3	16	48	36	.223

JOE ORSULAK 24 6-1 186 Bats L Throws L

A very disappointing season followed the outfielder's .300 rookie campaign of 1985 . . . Orsulak stood out when the club was hurting for outfielders, but he no longer is a big deal on a team brimming with young prospects . . . Collected two hits in three trips on final day in 1985 to record his first .300 season since he hit .315 for Greenwood (A) in 1981 . . . Born May 31, 1962, in Glen Ridge, N.J. . . . Nicknamed "Slak" . . . An All-State soccer goalie as a schoolboy . . . Sixth-round draft pick of Bucs in 1980 . . . Replaced Marvell Wynne as regular center fielder in 1985, but Barry Bonds entered the picture last year.

Year	Club	Pos.	G	AB	R	H	2B	3B	HR	RBI	SB	Avg.
1983	Pittsburgh	OF	7	11	0	2	0	0	0	1	0	.182
1984	Pittsburgh	OF	32	67	12	17	1	2	0	3	3	.254
1985	Pittsburgh	OF	121	397	54	119	14	6	0	21	24	.300
1986	Pittsburgh	OF	138	401	60	100	19	6	2	19	24	.249
	Totals		298	876	126	238	34	14	2	44	51	.272

R.J. REYNOLDS 26 6-0 183 Bats S Throws R

Along with Sid Bream, this outfielder gave the Bucs a shot in the arm when he was acquired from the Dodgers in the Bill Madlock deal . . . He batted .308 with his new club after the swap, but tailed off last year and saw limited playing time as the season progressed . . . Plagued by abdominal and hamstring problems with Dodgers in 1985 . . . An instant hit with Pirates after hitting safely in first nine games and in 27 of 31 with new club . . . Born April 19, 1960, in Sacramento, Cal. . . . Out of baseball three years before a JC coach convinced him to return . . . Nicknamed "Shoes" . . . Drafted by Dodgers on second round in January 1980.

Year	Club	Pos.	G	AB	R	H	2B	3B	HR	RBI	SB	Avg.
1983	Los Angeles	OF	24	55	5	13	0	0	2	11	5	.236
1984	Los Angeles	OF	73	240	24	62	12	2	2	24	7	.258
1985	L.A.-Pitt.	OF	104	337	44	95	15	7	3	42	18	.282
1986	Pittsburgh	OF	118	402	63	108	30	2	9	48	16	.269
	Totals		319	1034	136	278	57	11	16	125	46	.269

RICK REUSCHEL 37 6-3 240 **Bats R Throws R**

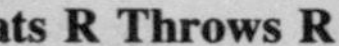

This old warhorse slipped from his Comeback-of-the-Year 1985 campaign, yet only Rick Rhoden was more effective as a Bucs' starter . . . Shoulder injury rendered him ineffective for most of the eighties until he bounced back with a 20-win season in 1985—six at Hawaii (AAA) and 14 with the Pirates . . . He hadn't won that many major-league games since 1979 and had totaled 14 victories from 1981-84 . . . Born May 16, 1949, in Quincy, Ill. . . . "Big Daddy" starred at Western Illinois before becoming a fixture on Cubs' staff in 1972 . . . Signed with Bucs as a free agent in February 1985 after other clubs turned their backs on him . . . Crowned his stirring comeback with a Gold Glove and Roberto Clemente Award in 1985.

Year	Club	G	IP	W	L	Pct.	SO	BB	H	ERA
1972	Chicago (NL)	21	129	10	8	.556	87	29	127	2.93
1973	Chicago (NL)	36	237	14	15	483	168	62	244	3.00
1974	Chicago (NL)	41	241	13	12	.520	160	83	262	4.29
1975	Chicago (NL)	38	234	11	17	.393	155	67	244	3.73
1976	Chicago (NL)	38	260	14	12	.538	146	64	260	3.46
1977	Chicago (NL)	39	252	20	10	.667	166	74	233	2.33
1978	Chicago (NL)	35	243	14	15	.483	115	54	235	3.41
1979	Chicago (NL)	36	239	18	12	.600	125	75	251	3.62
1980	Chicago (NL)	38	257	11	13	.458	140	76	281	3.40
1981	Chicago (NL)	13	86	4	7	.364	53	23	87	3.45
1981	New York (AL)	12	71	4	4	.500	22	10	75	2.66
1982	New York (AL)					Did Not Play				
1983	Chicago (NL)	4	20⅔	1	1	.500	9	10	18	3.92
1984	Chicago (NL)	19	92⅓	5	5	.500	43	23	123	5.17
1985	Pittsburgh	31	194	14	8	.636	138	52	153	2.27
1986	Pittsburgh	35	215⅔	9	16	.360	125	57	232	3.96
	Totals	436	2771⅔	162	155	.511	1652	759	2825	3.43

TOP PROSPECT

JIM NEIDLINGER 22 6-4 177 **Bats S Throws R**

A sizzling stretch drive for Nashua (AA) and the club's lack of great Triple-A prospects gives this young pitcher an edge, although he's probably one year away from the bigs . . . He was 4-6 with 3.25 ERA at midseason before becoming Eastern League's hottest pitcher . . . Born Sept. 14, 1964, in Vallejo, Cal. . . . He finished with 12-7 record and 2.42 ERA by going 8-1 in second half, including no-hitter . . . Promoted to Hawaii (AAA), he went 2-1 . . . Signed as free agent in 1984, out of Marin JC.

Johnny was a Ray of hope as ever afield and at bat.

MANAGER JIM LEYLAND: Received a contract extension despite a last-place finish and 64-98 mark as a rookie skipper . . . Pirates did show improvement in a transitional year, however, so he'll be better judged by what happens in 1987 . . . A feisty sort who didn't have the results to justify his cocky demeanor . . . Was named manager Nov. 20, 1985, after serving as third-base coach of the White Sox . . . Fulfilled a lifelong dream when he reached the bigs following 11 years as a minor-league manager . . . Born Dec. 15, 1944, in Toledo, Ohio

. . . Leyland promises aggressive baseball. "We're in the entertainment business," he notes. "As a manager, I may enjoy a 1-0 game, but the fans are bored by it." . . . He was a minor-league catcher from 1964-70 . . . Began his managerial career in the Detroit system in 1971 . . . His teams took or shared first five times in the minors before he joined the White Sox as a coach in 1982.

GREATEST ALL-TIME ROOKIE

The Brothers Waner performed a "Can you top this?" act in 1926 and 1927 and they rank as the best of the Bucs' rookies. Paul, alias "Big Poison", came on the scene first in 1926, belting a league-leading 22 triples, batting .336 and scoring 101 runs.

"Little Poison" Lloyd had something to shoot for in 1927, so he batted .355 and led the league with 133 runs. What Kiki Cuyler did in 1924 wasn't too shabby, either. Cuyler batted .354 with 94 runs and 85 RBI.

Gus Suhr made a smashing debut in 1930, with 26 doubles, 14 triples, 17 homers, a .286 average and 107 RBI. Ralph Kiner began a string of seven straight home-run titles by knocking 23 balls out of the park and notching 81 RBI in 1946.

The most successful Pirate rookie pitcher was Babe Adams. Way back in 1909, he was 12-3 with a tiny 1.11 ERA, including a 6-0 mark and two saves in relief.

ALL-TIME PIRATE SEASON RECORDS

BATTING: Arky Vaughan, .385, 1935
HRs: Ralph Kiner, 54, 1949
RBIs: Paul Waner, 131, 1927
STEALS: Omar Moreno, 96, 1980
WINS: Jack Chesbro, 28, 1902
STRIKEOUTS: Bob Veale, 276, 1965

ST. LOUIS CARDINALS

TEAM DIRECTORY: Chairman-Pres.: August A. Busch, Jr.; GM: Dal Maxvill; Senior VP: Stan Musial; Dir. Play. Pers.: Lee Thomas; Dir. Pub. Rel.: Jim Toomey; Trav. Sec.: C.J. Cherre; Mgr.: Whitey Herzog. Home: Busch Stadium (50,122). Field distances: 330, l.f. line; 414, c.f.; 330, r.f. line. Spring training: St. Petersburg, Fla.

SCOUTING REPORT

HITTING: St. Louis' slide in 1986 really doesn't require much analysis. The Redbirds went from a fearsome offense in their pennant-winning 1985 campaign to the worst attack in the NL last year. The Cardinals' .236 average was the worst in the league and, despite a league-leading 262 stolen bases, the club was dead

Todd Worrell won NL Rookie-of-the-Year honors.

last in runs scored (601). Moreover, the Cards' 58 homers were at least 52 fewer than any other NL team.

The short-circuited offense can be attributed to numerous slumps and Jack Clark's availability for only 65 games. Willie McGee, Tommy Herr and Terry Pendleton enjoyed career years in 1985, but were impotent at the dish for most of 1986. McGee mirrored the team collapse by plunging from .351 to .256, Herr's RBI total dipped from 110 to 61 and Vince Coleman's 107 steals didn't compensate for his paltry .232 average.

PITCHING: A slow start by John Tudor, Danny Cox's spring injury and the trade of Joaquin Andujar notwithstanding, the Cards' pitching was solid in 1986. The team ERA of 3.37 ranked fourth in the league and Bob Forsch enjoyed a marvelous comeback to top the staff in most categories. Tudor (13-7, 2.92) and Cox (12-13, 2.90) finished strong to augment Forsch (14-10, 3.25) and promising newcomer Greg Mathews (11-8, 3.65)

The bullpen by committee, a strength in 1985, went by the wayside when NL Rookie of the Year Todd Worrell (9-10, 2.08) set a rookie record with 36 saves. This is a decent staff that suffered from a lack of support last season.

FIELDING: Nobody does it better than the Cardinals, who build their defense around wunderkind shortstop Ozzie Smith, a perennial Gold Glover. "The Wizard" led the league with a .978 fielding percentage and center fielder McGee ranked first among the outfielders at .991. Herr also ranks among the best at his position.

The two liabilities last year were left fielder Coleman, who makes too many errors, and third baseman Pendleton, who slumped afield following a solid 1985. But the Cards are solid defensively down the middle, where it counts most.

OUTLOOK: Something was missing from the champs last year and it might have been Andujar's fiery demeanor. An horrendous start produced a 36-50 record at the All-Star break, but the pride of a champion surfaced during a 43-32 second half that created hope for 1987.

In 1986, as in 1982, people were talking dynasty because of the way Whitey Herzog's Redbirds were adapted to their park, using speed to humble opponents. But there's obviously more to the game than pitching and defense, because the 1986 Cards excelled in each department and failed miserably. The components for success remain, but the club needs a lot more punch than a healthy Clark can provide to compete with the Mets.

ST. LOUIS CARDINALS 1987 ROSTER

MANAGER Whitey Herzog
Coaches—Rich Hacker, Johnny Lewis, Nick Leyva, Dave Ricketts, Mike Roarke, Red Schoendienst

PITCHERS

No.	Name	1986 Club	W-L	IP	SO	ERA	B-T	Ht.	Wt.	Born
50	Arnold, Scott	St. Petersburg	10-5	136	84	2.71	R-R	6-2	210	8/18/62 Lexington, KY
		Arkansas	4-1	28	23	3.81				
43	Bargar, Greg	Louisville	3-4	68	65	3.56	R-R	6-2	185	1/27/59 Inglewood, CA
		St. Louis	0-2	27	12	5.60				
44	Buonantony, Rich	Louisville	7-6	108	81	5.58	R-R	6-4	205	11/28/62 Hoboken, NJ
39	Conroy, Tim	Louisville	1-0	8	6	2.25	L-L	6-1	185	4/3/60 Monroeville, PA
		St. Louis	5-11	115	79	5.23				
34	Cox, Danny	St. Louis	12-13	220	108	2.90	R-R	6-4	225	9/21/59 England
—	Dawley, Bill	Chicago (AL)	0-7	98	66	3.32	R-R	6-4	240	2/6/58 Norwich, CT
42	Dunn, Greg	Louisville	0-0	11	12	3.27	R-R	6-0	180	1/7/62 Atwater, CA
52	Fassero, Jeff	St. Petersburg	13-7	176	112	2.45	L-L	6-1	180	1/5/63 Springfield, IL
31	Forsch, Bob	St. Louis	14-10	230	104	3.25	R-R	6-3	200	1/13/50 Sacramento, CA
49	Horton, Rick	Springfield	0-0	2	2	0.00	L-L	6-2	195	7/30/59 Poughkeepsie, NY
		St. Louis	4-3	100	49	2.24				
32	Lahti, Jeff	St. Louis	0-0	2	3	0.00	R-R	6-0	180	10/8/56 Oregon City, OR
53	Mathews, Greg	Louisville	3-3	45	20	2.58	B-L	6-2	180	5/17/62 Harbor City, CA
		St. Louis	11-8	145	67	3.65				
37	Perry, Pat	Louisville	1-0	11	7	3.27	L-L	6-1	170	2/4/59 Taylorville, IL
		St. Louis	2-3	69	29	3.80				
47	Soff, Ray	Arkansas	3-2	21	14	1.27	R-R	6-0	185	10/31/58 Adrian, MI
		Louisville	3-2	43	30	1.90				
		St. Louis	4-2	38	22	3.29				
30	Tudor, John	St. Louis	137	219	107	2.92	L-L	6-0	185	2/2/54 Schenectady, NY
38	Worrell, Todd	St. Louis	9-10	104	73	2.08	R-R	6-5	200	9/28/59 Arcadia, CA

CATCHERS

No.	Name	1986 Club	H	HR	RBI	Pct.	B-T	Ht.	Wt.	Born
25	Lake, Steve	Iowa-Lou.	24	0	13	.245	R-R	6-1	190	3/14/57 Inglewood, CA
		Chi. (NL)-St. L.	20	2	14	.294				
10	LaValliere, Mike	St. Louis	71	3	30	.234	L-R	5-10	190	8/18/60 Charlotte, NC
19	Pagnozzi, Tom	Louisville	31	1	18	.292	R-R	6-1	190	7/30/62 Tucson, AZ

INFIELDERS

No.	Name	1986 Club	H	HR	RBI	Pct.	B-T	Ht.	Wt.	Born
26	Booker, Rod	Arkansas	48	0	20	.318	L-R	6-0	175	9/4/58 Los Angeles, CA
		Louisville	81	1	29	.280				
22	Clark, Jack	St. Louis	55	9	23	.237	R-R	6-3	205	11/10/55 New Brighton, PA
25	Fitzgerald, Mike	Springfield	148	19	93	.297	R-R	6-1	200	3/28/64 Savannah, GA
28	Herr, Tom	St. Louis	141	2	61	.252	B-R	6-0	185	4/4/56 Lancaster, PA
35	Laga, Mike	Detroit	9	3	8	.200	L-L	6-2	210	6/14/60 Ridgewood, NJ
		Nashville	9	2	7	.220				
		St. Louis	10	3	8	.217				
12	Lawless, Tom	St. Louis	11	0	3	.282	R-R	5-11	165	12/19/56 Erie, PA
15	Lindeman, Jim	Louisville	128	20	96	.251	R-R	6-1	200	1/10/62 Evanston, IL
		St. Louis	14	1	6	.255				
11	Oquendo, Jose	St. Louis	41	0	13	.297	B-R	5-10	160	7/4/63 Puerto Rico
9	Pendelton, Terry	St. Louis	138	1	59	.239	B-R	5-9	180	7/16/60 Los Angeles, CA
1	Smith, Ozzie	St. Louis	144	0	54	.280	B-R	5-10	150	12/26/54 Mobile, AL

OUTFIELDERS

No.	Name	1986 Club	H	HR	RBI	Pct.	B-T	Ht.	Wt.	Born
40	Carter, Dennis	Springfield	140	13	82	.270	R-R	6-4	200	11/20/64 Hinds County, MS
29	Coleman, Vince	St. Louis	139	0	29	.232	B-R	6-0	170	9/22/61 Jacksonville, FL
27	Ford, Curt	Louisville	59	4	31	.295	L-R	5-10	150	10/11/60 Jackson, MS
		St. Louis	53	2	29	.248				
21	Landrum, Tito	St. Louis	43	2	17	.210	R-R	5-11	175	10/25/54 Joplin, MO
51	McGee, Willie	St. Louis	127	7	48	.256	B-R	6-1	175	11/2/58 San Francisco, CA
33	Morris, John	Louisville	50	1	24	.235	L-L	6-1	185	2/23/61 Freeport, NY
		St. Louis	24	1	14	.240				
18	Van Slyke, Andy	St. Louis	137	13	61	.270	L-L	6-1	190	12/2/60 Utica, NY

CARDINAL PROFILES

TOM HERR 30 6-0 185 **Bats S Throws R**

After enjoying a career year in 1985, Herr took a nose dive last year and the Cardinals followed . . . Most notable dropoff was in average and RBI, because he plunged from among league's best to worst in each category . . . A horrid April set the tone, but he batted .307 in June and .304 in July to show signs of improvement before regressing down the stretch . . . Born April 4, 1956, in Lancaster, Pa. . . . In 1985, he became only the seventh second baseman in major-league history to top 100 RBI . . . Also became first player in 25 years to surpass 100 RBI without hitting at least 10 homers, Detroit's George Kell being the last . . . Four doubles in 1985 NL Championship Series tied a record . . . Batted .333 in playoffs before World Series slump gave an indication of things to come.

Year	Club	Pos.	G	AB	R	H	2B	3B	HR	RBI	SB	Avg.
1979	St. Louis	2B	14	10	4	2	0	0	0	1	1	.200
1980	St. Louis	2B-SS	76	222	29	55	12	5	0	15	9	.248
1981	St. Louis	2B	103	411	50	110	14	9	0	46	23	.268
1982	St. Louis	2B	135	493	83	131	19	4	0	36	25	.266
1983	St. Louis	2B	89	313	43	101	14	4	2	31	6	.323
1984	St. Louis	2B	145	558	67	154	23	2	4	49	13	.276
1985	St. Louis	2B	159	596	97	180	38	3	8	110	31	.302
1986	St. Louis	2B	152	559	48	141	30	4	2	61	22	.252
	Totals		873	3162	421	874	150	31	16	349	130	.276

WILLIE McGEE 28 6-1 175 **Bats S Throws R**

Slumped more than any of the Cardinals considering the level of excellence he attained as batting champion and MVP in 1985 . . . Injuries contributed to dramatic dip in average . . . Center fielder never really got going after doing nothing wrong in 1985 . . . His 1985 MVP campaign included league lead in hits and triples . . . Named *The Sporting News* NL Player of the Year . . . Average was the highest ever by a NL switch-hitter, topping .348 of Pete Rose and Frankie Frisch . . . Born Nov. 2, 1958, in San Francisco . . . Entered 1986 batting .311 from left side and .301 from right side . . . Didn't do job either way last year, but has too much talent not to bounce back if healthy . . . In Cardinals'

biggest steal since Lou Brock, he was acquired from Yankees for Bob Sykes prior to 1982 season.

Year	Club	Pos.	G	AB	R	H	2B	3B	HR	RBI	SB	Avg.
1982	St. Louis	OF	123	422	43	125	12	8	4	56	24	.296
1983	St. Louis	OF	147	601	75	172	22	8	5	75	39	.286
1984	St. Louis	OF	145	571	82	166	19	11	6	50	43	.291
1985	St. Louis	OF	152	612	114	216	26	18	10	82	56	.353
1986	St. Louis	OF	124	497	65	127	22	7	7	48	19	.256
	Totals		691	2703	379	806	101	52	32	311	181	.298

OZZIE SMITH 32 5-10 150 Bats S Throws R

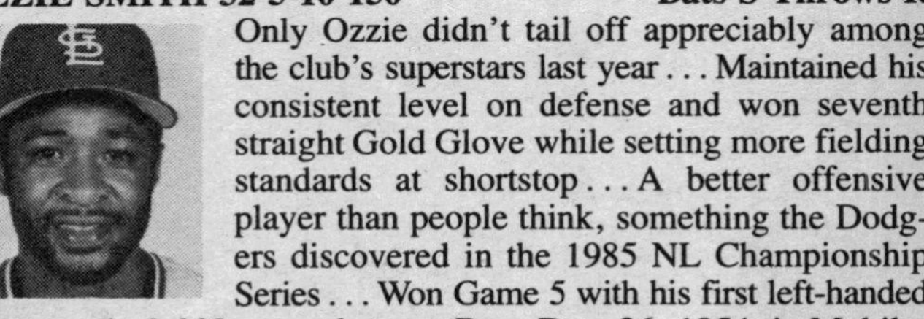

Only Ozzie didn't tail off appreciably among the club's superstars last year . . . Maintained his consistent level on defense and won seventh straight Gold Glove while setting more fielding standards at shortstop . . . A better offensive player than people think, something the Dodgers discovered in the 1985 NL Championship Series . . . Won Game 5 with his first left-handed home run in 3,009 pro at-bats . . . Born Dec. 26, 1954, in Mobile, Ala. . . . Known for his snappy clothes . . . Attended Cal Poly-San Luis Obispo . . . Padres' fourth-round pick in 1977 draft . . . Played only 68 minor-league games before becoming San Diego's shortstop . . . Complained of low pay by Padres and once threatened to augment salary as a gardener . . . First player to earn a million-dollar contract for his glove . . . Acquired for Garry Templeton prior to 1982 season.

Year	Club	Pos.	G	AB	R	H	2B	3B	HR	RBI	SB	Avg.
1978	San Diego	SS	159	590	69	152	17	6	1	46	40	.258
1979	San Diego	SS	156	587	77	124	18	6	0	27	28	.211
1980	San Diego	SS	158	609	67	140	18	5	0	35	57	.230
1981	San Diego	SS	110	450	53	100	11	2	0	21	22	.222
1982	St. Louis	SS	140	488	58	121	24	1	2	43	25	.248
1983	St. Louis	SS	159	552	69	134	30	6	3	50	34	.243
1984	St. Louis	SS	124	412	53	106	20	5	1	44	35	.257
1985	St. Louis	SS	158	537	70	148	22	3	6	54	31	.276
1986	St. Louis	SS	153	514	67	144	19	4	0	54	31	.280
	Totals		1317	4739	583	1169	179	38	13	374	303	.247

VINCE COLEMAN 25 6-0 170 Bats S Throws R

One wonders how many bases this guy would steal if he learned how to hit . . . Had a woeful season at plate in 1986, yet almost approached his rookie-record 110 steals of 1985 . . . Nobody steals them better, but Reds' Eric Davis may steal more, because he'll get on base more . . . Left fielder had 58 thefts by the All-Star break and didn't slow down . . . Born Sept. 22, 1961, in Jacksonville . . . Has a degree from Florida A&M . . . Considered NFL punting career, following footsteps of cousin Greg Coleman of the Vikings . . . A 10th-round draft choice in 1982 . . . One year later, he batted .350 with 145 steals for Macon (A) . . . Batting .143 at Louisville (AAA) when he joined Cards as an injury replacement in 1985 . . . That season ended on sour note when Busch Stadium tarpaulin machine caused leg injury that knocked him out of World Series.

Year	Club	Pos.	G	AB	R	H	2B	3B	HR	RBI	SB	Avg.
1985	St. Louis	OF	151	636	107	170	20	10	1	40	110	.267
1986	St. Louis	OF	154	600	94	139	13	8	0	29	107	.232
	Totals		305	1236	201	309	33	18	1	69	217	.250

ANDY VAN SLYKE 26 6-1 190 **Bats L Throws R**

Finished strong last year and firmly established himself as solid role player . . . Best power hitter on club with Jack Clark out . . . Right fielder batted .354 with 10 doubles in August . . . Perhaps the most underrated Redbird, because he has power, speed and a great arm . . . Successful on 34 of 40 steal attempts in 1985, his best season . . . Consistent in postseason, going 1-for-11 against both Dodgers and Royals . . . Born Dec. 21, 1960, in Utica, N.Y. . . . First-round pick in 1979 draft . . . Married during .363 season at Louisville (AAA) in 1983 and made four errors in first game back from brief honeymoon . . . Club's most versatile player, he can also play first and third.

Year	Club	Pos.	G	AB	R	H	2B	3B	HR	RBI	SB	Avg.
1983	St. Louis	OF-1B-3B	101	309	51	81	15	5	8	38	21	.262
1984	St. Louis	OF-1B-3B	137	361	45	88	16	4	7	50	28	.244
1985	St. Louis	OF-1B	146	424	61	110	25	6	13	55	34	.259
1986	St Louis	OF-1B	137	418	48	113	23	7	13	61	21	.270
	Totals		521	1512	205	392	79	22	41	204	104	.259

JACK CLARK 31 6-3 205 **Bats R Throws R**

Injury-plagued career followed form last season, when knee surgery limited first baseman to 65 games and virtually left Redbirds powerless . . . Got off to his usual slow start, yet led club in homers most of season . . . Ecstatic when Giants traded him prior to 1985 season because he wanted to be on a pennant-winner, and his bat made the dream come true . . . His two-out, ninth-inning homer in Game 6 of the NL Championship Series almost matched Bobby Thomson's in magnitude, sending Cards into World Series . . . Born Nov. 10, 1955, in New Brighton, Pa. . . . Proved that scouting isn't an exact science when he lasted until 13th round in 1973 and was picked as a pitcher . . . Set all-time Giant record with 46 doubles and a 26-game hitting streak in 1978 . . . Topped NL with 18 game-winning RBI in 1980 . . . Swapped to St. Louis for Dave LaPoint, David Green, Gary Rajsich and Jose Uribe on Feb. 1, 1985.

Year	Club	Pos.	G	AB	R	H	2B	3B	HR	RBI	SB	Avg.
1975	San Francisco.	OF-3B	8	17	3	4	0	0	0	2	1	.235
1976	San Francisco.	OF	26	102	14	23	6	2	2	10	6	.225
1977	San Francisco.	OF	136	413	64	104	17	4	13	51	12	.252
1978	San Francisco.	OF	156	592	90	181	46	8	25	98	15	.306
1979	San Francisco.	OF-3B	143	527	84	144	25	2	26	86	11	.273
1980	San Francisco.	OF	127	437	77	124	20	8	22	82	2	.284
1981	San Francisco.	OF	99	385	60	103	19	2	17	53	1	.268
1982	San Francisco.	OF	157	563	90	154	30	3	27	103	6	.274
1983	San Francisco.	OF-1B	135	492	82	132	25	0	20	66	5	.268
1984	San Francisco.	OF-1B	57	203	33	65	9	1	11	44	1	.320
1985	St. Louis	1B-OF	126	442	71	124	26	3	22	87	1	.281
1986	St. Louis	1B	65	232	34	55	12	2	9	23	1	.237
	Totals		1235	4405	702	1213	235	35	194	705	62	.275

JOHN TUDOR 33 6-0 185 Bats L Throws L

One of the best left-handers in the majors since joining the Cardinals in 1985 . . . Picked up where he left off in 1985 by posting a 3-1 record and a 2.08 ERA in April . . . That defeat against the Mets on April 27, however, snapped a 14-game winning streak dating back to July 1985 . . . Enjoyed a 4-1 August . . . Born Feb. 2, 1954, in Schenectady, N.Y. . . . Has degree in criminal justice from Georgia Southern . . . Drafted by Red Sox in 1976 and traded to Pirates after 1983 season . . . Came to Cardinals with Brian Harper for George Hendrick and Steve Barnard prior to 1985 season . . . Got off to a 1-7 start with St. Louis, but won 20 of last 21 decisions . . . Added three victories in postseason, blanking Royals in Game 4 of 1985 World Series.

Year	Club	G	IP	W	L	Pct.	SO	BB	H	ERA
1979	Boston	6	28	1	2	.333	11	9	39	6.43
1980	Boston	16	92	8	5	.615	45	31	81	3.03
1981	Boston	18	79	4	3	.571	44	28	74	4.56
1982	Boston	32	195⅔	13	10	.565	146	59	215	3.63
1983	Boston	34	242	13	12	.520	136	81	236	4.09
1984	Pittsburgh	32	212	12	11	.522	117	56	200	3.27
1985	St. Louis.	36	275	21	8	.724	169	49	209	1.93
1986	St. Louis.	30	219	13	7	.650	107	53	197	2.92
	Totals.	204	1342⅔	85	58	.594	775	366	1251	3.26

DANNY COX 27 6-4 225 **Bats R Throws R**

Overcame spring-training injury to finish strong, posting a 4-1 record and a 2.27 ERA in September . . . First full season was a bonus for the Cards as he won nine of first 11 decisions in 1985 . . . Won Game 3 of NL Championship Series, starting club from an 0-2 deficit to the pennant . . . Posted 1.20 ERA in World Series . . . Born Sept. 21, 1959, in Northhampton, England . . . Only third European-born pitcher to ever start a World Series game . . . All-American at Troy State . . . Drafted in 13th round in 1981 . . . Had distinction of pitching at every level of minors before reaching bigs in 1983.

Year	Club	G	IP	W	L	Pct.	SO	BB	H	ERA
1983	St. Louis	12	83	3	6	.333	36	23	92	3.25
1984	St. Louis	29	156⅓	9	11	.450	70	54	171	4.03
1985	St. Louis	35	241	18	9	.667	131	64	226	2.88
1986	St. Louis	32	220	12	13	.480	108	60	189	2.90
	Totals	108	700⅓	42	39	.519	345	201	678	3.19

BOB FORSCH 37 6-3 200 **Bats R Throws R**

For a guy who was supposed to be losing it, this veteran workhorse bounced back strong in 1986 . . . Along with Greg Mathews, he was the most pleasant surprise for the club in a down year . . . Was 2-1 with a 1.79 ERA in June and won four games in July . . . Born Jan. 13, 1950, in Sacramento, Cal. . . . A 38th-round draft choice in 1968, he has been a double-figure winner in nine of his 12 full major-league seasons . . . Pitched a no-hitter for Tulsa against Denver in 1973 and notched two more in majors: against Phillies in 1978 and Expos in 1983 . . . He and Ken are the only brothers to fire major-league no-hitters . . . A 1984 back injury left his future in doubt, but he has made it all the way back.

Year	Club	G	IP	W	L	Pct.	SO	BB	H	ERA
1974	St. Louis	19	100	7	4	.636	39	34	84	2.97
1975	St. Louis	34	230	15	10	.600	108	70	213	2.86
1976	St. Louis	33	194	8	10	.444	76	71	209	3.94
1977	St. Louis	35	217	20	7	.741	95	69	210	3.48
1978	St. Louis	34	234	11	17	.393	114	97	205	3.69
1979	St. Louis	33	219	11	11	.500	92	52	215	3.82
1980	St. Louis	31	215	11	10	.524	87	33	225	3.77
1981	St. Louis	20	124	10	5	.667	41	29	106	3.19
1982	St. Louis	36	233	15	9	.625	69	54	238	3.48
1983	St. Louis	34	187	10	12	.455	56	54	190	4.28
1984	St. Louis	16	52⅓	2	5	.286	21	19	64	6.02
1985	St. Louis	34	136	9	6	.600	48	47	132	3.90
1986	St. Louis	33	230	14	10	.583	104	68	211	3.25
	Totals	392	2371⅓	143	116	.552	950	697	2302	3.62

TODD WORRELL 27 6-5 200 **Bats R Throws R**

Captured NL Rookie-of-the-Year honors after winning saves title with 36 . . . Didn't pitch like a freshman after appearing in seven postseason games in 1985 . . . Pitcher of the Month in July with a 1-0 record, 1.17 ERA and eight saves in 12 games . . . Added eight more saves in August, No. 24 on Aug. 10 establishing major-league rookie record . . . Born Sept. 28, 1959, in Arcadia, Cal. . . . All-American at Biola College . . . First-round pick in 1982 draft . . . A starter until shortly before he joined Cardinals' bullpen committee in the second half of 1985 and went 3-0 with 11 saves and a 1.17 ERA in his final 17 games . . . Was 1-0 with a 1.42 ERA in four NL Championship Series games.

Year	Club	G	IP	W	L	Pct.	SO	BB	H	ERA
1985	St. Louis.	17	21⅔	3	0	1.000	17	7	17	2.91
1986	St. Louis.	74	103⅔	9	10	.474	73	41	86	2.08
	Totals.	91	125⅓	12	10	.545	90	48	103	2.23

TOP PROSPECT

JOE MAGRANE 22 6-6 225 **Bats L Throws L**

Made big strides at Arkansas (AA) and Louisville (AAA) last season to rate consideration for starting job in the bigs this year . . . In only second pro season, he was 8-4 with a 2.42 ERA at Arkansas and finished 9-6 with 2.06 ERA at Louisville . . . Strapping southpaw has exceptional control for his size . . . Standout at U. of Arizona and first-round draft pick in 1985 . . . Born July 2, 1964, in Des Moines, Iowa.

MANAGER WHITEY HERZOG: "The White Rat" has experienced the gamut of emotions the last two years . . . There was the exhilaration of a dramatic pennant-clinching victory in the 1985 NL Championship Series and a downhill slide that began after the Cardinals had taken a 3-1 World Series lead . . . Manager of the Year in 1985, when his club was picked to finish last and almost went all the way . . . Had earned similar honors with the 1976 Royals and the 1982 Redbirds . . . Born Nov. 9, 1931, in New Athens, Ill. . . . Best remembered for building 1982 club into a champion in his dual roles of manager

and GM . . . Was a major-league outfielder for eight years, batting .257 . . . Began managing with Texas in 1973 and won three straight division titles for Kansas City from 1976-78 . . . Is 991-849 as major-league manager.

GREATEST ALL-TIME ROOKIE

There are lots of strong candidates for the Cards' all-time rookie, but it's hard to ignore what slugger Johnny Mize, speedster Vince Coleman and pitcher Johnny Beazley did when they cracked the big time.

Hall of Famer Mize broke in with a bang in 1936 by belting 30 homers, eight triples and 19 home runs for a gaudy .577 slugging percentage. He batted .329 with 93 RBI. In 1985, Coleman swiped 110 bases, unprecedented for a rookie.

Beazley, like Coleman, helped the Cardinals to a pennant. In 1942, he was 21-6 with a 2.13 ERA and three saves. But his was only one of several outstanding pitching performances by Redbird rookies.

Before attaining fame with the Reds, Paul Derringer was 18-8 as a St. Louis freshman in 1931. Then came the Dean brothers. In 1932, Dizzy was 18-15 with a league-leading 191 strikeouts and four shutouts. Two years later, Daffy went 19-11 with five shutouts.

In 1941, Ernie White posted a 17-7 record and a 2.40 ERA. Harvey Haddix, who went on to no-hit immortality, was 20-9 with a 3.06 ERA and six shutouts as a rookie in 1953.

Among the hitters, Rogers Hornsby had 15 triples and a .313 average in 1916; Pepper Martin batted .300 in 1931; Wally Moon was the Rookie of the Year in 1954, batting .304 with 106 runs; Ray Jablonski had 21 homers and 112 RBI in 1953, and Bake McBride batted .309 to win Rookie-of-the-Year honors in 1974.

ALL-TIME CARDINAL SEASON RECORDS

BATTING: Rogers Hornsby, .424, 1924
HRs: Johnny Mize, 43, 1940
RBIs: Joe Medwick, 154, 1937
STEALS: Lou Brock, 118, 1974
WINS: Dizzy Dean, 30, 1934
STRIKEOUTS: Bob Gibson, 274, 1970

ATLANTA BRAVES

TEAM DIRECTORY: Chairman: Bill Bartholomay; Pres.: R.E. (Ted) Turner III; Exec. VP: Al Thornwell, Jr.; GM: Bobby Cox; Exec. Asst.: John Mullen; VP-Dir. Play. Dev.: Hank Aaron; Dir. Scouting: Paul Snyder; Dir. Pub. Rel.: Wayne Minshew; Trav. Sec.: Bill Acree; Mgr.: Chuck Tanner. Home: Atlanta Stadium (53,046). Field distances: 330, l.f. line; 402, c.f.; 330, r.f. line. Spring training: West Palm Beach, Fla.

SCOUTING REPORT

HITTING: The Braves continue to be a mystery at the plate. Playing in a park suited to robust hitting and possessing ample sluggers, Atlanta still managed to rank in a 10th-place tie in the NL with a .250 average and 11th in runs with 615.

The two biggest reasons for the 1986 offensive mediocrity were

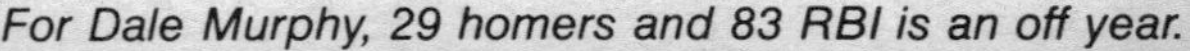

For Dale Murphy, 29 homers and 83 RBI is an off year.

a sub-par year by Dale Murphy (.265, 29 homers, 83 RBI) and an unexpected season-long slump by catcher Ozzie Virgil (.223, 15, 48), who figured to benefit from Fulton County Stadium's cozy dimensions. And the offensive picture for 1987 is clouded by the Braves' inability to re-sign free agent Bob Horner (.273, 27, 87) last winter.

On the plus side, Ken Griffey batted .308 after returning to the NL and Ted Simmons gave the club a credible bench with 18 RBI in a pinch. Glenn Hubbard (.230, 4, 36) and Rafael Ramirez (.240, 8, 33), though, tailed off sharply on offense.

PITCHING: The pitching was a horror story again in 1986, except for the development of rookie Paul Assenmacher (7-3, 2.50, 7 saves) and the return to form of reliever Gene Garber (5-5, 2.54, 24 saves) in the absence of Bruce Sutter.

Rick Mahler (14-18, 4.88) is the workhorse of the staff, but his hits-to-innings ratio (283 in 237⅔) was awful, so it appears Zane Smith (8-16, 4.05) or David Palmer (11-10, 3.65) is the logical candidate to become the new ace of a so-so staff. The bullpen is solid with Assenmacher, Garber and Jeff Dedmon, so if Sutter bounces back, the Braves' relief corps will rank with the best in the league.

FIELDING: This was the Braves' strongest area in 1986 and it still wasn't much to brag about. The strength is at third base, where Ken Oberkfell made only eight errors. Hubbard has tailed off as a second baseman and Ramirez and Andres Thomas had a combined total of 40 errors at shortstop. Murphy made six errors, but is solid in center.

OUTLOOK: The Braves always seem to be better on paper than on the field. For all of their hitting stars, they don't generate enough offense in a park designed for it. At least they were a winner at home (41-40) last season after a pattern of doing better on the road.

Chuck Tanner's clubs had a knack for finishing strong in his Pittsburgh days, but that magic didn't rub off in his maiden Atlanta season. The Braves finished 72-89 and were 30-43 after the All-Star break, hardly building momentum for what figures to be another long season in 1987. A return to form by Virgil and Murphy could improve the club, but the starting pitching remains shaky, as usual.

ATLANTA BRAVES 1987 ROSTER

MANAGER Chuck Tanner
Coaches—Tony Bartirome, Al Monchak, Russ Nixon, Johnny Sain, Bob Skinner, Willie Stargell

PITCHERS

No.	Name	1986 Club	W-L	IP	SO	ERA	B-T	Ht.	Wt.	Born
38	Acker, Jim	Toronto	2-4	60	32	4.35	R-R	6-2	212	9/24/58 Freer, TX
		Atlanta	3-8	95	37	3.79				
30	Assenmacher, Paul	Atlanta	7-3	68	56	2.50	L-L	6-3	195	12/10/60 Detroit, MI
61	Coffman, Kevin	Sumter	10-3	114	120	3.07	R-R	6-2	175	1/19/65 Austin, TX
		Durham	1-2	13	7	7.43				
		Greenville	3-4	49	43	4.44				
49	Dedmon, Jeff	Atlanta	6-6	100	58	2.98	L-R	6-2	200	3/4/60 Torrance, CA
26	Garber, Gene	Atlanta	5-5	78	56	2.54	R-R	5-10	172	11/13/47 Lancaster, PA
47	Glavine, Tom	Greenville	11-6	145	114	3.41	L-L	6-0	175	3/25/66 Concord, MA
		Richmond	1-5	40	12	5.63				
66	Kilner, John	Durham	6-8	141	89	4.53	L-L	6-0	170	6/20/65 Cleveland, OH
42	Mahler, Rick	Atlanta	14-18	238	137	4.88	R-R	6-1	202	8/5/53 Austin, TX
29	McMurtry, Craig	Greenville	1-1	15	12	6.00	R-R	6-5	192	11/5/59 Temple, TX
		Atlanta	1-6	80	50	4.74				
31	Olwine, Ed	Richmond	2-0	25	15	0.73	R-L	6-2	170	5/28/58 Greenville, OH
		Atlanta	0-0	48	37	3.40				
46	Palmer, David	Atlanta	11-10	210	170	3.65	R-R	6-1	205	10/19/57 Glens Falls, NY
45	Puleo, Charlie	Richmond	14-7	170	124	3.49	R-R	6-3	200	2/7/55 Glen Ridge, NJ
		Atlanta	1-2	24	18	2.96				
68	Siebert, Richard	Durham	11-9	151	104	5.47	R-R	6-2	165	10/13/63 E. Cleveland, OH
65	Smith, Pete	Greenville	1-8	105	64	5.85	R-R	6-2	183	2/27/66 Abington, MA
34	Smith, Zane	Atlanta	8-16	204	139	4.05	L-L	6-2	195	12/28/60 Madison, WI
40	Sutter, Bruce	Atlanta	2-0	19	16	4.34	R-R	6-2	195	1/8/53 Lancaster, PA
48	West, Matt	Richmond	Disabled list				B-R	6-4	195	1/13/60 Santa Monica, CA
59	Ziem, Steve	Greenville	7-2	75	54	4.70	R-R	6-2	210	10/24/61 Milwaukee, WI
		Richmond	8-5	96	48	3.08				

CATCHERS

No.	Name	1986 Club	H	HR	RBI	Pct.	B-T	Ht.	Wt.	Born
20	Benedict, Bruce	Atlanta	36	0	13	.225	R-R	6-2	195	8/15/55 Birmingham, AL
9	Virgil, Ozzie	Atlanta	80	15	48	.223	R-R	6-1	205	12/7/56 Puerto Rico

INFIELDERS

No.	Name	1986 Club	H	HR	RBI	Pct.	B-T	Ht.	Wt.	Born
63	Blauser, Jeff	Durham	128	13	52	.289	R-R	6-0	170	12/8/65 Los Gatos, CA
32	Gant, Ron	Durham	54	4	23	.234	R-R	6-0	172	3/2/65 Victoria, TX
17	Hubbard, Glenn	Atlanta	94	4	36	.230	R-R	5-7	170	9/25/57 Germany
24	Oberkfell, Ken	Atlanta	136	5	48	.270	L-R	6-1	210	5/4/56 Maryville, IL
28	Perry, Gerald	Richmond	125	10	75	.326	L-R	6-0	190	10/30/60 Savannah, GA
		Atlanta	19	2	11	.271				
16	Ramirez, Rafael	Atlanta	119	8	33	.240	R-R	5-11	190	2/18/59 Dominican Republic
12	Runge, Paul	Richmond	126	6	59	.275	R-R	6-0	175	5/21/58 Kingston, NY
		Atlanta	2	0	0	.250				
23	Simmons, Ted	Atlanta	32	4	25	.252	B-R	6-0	200	8/9/49 Highland Park, MI
14	Thomas, Andres	Atlanta	81	6	32	.251	R-R	6-1	185	11/10/63 Dom. Republic

OUTFIELDERS

No.	Name	1986 Club	H	HR	RBI	Pct.	B-T	Ht.	Wt.	Born
54	Denson, Drew	Durham	54	4	23	.234	R-R	6-5	210	12/16/65 Cincinnati, OH
22	Griffey, Ken	New York (AL)	60	9	26	.303	L-L	6-0	200	4/10/50 Donora, PA
		Atlanta	90	12	32	.308				
1	Hall, Albert	Richmond	119	3	41	.270	B-R	5-11	158	3/7/59 Birmingham, AL
		Atlanta	12	0	1	.240				
19	Harper, Terry	Atlanta	68	8	30	.257	R-R	6-1	205	8/19/55 Douglasville, GA
64	Hood, Dennis	Sumter	142	7	42	.253	R-R	6-2	170	7/3/66 Glendell, CA
36	Komminsk, Brad	Richmond	109	13	65	.234	R-R	6-2	205	4/4/61 Lima, OH
6	Motley, Darryl	Kansas City	44	7	20	.203	R-R	5-9	196	1/21/60 Muskogee, OK
		Omaha	18	0	8	.234				
		Atlanta	2	0	0	.200				
3	Murphy, Dale	Atlanta	163	29	83	.265	R-R	6-4	215	3/12/56 Portland, OR
62	Tubbs, Greg	Greenville	144	5	56	.269	R-R	5-9	178	8/31/62 Smithville, TN

BRAVE PROFILES

DALE MURPHY 31 6-4 215 Bats R Throws R

"Murf" enjoyed a good season, but center fielder fell below his superstar standards . . . There were too many dry spots in a streaky home-run year, even though his two halves were comparable . . . Did not play at Philadelphia on July 9, snapping his consecutive-game streak at 740 . . . After a cut hand endangered the streak, he kept it alive with a dramatic pinch-homer for 676 straight on April 30 . . . Connected for 250th homer on June 30 . . . Batted .344 in April and was NL Player of the Month in August, batting .337 with 10 homers and 30 RBI . . . Born March 12, 1956, in Portland, Ore. . . . Attended BYU and was first-round pick in 1974 . . . Youngest back-to-back MVP award winner in NL history.

Year	Club	Pos.	G	AB	R	H	2B	3B	HR	RBI	SB	Avg.
1976	Atlanta	C	19	65	3	17	6	0	0	9	0	.262
1977	Atlanta	C	18	76	5	24	8	1	2	14	0	.316
1978	Atlanta	C-1B	151	530	66	120	14	3	23	79	11	.226
1979	Atlanta	1B-C	104	384	53	106	7	2	21	57	6	.276
1980	Atlanta	OF-1B	156	569	98	160	27	2	33	89	9	.281
1981	Atlanta	OF-1B	104	369	43	91	12	1	13	50	14	.247
1982	Atlanta	OF	162	598	113	168	23	2	36	109	23	.281
1983	Atlanta	OF	162	589	131	178	24	4	36	121	30	.302
1984	Atlanta	OF	162	607	94	176	32	8	36	100	19	.290
1985	Atlanta	OF	162	616	118	185	32	2	37	111	10	.300
1986	Atlanta	OF	160	614	89	163	29	7	29	83	7	.265
	Totals		1360	5017	813	1388	214	32	266	822	129	.277

GLENN HUBBARD 29 5-7 170 Bats R Throws R

"Hub's" offensive production has been slipping since he led NL second basemen in RBI with 70 in 1983 . . . Weak bat is making it hard for Braves to justify sticking with him solely for his dependable glove . . . Set all-time Braves' mark for second baseman with .991 fielding percentage in 1981, but his error total soared to 19 last season . . . Despite .230 batting average, he managed to draw 66 walks to boost on-base percentage to .340 in 1986 . . . A battler . . . Born Sept. 25, 1957, in Hahn Air Force Base, West Germany . . . Played Little League ball in Taiwan before becoming four-sport prep star in Utah . . . Braves drafted him on 20th round in 1975 . . . Participated in a triple play against the Phillies in his second major-league game in 1978 . . . He's so sure-handed that teammates call the area around second base "The Dead Zone."

Year	Club	Pos.	G	AB	R	H	2B	3B	HR	RBI	SB	Avg.
1978	Atlanta	2B	44	163	15	42	4	0	2	13	2	.258
1979	Atlanta	2B	97	325	34	75	12	0	3	29	0	.231
1980	Atlanta	2B	117	431	55	107	21	3	9	43	7	.248
1981	Atlanta	2B	99	361	39	85	13	5	6	33	4	.235
1982	Atlanta	2B	145	532	75	132	25	1	9	59	4	.248
1983	Atlanta	2B	148	517	65	136	24	6	12	70	3	.263
1984	Atlanta	2B	120	397	53	93	27	2	9	43	4	.234
1985	Atlanta	2B	142	439	51	102	21	0	5	39	4	.232
1986	Atlanta	2B	143	408	42	94	16	1	4	36	3	.230
	Totals		1055	3573	429	866	163	18	59	365	31	.242

OZZIE VIRGIL 30 6-1 205 **Bats R Throws R**

Clubbed most homers by a Brave catcher since Vic Correll clouted 11 in 1975, but that was no consolation . . . Ozzie was supposed to hit a ton at Fulton County Stadium, adding more meat to the lineup, but instead suffered an horrendous slump . . . Did lots of damage with Phillies in 1984 and 1985 . . . Maybe Phillies knew something when they swapped him and Peter Smith for Steve Bedrosian and Milt Thompson prior to last season . . . Born Dec. 7, 1956, in Mayaguez, P.R. . . . Son of Seattle coach Ozzie Sr . . . Phillies' sixth-round pick in 1976 . . . Stole job from injured Bo Diaz in 1984 . . . Needs to improve this season to keep his job with Atlanta.

Year	Club	Pos.	G	AB	R	H	2B	3B	HR	RBI	SB	Avg.
1980	Philadelphia	C	1	5	1	1	1	0	0	0	0	.200
1981	Philadelphia	C	6	6	0	0	0	0	0	0	0	.000
1982	Philadelphia	C	49	101	11	24	6	0	3	8	0	.238
1983	Philadelphia	C	55	140	11	30	7	0	6	23	0	.214
1984	Philadelphia	C	141	456	61	119	21	2	18	68	1	.261
1985	Philadelphia	C	131	426	47	105	16	3	19	55	0	.246
1986	Atlanta	C	114	359	45	80	9	0	15	48	1	.223
	Totals		497	1493	176	359	60	5	61	202	2	.240

KEN OBERKFELL 30 6-1 210 **Bats L Throws R**

Played more to his potential than any of the regulars, ranking among league leaders in on-base percentage (.373) and walks (83) . . . Climbed to .300 by end of July, but gradually tailed off . . . His prowess at third base and at the plate forced Bob Horner to first base in 1985 . . . Born May 4, 1956, in Maryville, Ill. . . . Signed by Cardinals as free agent in 1975 . . .

Came up as second baseman, but shifted to third to accommodate Tom Herr . . . Topped NL in fielding at second and third with Redbirds . . . Batting .309 on June 15, 1984, when St. Louis traded him to Atlanta for Ken Dayley and Mike Jorgensen.

Year	Club	Pos.	G	AB	R	H	2B	3B	HR	RBI	SB	Avg.
1977	St. Louis	2B	9	9	0	1	0	0	0	1	0	.111
1978	St. Louis	2B-3B	24	50	7	6	1	0	0	0	0	.120
1979	St. Louis	2B-3B-SS	135	369	53	111	19	5	1	35	4	.301
1980	St. Louis	2B-3B	116	422	58	128	27	6	3	46	4	.303
1981	St. Louis	3B-SS	102	376	43	110	12	6	2	45	13	.293
1982	St. Louis	3B-2B	137	470	55	136	22	5	2	34	11	.289
1983	St. Louis	3B-2B-SS	151	488	62	143	26	5	3	38	12	.293
1984	St.L.-Atl.	3B-2B-SS	100	324	38	87	19	2	1	21	2	.269
1985	Atlanta	3B-2B	134	412	30	112	19	4	3	35	1	.272
1986	Atlanta	3B-2B	151	503	62	136	24	3	5	48	7	.270
	Totals		1059	3423	408	970	169	36	20	303	54	.283

KEN GRIFFEY 36 6-0 200 **Bats L Throws L**

Had outstanding year, combining to bat above .300 and belt 21 home runs for Yanks and Braves . . . Left fielder joined Atlanta on June 29 following a swap with the Yankees for Claudell Washington and Paul Zuvella . . . A lifetime .300 hitter in the NL, where he first attained stardom with Cincinnati . . . Batted .333 with 16 RBI in August . . . Born April 10, 1950, in Donora, Pa. . . . Became one of first baseball millionaires after being a 29th-round draft choice in 1969 . . . All-Star Game MVP and Reds' MVP in 1980 . . . A .313 hitter in nine NL Championship Series games.

Year	Club	Pos.	G	AB	R	H	2B	3B	HR	RBI	SB	Avg.
1973	Cincinnati	OF	25	86	19	33	5	1	3	14	4	.384
1974	Cincinnati	OF	88	227	24	57	9	5	2	19	9	.251
1975	Cincinnati	OF	132	463	95	141	15	9	4	46	16	.305
1976	Cincinnati	OF	148	562	111	189	28	9	6	74	34	.336
1977	Cincinnati	OF	154	585	117	186	35	8	12	57	17	.318
1978	Cincinnati	OF	158	614	90	177	33	8	10	63	23	.288
1979	Cincinnati	OF	95	380	62	120	27	4	8	32	12	.316
1980	Cincinnati	OF	146	544	89	160	28	10	13	85	23	.294
1981	Cincinnati	OF	101	396	65	123	21	6	2	34	12	.311
1982	New York (AL)	OF	127	484	70	134	23	2	12	54	10	.277
1983	New York (AL)	OF-1B	118	458	60	140	21	3	11	46	5	.306
1984	New York (AL)	OF-1B	120	399	44	109	20	1	7	56	2	.273
1985	New York (AL)	OF-1B	127	438	68	120	28	4	10	69	7	.274
1986	New York (AL)	OF	59	198	33	60	7	0	9	26	2	.303
1986	Atlanta	OF	80	292	36	90	15	3	12	32	12	.308
	Totals		1678	6126	983	1839	315	73	121	707	188	.300

ZANE SMITH 26 6-2 195 **Bats L Throws L**

Judging from 8-16 record and 4.05 ERA in his second full major-league season, you might not think this guy figures prominently in the Braves' plans . . . But he does . . . In fact, lots of clubs tried to pry him away during the winter, but Braves resisted offers . . . Drafted in third round in 1982, he arrived in majors ahead of schedule in 1984 . . . Born Dec. 28, 1960, in Madison, Wis. . . . Did not play baseball in high school, but did pitch for Indiana State . . . Knows how to change speeds and get the ground ball . . . Had two shutouts in only 18 starts in 1985 . . . Removal of cyst from his back cost him month on disabled list in 1985 . . . Pitching-poor Braves need him to grow up in a hurry.

Year	Club	G	IP	W	L	Pct.	SO	BB	H	ERA
1984	Atlanta	3	20	1	0	1.000	16	13	16	2.25
1985	Atlanta	42	147	9	10	.474	85	80	135	3.80
1986	Atlanta	38	204⅔	8	16	.333	139	105	209	4.05
	Totals	83	371⅔	18	26	.409	240	198	360	3.85

PAUL ASSENMACHER 26 6-3 195 **Bats L Throws L**

A pleasant surprise in a dismal season, the rookie made the jump from Double-A and was the best southpaw out of the Braves bullpen . . . Formed a solid one-two punch with Gene Garber to compensate for loss of Bruce Sutter . . . Solid finish gave him a streak of one earned run relinquished in an 11-game stretch in August and September . . . Born Dec. 10, 1960, in Detroit . . . Signed by Braves as free agent in 1983 . . . An undistinguished minor-league career until he was sent to the bullpen in 1985 . . . Sinkerballer finished 6-0 with four saves at Greenville (AA) in 1985.

Year	Club	G	IP	W	L	Pct.	SO	BB	H	ERA
1986	Atlanta	61	68⅓	7	3	.700	56	26	61	2.50

GENE GARBER 39 5-10 172 **Bats R Throws R**

He hadn't enjoyed great bullpen success since 1982, so who would have thought the side-winding veteran would have stepped in for Bruce Sutter and become a stopper once again last year? . . . But it happened as he saved 24 games in 1986, following a one-save season in 1985 . . . A 3-0, five-save May got him going and he enjoyed a solid August with eight saves . . . Born Nov. 13, 1947, in Lancaster, Pa. . . . Works on the family dairy farm during the winter . . . Attended Elizabethtown College and was Pirates' 13th-round draft pick in 1965 . . . Has career total of 194 saves . . . Stopped Pete Rose's record 44-game hitting streak in 1978 . . . Obtained from Phils for Dick Ruthven in June 1978.

Year	Club	G	IP	W	L	Pct.	SO	BB	H	ERA
1969	Pittsburgh	2	5	0	0	.000	3	1	6	5.40
1970	Pittsburgh	14	22	0	3	.000	7	10	22	5.32
1972	Pittsburgh	4	6	0	0	.000	3	3	7	7.50
1973	Kansas City	48	153	9	9	.500	60	49	164	4.24
1974	Kansas City	17	28	1	2	.333	14	13	35	4.82
1974	Philadelphia	34	48	4	0	1.000	27	31	39	2.06
1975	Philadelphia	71	110	10	12	.455	69	27	104	3.60
1976	Philadelphia	59	93	9	3	.750	92	30	78	2.81
1977	Philadelphia	64	103	8	6	.571	78	23	82	2.36
1978	Phil.-Atl.	65	117	6	5	.545	85	24	84	2.15
1979	Atlanta	68	106	6	16	.273	56	24	121	4.33
1980	Atlanta	68	82	5	5	.500	51	24	95	3.84
1981	Atlanta	35	59	4	6	.400	34	20	49	2.59
1982	Atlanta	69	119⅓	8	10	.444	68	32	100	2.34
1983	Atlanta	43	60⅔	4	5	.444	45	23	72	4.60
1984	Atlanta	62	106	3	6	.333	55	24	103	3.06
1985	Atlanta	59	97⅓	6	6	.500	66	25	98	3.61
1986	Atlanta	61	78	5	5	.500	56	20	76	2.54
	Totals	843	1393⅓	88	99	.471	869	403	1335	3.29

RICK MAHLER 33 6-1 202 **Bats R Throws R**

Finished poorly to become biggest loser in NL last year after being staff ace in 1985 . . . Streaky in 1986, going 6-0 in June and posting a 9-1 mark from May 3 to June 30 . . . A six-game losing streak followed . . . His 7-0 start in 1985 was among best in Braves' history, yet he finished only two games above .500 . . . Born Aug. 5, 1953, in Austin, Tex. . . . Attended Trinity U. . . . Non-drafted signee by Braves because of a shortage of pitchers on Kingsport rookie club in 1975 . . . Younger brother of pitcher Mickey Mahler . . . Flubbed first big chance with

Braves, but made it back following 12-7 stint at Richmond (AAA) in 1983.

Year	Club	G	IP	W	L	Pct.	SO	BB	H	ERA
1979	Atlanta	15	22	0	0	.000	12	11	28	6.14
1980	Atlanta	2	4	0	0	.000	1	0	2	2.25
1981	Atlanta	34	112	8	6	.571	54	43	109	2.81
1982	Atlanta	39	205⅓	9	10	.474	105	62	213	4.21
1983	Atlanta	10	14⅓	0	0	.000	7	9	16	5.02
1984	Atlanta	38	222	13	10	.565	106	62	209	3.12
1985	Atlanta	39	266⅔	17	15	.531	107	79	272	3.48
1986	Atlanta	39	237⅔	14	18	.438	137	95	283	4.88
	Totals	216	1084	61	59	.508	529	361	1132	3.85

DAVID PALMER 29 6-1 205 **Bats R Throws R**

Pitched better in first season with Braves than record showed . . . Best month was a 3-0 August . . . Good hits-to-innings ratio . . . Signed with Braves as a free agent in February 1985 . . . Underwent elbow surgery in 1980 and again in 1982, missing entire 1983 season with Expos before mounting comeback . . . Born Oct. 19, 1957, in Glens Falls, N.Y. . . . A 21st-round draft pick by Montreal in 1976 . . . Once went 37 straight innings without issuing a walk in minors . . . Knee surgery in 1979 began string of injury problems . . . Made tremendous comeback in 1984, firing a five-inning, rain-shortened perfect game against the Cardinals on April 21.

Year	Club	G	IP	W	L	Pct.	SO	BB	H	ERA
1978	Montreal	5	10	0	1	.000	7	2	9	2.70
1979	Montreal	36	123	10	2	.833	72	30	110	2.63
1980	Montreal	24	130	8	6	.571	73	30	124	2.98
1982	Montreal	13	73⅔	6	4	.600	46	36	60	3.18
1983	Montreal					Disabled list				
1984	Montreal	20	105⅓	7	3	.700	66	44	101	3.84
1985	Montreal	24	135⅔	7	10	.412	106	67	128	3.71
1986	Atlanta	35	209⅔	11	10	.524	170	102	181	3.65
	Totals	157	787⅓	49	36	.576	540	311	713	3.36

TOP PROSPECT

CHARLIE PULEO 32 6-3 200 **Bats R Throws R**

Granted, he has been around, having pitched for Mets and Reds, but he's new to the Braves and as good a prospect as they had on the graybeard Richmond (AAA) roster . . . Born Feb. 7, 1955, in Glen Ridge, N.J. . . . Puleo was 14-7 with 3.49 ERA for International League champs and had 2-0 record with 0.60 ERA in the playoffs, beating Tidewater, 8-1, and Rochester, 3-0 . . . Was 1-2 with 2.96 ERA in five games with Braves in September.

MANAGER CHUCK TANNER: Experienced a second straight dismal season in first year at helm of Braves . . . Probably more a case of lacking talent rather than touch, because "Chuckles" has a reputation for getting the most out of his players and finishing strong . . . That hasn't happened recently . . . His 1,263rd victory last year placed him 24th on the all-time list . . . Signed five-year contract with Ted Turner after ending nine-year association with Pirates . . . Born July 4, 1929, in New Castle, Pa. . . . Signed with Boston Braves as free agent in 1946 . . . Batted above .300 four times with minor-league Atlanta Crackers from 1951-54 before reaching Milwaukee in 1955 and homering in first at-bat . . . Began managing in 1966 and got first big-league job with White Sox in 1970 . . . Managed A's in 1976 before Charlie Finley traded him to Pirates for Manny Sanguillen . . . Guided 1979 Bucs to World Championship, sweeping Reds and downing Orioles in seven . . . Career major-league record is 1,271-1,262.

GREATEST ALL-TIME ROOKIE

It's only fair that the Boston Braves, Milwaukee Braves and Atlanta Braves each have their own top rookie. The three winners are Wally Berger (Boston), Rico Carty (Milwaukee) and Bob Horner (Atlanta).

Berger established a rookie home-run record with 38 in 1930, a mark tied by Frank Robinson 26 years later. Berger also had a .310 average, 27 doubles, 14 triples, 98 runs and 119 RBI.

Among the Boston pitchers, Kid Nichols was 27-19 with a 2.21 ERA and seven shutouts in 1890; Vic Willis was 24-13 with a 2.84 ERA in 1898, and Chet Nichols topped the National League with a 2.88 ERA in 1951.

Berger's biggest competition, however, came from second baseman Alvin Dark, whose all-around play helped the Braves to a pennant in 1948. Dark batted .322 that season and belted 39 doubles. Rookie Ed Mathews hit 25 home runs in 1952.

Nobody comes close to Carty among Milwaukee freshmen. Only an outrageous year by Richie Allen deprived Rico of league honors in 1964, when he batted a robust .330 with 22 home runs and 88 RBI.

Atlanta didn't have a great rookie until Horner went from Arizona State stardom into the Braves' lineup in 1978. Horner amassed 23 homers and 63 RBI in only 89 games and was named Rookie of the Year.

ALL-TIME BRAVE SEASON RECORDS

BATTING: Rogers Hornsby, .387, 1928
HRs: Eddie Mathews, 47, 1953
Hank Aaron, 47, 1971
RBIs: Eddie Mathews, 135, 1953
STEALS: Ralph Myers, 57, 1913
WINS: Vic Willis, 27, 1902
Charles Pittinger, 27, 1902
Dick Rudolph, 27, 1914
STRIKEOUTS: Phil Niekro, 262, 1977

Ol' sidewinder Gene Garber rescued Sutter-less Braves.

CINCINNATI REDS

TEAM DIRECTORY: Principal Owner-Pres.: Marge Schott; GM: Bill Bergesch; Scounting Dir.: Larry Doughty; VP-Play. Pers.: Sheldon Bender; VP-Publ.: Jim Ferguson; Trav. Sec.: Brad Del Barba; Mgr.: Pete Rose. Home: Riverfront Stadium (52,392). Field distances: 330, l.f. line; 404, c.f.; 330, r.f. line. Spring training: Tampa, Fla.

SCOUTING REPORT

HITTING: With a .254 average, the Reds ranked fifth in the NL in hitting last year and their 732 runs ranked third, so offense is not a problem. In fact, it could improve with Pete Rose no longer a regular and with Eric Davis having a chance to play more than 132 games.

Dave Parker (.273, 31 homers, 116 RBI) remains among the most dangerous hitters in the game, but the Reds' success could be tied to the awesome potential of Davis, who had a .271 average, 27 homers, 71 RBI and 80 stolen bases last season. He should continue to improve, along with newcomers Barry Larkin and Kal Daniels.

The same probably cannot be said of Buddy Bell (.278, 20, 75), who gave the Reds more than they could have expected in 1986. It's time for Nick Esasky (.230, 12, 41) to fish or cut bait at first base. If he cannot handle the daily grind, Parker might be ready for a shift to first to accommodate younger outfield talent.

PITCHING: Cincinnati's collective 3.91 ERA ranked ninth in the league last year, but there's hope for improvement because of some interesting developments. Ted Power (10-6, 3.70) was an emergency starter and came through sufficiently to make high-priced John Denny expendable.

The club also augmented the bullpen wizardry of John Franco (6-6, 2.94, 29 saves) with Ron Robinson (10-3, 3.24), so this is a decent staff and could be a great one if Mario Soto (5-10, 4.71), Bill Gullickson (15-12, 3.38) and Tom Browning (14-13, 3.81) pitch up to their capabilities.

FIELDING: It's difficult to get a reading on the Cincinnati defense because of all the recent changes, but shortstop Larkin has learned well from a master in Dave Concepcion and should form a solid double-play combination with Ron Oester. Bell displayed some of his former brilliance with a 10-error season at third and

Eric Davis has sights set on being a 30-30 man.

Eddie Milner and Davis can scoot with the best of the outfielders. Parker has lost a step in right, but his arm remains formidable.

OUTLOOK: A pitching improvement could make Rose's Reds a pennant winner. The confidence is there because of a strong second-half run. The Reds were struggling along at 40-44 at mid-season, but used a 46-32 second half to build momentum for 1987.

Cincinnati's slow start was reflected in a 44-46 mark against Western foes, but no NL West team played the East tougher (42-30). The Reds also didn't seem to mind where they played, going 43-38 at home and on the road. Big performances by the youngsters, another solid year by Parker and Davis' blossoming could make this club a big winner.

CINCINNATI REDS 1987 ROSTER

MANAGER Pete Rose

Coaches—Scott Breeden, Billy DeMars, Tommy Helms, Bruce Kimm, Tony Perez

PITCHERS

No.	Name	1986 Club	W-L	IP	SO	ERA	B-T	Ht.	Wt.	Born
32	Browning, Tom	Cincinnati	14-13	243	147	3.81	L-L	6-1	190	4/28/60 Casper, WY
47	Charlton, Norm	Vermont	10-6	137	96	2.83	B-L	6-2	190	1/6/63 Ft. Polk, LA
49	Dibble, Rob	Vermont	3-2	55	37	3.09	L-R	6-4	225	1/24/64 Bridgeport, CT
		Denver	1-0	7	3	5.40				
31	Franco, John	Cincinnati	6-6	101	84	2.94	L-L	5-10	175	9/17/60 Brooklyn, NY
52	Gray, Jeff	Vermont	14-2	84	65	2.35	R-R	6-1	180	4/10/63 Richmond, VA
34	Gullickson, Bill	Cincinnati	15-12	245	121	3.38	R-R	6-3	220	2/20/59 Marshall, MN
53	Kemp, Hugh	Denver	10-7	171	106	4.11	L-R	6-3	190	12/13/60 Nashville, TN
43	Landrum, Bill	Denver	1-3	36	36	3.47	R-R	6-2	185	8/17/58 Columbia, SC
		Cincinnati	0-0	13	14	6.75				
46	Murphy, Rob	Denver	3-4	43	36	1.90	L-L	6-2	205	5/26/60 Miami, FL
		Cincinnati	6-0	50	36	0.72				
35	Pacillo, Pat	Denver	11-6	148	111	4.32	R-R	6-2	205	7/23/63 Jersey City, NJ
48	Power, Ted	Cincinnati	10-6	129	95	3.70	R-R	6-4	225	1/31/55 Guthrie, OK
33	Robinson, Ron	Cincinnati	10-3	116	117	3.24	R-R	6-4	215	3/24/62 Woodlake, CA
59	Smith, Michael	Cedar Rapids	10-10	191	172	3.35	R-R	6-3	180	10/31/63 San Antonio, TX
36	Soto, Mario	Cincinnati	5-10	105	67	4.71	R-R	6-0	190	7/12/56 Dominican Republic
38	Terry, Scott	Cincinnati	1-2	56	32	6.14	R-R	5-11	195	11/21/59 Hobbs, NM
		Denver	1-2	19	13	2.33				
—	Williams, Frank	Phoenix	1-1	38	41	2.13	R-R	6-1	180	2/13/58 Seattle, WA
		San Francisco	3-1	52	33	1.20				

CATCHERS

No.	Name	1986 Club	H	HR	RBI	Pct.	B-T	Ht.	Wt.	Born
54	Berry, Mark	Tampa	140	4	73	.315	R-R	6-0	180	9/22/62 Lynnwood, CA
22	Butera, Sal	Cincinnati	27	2	16	.239	R-R	6-0	190	9/25/52 Richmond Hill, NY
6	Diaz, Bo	Cincinnati	129	10	56	.272	R-R	5-11	200	3/23/53 Venezuela
8	McGriff, Terry	Denver	99	9	54	.291	R-R	6-2	190	9/23/63 Ft. Pierce, FL
55	Oliver, Joe	Vermont	78	6	41	.277	R-R	6-3	210	7/24/65 Memphis, TN

INFIELDERS

No.	Name	1986 Club	H	HR	RBI	Pct.	B-T	Ht.	Wt.	Born
25	Bell, Buddy	Cincinnati	158	20	75	.278	R-R	6-2	185	8/27/51 Pittsburgh, PA
13	Concepcion, Dave	Cincinnati	81	3	30	.260	R-R	6-1	190	6/17/48 Venezuela
56	Harris, Lenny	Vermont	114	10	52	.253	R-R	5-10	190	10/28/64 Miami, FL
15	Larkin, Barry	Denver	136	10	51	.329	R-R	6-0	185	4/28/64 Cincinnati, OH
		Cincinnati	45	3	19	.283				
30	McClendon, Lloyd	Denver	112	24	88	.259	R-R	5-11	195	1/11/59 Gary, IN
16	Oester, Ron	Cincinnati	135	8	44	.258	B-R	6-2	190	5/5/56 Cincinnati, OH
17	Rowdon, Wade	Denver	60	8	37	.333	R-R	6-2	180	9/7/60 Riverhead, NY
		Cincinnati	20	0	10	.250				
14	*Rose, Pete	Cincinnati	119	107	2	.264	B-R	5-11	200	4/14/64 Cincinnati, OH
50	Sabo, Chris	Denver	118	10	60	.273	R-R	6-0	170	1/19/62 Detroit, MI
11	Stillwell, Kurt	Denver	7	0	2	.233	B-R	5-11	175	6/4/65 Thousand Oaks, CA
		Cincinnati	64	0	26	.229				
58	Treadway, Jeff	Vermont	41	1	16	.336	L-R	5-11	165	1/22/63 Columbus, GA
		Denver	67	3	23	.328				

OUTFIELDERS

No.	Name	1986 Club	H	HR	RBI	Pct.	B-T	Ht.	Wt.	Born
28	Daniels, Kal	Denver	49	8	32	.371	L-R	5-11	185	8/20/63 Vienna, GA
		Cincinnati	58	6	23	.320				
44	Davis, Eric	Cincinnati	115	27	71	.277	R-R	6-3	175	5/29/62 Los Angeles, CA
12	Esasky, Nick	Cincinnati	76	12	41	.230	R-R	6-3	210	2/24/60 Hialeah, FL
26	Garcia, Leo	Denver	147	4	57	.278	L-L	5-8	165	11/6/62 Dominican Republic
57	Jones, Chris	Cedar Rapids	117	20	78	.247	R-R	6-2	195	12/16/65 Utica, NY
29	Jones, Tracy	Cincinnati	30	2	10	.349	R-R	6-3	220	3/31/61 Hawthorne, CA
21	O'Neill, Paul	Cincinnati	0	0	0	.000	L-L	6-4	205	2/25/63 Columbus, OH
		Denver	49	5	27	.254				
39	Parker, Dave	Cincinnati	174	31	116	.273	L-R	6-5	230	6/9/51 Jackson, MS
9	Venable, Max	Cincinnati	31	2	15	.211	L-R	5-10	185	6/6/57 Phoenix, AZ

*Free agent as a player at press time

RED PROFILES

DAVE PARKER 35 6-5 230 **Bats L Throws R**

Only a torrid finish by Mike Schmidt deprived "The Cobra" of a second straight RBI crown ... Has averaged 112 RBI in three years with Reds, reviving his career ... Collected 1,000th RBI on May 20 ... Took 16 homers and 55 RBI into All-Star Game ... Erupted for eight homers and 25 RBI in July ... Reds signed him as free agent prior to 1984 season ... Born June 9, 1951, in Jackson, Miss. ... . Drafted in 14th round by Pirates in 1970, so it took 14 years for right fielder to realize his dream of playing in hometown ... Batted above .300 five years in a row with Bucs, including successive batting titles in 1977-78 ... MVP of NL in 1978 and All-Star Game in 1979 ... Deserved MVP honors in 1985 following best all-around season.

Year	Club	Pos.	G	AB	R	H	2B	3B	HR	RBI	SB	Avg.
1973	Pittsburgh	OF	54	139	17	40	9	1	4	14	1	.288
1974	Pittsburgh	OF-1B	73	220	27	62	10	3	4	29	3	.282
1975	Pittsburgh	OF	148	558	75	172	35	10	25	101	8	.308
1976	Pittsburgh	OF	138	537	82	168	28	10	13	90	19	.313
1977	Pittsburgh	OF-2B	159	637	107	215	44	8	21	88	17	.338
1978	Pittsburgh	OF	148	581	102	194	32	12	30	117	20	.334
1979	Pittsburgh	OF	158	622	109	193	45	7	25	94	20	.310
1980	Pittsburgh	OF	139	518	71	153	31	1	17	79	10	.295
1981	Pittsburgh	OF	67	240	29	62	14	3	9	48	6	.258
1982	Pittsburgh	OF	73	244	41	66	19	3	6	29	7	.270
1983	Pittsburgh	OF	144	552	68	154	29	4	12	69	12	.279
1984	Cincinnati	OF	156	607	73	173	28	0	16	94	11	.285
1985	Cincinnati	OF	160	635	88	198	42	4	34	125	5	.312
1986	Cincinnati	OF	162	637	89	174	31	3	31	116	1	.273
	Totals		1779	6727	978	2024	397	69	247	1093	140	.301

ERIC DAVIS 24 6-3 175 **Bats R Throws R**

Flashed his overwhelming potential last season with remarkable stats for only 415 official at-bats ... We're talking franchise player here ... Once Eric cuts down on strikeouts and avoids lengthy power slumps, the baseball world will be his oyster ... Center fielder batted .361 with five homers and 17 steals in June, yet didn't move into starting lineup for good until June 15 ... NL Player of the Month in July, batting .381 with six homers and 25 steals ... Two homers at Pittsburgh on Aug. 25 made him third man in history to hit 20 homers and steal 60 bases, joining Joe Morgan and Rickey Henderson ... Belted three homers against

Giants on Sept. 10, but went three weeks before his next one . . . Born May 29, 1962, in Los Angeles . . . Played sandlot ball with Darryl Strawberry and Chris Brown . . . Prep basketball star . . . Eighth-round draft pick in 1980.

Year	Club	Pos.	G	AB	R	H	2B	3B	HR	RBI	SB	Avg.
1984	Cincinnati	OF	57	174	33	39	10	1	10	30	10	.224
1985	Cincinnati	OF	56	122	26	30	3	3	8	18	16	.246
1986	Cincinnati	OF	132	415	97	115	15	3	27	71	80	.277
	Totals		245	711	156	184	28	7	45	119	106	.259

RON OESTER 30 6-2 190 **Bats S Throws R**

A switch-hitter who doesn't scare you from either side . . . Primarily in lineup for his glove . . . Indicated that 1985 average (.295) was a fluke by returning to earlier level last season . . . Only a zero-for-15 start kept him from a .300 season in 1985 because he batted .303 thereafter . . . Born May 5, 1956, in Cincinnati . . . One of several hometown athletes on the Reds . . . An all-state schoolboy in 1974, he was drafted by Reds in eighth round . . . Came up as a shortstop, but was shifted to second because of Dave Concepcion . . . His 21-game hitting streak in 1984 is Reds' longest since Pete Rose's record 44-game spree in 1978.

Year	Club	Pos.	G	AB	R	H	2B	3B	HR	RBI	SB	Avg.
1978	Cincinnati	SS	6	8	1	3	0	0	0	1	0	.375
1979	Cincinnati	SS	6	3	0	0	0	0	0	0	0	.000
1980	Cincinnati	2B-SS-3B	100	303	40	84	16	2	2	20	6	.277
1981	Cincinnati	2B-SS	105	354	45	96	16	7	5	42	2	.271
1982	Cincinnati	2B-SS-3B	151	549	63	143	19	4	9	47	5	.260
1983	Cincinnati	2B	157	549	63	145	23	5	11	58	2	.264
1984	Cincinnati	2B-SS	150	553	54	134	26	3	3	38	7	.242
1985	Cincinnati	2B	152	526	59	155	26	3	1	34	5	.295
1986	Cincinnati	2B	153	523	52	135	23	2	8	44	9	.258
	Totals		980	3368	377	895	149	26	39	284	36	.266

BUDDY BELL 35 6-2 185 **Bats R Throws R**

It took him a year, but Buddy finally got the hang of NL pitching down the stretch last season . . . After struggling during first half, he batted .319 in July and bashed 10 homers in August . . . Third baseman posted career high in home runs . . . Born Aug. 27, 1951, in Pittsburgh . . . Son of former Reds' slugger Gus Bell . . . He and his dad have combined total of 382 homers; only Berras have more . . . Indians' 16th-round draft pick in 1969 . . . Attained greatest success after 1978 swap to Texas . . . Acquired by Reds on July 19, 1985, for Duane Walker and Jeff Russell.

Year	Club	Pos.	G	AB	R	H	2B	3B	HR	RBI	SB	Avg.
1972	Cleveland	OF-3B	132	466	49	119	21	1	9	36	5	.255
1973	Cleveland	3B-OF	156	631	86	169	23	7	14	59	7	.268
1974	Cleveland	3B	116	423	51	111	15	1	7	46	1	.262
1975	Cleveland	3B	153	553	66	150	20	4	10	59	6	.271
1976	Cleveland	3B-1B	159	604	75	170	26	2	7	60	3	.281
1977	Cleveland	3B-OF	129	479	64	140	23	4	11	64	1	.292
1978	Cleveland	3B	142	556	71	157	27	8	6	62	1	.282
1979	Texas	3B-SS	162	670	89	200	42	3	18	101	5	.299
1980	Texas	3B-SS	129	490	76	161	24	4	17	83	3	.329
1981	Texas	3B-SS	97	360	44	106	16	1	10	64	3	.294
1982	Texas	3B-SS	148	537	62	159	27	2	13	67	5	.296
1983	Texas	3B	156	618	75	171	35	3	14	66	3	.277
1984	Texas	3B	148	553	88	174	36	5	11	83	2	.315
1985	Texas	3B	84	313	33	74	13	3	4	32	3	.236
1985	Cincinnati	3B	67	247	28	54	15	2	6	36	0	.219
1986	Cincinnati	3B	155	568	89	158	29	3	20	75	2	.278
	Totals		2133	8068	1046	2273	392	53	177	993	50	.282

BO DIAZ 34 5-11 200 — Bats R Throws R

Bounced back from injury-marred 1985 to enjoy a solid first full season as Reds' catcher . . . Batted .300 last two months to finish with respectable numbers . . . Obviously did a good job handling pitchers, which is main reason club acquired him and Greg Simpson in August 1985 swap with Phillies for Tom Foley, Alan Knicely and Fred Toliver . . . Born March 23, 1953, in Cua, Venezuela . . . As a youngster, Bo played on champion Little League team that missed trip to World Series because an earthquake devastated his town . . . Originally signed with Red Sox . . . Best years were 1982 and 1983, including a .333 World Series average for Phils in 1983.

Year	Club	Pos.	G	AB	R	H	2B	3B	HR	RBI	SB	Avg.
1977	Boston	C	2	1	0	0	0	0	0	0	0	.000
1978	Cleveland	C	44	127	12	30	4	0	2	11	0	.236
1979	Cleveland	C	15	32	0	5	2	0	0	1	0	.156
1980	Cleveland	C	76	207	15	47	11	2	3	32	1	.227
1981	Cleveland	C	63	182	25	57	19	0	7	38	2	.313
1982	Philadelphia	C	144	525	69	151	29	1	18	85	3	.288
1983	Philadelphia	C	136	471	49	111	17	0	15	64	1	.236
1984	Philadelphia	C	27	75	5	16	4	0	1	9	0	.213
1985	Phil.-Cin.	C	77	237	21	58	13	1	5	31	0	.245
1986	Cincinnati	C	134	474	50	129	21	0	10	56	1	.272
	Totals		718	2331	246	604	120	4	61	327	8	.259

BILL GULLICKSON 28 6-3 220 — Bats R Throws R

A 2-4 finish ruined what would have been an outstanding season in his Reds' debut . . . "Gully" still was the biggest winner on the club, thanks to a sensational August, when he was NL Pitcher of the Month with a 5-2 record and a 0.79 ERA . . . Beginning with a July 29 outing against San Diego, he remarkably made nine consecutive starts in which he yielded one earned run or less, yet twice was a 2-1 loser during that stretch . . . Born Feb. 20, 1959, in Marshall, Minn. . . . A diabetic, he does charity work to combat the disease . . . Expos' No. 1 pick in 1977 draft following a sensational schoolboy career which included 23-1 record and six no-hitters at Joliet (Ill.) Catholic . . . Traded to Reds with Sal Butera for Jay Tibbs, Andy McGaffigan, John Stuper and Dann Bilardello prior to 1986 season.

Year	Club	G	IP	W	L	Pct.	SO	BB	H	ERA
1979	Montreal	1	1	0	0	.000	0	0	2	0.00
1980	Montreal	24	141	10	5	.667	120	50	127	3.00
1981	Montreal	22	157	7	9	.438	115	34	142	2.81
1982	Montreal	34	236⅔	12	14	.462	155	61	231	3.57
1983	Montreal	34	242⅓	17	12	.586	120	59	230	3.75
1984	Montreal	32	226⅔	12	9	.571	100	37	230	3.61
1985	Montreal	29	181⅓	14	12	.538	68	47	187	3.52
1986	Cincinnati	37	244⅔	15	12	.556	121	60	245	3.38
	Totals	213	1430⅔	87	73	.544	799	348	1394	3.43

TOM BROWNING 26 6-1 190 Bats L Throws L

Didn't approach rookie 20-win success of 1985, but was a workhorse and gave the staff stability . . . Did best work in July, going 4-1 with a 3.00 ERA . . . Born April 28, 1960, in Casper, Wyo. . . . Reds' ninth-round draft choice in 1982 . . . Commanded attention with 8-1 start for Class-A Tampa in 1983, entered bigs one year later . . . Development of screwball vital to his progress . . . Fired a seven-inning no-hitter for Wichita against Iowa in 1984 . . . In 1985, he became first rookie 20-game winner in majors since Bob Grim of the Yankees in 1954 and Cincy's first 20-game winner since Jim Merritt in 1970 . . . An 11-game winning string was club's best in 30 years . . . Rookie Pitcher of the Year in the NL.

Year	Club	G	IP	W	L	Pct.	SO	BB	H	ERA
1984	Cincinnati	3	23⅓	1	0	1.000	14	5	27	1.54
1985	Cincinnati	38	261⅓	20	9	.690	155	73	242	3.55
1986	Cincinnati	39	243⅓	14	13	.519	147	70	225	3.81
	Totals	80	528	35	22	.614	316	148	494	3.58

JOHN FRANCO 26 5-10 175 Bat L Throws L

A third consecutive dazzling season for the relief ace following moderate success as a minor-league starter . . . Notched 29 saves in 1986, 11 more than he had totaled in his previous pro career . . . Took a 2.27 ERA and 14 saves into the All-Star Game . . . Born Sept 17, 1960, in Brooklyn, N.Y. . . . Attended St. John's and drafted by the Dodgers, who let him get away in a swap for Rafael Landestoy in May 1983 . . . Big mistake . . .

Topped major-league relievers in victories in 1985 . . . Had an 11-game winning streak, longest on the Reds in 30 years . . . In one 18-game streak in 1985, he yielded but one earned run in 34 innings.

Year	Club	G	IP	W	L	Pct.	SO	BB	H	ERA
1984	Cincinnati	54	79⅓	6	2	.750	55	36	74	2.61
1985	Cincinnati	67	99	12	3	.800	61	40	83	2.18
1986	Cincinnati	74	101	6	6	.500	84	44	90	2.94
	Totals	195	279⅓	24	11	.686	200	120	247	2.58

TED POWER 32 6-4 225 — Bats R Throws R

Necessity was the mother of invention when the Reds switched Power from the bullpen in an emergency move and found their most effective starter down the stretch . . . Ted had a 4-5 record and 10 saves when he ended a string of 229 straight relief appearances on Aug. 22, because of injuries to John Denny and Mario Soto . . . He was beaten by the Cubs that day, but reeled off six straight wins as a starter the rest of the way . . . He was 5-0 with a 2.22 ERA in September . . . Born Jan. 31, 1955, in Guthrie, Okla. . . . Attended Kansas State, once fanning 19 batters in a game . . . Drafted by Dodgers in fifth round in 1976 and became a big winner at Triple-A Albuquerque . . . Cincy purchased him from Albuquerque in 1982 . . . Transformed into reliever by Reds and became bullpen ace in 1985.

Year	Club	G	IP	W	L	Pct.	SO	BB	H	ERA
1981	Los Angeles	5	14	1	3	.250	7	7	16	3.21
1982	Los Angeles	12	33⅔	1	1	.500	15	23	38	6.68
1983	Cincinnati	49	111	5	6	.455	57	49	120	4.54
1984	Cincinnati	78	108⅔	9	7	.563	81	46	93	2.82
1985	Cincinnati	64	80	8	6	.571	42	45	65	2.70
1986	Cincinnati	56	129	10	6	.625	95	52	115	3.70
	Totals	264	476⅓	34	29	.539	297	222	447	3.72

RON ROBINSON 25 6-4 215 — Bats R Throws R

Complemented John Franco beautifully in Reds' bullpen, freeing Ted Power for starting duty and making John Denny expendable . . . Struck out 117 in 116⅔ innings, one of the finest ratios in the majors . . . Started strong, going 2-0 with 1.37 ERA in April . . . Was 3-0 with 1.66 ERA in June . . . Born March 24, 1962, in Woodlake, Cal. . . . Pitched four no-hitters as a high-school senior . . . Reds' No. 1 draft pick in 1980 . . . Almost exclusively a starter in minors, going 15-7 at Denver (AAA) before reaching Reds to stay in 1985 . . . Alternated between bullpen and rotation in 1985 and performed erratically, winning five in a row and dropping six straight . . . Thrived as full-time reliever last year and should provide formidable one-two punch with Franco for years to come.

Year	Club	G	IP	W	L	Pct.	SO	BB	H	ERA
1984	Cincinnati	12	39⅔	1	2	.333	24	13	35	2.72
1985	Cincinnati	33	108⅓	7	7	.500	76	32	107	3.99
1986	Cincinnati	70	116⅔	10	3	.769	117	43	110	3.24
	Totals	115	264⅔	18	12	.600	217	88	252	3.47

TOP PROSPECT

BARRY LARKIN 22 6-0 185 Bats R Throws R

The club's No. 1 draft choice in the June 1985 draft, he joined the lengthy list of hometown athletes to play for Reds . . . Groomed as successor to Dave Concepcion at shortstop . . . Attended the U. of Michigan . . . Born April 28, 1964, in Cincinnati . . . Batted .329 with 31 doubles, 10 triples and 10 home runs at Denver (AAA) . . . Regarded as No. 2 prospect in the American Association, behind Ruben Sierra of the Rangers . . . A member of 1984 U.S. Olympic squad.

MANAGER PETE ROSE 45 5-11 200 Bats S Throws R

Concentrated more on managing last year and did a splendid job . . . Reds were 40-44 and in fifth place at All-Star break, but they finished 46-32 and took second again . . . Though he suffered through worst year at the plate, Pete had a burst of glory against the Giants on Aug. 11. With four singles and a double, he set a league record with his 10th five-hit game . . . Removed himself from 40-man roster during winter, making him ineligible to play until May 15 in 1987 . . . Insists he'll remain active as pinch-hitter . . . Born April 14, 1941, in Cincinnati . . . There's really not much to say about a man who has done it all in a Hall-of-Fame career topped by all-time hits record . . . Owns most records for longevity after playing 24 years . . . Major-league marks include most doubles, singles, games, at-bats, winning games and 200-hit seasons . . . Only man to play more than 500 games at five different positions . . . Rejoined Reds in deal with Montreal for Tom Lawless on Aug. 16, 1984 . . . Holds NL record with 44-game hitting streak in 1978 . . . His managerial record is 195-70.

Year	Club	Pos.	G	AB	R	H	2B	3B	HR	RBI	SB	Avg.
1963	Cincinnati	2B-OF	157	623	101	170	25	9	6	41	13	.273
1964	Cincinnati	2B	136	516	64	139	13	2	4	34	4	.269
1965	Cincinnati	2B	162	670	117	209	35	11	11	81	8	.312
1966	Cincinnati	2B-3B	156	654	97	205	38	5	16	70	4	.313
1967	Cincinnati	OF-2B	148	585	86	176	32	8	12	76	11	.301
1968	Cincinnati	OF-2B-1B	149	626	94	210	42	6	10	49	3	.335
1969	Cincinnati	OF-2B	156	627	120	218	33	11	16	82	7	.348
1970	Cincinnati	OF	159	649	120	205	37	9	15	52	12	.316
1971	Cincinnati	OF	160	632	86	192	27	4	13	44	13	.304
1972	Cincinnati	OF	154	645	107	198	31	11	6	57	10	.307
1973	Cincinnati	OF	160	680	115	230	36	8	5	64	10	.338
1974	Cincinnati	OF	163	652	110	185	45	7	3	51	2	.284
1975	Cincinnati	3B-OF	162	662	112	210	47	4	7	74	0	.317
1976	Cincinnati	3B-OF	162	665	130	215	42	6	10	63	9	.323
1977	Cincinnati	3B	162	655	95	204	38	7	9	64	16	.311
1978	Cincinnati	3B-OF-1B	159	655	103	198	51	3	7	52	13	302
1979	Philadelphia . .	1B-3B-2B	163	628	90	208	40	5	4	59	20	.331
1980	Philadelphia . .	1B	162	655	95	185	42	1	1	64	12	.282
1981	Philadelphia . .	1B	107	431	73	140	18	5	0	33	4	.325
1982	Philadelphia . .	1B	162	634	80	172	25	4	3	54	8	.271
1983	Philadelphia . .	1B-OF	151	493	52	121	14	3	0	45	7	.245
1984	Mont.-Cin. . . .	1B-OF	121	374	43	107	15	2	0	34	1	.286
1985	Cincinnati	1B	119	405	60	107	12	2	2	46	8	.264
	Totals		3490	13816	2150	4204	738	133	160	1289	195	.304

John Franco won or saved 35 of Reds' 86 victories.

GREATEST ALL-TIME ROOKIE

Frank Robinson began his Hall-of-Fame career with a rookie-record-tying 38 home runs in 1956, so he's a landslide winner among Cincinnati yearlings.

Robby embellished his power demonstration with a .290 average, a .558 slugging percentage, 27 doubles, 83 RBI and a league-leading 122 runs scored for the power-laden Reds of the mid-fifties.

Pete Rose scored 101 runs and batted .273 as a rookie in 1963. Johnny Bench belted 40 doubles and 15 homers while batting .275 with 82 RBI as a freshman in 1968.

Among the pitchers, numerous Reds enjoyed significant achievements as rookies. In 1899, Noodles Hahn was 23-8 with a 2.68 ERA and a league-leading 145 strikeouts. In 1941, Elmer Riddle went 19-4 with a 2.24 ERA and four shutouts.

In 1964, Sammy Ellis broke in with a 10-3 mark and a 2.57 ERA. In relief, he was 7-2 with 14 saves, so he had a hand in 24 victories. Three years later, Gary Nolan was 14-8 with a 2.58 ERA, 206 strikeouts and five shutouts.

ALL-TIME RED SEASON RECORDS

BATTING: Cy Seymour, .377, 1905
HRs: George Foster, 52, 1977
RBIs: George Foster, 149, 1977
STEALS: Bob Bescher, 81, 1911
WINS: Adolfo Luque, 27, 1923
Bucky Walters, 27, 1939
STRIKEOUTS: Mario Soto, 274, 1982

HOUSTON ASTROS

TEAM DIRECTORY: Chairman: Dr. John J. McMullen; Pres.-GM: Dick Wagner; VP-Baseball Oper.: Fred Stanley; Special Asst.: Donald Davidson; Dir. Minor League Oper.: Fred Nelson; Dir. Pub. Rel.: Rob Matwick; Trav. Sec.: Barry Waters; Mgr.: Hal Lanier. Home: Astrodome (45,000). Field distances: 330, l.f. line; 380, l.c.; 400, c.f.; 380, r.c.; 300, r.f. line. Spring training: Kissimmee, Fla.

SCOUTING REPORT

HITTING: Because their pitching was so good last year, it didn't matter that the Astros ranked only eighth in runs (654) among NL teams. They scored enough to win their division, thanks to a batting order of line-drive hitters who capitalized on the Astrodome's spacious alleys.

Denny Walling (.312, 13 homers, 58 RBI) and Kevin Bass (.311, 20, 79) had career seasons and Jose Cruz (.278, 10, 72)

NL MVP runnerup Glenn Davis had 16 game-winning RBI.

came on strong following a slow start. Bill Doran (.276, 42 stolen bases) and Billy Hatcher (.258, 38 steals) set the table. But the biggest difference in the 1986 Astros was the presence of a hammer. First baseman Glenn Davis provided the knockout punch with 31 homers and 101 RBI and finished second in the MVP voting.

PITCHING: The Mets had better quality depth, but nobody in the NL had a better pitcher than Cy Young Award winner Mike Scott (18-10, 2.22), whose dominance almost carried the Astros into the World Series. In fact, Scott and his pitching cohorts played a game of can-you-top-this down the stretch, helping Houston overcome the pressures of a pennant race.

Scott heads a rotation of Bob Knepper (17-12, 3.14), Nolan Ryan (12-8, 3.34) and surprising Jim Deshaies (12-5, 3.25), who proved he belonged among such select company. Scott finished with 306 strikeouts and the rubber-armed Ryan (194 strikeouts) showed he still could throw heat with the best of them.

Dave Smith (4-7, 2.73) was the bullpen stopper with 33 saves and rookie Charlie Kerfeld (11-2, 2.59, 7 saves) glittered in long relief. The Astros' 3.15 team ERA was bettered only by the Mets, but no team matched Houston's 19 shutouts.

FIELDING: The Astros tied for third in NL in fielding percentage at .979. Nobody was the best at his position, but all of the Astros performed well afield. The shortstop duo of Craig Reynolds and Dickie Thon was especially tough, making a combined total of only 19 errors. Bass' fielding in right was worthy of Gold Glove acclaim and Doran is excellent at second.

OUTLOOK: It's tough to repeat in the NL West, but the Astros have a chance if their pitching holds up. Manager Hal Lanier did a fine job in his rookie season, making all the right moves, but the Astros were relatively injury-free while posting a club-record 96 victories.

It will take the same type of season for Houston to win the division again, because Ryan and Cruz definitely are on the down side of great careers. Youngsters like Bass, Davis and Doran, however, should keep the lineup solid and the club competitive.

The mark of a championship club is its consistency and the Astros definitely were that last year. Their 52-29 home record and 44-37 road mark ranked them second to the Mets. They also dominated their division at 56-34 and were a solid 49-25 in the second half. The odds are against a repeat, but Houston is too solid to bet against it.

HOUSTON ASTROS 1987 ROSTER

MANAGER Hal Lanier

Coaches—Yogi Berra, Matt Galante, Denis Menke, Les Moss, Gene Tenace

PITCHERS

No.	Name	1986 Club	W-L	IP	SO	ERA	B-T	Ht.	Wt.	Born
17	Andersen, Larry	Houston	2-1	77	42	3.03	R-R	6-3	205	5/6/53 Portland, OR
—	Childress, Rocky	Port.-Tuc.	5-10	83	40	7.45	R-R	6-2	195	2/18/62 Santa Rosa, CA
		Philadelphia	0-0	3	1	6.75				
43	Deshaies, Jim	Houston	12-5	144	128	3.25	L-L	6-4	222	6/23/60 Massena, NY
44	Darwin, Danny	Milwaukee	6-8	130	79	3.52	R-R	6-3	190	10/25/55 Bonham, TX
		Houston	5-2	54	40	2.32				
—	Edwards, Jeff	San Antonio	9-10	141	124	3.77	L-L	6-2	190	6/27/63 Nashville, TN
54	Friederich, Mike	Columbus	8-9	165	110	4.35	B-R	6-5	225	2/26/65 Windfield, IL
42	Funk, Tom	Columbus	6-2	64	57	2.53	L-L	6-2	200	3/13/62 Kansas, City, MO
		Houston	0-0	8	2	6.48				
38	Hernandez, Manny	Tucson	8-7	128	84	4.71	R-R	6-0	150	5/7/61 Dominican Republic
		Houston	2-3	28	9	3.90				
—	Kelley, Anthony	Columbus	14-4	193	126	3.63	R-R	6-2	205	3/4/62 Chicago, IL
37	Kerfield, Charlie	Houston	11-2	94	77	2.59	R-R	6-6	245	9/28/63 Knobnoster, MO
39	Knepper, Bob	Houston	17-12	258	143	3.14	L-L	6-2	210	5/25/54 Akron, OH
35	Lopez, Aurelio	Houston	3-3	78	44	3.46	R-R	6-0	225	9/5/48 Mexico
—	Mallicoat, Rob	Tucson	0-2	14	9	6.43	L-L	6-3	180	11/16/64 St. Helens, OR
		Columbus	0-6	58	52	4.81				
—	Meads, Dave	Asheville	4-3	54	50	1.99	L-L	6-0	175	1/7/64 Montclair, NJ
		Osceola	2-4	15	10	7.63				
		Columbus	1-1	22	26	4.43				
51	Montalvo, Rafael	Tucson	5-3	77	31	3.86	R-R	6-0	185	3/31/64 Puerto Rico
		Houston	0-0	1	0	9.00				
34	Ryan, Nolan	Houston	12-8	178	194	3.34	R-R	6-2	210	1/31/47 Refugio, TX
33	Scott, Mike	Houston	18-10	275	306	2.22	R-R	6-3	215	4/26/55 Santa Monica, CA
45	Smith, Dave	Houston	4-7	56	45	2.73	R-R	6-1	195	1/21/55 San Francisco, CA
52	Solano, Julio	Tucson	6-4	71	53	1.89	R-R	6-1	170	1/8/60 Dominican Republic
		Houston	3-1	32	21	7.59				

CATCHERS

No.	Name	1986 Club	H	HR	RBI	Pct.	B-T	Ht.	Wt.	Born
14	Ashby, Alan	Houston	81	7	38	.257	B-R	6-2	195	7/8/51 Long Beach, CA
7	Wine, Robbie	Tucson	79	10	44	.228	R-R	6-2	200	7/13/62 Philadelphia, PA
		Houston	3	0	0	.250				
INFIELDERS										
27	Davis, Glenn	Houston	152	31	101	.265	R-R	6-3	210	3/28/61 Jacksonville, FL
19	Doran, Bill	Houston	152	6	37	.276	B-R	6-0	175	5/28/58 Cincinnati, OH
3	Garner, Phil	Houston	83	9	41	.265	R-R	5-10	175	4/30/49 Jefferson City, TN
—	Jackson, Chuck	Tucson	137	11	62	.306	B-R	6-0	185	3/19/63 Seattle, WA
20	Pankovits, Jim	Houston	32	1	7	.283	R-R	5-10	175	8/6/55 Pennington Gap, VA
1	Pena, Bert	Tucson	119	11	60	.260	R-R	5-11	165	7/11/59 Puerto Rico
		Houston	6	0	2	.207				
12	Reynolds, Craig	Houston	78	6	41	.249	L-R	6-1	175	12/27/52 Houston, TX
10	Thon, Dickie	Houston	69	3	21	.248	R-R	5-11	175	6/20/58 South Bend, IN
29	Walling, Denny	Houston	119	13	58	.312	L-R	6-1	185	4/17/54 Neptune, NJ
OUTFIELDERS										
17	Bass, Kevin	Houston	184	20	79	.311	B-R	6-0	180	5/12/59 Redwood City, CA
9	Bullock, Eric	Tucson	58	3	21	.384	L-L	5-11	185	2/16/60 Los Angeles, CA
		Houston	1	0	1	.048				
25	Cruz, Jose	Houston	133	10	72	.278	L-L	6-0	185	8/8/47 Puerto Rico
24	Gainey, Ty	Tucson	126	17	63	.351	L-L	6-1	190	12/25/60 Cheraw, SC
		Houston	15	1	6	.300				
28	Hatcher, Billy	Houston	108	6	36	.258	R-R	5-9	175	10/4/60 Williams, AZ
11	Lopes, Davey	Chi.(NL)-Hou.	70	7	35	.275	R-R	5-9	170	5/3/46 Providence, RI
21	Puhl, Terry	Houston	42	3	14	.244	L-R	6-2	200	7/8/56 Canada
30	Walker, Tony	Tucson	16	0	8	.190	R-R	6-2	205	7/1/59 San Diego, CA
		Houston	20	2	10	.222				
—	Young, Gerald	Columbus	151	9	61	.280	B-R	6-2	185	10/22/64 Honduras

ASTRO PROFILES

KEVIN BASS 27 6-0 180 Bats S Throws R

Right fielder blossomed into an All-Star with a solid season, leading Astros' regulars in batting . . . A sensational June earned him NL Player-of-the-Month honors as he batted .378 with seven homers, 20 runs and 15 RBI . . . Average never dropped below .300 after July 21 . . . Also topped Houston regulars with a .292 average in NL Championship Series . . . Born May 12, 1959, in Redwood City, Cal. . . . Signed by Brewers as second-round pick in 1977 . . . Joined Astros with Mike Madden and Frank DiPino in 1982 deal that sent Don Sutton to Milwaukee . . . Terry Puhl's injury gave him big chance in 1985 and he has enjoyed two solid seasons as a regular . . . An improved offensive player who has above-average defensive ability . . . One of the Astros' many unsung stars.

Year	Club	Pos.	G	AB	R	H	2B	3B	HR	RBI	SB	Avg.
1982	Milwaukee	OF	18	9	4	0	0	0	0	0	0	.000
1982	Houston	OF	12	24	2	1	0	0	0	0	0	.042
1983	Houston	OF	88	195	25	46	7	3	2	18	2	.236
1984	Houston	OF	121	331	33	86	17	5	2	29	5	.260
1985	Houston	OF	150	539	72	145	27	5	16	68	19	.269
1986	Houston	OF	157	591	83	184	33	5	20	79	22	.311
	Totals		546	1689	219	462	84	18	40	195	48	.274

BILL DORAN 28 6-0 175 Bats S Throws R

Another unheralded player, he was the sparkplug for the Houston offense with his speed and also the key to the club's inner defense at second base . . . A .306 April triggered a solid season . . . Smooth and dependable, he became the first Houston player to swipe 40 bases since Cesar Cedeno in 1980 . . . Born May 28, 1958, in Cincinnati . . . Attended Miami of Ohio, where he was an All-American . . . Astros' sixth-round draft choice in 1979 . . . A .302 season at Tucson (AAA) in 1982 was his ticket to the bigs . . . Club MVP in 1985, when he tied Joe Morgan's club record of 14 homers by a second baseman . . . He'd be the best all-around second baseman in the league if it weren't for Ryne Sandberg.

Year	Club	Pos.	G	AB	R	H	2B	3B	HR	RBI	SB	Avg.
1982	Houston	2B	26	97	11	27	3	0	0	6	5	.278
1983	Houston	2B	154	535	70	145	12	7	8	39	12	.271
1984	Houston	2B-SS	147	548	92	143	18	11	4	41	21	.261
1985	Houston	2B	148	578	84	166	31	6	14	59	23	.287
1986	Houston	2B	145	550	92	152	29	3	6	37	42	.276
	Totals		620	2308	349	633	93	27	32	182	103	.274

JOSE CRUZ 39 6-0 185 **Bats L Throws L**

Injuries finally slowed down this vastly underrated player last year, but he was hot when the Astros needed him most . . . Lingering knee injury contributed to left fielder's .249 average, one homer and 31 RBI at All-Star break . . . With the help of a .327 August, he batted .309 with nine homers and 40 RBI in second half . . . Celebrated his 39th birthday with 1,000th RBI and 1,800th hit in Aug. 8 victory over Padres . . . Born Aug. 8, 1947, in Arroyo, P.R. . . . Named Astros' MVP four times and Puerto Rico's top athlete twice . . . Signed as free agent by Cardinals in 1967 and sold to Houston in 1974, launching a great career . . . Belted homer in his first game with Astros and has been a .295 lifetime hitter with them, topping .300 six times . . . Among Astros, only Glenn Davis had more game-winning RBI than Cruz' 12 last season.

Year	Club	Pos.	G	AB	R	H	2B	3B	HR	RBI	SB	Avg.
1970	St. Louis	OF	6	17	2	6	1	0	0	1	0	.353
1971	St. Louis	OF	83	292	46	80	13	2	9	27	6	.274
1972	St. Louis	OF	117	332	33	78	14	4	2	23	9	.235
1973	St. Louis	OF	132	406	51	92	22	5	10	57	10	.227
1974	St. Louis	OF-1B	107	161	24	42	4	3	5	20	4	.261
1975	Houston	OF	120	315	44	81	15	2	9	49	6	.257
1976	Houston	OF	133	439	49	133	21	5	4	61	28	.303
1977	Houston	OF	157	579	87	173	31	10	17	87	44	.299
1978	Houston	OF-1B	153	565	79	178	34	9	10	83	37	.315
1979	Houston	OF	157	558	73	161	33	7	9	72	36	.289
1980	Houston	OF	160	612	79	185	29	7	11	91	36	.302
1981	Houston	OF	107	409	53	109	16	5	13	55	5	.267
1982	Houston	OF	155	570	62	157	27	2	9	68	21	.275
1983	Houston	OF	160	594	85	189	28	8	14	92	30	.318
1984	Houston	OF	160	600	96	187	28	13	12	95	22	.312
1985	Houston	OF	141	544	69	163	34	4	9	79	16	.300
1986	Houston	OF	141	479	48	133	22	4	10	72	3	.278
	Totals		2189	7472	980	2147	372	90	153	1032	313	.287

GLENN DAVIS 26 6-3 210 **Bats R Throws R**

First baseman overcame rocky childhood to become stabilizing force in heart of Astros' batting order . . . Joined Jim Wynn as only Houston players to surpass 30 home runs in a season . . . Outstanding in the clutch, as evidenced by his 16 game-winning RBI and four game-winning homers in club's final at-bat . . . Did much of his long-ball damage in June and July, totaling 15 homers and 44 RBI those months . . . Also sizzled down the stretch as Astros pulled away, batting .321 in September . . . Earned considerable support for NL MVP in first full season as a major leaguer . . . Born March 28, 1961, in Jacksonville, Fla. . . .

Astros' No. 1 pick in secondary phase of January 1981 draft... Gave a preview of what was to come with 20 homers and 64 RBI in only 100 games in 1985... His homer off Dwight Gooden accounted for only run in Astros' 1-0 victory in Game 1 of NL Championship Series.

Year	Club	Pos.	G	AB	R	H	2B	3B	HR	RBI	SB	Avg.
1984	Houston	1B	18	61	6	13	5	0	2	8	0	.213
1985	Houston	1B-OF	100	350	51	95	11	0	20	64	0	.271
1986	Houston	1B	158	574	91	152	32	3	31	101	3	.265
	Totals		276	985	148	260	48	3	53	173	3	.264

DENNY WALLING 32 6-1 185 Bats L Throws R

Probably benefitted most from club's platoon system in 1986, registering highs in most offensive categories despite playing in only 130 games and getting only 382 at-bats... Also sparkled afield, making only five errors at third base... Batted .387 on 12-for-31 as a pinch-hitter and is the Astros' all-time leader with 70 pinch-hits... Thrived during the second half, batting .318 from the All-Star break to season's end... At his best down the stretch, with a .351 August and a .338 September... Born April 17, 1954, in Neptune, N.J.... Following an outstanding career at Clemson, he was the A's first-round draft pick in 1975 ... Traded to Houston for Willie Crawford in June 1977.

Year	Club	Pos.	G	AB	R	H	2B	3B	HR	RBI	SB	Avg.
1975	Oakland	OF	6	8	0	1	1	0	0	2	0	.125
1976	Oakland	OF	3	11	1	3	0	0	0	0	0	.273
1977	Houston	OF	6	21	1	6	0	1	0	6	0	.286
1978	Houston	OF	120	247	30	62	11	3	3	36	9	.251
1979	Houston	OF	82	147	21	48	8	4	3	31	3	.327
1980	Houston	1B-OF	100	284	30	85	6	5	3	29	4	.299
1981	Houston	1B-OF	65	158	23	37	6	0	5	23	2	.234
1982	Houston	OF-1B	85	146	22	30	4	1	1	14	4	.205
1983	Houston	1B-3B-OF	100	135	24	40	5	3	3	19	2	.296
1984	Houston	3B-1B-OF	87	249	37	70	11	5	3	31	7	.281
1985	Houston	3B-1B-OF	119	345	44	93	20	1	7	45	5	.270
1986	Houston	3B-1B-OF	130	382	54	119	23	1	13	58	1	.312
	Totals		903	2133	287	594	95	24	41	294	37	.278

MIKE SCOTT 31 6-3 215 Bats R Throws R

Nobody did it better than this split-finger fastball specialist in 1986... Cy Young Award season was capped by an unprecedented, division-clinching no-hitter against the Giants, Sept. 25 ... Added NL Championship Series MVP honors with two impeccable performances against Mets, winning, 1-0 and 3-1... Struck out an NLCS-record 14 batters in the shutout and became the only pitcher to complete two games in playoffs . . . Topped majors with 306 strikeouts and a 2.22 ERA, becoming only the fourth NL pitcher to fan 300 in a season . . . Born April 26, 1955, in Santa Monica, Cal. . . . Sensational 1986 season took off with a 3-1 June and was capped by a 4-1 September in which he fanned 57 in 39⅓ innings . . . Starred at Pepperdine and was Mets' second-round pick in 1976 . . . Traded to Houston for Danny Heep prior to 1983 season . . . Learned split-finger pitch from Roger Craig and rest is history . . . Mets accused him of throwing scuff-balls, vainly pleading their case to NL president Chub Feeney during playoffs.

Year	Club	G	IP	W	L	Pct.	SO	BB	H	ERA
1979	New York (NL)	18	52	1	3	250	21	20	59	5.37
1980	New York (NL)	6	29	1	1	.500	13	8	40	4.34
1981	New York (NL)	23	136	5	10	.333	54	34	130	3.90
1982	New York (NL)	37	147	7	13	.350	63	60	185	5.14
1983	Houston	24	145	10	6	.625	73	46	143	3.72
1984	Houston	31	154	5	11	.313	83	43	179	4.68
1985	Houston	36	221⅔	18	8	.692	137	80	194	3.29
1986	Houston	37	275⅓	18	10	.643	306	72	182	2.22
	Totals	212	1160	65	62	.512	750	363	1112	3.70

BOB KNEPPER 32 6-2 210 — Bats L Throws L

Paragon of frustration during the NL Championship Series . . . Unable to hold 4-0 and 3-0 leads in games eventually lost by Astros . . . Finished with a 3.52 ERA in NLCS despite eight shutout innings in Game 6 . . . His 17 victories tied career high and represented Astros' record for a lefty . . . Best month was April, when he was 4-0 with 1.27 ERA, one of the victories being his 100th . . . Also solid in June at 3-1 with 2.33 . . . Got off to a 9-2 start, then went 8-10 rest of the way . . . Tied Mike Scott for major-league shutout lead with five . . . Born May 25, 1954, in Akron, Ohio . . . Second-round pick of Giants in 1972 . . . Went 20-5 for Fresno (A) in 1974 and had great first full season with Giants in 1978 . . . Traded to Houston for Enos Cabell prior to the 1981 season.

Year	Club	G	IP	W	L	Pct.	SO	BB	H	ERA
1976	San Francisco	4	25	1	2	.333	11	7	26	3.24
1977	San Francisco	27	166	11	9	.550	100	72	151	3.36
1978	San Francisco	36	260	17	11	.607	147	85	218	2.63
1979	San Francisco	34	207	9	12	.429	123	77	241	4.65
1980	San Francisco	35	215	9	16	.360	103	61	242	4.10
1981	Houston	22	157	9	5	.643	75	38	128	2.18
1982	Houston	33	180	5	15	.250	108	60	193	4.45
1983	Houston	35	203	6	13	.316	125	71	202	3.19
1984	Houston	35	233⅔	15	10	.600	140	55	223	3.20
1985	Houston	37	241	15	13	.536	131	54	253	3.55
1986	Houston	40	258	17	12	.586	143	62	232	3.14
	Totals	338	2145⅔	114	118	.491	1206	642	2109	3.44

JIM DESHAIES 26 6-4 222 **Bats L Throws L**

Astros' search for a dependable No. 4 starter ended when he sparkled as a rookie last year . . . Enjoyed a 4-1 June and was blazing down the stretch . . . Established modern major-league mark by striking out first eight batters against Dodgers, Sept. 23 . . . That was his 10th victory, the most by a Houston rookie southpaw . . . Won 11 of his final 14 starts, concluding the season with 19 scoreless innings . . . Wasn't used by Hal Lanier in NLCS . . . Born June 23, 1960, in Massena, N.Y. . . . Attended LeMoyne College . . . Was 21st-round draft pick of the Yankees in 1982 . . . Posted 38-21 minor-league record for Yanks and was organization's top pitching prospect in 1984 . . . Traded to Astros with Neder de Jesus Horta for Joe Niekro on Sept. 15, 1985.

Year	Club	G	IP	W	L	Pct.	SO	BB	H	ERA
1984	New York (AL)	2	7	0	1	.000	5	7	14	11.57
1985	Houston	2	3	0	0	.000	2	0	1	0.00
1986	Houston	26	144	12	5	.706	128	59	124	3.25
	Totals	30	154	12	6	.667	135	66	139	3.56

DAVE SMITH 32 6-1 195 **Bats R Throws R**

Established club save records for single season (33) and career (100) in 1986 before faltering in NL Championship Series . . . Finished regular season with two wins and 16 saves in last 22 outings . . . Started record spree with a 2.25 ERA and seven saves in April . . . Had eight saves in a brilliant August during which he allowed no earned runs in 10⅓ innings . . . Tied NL mark with eighth save in eight appearances May 3 . . . Born Jan. 21, 1955, in San Francisco . . . Attended San Diego State . . . Houston's eighth-round draft choice in 1976 . . . Reached bigs to stay with solid rookie season in 1980 . . . Became Astros' stopper in 1985 and has made good on 60-of-70 save opportunities since then . . . Took 17 saves into All-Star Game . . . Lost Game 3 of NL Championship Series on ninth-inning homer by Len Dykstra, then blew lead in ninth inning of Game 6.

Year	Club	G	IP	W	L	Pct.	SO	BB	H	ERA
1980	Houston	57	103	7	5	.583	85	32	90	1.92
1981	Houston	42	75	5	3	.625	52	23	54	2.76
1982	Houston	49	63⅓	5	4	.556	28	31	69	3.84
1983	Houston	42	72⅔	3	1	.750	41	36	72	3.10
1984	Houston	53	77⅓	5	4	.556	45	20	60	2.21
1985	Houston	64	79⅓	9	5	.643	40	17	69	2.27
1986	Houston	54	56	4	7	.364	46	22	39	2.73
	Totals	361	526⅔	38	29	.567	337	181	453	2.61

NOLAN RYAN 40 6-2 210 **Bats R Throws R**

"The Express" was sidetracked by an elbow problem early last year, but he finished strong to help Astros seal a division title . . . Despite a 3-6 start with a 5.21 ERA, the rubber-armed right-hander had a fine season . . . After going on the disabled list the first time June 2, he was 9-2 with 2.24 ERA and 135 strikeouts in 109⅓ innings . . . Struck out 15 Expos July 22 for his highest single-game total with Houston . . . Averaged 9.8 strikeouts per nine innings, his highest figure since 1978 . . . Amazingly, he allowed more than five hits in only two of his last 23 starts . . . Permitted Mets one run in nine innings, but got no-decision in Game 5 of NL Championship Series . . . Holds major-league marks with 4,277 strikeouts and 162 games in which he has fanned 10 or more . . . Born Jan. 31, 1947, in Refugio, Tex. . . . Mets drafted him in fifth round in 1965 . . . Swapped to Angels as part of package for Jim Fregosi prior to 1972 season . . . Signed with Astros as a free agent in 1979 to be close to his Alvin, Tex., home . . . Has a record five major-league no-hitters.

Year	Club	G	IP	W	L	Pct.	SO	BB	H	ERA
1966	New York (NL)	2	3	0	1	.000	6	3	5	15.00
1968	New York (NL)	21	134	6	9	.400	133	75	93	3.09
1969	New York (NL)	25	89	6	3	.667	92	53	60	3.54
1970	New York (NL)	27	132	7	11	.389	125	97	86	3.41
1971	New York (NL)	30	152	10	14	.417	137	116	125	3.97
1972	California	39	284	19	16	.543	329	157	166	2.28
1973	California	41	326	21	16	.568	383	162	238	2.87
1974	California	42	333	22	16	.578	367	202	221	2.89
1975	California	28	198	14	12	.538	186	132	152	3.45
1976	California	39	284	17	18	.486	327	183	193	3.36
1977	California	37	299	19	16	.543	341	204	198	2.77
1978	California	31	235	10	13	.435	260	148	183	3.71
1979	California	34	223	16	14	.533	223	114	169	3.59
1980	Houston	35	234	11	10	.524	200	98	205	3.35
1981	Houston	21	149	11	5	.688	140	68	99	1.69
1982	Houston	35	250⅓	16	12	.571	245	109	196	3.16
1983	Houston	29	196⅓	14	9	.609	183	101	134	2.98
1984	Houston	30	183⅔	12	11	.522	197	69	143	3.04
1985	Houston	35	232	10	12	.455	209	95	205	3.80
1986	Houston	30	178	12	8	.600	194	82	119	3.34
	Totals	611	4115⅓	253	226	.528	4277	2268	2990	3.15

TOP PROSPECT

TY GAINEY 26 6-1 190 **Bats L Throws L**

After eight seasons in the minors, this might be Gainey's final chance to make the major-league roster . . . He squandered an opportunity last spring by reporting overweight, but he compensated with a stunning season at Tucson (AAA) . . . Born Dec. 25, 1960, in Cheraw, S.C. . . . Pacific Coast League batting champion at .351 hit .300 in brief stint with Astros . . . Also topped PCL with .616 slugging percentage, belting 22 doubles, 11 triples and 17 homers . . . Needs to handle inside pitches better if he's to succeed as a major-league hitter . . . A decent outfielder with good speed.

MANAGER HAL LANIER: Won division title in his first season as a manager and was named NL Manager of the Year . . . A winner throughout his career, he played on only one losing major-league club and managed only one loser in five minor-league seasons . . . Promised to bring an aggressive brand of ball to Houston when he succeeded Bob Lillis as manager after 1985 season, and he didn't disappoint . . . Shattered franchise victory record with 96 in regular season, then added a pair in NL Championship Series . . . Born July 4, 1942, in Denton, N.C. . . . Son of former major-league pitcher Max Lanier, he was nicknamed "Maxie" as a Giant player . . . Signed with Giants in 1961 and became their regular shortstop in 1965 . . . Had .228 career average, finishing up with Yankees in 1973 . . . Became manager in Cardinals' system and was St. Louis third-base coach under Whitey Herzog before joining Astros.

GREATEST ALL-TIME ROOKIE

As a relatively new franchise, Houston hasn't had lots of outstanding rookie performances, but one does stand out because it spawned a future Hall of Famer.

Little Joe Morgan made a big splash with the Astros in 1965 before attaining greater stardom as the man who made the champion Reds tick 10 years later.

Playing 157 games for the 1965 Astros, Morgan drew a league-leading 97 walks, batted .271, stole 20 bases, scored 100 runs

The Ks keep on coming for 40-year-old Nolan Ryan.

and reached double figures in doubles (22), triples (12) and home runs (14).

Two years later, Don Wilson, the greatest rookie pitcher in Houston history, enjoyed a banner season punctuated by a no-hitter against the Braves. He went 10-9 with a 2.79 ERA and three shutouts.

Also deserving of recognition is Glenn Davis, whose debut season in 1985 proved to be an indication of things to come. In merely 100 games, he hit 20 home runs with 64 RBI.

ALL-TIME ASTRO SEASON RECORDS

BATTING: Rusty Staub, .333, 1967
HRs: Jimmy Wynn, 37, 1967
RBIs: Bob Watson, 110, 1977
STEALS: Cesar Cedeno, 61, 1977
WINS: Joe Niekro, 21, 1979
STRIKEOUTS: J. R. Richard, 313, 1979

LOS ANGELES DODGERS

TEAM DIRECTORY: Pres.: Peter O'Malley; Exec. VP: Fred Claire; VP-Play. Pers.: Al Campanis; VP-Minor Leagues; Bill Schweppe; Dir. Publ.: Steve Brener; Trav. Sec.: Bill DeLury; Mgr.: Tom Lasorda. Home: Dodger Stadium (56,000) Field distances: 300, l.f. line; 370, l.c.; 395, c.f.; 370, r.c.; 330, r.f. line. Spring training: Vero Beach, Fla.

SCOUTING REPORT

HITTING: The Dodgers are desperate for a return to form by Pedro Guerrero and Mike Marshall. Without that, they are an ordinary club and a shadow of the Los Angeles teams that have dominated the NL West in recent years. The Dodgers were doomed when Guerrero was injured last spring and Marshall (.233, 19 homers, 53 RBI) added fuel to the flames by playing in only 103 games.

Their return to previous eminence, continued improvement by Steve Sax (.332, 6, 56) and Franklin Stubbs (.226, 23, 58) and comebacks by Mariano Duncan (.229), Ken Landreaux (.261, 4,

Fernando led NL in wins (21) and complete games (20).

29 in 103 games) and Bill Madlock (.280, 10, 60 in 111 games) could make the Dodgers formidable at the dish again. The Dodgers figure to improve on a .251 team batting average that ranked ninth in the league.

PITCHING: Even the pitching, perennially this club's strength, faltered last year as the Dodgers finished fifth in the league with a 3.76 ERA. The starting staff seems solid once again with Fernando Valenzuela (21-11, 3.14) leading the way, but it would help if Orel Hershiser (14-14, 3.85) recaptures his 1985 touch instead of merely being a .500 pitcher. Bob Welch (7-13, 3.28) and Rick Honeycutt (11-9, 3.32) can do better. A comeback by Alejandro Pena wouldn't hurt, either.

The bullpen was the biggest culprit last season as Tom Niedenfuer (6-6, 3.71, 11 saves) apparently was unable to recover from Jack Clark's pennant-winning homer. The Dodgers hope they've solved that problem with the offseason acquisitions of ex-Brewer Tim Leary and ex-Mariner Matt Young, who hopes to do what another ex-Seattle lefthander, Ed Vande Berg, couldn't do in his NL debut. Ken Howell (6-12, 3.87, 12 saves) is a potential bullpen ace.

FIELDING: The Dodgers had fielding problems in their glory days, but overcame them with pitching and hitting. The shoddy Dodger defense was exposed last year, as Los Angeles' .971 fielding percentage ranked last in the league and its 181 errors were at least 38 more than any other NL team. Catcher Mike Scioscia is a rock, but the inner defense suffers with Madlock at third and Duncan at short and the outfielders are merely adequate.

OUTLOOK: Time was when the Dodgers would fall back for a season and then come back strong the next, but that pattern depended on a fruitful farm system. The well apparently has run dry at Albuquerque, so this club may suffer despite a pitching staff that will keep it in most games.

The defense doesn't figure to improve, so the club must compensate with solid years from Guerrero, Marshall and Madlock at the plate. Sax developed into a standout last year, enjoying a career season with the bat and overcoming his throwing problems.

However, the starting pitchers are getting older, so it will take great hitting for a return to eminence. Also, Los Angeles isn't as mentally tough as it used to be, judging from a 27-54 road record, the worst in the league. The Dodgers, 73-89 in 1986, haven't had sub-.500 records in successive seasons since 1967 and 1968, but this team just might do it.

LOS ANGELES DODGERS 1987 ROSTER

MANAGER Tom Lasorda

Coaches—Joe Amalfitano, Mark Cresse, Manny Mota, Ron Perranoski, Bill Russell

PITCHERS

No.	Name	1986 Club	W-L	IP	SO	ERA	B-T	Ht.	Wt.	Born
52	Galvez, Balvino	Albuquerque	3-6	81	32	4.89	R-R	6-0	198	3/31/64 Dominican Republic
		Los Angeles	0-1	21	11	3.92				
55	Hershiser, Orel	Los Angeles	14-14	231	153	3.85	R-R	6-3	195	9/16/58 Buffalo, NY
57	Hillegas, Shawn	Albuquerque	1-5	47	43	6.17	R-R	6-2	208	8/21/64 Dos Palos, CA
		San Antonio	9-5	132	97	3.06				
51	Holton, Brian	Albuquerque	10-10	183	105	3.78	R-R	6-0	193	11/29/59 McKeesport, PA
		Los Angeles	2-3	24	24	4.44				
40	Honeycutt, Rick	Los Angeles	11-9	171	100	3.32	L-L	6-1	193	6/29/54 Chattanooga, TN
43	Howell, Ken	Los Angeles	6-12	98	104	3.87	R-R	6-3	228	11/28/60 Detroit, MI
—	Leary, Tim	Milwaukee	12-12	188	110	4.21	R-R	6-3	190	12/23/58 Santa Monica, CA
59	Livingston, Dennis	Albuquerque	3-5	49	40	4.93	R-L	6-0	185	12/23/62 Somerville, MA
		San Antonio	1-8	66	52	4.48				
54	Mayberry, Greg	San Antonio	1-2	18	10	4.58	L-R	6-3	223	9/11/65 Lynchburg, VA
49	Niedenfuer, Tom	Los Angeles	6-6	80	55	3.71	R-R	6-5	224	8/13/59 St. Louis Park, MN
26	Pena, Alejandro	Vero Beach	0-2	16	11	7.47	R-R	6-1	203	6/25/59 Dominican Republic
		Los Angeles	1-2	70	46	4.89				
41	Reuss, Jerry	Los Angeles	2-6	74	29	5.84	L-L	6-5	227	6/19/49 St. Louis, MO
36	Scott, Tim	Vero Beach	5-4	95	37	3.40	R-R	6-2	193	11/16/66 Hanford, CA
34	Valenzuela, Fernando	Los Angeles	21-11	269	242	3.14	L-L	5-11	200	11/1/60 Mexico
35	Welch, Bob	Los Angeles	7-13	236	183	3.28	R-R	6-3	192	11/3/56 Detroit, MI
—	Young, Matt	Seattle	8-6	104	82	3.82	L-L	6-3	205	8/9/58 Pasadena, CA

CATCHERS

No.	Name	1986 Club	H	HR	RBI	Pct.	B-T	Ht.	Wt.	Born
45	Debus, Jon	Albuquerque	61	14	50	.262	R-R	6-2	219	8/31/58 Chicago Heights, IL
15	Reyes, Gilberto	Albuquerque	70	7	36	.229	R-R	6-2	203	12/10/63 Dom. Republic
14	Scioscia, Mike	Los Angeles	94	5	26	.251	L-R	6-2	220	11/27/58 Upper Darby, PA
29	Trevino, Alex	Los Angeles	53	4	26	.262	R-R	5-11	179	8/26/57 Mexico

INFIELDERS

No.	Name	1986 Club	H	HR	RBI	Pct.	B-T	Ht.	Wt.	Born
10	Anderson, Dave	Los Angeles	53	1	15	.245	R-R	6-2	184	8/1/60 Louisville, KY
25	Duncan, Mariano	Los Angeles	93	8	30	.229	B-R	6-0	182	3/13/63 Dominican Republic
27	Francois, Manuel	San Antonio	5	0	1	.263	B-R	5-10	165	5/28/66 Dominican Republic
		Bakersfield	39	1	5	.253				
33	Hamilton, Jeff	Albuquerque	90	10	42	.313	R-R	6-3	205	3/19/64 Flint, MI
		Los Angeles	33	5	19	.224				
12	Madlock, Bill	Los Angeles	106	10	60	.280	R-R	5-11	210	1/12/51 Memphis, TN
3	Sax, Stave	Los Angeles	210	6	56	.332	R-R	5-11	185	1/29/60 W. Sacramento, CA
20	See, Larry	Albuquerque	155	27	106	.289	R-R	6-0	204	6/20/60 Norwalk, CA
		Los Angeles	5	0	2	.250				
38	Shipley, Craig	Albuquerque	59	0	16	.291	B-R	6-0	168	1/7/63 Australia
		Los Angeles	3	0	4	.111				
7	Woodson, Tracy	San Antonio	133	18	90	.269	R-R	6-3	216	10/5/62 Richmond, VA

OUTFIELDERS

No.	Name	1986 Club	H	HR	RBI	Pct.	B-T	Ht.	Wt.	Born
46	Bryant, Ralph	Albuquerque	80	19	55	.237	L-R	6-2	202	5/20/61 Ft. Gaines, GA
		Los Angeles	19	6	13	.253				
47	Gonzalez, Jose	Albuquerque	84	6	37	.277	R-R	6-2	196	11/23/64 Dom. Republic
		Los Angeles	20	2	6	.215				
28	Guerrero, Pedro	Los Angeles	15	5	10	.246	R-R	6-0	195	6/29/56 Dominican Republic
44	Landreaux, Ken	Los Angeles	74	4	29	.261	L-R	5-11	184	12/22/54 Los Angeles, CA
5	Marshall, Mike	Los Angeles	77	19	53	.233	R-R	6-5	220	1/12/60 Libertyville, IL
17	Matuszek, Len	Los Angeles	52	9	28	.261	L-R	6-2	202	9/27/54 Toledo, OH
22	Stubbs, Franklin	Los Angeles	95	23	58	.226	L-L	602	215	10/21/60 Laurinburg, NC
21	Williams, Reggie	Los Angeles	84	4	32	.277	R-R	5-10	193	8/29/60 Memphis, TN

DODGER PROFILES

STEVE SAX 27 5-11 185 Bats R Throws R

Enjoyed a dream season in 1986, one which left him just shy of a batting title . . . Had the season gone one more week, the second baseman may have won it . . . Remarkably consistent, he began with a .333 April, warmed up to .348 in July and sizzled in September . . . Final month produced a .400 average, NL Player-of-the-Month honors and a 25-game hitting streak, longest since Willie Davis' 25-gamer in 1971 . . . Born Jan. 29, 1960, in Sacramento, Cal. . . . Club's ninth-round selection in 1978 draft . . . Batting champ of Texas League (AA) with a .346 at San Antonio in 1981, so he skipped Triple-A and promptly won NL Rookie-of-the-Year honors in 1982 . . . Collected run-scoring single last year to boost All-Star Game average to .600.

Year	Club	Pos.	G	AB	R	H	2B	3B	HR	RBI	SB	Avg.
1981	Los Angeles	2B	31	119	15	33	2	0	2	9	5	.277
1982	Los Angeles	2B	150	638	88	180	23	7	4	47	49	.282
1983	Los Angeles	2B	155	623	94	175	18	5	5	41	56	.281
1984	Los Angeles	2B	145	569	70	138	24	4	1	35	34	.243
1985	Los Angeles	2B-3B	136	488	62	136	8	4	1	42	27	.279
1986	Los Angeles	2B	157	633	91	210	43	4	6	56	40	.332
	Totals		774	3070	420	872	118	24	19	230	211	.284

FRANKLIN STUBBS 26 6-2 215 Bats L Throws L

First full season demonstrated his versatility and power . . . If he ever learns to hit for average, he could be a star, but the Dodgers no longer are cranking out great all-around players as they once did . . . June was only real good month, with .310 average, nine homers and 17 RBI . . . Left fielder belted 13 homers in 45 games in June and July . . . Born Oct. 21, 1960, in Laurinburg, N.C. . . . All-American at Virginia Tech, hitting 59 homers in three years . . . Drafted No. 1 in 1982 . . . On June 2, 1983, he hit four home runs in a game for Triple-A Albuquerque against Phoenix . . . Reached Dodgers to stay after belting 32 homers for Albuquerque in 1985 . . . Will probably shift to first in 1987, replacing traded Greg Brock.

Year	Club	Pos.	G	AB	R	H	2B	3B	HR	RBI	SB	Avg.
1984	Los Angeles	1B-OF	87	217	22	42	2	3	8	17	2	.194
1985	Los Angeles	1B	10	9	0	2	0	0	0	2	0	.222
1986	Los Angeles	OF-1B	132	420	55	95	11	1	23	58	7	.226
	Totals		229	646	77	139	13	4	31	77	9	.215

MIKE SCIOSCIA 28 6-2 220 **Bats L Throws R**

Ankle injury and a September slump ruined what might have been a solid season, dropping him way below lifetime average . . . Biggest asset is his defense, including a reputation for blocking the plate as well as anyone . . . Enjoyed a .281 April and was batting .280 in June when he went on disabled list . . . Returned on July 14 and batted .385 that month before tailing off sharply . . . Born Nov. 27, 1958, in Upper Darby, Pa. . . . Club's No. 1 draft pick in 1976 . . . A solid Triple-A hitter, he joined Dodgers to stay after posting .336 and .331 averages at Albuquerque in 1979 and 1980 . . . Career threatened by rotator-cuff injury in 1983, but he recovered to have outstanding season in 1985.

Year	Club	Pos.	G	AB	R	H	2B	3B	HR	RBI	SB	Avg.
1980	Los Angeles	C-3B	54	134	8	34	5	1	1	8	1	.254
1981	Los Angeles	C	93	290	27	80	10	0	2	29	0	.276
1982	Los Angeles	C	129	365	31	80	11	1	5	38	2	.219
1983	Los Angeles	C	12	35	3	11	3	0	1	7	0	.314
1984	Los Angeles	C	114	341	29	93	18	0	5	38	2	.273
1985	Los Angeles	C	141	429	47	127	26	3	7	53	3	.296
1986	Los Angeles	C	122	374	36	94	18	1	5	26	3	.251
	Totals		665	1968	181	519	91	6	26	199	11	.264

MIKE MARSHALL 27 6-5 220 **Bats R Throws R**

A stiff back destroyed his season after he collected 13 homers and 37 RBI the first two months . . . Had 17 homers at midseason, only two thereafter . . . Right fielder didn't play regularly from June 27 until early August, going into a 4-for-58 tailspin . . . An extremely frustrating season for a man with the tools to be one of the league's best sluggers, as he demonstrated in 1985 . . . Born Jan. 12, 1960, in Libertyville, Ill. . . . Sixth-round selection in 1978 draft . . . "Big Foot" was an awesome minor-league slugger . . . In 1981, he became first Pacific Coast League triple-crown winner since Steve Bilko in 1956, batting .373 with 34 homers and 137 RBI for Albuquerque (AAA) . . . Named Minor League Player of the Year.

Year	Club	Pos.	G	AB	R	H	2B	3B	HR	RBI	SB	Avg.
1981	Los Angeles	1B-OF	14	25	2	5	3	0	0	1	0	.200
1982	Los Angeles	OF-1B	49	95	10	23	3	0	5	9	2	.242
1983	Los Angeles	OF-1B	140	465	47	132	17	1	17	65	7	.284
1984	Los Angeles	1B-OF	134	495	69	127	27	0	21	65	4	.257
1985	Los Angeles	OF-1B	135	518	72	152	27	2	28	95	3	.293
1986	Los Angeles	OF-1B	103	330	47	77	11	0	19	53	4	.233
	Totals		575	1928	247	516	88	3	90	288	20	.268

BILL MADLOCK 36 5-11 210 Bats R Throws R

Two stints on disabled list reduced "Mad Dog's" effectiveness in first full season with Dodgers and resulted in third straight sub-par year at the plate for the lifetime .300 hitter . . . Third baseman salvaged a disaster by batting .340 in August and .341 in July after being under .240 at midseason . . . Born Jan. 12, 1951, in Memphis, Tenn. . . . Fifth-round draft choice of Washington Senators in January 1970 . . . Winner of four NL batting crowns, two each with Cubs and Pirates . . . Joined Bucs in 1979 and was the catalyst for a pennant drive, batting .328 after a .261 start with Giants . . . Batted .375 in 1979 World Series against O's . . . Joined Dodgers in exchange for Sid Bream, R.J. Reynolds and Cecil Espy in August 1985 . . . Batted .360 for Dodgers, including a 17-game hitting streak for division champs.

Year	Club	Pos.	G	AB	R	H	2B	3B	HR	RBI	SB	Avg.
1973	Texas	3B	21	77	16	27	5	3	1	5	3	.351
1974	Chicago (NL)	3B	128	453	65	142	21	5	9	54	11	.313
1975	Chicago (NL)	3B	130	514	77	182	29	7	7	64	9	.354
1976	Chicago (NL)	3B	142	514	68	174	36	1	15	84	15	.339
1977	San Francisco	2B-3B	140	533	70	161	28	1	12	46	13	.302
1978	San Francisco	2B-1B	122	447	76	138	26	3	15	44	16	.309
1979	SF-Pitts.	3B-2B-1B	154	560	85	167	26	5	14	85	32	.298
1980	Pittsburgh	3B-1B	137	494	62	137	22	4	10	53	16	.277
1981	Pittsburgh	3B	82	279	35	95	23	1	6	45	18	.341
1982	Pittsburgh	3B-1B	154	568	92	181	33	3	19	95	18	.319
1983	Pittsburgh	3B	130	473	68	153	21	0	12	68	3	.323
1984	Pittsburgh	3B-1B	103	403	38	102	16	0	4	44	3	.253
1985	Pitt.-L.A.	3B-1B	144	513	69	141	27	1	12	56	10	.275
1986	Los Angeles	3B	111	379	38	106	17	0	10	60	3	.280
	Totals		1698	6207	859	1906	330	34	146	803	170	.307

PEDRO GUERRERO 30 6-0 195 Bats R Throws R

Path to greatness was interrupted by a ruptured tendon below left knee in spring training last year . . . Rehabilitation was slow following April 4 surgery, so "Pete" missed virtually the entire season . . . His loss was main reason for club's sorry showing . . . There was some clubhouse sniping because he took so long to return to action . . . Left fielder had only seven at-bats before being disabled again on Aug. 11 . . . Reactivated on Sept. 3 and showed signs of former prowess down stretch, hitting five home runs . . . Born June 29, 1956, in San Pedro de Macoris, Dominican Republic. . . . Signed by Indians and sent to Dodgers for Bruce Ellingsen on April 4, 1974.

Year	Club	Pos.	G	AB	R	H	2B	3B	HR	RBI	SB	Avg.
1978	Los Angeles......	1B	5	8	3	5	0	1	0	1	0	.625
1979	Los Angeles......	OF-1B-3B	25	62	7	15	2	0	2	9	2	.242
1980	Los Angeles......	OF-INF	75	183	27	59	9	1	7	31	2	.322
1981	Los Angeles......	OF-3B-1B	98	347	46	104	17	2	12	48	5	.300
1982	Los Angeles......	OF-3B	150	575	87	175	27	5	32	100	22	.304
1983	Los Angeles......	3B-1B	160	584	87	174	28	6	32	103	23	.298
1984	Los Angeles......	OF-3B-1B	144	535	85	162	29	4	16	72	9	.303
1985	Los Angeles......	OF-3B-1B	137	487	99	156	22	2	33	87	12	.320
1986	Los Angeles......	OF	31	61	7	15	3	0	5	10	0	.246
	Totals..........		825	2842	448	865	137	21	139	461	75	.304

FERNANDO VALENZUELA 26 5-11 200 Bats L Throws L

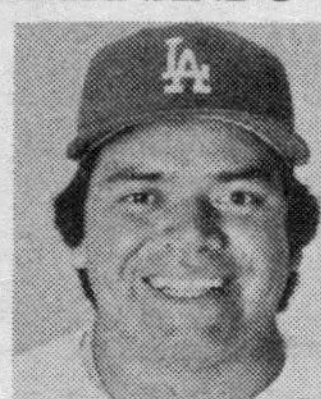

With 99 victories at age 25, he's heading for some big career numbers . . . His league-leading 21 victories last year were the most for a Dodger pitcher since Don Sutton won that number in 1976 . . . Surprisingly, it was his first 20-win season and the first by a Dodger since Tommy John in 1977 . . . Born Nov. 1, 1960, in Navajoa Sonora, Mexico . . . Started 1986 with a 3-1 April and posted a 4-1 July . . . Entered All-Star Game at 11-6 and proceeded to tie Carl Hubbell's strikeout mark by fanning five straight AL batters . . . Signed by the Dodgers in 1978, he was 16-20 in two minor-league seasons before career took off . . . Promoted to LA in 1980, he didn't yield an earned run in 17⅔ innings over 10 games . . . His 1981 Rookie-of-the-Year season included eight shutouts . . . Runnerup to Astros' Mike Scott in 1986 Cy Young race.

Year	Club	G	IP	W	L	Pct.	SO	BB	H	ERA
1980	Los Angeles..........	10	18	2	0	1.000	16	5	8	0.00
1981	Los Angeles..........	25	192	13	7	.650	180	61	140	2.48
1982	Los Angeles..........	37	285	19	13	.594	199	83	247	2.87
1983	Los Angeles..........	35	257	15	10	.600	189	99	245	3.75
1984	Los Angeles..........	34	261	12	17	.414	240	106	218	3.03
1985	Los Angeles..........	35	272⅓	17	10	.630	208	101	211	2.45
1986	Los Angeles..........	34	269⅓	21	11	.656	242	85	226	3.14
	Totals..............	210	1554⅔	99	68	.593	1274	540	1295	2.94

OREL HERSHISER 28 6-3 195 Bats R Throws R

Following a phenomenal 1985, Orel was merely mortal last season . . . Although he was previously unbeaten against Giants, he lost to them on Oct. 3 for a .500 finish after being 16 games over in 1985 . . . Went 3-2 with a 2.06 ERA in April and 2-1, 2.55 in May before his season corroded . . . Dodgers were blanked in six of his starts . . . Just the opposite of 1985, when everything went right, including an 11-0 record at Dodger Stadium . . . Born Sept. 16, 1958, in Buffalo, N.Y. . . . Played hockey for Philadelphia Flyers' junior team . . . Attended Bowling Green . . . A 17th-round draft bargain for LA in 1979 . . . A late bloomer, he was merely 35-29 in minors before making it big.

Year	Club	G	IP	W	L	Pct.	SO	BB	H	ERA
1983	Los Angeles.	8	8	0	0	.000	5	6	7	3.38
1984	Los Angeles.	45	189⅔	11	8	.579	150	50	160	2.66
1985	Los Angeles.	36	239⅔	19	3	.864	157	68	179	2.03
1986	Los Angeles.	35	231⅓	14	14	.500	153	86	213	3.85
	Totals	124	668⅔	44	25	.638	465	210	559	2.85

RICK HONEYCUTT 32 6-1 193 **Bats L Throws L**

Survived the Dodgers' slide to register respectable statistics . . . Topped NL pitchers with a 2.09 ERA at the All-Star break, but didn't have many wins to show for it . . . Born June 29, 1954, in Chattanooga, Tenn. . . . All-American first baseman at Tennessee . . . Pirates' 17th-round draft pick in 1976 . . . As a Niagara Falls rookie in 1976, he was 5-3 with a 2.60 ERA and batted .301 . . . Texas League ERA champ (2.47) for Shreveport (AA) in 1977 . . . Joined Mariners that season and pitched for Texas before being traded to Dodgers in August 1983 for Dave Stewart and Ricky Wright.

Year	Club	G	IP	W	L	Pct.	SO	BB	H	ERA
1977	Seattle	10	29	0	1	.000	17	11	26	4.34
1978	Seattle	26	134	5	11	.313	50	49	150	4.90
1979	Seattle	33	194	11	12	.478	83	67	201	4.04
1980	Seattle	30	203	10	17	.370	79	60	221	3.95
1981	Texas	20	128	11	6	.647	40	17	120	3.30
1982	Texas	30	164	5	17	.227	64	54	201	5.27
1983	Texas	25	174⅔	14	8	.636	56	37	168	2.42
1983	Los Angeles.	9	39	2	3	.400	18	13	46	5.77
1984	Los Angeles.	29	183⅔	10	9	.526	75	51	180	2.84
1985	Los Angeles.	31	142	8	12	.400	67	49	141	3.42
1986	Los Angeles.	32	171	11	9	.550	100	45	164	3.32
	Totals	275	1562⅓	87	105	.453	649	453	1618	3.76

BOB WELCH 30 6-3 192 **Bats R Throws R**

It seemed like it would be a banner season for Welch when he was 3-1 with a 1.44 ERA in April, but he was 4-12 the rest of the way, mirroring the club's flop . . . Born Nov. 3, 1956, in Detroit . . . All-American at Eastern Michigan . . . Dodgers' No. 1 pick in 1977 draft . . . Was in bigs to stay one year later, having more trouble with liquor than NL hitters . . . Remembered for duels with Reggie Jackson in 1978 World Series . . .

Plagued by arm trouble in 1979 and 1985, but has overcome problems to register 100 major-league wins.

Year	Club	G	IP	W	L	Pct.	SO	BB	H	ERA
1978	Los Angeles	23	111	7	4	.636	66	26	92	2.03
1979	Los Angeles	25	81	5	6	.455	64	32	82	4.00
1980	Los Angeles	32	214	14	9	.609	141	79	190	3.28
1981	Los Angeles	23	141	9	5	.643	88	41	141	3.45
1982	Los Angeles	36	235⅔	16	11	.593	176	81	199	3.36
1983	Los Angeles	31	204	15	12	.556	156	72	164	2.65
1984	Los Angeles	31	178⅔	13	13	.500	126	58	191	3.78
1985	Los Angeles	23	167⅓	14	4	.778	96	35	141	2.31
1986	Los Angeles	33	235⅔	7	13	.350	183	55	227	3.28
	Totals	257	1568⅓	100	77	.565	1096	479	1427	3.13

TOP PROSPECT

JEFF HAMILTON 23 6-3 205 **Bats R Throws R**

Didn't hit especially well following his recall from Albuquerque (AAA) June 27, but he's rated the club's best prospect for 1987 because he may be the regular third baseman . . . Born March 19, 1964, in Flint, Mich. . . . Was batting .313 with 10 homers and 42 RBI at time of his recall from PCL . . . Rangy youngster had playing time because of Bill Madlock's aches and pains . . . Hit first two major-league homers in consecutive at-bats, July 24 and 26 at Pittsburgh . . . Hit .224 with five homers and 19 RBI in 147 at-bats as Dodger.

MANAGER TOM LASORDA: The fun-loving, hearty-eating, hot-tempered round man people love to hate had more frowns than smiles during a pathetic season that was doomed when Pedro Guerrero went down for the count at Vero Beach . . . Tommy's steel-lined stomach was surely tested, yet there was no indigestion for a man who downs the chow with the best of them . . . The fifth-place finish was the poorest of his career, which includes five division titles, three pennants and one World Series (1981) since he got Dodger job in 1977 . . . Born Sept. 22, 1927, in Norristown, Pa. . . . Pitched in Dodgers' system and was 107-57 in Triple-A career at Montreal . . . Won five pennants in eight seasons of minor-league managing . . . Has served Dodgers for 37 seasons, leaving no doubt why he bleeds blue . . . Last season, he bled red, too . . . Has an 853-716 record with Dodgers.

GREATEST ALL-TIME ROOKIE

The Dodgers have had 11 Rookie-of-the-Year winners since 1947, but Jackie Robinson heads the list because of his impact on the game. It can safely be said that no other rookie had to endure what Robinson, the first black in the majors, encountered in 1947.

He was under a looking glass the entire season, yet he shrugged off the pressure, turned the other cheek and batted .297 with 31 doubles, 125 runs and a league-leading 29 stolen bases, helping the Dodgers to a pennant.

Other notable Brooklyn rookies included Jeff Pfeffer, who was 23-12 with a 1.97 ERA and four saves in 1914, and Dazzy Vance, who registered a league-leading 134 strikeouts and five shutouts while posting an 18-12 record in 1922.

The Boys of Summer had three outstanding rookies. Don Newcombe was 17-8 with five shutouts in 1949; Joe Black went 15-4 with 15 saves and a 2.15 ERA in 1952, and Junior Gilliam belted a league-leading 17 triples, scored 125 runs and walked 100 times in 1953.

Among the LA rookie gems have been Frank Howard, who cracked 23 homers in 1960; Rick Sutcliffe, who went 17-10 in 1979, and Fernando Valenzuela, who was 13-7 with a 2.48 ERA and a league-leading eight shutouts in strike-shortened 1981.

ALL-TIME DODGER SEASON RECORDS

BATTING: Babe Herman, .393, 1930
HRs: Duke Snider, 43, 1956
RBIs: Tommy Davis, 153, 1962
STEALS: Maury Wills, 104, 1962
WINS: Joe McGinnity, 29, 1900
STRIKEOUTS: Sandy Koufax, 382, 1965

SAN DIEGO PADRES

TEAM DIRECTORY: Owner: Joan Kroc; Pres.: Ballard Smith; Exec. VP-Chief Oper. Off.: Dick Freeman; VP-Baseball Oper.: Jack McKeon; Senior VP: Elten Schiller; Adm. Minor Leagues/ Scouting: Tom Romensko; Dir. Pub. Rel.: Bill Beck; Trav. Sec.: John Mattei; Mgr.: Larry Bowa. Home: San Diego Jack Murphy Stadium (58,433). Field distances: 327, l.f. line; 405, c.f.; 327, r.f. line. Spring training: Yuma, Ariz.

SCOUTING REPORT

HITTING: Start with Tony Gwynn (.329, 14 homers, 59 RBI) and hope Steve Garvey (.255, 21, 81) has one more good year remaining. Otherwise, there aren't too many dependable positives in a Padre offense that will have a new look in 1987. Terry Kennedy and Kevin McReynolds, who had a combined total of 38 homers and 153 RBI, were swapped over the winter, so patience will be required until a rash of newcomers blends into the attack.

Gwynn could suffer if Garvey continues his downward trend

Tony Gwynn shared NL lead in runs with 107.

or the newcomers don't blossom immediately, because Gwynn isn't as likely to see as many good pitches. With ex-Met property Stan Jefferson and Benito Santiago figuring to start in center and behind the plate respectively and second-year player Kevin Mitchell (.277, 12, 43), another ex-Met, at third, it will be difficult to gauge the San Diego offense until some games are played.

PITCHING: A staff that ranked among the majors' best in a pennant-winning 1984 season slumped to a 3.99 ERA last season, 11th in the league. To make matters worse, LaMarr Hoyt (8-11, 5.15) was released by the Padres after being involved in another winter brush with the law.

There's quality in starters Eric Show (9-5, 2.97), Dave Dravecky (9-11, 3.07) and Andy Hawkins (10-8, 4.30), but someone like Ed Whitson must come through to give the rotation depth. Rookie Jimmy Jones (2-0, 2.50) or former Oriole Storm Davis (9-12, 3.62) could provide the answer.

The bullpen is solid with Goose Gossage (5-7, 4.45, 21 saves), Craig Lefferts (9-8, 3.09, 4 saves) and Lance McCullers (10-10, 2.78, 5 saves), who appears headed for stardom. The Padres have all the pieces for a decent staff, but they haven't fit together properly the last two years.

FIELDING: Tim Flannery (three errors) did a fine job at second base in what may have been his finest major-league season, Garry Templeton can still do the job at short and Gwynn (19 assists) is a solid right fielder, but the rest of the defense could use some patching.

Garvey has become statuesque at first base, losing a step, and Graig Nettles and Jerry Royster had a combined total of 24 errors at third. Mitchell isn't known for his glove and Santiago made five errors in 17 games behind the plate, so it remains to be seen how the newcomers develop afield.

OUTLOOK: Trader Jack McKeon built for the future by sending McReynolds to the Mets in an eight-player deal that netted Jefferson, Mitchell and Shawn Abner, so don't expect too much, too soon from this young club. Rookie manager Larry Bowa will inject some life into the passive Padres, but that won't be enough to avoid another losing season on the heels of last year's 74-88 finish.

It'll be interesting to see how Gwynn responds without veteran help in the batting order or whether Garvey can return to his previous level of consistency. The progress of Mitchell, Jefferson and Santiago, however, will make this an interesting season.

SAN DIEGO PADRES 1987 ROSTER

MANAGER Larry Bowa

Coaches—Sandy Alomar, Galen Cisco, Harry Dunlop, Deacon Jones, Greg Riddoch

PITCHERS

No.	Name	1986 Club	W-L	IP	SO	ERA	B-T	Ht.	Wt.	Born
52	Bitker, Joe	Beaumont	7-7	115	93	3.53	R-R	6-1	175	2/12/64 Glendale, CA
		Las Vegas	2-0	27	19	3.29				
51	Booker, Greg	Las Vegas	8-9	129	71	5.25	R-R	6-6	223	6/22/60 Lynchburg, VA
		San Diego	1-0	11	7	1.64				
34	Davis, Storm	Baltimore	9-12	154	96	3.62	R-R	6-4	200	12/26/61 Dallas, TX
43	Dravecky, Dave	San Diego	9-11	161	87	3.07	R-L	6-1	193	2/14/58 Youngstown, OH
49	Ford, Rusty	Beaumont	2-9	82	63	3.72	R-R	6-4	200	12/15/61 Texarkana, TX
54	Gossage, Rich	San Diego	5-7	65	63	4.45	R-R	6-3	220	7/5/51 Colorado Springs, CO
40	Hawkins, Andy	San Diego	10-8	209	117	4.30	R-R	6-3	205	1/21/60 Waco, TX
25	Hayward, Ray	Las Vegas	9-11	136	100	4.63	L-L	6-1	190	4/27/61 Enid, OK
		San Diego	0-2	10	6	9.00				
45	Jones, Jimmy	Las Vegas	9-10	158	114	4.40	R-R	6-2	175	4/20/64 Dallas, TX
		San Diego	2-0	18	15	2.50				
37	Lefferts, Craig	San Diego	9-8	108	72	3.09	L-L	6-1	190	9/29/57 West Germany
41	McCullers, Lance	San Diego	10-10	136	92	2.78	B-R	6-1	215	3/8/64 Tampa, FL
30	Show, Eric	San Diego	9-5	136	94	2.97	R-R	6-1	179	5/19/56 Riverside, CA
53	Sierra, Candy	Beaumont	4-5	91	59	4.86	R-R	6-2	190	3/27/67 Puerto Rico
50	Vosberg, Ed	Las Vegas	7-8	130	93	4.72	L-L	6-1	190	9/28/61 Tucson, AZ
		San Diego	0-1	14	8	6.59				
32	Whitson, Ed	New York (AL)	5-2	37	27	7.54	R-R	6-3	195	5/19/55 Johnson City, TN
		San Diego	1-7	76	46	5.59				
26	Wojna, Ed	Las Vegas	12-7	175	102	3.59	R-R	6-1	185	8/20/60 Bridgeport, CT
		San Diego	2-2	39	19	3.23				

CATCHERS

No.	Name	1986 Club	H	HR	RBI	Pct.	B-T	Ht.	Wt.	Born
46	Alomar, Sandy	Beaumont	83	4	27	.240	R-R	6-5	200	6/18/66 Puerto Rico
15	Bochy, Bruce	San Diego	32	8	22	.252	R-R	6-4	234	4/16/55 France
27	Parent, Mark	Las Vegas	77	5	40	.288	R-R	6-5	215	9/16/61 Ashland, OR
		San Diego	2	0	0	.143				
16	Santiago, Benito	Las Vegas	125	17	71	.287	R-R	6-1	180	3/9/65 Puerto Rico
		San Diego	18	3	6	.290				

INFIELDERS

No.	Name	1986 Club	H	HR	RBI	Pct.	B-T	Ht.	Wt.	Born
12	Asadoor, Randy	Las Vegas	111	13	52	.281	R-R	6-1	185	10/20/62 Fresno, CA
		San Diego	20	0	7	.364				
11	Flannery, Tim	San Diego	103	3	28	.280	L-R	5-11	180	9/29/57 Tulsa, OK
6	Garvey, Steve	San Diego	142	21	81	.255	R-R	5-10	190	12/22/48 Tampa, FL
20	Green, Gary	Las Vegas	104	0	40	.249	R-R	6-3	175	1/14/62 Pittsburgh, PA
		San Diego	7	0	2	.212				
—	Mitchell, Kevin	New York (NL)	91	12	43	.277	R-R	5-11	210	1/13/62 San Diego, CA
5	Ready, Randy	Milwaukee	15	1	4	.190	R-R	5-11	180	1/8/60 San Mateo, CA
		San Diego	0	0	0	.000				
		Las Vegas	14	1	8	.368				
17	Rodriguez, Ed	Las Vegas	93	4	32	.301	R-R	5-11	175	8/14/60 Puerto Rico
1	Templeton, Garry	San Diego	126	2	44	.247	B-R	6-0	192	3/24/56 Lockey, TX

OUTFIELDERS

No.	Name	1986 Club	H	HR	RBI	Pct.	B-T	Ht.	Wt.	Born
—	Abner, Shawn	Jackson	136	14	76	.266	R-R	6-1	190	6/17/66 Hamilton, OH
47	Byers, Randell	Beaumont	123	11	50	.266	L-L	6-2	180	10/2/64 Bridgeton, NJ
19	Gwynn, Tony	San Diego	211	14	59	.329	L-L	5-11	206	5/9/60 Los Angeles, CA
—	Jefferson, Stan	Tidewater	107	2	36	.290	B-R	5-11	175	12/4/62 New York, NY
		New York (NL)	5	1	3	.208				
8	Kruk, John	Las Vegas	13	0	9	.464	L-L	5-10	190	2/9/61 Charleston, WV
		San Diego	86	4	38	.309				
14	Martinez, Carmelo	San Diego	58	9	25	.238	R-R	6-2	210	7/28/60 Puerto Rico
44	Parsons, Scott	Reno	87	13	63	.401	R-R	6-5	190	1/25/62 Livingston, NJ
		Beaumont	72	5	42	.350				
21	Steels, James	Las Vegas	148	8	64	.307	L-L	5-10	180	5/30/61 Jackson, MS
7	Wynne, Marvell	San Diego	76	7	37	.264	L-L	5-11	176	12/17/59 Chicago, IL

PADRE PROFILES

STEVE GARVEY 38 5-10 190 **Bats R Throws R**

Posted lowest batting average since 1971, yet hammered most home runs since 1980 last season . . . Apparently is being eased out of regular status to make room for John Kruk at first base . . . Holds NL endurance record with 1,207 straight games and had a 305-gamer snapped last season . . . The paragon of consistency as Dodger first baseman from 1974-80, notching 200 hits and batting above .300 six of seven years . . . Born Dec. 22, 1948, in Tampa, Fla. . . . Best month in 1986 was August, when he batted .319 with six homers . . . Played defensive back at Michigan State . . . Collected 2,500th hit last year . . . NL and All-Star Game MVP in 1974 . . . Signed with Padres as free agent in 1983 and was off to great start with new club before suffering a dislocated thumb . . . NL version of Mr. October with .356 average in 22 NL Championship Series games and .319 mark in five World Series . . . A .393 hitter in All-Star Games . . . Dodgers' first-round draft choice in 1968.

Year	Club	Pos.	G	AB	R	H	2B	3B	HR	RBI	SB	Avg.
1969	Los Angeles	3B	3	3	0	1	0	0	0	0	0	.333
1970	Los Angeles	3B-2B	34	93	8	25	5	0	1	6	1	.269
1971	Los Angeles	3B	81	225	27	51	12	1	7	26	1	.227
1972	Los Angeles	3B-1B	96	294	36	79	14	2	9	30	4	.269
1973	Los Angeles	1B-OF	114	349	37	106	17	3	8	50	0	.304
1974	Los Angeles	1B	156	642	95	200	32	3	21	111	5	.312
1975	Los Angeles	1B	160	659	85	210	38	6	18	95	11	.319
1976	Los Angeles	1B	162	631	85	200	37	4	13	80	19	.317
1977	Los Angeles	1B	162	646	91	192	25	3	33	115	9	.297
1978	Los Angeles	1B	162	639	89	202	36	9	21	113	10	.316
1979	Los Angeles	1B	162	648	92	204	32	1	28	110	3	.315
1980	Los Angeles	1B	163	658	78	200	27	1	26	106	6	.304
1981	Los Angeles	1B	110	431	63	122	23	1	10	64	3	.283
1982	Los Angeles	1B	162	625	66	176	35	1	16	86	5	.282
1983	San Diego	1B	100	388	76	114	22	0	14	59	4	.294
1984	San Diego	1B	161	617	72	175	27	2	8	86	1	.284
1985	San Diego	1B	162	654	80	184	34	6	17	81	0	.281
1986	San Diego	1B	155	557	58	142	22	0	21	81	1	.255
	Totals		2305	8759	1138	2583	438	43	271	1299	83	.295

TONY GWYNN 26 5-11 206 **Bats L Throws L**

Just missed in his bid for a second batting title last year, but led league with 210 hits and established club record for runs scored . . . Topped NL with .341 average at the All-Star break, but a poor September trip made him less effective in second half . . . Batted .322 in April, .349 in June and .341 in August . . . Right fielder hasn't posted a batting average below .300 since he reached the bigs to stay in 1983 . . . Born May 9, 1960, in Los Angeles . . . Started at point guard at San Diego State and was drafted by NBA Clippers . . . Third-round draft pick of Padres in 1981, he won batting title at Walla Walla (Wash.) as a pro rookie and was named MVP of the Northwest Rookie League . . . Finished 1981 batting .462 for Amarillo (AA).

Year	Club	Pos.	G	AB	R	H	2B	3B	HR	RBI	SB	Avg.
1982	San Diego	OF	54	190	33	55	12	2	1	17	8	.289
1983	San Diego	OF	86	304	34	94	12	2	1	37	7	.309
1984	San Diego	OF	158	606	88	213	21	10	5	71	33	.351
1985	San Diego	OF	154	622	90	197	29	5	6	46	14	.317
1986	San Diego	OF	160	642	107	211	33	7	14	59	37	.329
	Totals		612	2364	352	770	107	26	27	230	99	.326

KEVIN MITCHELL 25 5-11 210 Bats R Throws R

Met rookie surprise of 1986 has returned home to San Diego area . . . Along with prospects Stanley Jefferson and Shawn Abner, he was part of eight-player deal that sent Kevin McReynolds and Gene Walter to New York in December . . . Popular, muscular utility man finished third in NL Rookie-of-the-Year balloting . . . Played all three outfield spots, shortstop, third and first for Mets last season . . . Makes up for shaky glove with potent bat . . . His torrid first half last season made George Foster expendable, but he slumped after being installed as semi-regular . . . Nicknamed "World" . . . Born Jan. 13, 1962, in San Diego and still lives there . . . Father played basketball with Graig Nettles at San Diego State and now Mitch is expected to take over for Nettles at third base for Padres . . . Had 12 homers in only 328 at-bats . . . Mets signed him as free agent in 1980.

Year	Club	Pos.	G	AB	R	H	2B	3B	HR	RBI	SB	Avg.
1984	New York (NL)	3B	7	14	0	3	0	0	0	1	0	.214
1986	New York (NL)	1B-3B-OF	108	328	51	91	22	2	12	43	3	.277
	Totals		115	342	51	94	22	2	12	44	3	.275

GARRY TEMPLETON 31 6-0 192 Bats S Throws R

Once regarded as the cornerstone for the Cardinals' future success and the finest shortstop in the NL, "Tempy" is merely very good these days . . . Fell off considerably last year after earning team MVP honors in 1985 . . . A series of injuries rendered him merely mortal and hampered his speed . . . Born March 24, 1956, in Lockey, Tex. . . . Cardinals' first-round pick in 1974 . . . Led NL in triples three years in a row, 1977-79, his 19 in '79 being the most since Willie Mays' 20 in 1957 . . . Set record for switch-hitters with at least 100 hits from each side in

1979 . . . Problems with Whitey Herzog prefaced his departure from St. Louis . . . Was traded to Padres for Ozzie Smith on Feb. 11, 1982 . . . Batted .333 in NL Championship Series and .316 in World Series in 1984.

Year	Club	Pos.	G	AB	R	H	2B	3B	HR	RBI	SB	Avg.
1976	St. Louis	SS	53	213	32	62	8	2	1	17	11	.291
1977	St. Louis	SS	153	621	94	200	19	18	8	79	28	.322
1978	St. Louis	SS	155	647	82	181	31	13	2	47	34	.280
1979	St. Louis	SS	154	672	105	211	32	19	9	62	26	.314
1980	St. Louis	SS	118	504	83	161	19	9	4	43	31	.319
1981	St. Louis	SS	80	333	47	96	16	8	1	33	8	.288
1982	San Diego	SS	141	563	76	139	25	8	6	64	27	.247
1983	San Diego	SS	126	460	39	121	20	2	3	40	16	.263
1984	San Diego	SS	148	493	40	127	19	3	2	35	8	.258
1985	San Diego	SS	148	546	63	154	30	2	6	55	16	.282
1986	San Diego	SS	147	510	42	126	21	2	2	44	10	.247
	Totals		1423	5562	703	1578	240	86	44	519	215	.284

DAVE DRAVECKY 29 6-1 193 **Bats R Throws L**

Experienced first losing season in the majors last year, but wasn't blessed with good support . . . Opened season with a 2-1 record and a 0.75 ERA in April, then got little help . . . Victory total never seems commensurate with solid ERA and hits-to-innings ratio . . . Born Feb. 14, 1958, in Youngstown, Ohio . . . Attended Youngstown State and was drafted in 21st round by Pirates in 1978 . . . Traded to the Padres for outfielder Bobby Mitchell on April 5, 1981, and has served his present club in dual role of starter and reliever . . . Mostly came out of the bullpen in 1984 and was instrumental in championship season . . . Didn't yield a run in 10⅔ innings of postseason play against Cubs and Tigers.

Year	Club	G	IP	W	L	Pct.	SO	BB	H	ERA
1982	San Diego	31	105	5	3	.625	59	33	86	2.57
1983	San Diego	28	183⅔	14	10	.583	74	44	181	3.58
1984	San Diego	50	156⅔	9	8	.529	71	51	125	2.93
1985	San Diego	34	214⅔	13	11	.542	105	57	200	2.93
1985	San Diego	34	214⅔	13	11	.542	105	57	200	2.93
1986	San Diego	26	161⅓	9	11	.450	87	54	149	3.07
	Totals	169	821⅓	50	43	.538	396	239	741	3.06

RICH GOSSAGE 35 6-3 220 **Bats R Throws R**

Drew a suspension from Padres last year for knocking owner's hamburgers after pitching like one much of the year . . . Notched 21 saves, but only six came after the All-Star break . . . No longer a fearsome fireman, as evidenced by losing record and high ERA . . . Born July 5, 1951, in Colorado Springs, Colo. . . . "Goose" attended Southern Colorado State and was a ninth-round pick by the White Sox in 1970 draft . . . Outrageous second pro season produced 18-2 record, 1.38 ERA and seven shutouts at Appleton (Wis.) in 1971 . . . A reliever most of career, he completed 15 of 29 starts for Sox in 1976 . . . Attained bullpen stardom with Yankees before signing with Padres as free agent prior to 1984 season . . . Has 278 career saves . . . Has 1-0 record with 2.63 ERA and two saves in eight World Series games.

Year	Club	G	IP	W	L	Pct.	SO	BB	H	ERA
1972	Chicago (AL)	36	80	7	1	.875	57	44	72	4.28
1973	Chicago (AL)	20	50	0	4	.000	33	37	57	7.38
1974	Chicago (AL)	39	89	4	6	.400	64	47	92	4.15
1975	Chicago (AL)	62	142	9	8	.529	130	70	99	1.84
1976	Chicago (AL)	31	224	9	17	.346	135	90	214	3.94
1977	Pittsburgh	72	133	11	9	.550	151	49	78	1.62
1978	New York (AL)	63	134	10	11	.476	122	59	87	2.01
1979	New York (AL)	36	58	5	3	.625	41	19	48	2.64
1980	New York (AL)	64	99	6	2	.750	103	37	74	2.27
1981	New York (AL)	32	47	3	2	.600	48	14	22	0.77
1982	New York (AL)	56	93	4	5	.444	102	28	63	2.23
1983	New York (AL)	57	87⅓	13	5	.722	90	25	82	2.27
1984	San Diego	62	102⅓	10	6	.625	84	36	75	2.90
1985	San Diego	50	79	5	3	.625	52	17	64	1.82
1986	San Diego	45	64⅔	5	7	.417	63	20	69	4.45
	Totals	725	1482⅓	101	89	.532	1275	592	1196	2.87

ANDY HAWKINS 27 6-3 205 **Bats R Throws R**

It would have been asking a lot of "Hawk" to duplicate his surprising 1985, and he didn't come close . . . That dream season included an 11-0 start, best in the NL since reliever Elroy Face went 17-0 in 1959 . . . Slumped to very ordinary 10-8, 4.30 level last season . . . Born Jan. 21, 1960, in Waco, Tex . . . Club's first-round draft pick in 1978 . . . Unspectacular minor-league career until he reached Hawaii (AAA) in 1982, where he fired league-leading six shutouts in only 18 starts . . . Set tone for 1985 with a solid postseason in 1984 . . . Didn't yield a run in three NL Championship Series relief appearances and relinquished one run and four hits in 12 World Series innings.

Year	Club	G	IP	W	L	Pct.	SO	BB	H	ERA
1982	San Diego	15	63⅔	2	5	.286	25	27	66	4.10
1983	San Diego	21	119⅔	5	7	.417	59	48	106	2.93
1984	San Diego	36	146	8	9	.471	77	72	143	4.68
1985	San Diego	33	228⅔	18	8	.692	69	65	229	3.15
1986	San Diego	37	209⅓	10	8	.556	117	75	218	4.30
	Totals	142	767⅓	43	37	.538	347	287	762	3.80

ERIC SHOW 30 6-1 179 — Bats R Throws R

Two stints on the disabled list with elbow problems retarded what otherwise might have been a solid season . . . A 3-1 June with a 2.45 ERA represented one-third of his victory total . . . Posted a winning record for the fifth straight season as a San Diego starter . . . Has the equipment to be a big winner, yet has barely totaled 20 victories the last two years . . . He has been accused of thinking too much instead of letting talent guide him . . . Also was accused of talking too much two years ago, when his right-wing political views caused a stir . . . Born May 19, 1956, in Riverside, Cal. . . . A physics major at UC-Riverside who plays jazz guitar . . . An 18th-round draft pick in 1978, he has never had a losing season.

Year	Club	G	IP	W	L	Pct.	SO	BB	H	ERA
1981	San Diego	15	23	1	3	.250	22	9	17	3.13
1982	San Diego	47	150	10	6	.625	88	48	117	2.64
1983	San Diego	35	200⅔	15	12	.556	120	74	201	4.17
1984	San Diego	32	206⅔	15	9	.625	104	88	175	3.40
1985	San Diego	35	233	12	11	.522	141	87	212	3.09
1986	San Diego	24	136⅓	9	5	.643	94	69	109	2.97
	Totals	188	949⅔	62	46	.574	569	375	831	3.30

LANCE McCULLERS 23 6-1 215 — Bats S Throws R

With Goose Gossage on the fade, this guy looms as bullpen closer of future for Padres . . . Hard thrower struck out 92 in 136 innings last season en route to .500 record and five saves . . . Got break when he was promoted to replace injured Gossage in 1985 . . . Earned saves in first three major-league appearances and didn't allow an earned run in first 11⅓ innings . . . Made only 10 relief appearances in his 89 games as minor leaguer . . . Born March 8, 1964, in Tampa, Fla. . . . Played against Mets' Dwight Gooden and Montreal's Floyd Youmans in high school . . . Drafted by Phillies in second round in 1982 . . . Traded to Padres with Darren Burroughs, Marty Decker and Ed Wojna for Sixto Lezcano and Steve Fireovid in August 1983 . . . Should make jump from set-up man to finisher very soon . . . Actually resembles the husky Gossage and is known as "Little Goose".

Year	Club	G	IP	W	L	Pct.	SO	BB	H	ERA
1985	San Diego	21	35	0	2	.000	27	16	23	2.31
1986	San Diego	70	136	10	10	.500	92	58	103	2.78
	Totals	91	171	10	12	.454	119	74	126	2.68

TOP PROSPECTS

JIMMY JONES 22 6-2 175 **Bats R Throws R**
No rookie pitcher since the Giants' Juan Marichal in 1960 had a finer major-league debut than Jones. Like Marichal, Jones fired a one-hitter in his maiden start, shackling the Astros, 5-0 . . . Born April 20, 1964, in Dallas . . . For an encore, Jones combined with Goose Gossage on a five-hit, 3-2 victory over the Dodgers, fanning nine in seven innings . . . Promoted after going 9-10 at Las Vegas (AAA) . . . Yielded 10 hits, struck out 15 in 18 innings and was 2-0 as Padre . . . Never won more than seven games in a season until last year . . . Drafted in first round of June 1982 lottery.

BENITO SANTIAGO 22 6-1 180 **Bats R Throws R**
Swapping of Terry Kennedy to Orioles gives this young catcher a chance to start . . . Posted .290 average with three homers in a 17-game stint last year . . . Born March 9, 1965, in Ponce, P.R. . . . Signed as free agent in 1982 and began professional career at age 18 . . . Batted .298 as a Texas League All-Star for Beaumont (AA) in 1985 and .287 with 17 homers at Las Vegas (AAA) prior to promotion last year.

STANLEY JEFFERSON 24 5-11 175 **Bats S Throws R**
Former Met farmhand who was acquired in Kevin McReynolds deal figures to win center-field job . . . Injury-plagued 1986 season saw him hit .290 with 2 homers and 36 RBI for Tidewater (AAA) . . . Hit .208 in 24 at-bats with Mets in September . . . Born Dec. 4, 1962, in New York, N.Y. . . . Drafted by Mets in first round in 1983 . . . Had 144 stolen bases in four minor-league seasons . . . Hit .500 for Mets in spring of 1986, making strong bid to jump from Double-A to majors.

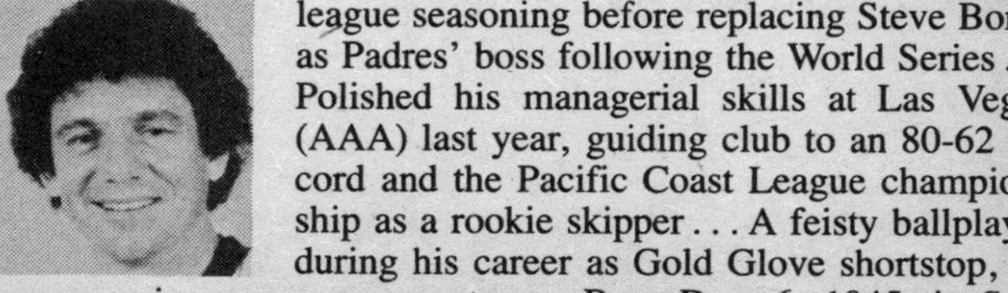

MANAGER LARRY BOWA: Had only one year of minor-league seasoning before replacing Steve Boros as Padres' boss following the World Series . . . Polished his managerial skills at Las Vegas (AAA) last year, guiding club to an 80-62 record and the Pacific Coast League championship as a rookie skipper . . . A feisty ballplayer during his career as Gold Glove shortstop, he is aggressive as a manager, too . . . Born Dec. 6, 1945, in Sacramento, Cal. . . . Signed as free agent by Phillies in 1965 and went on to become best-fielding shortstop in major-league history . . . Holds single-season and lifetime fielding percentage records with a .991 mark in 1979 and a .980 mark lifetime . . . His 2,222 games at short are the most in NL history . . . Led league in fielding six times . . . Traded to Cubs with Ryne Sandberg for Ivan DeJesus prior to 1983 season . . . Finished playing career with Mets in 1985 . . . Compiled .260 lifetime average.

GREATEST ALL-TIME ROOKIE

The Padres haven't been blessed with many great first-year players, so reliever Butch Metzger stands alone as San Diego's top rookie for sharing Rookie-of-the-Year honors in 1976.

Metzger came to the Padres in a swap with the Giants that also brought Tito Fuentes to San Diego and sent Derrel Thomas to San Francisco.

After going 1-0 in both 1974 and 1975, Metzger blossomed as a full-time reliever in 1976, posting an 11-4 record and a 2.93 ERA. His 12 consecutive victories in relief at the start of his career are a major-league record.

Outfielder Kevin McReynolds also enjoyed a solid first full season. After playing only 39 games in 1983, he batted .278 with 20 homers and 75 RBI in 1984, as San Diego captured its first pennant.

ALL-TIME PADRE SEASON RECORDS

BATTING: Tony Gwynn, .351, 1984
HRs: Nate Colbert, 38, 1970
RBIs: Dave Winfield, 118, 1979
STEALS: Alan Wiggins, 70, 1984
WINS: Randy Jones, 22, 1976
STRIKEOUTS: Clay Kirby, 231, 1971

SAN FRANCISCO GIANTS

TEAM DIRECTORY: Owner: Bob Lurie; Pres.-GM: Al Rosen; Exec. VP-Adm.: Corey Busch; VP-Baseball Oper.: Bob Kennedy; VP-Business Oper.: Pat Gallagher; Asst. GM: Ralph Nelson; Dir. Scouting: Bob Fontaine; Dir. Pub. Rel.: Duffy Jennings; Dir. Community Services: Dave Craig; Trav. Sec.: Dirk Smith; Mgr.: Roger Craig. Home: Candlestick Park (58,000). Field distances: 335, l.f. line; 365, l.c.; 400, c.f.; 365, l.c.; 335, r.f. line. Spring training: Scottsdale, Ariz.

SCOUTING REPORT

HITTING: The Giants tied for seventh in the NL in batting (.253) last year, but that represented a great improvement over the woeful, last-place offense they mustered in 1985. They also ranked fourth

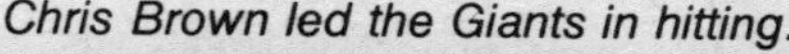

Chris Brown led the Giants in hitting.

in runs scored (698), quite a feat considering the absence of Jeffrey Leonard (.279, 6 homers, 42 RBI) and Chris Brown (.317, 7, 49) down the stretch.

With Leonard, Brown and second-year man Will Clark (.287, 11, 41) healthy for an entire season, the offense could improve. Candy Maldonado, the most effective pinch-hitter in the league last year, could provide a power boost as a regular after notching 18 homers and 85 RBI in a mostly reserve role. The Giants obtained Eddie Milner (.259, 15, 47) from the Reds in January amid rumors that Chili Davis (.278, 13, 70) and Dan Gladden (.276, 4, 29) were on the trading block.

PITCHING: Right-hander Mike Krukow (20-9, 3.05) heads a deep, but erratic starting rotation. After Krukow, there are numerous candidates, but none is a proven winner. A lot hinges on the return of injured former ERA king Atlee Hammaker and Roger Mason.

They will start if healthy and may be joined by Mike LaCoss (10-13, 3.57), Kelly Downs (4-4, 2.75) and Mark Davis (5-7, 2.99, 4 saves), who pitched in relief last year. The bullpen is solid with Scott Garrelts (13-9, 3.11, 10 saves) returning to his former job as the ace and Jeff Robinson and Greg Minton in subordinate roles.

FIELDING: The Giants made the fewest number of errors they had made in nearly 20 years last season, yet still ranked 11th with a .977 fielding percentage. Still, there are more strengths than weaknesses, especially in the solid double-play combination of shortstop Jose Uribe and second baseman Robby Thompson.

Bob Brenly topped the catchers with a .995 fielding percentage and outfielders Leonard and Maldonado possess strong and accurate arms. An injury contributed to Brown's slump at third base, but he has the potential to be the best in the league with a glove.

OUTLOOK: Pride was restored by manager Roger Craig last season, but this is a club unaccustomed to winning, so it's walking a tightrope. If things break right, the Giants could be a contender, but there are enough pitching question marks to warrant caution.

The Giants are in dire need of a leadoff batter to get the offense in gear and it remains to be seen if Maldonado will flourish as a regular. Brown and Leonard have the potential for stardom, but have had trouble going the distance.

Despite their chronic complaints about Candlestick Park, the Giants were a solid 46-35 at home. They'll have to improve on the road (37-44), in the second half (34-38) and against the East (34-38) if they're to be taken seriously.

SAN FRANCISCO GIANTS 1987 ROSTER

MANAGER Roger Craig

Coaches—Bill Fahey, Bob Lillis, Jose Morales, Norm Sherry, Don Zimmer

PITCHERS

No.	Name	1986 Club	W-L	IP	SO	ERA	B-T	Ht.	Wt.	Born
40	Berenguer, Juan	San Francisco	2-3	73	72	2.70	R-R	5-11	215	11/30/54 Panama
26	Bockus, Randy	Phoenix	11-6	123	55	4.26	L-R	6-3	195	10/5/60 Canton, OH
		San Francisco	0-0	7	4	2.57				
—	Burkett, John	Fresno	0-3	25	14	5.47	R-R	6-2	175	11/18/64 New Brighton, PA
		Shreveport	10-6	129	73	2.66				
13	Davis, Mark	San Francisco	5-7	84	90	2.99	L-L	6-4	205	10/19/60 Livermore, CA
37	Downs, Kelly	Phoenix	8-5	108	68	3.42	R-R	6-4	200	10/25/60 Ogden, UT
		San Francisco	4-4	88	64	2.75				
—	Ferran, George	Shreveport	16-1	153	146	2.29	R-R	6-1	165	8/27/64 Boston, MA
—	Freeland, Dean	Clinton	7-7	142	129	2.85	R-R	6-0	180	2/25/65 Milwaukee, WI
		Shreveport	1-2	33	21	3.78				
50	Garrelts, Scott	San Francisco	13-9	174	125	3.11	R-R	6-4	195	10/30/61 Urbana, IL
51	Gott, Jim	San Francisco	0-0	13	9	7.62	R-R	6-4	220	8/3/59 Hollywood, CA
		Phoenix	0-0	3	2	6.75				
46	Grant, Mark	Phoenix	14-7	182	93	4.90	R-R	6-2	200	10/24/63 Aurora, IL
		San Francisco	0-1	10	5	3.60				
18	Hammaker, Atlee	San Francisco	Disabled List				B-L	6-2	195	1/24/58 Carmel, CA
39	Krukow, Mike	San Francisco	20-9	245	178	3.05	R-R	6-4	205	1/21/52 Long Beach, CA
29	LaCoss, Mike	San Francisco	10-13	204	86	3.57	R-R	6-4	190	5/30/56 Glendale, CA
48	Mason, Roger	San Francisco	3-4	60	43	4.80	R-R	6-6	215	9/18/58 Bellaire, MI
		Phoenix	1-0	6	2	0.00				
—	Medvin, Scott	Shreveport	8-6	94	68	2.40	R-R	6-0	190	9/16/61 North Olmstead, OH
38	Minton, Greg	San Francisco	4-4	69	34	3.93	B-R	6-2	190	7/29/51 Lubbock, TX
45	Mulholland, Terry	Phoenix	8-5	111	77	4.46	R-L	6-3	200	3/9/63 Uniontown, PA
		San Francisco	1-7	55	27	4.94				
49	Robinson, Jeff	San Francisco	6-3	104	90	3.36	R-R	6-4	200	12/13/60 Santa Ana, CA
—	Ward, Colin	Phoenix	8-11	123	93	5.14	L-L	6-3	190	11/22/60 Los Angeles, CA
		Shreveport	1-1	25	17	2.55				

CATCHERS

No.	Name	1986 Club	H	HR	RBI	Pct.	B-T	Ht.	Wt.	Born
15	Brenly, Bob	San Francisco	116	16	62	.246	R-R	6-2	200	2/25/54 Coshocton, OH
7	Melvin, Bob	San Francisco	60	5	25	.224	R-R	6-4	205	10/28/61 Palo Alto, CA
12	Ouellette, Phil	Phoenix	89	7	39	.308	B-R	6-0	185	11/10/61 Salem, OR
		San Francisco	4	0	0	.174				
—	Sasser, Mackey	Shreveport	129	5	72	.293	L-R	6-1	190	8/3/62 Fort Gaines, GA

INFIELDERS

No.	Name	1986 Club	H	HR	RBI	Pct.	B-T	Ht.	Wt.	Born
35	Brown, Chris	San Francisco	132	7	49	.317	R-R	6-2	210	8/15/61 Jackson, MS
22	Clark, Will	San Francisco	117	11	41	.287	L-L	6-1	185	3/13/64 New Orleans, LA
		Phoenix	5	0	1	.250				
—	Escobar, Angel	Shreveport	149	2	46	.276	B-R	6-0	160	5/12/65 Venezuela
—	Perezchica, Tony	Fresno	126	9	54	.279	R-R	5-10	160	4/20/66 Mexico
—	Speier, Chris	Chicago (NL)	44	6	23	.284	R-R	6-1	180	6/28/50 Alameda, CA
16	Spilman, Harry	Detroit	12	3	8	.245	L-R	6-1	190	7/18/54 Albany, GA
		San Francisco	27	2	22	.287				
6	Thompson, Robby	San Francisco	149	7	47	.271	R-R	5-11	170	5/10/62 West Palm Beach, FL
23	Uribe, Jose	San Francisco	101	3	43	.223	B-R	5-10	165	1/21/60 Dominican Republic
41	Woodard, Mike	Phoenix	79	0	27	.319	L-R	5-9	160	3/2/60 Melrose Park, IL
		San Francisco	20	1	5	.253				

OUTFIELDERS

No.	Name	1986 Club	H	HR	RBI	Pct.	B-T	Ht.	Wt.	Born
1	Aldrete, Mike	Phoenix	59	6	35	.371	L-L	5-11	180	1/29/61 Carmel, CA
		San Francisco	54	2	25	.250				
—	Cockrail, Alan	Shreveport	113	14	78	.258	R-R	6-2	215	12/5/62 Kansas, City, KS
30	Davis, Chili	San Francisco	146	13	70	.278	B-R	6-3	195	1/17/60 Jamaica
32	Gladden, Dan	San Francisco	97	4	29	.276	R-R	5-11	180	7/7/57 San Jose, CA
		Phoenix	9	0	0	.333				
9	Kutcher, Randy	Phoenix	72	11	39	.346	R-R	5-11	175	4/20/60 Anchorage, AK
		San Francisco	44	7	16	.237				
20	Leonard, Jeffrey	San Francisco	95	6	42	.279	R-R	6-3	200	9/22/55 Philadelphia, PA
21	Maldonado, Candy	San Francisco	102	18	85	.252	R-R	6-0	190	9/5/60 Puerto Rico
20	Milner, Eddie	Cincinnati	110	15	47	.259	L-L	5-11	175	5/21/55 Columbus, OH
—	Reid, Jessie	Phoenix	115	14	61	.269	L-L	6-1	200	6/1/62 Honolulu, HI
8	Youngblood, Joel	San Francisco	47	5	28	.255	R-R	5-11	175	8/28/51 Houston, TX

GIANT PROFILES

CHRIS BROWN 25 6-2 210 **Bats R Throws R**

Brittle third baseman gets little sympathy when he's hurt because of crybaby reputation . . . A sore shoulder hampered his effectiveness in the second half, yet he still managed to lead club with .317 average . . . Started strong with a .349 April and a .337 June, taking a .338 average into the All-Star Game, where he doubled in his debut . . . Born Aug. 15, 1961, in Jackson, Miss. . . . Played high-school ball with Darryl Strawberry at Crenshaw High in LA . . . Second-round draft choice in 1979 . . . Became a better hitter in majors after six-year minor-league career . . . Moves extremely well for his size and is an outstanding fielder . . . Has a career .358 average in the bigs with runners in scoring position.

Year	Club	Pos.	G	AB	R	H	2B	3B	HR	RBI	SB	Avg.
1984	San Francisco.....	3B	23	84	6	24	7	0	1	11	2	.286
1985	San Francisco.....	3B	131	432	50	117	20	3	16	61	2	.271
1986	San Francisco.....	3B	116	416	57	132	16	3	7	49	13	.317
	Totals..........		270	932	113	273	43	6	24	121	17	.293

BOB BRENLY 33 6-2 200 **Bats R Throws R**

Overcame sluggish start with hot September to finish with decent power figures . . . Also withstood challenge of newcomer Bob Melvin to keep catching job because Melvin didn't hit . . . Increased pitchouts made him better behind the plate . . . Batted .277 with seven homers and 19 RBI in September . . . Had two memorable final-month performances . . . Matched a record with a four-error inning at third base before belting game-winning homer against Braves . . . Two weeks later, he doubled in the 16th to down the Dodgers in a 5:45 marathon . . . Born Feb. 25, 1954, in Coshocton, Ohio . . . All-American at Ohio U., where he tied some of Mike Schmidt's records . . . Became first catcher in 91 years to lead Giants in homers in 1985.

Year	Club	Pos.	G	AB	R	H	2B	3B	HR	RBI	SB	Avg.
1981	San Francisco.....	C-3B-OF	19	45	5	15	2	1	1	4	0	.333
1982	San Francisco.....	C	65	180	26	51	4	1	4	15	6	.283
1983	San Francisco.....	C-1B-OF	104	281	36	63	12	2	7	34	10	.224
1984	San Francisco.....	C-1B-OF	145	506	74	147	28	0	20	80	6	.291
1985	San Francisco.....	C-1B-3B	133	440	41	97	16	1	19	56	1	.220
1986	San Francisco.....	C-1B-3B	149	472	60	116	26	0	16	62	10	.246
	Totals..........		615	1924	242	489	88	5	67	251	33	.254

WILL CLARK 23 6-1 185 Bats L Throws L

Played only 65 minor-league games at Class-A Fresno before landing the first-base job last spring . . . Didn't disappoint, although an elbow injury sidelined him for more than one month and reduced his numbers . . . Made a sensational debut with a home run off Nolan Ryan in his first big-league at-bat . . . Also homered in his pro debut for Fresno in 1985 . . . Has a flair for the dramatic and was nicknamed "The Thrill" by Bob Brenly . . . Born March 13, 1964, in New Orleans, La. . . . An All-American at Mississippi State and a star on 1984 U.S. Olympic squad who hit three homers in a Fenway Park exhibition game . . . No. 1 draft pick in 1985 and second player chosen overall.

Year	Club	Pos.	G	AB	R	H	2B	3B	HR	RBI	SB	Avg.
1986	San Francisco.	1B	111	408	66	117	27	2	11	41	4	.287

ROBBY THOMPSON 24 5-11 170 Bats R Throws R

An even bigger surprise than Will Clark, this scrappy and unheralded second baseman made the jump from Double-A, winning the job in spring training . . . Had a much better season with the Giants than he did in three years in lower minors . . . Hot finish placed him in Rookie-of-the-Year contention . . . A gamer who frequently played hurt, Robby topped NL with 18 sacrifice hits . . . Made only two throwing errors all season and his glove was glue . . . Reminiscent of Eddie Stanky . . . Born May 10, 1962, in West Palm Beach, Fla. . . . Attended U. of Florida and was Giants' top choice in secondary phase of 1983 draft.

Year	Club	Pos.	G	AB	R	H	2B	3B	HR	RBI	SB	Avg.
1986	San Francisco.	2B-SS	149	549	73	149	27	3	7	47	12	.271

CHILI DAVIS 27 6-3 195 Bats S Throws R

Suffered from an attitude problem last year . . . Even when he was going well in the first half, he wasn't happy because he wanted out of Candlestick Park . . . The club's improvement didn't change his mind, so it's possible new surroundings will greet the right fielder this year . . . If not, the Giants surely will lose him to free agency at the end of 1987 . . . Took a .294 average and 55 RBI into the All-Star Game, but did little damage thereafter . . . Born Jan. 17, 1960, in Kingston, Jamaica, but was reared in Los Angeles . . . An 11th-round draft pick in 1978, he was a highly-touted rookie by 1982 and a star by 1984.

Year	Club	Pos.	G	AB	R	H	2B	3B	HR	RBI	SB	Avg.
1981	San Francisco.	OF	8	15	1	2	0	0	0	0	2	.133
1982	San Francisco.	OF	154	641	86	167	27	6	19	76	24	.261
1983	San Francisco.	OF	137	486	54	113	21	2	11	59	10	.233
1984	San Francisco.	OF	137	499	87	157	21	6	21	81	12	.315
1985	San Francisco.	OF	136	481	53	130	25	2	13	56	15	.270
1986	San Francisco.	OF	153	526	71	146	28	3	13	70	16	.278
	Totals		725	2648	352	715	122	19	77	342	79	.270

JEFF LEONARD 31 6-3 200 **Bats R Throws R**

"Hac Man" was heading for his greatest season when a wrist injury limited him to 89 games . . . Should have sat down sooner, but left fielder's gameness exemplified the club's new attitude in 1986 . . . League leader with 11 game-winning RBI at All-Star break, but injury prevented him from pulling the ball and he succumbed to surgery one month later . . . Born Sept. 22, 1955, in Philadelphia . . . Signed with the Dodgers as a free agent in 1973 . . . Pacific Coast League Player of the Year in 1978, batting .365 for Albuquerque (AAA), but was dealt to Astros . . . Received some recognition as a rookie with Houston in 1980, but was swapped to the Giants along with Dave Bergman for Mike Ivie in 1981.

Year	Club	Pos.	G	AB	R	H	2B	3B	HR	RBI	SB	Avg.
1977	Los Angeles	OF	11	10	1	3	0	1	0	2	0	.300
1978	Houston	OF	8	26	2	10	2	0	0	4	0	.385
1979	Houston	OF	134	411	47	119	15	5	0	47	23	.290
1980	Houston	OF	88	216	29	46	7	5	3	20	4	.213
1981	Hou.-S.F.	OF-1B	44	145	21	42	12	4	4	29	5	.290
1982	San Francisco.	OF-1B	80	278	32	72	16	1	9	49	18	.259
1983	San Francisco.	OF	139	516	74	144	17	7	21	87	26	.279
1984	San Francisco.	OF	136	514	76	155	27	2	21	86	17	.302
1985	San Francisco.	OF	133	507	49	122	20	3	17	62	11	.241
1986	San Francisco.	OF	89	341	48	95	11	3	6	42	16	.279
	Totals		862	2964	379	808	127	31	81	428	120	.273

CANDY MALDONADO 26 6-0 190 **Bats R Throws R**

Giants received much more than they expected when they acquired Candy from the Dodgers for Alex Trevino after the 1985 season . . . He couldn't find a job in the Giant outfield, but made an impact with a club-record 17 pinch-hits . . . Topped major-league pinch-hitters with four homers and 20 RBI, though he was a regular the final two months . . . His fourth pinch-homer, on July 1, tied the Giant record . . . Broke pinch-hit mark when he collected his 15th pinch RBI on Aug. 9 . . . Two homers, including a grand slam, on final day gave him club lead in homers and RBI despite limited at-bats . . . Born Sept. 5, 1960, in Humacao, Puerto Rico. . . . Signed with Dodgers as free agent in 1978 . . . In 545 at-bats with LA, he totaled 11 homers and 53 RBI, far below his one-season outburst with Giants.

Year	Club	Pos.	G	AB	R	H	2B	3B	HR	RBI	SB	Avg.
1981	Los Angeles......	OF	11	12	0	1	0	0	0	0	0	.083
1982	Los Angeles......	OF	6	4	0	0	0	0	0	0	0	.000
1983	Los Angeles......	OF	42	62	5	12	1	1	1	6	0	.194
1984	Los Angeles......	OF-3B	116	254	25	68	14	0	5	28	0	.268
1985	Los Angeles......	OF	121	213	20	48	7	1	5	19	1	.225
1986	San Francisco.....	OF	133	405	49	102	31	3	18	85	4	.252
	Totals..........		429	950	99	231	53	5	29	138	5	.243

SCOTT GARRELTS 25 6-4 195 — Bats R Throws R

Demonstrated his versatility by starting and relieving last season . . . Club's bullpen ace of 1985 entered rotation at start of season and was 1-1 with 1.91 ERA in May . . . When right-handed relievers were erratic, he returned to the bullpen for good at midseason and again prospered . . . In final 16 games, Scotty's heater produced three wins and six saves as he yielded four earned runs in 30 innings (1.20 ERA) . . . Born Oct. 30, 1961, in Urbana, Ill. . . . Once fanned 22 batters in a seven-inning prep game . . . Club's top pick in 1979 draft . . . Plagued by control problems much of career, but rectified them by always pitching out of the stretch . . . Posted 24-inning scoreless streak in 1985.

Year	Club	G	IP	W	L	Pct.	SO	BB	H	ERA
1982	San Francisco	1	2	0	0	.000	4	2	3	13.50
1983	San Francisco	5	35⅔	2	2	.500	16	19	33	2.52
1984	San Francisco	21	43	2	3	.400	32	34	45	5.65
1985	San Francisco	74	105⅔	9	6	.600	106	58	76	2.30
1986	San Francisco	53	173⅔	13	9	.591	125	74	144	3.11
	Totals..............	154	360	26	20	.565	283	187	301	3.18

MIKE KRUKOW 35 6-4 205 — Bats R Throws R

Capped brilliant season by becoming Giants' first 20-game winner since 1973 with victory over the Dodgers on Oct. 5 . . . Fell behind, 2-0, but tied game with a run-scoring single and a squeeze bunt . . . Placed 20 wins in jeopardy by suffering rib injury in a brawl at St. Louis that cost him at least three starts . . . Bounced back strong and was NL Pitcher of the Month with a 6-0 record and a 1.37 ERA in September . . . Took an 11-5 mark into the All-Star Game and fired a perfect inning . . . Born Jan. 21, 1952, in Long Beach, Cal. . . . Attended Cal Poly-San Luis Obispo and drafted in eighth round by Cubs in 1973 . . . Acquired by Giants from Phillies in 1982 with Mark Davis for Joe Morgan and Al Holland.

Year	Club	G	IP	W	L	Pct.	SO	BB	H	ERA
1976	Chicago (NL)	2	4	0	0	.000	1	2	6	9.00
1977	Chicago (NL)	34	172	8	14	.364	106	61	195	4.40
1978	Chicago (NL)	27	138	9	3	.750	81	53	125	3.91
1979	Chicago (NL)	28	165	9	9	.500	119	81	172	4.20
1980	Chicago (NL)	34	205	10	15	.400	130	80	200	4.39
1981	Chicago (NL)	25	144	9	9	.500	101	55	146	3.69
1982	Philadelphia	33	208	13	11	.542	138	82	211	3.12
1983	San Francisco	31	184⅓	11	11	.500	136	76	189	3.95
1984	San Francisco	35	199⅓	11	12	.478	141	78	234	4.56
1985	San Francisco	28	194⅔	8	11	.419	150	49	176	3.38
1986	San Francisco	34	245	20	9	.690	178	55	204	3.05
	Totals	311	1859⅓	108	104	.509	1281	672	1858	3.84

MARK DAVIS 26 6-4 205 **Bats L Throws L**

A pitcher with tremendous potential that has gone unfulfilled for a variety of reasons . . . Teams tried to pry him loose over the winter, but Giants won't let him get away . . . He's on verge of breakthrough season because of great stuff and the split-finger fastball . . . Giants are so confident he'll become a big winner, they're toying with making him a starter again if they find a lefty reliever to augment stable of right-handers . . . Born Oct. 19, 1960, in Livermore, Cal. . . . Phillies first pick in secondary phase of June 1979 draft . . . Went 30-15 in first two years of pro ball, but progress through Phillies' system was stunted by arm trouble . . . Joined Giants with Mike Krukow in December 1982 deal involving Joe Morgan and Al Holland . . . Lost 17 games as a starter in 1984, but was switched to bullpen and topped major-league firemen with 128 strikeouts in 1985 . . . Limited left-handed hitters to .115 average last year and .185 mark in 1985.

Year	Club	G	IP	W	L	Pct.	SO	BB	H	ERA
1980	Philadelphia	2	7	0	0	.000	5	5	4	2.57
1981	Philadelphia	9	43	1	4	.200	29	24	49	7.74
1983	San Francisco	20	111	6	4	.600	83	50	93	3.49
1984	San Francisco	46	174⅔	5	17	.227	124	54	201	5.36
1985	San Francisco	77	114⅓	5	12	.294	131	41	89	3.54
1986	San Francisco	67	84⅓	5	7	.417	90	34	63	2.99
	Totals	221	534⅓	22	44	.333	462	208	499	4.36

TOP PROSPECT

KELLY DOWNS 26 6-4 200 **Bats R Throws R**
An injury to Greg Minton gave Downs a big break, prompting his recall from Phoenix (AAA) July 27 . . . Victimized by poor support, he started 0-4, then won four straight decisions for 4-4 record with 2.75 ERA . . . Born Oct. 25, 1960, in Ogden, Utah . . . Began career with Phillies and was acquired in Al Oliver deal . . . Was 8-5 with a 3.42 ERA at Phoenix last year . . . Expected to be in starting rotation this season.

MANAGER ROGER CRAIG: Nicknamed "Hum Baby" by his players after his positive attitude and direction led them out of the wilderness . . . Giants became only eighth club in history to rebound with a winning record following 100 defeats and Craig was primarily responsible . . . He made club very competitive, as evidenced by success against Mets and Astros, despite key injuries . . . Giants were in first place at the All-Star break, but patchwork lineups eventually caught up with club, which played under .500 the second half . . . Born Feb. 17, 1930, in Durham, N.C . . . Attended N.C. State . . . Signed with Dodgers in 1950 and won 74 major-league games, despite first two years with infant Mets in which he went 15-46 . . . Foremost expert on teaching the split-finger fastball was instrumental in success of Jack Morris and Mike Scott, among others . . . Enjoys riding horses on his ranch near San Diego . . . Managed Padres in 1978 and 1979 before becoming pitching coach of Tigers . . . Has 232-271 record as major-league manager.

GREATEST ALL-TIME ROOKIE

To give each era its due, Giant rookies representing the New York and San Francisco eras will be crowned. The winners are—drum roll, please—Bobby Thomson of the Polo Grounders and Orlando Cepeda of the West Coast variety, edging Hoyt Wilhelm and Willie McCovey, respectively.

Thomson, a sturdy Scot better known for his pennant-clinching homer in 1951, enjoyed an awesome rookie season in 1947, yet was overshadowed by Jackie Robinson's breaking of the color line across the river in Brooklyn. Thomson had 26 doubles, 29 homers, 105 runs, 85 RBI, a .283 average and a .508 slugging percentage.

Four years later, Willie Mays gained considerable attention for his 20 homers and 68 RBI in 121 games as the Giants won a pennant in miraculous fashion.

A handful of New York pitchers were even more dazzling in their debuts. Christy Mathewson was 20-17 with a 2.41 ERA in 1901; Jeff Tesreau was 16-7 with a 1.96 ERA in 1912; Cliff Melton went 20-9 with a 2.61 ERA and seven saves in 1937; Larry Jansen broke in with a 21-5 record in 1947, and the knuckleballing Wilhelm was 15-3 with 11 saves and a league-leading 71 games in 1952.

Of the moderns, Cepeda had the most memorable debut season, in 1958. The Baby Bull had a league-leading 38 doubles, 25 homers, 96 RBI and a .312 average. One year later, McCovey started his Hall-of-Fame career with four hits off Robin Roberts and finished with a .354 average and 13 homers in 52 games.

ALL-TIME GIANT SEASON RECORDS

BATTING: Bill Terry, .401, 1930
HRs: Willie Mays, 52, 1965
RBIs: Mel Ott, 151, 1929
STEALS: George Burns, 62, 1914
WINS: Christy Mathewson, 37, 1908
STRIKEOUTS: Christy Mathewson, 267, 1903

ALL-TIME MAJOR LEAGUE RECORDS

National	American
Batting (Season)	
Average	
.438 Hugh Duffy, Boston, 1894	.422 Napoleon Lajoie, Phila., 1901
.424 Rogers Hornsby, St. Louis, 1924	
At Bat	
701 Juan Samuel, Phila., 1984	705 Willie Wilson, Kansas City, 1980
Runs	
196 William Hamilton, Phila., 1894	177 Babe Ruth, New York, 1921
158 Chuck Klein, Phila., 1930	
Hits	
254 Frank J. O'Doul, Phila., 1929	257 George Sisler, St. Louis, 1920
254 Bill Terry, New York, 1930	
Doubles	
64 Joseph M. Medwick, St. L., 1936	67 Earl W. Webb, Boston, 1931
Triples	
36 J. Owen Wilson, Pitts., 1912	26 Joseph Jackson, Cleve., 1912
	26 Samuel Crawford, Detroit, 1914
Home Runs	
56 Hack Wilson, Chicago, 1930	61 Roger Maris, New York, 1961 (162-game schedule)
	60 Babe Ruth, New York, 1927
Runs Batted In	
190 Hack Wilson, Chicago, 1930	184 Lou Gehrig, New York, 1931
Stolen Bases	
118 Lou Brock, St. Louis, 1974	130 Rickey Henderson, Oakland, 1982
Bases on Balls	
148 Eddie Stanky, Brooklyn, 1945	170 Babe Ruth, New York, 1923
148 Jim Wynn, Houston, 1969	
Strikeouts	
189 Bobby Bonds, S.F., 1970	175 Dave Nicholson, Chicago, 1963
	175 Gorman Thomas, Milwaukee, 1979
Pitching (Season)	
Games	
106 Mike Marshall, L.A., 1974	88 Wilbur Wood, Chicago, 1968
Innings Pitched	
434 Joseph J. McGinnity, N.Y., 1903	464 Edward Walsh, Chicago, 1908
Victories	
37 Christy Mathewson, N.Y., 1908	41 Jack Chesbro, New York, 1904
Losses	
29 Victor Willis, Boston, 1905	26 John Townsend, Wash., 1904
	26 Robert Groom, Wash., 1909
Strikeouts	
(Lefthander)	
382 Sandy Koufax, Los Angeles, 1965	343 Rube Waddell, Phila., 1904
(Righthander)	
313 J.R. Richard, Houston, 1979	383 Nolan Ryan, Cal., 1973
Bases on Balls	
185 Sam Jones, Chicago, 1955	208 Bob Feller, Cleveland, 1938
Earned-Run Average (Minimum 200 Innings)	
1.12 Bob Gibson, St. L., 1968	1.01 Hubert Leonard, Boston, 1914
Shutouts	
16 Grover C. Alexander, Phila., 1916	13 John W. Coombs, Phila., 1910

INSIDE THE AMERICAN LEAGUE

By TOM PEDULLA
Gannett Newspapers

PREDICTED ORDER OF FINISH

East	West
Toronto Blue Jays	Texas Rangers
New York Yankees	Kansas City Royals
Cleveland Indians	California Angels
Boston Red Sox	Oakland A's
Detroit Tigers	Minnesota Twins
Milwaukee Brewers	Chicago White Sox
Baltimore Orioles	Seattle Mariners

Playoff winner: Texas

EAST DIVISION

	Team	Owner	1986	Morning Line Manager
1	**BLUE JAYS** Blue & white Return to '85 form	R. Howard Webster	W 86 L 76	5-2 Jimy Williams
2	**YANKEES** Navy blue pinstripes Owner misses Derby again	George Steinbrenner	W 90 L 72	3-1 Lou Piniella
3	**INDIANS** Red, white & blue Surprise contender	Richard & David Jacobs	W 84 L 78	9-2 Pat Corrales
4	**RED SOX** Red, white & blue Used up last race	Jean Yawkey	W 95 L 66	5-1 John McNamara
5	**TIGERS** Navy, orange & white Old mare ain't what she used to be	Tom Monaghan	W 87 L 75	10-1 Sparky Anderson
6	**BREWERS** Blue, gold & white New jockey needs time	Bud Selig	W 77 L 84	25-1 Tom Trebelhorn
7	**ORIOLES** Black & orange Overmatched in this field	Edward Bennett Williams	W 73 L 89	50-1 Cal Ripken Sr.

BLUE JAYS rallied after breaking slowly last time out and regain top spot this time. **YANKEES** drop back after they hook the leader. Long-shot **INDIANS** continue to improve. Defending champ **RED SOX** falter. **TIGERS** no threat here, while **BREWERS** need a few races over the track. Orioles make early run, but soon fall to back of pack.

CANADIAN STAKES

87th Running. American League Race. Distance: 162 games plus playoff. Payoff (based on '86): $86,254 per winning player, World Series: $74,985 per losing player, World Series. A field of 14 entered in two divisions.

Track Record: 111 wins—Cleveland, 1954

WEST DIVISION	Owner		Morning Line Manager
1 **RANGERS** Ready for the roses	Eddie Chiles Red, white & blue	1986 W 87 L 75	5-2 Bobby Valentine
2 **ROYALS** Remember '85	Ewing Kauffman Royal blue & white	1986 W 76 L 86	3-1 Dick Howser
3 **ANGELS** Cowboy Autry needs horse	Gene Autry Red, white & navy	1986 W 92 L 70	7-2 Gene Mauch
4 **A's** Jockey on new mount	Roy Eisenhardt Forest green, gold & white	1986 W 76 L 86	6-1 Tony LaRussa
5 **TWINS** Long shot at best	Carl Pohlad Scarlet, white & blue	1986 W 71 L 91	15-1 Tom Kelly
6 **WHITE SOX** No sign of improvement	E. Einhorn/J. Reinsdorf Navy, white & scarlet	1986 W 72 L 90	20-1 Jim Fregosi
7 **MARINERS** Can see them all	George Argyros Blue, gold & white	1986 W 67 L 95	40-1 Dick Williams

RANGERS still a bit green, but have talent to top field. **ROYALS** make a run for it, with defending champ **ANGELS** pressing the top two. **A's** best of rest. **TWINS** ready to improve. **WHITE SOX** and **MARINERS** no factors in this event.

BALTIMORE ORIOLES

TEAM DIRECTORY: Chairman: Edward Bennett Williams; Exec. VP-GM: Hank Peters; VP: Jack Dunn III; VP: Joseph P. Hamper, Jr.; VP: Robert Aylward; Spec. Asst. to Pres.: R. Douglas Melvin; Dir. Scouting-Play. Dev.: Tom Giordano; Dir. Pub. Rel.: Bob Brown; Trav. Sec.: Philip Itzoe; Mgr.: Cal Ripken Sr. Home: Memorial Stadium (53,208). Field distances: 309, l.f. line; 385, l.c.; 405, c.f.; 385, r.c.; 309, r.f. line. Spring training: Miami, Fla.

SCOUTING REPORT

HITTING: The Orioles took a dip in almost every department in 1986 and offense was no exception. After leading the league in homers and slugging percentage in 1985, Baltimore ranked sixth in homers (169), 10th in slugging percentage (.395), eighth in batting average (.258) and 11th in runs (708).

Having Eddie Murray (.305, 17 homers, 84 RBI) and Cal Ripken Jr. (.282, 25, 81) in the middle of the order should make the Orioles' attack more formidable than that, but Murray must put his feud with club owner Edward Bennett Williams behind him and boost his power numbers to their usual levels.

Fred Lynn (.287, 23, 67), Lee Lacy (.287, 11, 47) and Larry Sheets (.272, 18, 60) are three more potentially solid run producers, though Lynn's problem continues to be staying healthy.

The Orioles hope the acquisition of Terry Kennedy from the Padres for pitcher Storm Davis will give them increased production from the catcher's spot, especially if a change of scenery helps Kennedy improve on his .264 batting average, 12 homers and 57 RBI of last season.

PITCHING: The days in which the Orioles dominated in this category are long gone. This is a poor staff that may well deteriorate further.

Mike Boddicker (14-12, 4.70) has endured dreadful slides after fast starts each of the last two seasons and injury-prone Mike Flanagan (7-11, 4.24) posted his first losing record in a full major-league season. Scott McGregor (11-15, 4.52) and Ken Dixon (11-13, 4.58) have gopher-ball problems, yielding 35 and 33 home runs respectively last season. One bright spot is left-hander Eric Bell, who pitched impressively after his promotion late last season.

The bullpen is anchored by hard-throwing right-hander Don

Cal Ripken Sr. will manage Cal Jr. and rest of Birds.

Aase (6-7, 2.98), who might be hard-pressed to perform an encore to a 1986 season in which he set a club record with 34 saves.

Baltimore must find a way to revitalize a staff that ranked 10th in the AL in ERA (4.30) and yielded the third-highest total of homers (177).

FIELDING: The Orioles used to be renown as one of the most fundamentally sound teams in the majors. Not any more. Last season, the O's ranked 10th in the league in fielding percentage at .978.

Murray may have slipped a little at first base, but he is still solid. Kennedy has a reputation for being a liability behind the plate. There are still holes at second base, where the erratic Alan Wiggins wound up as a well-paid minor leaguer, and third base, where hefty Floyd Rayford proved inadequate. Jackie Gutierrez might get a shot at third and Billy Ripken, Cal Jr.'s brother, might win a job at second.

OUTLOOK: New manager Cal Ripken Sr., the former third-base coach, has waited 30 years for this opportunity. Soon, he may wish it never came. The Orioles' pitching staff drove Earl Weaver into retirement for a second time and it desperately needs an overhaul on the heels of the club's first losing season (73-89) since 1967 and its only last-place finish. Another miserable season seems imminent.

BALTIMORE ORIOLES 1987 ROSTER

MANAGER Cal Ripken, Sr.
Coaches—Terry Crowley, Elrod Hendricks, Frank Robinson, Mark Wiley, Jimmy Williams

PITCHERS

No.	Name	1986 Club	W-L	IP	SO	ERA	B-T	Ht.	Wt.	Born
41	Aase, Don	Baltimore	6-7	82	67	2.98	R-R	6-3	220	9/8/54 Orange, CA
57	Arnold, Tony	Rochester	4-3	88	49	1.95	R-R	6-0	185	5/3/59 El Paso, TX
		Baltimore	0-2	25	7	3.55				
45	Bell, Eric	Charlotte	9-6	130	104	3.05	L-L	6-0	165	10/27/63 Modesto, CA
		Rochester	7-3	77	59	3.05				
		Baltimore	1-2	23	18	5.01				
52	Boddicker, Mike	Baltimore	14-12	218	175	4.70	R-R	5-11	182	8/23/57 Cedar Rapids, IA
42	Bordi, Rich	Baltimore	6-4	107	83	4.46	R-R	6-7	220	4/18/59 San Francisco, CA
39	Dixon, Ken	Baltimore	11-13	202	170	4.58	B-R	5-11	192	10/17/60 Monroe, VA
46	Flanagan, Mike	Baltimore	7-11	172	96	4.24	L-L	6-0	194	12/16/51 Manchester, NH
54	Habyan, John	Rochester	12-7	157	93	4.29	R-R	6-2	195	1/29/64 Bayshore, NY
		Baltimore	1-3	26	14	4.44				
47	Havens, Brad	Baltimore	3-3	71	57	4.56	L-L	6-1	196	11/17/59 Highland Park, MI
13	Jones, Odell	Rochester	7-3	84	69	3.66	R-R	6-3	185	1/13/53 Tulare, CA
		Baltimore	2-2	49	32	3.83				
48	Kinnunen, Mike	Rochester	1-3	54	43	2.35	L-L	6-1	205	4/1/58 Seattle, WA
		Baltimore	0-0	7	1	6.43				
23	Martinez, Tippy	Baltimore	0-2	16	11	5.63	L-L	5-10	179	5/31/50 LaJunta, CO
		Rochester	0-1	6	4	6.00				
16	McGregor, Scott	Baltimore	11-15	203	95	4.52	B-L	6-1	190	1/18/54 Inglewood, CA
—	Skinner, Mike	Rochester	10-8	161	96	4.18	R-R	6-1	193	8/5/64 Teaneck, NJ
—	Telanantez, Greg	Hagerstown	12-6	149	124	4.36	R-R	6-2	190	10/17/65 Idaho Falls, ID
—	Williamson, Mark	Las Vegas	10-3	104	81	3.36	R-R	6-0	155	7/21/59 Lemon Grove, CA

CATCHERS

No.	Name	1986 Club	H	HR	RBI	Pct.	B-T	Ht.	Wt.	Born
15	Kennedy, Terry	San Diego	114	12	57	.264	L-R	6-4	224	6/4/56 Euclid, OH
26	Nichols, Carl	Charlotte	118	14	72	.269	R-R	6-0	184	10/14/62 Los Angeles, CA
		Baltimore	0	0	0	.000				
6	Rayford, Floyd	Baltimore	37	8	19	.174	R-R	5-10	220	7/27/57 Memphis, TN
		Rochester	16	2	7	.258				

INFIELDERS

No.	Name	1986 Club	H	HR	RBI	Pct.	B-T	Ht.	Wt.	Born
7	Burleson, Rick	California	77	5	29	.284	R-R	5-10	160	4/29/51 Lynwood,Ca
—	Gonzalez, Rene	Indianapolis	108	3	43	273	R-R	6-2	180	9/3/61 Austin, TX
		Montreal	3	0	0	.115				
11	Gutierrez, Jackie	Baltimore	27	0	4	.186	R-R	6-1	175	6/27/60 Columbia
		Rochester	60	1	22	.303				
—	Hudler, Rex	Baltimore	0	0	0	.000	R-R	6-2		9/2/60 Tempe, AZ
		Rochester	57	2	13	.260				
30	Jones, Ricky	Rochester	111	9	56	.251	R-R	6-3	186	6/4/59 Tupelo, MS
		Baltimore	6	0	4	.182				
33	Murray, Eddie	Baltimore	151	17	84	.305	B-R	6-2	215	2/24/56 Los Angeles, CA
—	Ripken, Bill	Charlotte	142	5	62	.268	R-R	6-1	178	12/16/64 Havre de Grace, MD
8	Ripken, Cal	Baltimore	177	25	81	.282	R-R	6-4	218	8/24/60 Havre de Grace, MD
—	Smith, D. L.	Charlotte	72	5	34	.242	R-R	6-2	185	10/20/62 Lynwood, CA
28	Traber, Jim	Rochester	90	12	55	.279	L-L	6-0	215	12/26/61 Columbus, OH
		Baltimore	54	13	44	.255				
2	Wiggins, Alan	Baltimore	60	0	11	.251	B-R	6-2	164	2/17/58 Los Angeles, CA
		Rochester	9	0	3	.205				

OUTFIELDERS

No.	Name	1986 Club	H	HR	RBI	Pct.	B-T	Ht.	Wt.	Born
12	Beniquez, Juan	Baltimore	103	6	36	.300	R-R	5-11	175	5/13/50 Puerto Rico
—	Dodd, Tom	Charlotte	129	28	100	.323	R-R	6-0	190	8/15/58 Portland, OR
		Baltimore	3	1	2	.231				
		Rochester	8	2	6	.163				
9	Dwyer, Jim	Baltimore	39	8	31	.244	L-L	5-10	182	1/3/50 Evergreen Park, IL
38	Gerhart, Ken	Rochester	124	28	72	.274	R-R	6-0	185	5/19/61 Charleston, SC
		Baltimore	16	1	7	.232				
27	Lacy, Lee	Baltimore	141	11	47	.287	R-R	6-1	195	4/10/49 Longview, TX
19	Lynn, Fred	Baltimore	114	23	67	.287	L-L	6-1	195	2/3/52 Chicago, IL
—	Padget, Chris	Charlotte	152	22	96	.324	L-R	6-1	190	9/20/62 Rochester, NY
18	Sheets, Larry	Baltimore	92	18	60	.272	L-R	6-3	225	12/6/59 Staunton, VA
37	Shelby, John	Baltimore	92	11	49	.228	B-R	6-1	178	2/23/58 Lexington, KY
43	Young, Mike	Baltimore	93	9	42	.252	B-R	6-2	198	3/20/60 Oakland, CA

ORIOLE PROFILES

EDDIE MURRAY 31 6-2 215  **Bats S Throws R**

Tumultuous season for the usually soft-spoken first baseman . . . Stung by criticism from owner Edward Bennett Williams that he had a bad year and should consider more offseason conditioning, he responded with trade request . . . Suffered career lows in runs, hits, home runs and RBI for a full season . . . Had one home run in last 32 games at Memorial Stadium . . . Placed fourth in AL with .396 on-base percentage . . . Led club in average (.305) and RBI (84) . . . Had glittering .363 mark with runners in scoring position (45-for-124) . . . Became first player to reach 1,000 RBI in first 10 seasons since Frank Robinson got 1,000th for Cincinnati in 1965 . . . Batted .400 over last 13 games . . . Missed 25 games due to pulled left hamstring . . . Selected for All-Star Game for seventh time . . . Born Feb. 24, 1956, in Los Angeles . . . Selected by Orioles in third round of June 1973 draft . . . Earned three straight Gold Gloves from 1982-84 . . . A natural righty, he turned to switch-hitting in 1975, while in minors . . . First official captain in modern Orioles' history . . . Appeared to have slowed down in the field . . . Might be time for change of scenery.

Year	Club	Pos.	G	AB	R	H	2B	3B	HR	RBI	SB	Avg.
1977	Baltimore.	OF-1B	160	611	81	173	29	2	27	88	0	.283
1978	Baltimore.	1B-3B	161	610	85	174	32	3	27	95	6	.285
1979	Baltimore.	1B	159	606	90	179	30	2	25	99	10	.295
1980	Baltimore.	1B	158	621	100	186	36	2	32	116	7	.300
1981	Baltimore.	1B	99	378	57	111	21	2	22	78	2	.294
1982	Baltimore.	1B	151	550	87	174	30	1	32	110	7	.316
1983	Baltimore.	1B	156	582	115	178	30	3	33	111	5	.306
1984	Baltimore.	1B	162	588	97	180	26	3	29	110	10	.306
1985	Baltimore.	1B	156	583	111	173	37	1	31	124	5	.297
1986	Baltimore.	1B	137	495	61	151	25	1	17	84	3	.305
	Totals		1499	5624	884	1679	296	20	275	1015	55	.299

CAL RIPKEN Jr. 26 6-4 218 **Bats R Throws R**

Can't budge him from the lineup . . . Lanky shortstop has played 765 consecutive games, beginning May 28, 1982, and 6,947 consecutive innings, starting June 5, 1982 . . . Might be more productive with occasional rest . . . Will new manager Cal Ripken Sr. insist he take a day off? . . . Covers a lot of ground, but that's deceptive because he plays very deep . . . Led club with 25 home runs, a level he's reached in all five major-league seasons . . . Tied for AL lead with 16 game-winning RBI . . . Topped all AL shortstops in home runs and RBI for fourth consecutive year . . . Headed all AL vote-getters for All-Star Game with 1,486,806 . . . Paced all AL shortstops with 482 assists . . . Born Aug. 24, 1960, in Havre de Grace, Md. . . . Selected by Orioles in second round of June 1978 draft . . . Brother, Billy, is second baseman in Orioles' organization.

Year	Club	Pos.	G	AB	R	H	2B	3B	HR	RBI	SB	Avg.
1981	Baltimore.	SS-3B	23	39	1	5	0	0	0	0	0	.128
1982	Baltimore.	SS-3B	160	598	90	158	32	5	28	93	3	.264
1983	Baltimore.	SS	162	663	121	211	47	2	27	102	0	.318
1984	Baltimore.	SS	162	641	103	195	37	7	27	86	2	.304
1985	Baltimore.	SS	161	642	116	181	32	5	26	110	2	.282
1986	Baltimore.	SS	162	627	98	177	35	1	25	81	4	.282
	Totals		830	3210	529	927	183	20	133	472	11	.289

FRED LYNN 35 6-1 195 **Bats L Throws L**

Tremendously talented player who frequently leaves the lineup with injuries . . . Last year no exception . . . Major problems were sprained right ankle and tendinitis in right shoulder . . . Caused him to miss 49 games and Orioles were 15-34 without their regular center fielder . . . Hit 23 homers for third straight year . . . Has surpassed 20 home runs for five consecutive seasons . . . Born Feb. 3, 1952, in Chicago . . . Played out option with California and signed five-year contract as free agent on Dec. 11, 1984 . . . Originally selected by Boston in second round of June 1973 draft . . . Avid fresh-water fisherman . . . Had bass pond built at his home so he could study living habits of fish . . . Best season by far was 1979, when he batted league-leading .333 for Boston with 39 homers, 122 RBI . . . Orioles have to be wondering about wisdom of this free-agent investment.

Year	Club	Pos.	G	AB	R	H	2B	3B	HR	RBI	SB	Avg.
1974	Boston	OF	15	43	5	18	2	2	2	10	0	.419
1975	Boston	OF	145	528	103	175	47	7	21	105	10	.331
1976	Boston	OF	132	507	76	159	32	8	10	65	14	.314
1977	Boston	OF	129	497	81	129	29	5	18	76	2	.260
1978	Boston	OF	150	541	75	161	33	3	22	82	3	.298
1979	Boston	OF	147	531	116	177	42	1	39	122	2	.333
1980	Boston	OF	110	415	67	125	32	3	12	61	12	.301
1981	California.	OF	76	256	28	56	8	1	5	31	1	.219
1982	California.	OF	138	472	89	141	38	1	21	86	7	.299
1983	California.	OF	117	437	56	119	20	3	22	74	2	.272
1984	California.	OF	142	517	84	140	28	4	23	79	2	.271
1985	Baltimore.	OF	124	448	59	118	12	1	23	68	7	.263
1986	Baltimore.	OF	112	397	67	114	13	1	23	67	2	.287
	Totals		1537	5589	906	1632	336	40	241	926	64	.292

LEE LACY 37 6-1 195 **Bats R Throws R**

Hard-hitting outfielder beginning to show his age . . . Missed 25 of the last 31 games due to strained muscles in rib cage area . . . Hit only .268 before All-Star break . . . Rebounded to bat .400 in first 27 games after the break . . . Hit leadoff occasionally, contributing to career-high 77 runs . . . Smacked three home runs against the Yankees on June 8 . . . Born April 10, 1949, in Longview, Tex. . . . Signed by Baltimore to four-year, free-agent contract in December 1984 after finishing second in NL batting race with .321 average for Pittsburgh . . . Originally selected by Los Angeles in second round of February 1969 draft as an infielder . . . Didn't begin playing outfield until 1975.

Year	Club	Pos.	G	AB	R	H	2B	3B	HR	RBI	SB	Avg.
1972	Los Angeles	2B	60	243	34	63	7	3	0	12	5	.259
1973	Los Angeles	2B	57	135	14	28	2	0	0	8	2	.207
1974	Los Angeles	2B-3B	48	78	13	22	6	0	0	8	2	.282
1975	Los Angeles	SS-2B-OF	101	306	44	96	11	5	7	40	5	.314
1976	Atl.-L.A.	2B-OF-3B	103	338	42	91	11	3	3	34	3	.269
1977	Los Angeles	OF-2B-3B	75	169	28	45	7	0	6	21	4	.266
1978	Los Angeles	OF-2B-3B	103	245	29	64	16	4	13	40	7	.261
1979	Pittsburgh	OF-2B	84	182	17	45	9	3	5	15	6	.247
1980	Pittsburgh	OF-3B	109	278	45	93	20	4	7	33	18	.335
1981	Pittsburgh	OF-3B	78	213	31	57	11	4	2	10	24	.268
1982	Pittsburgh	OF-3B	121	359	66	112	16	3	5	31	40	.312
1983	Pittsburgh	OF	108	288	40	87	12	3	4	13	31	.302
1984	Pittsburgh	OF-2B	138	474	66	152	26	3	12	70	21	.321
1985	Baltimore	OF	121	492	69	144	22	4	9	48	10	.293
1986	Baltimore	OF	130	491	77	141	18	0	11	47	4	.287
	Totals		1436	4291	615	1240	194	39	84	430	182	.289

TERRY KENNEDY 30 6-4 224 **Bats L Throws R**

Disenchantment with former manager Dick Williams led to his distress in the past, but what was the excuse last year? . . . Maybe a change of venue will help . . . Padres got tired of waiting for "Teke" to fullfill superstar potential and dealt him and Mark Williamson to Orioles for Storm Davis on Oct. 30 . . . The guy has some left-handed pop and he's improved his catching skills, yet something is missing . . . Born June 4, 1956, in Euclid, Ohio . . . Son of former major leaguer Bob Kennedy . . . Attended Florida State, where he was collegiate Player of the Year with 32 homers and .348 average . . . Cardinals' first-round draft choice in 1977, he was traded to Padres in 1980 mega-deal for Rollie Fingers.

Year	Club	Pos.	G	AB	R	H	2B	3B	HR	RBI	SB	Avg.
1978	St. Louis	C	10	29	0	5	0	0	0	2	0	.172
1979	St. Louis	C	33	109	11	31	7	0	2	17	0	.284
1980	St. Louis	C-OF	84	248	28	63	12	3	4	34	0	.254
1981	San Diego	C	101	382	32	115	24	1	2	41	0	.301
1982	San Diego	C-1B	153	562	75	166	42	1	21	97	1	.295
1983	San Diego	C-1B	149	549	47	156	27	2	17	98	1	.284
1984	San Diego	C	148	530	54	127	16	1	14	57	1	.240
1985	San Diego	C-1B	143	532	54	139	27	1	10	74	0	261
1986	San Diego	C-1B	141	432	46	114	22	1	12	57	0	.264
	Totals		962	3373	347	916	177	10	82	477	3	.272

MIKE BODDICKER 29 5-11 182 — Bats R Throws R

Spent winter of discontent after disastrous finish . . . Ended with seven-game losing streak . . . Did not win after Aug. 4 . . . Did not win at Memorial Stadium after July 25 . . . Placed on 15-day disabled list after tearing ligament in middle finger of right hand on April 19 . . . Word is he was unable to effectively throw his slider by end of season due to soreness in that finger . . . Jumped out to 10-1 record with 3.48 ERA after first 12 starts . . . Rode six-game winning streak from May 25 to June 20 . . . Went 4-8 in final 18 starts . . . Gave up 32 first-inning runs . . . Born in Cedar Rapids, Iowa, on Aug. 23, 1957 . . . Chosen by Baltimore in sixth round of June 1978 draft . . . Spends most of offseason in Norway, Iowa (pop. 633) . . . Has worked at grain elevator operation in Norway in recent winters . . . Named AL Rookie of the Year by *The Sporting News* in 1983 . . . In 1984, he was first Oriole to win ERA crown and lead league in victories.

Year	Club	G	IP	W	L	Pct.	SO	BB	H	ERA
1980	Baltimore	1	7	0	1	.000	4	5	6	6.43
1981	Baltimore	2	6	0	0	.000	2	2	6	4.50
1982	Baltimore	7	25⅔	1	0	1.000	20	12	25	3.51
1983	Baltimore	27	179	16	8	.667	120	52	141	2.77
1984	Baltimore	34	261⅓	20	11	.645	128	81	218	2.79
1985	Baltimore	32	203⅓	12	17	.414	135	89	227	4.07
1986	Baltimore	33	218⅓	14	12	.538	175	74	214	4.70
	Totals	136	900⅔	63	49	.563	584	315	837	3.60

DON AASE 32 6-3 220 — Bats R Throws R

Bullpen ace had career year that will be hard to duplicate . . . Set club record with 34 saves . . . Total represented most saves in history for a last-place team . . . Converted 34 of 43 save opportunities . . . Selected as Most Valuable Oriole . . . Saved AL victory in first All-Star Game appearance, getting game-ending double play . . . Hard thrower who was very strong at start of season, allowing one earned run in 19 appearances... Weakened as summer wore on... Went without a save from Aug. 23 to Sept. 17... Born in Orange, Cal., on Sept. 8, 1954... Played out option with California and signed four-year contract as free agent with Baltimore on Dec. 13, 1984... Missed most of two seasons with elbow injury suffered in 1982... Surgery, in which tendon from left wrist was transplanted to right elbow, saved career... Began career as mediocre starting pitcher, compiling 30-32 record... Became full-time reliever in late 1980.

Year	Club	G	IP	W	L	Pct.	SO	BB	H	ERA
1977	Boston	13	92	6	2	.750	49	19	85	3.13
1978	California	29	179	11	8	.579	93	80	185	4.02
1979	California	37	185	9	10	.474	96	77	200	4.82
1980	California	40	175	8	13	.381	74	66	193	4.06
1981	California	39	65	4	4	.500	38	24	56	2.35
1982	California	24	52	3	3	.500	40	23	45	3.46
1983	California					Disabled List				
1984	California	23	39	4	1	.800	28	19	30	1.62
1985	Baltimore	54	88	10	6	.625	67	35	83	3.78
1986	Baltimore	66	81⅔	6	7	.462	67	28	71	2.98
	Totals	325	956⅔	61	54	.530	552	371	948	3.74

MIKE FLANAGAN 36 6-0 194 Bats L Throws L

Endured his first losing record in a full major-league season, going 7-11... Probably has enjoyed last winning season... Did not win after Aug. 23... Posted one win in first 13 starts and was 1-5 through June 26... With 136 victories, he ranks fourth on club's all-time win list... Disabled from May 31 through June 18 with tendinitis in left elbow... Was fourth trip to DL in last six years... Born Dec. 16, 1951, in Manchester, N.H.... Tabbed by Orioles in seventh round of June 1973 draft ... Father, Edward, pitched in Red Sox system... Left-hander possesses one of league's best pickoff moves... Landslide Cy Young Award winner in 1979 after going 23-9... Placed sixth that year in MVP balloting... Poor results in 1986 not all his doing as Birds scored three runs or less in 14 of his 28 starts.

Year	Club	G	IP	W	L	Pct.	SO	BB	H	ERA
1975	Baltimore	2	10	0	1	.000	7	6	9	2.70
1976	Baltimore	20	85	3	5	.375	56	33	83	4.13
1977	Baltimore	36	235	15	10	.600	149	70	235	3.64
1978	Baltimore	40	281	19	15	.559	167	87	271	4.04
1979	Baltimore	39	266	23	9	.781	190	70	245	3.08
1980	Baltimore	37	251	16	13	.552	128	71	278	4.12
1981	Baltimore	20	116	9	6	.600	72	37	108	4.19
1982	Baltimore	36	236	15	11	.577	103	76	233	3.97
1983	Baltimore	20	125⅓	12	4	.750	50	31	135	3.30
1984	Baltimore	34	226⅔	13	13	.500	115	81	213	3.53
1985	Batimore	15	86	4	5	.444	42	28	101	5.13
1986	Baltimore	29	172	7	11	.389	96	66	179	4.24
	Totals	328	2090	136	103	.569	1175	656	2090	3.84

KEN DIXON 26 5-11 192 Bats S Throws R

Another Baltimore pitcher who failed late in season . . . Won one of last 10 starts, defeating Milwaukee on Sept. 19 . . . Gave up 33 home runs . . . In one sorry stretch, from April 27 through June 4, he surrendered 17 home runs in 48⅓ innings . . . Hasn't learned to mix speeds . . . Throws everything hard and doesn't have blazing speed to get away with it . . . Fanned career-high 13 batters against Chicago White Sox on July 11 . . . Failed to complete five innings in nine of 33 starts . . . Born Oct. 17, 1960, in Monroe, Va., and still lives there . . . Selected by Baltimore in third round of June 1980 draft . . . Rejected football scholarship to Virginia Tech.

Year	Club	G	IP	W	L	Pct.	SO	BB	H	ERA
1984	Baltimore	2	13	0	1	.000	8	4	14	4.15
1985	Baltimore	34	162	8	4	.667	108	64	144	3.67
1986	Baltimore	35	202⅓	11	13	.458	170	83	194	4.58
	Totals	71	377⅓	19	18	.514	286	151	352	4.17

SCOTT McGREGOR 33 6-1 190 Bats S Throws L

Results made it obvious his best years are behind him . . . Tied club record by surrendering 35 home runs . . . Robin Roberts allowed 35 in 1963 . . . Knocked out nine times before fifth inning, 17 times in last two years . . . Suffered first losing year since 1977 rookie campaign . . . Not entirely his fault as Orioles scored 30 runs in his 15 defeats . . . Had one win in 10 starts from June 10 through July 23, going 1-6 . . . Born Jan. 18, 1954, in Inglewood, Cal. . . . Obtained June 15, 1976, in 10-player blockbuster trade with Yankees . . . Is 7-14 lifetime vs. former team, losing nine of last 10 decisions.

Year	Club	G	IP	W	L	Pct.	SO	BB	H	ERA
1976	Baltimore	3	15	0	1	.000	6	5	17	3.60
1977	Baltimore	29	114	3	5	.375	55	30	119	4.42
1978	Baltimore	35	233	15	13	.536	94	47	217	3.32
1979	Baltimore	27	175	13	6	.684	81	23	165	3.34
1980	Baltimore	36	252	20	8	.714	119	58	254	3.32
1981	Baltimore	24	160	13	5	.722	82	40	167	3.26
1982	Baltimore	37	226⅓	14	12	.538	84	52	238	4.61
1983	Baltimore	36	260	18	7	.720	86	45	271	3.18
1984	Baltimore	30	196⅓	15	12	.556	67	54	216	3.94
1985	Baltimore	35	204	14	14	.500	86	65	226	4.81
1986	Baltimore	34	203	11	15	.423	95	57	216	4.52
	Totals	326	2038⅔	136	98	.581	855	476	2106	3.84

TOP PROSPECT

KEN GERHART 25 6-0 185 **Bats R Throws R**
One of the few bright prospects in Orioles' organization . . . Major-league debut nothing to remember . . . Fanned in all four at-bats against Detroit on Sept. 14 . . . Rebounded to start seven-game hitting streak . . . Outfielder tried as leadoff man by Orioles . . . Finished with .232 average in 20 games . . . Led International League in home runs (28) and total bases (232) . . . Was fifth in league with 72 RBI . . . Born May 19, 1961, in Charleston, S.C. . . . Baltimore's fifth-round draft choice in June 1982.

MANAGER CAL RIPKEN Sr.: Third-base coach was named to replace Earl Weaver as manager on Oct. 6, after Weaver retired a second time . . . Only the eighth Oriole manager in 32 years . . . Managed in O's farm system from 1961-74, longest tenure of any minor-league skipper in club's history . . . Has spent 30 years in Oriole organization . . . Has managed at every level except rookie league and has endured only one losing season . . . Father of shortstop Cal Ripken Jr., making him third father to manage son in major-league history . . . Others were Connie Mack and son Earle with Philadelphia A's in 1910, 1911 and 1914 and Yogi Berra and son Dale with the Yankees in 1985 . . . Another of Ripken's sons, Billy, played second base for Orioles' affiliate in Charlotte (AA) . . . Ripken Sr. never played in the majors . . . Was a catcher during eight-year minor-league career and occasionally pitched or played outfield or third base . . . Was twice passed over for Oriole managerial job, when Weaver retired for the first time at the end of the 1982 season and again when Joe Altobelli was fired during the 1985 campaign and Weaver returned . . . Born Dec. 17, 1935, in Aberdeen, Md., and still lives there.

GREATEST ALL-TIME ROOKIE

The Yankees know too well what kind of a rookie year Eddie Murray had in 1977. It's indelibly noted in their scorebook and in the memories of the pitchers who faced him.

That was the year Murray established himself as a Yankee tormentor by driving in the winning run in five of the Orioles' eight victories over the Yankees and amassing four home runs and 15 RBI in 15 games against them. Murray didn't fare badly against the rest of the league, either.

The Los Angeles native was selected as the fourth Rookie of the Year in Orioles' history. He slammed 27 home runs, tying Lee May for the club lead and establishing an Oriole rookie record. Murray led the club in games (160), at-bats (611) and extra-base hits (58). He placed second in runs (81), hits (173) and doubles (29). He was third on the club with 88 RBI despite what has been a career-high 104 strikeouts.

Murray played primarily as a designated hitter as a rookie. He would soon displace May at first base and emerge as a Gold Glove performer there.

ALL-TIME ORIOLE SEASON RECORDS

BATTING: Ken Singleton, .328, 1977
HRs: Frank Robinson, 49, 1966
RBIs: Jim Gentile, 141, 1961
STEALS: Luis Aparicio, 57, 1964
WINS: Steve Stone, 25, 1980
STRIKEOUTS: Dave McNally, 202, 1968

BOSTON RED SOX

TEAM DIRECTORY: Pres.: Jean R. Yawkey; Chief Exec. Off.-Chief Oper. Off.: Haywood Sullivan; Gen. Partner: Edward (Buddy) LeRoux; VP-GM: Lou Gorman; VP-Dir. Play. Dev.: Edward Kenney; Dir. Scouting: Eddie Kasko; Dir. Pub. Rel.: Dick Bresciani; Trav. Sec.: Jack Rogers; Mgr.: John McNamara. Home: Fenway Park (33,583). Field distances: 315, l.f. line; 379, l.c.; 390, c.f.; 420, r.c. corner; 380, r.c.; 302, r.f. line. Spring training: Winter Haven, Fla.

SCOUTING REPORT

HITTING: The Red Sox feature baseball's best pure hitter in three-time AL batting champion Wade Boggs (.357, 8 homers, 71 RBI, 107 runs, .453 on-base percentage) and four outstanding RBI men in Jim Rice (.324, 20, 110), Bill Buckner (.267, 18, 102), Dwight Evans (.259, 26, 97) and Don Baylor (.238, 31, 94). Rice cut down on his swing and hit into fewer ground-ball double plays and Buckner has learned to pull the ball more frequently.

Marty Barrett (.286, 4, 60) emerged as a star in the postseason,

Bruce Hurst beat the Mets twice in World Series.

capturing MVP honors in the AL Championship Series, and he combined with Boggs to give the Red Sox a solid pair of table-setters. Boston needs a catcher to replace likely free-agent defector Rich Gedman (.258, 16, 65) and a big year from postseason standout Dave Henderson.

Boston, a team that has traditionally relied on the long ball, ranked only 11th in the league in homers (144) last season, third in batting average (.271), fifth in runs (794) and last in stolen bases (41), so there's certainly room for offensive improvement, particularly from the center-field position.

PITCHING: Cy Young Award winner Roger Clemens (24-4, 2.48), the first starting pitcher to win the AL MVP award in 15 years, never allowed the Red Sox to go into a prolonged tailspin, but can the right-hander dominate again in 1987?

Left-hander Bruce Hurst (13-8, 2.99) showed he is capable of being a big winner during a magnificent postseason and flammable Dennis "Oil Can" Boyd (16-10, 3.78) is successful when he contains his emotions. The rest of the rotation is uncertain with the departure of Tom Seaver and the post-injury decline of Al Nipper.

Right-hander Calvin Schiraldi (4-2, 1.41) became the bullpen stopper, registering nine saves following his promotion from Pawtucket at the start of August. But how will the youngster react to his disastrous postseason? Sinkerballer Bob Stanley (6-6, 4.37, 16 saves) and left-hander Joe Sambito (2-0, 4.84, 12 saves), who specializes in retiring lefty hitters, complement Schiraldi.

FIELDING: The Red Sox' defense is not typical of champions, although Evans is still exceptional in right and Boggs has turned himself into an above-average third baseman. Gedman will be missed behind the plate. First baseman Buckner, who allowed Mookie Wilson's grounder to slip through his legs for a decisive error in Game 6 of the World Series, and shortstop Spike Owen, who was tentative throughout the postseason, are nothing special.

OUTLOOK: Except for the World Series, everything went right for the Red Sox. They won their first division title since 1975 with a 95-66 record and returned from the brink to stun the Angels in the ALCS. It won't happen again.

There are several pitching questions, including whether Clemens will be able to escape the Cy Young jinx. John McNamara's Red Sox lack speed, usually advancing one painstaking base at a time, and are lacking defensively, so a return to the middle of the pack seems likely.

BOSTON RED SOX 1987 ROSTER

MANAGER John McNamara
Coaches—Bill Fischer, Walt Hriniak, Joe Morgan, Rac Slider

PITCHERS

No.	Name	1986 Club	W-L	IP	SO	ERA	B-T	Ht.	Wt.	Born
23	Boyd, Oil Can	Boston	16-10	214	129	3.78	R-R	6-1	144	10/6/59 Meridian, MS
21	Clemens, Roger	Boston	24-4	254	238	2.48	R-R	6-4	215	8/4/62 Dayton, OH
28	Crawford, Steve	Pawtucket	1-1	6	2	6.00	R-R	6-5	236	4/29/58 Pryor, OK
		Boston	0-2	57	32	3.92				
—	Curry, Steve	New Britain	11-9	177	94	2.79	R-R	6-6	195	9/13/65 Winter Park, FL
44	Gardner, Wes	Boston	0-0	1	1	9.00	R-R	6-4	195	4/29/61 Benton, AR
47	Hurst, Bruce	Boston	13-8	174	167	2.99	L-L	6-3	207	3/24/58 St. George, UT
—	Johnson, Mitch	Pawtucket	4-5	85	36	5.21	R-R	6-5	218	8/2/62 Columbia, PA
—	Leister, John	Pawtucket	8-7	135	78	4.08	R-R	6-2	200	1/3/61 San Antonio, TX
48	Lollar, Tim	Boston	2-0	43	28	6.91	L-L	6-3	204	3/17/56 Poplar Bluff, MO
—	Manzanillo, Josia	Winter Haven	13-5	143	102	2.27	R-R	6-1	190	10/16/67 Dom. Republic
49	Nipper, Al	Boston	10-12	159	79	5.38	R-R	6-0	194	4/2/59 San Diego, CA
—	Rochford, Mike	Pawtucket	11-10	171	70	3.53	L-L	6-4	205	3/14/63 Methuen, MA
43	Sambito, Joe	Boston	2-0	45	30	4.84	L-L	6-1	190	6/28/52 Brooklyn, NY
31	Schiraldi, Calvin	Pawtucket	4-3	44	59	2.86	R-R	6-4	200	6/16/62 Houston, TX
		Boston	4-2	51	55	1.41				
19	Sellers, Jeff	Pawtucket	7-4	106	74	3.74	R-R	6-0	181	5/11/64 Compton, CA
		Boston	3-7	82	51	4.94				
46	Stanley, Bob	Boston	6-6	82	54	4.37	R-R	6-4	220	11/10/54 Portland, ME
—	Stewart, Hector	New Britain	7-6	69	46	1.97	L-L	6-2	210	9/30/63 Puerto Rico
53	Stewart, Sam	Boston	4-1	64	47	4.38	R-R	6-3	223	10/28/54 Asheville, NC
42	Woodward, Rob	Pawtucket	9-6	128	73	3.17	R-R	6-3	202	9/28/62 Hanover, NH
		Boston	2-3	36	14	5.30				

CATCHERS

No.	Name	1986 Club	H	HR	RBI	Pct.	B-T	Ht.	Wt.	Born
50	Sax, Dave	Pawtucket	93	9	49	.289	R-R	6-0	185	9/22/58 Sacramento, CA
		Boston	5	1	1	.455				
—	Sheaffer, Danny	Pawtucket	90	2	30	.340	R-R	6-0	190	8/21/61 Jacksonville, FL
15	Sullivan, Marc	Boston	23	1	14	.193	R-R	6-4	213	7/25/58 Quincy, MA

INFIELDERS

No.	Name	1986 Club	H	HR	RBI	Pct.	B-T	Ht.	Wt.	Born
17	Barrett, Marty	Boston	179	4	60	.286	R-R	5-10	176	6/23/58 Arcadia, CA
26	Boggs, Wade	Boston	207	8	71	.357	L-R	6-2	197	6/15/58 Omaha, NE
6	Buckner, Bill	Boston	168	18	102	.267	L-L	6-1	182	12/14/49 Vallejo, CA
27	Dodson, Pat	Pawtucket	112	27	102	.269	L-L	6-4	210	10/11/59 Santa Monica, CA
		Boston	5	1	3	.417				
—	Horn, Sam	Pawtucket	15	3	14	.195	L-L	6-5	215	11/2/63 Dallas, TX
		New Britain	85	8	46	.246				
5	Owen, Spike	Sea.-Bos.	122	1	45	.231	B-R	5-10	165	4/19/61 Cleburne, TX
—	Reed, Jody	New Britain	50	0	11	.229	R-R	5-9	170	7/26/62 Tampa, FL
		Pawtucket	64	1	30	.282				
7	Romero, Ed	Boston	49	2	23	.210	R-R	5-11	150	12/9/57 Puerto Rico

OUTFIELDERS

No.	Name	1986 Club	H	HR	RBI	Pct.	B-T	Ht.	Wt.	Born
25	Baylor, Don	Boston	139	31	94	.238	R-R	6-1	210	6/28/49 Austin, TX
—	Benzinger, Todd	Pawtucket	79	11	32	.252	B-R	6-1	185	2/11/63 Dayton, KY
—	Burks, Ellis	New Britain	126	14	55	.273	R-R	6-2	175	9/11/64 Vicksburg, MS
24	Evans, Dwight	Boston	137	26	97	.259	R-R	6-3	204	11/3/51 Santa Monica, CA
39	Greenwell, Mike	Pawtucket	96	18	59	.300	L-R	6-0	189	7/18/63 Louisville, KY
		Boston	11	0	4	.314				
40	Henderson, Dave	Sea.-Bos.	103	15	47	.255	R-R	6-2	220	7/21/58 Dos Palos, CA
14	Rice, Jim	Boston	200	20	110	.324	R-R	6-2	217	3/8/53 Anderson, SC
16	Romine, Kevin	Pawtucket	75	4	32	.292	R-R	5-11	191	5/23/61 Exeter, NH
		Boston	9	0	2	.257				
55	Tarver, LaSchelle	Pawtucket	120	2	26	.320	L-L	5-11	165	1/30/59 Modesto, CA
		Boston	3	0	1	.120				

RED SOX PROFILES

WADE BOGGS 28 6-2 197 **Bats L Throws R**

Won AL batting title for third time in last four seasons by batting .357 . . . Forced to sit out potential head-to-head confrontation with runnerup, Yankees' Don Mattingly, in last four regular-season games due to torn right hamstring . . . Produced more than 200 hits for a club-record fourth straight year . . . Set career highs in doubles (47) and walks (105) and tied career best with eight homers . . . First major leaguer to get 200 hits and 100 walks in same season since Stan Musial in 1953 . . . Batted .359 with runners in scoring position . . . Put together 20-game hitting streak from Aug. 29 through Sept. 18 . . . Enjoyed two five-hit games and six four-hit games . . . Led AL third basemen with 121 putouts and sparkled defensively in postseason . . . Batted only .233 in AL Championship Series, but rebounded to hit .290 in World Series . . . Born June 15, 1958, in Omaha, Neb. . . . Red Sox' seventh-round pick in June 1976 draft . . . Overcame personal tragedy last June, when his mother died in an auto accident.

Year	Club	Pos.	G	AB	R	H	2B	3B	HR	RBI	SB	Avg.
1982	Boston	1B-3B-OF	104	338	51	118	14	1	5	44	1	.349
1983	Boston	3B	153	582	100	210	44	7	5	74	3	.361
1984	Boston	3B	158	625	109	203	31	4	6	55	3	.325
1985	Boston	3B	161	653	107	240	42	3	8	78	2	.368
1986	Boston	3B	149	580	107	207	47	2	8	71	0	.357
	Totals		725	2778	474	978	178	17	32	322	9	.352

JIM RICE 34 6-2 217 **Bats R Throws R**

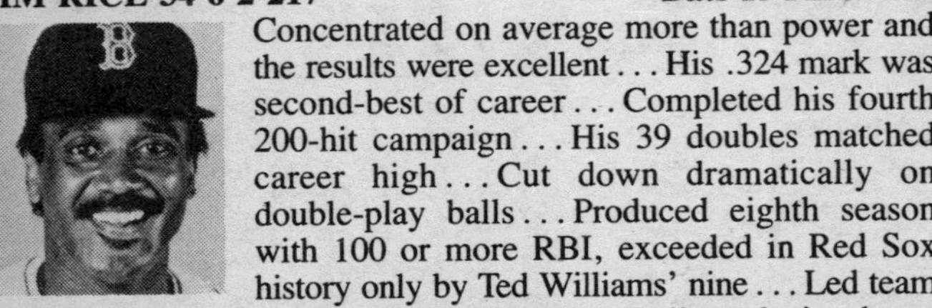

Concentrated on average more than power and the results were excellent . . . His .324 mark was second-best of career . . . Completed his fourth 200-hit campaign . . . His 39 doubles matched career high . . . Cut down dramatically on double-play balls . . . Produced eighth season with 100 or more RBI, exceeded in Red Sox history only by Ted Williams' nine . . . Led team with 40 game-tying and go-ahead RBI . . . Delivered nine homers, including two grand slams, and 32 RBI in 24 games from Aug. 20 through Sept. 14 . . . Ranked third among AL outfielders with 16 assists . . . Better left fielder than he is given credit for . . . Eight-time All-Star . . . Batted .333, but did not drive in a run in World Series . . . Belted two homers and knocked in six runs in AL Championship Series despite .161 average . . . Born March 8,

1953, in Anderson, S.C. . . . Red Sox' first pick in June 1971 draft . . . An avid golfer with tremendous driving prowess.

Year	Club	Pos.	G	AB	R	H	2B	3B	HR	RBI	SB	Avg.
1974	Boston.	OF	24	67	6	18	2	1	1	13	0	.269
1975	Boston.	OF	144	564	92	174	29	4	22	102	10	.309
1976	Boston.	OF	153	581	75	164	25	8	25	85	8	.282
1977	Boston.	OF	160	644	104	206	29	15	39	114	5	.320
1978	Boston.	OF	163	677	121	213	25	15	46	139	7	.315
1979	Boston.	OF	158	619	117	201	39	6	39	130	9	.325
1980	Boston.	OF	124	504	81	148	22	6	24	86	8	.294
1981	Boston.	OF	108	451	51	128	18	1	17	62	2	.284
1982	Boston.	OF	145	573	86	177	24	5	24	97	0	.309
1983	Boston.	OF	155	626	90	191	34	1	39	126	0	.305
1984	Boston.	OF	159	657	98	184	25	7	28	122	4	.280
1985	Boston.	OF	140	546	85	159	20	3	27	103	2	.291
1986	Boston.	OF	157	618	98	200	39	2	20	110	0	.324
	Totals.		1790	7127	1104	2163	331	74	351	1289	55	.303

MARTY BARRETT 28 5-10 176 Bats R Throws R

Rousing postseason performance capped an excellent year . . . Second baseman was named Most Valuable Player of AL Championship Series, when he batted .367 with five RBI . . . Hit .433 in World Series . . . Established a record with 24 postseason hits . . . Reached career highs in games (158), hits (179), doubles (39), runs (94), RBI (60) and walks (65) . . . Struck out only 31 times in 713 plate appearances . . . Hit .313 with men in scoring position . . . Led AL second basemen who played at least 100 games with 450 assists and ranked second in total chances with 767 . . . Born June 23, 1958, in Arcadia, Cal. . . . Boston's first pick in secondary phase of June 1979 draft . . . Brother, Charlie, pitched in Dodgers' system and another brother, Tom, is second baseman in Phillies' organization . . . Played one year at Arizona State.

Year	Club	Pos.	G	AB	R	H	2B	3B	HR	RBI	SB	Avg.
1982	Boston	2B	8	18	0	1	0	0	0	0	0	.056
1983	Boston	2B	33	44	7	10	1	1	0	2	0	.227
1984	Boston	2B	139	475	56	144	23	3	3	45	5	.303
1985	Boston	2B	156	534	59	142	26	0	5	56	7	.266
1986	Boston	2B	158	625	94	179	39	4	4	60	15	.286
	Totals		494	1696	216	476	89	8	12	163	27	.281

DON BAYLOR 37 6-1 210 Bats R Throws R

Acquisition of Baylor from Yankees for Mike Easler on March 28 was a key to Red Sox' first pennant since 1975 . . . Designated hitter led on the field, where he had 31 home runs and 94 RBI, and off the field, where he was judge of a kangaroo court that fined players for missed fundamentals . . . Burly batter who crowds plate and refuses to give ground . . . Was hit by pitch

35 times in 1986, breaking own record and extending AL career mark to 227 . . . Played in 160 games, his most since 1979, when he was AL MVP with Angels . . . Ranked third on Sox with 27 game-tying and go-ahead RBI . . . Born June 28, 1949, in Austin, Tex. . . . Began career as Baltimore's second-round choice in June 1967 draft . . . Batted .346 in AL Championship Series . . . His two-run homer triggered four-run ninth in Game 5 as Bosox avoided elimination . . . Was frustrated by World Series rule that allows for DH only in AL park . . . Batted .182 and was not a factor vs. Mets.

Year	Club	Pos.	G	AB	R	H	2B	3B	HR	RBI	SB	Avg.
1970	Baltimore	OF	8	17	4	4	0	0	0	4	1	.235
1971	Baltimore	OF	1	2	0	0	0	0	0	1	0	.000
1972	Baltimore	OF-1B	102	319	33	81	13	3	11	38	24	.254
1973	Baltimore	OF-1B	118	405	64	116	20	4	11	51	32	.286
1974	Baltimore	OF-1B	137	489	66	133	22	1	10	59	29	.272
1975	Baltimore	OF-1B	145	524	79	148	21	6	25	76	32	.282
1976	Oakland	OF-1B	157	595	85	147	25	1	15	68	52	.247
1977	California	OF-1B	154	561	87	141	27	0	25	75	26	.251
1978	California	OF-1B	158	591	103	151	26	0	34	99	22	.255
1979	California	OF-1B	162	628	120	186	33	3	36	139	22	.296
1980	California	OF	90	340	39	85	12	2	5	51	6	.250
1981	California	1B-OF	103	377	52	90	18	1	17	66	3	.239
1982	California	DH	157	608	80	160	24	1	24	93	10	.263
1983	New York (AL)	OF-1B	144	534	82	162	33	3	21	85	17	.303
1984	New York (AL)	OF	134	493	84	129	29	1	27	89	1	.262
1985	New York (AL)	DH	142	477	70	110	24	1	23	91	0	.231
1986	Boston	1B	160	585	93	139	23	1	31	94	3	.238
	Totals		2072	7546	1141	1982	350	28	315	1179	280	.263

BILL BUCKNER 37 6-1 182 **Bats L Throws L**

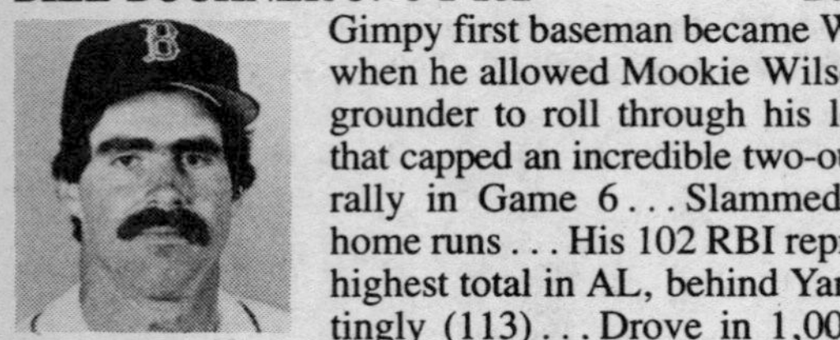

Gimpy first baseman became World Series goat when he allowed Mookie Wilson's 10th-inning grounder to roll through his legs for an error that capped an incredible two-out, three-run Met rally in Game 6 . . . Slammed career-high 18 home runs . . . His 102 RBI represented second-highest total in AL, behind Yankees' Don Mattingly (113) . . . Drove in 1,000th run in New York June 17 . . . Led AL first basemen with 157 assists . . . Struck out only 25 times in 681 plate appearances . . . Hit only .242 with runners in scoring position, but .344 in last two months . . . Hit .187 in nightmarish World Series . . . Struggled in AL Championship Series as well, hitting .214 . . . Wore high-top shoes to protect strained Achilles tendon . . . Given his assorted leg problems, it was an accomplishment that he played . . . Born Dec. 14, 1949, in Vallejo, Cal. . . . Began career as Dodgers' second-round pick in June 1968 draft . . . Acquired by Boston from Cubs for Dennis Eckersley and Mike Brumley on May 25, 1984.

Year	Club	Pos.	G	AB	R	H	2B	3B	HR	RBI	SB	Avg.
1969	Los Angeles.	PH	1	1	0	0	0	0	0	0	0	.000
1970	Los Angeles.	OF-1B	28	68	6	13	3	1	0	4	0	.191
1971	Los Angeles.	OF-1B	108	358	37	99	15	1	5	41	4	.277
1972	Los Angeles.	OF-1B	105	383	47	122	14	3	5	37	10	.319
1973	Los Angeles.	1B-OF	140	575	68	158	20	0	8	46	12	.275
1974	Los Angeles.	OF-1B	145	580	83	182	30	3	7	58	31	.314
1975	Los Angeles.	OF	92	288	30	70	11	2	6	31	8	.243
1976	Los Angeles.	1B-OF	154	642	76	193	28	4	7	60	28	.301
1977	Chicago (NL)	1B	122	426	40	121	27	0	11	60	7	.284
1978	Chicago (NL)	1B	117	446	47	144	26	1	5	74	7	.323
1979	Chicago (NL)	1B	149	591	72	168	34	7	14	66	9	.284
1980	Chicago (NL)	1B-OF	145	578	69	187	41	3	10	68	1	.324
1981	Chicago (NL)	1B	106	421	45	131	35	3	10	75	5	.311
1982	Chicago (NL)	1B	161	657	93	201	34	5	15	105	15	.306
1983	Chicago (NL)	1B-OF	153	626	79	175	38	6	16	66	12	.280
1984	Chicago (NL)	1B-OF	21	43	3	9	0	0	0	2	0	.209
1984	Boston	1B	114	439	51	122	21	2	11	67	2	.278
1985	Boston	1B	162	673	89	201	46	3	16	110	18	.299
1986	Boston	1B	153	629	73	168	39	2	18	102	6	.267
	Totals.		2176	8424	1008	2464	462	46	164	1072	175	.292

DWIGHT EVANS 35 6-3 204 Bats R Throws R

Began strong season by slugging first pitch from Detroit's Jack Morris for a home run Opening Day . . . Ranked second on club with 26 home runs and third with 97 RBI . . . Clouted seven homers in September . . . Worst month was May, when he hit .196 . . . Totalled 37 RBI in 30 games from June 17 to July 21 . . . Ranked second in AL behind teammate Wade Boggs with 97 walks . . . Made only five errors, two after July 13 . . . Arm is still above average, but not the gun it once was . . . Moved past Bobby Doerr into third place on Sox' all-time list in games played . . . Batted .308 with two homers and nine RBI in World Series after disappointing .214 showing in AL Championship Series . . . Drove in three runs in Game 7 of World Series . . . Born Nov. 3, 1951, in Santa Monica, Cal. . . . Red Sox' fifth selection in June 1969 draft.

Year	Club	Pos.	G	AB	R	H	2B	3B	HR	RBI	SB	Avg.
1972	Boston	OF	18	57	2	15	3	1	1	6	0	.263
1973	Boston	OF	119	282	46	63	13	1	10	32	5	.223
1974	Boston	OF	133	463	60	130	19	8	10	70	4	.281
1975	Boston	OF	128	412	61	113	24	6	13	56	3	.274
1976	Boston	OF	146	501	61	121	34	5	17	62	6	.242
1977	Boston	OF	73	230	39	66	9	2	14	36	4	.287
1978	Boston	OF	147	497	75	123	24	2	24	63	8	.247
1979	Boston	OF	152	489	69	134	24	1	21	58	6	.274
1980	Boston	OF	148	463	72	123	37	5	18	60	3	.266
1981	Boston	OF	108	412	84	122	19	4	22	71	3	.296
1982	Boston	OF	162	609	122	178	37	7	32	98	3	.292
1983	Boston	OF	126	470	74	112	19	4	22	58	3	.238
1984	Boston	OF	162	630	121	186	37	8	32	104	3	.295
1985	Boston	OF	159	617	110	162	29	1	29	78	7	.263
1986	Boston	OF	152	529	86	137	33	2	26	97	3	.259
	Totals.		1933	6661	1082	1785	361	57	291	949	61	.268

Marty Barrett had a whale of a World Series.

ROGER CLEMENS 24 6-4 215 **Bats R Throws R**

Cy Young winner and AL MVP began 14-0, the fifth-best start in major-league history . . . Led AL with 24 wins and 2.48 ERA . . . Placed second in AL to Seattle's Mark Langston with 238 strikeouts . . . Set major-league record for strikeouts in a nine-inning game with 20 against Seattle on April 29 . . . Incredibly, he walked none in that game . . . Fourteen of his victories came after a Sox loss . . . Limited opponents to .195 average . . . Won last seven decisions in regular season . . . Victory total was highest by Sox pitcher since Mel Parnell went 25-7 in 1949 . . . Was not overpowering in postseason . . . Went 1-1 with 4.37 ERA in two AL Championship Series starts . . . Posted 3.18 ERA and didn't get a decision in World Series . . . Was All-Star Game MVP and winning pitcher with three perfect innings . . . Born Aug. 4, 1962, in Dayton, Ohio . . . Red Sox' first pick (19th overall) in June 1983 draft . . . Drafted by Mets in June 1981, but did not sign . . . Was plagued by injuries in 1984 and 1985 . . . Underwent surgery on his right shoulder on Aug. 30, 1985 . . . Winning pitcher for Texas in 1983 College World Series title game.

Year	Club	G	IP	W	L	Pct.	SO	BB	H	ERA
1984	Boston	21	133⅓	9	4	.692	126	29	146	4.32
1985	Boston	15	98⅓	7	5	.583	74	37	83	3.29
1986	Boston	33	254	24	4	.857	238	67	179	2.48
	Totals	69	485⅔	40	13	.755	438	133	408	3.15

BRUCE HURST 29 6-3 207 **Bats L Throws L**

World Series hero until he tired and had to leave after six innings of Game 7, with the score tied at 3-3 . . . Pitched eight scoreless innings to win World Series opener, 1-0, and returned to win Game 5, 4-2, with strong complete-game effort . . . Use of forkball as a third pitch has helped him come into his own . . . Gained career-high 13 wins despite being sidelined from May 31 to July 18 with a groin injury . . . Was leading AL in strikeouts at time of injury . . . AL Pitcher of the Month in September with 5-0 mark and 1.07 ERA . . . Defied belief that left-handers can't win at Fenway Park by going 8-3 with 2.37 ERA in 14 starts there . . . All four of his shutouts were at Fenway . . . Born March 24, 1958, in St. George, Utah . . . Red Sox' first pick in June 1976 draft.

Year	Club	G	IP	W	L	Pct.	SO	BB	H	ERA
1980	Boston	12	31	2	2	.500	16	16	39	9.00
1981	Boston	5	23	2	0	1.000	11	12	23	4.30
1982	Boston	28	117	3	7	.300	53	40	161	5.77
1983	Boston	33	211⅓	12	12	.500	115	62	241	4.09
1984	Boston	33	218	12	12	.500	136	88	232	3.92
1985	Boston	35	229⅓	11	13	.458	189	70	243	4.51
1986	Boston	25	174⅓	13	8	.619	167	50	169	2.99
	Totals	171	1004	55	54	.505	687	338	1108	4.31

DENNIS BOYD 27 6-1 144 **Bats R Throws R**

Difficult, emotionally-charged season ended with manager John McNamara's decision to bypass him in favor of Bruce Hurst in World Series Game 7 . . . Rollercoaster ride began July 10, when he was suspended for throwing a temper tantrum in clubhouse . . . "Oil Can" was upset that he had been left off All-Star staff despite 11-6 record . . . Reinstated only to be suspended again, after altercation with police, who followed pitcher on tip he had been involved in a drug deal . . . Eventually hospitalized for complete evaluation, including drug testing . . . Rejoined Red Sox for good on Aug. 1 . . . Won a career-high 16 games . . . Pitched into seventh inning in 24 of 30 regular-season starts . . . Was winning pitcher when Boston beat Toronto to clinch first divisional title since 1975 . . . Charged with 7-1 loss in Game 3 in only World Series outing . . . Was 1-1 with 4.61 ERA in two AL Championship Series starts . . . Born Oct. 6, 1959, in Meridian, Miss. . . . Boston's 16th-round pick in June 1980 draft . . . Father, Willie James, played for Homestead Grays . . . One of 14 children . . . Flamboyant performer who can't escape trouble.

Year	Club	G	IP	W	L	Pct.	SO	BB	H	ERA
1982	Boston	3	8	0	1	.000	2	2	11	5.40
1983	Boston	15	99	4	8	.333	43	23	103	3.28
1984	Boston	29	197⅔	12	12	.500	134	53	207	4.37
1985	Boston	35	272⅓	15	13	.536	154	67	273	3.70
1986	Boston	30	214⅓	16	10	.615	129	45	222	3.78
	Totals	112	791⅓	47	44	.516	462	190	816	3.86

TOP PROSPECT

MIKE GREENWELL 23 6-0 189 **Bats L Throws R**
Red Sox showed faith in this guy as manager John McNamara made him his top pinch-hitter in World Series . . . Outfielder couldn't deliver, however, going 0-for-4 with two strikeouts . . . Batted .300 in 89 games for Pawtucket (AAA) with 18 homers, 59 RBI before July 24 recall . . . Hit .314 for Red Sox in 31 games . . . Started only four times . . . An International League All-Star . . . Forty of his 96 hits for Pawtucket were for extra bases, giving him a slugging percentage of .541 . . . Born July 18, 1963, in Louisville, Ky. . . . Selected in third round of June 1982 draft.

MANAGER JOHN McNAMARA: His steady hand and command of pitching staff had much to do with Red Sox' first pennant since 1975 . . . Club never let down, despite horde of critics who awaited a flop . . . Spirited manager who climbed into stands with his players when a Yankee Stadium fan stole outfielder Jim Rice's cap . . . Minor-league catcher who batted .239 with seven home runs during 14-year minor-league career . . . At 26, he became player-manager for Lewiston club in Northwest League in 1959 . . . Continued playing until 1967 . . . Named a coach with Kansas City A's in 1968, when they moved to Oakland . . . Became A's manager in 1969 . . . Managed San Diego from 1974

through May 28, 1977 . . . Piloted Cincinnati from 1979 through July 20, 1982, leading Reds to NL West title in 1979 . . . His Reds' had best overall record in baseball at 66-42 in strike-interrupted 1981, but they missed out on postseason play due to special format . . . Still bitter about that snub . . . Managed California in 1983 and '84 before moving on to Boston . . . Born June 4, 1932, in Sacramento, Cal. . . . Composite managerial record is 927-962.

GREATEST ALL-TIME ROOKIE

The Red Sox said he needed more seasoning in 1938 and Ted Williams wound up in Minneapolis. He was ready, very ready, in 1939, when he batted .327, with 31 home runs and a league-leading 145 RBI.

That was only a hint of what was to come for the left-handed-hitting outfielder, who raised his average to .344 the following year and posted a remarkable .406 mark in 1941.

Going into the final day of that 1941 season, Williams' average stood at .3996 and manager Joe Cronin offered to keep him on the bench to protect the .400 he had before a doubleheader against the Philadelphia A's. Williams would have none of that. He played in both games and tacked the final six points onto his average with six hits in eight at-bats.

That was the first of six batting titles. Twice—in 1942 and 1947—he won the triple crown. He was passed over for the MVP award in both of those seasons and also in 1941, his .406 season, when Joe DiMaggio won it for hitting safely in a record 56 straight games. Williams did win MVP crowns in 1946 and 1949.

When he won the 1958 batting title with a .328 average, he was 40 years old, the oldest batting champion ever. Acknowledged as the greatest pure hitter in baseball history, Williams retired at the age of 42 with a career average of .344 and 521 home runs.

ALL-TIME RED SOX SEASON RECORDS

BATTING: Ted Williams, .406, 1941
HRs: Jimmie Foxx, 50, 1938
RBIs: Jimmie Foxx, 175, 1938
STEALS: Tommy Harper, 54, 1973
WINS: Joe Wood, 34, 1912
STRIKEOUTS: Joe Wood, 258, 1912

CLEVELAND INDIANS

TEAM DIRECTORY: Owners: Richard Jacobs, David Jacobs; Pres.-Chief Exec. Officer: Peter Bavasi; Sr. VP-Baseball Adm./Play. Dev.: Dan O'Brien; VP-Baseball Adm.: Joe Klein; Dir. Play. Dev.-Scouting: Jeff Scott; Dir. Pub. Rel.: Rick Minch; Trav. Sec.: Mike Seghi; Mgr.: Pat Corrales. Home: Cleveland Municipal Stadium (74,208). Field distances: 320, l.f. line; 377, l.c.; 400, c.f.; 395, r.c.; 320, r.f. line. Spring training: Tucson, Ariz.

SCOUTING REPORT

HITTING: A potent lineup that led the AL in average (.284), runs (831) and stolen bases (141) makes the Indians legitimate contenders at long last.

Joe Carter, acquired from the Cubs in the Rick Sutcliffe deal in 1984, has emerged as a dominant offensive player. The left fielder became the first Indian to hit 20 or more homers (29), drive in 100 or more runs (a major-league-leading 121) and steal 20 or more bases (29) last season.

Carter, who batted .302, is one of four .300 hitters returning to the Cleveland lineup. The others are Pat Tabler (.326, 6 homers, 48 RBI), Julio Franco (.306, 10, 74) and switch-hitting Tony Bernazard (.301, 17, 73), who found a home in the leadoff spot. Mel Hall (.296, 18, 77) and Brook Jacoby (.288, 17, 80) more than compensated for the decline of DH Andre Thornton. And this season, the Indians will have Cory Snyder (.272, 24, 69) for the full season. Last year, he didn't join the Indians until June 3.

PITCHING: This will be the Indians' downfall. Only Seattle and Minnesota posted higher team ERAs than Cleveland's 4.58 in 1986.

Some outside help is probably required, but there is hope for improvement by some of the younger members of the staff. Developing knuckleballer Tom Candiotti (16-12, 3.57) led the AL with 17 complete games and appeared to benefit from the presence of a knuckleballing mentor in Phil Niekro (11-11, 4.32), who has won 311 games and counting. Ken Schrom (14-7, 4.54) struggled after a torrid stretch that earned him an All-Star berth. Ernie Camacho (2-4, 4.08, 20 saves) is the mainstay in the bullpen.

Cleveland must hope for the rapid maturity of left-hander Greg Swindell (5-2, 4.23), who jumped to the parent club from Class-A Waterloo last season and has the makings of a great one, and

Joe Carter emerged as star with 29 homers and 121 RBI.

Scott Bailes, another promising lefty, who had 10 wins and seven saves as a starter and reliever in 1986.

FIELDING: Like the pitching staff, the Indians' defense tends to be porous, as witnessed by Cleveland's league-high 157 errors last season. Third baseman Jacoby (25 errors), shortstop Franco (19 errors) and second baseman Bernazard (17 errors) were the chief offenders, although Franco's total represented an improvement of 17 from his 1985 total.

On the positive side of the ledger, Brett Butler is a near-flawless, if unspectacular center fielder.

OUTLOOK: Before the Indians' fifth-place finish last season at 84-78, they had wound up last or next-to-last every year since 1977. Pat Corrales' club still doesn't have enough pitching and must fill a hole behind the plate, but a franchise that hasn't brought home a pennant since 1954 finally put a charge into the Cleveland fans in 1986.

The front office's work won't be done until some quality arms are acquired without sacrificing too much of the Indians' young offensive talent, but this is a team headed in the right direction.

CLEVELAND INDIANS 1987 ROSTER

MANAGER Pat Corrales
Coaches—Jack Aker, Bobby Bonds, Doc Edwards, Johnny Goryl

PITCHERS

No.	Name	1986 Club	W-L	IP	SO	ERA	B-T	Ht.	Wt.	Born
43	Bailes, Scott	Cleveland	10-10	113	60	4.95	L-L	6-2	175	12/18/61 Chillicothe, OH
13	Camacho, Ernie	Cleveland	2-4	57	36	4.08	R-R	6-1	180	2/1/56 Salinas, CA
49	Candiotti, Tom	Cleveland	16-12	252	167	3.57	R-R	6-3	205	8/31/57 Walnut Creek, CA
36	Easterly, Jamie	Cleveland	0-2	18	9	7.64	L-L	5-10	180	2/17/53 Houston, TX
52	Farrell, John	Waterbury	9-10	173	104	3.06	R-R	6-4	210	8/4/62 Monmouth Park, NJ
46	Jones, Doug	Maine	5-6	116	98	2.09	R-R	6-2	190	6/24/57 Covina, CA
		Cleveland	1-0	18	12	2.50				
41	Murphy, Mike	Waterbury	8-7	118	62	3.58	R-R	6-4	230	2/15/63 Bronx, NY
35	Niekro, Phil	Cleveland	11-11	210	81	4.32	R-R	6-1	193	4/1/39 Blaine, OH
33	Oelkers, Bryan	Maine	4-4	52	28	2.42	L-L	6-3	192	3/11/61 Spain
		Cleveland	3-3	69	33	4.70				
56	Roberts, Scott	Maine	4-7	66	48	4.25	R-R	6-4	200	10/7/59 Seattle, WA
34	Roman, Jose	Maine	4-5	96	76	4.23	R-R	6-0	175	5/21/63 Dominican Republic
		Cleveland	1-2	22	9	6.55				
18	Schrom, Ken	Cleveland	14-7	206	87	4.54	R-R	6-2	195	11/23/54 Grangeville, ID
37	Schulze, Don	Maine	0-1	10	7	6.30	R-R	6-3	225	9/27/62 Roselle, IL
		Cleveland	4-4	85	33	5.00				
21	Swindell, Greg	Waterloo	2-1	18	16	1.00	R-L	6-2	225	1/2/65 Houston, TX
		Cleveland	5-2	62	46	4.23				
54	Waddell, Tom	Maine	0-0	8	4	6.75	R-R	6-1	190	9/17/58 Scotland
31	Wardle, Curt	Maine	7-10	113	71	4.14	L-L	6-5	220	11/16/60 Downey, CA
22	Wills, Frank	Maine	4-3	31	21	2.87	R-R	6-2	202	10/26/58 New Orleans, LA
		Cleveland	3-4	40	32	4.91				
42	Yett, Rich	Maine	0-0	6	2	4.50	R-R	6-1	170	10/6/62 Pomona, CA
		Cleveland	5-3	79	50	5.15				

CATCHERS

No.	Name	1986 Club	H	HR	RBI	Pct.	B-T	Ht.	Wt.	Born
6	Allanson, Andy	Cleveland	66	1	29	.225	R-R	6-5	215	12/22/61 Richmond, VA
23	Bando, Chris	Cleveland	68	2	26	.268	B-R	6-0	195	2/4/56 Cleveland, OH

INFIELDERS

No.	Name	1986 Club	H	HR	RBI	Pct.	B-T	Ht.	Wt.	Born
16	Bell, Jay	Waterbury	137	7	74	.277	R-R	6-1	180	12/11/65 Eglin AFB, FL
		Cleveland	5	1	4	.357				
4	Bernazard, Tony	Cleveland	169	17	73	.301	B-R	5-9	160	8/24/56 Puerto Rico
14	Franco, Julio	Cleveland	183	10	74	.306	R-R	6-0	160	8/23/61 Dom. Republic
26	Jacoby, Brook	Cleveland	168	17	80	.288	R-R	5-11	175	11/23/59 Philadelphia, PA
17	Noboa, Junior	Maine	114	4	32	.286	R-R	5-10	160	11/10/64 Dom. Republic
10	Tabler, Pat	Cleveland	154	6	48	.326	R-R	6-2	200	2/2/58 Hamilton, OH
29	Thornton, Andre	Cleveland	92	17	66	.229	R-R	6-2	205	8/13/49 Tuskegee, AL
24	Williams, Eddie	Cleveland	1	0	1	.143	R-R	6-0	175	11/1/64 Shreveport, LA

OUTFIELDERS

No.	Name	1986 Club	H	HR	RBI	Pct.	B-T	Ht.	Wt.	Born
50	Brito, Bernardo	Waterbury	118	18	75	.246	R-R	6-1	190	12/4/63 Dominican Republic
2	Butler, Brett	Cleveland	163	4	51	.278	L-L	5-10	160	6/15/57 Los Angeles, CA
30	Carter, Joe	Cleveland	200	29	121	.302	R-R	6-3	215	3/7/60 Oklahoma City, OK
8	Castillo, Carmen	Cleveland	57	8	32	.278	R-R	6-1	185	6/8/58 Dominican Republic
12	Clark, Dave	Maine	99	19	59	.279	L-R	6-2	198	9/3/62 Tupelo, MS
		Cleveland	16	3	9	.276				
15	Gallagher, Dave	Maine	145	8	44	.292	R-R	6-0	165	9/20/60 Trenton, NJ
27	Hall, Mel	Cleveland	168	17	80	.288	L-L	6-1	185	9/16/60 Lyons, NY
20	Nixon, Otis	Cleveland	25	0	8	.263	B-R	6-2	180	1/9/59 Evergreen, NC
57	Roman, Miguel	Waterbury	127	6	53	.266	R-R	6-2	170	6/18/64 Dominican Republic
28	Snyder, Cory	Maine	58	9	32	.302	R-R	6-3	175	11/11/62 Inglewood, CA
		Cleveland	113	24	69	.272				

INDIAN PROFILES

JOE CARTER 27 6-3 215

Bats R Throws R

Stayed injury-free for first time and results were startling . . . Left fielder led majors with 121 RBI and topped Indians with 29 homers . . . Became first Indian to record at least 20 homers, steal 20 bases and drive in 100 runs in same season . . . His 121 RBI were most by an Indian since Larry Doby's 126 in 1954 . . . First Indian to lead league in RBI since Rocky Colavito's 108 in 1965 . . . Rode 21-game hit streak, second longest in AL, that started May 17 . . . Had problems with wrist in 1985 and with knee in 1984 . . . Born March 7, 1960, in Oklahoma City, Okla. . . . Second choice in nation, by Chicago Cubs, in June 1981 draft . . . Acquired with Mel Hall, Don Schulze and Darryl Banks on June 13, 1984, for Rick Sutcliffe, Ron Hassey, George Frazier and Pookie Bernstine . . . Honored as College Player of the Year by *The Sporting News* in 1981 with Wichita State . . . Rookie of the Year in the American Association in 1983, with Iowa.

Year	Club	Pos.	G	AB	R	H	2B	3B	HR	RBI	SB	Avg.
1983	Chicago (NL)	OF	23	51	6	9	1	1	0	1	1	.176
1984	Cleveland	OF-1B	66	244	32	67	6	1	13	41	2	.275
1985	Cleveland	OF-1B-2B-3B	143	489	64	128	27	0	15	59	24	.262
1986	Cleveland	OF-1B	162	663	108	200	36	9	29	121	29	.302
	Totals		394	1447	210	404	70	11	57	222	56	.279

CORY SNYDER 24 6-3 175

Bats R Throws R

Output was outstanding considering he didn't make major-league debut until June 13 . . . Tripled against Minnesota in second major-league at-bat . . . His 24 homers were most by an Indian rookie since Al Rosen's 37 in 1950 . . . With 69 RBI, he was one of seven Indians with 65 or more . . . Hit in 17 straight games from Sept. 12-29, longest streak by a Cleveland rookie since Chris Chambliss' 19-game streak in 1971 . . . Big swinger who must reduce strikeout total . . . Lack of patience evident in that he drew only 16 walks . . . Can play third base and shortstop but spent most of time in right field . . . Born Nov. 11, 1962, in Inglewood, Cal. . . . Chosen by Cleveland in first round (fourth pick) of June 1984 draft . . . Batted .400 with two home runs and seven RBI in 1984 Olympics . . . Set a number of records at BYU.

Year	Club	Pos.	G	AB	R	H	2B	3B	HR	RBI	SB	Avg.
1986	Cleveland	OF	103	416	58	113	21	1	24	69	2	.272

JULIO FRANCO 25 6-0 160 **Bats R Throws R**

Defensive improvement was a welcome development because there has never been any doubt about shortstop's offensive ability . . . Committed 17 fewer errors, lowering total to 19 . . . Had 28-game errorless string May 28 to July 1 . . . Achieved at least 180 hits for third straight season, most by an Indian since Earl Averill had six straight of 180 or better from 1929-34 . . . Only negative note was club record he set by grounding into 30 double plays . . . Born Aug. 23, 1961, in San Pedro de Macoris, Dominican Republic . . . Traded to Cleveland with Jerry Willard, Jay Baller, George Vukovich and Manny Trillo by Philadelphia for Von Hayes on Dec. 9, 1982 . . . Finished second in 1983 voting for AL Rookie of the Year, behind Ron Kittle of the Chicago White Sox . . . Led club as a rookie with 80 RBI and 153 hits.

Year	Club	Pos.	G	AB	R	H	2B	3B	HR	RBI	SB	Avg.
1982	Philadelphia	SS-3B	16	29	3	8	1	0	0	3	0	.276
1983	Cleveland.	SS	149	560	68	153	24	8	8	80	32	.273
1984	Cleveland.	SS	160	658	82	188	22	5	3	79	19	.286
1985	Cleveland.	SS-2B	160	636	97	183	33	4	6	90	13	.288
1986	Cleveland.	SS	149	599	80	183	30	5	10	74	10	.306
	Totals		634	2482	330	715	110	22	27	326	74	.288

TONY BERNAZARD 30 5-9 160 **Bats S Throws R**

Second baseman's career was buoyed by shift to leadoff position on June 21 . . . Batted .299 in 82 games at top of the order with 13 homers and 51 RBI . . . That led to these career highs: average (.301), home runs (17), RBI (73), game-winning RBI (11), doubles (28), hits (169) and at-bats (562) . . . Set Indian record for home runs by a switch-hitter . . . First Indian in history to homer from both sides of the plate in a game . . . Did it on July 1 against Oakland . . . His 73 RBI were most by an Indian second baseman since Joe Gordon's 84 in 1949 . . . Born Aug. 24, 1956, in Caguas, Puerto Rico . . . Originally signed as free agent by Montreal in 1973 . . . Obtained from Seattle for Jack Perconte and Gorman Thomas on Dec. 7, 1983 . . . Re-signed as free agent to two-year contract prior to last season.

Year	Club	Pos.	G	AB	R	H	2B	3B	HR	RBI	SB	Avg.
1979	Montreal	2B	22	40	11	12	2	0	1	8	1	.300
1980	Montreal	2B-SS	82	183	26	41	7	1	5	18	9	.224
1981	Chicago (AL)	2B-SS	106	384	53	106	14	4	6	34	4	.276
1982	Chicago (AL)	2B-SS	137	540	90	138	25	9	11	56	11	.256
1983	Chicago (AL)-Seattle	2B	139	533	65	141	34	3	8	56	23	.265
1984	Cleveland.	2B	140	439	44	97	15	4	2	38	20	.221
1985	Cleveland.	2B-SS	153	500	73	137	26	3	11	59	17	.274
1986	Cleveland.	2B	146	562	88	169	28	4	17	73	17	.301
	Totals		925	3181	450	841	151	28	61	342	102	.264

BRETT BUTLER 29 5-10 160 **Bats L Throws L**

Recovered from a dismal first half to salvage solid season . . . Produced a .245 average in first half, then came on in last 31 games to bat .381, boosting average to .278 . . . Tied for eighth in league with 32 steals . . . Led majors with 14 triples, second straight year he reached that total . . . Errorless string of 110 games, started on Sept. 1, 1985, ran until July 10 . . . Born June 15, 1957, in Los Angeles . . . Acquired as one of three players to be named later in Aug. 28, 1983, deal that sent Len Barker to Atlanta . . . Indians also received Brook Jacoby and Rick Behenna . . . Produced 24 bunt hits in 50 attempts . . . Became only Indian to steal 50 or more bases and score 100 or more runs in same season in 1984 . . . International League MVP at Richmond (AAA) in 1981, when he batted .335 and finished second in league batting race by one point to Pawtucket's Wade Boggs.

Year	Club	Pos.	G	AB	R	H	2B	3B	HR	RBI	SB	Avg.
1981	Atlanta	OF	40	126	17	32	2	3	0	4	9	.254
1982	Atlanta	OF	89	240	35	52	2	0	0	7	21	.217
1983	Atlanta	OF	151	549	84	154	21	13	5	37	39	.281
1984	Cleveland.	OF	158	602	108	162	25	9	3	49	52	.269
1985	Cleveland.	OF	152	591	106	184	28	14	5	50	47	.311
1986	Cleveland.	OF	161	587	92	163	17	14	4	51	32	.278
	Totals		751	2695	442	747	95	53	17	198	200	.277

BROOK JACOBY 27 5-11 175  **Bats R Throws R**

Third baseman was recognized with his first selection to All-Star team . . . Established career high with .288 average . . . Had 83 runs, 168 hits, 30 doubles, four triples and nine game-winning RBI . . . Batted .297 with men in scoring position . . . Totaled 50 multi-hit games . . . His 137 strikeouts broke Bobby Bonds' club record of 135, set in 1979 . . . Born Nov. 23, 1959, in Philadelphia . . . Acquired as one of three players to be named later in Aug. 28, 1983, deal that sent Len Barker to Atlanta . . . International League Rookie of the Year in 1982, leading Richmond to first league title in 15 years . . . Nicknamed "Quiet One" . . . Father, Brook Sr., played in Cleveland and Philadelphia organizations.

Year	Club	Pos.	G	AB	R	H	2B	3B	HR	RBI	SB	Avg.
1981	Atlanta	3B	11	10	0	2	0	0	0	1	0	.200
1983	Atlanta	3B	4	8	0	0	0	0	0	0	0	.000
1984	Cleveland.	3B-SS	126	439	64	116	19	3	7	40	3	.264
1985	Cleveland.	3B-2B	161	606	72	166	26	3	20	87	2	.274
1986	Cleveland.	3B	158	583	83	168	30	4	17	80	2	.288
	Totals		460	1646	219	452	75	10	44	208	7	.275

PAT TABLER 29 6-2 200 **Bats R Throws R**

Always a clutch hitter, he displayed more consistency in 1986, producing career highs in average (.326), hits (154) and doubles (29) . . . His .326 mark ranked fourth in AL and was the highest average by an Indian since Miguel Dilone hit .341 in 1980 . . . Owns remarkable .533 career average in bases-loaded situations (24-for-45) with two homers and 57 RBI . . . Tribe's leading hitter with runners in scoring position at .306 . . . Went on 15-day disabled list on June 11 with hematoma on right thigh . . . Hitting .258 on July 20, he batted .392 the rest of the way . . . Born Feb. 2, 1958, in Hamilton, Ohio . . . Yankees' top choice and 16th pick overall in June 1976 draft . . . Acquired by Cleveland from White Sox for Jerry Dybzinski on April 1, 1983 . . . An All-American in baseball and basketball at McNicholas High School in Cincinnati, he was that city's Player of the Year in 1976.

Year	Club	Pos.	G	AB	R	H	2B	3B	HR	RBI	SB	Avg.
1981	Chicago (NL)	2B	35	101	11	19	3	1	1	5	0	.188
1982	Chicago (NL)	3B	25	85	9	20	4	2	1	7	0	.235
1983	Cleveland	3B-OF-2B	124	430	56	125	23	5	6	65	2	.291
1984	Cleveland	1B-OF-3B-2B	144	473	66	137	21	3	10	68	3	.290
1985	Cleveland	1B-3B-2B	117	404	47	111	18	3	5	59	0	.275
1986	Cleveland	1B-3B	130	473	61	154	29	2	6	48	3	.326
	Totals		575	1966	250	566	98	16	29	252	8	.288

PHIL NIEKRO 48 6-1 193 **Bats R Throws R**

One of the world's great geriatric wonders . . . Knuckleballer tied for third with Gaylord Perry on all-time list with 690 starts . . . Tied for 12th all time in victories with 311 . . . Superb competitor worked into seventh inning in 21 of 31 starts . . . Has pitched against every team in majors except Atlanta . . . Born April Fools' Day, 1939, in Blaine, Ohio . . . Released by Atlanta on Oct. 7, 1983, after he refused to retire . . . Released by pitching-poor Yankees on March 28, 1986, and claimed on waivers by Cleveland . . . Five-time All-Star . . . Won four Gold Gloves . . . Became 18th player to win 300 games on final day of 1985 season, in his fifth try . . . It was an 8-0 blanking of Toronto and he replaced Satchel Paige as the oldest pitcher to throw a shutout . . . Didn't use his knuckleball in that game until he fanned final batter, Jeff Burroughs. . . . Originally signed as free agent by old Milwaukee Braves on July 19, 1958 . . . Likes to write poetry in offseason . . . An avid fisherman.

Year	Club	G	IP	W	L	Pct.	SO	BB	H	ERA
1964	Milwaukee	10	15	0	0	.000	8	7	15	4.80
1965	Milwaukee	41	75	2	3	.400	40	26	73	2.88
1966	Atlanta	28	50	4	3	.571	17	23	48	4.14
1967	Atlanta	46	207	11	9	.550	129	55	164	1.87
1968	Atlanta	37	257	14	12	.538	140	45	228	2.50
1969	Atlanta	40	284	23	13	.639	193	57	235	2.57
1970	Atlanta	34	230	12	18	.400	168	68	222	4.27
1971	Atlanta	42	269	15	14	.517	173	70	248	2.98
1972	Atlanta	38	282	16	12	.571	164	53	254	3.06
1973	Atlanta	42	245	13	10	.565	131	89	214	3.31
1974	Atlanta	41	302	20	13	.606	195	88	249	2.38
1975	Atlanta	39	276	15	15	.500	144	72	285	3.20
1976	Atlanta	38	271	17	11	.607	173	101	249	3.29
1977	Atlanta	44	330	16	20	.444	262	164	315	4.04
1978	Atlanta	44	334	19	18	.514	248	102	295	2.88
1979	Atlanta	44	342	21	20	.512	208	113	311	3.39
1980	Atlanta	40	275	15	18	.455	176	85	256	3.63
1981	Atlanta	22	139	7	7	.500	62	56	120	3.11
1982	Atlanta	35	234⅓	17	4	.810	144	73	225	3.61
1983	Atlanta	34	201⅔	11	10	.524	128	105	212	3.97
1984	New York (AL)	32	215⅔	16	8	.667	136	76	219	3.09
1985	New York (AL)	33	220	16	12	.571	149	120	203	4.09
1986	Cleveland	34	210⅓	11	11	.500	81	95	241	4.32
	Totals	838	5265	311	261	.544	3278	1743	4881	3.27

ERNIE CAMACHO 31 6-1 180 **Bats R Throws R**

Rebounded strongly after making only two appearances in 1985 due to elbow miseries . . . Led club with 20 saves and tied for sixth in AL . . . Converted 20 of 31 save opportunities. . . . First Indian to have at least two seasons with 20 or more saves . . . Born Feb. 1, 1956, in Salinas, Cal. . . . Obtained from Milwaukee on June 6, 1983, with Gorman Thomas and Jamie Easterly for Rick Manning and Rick Waits . . . Holds Indian record for saves with 23 in 1984 . . . Originally selected by Pittsburgh in 12th round of June 1975 draft . . . Extremely hard thrower whose biggest problem is staying healthy . . . Was disabled for two weeks last May with tender right shoulder.

Year	Club	G	IP	W	L	Pct.	SO	BB	H	ERA
1980	Oakland	5	12	0	0	.000	9	5	20	6.75
1981	Pittsburgh	7	22	0	1	.000	11	15	23	4.91
1983	Cleveland	4	5⅓	0	1	.000	2	2	5	5.06
1984	Cleveland	69	100	5	9	.357	48	37	83	2.43
1985	Cleveland	2	3⅓	0	1	.000	2	1	4	8.10
1986	Cleveland	51	57⅓	2	4	.333	36	31	60	4.08
	Totals	138	200	7	16	.304	108	91	195	3.60

TOM CANDIOTTI 29 6-3 205 **Bats R Throws R**

May be on his way to becoming game's premier knuckleball pitcher and one of the finest pitchers, period . . . Led club in victories with 16-12 mark and in ERA at 3.57 . . . Led AL with 17 complete games, first Indian to do so since Gaylord Perry in 1973 . . . Was sixth in AL with 252⅓ innings pitched . . . Still learning to master knuckleball with help of teammate Phil Niekro . . . Tied for third in AL with three shutouts . . . Admits he was marginal major leaguer before developing knuckleball . . . Pitch became essential when he had elbow surgery in 1981 . . . Born Aug. 31, 1957, in Walnut Creek, Cal. . . . Signed by Indians as free agent on Dec. 12, 1985.

Year	Club	G	IP	W	L	Pct.	SO	BB	H	ERA
1983	Milwaukee	10	55⅔	4	4	.500	21	16	62	3.23
1984	Milwaukee	8	32⅓	2	2	.500	23	10	38	5.29
1986	Cleveland	36	252⅓	16	12	.571	167	106	234	3.57
	Totals	54	340⅓	22	18	.550	211	132	334	3.68

SCOTT BAILES 25 6-2 175 **Bats L Throws L**

Biggest debate on Bailes concerns whether he should start or relieve . . . Shows ability in both roles . . . Made first 51 appearances as a reliever, going 8-7 with seven saves and 4.68 ERA . . . Made first major-league start on Aug. 10 at Baltimore and defeated Orioles, 6-3 . . . Went 2-3 with a 5.76 ERA as a starter . . . Much prefers to start . . . Led club with 62 appearances . . . Born Dec. 18, 1961, in Chillicothe, Ohio . . . Selected by Pittsburgh in fourth round of June 1982 draft . . . Obtained from Pirates as the player to be named later in May 29, 1985, deal that sent Johnnie LeMaster to Pittsburgh . . . Named an Eastern League All-Star with 9-6 record and nine saves at Nashua and Waterbury (AA) in 1985.

Year	Club	G	IP	W	L	Pct.	SO	BB	H	ERA
1986	Cleveland	62	112⅔	10	10	.500	60	43	123	4.95

TOP PROSPECT

GREG SWINDELL 22 6-2 225 **Bats R Throws L**

Look for a big year from Swindell in his first full major-league season . . . Went 5-2 with 4.23 ERA after late-season promotion, despite being pounded in his major-league debut by Boston in a 24-5 thrashing on Aug. 21 . . . Second player chosen in June 1986 draft after brilliant career at Texas, where he was 43-8 with 1.92 ERA in three seasons . . . Was 2-1 with 1.00 ERA at Waterloo (A) of Midwest League . . . Born Jan. 2, 1965, in Houston.

Yanks were knuckleheads for letting Phil Niekro go.

MANAGER PAT CORRALES: Due much credit for resurgence of the Indians, whose 84-78 record marked a 24-game improvement . . . Composite major-league managerial record improved to 541-578 . . . Made do with a patchwork pitching staff . . . Managerial career began in 1975 with Alexandria (AA) of Texas League . . . Took over Texas Rangers in 1979 after three seasons as a coach . . . Dismissed by Texas after 1980 and hired by Philadelphia in 1982 . . . Was out of work again in 1983, when Phillies fired him . . . On July 31, 1983, he was hired by Indians, joining John McGraw, Rogers Hornsby and Bill Virdon as only men to manage in both leagues in same season . . . Born March 20, 1941, in Los Angeles . . . Of Mexican-Indian descent . . . Was a catcher for Cardinals, Reds and Padres.

GREATEST ALL-TIME ROOKIE

Al Rosen's first full major-league season came in 1950 and his last was in 1956. But what Rosen's career lacked in length it made up for in quality.

Rosen led the league in home runs with 37 in 1950 and knocked in 116 runs, the first of five times he would reach the century mark in RBI. He batted .287 and scored 100 runs, the first of three times he would score at least that many. Rosen was a well-rounded performer and he led AL third basemen in assists his first year as an Indian.

Rosen compiled a .285 career average and enjoyed his greatest year in 1953, when he established career highs in batting average (.336) and home runs (43) and was named American League Most Valuable Player.

ALL-TIME INDIAN SEASON RECORDS

BATTING: Joe Jackson, .408, 1911
HRs: Al Rosen, 43, 1953
RBIs: Hal Trosky, 162, 1936
STEALS: Miguel Dilone, 61, 1980
WINS: Jim Bagby, 31, 1920
STRIKEOUTS: Bob Feller, 348, 1946

DETROIT TIGERS

TEAM DIRECTORY: Chairman: John E. Fetzer; Vice-Chairman: Tom Monaghan; Pres.-Chief Exec. Off.: Jim Campbell; VP-Operations: William Haase; VP-GM: William Lajoie; VP-Play. Procurement/Dev.: Joe McDonald; Dir. Pub. Rel.: Dan Ewald; Trav. Sec.: Bill Brown; Mgr.: Sparky Anderson. Home: Tiger Stadium (52,806). Field distances: 340, l.f. line; 365, l.c.; 440, c.f.; 370, r.c.; 325, r.f. line. Spring training: Lakeland, Fla.

Jack Morris couldn't escape the Tigers' den.

SCOUTING REPORT

HITTING: The Tigers topped the AL with 198 home runs and are capable of doing it again. Much of the power stems from an all-20-home-run-hitting infield—first baseman Darrell Evans (.241, 29, 85), second baseman Lou Whitaker (.269, 20, 73), third baseman Darnell Coles (.273, 20, 86) and shortstop Alan Trammell (.277, 21, 75).

Outfielder Kirk Gibson (.268, 28, 86) is the Tigers' greatest all-around threat and must only stay healthy—an injured left ankle and a dog bite sidelined him at different times in 1986—to improve on his performance of last year. But how will the Tigers compensate for the likely defection of free agent Lance Parrish (.257, 22, 62), who was greatly missed when he was sidelined by a back problem last summer?

PITCHING: The staff is mediocre after ace Jack Morris (21-8, 3.27), who agreed to arbitration after finding no takers as a free agent last winter.

Frank Tanana (12-9, 4.16) and well-shopped Walt Terrell (15-12, 4.56) are capable, but not potential big winners. If right-hander Dan Petry can recover from an elbow problem—he was 1-5 after arthroscopic surgery last June 10—it would provide a tremendous lift.

Left-hander Willie Hernandez (8-7, 3.55, 24 saves) and his screwball are not as dependable as a couple of seasons ago. The Tigers think Eric King (11-4, 3.51, 3 saves) can be the answer.

FIELDING: The Tigers ranked third in the AL with a .982 fielding percentage and are testimony to the value of strength up the middle. Trammell and Whitaker, double-play partners for a decade, form an impeccable combination. Chet Lemon is very capable in center. Coles, although he made a team-high 23 errors, established himself at third base and will continue to improve.

OUTLOOK: No one can put a finger on it, but Sparky Anderson's Tigers have lost some essential ingredients since winning the world championship in 1984. The feeling is the Tigers played above their heads that year and have played somewhat below their abilities the last two summers. Lack of quality pitching and the loss of Parrish make Detroit an also-ran in a tough division and unlikely to improve upon last year's 87-75 finish.

DETROIT TIGERS 1987 ROSTER

MANAGER Sparky Anderson
Coaches—Billy Consolo, Alex Grammas, Billy Muffett, Vada Pinson, Dick Tracewski

PITCHERS

No.	Name	1986 Club	W-L	IP	SO	ERA	B-T	Ht.	Wt.	Born
22	Barlow, Ricky	Glens Falls	5-8	89	73	2.63	R-R	6-2	170	3/21/63 Woodville, TX
43	Cary, Chuck	Detroit	1-2	32	21	3.41	L-L	6-4	210	3/30/60 Whittier, CA
		Nashville	1-4	26	19	5.47				
48	Gibson, Paul	Glens Falls	3-1	20	21	1.37	R-L	6-0	165	1/4/60 Southampton, NY
		Nashville	5-6	113	91	3.97				
39	Henneman, Mike	Nashville	2-5	58	39	2.95	R-R	6-4	195	12/11/61 St. Charles, MO
21	Hernandez, Willie	Detroit	8-7	89	77	3.55	L-L	6-2	185	11/14/54 Puerto Rico
45	Kelly, Bryan	Nashville	5-5	101	74	4.62	R-R	6-2	195	2/24/59 Silver Spring, MD
		Detroit	1-2	20	18	4.50				
25	King, Eric	Nashville	3-2	38	38	3.52	R-R	6-2	180	4/10/64 Oxnard, CA
		Detroit	11-4	138	79	3.51				
42	Madden, Morris	Glens Falls	7-5	91	64	4.04	L-L	6-0	155	8/31/60 Laurens, SC
47	Morris, Jack	Detroit	21-8	267	223	3.27	R-R	6-3	200	5/16/55 St. Paul, MN
49	O'Neal, Randy	Detroit	3-7	123	68	4.33	R-R	6-2	195	8/30/60 Ashland, KY
		Nashville	1-2	28	15	4.76				
27	Pacella, John	Nashville	7-6	68	55	2.90	R-R	6-3	200	9/15/56 Brooklyn, NY
		Detroit	0-0	11	5	4.09				
46	Petry, Dan	Lakeland	1-1	10	6	3.97	R-R	6-4	200	11/13/58 Palo Alto, CA
		Detroit	5-10	116	56	4.66				
44	Robinson, Jeff	Nashville	10-7	150	72	4.38	R-R	6-6	210	12/14/61 Ventura, CA
28	Tanana, Frank	Detroit	12-9	188	119	4.16	L-L	6-3	195	7/3/53 Detroit, MI
35	Terrell, Walt	Detroit	15-12	217	93	4.56	L-R	6-2	205	5/11/58 Jeffersonville, IN
40	Thurmond, Mark	San Diego	3-7	71	32	6.50	L-L	6-0	195	9/12/56 Houston, TX
		Detroit	4-1	52	17	1.92				

CATCHERS

No.	Name	1986 Club	H	HR	RBI	Pct.	B-T	Ht.	Wt.	Born
32	Harper, Brian	Nashville	83	11	45	.262	R-R	6-2	195	10/16/59 Los Angeles, CA
		Detroit	5	0	3	.139				
8	Heath, Mike	St. Louis	39	4	25	.205	R-R	5-11	180	2/5/55 Tampa, FL
		Detroit	26	4	11	.265				
12	Lowry, Dwight	Nashville	14	1	6	.246	L-R	6-3	210	10/23/57 Robeson County, NC
		Detroit	46	3	18	.307				
33	Nokes, Matt	Nashville	122	10	71	.285	L-R	6-1	185	10/31/63 San Diego, CA
		Detroit	8	1	2	.333				
10	Palacios, Rey	Glens Falls	116	16	66	.252	R-R	5-10	190	11/8/62 Brooklyn, NY

INFIELDERS

No.	Name	1986 Club	H	HR	RBI	Pct.	B-T	Ht.	Wt.	Born
9	Baker, Doug	Detroit	3	0	0	.125	B-R	5-9	165	4/3/61 Fullerton, CA
		Nashville	101	2	40	.274				
14	Bergman, Dave	Detroit	30	1	9	.231	L-L	6-2	190	6/6/53 Evanston, IL
16	Brookens, Tom	Detroit	76	3	25	.270	R-R	5-10	170	8/10/53 Chambersburg, PA
18	Chavez, Pedro	Nashville	107	2	43	.258	R-R	5-11	160	2/23/62 Venezuela
19	Coles, Darnell	Detroit	142	20	86	.273	R-R	6-1	185	6/2/62 San Bernardino, CA
41	Evans, Darrell	Detroit	122	29	85	.241	L-R	6-2	205	5/26/47 Pasadena, CA
29	Hermann, Jeff	Lakeland	20	6	11	.256	L-R	6-5	220	10/8/63 Joliet, IL
		Glens Falls	58	2	31	.235				
20	Rivera, German	Nashville	151	14	84	.298	R-R	6-2	195	7/6/59 Puerto Rico
3	Trammell, Alan	Detroit	159	21	75	.277	R-R	6-0	175	2/21/58 Garden Grove, CA
1	Whitaker, Lou	Detroit	157	20	73	.269	L-R	5-11	160	5/12/57 Brooklyn, NY

OUTFIELDERS

No.	Name	1986 Club	H	HR	RBI	Pct.	B-T	Ht.	Wt.	Born
37	Fields, Bruce	Nashville	141	1	53	.368	L-R	6-0	185	10/6/60 Cleveland, OH
		Detroit	12	0	6	.279				
23	Gibson, Kirk	Detroit	118	28	86	.268	L-L	6-3	215	5/28/57 Pontiac, MI
30	Grubb, John	Nashville	5	1	3	.179	L-R	6-3	180	8/4/48 Richmond, VA
		Detroit	70	13	51	.333				
31	Herndon, Larry	Detroit	70	8	37	.247	R-R	6-3	200	11/3/53 Sunflower, MS
34	Lemon, Chet	Detroit	101	12	53	.251	R-R	6-0	190	2/12/55 Jackson, MS
15	Sheridan, Pat	Nashville	10	1	5	.286	L-R	6-3	175	12/4/57 Ann Arbor, MI
		Detroit	56	6	19	.237				
38	Tolman, Tim	Nashville	144	11	71	.298	R-R	6-0	195	4/20/56 Santa Monica, CA
		Detroit	6	0	2	.176				

TIGER PROFILES

KIRK GIBSON 29 6-3 215 **Bats L Throws L**

Right fielder's production was curtailed by injuries last season . . . Suffered ligament damage in left ankle April 22 in Boston and was disabled until June 2 . . . Off to great start before injury, batting .359 . . . Belted two home runs on Opening Day and had five-RBI game . . . Missed three games in September when bitten by his dog . . . Still reached 20 home runs and 20 stolen bases for third consecutive season . . . Shared club RBI lead with Darnell Coles at 86 . . . Smashed five home runs in five games Sept. 6-11 . . . Born May 28, 1957, in Pontiac, Mich. . . . Tigers' first-round selection (12th pick) in June 1978 draft . . . One of baseball's great all-around athletes . . . All-American flanker at Michigan State, setting school records with 112 catches, 2,347 yards and 24 touchdown receptions . . . Walloped 523-foot home run in 1983 that cleared right-field roof of Tiger Stadium and landed on a lumberyard roof across Trumbull Avenue . . . MVP of 1984 AL Championship Series, batting .417 with .500 on-base percentage.

Year	Club	Pos.	G	AB	R	H	2B	3B	HR	RBI	SB	Avg.
1979	Detroit	OF	12	38	3	9	3	0	1	4	3	.237
1980	Detroit	OF	51	175	23	46	2	1	9	16	4	.263
1981	Detroit	OF	83	290	41	95	11	3	9	40	17	.328
1982	Detroit	OF	69	266	34	74	16	2	8	35	9	.278
1983	Detroit	OF	128	401	60	91	12	9	15	51	14	.227
1984	Detroit	OF	149	531	92	150	23	10	27	91	29	.282
1985	Detroit	OF	154	581	96	167	37	5	29	97	30	.287
1986	Detroit	OF	119	441	84	118	11	2	28	86	34	.268
	Totals		765	2723	433	750	115	32	126	420	140	.275

DARRELL EVANS 39 6-2 205 **Bats L Throws R**

Slugging first baseman is making few concessions to age . . . Led Detroit with 29 home runs . . . With 85 RBI, he was one off team lead shared by Kirk Gibson and Darnell Coles . . . Hit in eight straight games June 25 to July 3, with five homers, 12 RBI . . . Went 16 games without a home run May 23 to June 10 . . . Clouted homers in three successive games to begin July . . . Cool spell soon followed in which Evans went homerless from July 9 to Aug. 3 . . . Born May 26, 1947, in Pasadena, Cal. . . . Signed as free agent on Dec. 16, 1983 . . . In 1985, he became first Detroit home-run champ since Hank Greenberg had 44 in 1946 . . . First Tiger left-handed-hitting home-run king since Ty Cobb had nine in 1909 . . . First major leaguer to hit 40 homers in each league . . . Oldest player ever to win AL home-run title.

Year	Club	Pos.	G	AB	R	H	2B	3B	HR	RBI	SB	Avg.
1969	Atlanta	3B	12	26	3	6	0	0	0	1	0	.231
1970	Atlanta	3B	12	44	4	14	1	1	0	9	0	.318
1971	Atlanta	3B-OF	89	260	42	63	11	1	12	38	2	.242
1972	Atlanta	3B	125	418	67	106	12	0	19	71	4	.254
1973	Atlanta	3B-1B	161	595	114	167	25	8	41	104	6	.281
1974	Atlanta	3B	160	571	99	137	21	3	25	79	4	.240
1975	Atlanta	3B-1B	156	567	82	138	22	2	22	73	12	.243
1976	Atl.-S.F.	1B-3B	136	396	53	81	9	1	11	46	9	.205
1977	San Francisco...	OF-1B-3B	144	461	64	117	18	3	17	72	9	.254
1978	San Francisco...	3B	159	547	82	133	24	2	20	78	4	.243
1979	San Francisco...	3B	160	562	68	142	23	2	17	70	6	.253
1980	San Francisco...	3B-1B	154	556	69	147	23	0	20	78	17	.264
1981	San Francisco...	3B-1B	102	357	51	92	13	4	12	48	2	.258
1982	San Francisco...	3B-1B-SS	141	465	64	119	20	4	16	61	5	.256
1983	San Francisco...	1B-3B-SS	142	523	94	145	29	3	30	82	6	.277
1984	Detroit	3B-1B	131	401	60	93	11	1	16	63	2	.232
1985	Detroit	1B-3B	151	505	81	125	17	0	40	94	0	.248
1986	Detroit	1B-3B	151	507	78	122	15	0	29	85	3	.241
	Totals		2286	7761	1175	1947	294	35	347	1152	91	.251

ALAN TRAMMELL 29 6-0 175 Bats R Throws R

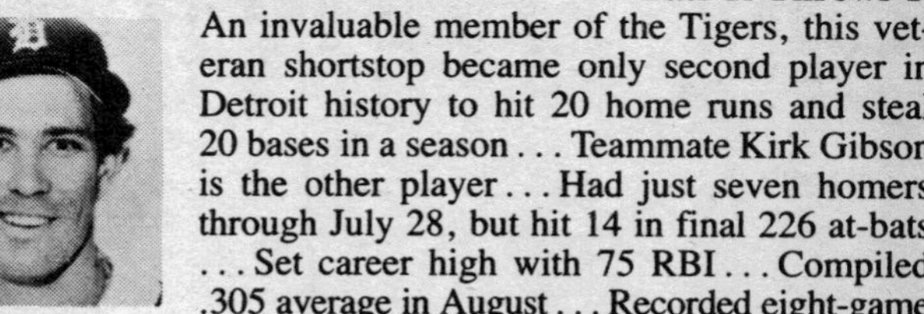

An invaluable member of the Tigers, this veteran shortstop became only second player in Detroit history to hit 20 home runs and steal 20 bases in a season . . . Teammate Kirk Gibson is the other player . . . Had just seven homers through July 28, but hit 14 in final 226 at-bats . . . Set career high with 75 RBI . . . Compiled .305 average in August . . . Recorded eight-game batting streak Aug. 12-20, six of those multi-hit efforts . . . Born Feb. 21, 1958, in Garden Grove, Cal. . . . Detroit's second-round pick in June 1976 draft . . . World Series MVP in 1984, when he led in average (.450), hits (nine) and total bases (16) . . . Might be greater player if not for various injuries in his career, most severe being a nagging problem with right shoulder.

Year	Club	Pos.	G	AB	R	H	2B	3B	HR	RBI	SB	Avg.
1977	Detroit	SS	19	43	6	8	0	0	0	0	0	.186
1978	Detroit	SS	139	448	49	120	14	6	2	34	3	.268
1979	Detroit	SS	142	460	68	127	11	4	6	50	17	.276
1980	Detroit	SS	146	560	107	168	21	5	9	65	12	.300
1981	Detroit	SS	105	392	52	101	15	3	2	31	10	.258
1982	Detroit	SS	157	489	66	126	34	3	9	57	19	.258
1983	Detroit	SS	142	505	83	161	31	2	14	66	30	.319
1984	Detroit	SS	139	555	85	174	34	5	14	69	19	.314
1985	Detroit	SS	149	605	79	156	21	7	13	57	14	.258
1986	Detroit	SS	151	574	107	159	33	7	21	75	25	.277
	Totals		1289	4631	702	1300	214	42	90	504	149	.281

LOU WHITAKER 29 5-11 160 **Bats L Throws R**

A favorite of Detroit fans, smooth second baseman is greeted by cries of "Lou! Lou!" whenever he steps to the plate . . . Earned fourth All-Star selection and drilled two-run home run off NL ace Dwight Gooden for game-winning RBI . . . Enjoyed second straight season with 20 or more homers, slamming No. 20 on last weekend of season . . . Put together Detroit's longest hitting streak, 16 games, from July 24 to Aug. 9 . . . Had streaks of 10 games or more three times . . . Born May 12, 1957, in Brooklyn, N.Y. . . . Detroit's fifth-round selection in June 1975 draft . . . AL Rookie of the Year in 1978 . . . Delivered three hits in first major-league game on Sept. 9, 1977 . . . Began career as third baseman in the minors, but switched to second when he was MVP of Florida State League in 1976.

Year	Club	Pos.	G	AB	R	H	2B	3B	HR	RBI	SB	Avg.
1977	Detroit	28	11	32	5	8	1	0	0	2	2	.250
1978	Detroit	2B	139	484	71	138	12	7	3	58	7	.285
1979	Detroit	2B	127	423	75	121	14	8	3	42	20	.286
1980	Detroit	2B	145	477	68	111	19	1	1	45	8	.233
1981	Detroit	2B	109	335	48	88	14	4	5	36	5	.263
1982	Detroit	2B	152	560	76	160	22	8	15	65	11	.286
1983	Detroit	2B	161	643	94	206	40	6	12	72	17	.320
1984	Detroit	2B	143	558	90	161	25	1	13	56	6	.289
1985	Detroit	2B	152	609	102	170	29	8	21	73	6	.279
1986	Detroit	2B	144	584	95	157	26	6	20	73	13	.269
	Totals		1283	4705	724	1320	202	49	93	522	95	.281

CHET LEMON 32 6-0 190 **Bats R Throws R**

On downside of solid career . . . His 12 home runs last season represented his lowest total since his final year with the White Sox in 1981 . . . Connected three times in first 263 at-bats . . . Hit nine in next 115 at-bats . . . Enjoyed great May with .429 average, including 14-game hitting streak . . . Had eight-game streak in April . . . Born Feb. 12, 1955, in Jackson, Miss. . . . Obtained from White Sox for Steve Kemp on Nov. 27, 1981 . . . Best season was 1979, when he batted career-high .318 with

17 homers and career-high 86 RBI . . . Once an exceptional center fielder, now merely average.

Year	Club	Pos.	G	AB	R	H	2B	3B	HR	RBI	SB	Avg.
1975	Chicago (AL)	3B-OF	9	35	2	9	2	0	0	1	1	.257
1976	Chicago (AL)	OF	132	451	46	111	15	5	4	38	13	.246
1977	Chicago (AL)	OF	150	553	99	151	38	4	19	67	8	.273
1978	Chicago (AL)	OF	105	357	51	107	24	6	13	55	5	.300
1979	Chicago (AL)	OF	148	556	79	177	44	2	17	86	7	.318
1980	Chicago (AL)	OF-2B	147	514	76	150	32	6	11	51	6	.292
1981	Chicago (AL)	OF	94	328	50	99	23	6	9	50	5	.302
1982	Detroit	OF	125	436	75	116	20	1	19	52	1	.266
1983	Detroit	OF	145	491	78	125	21	5	24	69	0	.255
1984	Detroit	OF	141	509	77	146	34	6	20	76	5	.287
1985	Detroit	OF	145	517	69	137	28	4	18	68	0	.265
1986	Detroit	OF	126	403	45	101	21	3	12	53	2	.251
	Totals		1467	5150	747	1429	302	48	166	666	53	.277

ERIC KING 22 6-2 180 — Bats R Throws R

Has the talent to develop into top reliever . . . Worked final 10 games in relief with Tigers and was 3-0 with 1.25 ERA and three saves out of the bullpen, compared to 8-4 and 4.31 in 16 starts . . . Contract purchased from Nashville (AAA) on May 14 . . . Pitched 5⅓ innings of one-hit relief in major-league debut against Texas on May 15 . . . Won first four decisions from May 21 to June 9 . . . Eleven wins were most by Tiger rookie since Dave Rozema's 15 in 1977 . . . Born April 10, 1964, in Oxnard, Cal. . . . Was selected by the Giants in June 1983 draft after outstanding career at Royal High School in Simi Valley, Cal. . . . Went 5-10 with a 3.36 ERA at Clinton (A) in 1984 and was 5-3 with a 2.32 ERA at Shreveport (AA) in 1985, when a sore arm limited him to 15 games . . . In the fall of 1985, Tigers acquired him from the Giants with Dave LaPoint and Matt Nokes for Juan Berenguer, Bob Melvin and Scott Medvin . . . Was 3-2 with a 3.52 ERA in six games at Nashville before moving up to the bigs.

Year	Club	G	IP	W	L	Pct.	SO	BB	H	ERA
1986	Detroit	33	138⅓	11	4	.733	79	63	108	3.51

JACK MORRIS 31 6-3 200 — Bats R Throws R

The major-league leader in victories since 1979 enjoyed his finest season yet, establishing career bests with 21 victories, 3.27 ERA and six shutouts . . . Did not lose after Aug. 21 . . . Won last six decisions . . . Was 14-2 after July 9 . . . Hurled three consecutive shutouts in July, blanking Kansas City, Minnesota and Texas . . . Gave up club-high 40 homers . . . Has led Tigers in innings pitched and victories for eight consecutive seasons . . . Has 140 wins since 1979 . . . Born May 16, 1955, in St. Paul, Minn. . . . Detroit's fifth selection in June 1978 draft . . . Has logged at least 197 innings for eight consecutive years . . . Outspoken critic of Detroit management who reluctantly re-signed with Tigers last winter.

Year	Club	G	IP	W	L	Pct.	SO	BB	H	ERA
1977	Detroit	7	46	1	1	.500	28	23	38	3.72
1978	Detroit	28	106	3	5	.375	48	49	107	4.33
1979	Detroit	27	198	17	7	.708	113	59	179	3.27
1980	Detroit	36	250	16	15	.516	112	87	252	4.18
1981	Detroit	25	198	14	7	.667	97	78	153	3.05
1982	Detroit	37	266⅓	17	16	.515	135	96	247	4.06
1983	Detroit	37	293⅔	20	13	.606	232	83	257	3.34
1984	Detroit	35	240⅓	19	11	.633	148	87	221	3.60
1985	Detroit	35	257	16	11	.593	191	110	212	3.33
1986	Detroit	35	267	21	8	.724	223	82	229	3.27
	Totals	302	2122⅓	144	94	.605	1327	754	1895	3.57

FRANK TANANA 33 6-3 195 **Bats L Throws L**

Born in Detroit on July 3, 1953, Tanana welcomed first full season in Motor City . . . Got off to rousing start in 1986, winning four straight in April . . . Cooled suddenly and dropped three straight May 10 to June 1 . . . Streaky campaign continued when he won five in a row June 7 to Aug. 5 . . . Victim of poor support in number of losses . . . Possessed overpowering fastball early in career . . . Learned to survive on finesse . . . Obtained June 20, 1985, from Texas for Duane James . . . Struck out league-leading 269 batters in 1975 with California . . . Fanned 261 the next year.

Year	Club	G	IP	W	L	Pct.	SO	BB	H	ERA
1973	California	4	26	2	2	.500	22	8	20	3.12
1974	California	39	269	14	19	.424	180	77	262	3.11
1975	California	34	257	16	9	.640	269	73	211	2.63
1976	California	34	288	19	10	.655	261	73	212	2.44
1977	California	31	241	15	9	.625	205	61	201	2.54
1978	California	33	239	18	12	.600	137	60	239	3.65
1979	California	18	90	7	5	.583	46	25	93	3.90
1980	California	32	204	11	12	.478	113	45	223	4.15
1981	Boston	24	141	4	10	.286	78	43	142	4.02
1982	Texas	30	194⅓	7	18	.280	87	55	199	4.21
1983	Texas	29	159⅓	7	9	.438	108	49	144	3.16
1984	Texas	35	246⅓	15	15	.500	141	81	234	3.25
1985	Texas-Detroit	33	215	12	14	.462	159	57	220	4.27
1986	Detroit	32	188⅓	12	9	.571	119	65	196	4.16
	Totals	408	2758⅓	159	153	.510	1925	772	2596	3.40

WILLIE HERNANDEZ 32 6-2 185 Bats L Throws L

Still a capable reliever, but can no longer shoulder bullpen burden alone . . . Converted 24 of 31 save opportunities to lead Tigers in saves for third time in three years with them . . . Finished fourth in AL in saves . . . One of only two pitchers in league with at least 20 saves for three straight years, other being Yankees' Dave Righetti . . . Was booed by hometown fans after terrible August . . . Allowed 10 earned runs in 13⅓ innings for 6.75 ERA . . . Named to All-Star staff for third time . . . Born Nov. 14, 1954, in Aguada, Puerto Rico . . . Obtained from Philadelphia with Dave Bergman for Glenn Wilson and John Wockenfuss on March 24, 1984 . . . Trade was key to 1984 World Championship . . . Screwballer became second Tiger to win Cy Young Award, succeeding in 32 of 33 save situations . . . May be wearing down due to heavy use . . . Has appeared in at least 64 games each of last five years.

Year	Club	G	IP	W	L	Pct.	SO	BB	H	ERA
1977	Chicago (NL)	67	110	8	7	.533	78	28	94	3.03
1978	Chicago (NL)	54	60	8	2	.800	38	35	57	3.75
1979	Chicago (NL)	51	79	4	4	.500	53	39	85	5.01
1980	Chicago (NL)	53	108	1	9	.100	75	45	115	4.42
1981	Chicago (NL)	12	14	0	0	.000	13	8	14	3.86
1982	Chicago (NL)	75	75	4	6	.400	54	24	74	3.00
1983	Chi (NL)-Phil.	74	115⅓	9	4	.692	93	32	109	3.28
1984	Detroit	80	140⅓	9	3	.750	112	36	96	1.92
1985	Detroit	74	106⅔	8	10	.444	76	14	82	2.70
1986	Detroit	64	88⅔	8	7	.533	77	21	87	3.55
	Totals	604	897	59	52	.532	669	282	813	3.30

WALT TERRELL 28 6-2 205 Bats L Throws R

Bulldog on the mound who hates to leave a game . . . Made 30 or more starts for third consecutive year . . . Registered career-high nine complete games with two shutouts . . . No-hit bid against California on Aug. 20 lasted for 8⅔ innings before clean double by rookie Wally Joyner . . . Closed season by winning three straight . . . Up-and-down campaign highlighted by five-game winning streak, part of 6-1 start . . . Unfortunately for Terrell, that was followed by four-game losing streak . . . Best stretch came when he worked three consecutive complete games May 14, 20 and 25 . . . Blanked Seattle and stopped Oakland, 2-1, on four-hitter . . . Hasn't demonstrated more than .500 ability . . . Born May 11, 1958, in Jeffersonville, Ind. . . . Obtained from New York Mets for Howard Johnson on Dec. 7, 1984 . . .

Had clashed with Mets' manager Dave Johnson over his removal in certain situations.

Year	Club	G	IP	W	L	Pct.	SO	BB	H	ERA
1982	New York (NL)	3	21	0	3	.000	8	14	22	3.43
1983	New York (NL)	21	133⅔	8	8	.500	59	55	123	3.57
1984	New York (NL)	33	215	11	12	.478	114	80	232	3.52
1985	Detroit	34	229	15	10	.600	130	95	221	3.85
1986	Detroit	34	217⅓	15	12	.556	93	98	199	4.56
	Totals	125	816	49	45	.521	404	342	797	3.89

TOP PROSPECT

BRUCE FIELDS 26 6-0 185 **Bats L Throws R**

Seems strange to describe this outfielder as a top prospect because he's a nine-year minor leaguer . . . But he showed he's ready for major-league duty by leading American Association with .368 average, netting 141 hits in 383 at-bats . . . Scored 57 runs and knocked in 53 more in 116 games . . . Had just one home run . . . Impressed Tigers in September, batting .279 in 16 games . . . Born Oct. 6, 1960, in Cleveland . . . Tigers' seventh pick in June 1978 draft.

MANAGER SPARKY ANDERSON: Directed Tigers to third-place finish for second straight year . . . Record of 87-75 represented slight improvement from 84-77 mark of 1985 . . . Some discontentment in Detroit following dramatic dropoff from 104-victory World Championship season in '84 . . . Composite major-league record is 1,513-1,122 . . . Has 650-536 record since he took over Tigers on June 14, 1979 . . . Takes great pride in having won World Championships in both leagues . . . Piloted Cincinnati to 863-586 record from 1970-78, winning two World Series, four pennants and five NL West titles . . . Born Feb. 22, 1934, in Bridgewater, S.D. . . . Played in minors for six seasons before joining Phillies as an infielder in 1959 . . . Hit .218 in only major-league season . . . Managed for four years in minors and coached for San Diego in 1969 . . . Beloved by media for his willingness to spout opinions . . . Many players he trumpeted were released soon afterward.

GREATEST ALL-TIME ROOKIE

Mark Fidrych's rookie year in 1976 was a delightful time for the Tigers. "The Bird" made it so.

Fidrych, given his nickname in the minor leagues because he resembled the Sesame Street character, was a joy to fans for his pitching brilliance and his peculiar habits.

Here was a pitcher who talked to the ball, who sprinted to and from the mound, who sank to his knees to groom the soil, who hurried over to teammates to thank them for fine plays. Here was a winner.

In fact, Fidrych's 19 victories represented the highest total by a Detroit rookie in 68 seasons and he lost only nine. The right-hander from Worcester, Mass., became only the second Rookie of the Year in Tigers' history, leading the league in ERA (2.34), complete games (24) and fielding percentage (1.000). Fidrych handled 78 chances flawlessly.

Alas, Fidrych's story ended tragically. He fell victim to a rotator-cuff injury, was limited to 11 starts and a 6-4 mark in 1977 and, in the three ineffective years that followed, he posted a 4-6 record. His career officially ended in 1980, but he was really finished after that one, stunning rookie season.

ALL-TIME TIGER SEASON RECORDS

BATTING: Ty Cobb, .420, 1911
HRs: Hank Greenberg, 58, 1938
RBIs: Hank Greenberg, 183, 1937
STEALS: Ty Cobb, 96, 1915
WINS: Denny McLain, 31, 1968
STRIKEOUTS: Mickey Lolich, 308, 1971

MILWAUKEE BREWERS

TEAM DIRECTORY: Pres.: Allan (Bud) Selig; Exec. VP-GM: Harry Dalton; Asst. GM: Walter Shannon; Spec. Assts. to GM: Dee Fondy, Sal Bando; Farm Dir.: Bruce Manno; Dir. Publ.: Tom Skibosh; Trav. Sec.: Jimmy Bank; Mgr.: Tom Trebelhorn. Home: Milwaukee County Stadium (53,192). Field distances: 315, l.f. line; 362, l.f.; 392, l.c.; 402, c.f.; 392, r.c.; 362, r.f.; 315, r.f. line, Spring training: Chandler, Ariz.

SCOUTING REPORT

HITTING: These Brewers don't remind you of "Harvey's Wallbangers." Milwaukee ranked 10th in the AL in average (.255) and, more significantly, 12th in runs (667) and next-to-last in home runs (127) in 1986.

Rob Deer, who had 33 homers and 86 RBI, will have the pitchers' attention after an eye-opening AL debut season. This slugger must work on reducing his strikeout total after fanning a club-record 179 times last season. The Brewers did add more sock over the winter by obtaining first baseman Greg Brock (.234, 16 homers, 52 RBI) from Los Angeles for pitcher Tim Leary. Brock displaces declining veteran Cecil Cooper (.258, 12, 75), who will be used as a designated hitter.

Veterans Robin Yount (.312, 9, 46), Paul Molitor (.281, 9, 55) and Jim Gantner (.274, 7, 38) remain key figures in the attack. Youngsters to watch include B.J. Surhoff, the first player picked in the June 1985 draft, and Glenn Braggs, who looks to rebound after hitting a disappointing .237 in 58 games.

PITCHING: Screwballing Teddy Higuera (20-11, 2.79, team-record 207 strikeouts) may be among the toughest pitchers in baseball. Juan Nieves (11-12, 4.92) dropped eight straight before winning on the last day of the season in relief. The Brewers' staff led the AL with a 3.88 ERA as of Aug. 29 before weakening and finishing fifth with a 4.01 mark.

Milwaukee was 59-2 when it held the lead after seven innings, a record that speaks well of the bullpen. Revived veteran Mark Clear (5-5, 2.20, 16 saves) and Dan Plesac (10-7, 2.97, 14 saves), a hard-throwing left-hander who made the leap from Double-A ball, are a solid tandem.

FIELDING: The Brewers didn't treat their pitchers well. They made 146 errors in 161 games, including 40 in the last 34 games.

Teddy Higuera went 20-11 with a 2.79 ERA.

Only Seattle and Cleveland had poorer fielding percentages than Milwaukee's .976.

Shortstop Ernest Riles is a major concern after committing 20 errors in 145 games on the heels of 21 errors as a rookie in 1985. New manager Tom Trebelhorn is switching Deer from right field to left and Braggs from left to right.

OUTLOOK: Milwaukee's 77-84 finish drove George Bamberger back into retirement, but help is on the way. The Brewers received Organization-of-the-Year honors for the second straight season, emerging as the only franchise to have all of its minor-league affiliates compile winning records in 1986. Trebelhorn, a substitute teacher in the offseason, will start to reap the talent from the minors, but the Brewers are still a couple of years away from feeling the full impact. In 1987, the growing pains will continue.

MILWAUKEE BREWERS 1987 ROSTER

MANAGER Tom Trebelhorn
Coaches—Andy Etchebarren, Larry Haney, Chuck Hartenstein, Dave Hilton, Tony Muser

PITCHERS

No.	Name	1986 Club	W-L	IP	SO	ERA	B-T	Ht.	Wt.	Born
63	Aldrich, Jay	El Paso	3-3	54	34	3.64	R-R	6-3	210	4/14/61 Alexandria, LA
30	Birkbeck, Mike	Vancouver	12-6	134	81	4.62	R-R	6-2	185	3/10/61 Orrville, OH
		Milwaukee	1-1	22	13	4.50				
29	Bosio, Chris	Vancouver	7-3	67	59	2.28	R-R	6-3	220	4/3/63 Carmichael, CA
		Milwaukee	0-4	35	29	7.01				
34	Ciardi, Mark	Vancouver	9-8	168	106	4.06	R-R	6-0	180	8/19/61 New Brunswick, NJ
25	Clear, Mark	Milwaukee	5-5	74	85	2.20	R-R	6-4	204	5/27/56 Los Angeles, CA
48	Clutterbuck, Bryan	Vancouver	8-5	115	63	4.60	R-R	6-4	225	12/17/59 Detroit, MI
		Milwaukee	0-1	57	38	4.29				
49	Higuera, Ted	Milwaukee	20-11	248	207	2.79	B-L	5-10	178	11/9/58 Mexico
28	Johnson, John Henry	Vancouver	2-0	32	35	0.28	L-L	6-2	210	8/21/56 Houston, TX
		Milwaukee	2-1	44	42	2.66				
35	Jones, Al	Buffalo	2-0	47	31	4.56	R-R	5-11	180	2/10/59 Charleston, MS
		Vancouver	2-0	24	22	1.50				
41	Knudson, Mark	Houston	1-5	43	20	4.22	R-R	6-5	215	10/28/60 Denver, CO
		Tucson	5-5	94	55	3.93				
		Vancouver	1-1	13	8	5.68				
		Milwaukee	0-1	18	9	7.64				
61	Madrid, Alex	El Paso	12-9	158	99	6.02	R-R	6-3	198	4/18/63 Springerville, AZ
32	Murphy, Dan	El Paso	9-2	116	89	4.41	R-R	6-2	195	9/18/64 Artesia, CA
20	Nieves, Juan	Milwaukee	11-12	185	116	4.92	L-L	6-3	175	1/5/65 Puerto Rico
—	Palacios, Vincente	Aguascalientes	5-14	139	121	4.41	R-R	6-3	165	7/19/63 Mexico
37	Plesac, Dan	Milwaukee	10-7	91	75	2.97	L-L	6-5	210	2/4/62 Gary, IN
51	Serna, Ramon	Monterrey	12-8	148	94	3.88	R-R	6-0	189	12/1/62 Mexico
46	Wegman, Bill	Milwaukee	5-12	198	82	5.13	R-R	6-5	200	12/19/62 Cincinnati, OH

CATCHERS

No.	Name	1986 Club	H	HR	RBI	Pct.	B-T	Ht.	Wt.	Born
—	O'Brien, Charlie	Vancouver	2	0	1	.118	R-R	6-2	190	5/1/61 Tulsa, OK
		El Paso	109	15	74	.324				
21	Schroeder, Bill	El Paso	6	1	2	.231	R-R	6-2	200	9/7/58 Baltimore, MD
		Milwaukee	46	7	19	.212				

INFIELDERS

No.	Name	1986 Club	H	HR	RBI	Pct.	B-T	Ht.	Wt.	Born
9	Adduci, Jim	Vancouver	144	4	53	.339	L-L	6-4	200	8/9/59 Chicago, IL
		Milwaukee	1	0	0	.091				
—	Brock, Greg	Los Angeles	76	16	52	.234	L-R	6-3	210	6/14/57 McMinnville, OR
3	Castillo, Juan	Vancouver	14	0	4	.192	B-R	5-11	155	1/25/62 Dominican Republic
		Milwaukee	9	0	5	.167				
15	Cooper, Cecil	Milwaukee	140	12	75	.258	L-L	6-2	190	12/20/49 Brenham, TX
2	Diaz, Edgar	Vancouver	14	0	4	.192	R-R	6-0	160	2/6/64 Puerto Rico
		Milwaukee	3	0	0	.231				
17	Gantner, Jim	Milwaukee	136	7	38	.274	L-R	5-11	175	1/5/54 Eden, WI
32	Kiefer, Steve	Vancouver	114	15	69	.268	R-R	6-0	185	10/13/50 Chicago, IL
		Milwaukee	0	0	0	.000				
23	Meyer, Joey	Vancouver	115	24	98	.258	R-R	6-3	260	5/10/62 Honolulu, HI
4	Molitor, Paul	Milwaukee	123	9	55	.281	R-R	6-0	175	8/22/56 St. Paul, MN
58	Pyznarski, Tim	Las Vegas	153	23	119	.326	R-R	6-2	205	2/4/60 Chicago, IL
		San Diego	10	0	0	.238				
1	Riles, Ernest	Milwaukee	132	9	47	.252	L-R	6-1	180	10/2/60 Bainbridge, GA
13	Robidoux, Billy Joe	Beloit	4	0	2	.250	L-R	6-1	200	1/13/64 Ware, MA
		El Paso	37	10	34	.325				
		Milwaukee	41	1	21	.227				
57	Sveum, Dale	Vancouver	31	1	23	.295	B-R	6-3	185	11/23/63 Richmond, CA
		Milwaukee	78	7	35	.246				

OUTFIELDERS

No.	Name	1986 Club	H	HR	RBI	Pct.	B-T	Ht.	Wt.	Born
26	Braggs, Glenn	Vancouver	117	15	75	.360	R-R	6-3	210	10/17/62 San Bernardino, CA
		Milwaukee	51	4	18	.237				
45	Deer, Rob	Milwaukee	108	33	86	.232	R-R	6-3	210	9/29/60 Orange, CA
16	Felder, Mike	Vancouver	40	1	15	.261	B-R	5-8	160	11/18/62 Richmond, CA
		El Paso	14	0	2	.452				
		Milwaukee	37	1	13	.239				
14	James, Dion	Vancouver	137	6	55	.282	L-L	6-1	170	11/9/62 Philadelphia, PA
28	Manning, Rick	Milwaukee	52	8	27	.254	L-R	6-1	180	9/2/54 Niagara Falls, NY
19	Yount, Robin	Milwaukee	163	9	46	.312	R-R	6-0	180	9/16/55 Danville, IL

BREWER PROFILES

ROBIN YOUNT 31 6-0 180 **Bats R Throws R**

According to new manager Tom Trebelhorn, center fielder played at about 85 percent last season . . . If that was the case, other players would like to have his 85 percent . . . Led club with .312 average . . . Hit .408 in April, .375 through May and .330 through All-Star break . . . Fell off to .247 in July . . . Batted just .248 against left-handers compared to .332 against righties . . . Passed 2,000 career hits . . . Played 1,800th game of career on 31st birthday . . . Born Sept. 16, 1955, in Danville, Ill. . . . Chosen by Brewers in first round (third pick) of June 1973 draft and played only one season in minors . . . Brewers' regular shortstop by age 19 . . . Voted AL MVP in 1982, when he became first shortstop to lead league in slugging percentage and total bases . . . Converted into center fielder due to injury to throwing arm.

Year	Club	Pos.	G	AB	R	H	2B	3B	HR	RBI	SB	Avg.
1974	Milwaukee	SS	107	344	48	86	14	5	3	26	7	.250
1975	Milwaukee	SS	147	558	67	149	28	2	8	52	12	.267
1976	Milwaukee	SS-OF	161	638	59	161	19	3	2	54	16	.252
1977	Milwaukee	SS	154	605	66	174	34	4	4	49	16	.288
1978	Milwaukee	SS	127	502	66	147	23	9	9	71	16	.293
1979	Milwaukee	SS	149	577	72	154	26	5	8	51	11	.267
1980	Milwaukee	SS	143	611	121	179	49	10	23	87	20	.293
1981	Milwaukee	SS	96	377	50	103	15	5	10	49	4	.273
1982	Milwaukee	SS	156	635	129	210	46	12	29	114	14	.331
1983	Milwaukee	SS	149	578	102	178	42	10	17	80	12	.308
1984	Milwaukee	SS	160	624	105	186	27	7	16	80	14	.298
1985	Milwaukee	OF-1B	122	466	76	129	26	3	15	68	10	.277
1986	Milwaukee	OF	140	522	82	163	31	7	9	46	14	.312
	Totals		1811	7037	1043	2019	380	82	153	827	166	.287

ROB DEER 26 6-3 210 **Bats R Throws R**

Made club as a non-roster player in spring training and wound up leading Brewers with 33 home runs and 86 RBI . . . An all-or-nothing slugger who struck out 179 times, breaking Gorman Thomas' club record of 175 set in 1979 . . . Deer is vulnerable to the slider away . . . Batted only .214 against right-handers compared to .279 against left-handers . . . Tied club record with four strikeouts in a game, against Boston's Roger Clemens on June 6 . . . Born Sept. 29, 1960, in Orange, Cal. . . . Obtained from San Francisco on Dec. 18, 1985, for Dean Freeland and Eric Pilkington . . . Right fielder was selected in fourth round of June 1978 draft by San Francisco . . .

Attended Fresno City College . . . Works in his father's construction business in offseason.

Year	Club	Pos.	G	AB	R	H	2B	3B	HR	RBI	SB	Avg.
1984	San Francisco	OF	13	24	5	4	0	0	3	3	1	.167
1985	San Francisco	OF-1B	78	162	22	30	5	1	8	20	0	.185
1986	Milwaukee	OF	134	466	75	108	17	3	33	86	5	.232
	Totals		225	652	102	142	22	4	44	109	6	.218

JIM GANTNER 33 5-11 175 Bats L Throws R

Rebounded from one of worst years of career to complete more typical season . . . Boosted average 20 points to .274 . . . Made only 10 errors . . . Didn't commit an error in first 30 games . . . Enjoyed 42-game errorless stretch from June 29 to Aug. 16 . . . Struggled against left-handers with .219 average compared to .293 against right-handers . . . Put together nine-game batting streak April 19-30 . . . Stroked 1,000th career hit on July 11 against Seattle . . . Second baseman was born Jan. 5, 1954, in Eden, Wis. . . . Picked by Brewers in 12th round of June 1974 draft.

Year	Club	Pos.	G	AB	R	H	2B	3B	HR	RBI	SB	Avg.
1976	Milwaukee	3B	26	69	6	17	1	0	0	7	1	.246
1977	Milwaukee	3B	14	47	4	14	1	0	1	2	2	.298
1978	Milwaukee	2B-3B-SS-1B	43	97	14	21	1	0	1	8	2	.216
1979	Milwaukee	3B-2B-SS-P	70	208	29	59	10	3	2	22	3	.284
1980	Milwaukee	3B-2B-SS	132	415	47	117	21	3	4	40	11	.282
1981	Milwaukee	2B	107	352	35	94	14	1	2	33	3	.267
1982	Milwaukee	2B	132	447	48	132	17	2	4	43	6	.295
1983	Milwaukee	2B	161	603	85	170	23	8	11	74	5	.282
1984	Milwaukee	2B	153	613	61	173	27	1	3	56	6	.282
1985	Milwaukee	2B-3B-SS	143	523	63	133	15	4	5	44	11	.254
1986	Milwaukee	2B	139	497	58	136	25	1	7	38	13	.274
	Totals		1120	3871	450	1066	155	23	40	367	63	.275

ERNEST RILES 26 6-1 180 Bats L Throws R

Suffered sophomore jinx after exciting rookie season . . . Average tumbled 34 points to .252 . . . Brewers were sorely disappointed by that, because he's not a great fielding shortstop . . . Made 20 errors . . . Committed only three errors in first 63 games, but made five in July and six in 25 games in August . . . Hit in 10 straight games May 18-30 . . . Had greatest problems with southpaws, batting .207 against them compared to .265 against right-handers . . . Born Oct. 2, 1960, in Whigham, Ga. . . . Brewers selected him third in secondary phase of January 1981 draft . . . Could do without nickname—"E."

Year	Club	Pos.	G	AB	R	H	2B	3B	HR	RBI	SB	Avg.
1985	Milwaukee	SS	116	448	54	128	12	7	5	45	2	.286
1986	Milwaukee	SS	145	524	69	132	24	2	9	47	7	.252
	Totals		261	972	123	260	36	9	14	92	9	.267

PAUL MOLITOR 30 6-0 175 **Bats R Throws R**

Third baseman has been hampered by injuries throughout career and again was unable to stay healthy . . . Problem this time was severely pulled hamstring that put him on DL from May 10-30 . . . Re-injured leg June 5, requiring another trip to DL . . . Did not come off for good until July 8 . . . Played well when healthy . . . Compiled 12-game hitting streak Aug. 7-19 . . . Hit in 16 of 18 games Aug. 7-27 . . . Stole home against California on May 2, first time a Brewer stole home since 1978 . . . Played in 1,000th game . . . Born Aug. 22, 1956, in St. Paul, Minn. . . . Top pick overall in June 1977 draft . . . Spent only one season in minors . . . Captured Midwest League batting title and MVP award for Burlington (A) in 1977 . . . Excelled in 1982 World Series, batting .355 and collecting five hits in one game against St. Louis.

Year	Club	Pos.	G	AB	R	H	2B	3B	HR	RBI	SB	Avg.
1978	Milwaukee	2B-SS-3B	125	521	73	142	26	4	6	45	30	.273
1979	Milwaukee	2B-SS	140	584	88	188	27	16	9	62	33	.322
1980	Milwaukee	2B-SS-3B	111	450	81	137	29	2	9	37	34	.304
1981	Milwaukee	OF	64	251	45	67	11	0	2	19	10	.267
1982	Milwaukee	3B-SS	160	666	136	201	26	8	19	71	41	.302
1983	Milwaukee	3B	152	608	95	164	28	6	15	47	41	.269
1984	Milwaukee	3B	13	46	3	10	1	0	0	6	1	.217
1985	Milwaukee	3B	140	576	93	171	28	3	10	48	21	.297
1986	Milwaukee	3B	105	437	62	123	24	6	9	55	20	.281
	Totals		1010	4139	676	1203	200	45	79	390	231	.291

GREG BROCK 29 6-3 205 **Bats L Throws R**

Slugging first baseman who never fulfilled big billing in Los Angeles gets fresh start with Brewers . . . Power-poor Milwaukee acquired him from Dodgers for Tim Leary and minor-leaguer Tim Crews in December . . . Disappointing 1986 season included June surgery to remove cartilage from left knee . . . Got off to terrible start, batting .189 in April and .214 in May . . . Heated up in August, batting .300, with four home runs, 15 RBI . . . Belted four homers in as many games in early June

. . . Born June 14, 1957, in McMinnville, Ore. . . . Set club records at Albuquerque (AAA) with 44 homers, 138 RBI in 1982 . . . Replaced long-time Dodger star Steve Garvey in 1983 . . . LA scouting director Ben Wade once labelled him "the best power-hitting prospect Dodgers have had since Duke Snider." . . . Dodgers drafted him in 13th round in 1979.

Year	Club	Pos.	G	AB	R	H	2B	3B	HR	RBI	SB	Avg.
1982	Los Angeles	1B	18	17	1	2	1	0	0	1	0	.118
1983	Los Angeles	1B	146	455	64	102	14	2	20	67	5	.224
1984	Los Angeles	1B	88	271	33	61	6	0	14	34	8	.225
1985	Los Angeles	1B	129	438	64	110	19	0	21	66	4	.251
1986	Los Angeles	1B	115	325	33	76	13	0	16	52	2	.234
	Totals		496	1506	195	351	53	2	71	219	19	.233

TEDDY HIGUERA 28 5-10 178 — Bats S Throws L

Described by AL batting champ Wade Boggs of Boston and Yankees' Don Mattingly as league's toughest left-hander . . . Impossible to dispute that . . . Higuera became third Brewer pitcher to win 20 games, others being Mike Caldwell (22 in 1978) and Jim Colborn (20 in 1973) . . . Established club record with 207 strikeouts, surpassing Marty Pattin's 169 in 1971 . . . Participated in first All-Star Game and allowed one hit in three innings . . . Born Nov. 9, 1958, in Los Mochis, Sinaloa, Mexico . . . Brewers purchased his contract from Juarez of Mexican League . . . Led all pitchers there with 222 innings and 165 strikeouts in 1983 . . . Placed second in AL Rookie-of-the-Year voting in 1985 . . . Almost impossible to beat at County Stadium, where he went 10-3 with 1.79 ERA in 16 games.

Year	Club	G	IP	W	L	Pct.	SO	BB	H	ERA
1985	Milwaukee	32	212⅓	15	8	.652	127	63	186	3.90
1986	Milwaukee	34	248⅓	20	11	.645	207	74	226	2.79
	Totals	66	460⅔	35	19	.648	334	137	412	3.30

JUAN NIEVES 22 6-3 175 — Bats L Throws L

Belief in him as a quality starter remains unshaken despite disastrous second half . . . Suffered eight-game losing streak Aug. 6 to Sept. 27 . . . Received some solace when he won in relief, pitching 3⅓ scoreless innings on last day of season to defeat Toronto . . . Won first major-league game and started five-game winning streak on May 2 with 5-4 defeat of California . . . Next victory was a 10-0 shutout of Seattle . . . Posted three shutouts in all, two against Seattle . . . Was 0-3 in August with 10.42 ERA . . . Born Jan. 5, 1965, in Santurce, Puerto Rico . . . One of most sought-after players in the country when he was signed by Brewers as a free agent in 1983 . . . Attended prep school in Avon, Conn., where he was 19-1 with 1.05 ERA and 288 strikeouts in 196 innings.

Year	Club	G	IP	W	L	Pct.	SO	BB	H	ERA
1986	Milwaukee	35	184⅔	11	12	.478	116	77	224	4.92

DAN PLESAC 25 6-5 210 **Bats L Throws L**

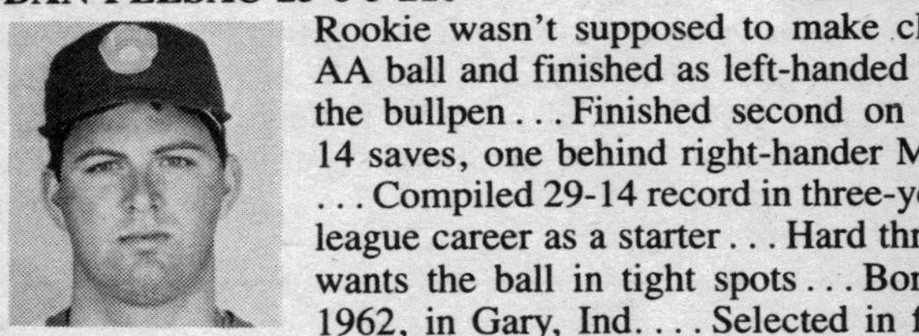

Rookie wasn't supposed to make club out of AA ball and finished as left-handed stopper in the bullpen . . . Finished second on club with 14 saves, one behind right-hander Mark Clear . . . Compiled 29-14 record in three-year minor-league career as a starter . . . Hard thrower who wants the ball in tight spots . . . Born Feb. 4, 1962, in Gary, Ind. . . . Selected in first round of June 1983 draft . . . All-American in basketball and baseball in high school . . . All-American in baseball at North Carolina State.

Year	Club	G	IP	W	L	Pct.	SO	BB	H	ERA
1986	Milwaukee	51	91	10	7	.588	75	29	81	2.97

MARK CLEAR 30 6-4 204 **Bats R Throws R**

Brewers placed trust in Clear, making him No. 1 man in the pen, and he responded . . . Led club with 15 saves and 2.20 ERA . . . Save total matched that of previous three seasons combined . . . ERA was more than a run and a half lower than in 1985 . . . Obtained from Boston for Ed Romero on Dec. 10, 1985 . . . Originally selected by Philadelphia in eighth round of June 1974 draft . . . Nicknamed "Horse" . . . Difference in Clear was ability to get curveball over and an improved fastball . . . Increased workload aided his control . . . Was almost untouchable at County Stadium, going 5-2 with six saves and 0.86 ERA . . . Was 0-3 with nine saves and 3.98 ERA on road . . . Born May 27, 1956, in Los Angeles.

Year	Club	G	IP	W	L	Pct.	SO	BB	H	ERA
1979	California	52	109	11	5	.688	98	68	87	3.63
1980	California	58	106	11	11	.500	105	65	82	3.31
1981	Boston	34	77	8	3	.727	82	51	69	4.09
1982	Boston	55	105	14	9	.609	109	61	92	3.00
1983	Boston	48	96	4	5	.444	81	68	101	6.28
1984	Boston	47	67	8	3	.727	76	70	47	4.03
1985	Boston	41	55⅔	1	3	.250	55	50	45	3.72
1986	Milwaukee	59	73⅔	5	5	.500	85	36	53	2.20
	Totals	394	689⅓	62	44	.585	691	469	576	3.80

TOP PROSPECT

B.J. SURHOFF 22 6-1 198 **Bats L Throws R**
Top pick overall in June 1985 draft is about ready to take over Brewers' full-time catching duties . . . Batted .309 in 115 games with Vancouver (AAA), totaling 141 hits, five homers and 59 RBI . . . Sported .396 slugging percentage and .349 on-base percentage . . . Excellent speed for a catcher . . . Batted .303 as member of 1984 Olympic team . . . Named College Player of the Year in 1985 by *The Sporting News* . . . Set University of North Carolina record with .392 career average . . . Brother, Rich, is in Chicago Cubs' system . . . Father, Dick, played for NBA's New York Knickerbockers . . . Born Aug. 4, 1964, in Bronx, N.Y.

MANAGER TOM TREBELHORN: Signed a one-year contract

to manage Brewers on Oct. 1, succeeding George Bamberger . . . Managed Vancouver (AAA) to Pacific Coast League championship in 1985 . . . Coached first base for Brewers in 1984 under Rene Lachemann . . . Was scheduled to handle Brewers' Helena farm club in Pioneer League in 1986 but became third-base coach after Tony Muser was injured in clubhouse explosion during spring training . . . Born Jan. 27, 1948, in Portland . . . Played baseball and basketball at Portland State . . . All-Conference catcher his senior year . . . Played in the Northwest League in 1971 and 1972 . . . Oakland A's purchased his contract in 1973 and he played two seasons in Oakland system before retiring with .241 career average . . . Has been substitute teacher in Portland, Ore., school system in offseason.

GREATEST ALL-TIME ROOKIE

It is a long way from Los Mochis, Sinaloa, Mexico, to Milwaukee, but that is where fortune has taken Teddy Higuera. And Brewer fans couldn't be happier that he made the trip.

Higuera was *The Sporting News* American League Rookie Pitcher of the Year in 1985 and placed second in overall Rookie-of-the-Year balloting to shortstop Ozzie Guillen of the Chicago White Sox.

After a slow start, Higuera came on to finish at 15-8 with a 3.90 ERA, leading the 71-90 Brewers in victories, starts (30) and shutouts (two) and allowing the fewest hits per nine innings (7.8). His 15 wins also established a club mark for a rookie, besting Bill Parsons' 13 in 1972.

Higuera developed rapidly as his knowledge of the league widened. He was 9-1 with a 3.25 ERA from July 7 to Sept. 11 and he went seven or more innings in 13 of his final 17 starts, going 10-1 with a 2.45 ERA in those games.

Not a bad start for a pitcher who toiled five seasons in the Mexican League before getting his shot at the majors.

ALL-TIME BREWER SEASON RECORDS

BATTING: Cecil Cooper, .352, 1980
HRs: Gorman Thomas, 45, 1979
RBIs: Cecil Cooper, 126, 1983
STEALS: Paul Molitor, 41, 1982, 1983
WINS: Mike Caldwell, 22, 1978
STRIKEOUTS: Ted Higuera, 207, 1986

NEW YORK YANKEES

TEAM DIRECTORY: Principal Owner: George Steinbrenner III; Adm. VP-Treas.: David Weidler; VP-GM: Woody Woodward; VP-Baseball Oper.: Bob Quinn; Dir. Minor League Oper.: Bobby Hofman; Dir. Scouting: Brian Sabean; Dir. Media Rel.: Harvey Greene; Trav. Sec.: Bill Kane; Mgr.: Lou Piniella. Home: Yankee Stadium (57,545). Field distances: 312, l.f. line; 379, l.f.; 411, l.c.; 410, c.f.; 385, r.c.; 310, r.f. line. Spring training: Fort Lauderdale, Fla.

SCOUTING REPORT

HITTING: Only three AL clubs generated more runs than the Yankees' 797, only one posted a higher average than their .271 mark and two had more homers than their 188 in 1986. This hard-to-match attack is highlighted by Don Mattingly (.352, 31 homers, 113 RBI), simply the best player of his time, and Rickey Henderson (.263, 28, 74, 87 stolen bases), one of the best leadoff hitters and base-stealers of all time.

Throw in Dave Winfield (.262, 24, 104) and developing youngsters Dan Pasqua (.293, 16, 45) and Mike Pagliarulo (.238, 28, 71) and it's obvious that the Yankees can get by with a minimal offensive contribution from catcher and shortstop. The signing of Texas free agent Gary Ward (.316, 5, 51 RBI in 105 games) provides a righthanded designated hitter and platoon left fielder to complement lefthanded hitters Claudell Washington (.237, 6, 16 RBI in 54 games) and Pasqua.

PITCHING: The 1986 staff limped home with a 4.11 ERA, the ninth-highest mark in the AL, and kept the Yankees from challenging the Red Sox in the East. However, the Yanks strengthened themselves considerably in the offseason with the acquisition of former Pirate Rick Rhoden (15-12, 2.84), former Phil Charlie Hudson (7-10, 4.94) and former Angel Ron Romanick. Of course, Dennis Rasmussen (18-6, 3.88) must prove his stellar 1986 performance was no fluke. Also, the Yanks must replace likely free-agent defector Ron Guidry (9-12, 3.98).

Dave Righetti (8-8, 2.45) has to be regarded as the game's premier reliever after earning a major-league-record 46 saves. Cecilio Guante (5-2, 3.35, 4 saves), also acquired from the Pirates in the Rhoden deal, should prove a fine addition in the set-up role vacated by the enigmatic Brian Fisher.

FIELDING: Mattingly is a two-time Gold Glove winner at first base, Pagliarulo is on the verge of becoming a Gold Glover at

Dave Righetti set all-time saves record with 46.

third, Willie Randolph is a steady second baseman and Wayne Tolleson an adequate shortstop, although the Yankees are concerned about his ability to sustain a high performance level throughout an entire season. Joel Skinner must prove that he is a major-league hitter, but there is no doubt about his ability as a catcher. Winfield and Henderson are defensive assets and they can chew up ground in right and center respectively.

OUTLOOK: This is a team of stars, but chemistry has been lacking while the Yankees have placed second each of the last two years. Players are unsettled by the involvement of owner George Steinbrenner and by the pressure-filled atmosphere that goes with being a Yankee. The talent is there to improve on last year's 90-72 finish, but, as manager Lou Piniella knows, talent isn't always enough.

NEW YORK YANKEES 1987 ROSTER

MANAGER Lou Piniella

Coaches—Mark Connor, Mike Ferraro, Stump Merrill, Jeff Torborg, Jay Ward

PITCHERS

No.	Name	1986 Club	W-L	IP	SO	ERA	B-T	Ht.	Wt.	Born
68	Arnsberg, Brad	Columbus	8-12	177	96	4.21	R-R	6-4	205	8/20/63 Seattle, WA
		New York (AL)	0-0	8	3	3.38				
43	*Burns, Britt	New York (AL)	Disabled list				R-L	6-5	218	6/8/59 Houston, TX
54	Clements, Pat	Pittsburgh	0-4	61	31	2.80	R-L	6-0	180	2/2/62 McCloud, CA
—	Filson, Pete	Buffalo	14-3	139	80	2.26	B-L	6-2	185	9/28/58 Darby, PA
		Min.-Chi. (AL)	0-1	18	8	6.00				
64	Fulton, Bill	Albany	6-6	80	46	4.73	R-R	6-3	195	10/22/63 Pittsburgh, PA
		Columbus	4-6	75	36	3.84				
38	Guante, Cecilio	Pittsburgh	5-2	78	63	3.35	R-R	6-3	205	2/2/60 Dominican Republic
—	Hudson, Charles	Philadelphia	7-10	144	82	4.94	R-R	6-3	190	3/16/59 Ennis, TX
25	John, Tommy	New York (AL)	5-3	71	28	2.93	L-L	6-3	203	5/22/43 Terre Haute, IN
56	Leiter, Al	Ft. Lauderdale	4-8	118	101	4.05	L-L	6-2	200	10/23/65 Toms River, NJ
39	Niekro, Joe	New York (AL)	9-10	126	59	4.87	R-R	6-1	195	11/7/44 Martins Ferry, OH
47	Pulido, Alfonso	Columbus	5-8	96	28	2.92	L-L	5-11	170	1/23/57 Mexico
		New York (AL)	1-1	31	13	4.70				
45	Rasmussen, Dennis	New York (AL)	18-6	202	131	3.88	L-L	6-7	225	4/18/59 Los Angeles, CA
34	Rhoden, Rick	Pittsburgh	15-12	254	159	2.84	R-R	6-4	203	5/16/53 Boynton Beach, FL
19	Righetti, Dave	New York (AL)	8-8	107	83	2.45	L-L	6-3	198	11/28/58 San Jose, CA
28	Scurry, Rod	New York (AL)	1-2	39	36	3.66	L-L	6-2	180	3/17/56 Sacramento, CA
43	Stoddard, Tim	San Diego	1-3	45	47	3.77	R-R	6-7	253	1/24/53 East Chicago, IN
		New York (AL)	4-1	49	34	3.83				
35	Tewksbury, Bob	Columbus	1-0	10	4	2.70	R-R	6-4	200	11/30/60 Concord, NH
		New York (AL)	9-5	130	49	3.31				

CATCHERS

No.	Name	1986 Club	H	HR	RBI	Pct.	B-T	Ht.	Wt.	Born
58	Espino, Juan	Columbus	54	5	21	.302	R-R	6-1	190	3/16/56 Dominican Republic
		New York (AL)	6	0	5	.162				
27	Lombardi, Phil	Columbus	81	8	28	.292	R-R	6-2	200	2/20/63 Abilene, TX
		New York (AL)	10	2	6	.278				
59	Lyden, Mitch	Albany	48	8	29	.302	R-R	6-3	200	12/14/64 Portland, OR
		Columbus	0	0	0	.000				
12	Skinner, Joel	Chi. (AL)-NY (AL)	73	5	37	.232	R-R	6-4	204	2/21/61 La Jolla, CA

INFIELDERS

No.	Name	1986 Club	H	HR	RBI	Pct.	B-T	Ht.	Wt.	Born
61	Destrade, Orestes	Columbus	99	19	56	.276	B-R	6-4	210	5/8/62 Cuba
23	Mattingly, Don	New York (AL)	238	31	113	.352	L-L	5-11	185	4/20/61 Evansville, IN
13	Pagliarulo, Mike	New York (AL)	120	28	71	.238	L-R	6-2	195	3/15/60 Medford, MA
30	Randolph, Willie	New York (AL)	136	5	50	.276	R-R	5-11	166	7/6/54 Holly Hill, SC
—	Sakata, Lenn	Oakland	12	0	5	.353	R-R	5-9	160	6/8/53 Honolulu, HI
2	Tolleson, Wayne	Chi. (AL)-NY (AL)	126	3	43	.265	B-R	5-9	160	9/22/55 Spartanburg, SC
26	Zuvella, Paul	Rich.-Col.	101	2	31	.302	R-R	6-0	178	10/31/58 San Mateo, CA
		New York (AL)	4	0	2	.083				

OUTFIELDERS

No.	Name	1986 Club	H	HR	RBI	Pct.	B-T	Ht.	Wt.	Born
60	Buhner, Jay	Ft. Lauderdale	42	7	31	.304	R-R	6-3	205	8/13/64 Louisville, KY
46	Cotto, Henry	Columbus	89	7	48	.248	R-R	6-2	178	1/5/61 Bronx, NY
		New York (AL)	17	1	6	.213				
24	Henderson, Rickey	New York (AL)	160	28	74	.263	R-L	5-10	195	12/25/58 Chicago, IL
53	Hughes, Keith	Albany	99	7	37	.307	L-L	6-3	205	9/12/63 Bryn Mawr, PA
		Columbus	1	0	0	.125				
57	Kelly, Roberto	Albany	87	2	43	.291	R-R	6-2	185	10/1/64 Panama
33	Kittle, Ron	Chi. (AL)-NY (AL)	82	21	60	.218	R-R	6-4	220	1/5/58 Gary, IN
21	Pasqua, Dan	Columbus	32	6	20	.291	L-L	6-0	203	10/17/61 Yonkers, NY
		New York (AL)	82	16	45	.293				
—	Ward, Gary	Texas	120	5	51	.316	R-R	6-2	202	12/6/53 Los Angeles, CA
18	Washington, Claudell	Atlanta	37	5	14	.270	L-L	6-0	190	8/31/54 Los Angeles, CA
		New York (AL)	32	6	16	.237				
31	Winfield, Dave	New York (AL)	148	24	104	.262	R-R	6-6	220	10/3/51 St. Paul, MN

*Free agent at press time listed with 1986 team

YANKEE PROFILES

DON MATTINGLY 25 5-11 185 Bats L Throws L

Established Yankee records with 238 hits, breaking mark of 231 set by Hall of Famer Earle Combs, and with 53 doubles, breaking Lou Gehrig's standard by one . . . Both records had stood since 1927 . . . Produced 200 hits for third consecutive season . . . Only other Yankee to do that was Gehrig, 1930-32 . . . Put together longest hitting streak in AL, career-high 24 games . . . Batted .430 (43-for-97) in that stretch . . . His .352 batting average left him five points short of Boston's Wade Boggs . . . His pursuit of batting title was hurt by Boggs' decision to sit out last four games due to injured right hamstring . . . First baseman became a left-handed third baseman for three games as an emergency fill-in . . . Turned first chance into a double play . . . Born April 20, 1961, in Evansville, Ind., and still lives there . . . Selected by New York Yankees in 19th round of June 1979 draft . . . In 1984, his first full major-league season, he became first Yankee to win batting championship since Mickey Mantle in 1956, finishing with .343 average, three points ahead of teammate Dave Winfield . . . Was AL MVP in 1985 . . . No one way to pitch to him. Tends to study first pitch and adjust from there . . . Only area for improvement is base-running . . . Won second Gold Glove in 1986.

Year	Club	Pos.	G	AB	R	H	2B	3B	HR	RBI	SB	Avg.
1982	New York (AL)	OF-1B	7	12	0	2	0	0	0	1	0	.167
1983	New York (AL)	OF-1B-2B	91	279	34	79	15	4	4	32	0	.283
1984	New York (AL)	1B-OF	153	603	91	207	44	2	23	110	1	.343
1985	New York (AL)	1B	159	652	107	211	48	3	35	145	2	.324
1986	New York (AL)	1B	162	677	117	238	53	2	31	113	0	.352
	Totals		572	2223	349	737	160	11	93	401	3	.332

RICKEY HENDERSON 28 5-10 195 Bats R Throws L

One of the premier leadoff hitters in history . . . With league-leading 130 runs, he went above century mark for fifth consecutive season and sixth time in seven full major-league campaigns . . . Only interruption was strike-shortened 1981 . . . Paced AL in stolen bases with 87, breaking own Yankee record by seven . . . Has led AL in that category since start of career . . . Center fielder set career high in home runs for third consecutive year with 28 . . . Broke own AL record for leadoff homers with nine, two shy of major-league mark recorded by Bobby Bonds with San

Francisco in 1973 . . . Smashed Lou Brock's single-season stolen-base record with 130 thefts in 1982 . . . As great as Henderson is, feeling persists he could be better . . . Increasingly careless on base-paths . . . Born Christmas Day, 1958, in Chicago . . . Selected by Oakland in fourth round of June 1976 draft . . . Acquired from Oakland with Bert Bradley for Jay Howell, Jose Rijo, Eric Plunk, Tim Birtsas and Stan Javier on Dec. 8, 1984.

Year	Club	Pos.	G	AB	R	H	2B	3B	HR	RBI	SB	Avg.
1979	Oakland.	OF	89	351	49	96	13	3	1	26	33	.274
1980	Oakland.	OF	158	591	111	179	22	4	9	53	100	.303
1981	Oakland.	OF	108	423	89	135	18	7	6	35	56	.319
1982	Oakland.	OF	149	536	119	143	24	4	10	51	130	.267
1983	Oakland.	OF	145	513	105	150	25	7	9	48	108	.292
1984	Oakland.	OF	142	502	113	147	27	4	16	58	66	.293
1985	New York (AL)	OF	143	547	146	172	28	5	24	72	80	.314
1986	New York (AL)	OF	153	608	130	160	31	5	28	74	87	.263
	Totals		1087	4071	862	1182	188	39	103	417	660	.290

WILLIE RANDOLPH 32 5-11 166 Bats R Throws R

Became club's all-time leader in games played at second base with 1,459 . . . Co-captain with Ron Guidry . . . With 232 stolen bases, he needs one to tie Roy White for second on all-time Yankee list . . . Finished strong after an unusually shaky first half . . . Guilty of team-high 15 errors in first 81 games . . . Four-time All-Star still turns double play better than anyone . . . Netted nine game-winning RBI, including one in each of his last two starts . . . Fifty RBI represented his best total since he had 61 in 1979 . . . Enjoyed 33 multiple-hit games . . . Born July 6, 1954, in Holly Hill, S.C. . . . Grew up in Brownsville section of Brooklyn, N.Y. . . . Seventh-round draft choice of Pittsburgh in June 1972 . . . Yankees acquired him from Pittsburgh with pitchers Ken Brett and Dock Ellis for pitcher Doc Medich on Dec. 11, 1975 . . . Received James P. Dawson Award as top rookie in Yankee camp in 1976.

Year	Club	Pos.	G	AB	R	H	2B	3B	HR	RBI	SB	Avg.
1975	Pittsburgh	2B-3B	30	61	9	10	1	0	0	3	1	.164
1976	New York (AL) . .	2B	125	430	59	115	15	4	1	40	37	.267
1977	New York (AL) . .	2B	147	551	91	151	28	11	4	40	13	.274
1978	New York (AL) . .	2B	134	499	87	139	18	6	3	42	36	.279
1979	New York (AL) . .	2B	153	574	98	155	15	13	5	61	33	.270
1980	New York (AL) . .	2B	138	513	99	151	23	7	7	46	30	.294
1981	New York (AL) . .	2B	93	357	59	83	14	3	2	24	14	.232
1982	New York (AL) . .	2B	144	553	85	155	21	4	3	36	16	.280
1983	New York (AL) . .	2B	104	420	73	117	21	1	2	38	12	.279
1984	New York (AL) . .	2B	142	564	86	162	24	2	2	31	10	.287
1985	New York (AL) . .	2B	143	497	75	137	21	2	5	40	16	.276
1986	New York (AL) . .	2B	141	492	76	136	15	2	5	50	15	.276
	Totals		1494	5511	897	1511	216	55	39	451	233	.274

DAVE WINFIELD 35 6-6 220 **Bats R Throws R**

Hit career-low .262, 22 points below career average entering season . . . Never fully recovered from .222 first half . . . Despite disturbing average, he finished with 24 home runs and 104 RBI . . . Surpassed 100 RBI for fifth consecutive season . . . Last Yankee to enjoy so many consecutive RBI seasons was Joe DiMaggio, who ran off seven straight from 1936-42 . . . Became 54th player to achieve 300 home runs with two-run blast against Seattle on Aug. 20 . . . Ten-time All-Star has had flaps with owner George Steinbrenner, who seeks more clutch production from him . . . Appeared to lose a step last season, although he remained an outstanding right fielder . . . Unorthodox, undisciplined hitter who will chase bad breaking balls . . . Born Oct. 3, 1951, in St. Paul, Minn. . . . Selected by San Diego in first round (fourth pick) of June 1969 draft . . . Signed 10-year, $23-million pact as free agent with Yankees on Dec. 15, 1980 . . . Batted career-high .340 in 1984, losing race to teammate Don Mattingly on last day . . . Heads Winfield Foundation, which performs various community services.

Year	Club	Pos.	G	AB	R	H	2B	3B	HR	RBI	SB	Avg.
1973	San Diego	OF-1B	56	141	9	39	4	1	3	12	0	.277
1974	San Diego	OF	145	498	57	132	18	4	20	75	9	.265
1975	San Diego	OF	143	509	74	136	20	2	15	76	23	.267
1976	San Diego	OF	137	492	81	139	26	4	13	69	26	.283
1977	San Diego	OF	157	615	104	169	29	7	25	92	16	.275
1978	San Diego	OF-1B	158	587	88	181	30	5	24	97	21	.308
1979	San Diego	OF	159	597	97	184	27	10	34	118	15	.308
1980	San Diego	OF	162	558	89	154	25	6	20	87	23	.276
1981	New York (AL) . .	OF	105	388	52	114	25	1	13	68	11	.294
1982	New York (AL) . .	OF	140	539	84	151	24	8	37	106	5	.280
1983	New York (AL) . .	OF	152	598	99	169	26	8	32	116	15	.283
1984	New York (AL) . .	OF	141	567	106	193	34	4	19	100	6	.340
1985	New York (AL) . .	OF	155	633	105	174	34	6	26	114	19	.275
1986	New York (AL) . .	OF	154	565	90	148	31	5	24	104	6	.262
	Totals		1964	7287	1135	2083	353	71	305	1234	195	.286

DAN PASQUA 25 6-0 203 **Bats L Throws L**

Continued to progress as he seeks to establish himself as an everyday player . . . Lost his spot on club with .104 average in spring training . . . Was recalled from Columbus (AAA) on May 18 after batting .291 with six homers and 20 RBI . . . Above-average outfielder with powerful arm . . . Showed more patience at the plate, leading to a jump in average . . . Must improve concentration, especially on basepaths . . . Yanks are concerned about his tendency to gain weight quickly . . . Born Oct.

17, 1961, in Yonkers, N.Y. . . . Yankees' third-round pick in June 1982 draft . . . Outstanding minor-league career highlighted by 1985 campaign, when he was named International League Rookie of the Year and MVP . . . Batted .321 with 18 homers and 69 RBI with Columbus . . . Appalachian League Player of the Year in 1982.

Year	Club	Pos.	G	AB	R	H	2B	3B	HR	RBI	SB	Avg.
1985	New York (AL)	OF	60	148	17	31	3	1	9	25	0	.209
1986	New York (AL)	OF	102	280	44	82	17	0	16	45	2	.293
	Totals		162	428	61	113	20	1	25	70	2	.264

MIKE PAGLIARULO 27 6-2 195 Bats L Throws R

A potentially great season was spoiled by a late-season swoon . . . Collected 18 home runs, 40 RBI in first half . . . Did not hit a home run after Aug. 24 . . . Drought covered 99 at-bats and 31 games . . . Ended with six hits in last 56 at-bats . . . An extremely hard worker who appeared to drive himself to exhaustion . . . Twice took batting practice after games . . . Too aggressive at the plate sometimes . . . Was platooned at third base to start the season after poor spring training . . . Still must prove he can handle left-handers . . . Born March 15, 1960, in Medford, Mass. . . . Selected by Yankees in sixth round of June 1981 draft . . . Father, Charles, was an infielder in Chicago Cubs' organization . . . An exceptional fielder, prompting comparisons to former Yankee third baseman Graig Nettles . . . Suffered broken nose when he was hit by fastball from Oakland's Curt Young on June 1 . . . Sat out one game, then homered in each of next three.

Year	Club	Pos.	G	AB	R	H	2B	3B	HR	RBI	SB	Avg.
1984	New York (AL)	3B	67	201	24	48	15	3	7	34	0	.239
1985	New York (AL)	3B	138	380	55	91	16	2	19	62	0	.239
1986	New York (AL)	3B	149	504	71	120	24	3	28	71	4	.238
	Totals		354	1085	150	259	55	8	54	167	4	.239

DAVE RIGHETTI 28 6-3 198 Bats L Throws L

Dispelled lingering doubts about conversion into a reliever by posting major-league record 46 saves . . . Dan Quisenberry (1983) and Bruce Sutter (1984) had shared the mark with 45 . . . Righetti reached 46 by preserving wins in both games of a doubleheader against Boston at Fenway Park on next-to-last day of season . . . Third on all-time Yankee list with 107 saves . . . Made switch to bullpen in 1984 . . . Was reluctant to do so with memory of July 4, 1983, no-hitter against Boston at Yankee Stadium still fresh . . . Righetti's no-hitter represented first by Yankee pitcher since Don Larsen's perfect game in 1956 World Series . . . Named to All-Star staff for first time . . . Extremely confident pitcher who challenges hitters . . . Born Nov. 28, 1958, in San Jose, Cal. . . . Father, Leo, was Yankee minor-league shortstop . . . First time dad saw son pitch was when Yanks clinched 1981 AL Championship Series . . . Selected by Texas in first round (ninth pick) of January 1977 draft . . . Acquired from Texas on Nov. 10, 1978, as key man in 10-player deal . . . Named AL Rookie of the Year in 1981.

Year	Club	G	IP	W	L	Pct.	SO	BB	H	ERA
1979	New York (AL)	3	17	0	1	.000	13	10	10	3.71
1981	New York (AL)	15	105	8	4	.667	89	38	75	2.06
1982	New York (AL)	33	183	11	10	.524	163	108	155	3.79
1983	New York (AL)	31	217	14	8	.636	169	67	194	3.44
1984	New York (AL)	64	96⅓	5	6	.455	90	37	79	2.34
1985	New York (AL)	74	107	12	7	.632	92	45	96	2.78
1986	New York (AL)	74	106⅔	8	8	.500	83	35	88	2.45
	Totals	294	832	58	44	.569	699	340	697	3.01

DENNIS RASMUSSEN 27 6-7 225 Bats L Throws L

Finally came into his own, doubling his career high with 18 victories . . . Finished second in the league to Boston's Roger Clemens with .750 winning percentage . . . Led Yanks with 31 starts and 202 innings . . . Missed two turns after being struck by a line drive off bat of Texas' Toby Harrah on July 22, suffering severe bruise above left elbow . . . Won seven straight from June 14 to July 22 . . . Streak highlighted by first major-league shutout, an 8-0 three-hitter over Chicago . . . Developed poise and maturity . . . Wisely threw more fastballs and fewer damaging slow curves last season . . . Left with dislocated pinky in last start . . . Spent most of 1985 season with Columbus (AAA) after 0-3 start . . . Didn't get along with then-manager Billy Martin . . . Selected by California in first round (17th pick) of June 1980 draft . . . Yanks twice traded for him, the second time acquiring Rasmussen from San Diego for Graig Nettles and Darin Cloninger on March 30, 1984 . . . Born April 18, 1959, in Los Angeles . . . Played basketball at Creighton, which enabled him to oppose Indiana State's Larry Bird.

Year	Club	G	IP	W	L	Pct.	SO	BB	H	ERA
1983	San Diego	4	13⅔	0	0	.000	13	8	10	1.98
1984	New York (AL)	24	147⅔	9	6	.600	110	60	127	4.57
1985	New York (AL)	22	101⅔	3	5	.375	63	42	97	3.98
1986	New York (AL)	31	202	18	6	.750	131	74	160	3.88
	Totals	81	465	30	17	.638	317	184	394	4.06

Rickey Henderson led AL in runs and stolen bases.

JOE NIEKRO 42 6-1 195 **Bats R Throws R**

Suffered disappointing campaign after being re-signed as free agent to three-year contract... First blow came in spring training, when Yankees released his brother, Phil... Never recovered emotionally from that... Won first four decisions for best start of career... Was 7-3 on June 10 when season suddenly soured... Niekro won once from June 10 until Aug. 30... Later revealed he had developed sore shoulder in June . . . Injury was diagnosed as frayed rotator cuff . . . Failed to work as much as six innings in any of last 12 starts . . . Generally fell behind hitters with knuckleball and was hurt by fastball and slider . . . Did not pitch after Sept. 6 . . . This 213-game winner failed to finish in double figures in victories for only second time in last 10 years . . . Winning pitcher for Houston in one-game NL West playoff against Los Angeles in 1980 . . . Was runnerup in NL Cy Young Award balloting in 1979 . . . Born Nov. 7, 1944, in Martins Ferry, Ohio . . . Was third-round draft choice of the Cubs in June 1966.

Year	Club	G	IP	W	L	Pct.	SO	BB	H	ERA
1967	Chicago (NL)	35	170	10	7	.588	77	32	171	3.34
1968	Chicago (NL)	34	177	14	10	.583	65	59	204	4.32
1969	Chi. (NL)-S.D.	41	221	8	18	.308	62	51	237	3.71
1970	Detroit	38	213	12	13	.480	101	72	221	4.06
1971	Detroit	31	122	6	7	.462	43	49	136	4.50
1972	Detroit	18	47	3	2	.600	24	8	62	3.83
1973	Atlanta	20	24	2	4	.333	12	11	23	4.13
1974	Atlanta	27	43	3	2	.600	31	18	36	3.56
1975	Houston	40	88	6	4	.600	54	39	79	3.07
1976	Houston	36	118	4	8	.333	77	56	107	3.36
1977	Houston	44	181	13	8	.619	101	64	155	3.03
1978	Houston	35	203	14	14	.500	97	73	190	3.86
1979	Houston	38	264	21	11	.656	119	107	221	3.00
1980	Houston	37	256	20	12	.625	127	79	268	3.55
1981	Houston	24	166	9	9	.500	77	47	150	2.82
1982	Houston	35	270	17	12	.586	130	64	224	2.47
1983	Houston	38	263⅔	15	14	.517	152	101	238	3.48
1984	Houston	38	248⅓	16	12	.571	127	89	223	3.04
1985	Houston	32	213	9	12	.429	117	99	197	3.72
1985	New York (AL)	3	12⅓	2	1	.667	4	8	14	5.84
1986	New York (AL)	25	125⅔	9	10	.474	59	63	139	4.87
	Totals	670	3426	213	190	.529	1656	1189	3295	3.50

RICK RHODEN 33 6-4 203 **Bats R Throws R**

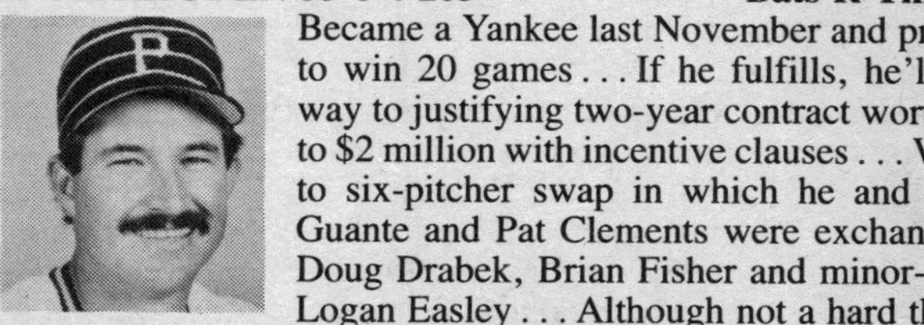

Became a Yankee last November and promised to win 20 games . . . If he fulfills, he'll be on way to justifying two-year contract worth close to $2 million with incentive clauses . . . Was key to six-pitcher swap in which he and Cecilio Guante and Pat Clements were exchanged for Doug Drabek, Brian Fisher and minor-leaguer Logan Easley . . . Although not a hard thrower, he has a good fastball that some protest he scuffs . . . Giant catcher Bob Brenly suggested umpires allow him to take a work bench to mound . . . Eight-year Pirate was NL Pitcher of the Month for May with 5-1 record and 1.99 ERA . . . Made All-Star team and followed with 5-1, 2.73 August en route to 15-12, 2.84 for the year . . . Born May 16, 1953, in Boynton Beach, Fla. . . . Wore leg brace as youngster . . . First-round draft pick of Dodgers in June 1971 . . . Traded to Bucs in 1979 for Jerry Reuss.

Year	Club	G	IP	W	L	Pct.	SO	BB	H	ERA
1974	Los Angeles	4	9	1	0	1.000	7	4	5	2.00
1975	Los Angeles	26	99	3	3	.500	40	32	94	3.09
1976	Los Angeles	27	181	12	3	*.800	77	53	165	2.98
1977	Los Angeles	31	216	16	10	.615	122	63	223	3.75
1978	Los Angeles	30	165	10	8	.556	79	51	160	3.65
1979	Pittsburgh	1	5	0	1	.000	2	2	5	7.20
1980	Pittsburgh	20	127	7	5	.583	70	40	133	3.83
1981	Pittsburgh	21	136	9	4	.692	76	53	147	3.90
1982	Pittsburgh	35	230⅓	11	14	.440	128	70	239	4.14
1983	Pittsburgh	36	244⅓	13	13	.500	153	68	256	3.09
1984	Pittsburgh	33	238⅓	14	9	.609	136	62	216	2.72
1985	Pittsburgh	35	213⅓	10	15	.400	128	69	254	4.47
1986	Pittsburgh	34	253⅔	15	12	.556	159	76	211	2.84
	Totals	333	2118	121	97	.555	1177	643	2108	3.48

TOP PROSPECT

SCOTT NIELSEN 28 6-1 190 Bats R Throws R

Will receive a long look in spring training after mixed 1986 results . . . Contract purchased from Columbus on July 4, following 4-0 start in rehabilitation assignment at Fort Lauderdale (A) and 9-3 mark at Columbus (AAA) . . . Won first two major-league starts, including rare shutout at Minnesota's Metrodome on July 12 . . . Then was routed in three straight starts, permitting 25 earned runs in 7⅓ innings . . . Optioned to Columbus on July 30 . . . Pitched well after recall in September, winning last two starts, including five-hit shutout of Boston . . . Wound up 4-4 with 4.02 ERA as Yank . . . Born Dec. 18, 1958, in Salt Lake City, Utah . . . Sixth-round choice of Seattle in June 1983 draft . . . Acquired by Yankees from Seattle with Eric Parent for Larry Milbourne on Feb. 14, 1984.

MANAGER LOU PINIELLA: Stepped into the most difficult job in baseball as a rookie manager and did well, piloting Yankees to 90-72 record . . . Despite minimal contact with George Steinbrenner for one long stretch and uncertainty over whether he'd be retained, he received a two-year contract and substantial raise over his $200,000, first-year salary in October . . . Showed more patience with starting pitchers as year progressed . . . Injuries to pitching staff forced him to start five rookies at one time or another . . . Went through six shortstops and four catchers . . . Got effort from his players to the end as Yanks swept

a season-ending four-game series in Boston to secure second straight second-place finish . . . Piniella didn't go to a set lineup until early August and admitted that was too late . . . Retired as player on June 17, 1984, with .291 average in 1,747 games . . . Named AL Rookie of the Year for Kansas City in 1969 . . . Outfielder was traded to Yankees with Ken Wright for Lindy McDaniel before 1974 season . . . Spent last 11 years with New York, batting .295 . . . Hit .305 in five AL Championship Series, .319 in four World Series . . . Known as "Sweet Lou" by fans, who responded to his fiery nature . . . Born Aug. 28, 1943, in Tampa, Fla.

GREATEST ALL-TIME ROOKIE

He was one of nine children born to an immigrant fisherman from Southern Italy, but the smell of fish nauseated him. Joe DiMaggio made sure he didn't have to spend his life on a fishing boat. His way out was the baseball field.

When the Yankees bought him from the San Francisco Seals of the Pacific Coast League in 1936 for $25,000 and five minor leaguers, DiMaggio brought with him a record of having hit safely in 61 consecutive games. But injuries made him a question mark to most major-league teams.

For the Yankees, he was a steal. After missing the first 17 games because he had burned himself under a diathermy machine, the 21-year-old rookie center fielder went on to hit .323, drive in 125 runs and belt 29 homers.

Afield, right from the beginning, his trademark was making the hardest catches look easy with his grace.

DiMaggio won the home-run crown in his second season, 1937, with 46 homers and gained batting titles in 1939 and 1940 with marks of .381 and .352, respectively, in the course of a Hall-of-Fame career that ended in 1951.

He is best remembered, of course, for the batting streak that extended from May 15 through July 16, 1941. Fifty-six games. It's one record that may never be broken.

ALL-TIME YANKEE SEASON RECORDS

BATTING: Babe Ruth, .393, 1923
HRs: Roger Maris, 61, 1961
RBIs: Lou Gehrig, 184, 1931
STEALS: Rickey Henderson, 87, 1986
WINS: Jack Chesbro, 41, 1904
STRIKEOUTS: Ron Guidry, 248, 1978

TORONTO BLUE JAYS

TEAM DIRECTORY: Chairman: R. Howard Webster; Vice-Chairman/Chief Exec. Off: N.E. (Peter) Hardy; Exec. VP-Baseball: Pat Gillick; VP-Bus. Oper.: Paul Beeston; VP-Baseball: Al LaMacchia; VP-Baseball: Bob Mattick; VP-Finance: Bob Nicholson; Dir. Pub. Rel.: Howard Starkman; Trav. Sec.: Ken Carson; Mgr.: Jimy Williams. Home: Exhibition Stadium (43,737). Field distances: 330, l.f. line; 375, l.c.; 400, c.f.; 375, r.c.; 330, r.f. line. Spring training: Dunedin, Fla.

SCOUTING REPORT

HITTING: The Blue Jays' slip from the top of the AL East in 1986 couldn't be attributed to a lack of offensive production. They ranked second to Cleveland in the AL in runs scored with 809, ranked fourth in batting average at .269 and fourth in home runs with 181.

When you think of the Toronto lineup, outfielders Jesse Barfield, Lloyd Moseby and George Bell spring to mind. That trio of young sluggers produced a total of 92 homers and 302 RBI last season. Barfield paced the AL with a career-high 40 homers, placed second in the league in slugging percentage at .559 and hit .289. He and Bell both set a club record by driving in 108 runs

Jesse Barfield showed Blue Jays the way with 40 homers.

in 1986. Bell, who batted .309 with 31 homers, also set a club mark with 15 game-winning RBI. Moseby (.253, 21 homers, 86 RBI) is no slouch at the plate, either.

Tony Fernandez, another big offensive weapon, set a record for major-league shortstops with 213 hits en route to a .310 average and a seventh-place finish in the AL batting race. Fernandez' lone weakness as a table-setter was his inability to draw many walks (27 in 727 plate appearances), but his above-average power (10 homers, 65 RBI) more than compensated for that shortcoming.

The production of the third-base platoon, Garth Iorg (.260, 3, 44) and Rance Mulliniks (.259, 11, 45), dipped somewhat. The Blue Jays are hoping Cecil Fielder can put up some decent numbers as the DH.

PITCHING: Dave Stieb makes or breaks this staff. Last year, he broke it. Stieb dropped his first six decisions and pitched so poorly that the release date of his autobiography, *Tomorrow, I'll Be Perfect*, was delayed. The right-hander earned a career-low seven victories against 12 defeats and his ERA ballooned to a career-high 4.74.

Right-hander Jim Clancy (14-14, 3.94) failed to fill the void, dropping his last seven decisions. However, Jimmy Key (14-11, 3.57) and John Cerutti (9-4, 4.15) proved to be capable left-handers. Right-handers Tom Henke (9-5, 3.35, 27 saves) and Mark Eichhorn (14-6, 1.72, 10 saves) are formidable in the bullpen.

FIELDING: The Blue Jays need only to repeat their steady performance of last season, when they paced the AL with a .984 fielding percentage. Their 100 errors in 1986 represented the lowest total for a full season since Baltimore committed 95 in 1980.

Barfield was guilty of only three errors, topped AL outfielders with 20 assists and won a Gold Glove in right. Left fielder Bell was runnerup to Barfield with 17 assists and Fernandez led AL shortstops in fielding percentage at .983 and won his first Gold Glove.

OUTLOOK: After slipping 13 games off their 99-victory pace of 1985, when they won their first division title, the Blue Jays may be ready to win again. Last season, they lost 18 of their first 30 games under rookie manager Jimy Williams, but then became a contender. The performances of first baseman Willie Upshaw (.251, 9, 60) and second baseman Damaso Garcia (.281, 6, 46) have been declining. But, if Stieb regains his form as one of the game's premier pitchers, the Blue Jays could be playing baseball into October this season.

TORONTO BLUE JAYS 1987 ROSTER

MANAGER Jimy Williams
Coaches—Cito Gaston, John McLaren, Billy Smith, John Sullivan, Al Widmar

PITCHERS

No.	Name	1986 Club	W-L	IP	SO	ERA	B-T	Ht.	Wt.	Born
32	Aquino, Luis	Syracuse	3-7	84	60	2.88	R-R	6-1	175	5/19/65 Puerto Rico
		Toronto	1-1	11	5	6.35				
36	Caudill, Bill	Toronto	2-4	36	32	6.19	R-R	6-1	210	7/13/56 Santa Monica, CA
18	Clancy, Jim	Toronto	14-14	219	126	3.94	R-R	6-4	215	12/18/55 Chicago, IL
55	Cerutti, John	Syracuse	1-3	44	22	4.12	L-L	6-2	195	4/28/60 Albany, NY
		Toronto	9-4	145	89	4.15				
25	Davis, Steve	Syracuse	5-7	105	80	5.59	L-L	6-1	183	8/4/60 San Antonio, TX
		Toronto	0-0	4	5	17.18				
38	Eichhorn, Mark	Toronto	14-6	157	166	1.72	R-R	6-3	200	11/21/60 San Jose, CA
39	Gordon, Don	Syracuse	8-5	109	62	2.89	R-R	6-1	175	10/10/59 New York, NY
		Toronto	0-1	22	13	7.06				
50	Henke, Tom	Toronto	9-5	91	118	3.35	R-R	6-5	215	12/21/57 Kansas City, MO
33	Johnson, Joe	Atlanta	6-7	87	49	4.97	R-R	6-2	195	10/30/61 Brookline, MA
		Toronto	7-2	88	39	3.89				
22	Key, Jimmy	Toronto	14-11	232	141	3.57	R-L	6-1	185	4/22/61 Huntsville, AL
46	Lavelle, Gary	Toronto	Disabled list				R-L	6-1	217	1/3/49 Scranton, PA
—	Mesa, Jose	Ventura	10-6	142	113	3.86	R-R	6-3	170	5/22/66 Dominican Republic
		Knoxville	2-2	41	30	4.35				
35	Musselman, Jeff	Ventura	7-7	155	165	3.03	L-L	6-0	180	6/21/63 Doylestown, PA
		Knoxville	5-1	41	38	2.83				
		Toronto	0-0	5	4	10.13				
—	Nunez, Jose	Memphis	2-6	48	36	5.36	R-R	6-3	175	I/13/64 Dom. Republic
		Ft. Myers	8-2	87	59	2.47				
37	Stieb, Dave	Toronto	7-12	205	127	4.74	R-R	6-1	195	7/22/57 Santa Ana, CA
31	Ward, Duane	Attlanta	0-1	16	8	7.31	R-R	6-4	205	5/28/64 Park View, NM
		Rich.-Syr.	7-5	118	67	3.98				
		Toronto	0-1	2	1	13.50				

CATCHERS

No.	Name	1986 Club	H	HR	RBI	Pct.	B-T	Ht.	Wt.	Born
54	Hearron, Jeff	Syracuse	79	7	36	.247	R-R	6-1	195	11/19/61 Long Beach, CA
		Toronto	5	0	4	.217				
—	Myers, Greg	Ventura	133	20	79	.295	L-R	6-2	202	4/14/66 Riverside, CA
—	Stark, Matt	Knoxville	125	17	72	.295	R-R	6-4	225	1/21/65 Whittier, CA
12	Whitt, Ernie	Toronto	106	16	56	.268	L-R	6-2	200	6/13/52 Detroit, MI

INFIELDERS

No.	Name	1986 Club	H	HR	RBI	Pct.	B-T	Ht.	Wt.	Born
1	Fernandez, Tony	Toronto	213	10	65	.310	B-R	6-2	165	8/6/62 Dominican Republic
23	Fielder, Cecil	Syracuse	91	18	68	.280	R-R	6-3	230	9/21/63 Los Angeles, CA
		Toronto	13	4	13	.157				
7	Garcia, Damaso	Toronto	119	6	46	.281	R-R	6-0	183	2/7/57 Dominican Republic
—	Garcia, Santiago	Ventura	124	9	61	.306	R-R	6-0	165	12/8/65 Dominican Republic
17	Gruber, Kelly	Syracuse	28	5	15	.196	R-R	6-0	180	2/26/62 Houston, TX
14	Infante, Alexis	Syracuse	53	0	15	.275	R-R	5-10	175	12/4/62 Venezuela
16	Iorg, Garth	Toronto	85	3	44	.260	R-R	5-11	170	10/12/54 Arcata, CA
4	Lee, Manny	Knoxville	43	0	11	.272	B-R	5-9	151	6/17/55 Dominican Republic
		Syracuse	58	1	19	.246				
		Toronto	16	1	7	.205				
—	Liriano, Nelson	Knoxville	159	7	59	.285	B-R	5-10	165	6/3/64 Dominican Republic
19	McGriff, Fred	Syracuse	121	19	74	.259	L-L	6-3	200	10/31/63 Tampa, FL
		Toronto	1	0	0	.200				
5	Mulliniks, Rance	Toronto	90	11	45	.259	L-R	6-0	175	1/15/56 Tulare, CA
10	Sharperson, Mike	Syracuse	150	4	45	.289	R-R	6-1	175	11/4/61 Orangeburg, SC
26	Upshaw, Willie	Toronto	144	9	60	.251	L-L	6-0	192	4/27/57 Blanco, TX

OUTFIELDERS

No.	Name	1986 Club	H	HR	RBI	Pct.	B-T	Ht.	Wt.	Born
29	Barfield, Jesse	Toronto	170	40	108	.289	R-R	6-1	200	10/29/59 Joliet, IL
11	Bell, George	Toronto	198	31	108	.309	R-R	6-1	190	10/21/59 Dom. Republic
6	Campusano, Sil	Knoxville	126	14	59	.256	R-R	6-0	160	12/31/66 Dom. Republic
—	Ducey, Rob	Ventura	60	12	38	.337	L-R	6-2	173	5/24/65 Canada
		Knoxville	106	11	58	.308				
20	Green, Otis	Syracuse	135	5	53	.281	L-L	6-2	160	3/11/64 Miami, FL
30	Hill, Glenallen	Knoxville	158	31	97	.277	R-R	6-2	205	3/22/65 Santa Cruz, CA
9	Leach, Rick	Toronto	76	5	39	.309	L-L	6-0	195	5/4/57 Ann Arbor, MI
15	Moseby, Lloyd	Toronto	149	21	86	.253	L-R	6-3	205	11/5/59 Portland, AR
28	Thornton, Lou	Syracuse	60	2	28	.260	L-R	6-0	175	4/26/63 Montgomery, AL

BLUE JAY PROFILES

JESSE BARFIELD 27 6-1 200 — Bats R Throws R

Led AL with 40 home runs, 13 above 1985 career high . . . Placed second to Yankees' Don Mattingly with .559 slugging percentage . . . Tied for fourth with 108 RBI, sharing team lead with George Bell . . . Right fielder led AL outfielders with 20 assists . . . Went first 15 games without a home run. . . . Amassed 10 RBI in two games, including a six-RBI effort on May 17 against Cleveland . . . Born Oct. 29, 1959, in Joliet, Ill. . . . Toronto's ninth-round selection in June 1977 draft . . . Struck out 146 times, breaking own club record set in 1985 . . . In 1985, he became first Toronto player to have 20 homers and 20 RBI in same season . . . In 1982, he set club rookie marks in home runs (18) and slugging percentage (.426).

Year	Club	Pos.	G	AB	R	H	2B	3B	HR	RBI	SB	Avg.
1981	Toronto	OF	25	95	7	22	3	2	2	9	4	.232
1982	Toronto	OF	139	394	54	97	13	2	18	58	1	.246
1983	Toronto	OF	128	388	58	98	13	3	27	68	2	.253
1984	Toronto	OF	110	320	51	91	14	1	14	49	8	.284
1985	Toronto	OF	155	539	94	156	34	9	27	84	22	.289
1986	Toronto	OF	158	589	107	170	35	2	40	108	8	.289
	Totals		715	2325	371	634	112	19	128	376	45	.273

LLOYD MOSEBY 27 6-3 205 — Bats L Throws R

Center fielder's continuing development was recognized with selection to his first All-Star Game . . . Set career high with 21 home runs after clubbing 18 each of last three seasons . . . Struck out 122 times, matching career high of 1984 . . . Hit .319 in May with four home runs, 19 RBI . . . Had terrible July, batting .170 . . . Rebounded to hit .309 in August . . . Born Nov. 5, 1959, in Portland, Ark. . . . High-school All-American in baseball and basketball . . . Nicknamed "Shaker" for his elusive moves as schoolboy cager in Oakland . . . Finished second in Florida State League in batting (.332) and homers (18) while playing for Dunedin (A) in 1979.

Year	Club	Pos.	G	AB	R	H	2B	3B	HR	RBI	SB	Avg.
1980	Toronto	OF	114	389	44	89	24	1	9	46	4	.229
1981	Toronto	OF	100	378	36	88	16	2	9	43	11	.233
1982	Toronto	OF	147	487	51	115	20	9	9	52	11	.236
1983	Toronto	OF	151	539	104	170	31	7	18	81	27	.315
1984	Toronto	OF	158	592	97	166	28	15	18	92	39	.280
1985	Toronto	OF	152	584	92	151	30	7	18	70	37	.259
1986	Toronto	OF	152	589	89	149	24	5	21	86	32	.253
	Totals		974	3558	513	928	173	46	102	470	161	.261

GEORGE BELL 27 6-1 190 Bats R Throws R

Known for hot temper and it's proven costly . . . Bid for 200 hits short-circuited by two-game suspension last weekend of season for making physical contact with umpire Al Clark . . . Finished with 198 hits . . . Improved RBI total for third consecutive year with 108 . . . Tied for club lead with Jesse Barfield in that category . . . Also set career high with 31 home runs . . . Left fielder placed second in league in outfielder assists to Barfield with 17 . . . Suffered 0-for-26 drought May 8-14 . . . Got off to rousing .361 start in April . . . A clutch hitter who broke Willie Upshaw's club record with 15 game-winning RBI . . . Born Oct. 21, 1959, in San Pedro de Macoris, Dominican Republic, and still lives there . . . Plucked from Phillies' organization in major-league draft on Dec. 8, 1980.

Year	Club	Pos.	G	AB	R	H	2B	3B	HR	RBI	SB	Avg.
1981	Toronto	OF	60	163	19	38	2	1	5	12	3	.233
1983	Toronto	OF	39	112	5	30	5	4	2	17	1	.268
1984	Toronto	OF-3B	159	606	85	177	39	4	26	87	11	.292
1985	Toronto	OF-1B	157	607	87	167	28	6	28	95	21	.275
1986	Toronto	OF	159	641	101	198	38	6	31	108	7	.309
	Totals		574	2129	297	610	112	21	92	319	43	.287

TONY FERNANDEZ 24 6-2 165 Bats S Throws R

Emerged as finest all-around shortstop in AL . . . Led Jays with .310 average . . . First Toronto player in club history to surpass 200 hits in a season (213) . . . Set club record with 161 singles . . . Has played in 327 consecutive games . . . Development allowed club to trade Alfredo Griffin before 1985 season . . . Born Aug. 6, 1962, in San Pedro de Macoris, Dominican Republic, and still lives there . . . One of 11 children . . . Made first appearance in All-Star Game . . . Signed as free agent April 24, 1979 for 1980 season . . . International League All-Star shortstop for Syracuse (AAA) in 1982 and 1983 . . . Missed all of spring training in 1984 with broken bone in left hand suffered in preceding August . . . Established himself as Blue Jays' leadoff hitter . . . Has great range and strong arm . . . Played 33 errorless games from July 7 to Aug. 13.

Year	Club	Pos.	G	AB	R	H	2B	3B	HR	RBI	SB	Avg.
1983	Toronto	SS	15	34	5	9	1	1	0	2	0	.265
1984	Toronto	SS-3B	89	233	29	63	5	3	3	19	5	.270
1985	Toronto	SS	161	564	71	163	31	10	2	51	13	.289
1986	Toronto	SS	163	687	91	213	33	9	10	65	25	.310
	Totals		428	1518	196	448	70	23	15	137	43	.295

MARK EICHHORN 26 6-3 200 **Bats R Throws R**

Attended spring training as non-roster player and wound up setting club rookie records for wins (14), innings pitched (157) and relief appearances (69) . . . Finished with glittering 1.72 ERA, falling five innings short of qualifying for AL title . . . Reliever shared team lead in wins with starter Jimmy Key . . . Established himself with brilliant April, allowing one run in first 18⅔ innings . . . Changed from overhand to sidearm delivery in 1984 . . . Baffled major-league hitters with motion and assortment of breaking pitches . . . Born Nov. 21, 1960, in San Jose, Cal. . . . Jays' second-round selection in January 1979 draft . . . Only negative note of rookie year came when he was spiked by Detroit's Darnell Coles on June 14 while covering first base and landed on disabled list.

Year	Club	G	IP	W	L	Pct.	SO	BB	H	ERA
1982	Toronto	7	38	0	3	.000	16	14	40	5.45
1986	Toronto	69	157	14	6	.700	166	45	105	1.72
	Totals	76	195	14	9	.609	182	59	145	2.45

JIMMY KEY 25 6-1 185 **Bats L Throws L**

Recovered from disastrous start to salvage good season . . . Tied for club lead with rookie reliever Mark Eichhorn with 14 wins . . . Was 0-3 with 13.27 ERA after first six starts . . . Did not win until May 11 at Seattle . . . Rebounded to take five straight from June 12 to July 7 . . . Has emerged as one of best fielding pitchers in AL . . . Battled Boston's Roger Clemens three times and rose to occasion with 1-1 record and 1.93 ERA . . . Born April 22, 1961, in Huntsville, Ala. . . . Toronto's third-round selection in June 1982 draft . . . Drafted by Cincinnati in June 1979 but did not sign . . . In 1985, he became first Blue Jays' starting left-hander to win since Paul Mirabella beat Boston on Oct. 4, 1980 . . . Clemson's MVP in 1982 as he went 9-3 with 2.79 ERA . . . Retired first 16 batters he faced as a rookie in 1984 . . . Used in relief, he made 63 appearances in first season.

Year	Club	G	IP	W	L	Pct.	SO	BB	H	ERA
1984	Toronto	63	62	4	5	.444	44	32	70	4.65
1985	Toronto	35	212⅔	14	6	.700	85	50	188	3.00
1986	Toronto	36	232	14	11	.560	141	74	222	3.57
	Totals	134	506⅔	32	22	.593	270	156	480	3.46

TOM HENKE 29 6-5 215 **Bats R Throws R**

Proved rookie season was no fluke by leading Toronto in saves for second straight year with 27 . . . Finished strong, posting seven saves in September . . . As with most bullpen closers, he is best used for one or two innings . . . Ran into trouble early in season when pressed into longer service . . . No mystery to this hard thrower . . . Overpowered batters for 118 strikeouts in 91⅓ innings . . . Born Dec. 21, 1957, in Kansas City, Mo. . . . Selected by Rangers in fourth round of June 1980 draft . . . Was going nowhere with Texas when Toronto obtained him with January 1985 compensation pool pick.

Year	Club	G	IP	W	L	Pct.	SO	BB	H	ERA
1982	Texas	8	15⅔	1	0	1.000	9	8	14	1.15
1983	Texas	8	16	1	0	1.000	17	4	16	3.38
1984	Texas	25	28⅓	1	1	.500	25	20	36	6.35
1985	Toronto	28	40	3	3	.500	42	8	29	2.03
1986	Toronto	63	91⅓	9	5	.643	118	32	63	3.35
	Totals	132	191⅓	15	9	.625	211	72	158	3.34

DAVE STIEB 29 6-1 195 **Bats R Throws R**

Career took alarming downward turn . . . Failed to win in double figures for first time since rookie season in 1979 and his seven wins were a career low . . . After winning ERA title with 2.48 mark in 1985, he saw his 1986 ERA swell to career-high 4.74 . . . Stieb's failures became especially embarrassing because his autobiography, *Tomorrow I'll Be Perfect*, was due for release at beginning of season . . . Began season with six straight losses . . . Relief appearance on July 12 against Oakland snapped string of 189 consecutive starts . . . Born July 22, 1957, in Santa Ana, Cal. . . . Toronto's fifth-round pick in June 1978 draft. . . . Jays' all-time victory leader entering season . . . Big difference was loss of his sharp-breaking slider . . . A moody performer who is sensitive to criticism . . . Music lover with extensive guitar collection.

Year	Club	G	IP	W	L	Pct.	SO	BB	H	ERA
1979	Toronto	18	129	8	8	.500	52	48	139	4.33
1980	Toronto	34	243	12	15	.444	108	83	232	3.70
1981	Toronto	25	184	11	10	.524	89	61	148	3.18
1982	Toronto	38	288⅓	17	14	.548	141	75	271	3.25
1983	Toronto	36	278	17	12	.586	187	93	223	3.04
1984	Toronto	35	267	16	8	.667	198	88	215	2.83
1985	Toronto	36	265	14	13	.519	167	96	206	2.48
1986	Toronto	37	205	7	12	.368	127	87	239	4.74
	Totals	259	1859⅓	102	92	.526	1069	631	1673	3.34

JIM CLANCY 31 6-4 215 Bats R Throws R

Improved dramatically after injury-plagued 1985 campaign . . . Worked more than 200 innings for fourth time in last five years . . . Was at his best in midseason, winning six straight from June 25 through July 28 . . . String included 2-0 shutout of California and 6-0 blanking of Kansas City . . . Went 5-0 in July with 1.54 ERA in five games . . . Became first pitcher in Toronto history to go over 100 career wins with his shutout of KC on July 28 . . . Born Dec. 18, 1955, in Chicago . . . Acquired from Texas on Nov. 5, 1976, in AL expansion draft . . . Gutsy pitcher who perseveres despite injury problems.

Year	Club	G	IP	W	L	Pct.	SO	BB	H	ERA
1977	Toronto	13	77	4	9	.308	44	47	80	5.03
1978	Toronto	31	194	10	12	.455	106	91	199	4.08
1979	Toronto	12	64	2	7	.222	33	31	65	5.48
1980	Toronto	34	251	13	16	.448	152	128	217	3.30
1981	Toronto	22	125	6	12	.333	56	64	126	4.90
1982	Toronto	40	266⅔	16	14	.533	139	77	251	3.71
1983	Toronto	34	223	15	11	.577	99	61	238	3.91
1984	Toronto	36	219⅔	13	15	.464	118	88	249	5.12
1985	Toronto	23	128⅔	9	6	.600	66	37	117	3.78
1986	Toronto	34	219⅓	14	14	.500	126	63	202	3.94
	Totals	279	1768⅓	102	116	.468	939	687	1744	4.13

JOHN CERUTTI 26 6-2 195 Bats L Throws L

Left-hander failed to make the club out of spring training but wound up as one of Toronto's most reliable starters . . . Recalled on May 16 despite 1-3 record with 4.12 ERA for Syracuse . . . Gained first major-league win May 25, working eight innings in 8-1 decision over Cleveland . . . Gained first major-league shutout on June 25, 8-0 over Milwaukee . . . Enjoyed pair of four-game winning streaks . . . Born April 28, 1960, in Albany, N.Y. . . . First-round selection (21st pick) by Toronto in June 1981 . . . Most scouted player in Amherst College history . . . Compiled 29-5 record and 1.95 ERA for Amherst.

Year	Club	G	IP	W	L	Pct.	SO	BB	H	ERA
1985	Toronto	4	6⅔	0	2	.000	5	4	10	5.40
1986	Toronto	34	145⅓	9	4	.692	89	47	150	4.15
	Totals	38	152	9	6	.600	94	51	160	4.20

TOP PROSPECT

TODD STOTTLEMYRE 21 6-3 185 Bats L Throws R
Chosen by Toronto in first round of June 1985 draft and did nothing to disappoint Jays . . . Son of Mel Stottlemyre, former Yankee pitcher and current Mets' pitching coach . . . Began pro career with Ventura (A) and compiled 9-4 record with 2.43 ERA in 17 starts . . . Fanned 104 batters in 103⅔ innings . . . Earned promotion to Knoxville (AA), where he went 8-7 with 4.18 ERA in 18 starts . . . Born May 20, 1965, in Yakima, Wash.

MANAGER JIMY WILLIAMS: Received one-year contract extension after Toronto finished fourth in AL East with 86-76 record . . . Perhaps most impressive element of Williams' rookie campaign as manager was that he held club together after terrible start and Jays moved back into contention . . . Tries to stay close to his players and regularly throws batting practice . . . Named as manager after the 1985 season when Bobby Cox left to become GM at Atlanta . . . Served as Jays' third-base coach for six seasons . . . Managed in California organization from 1974-79 . . . Major-league career as shortstop consisted of 14 games in which he hit .214 with St. Louis in 1966 and 1967 . . . Born Oct. 4, 1943, in Arroyo Grande, Cal. . . . Graduated from Fresno State, where he majored in animal science.

GREATEST ALL-TIME ROOKIE

Toronto won 53 games, lost 109 and finished in last place in the American League East in 1979, 50½ games off the pace. Not a year to remember for Blue Jays fans—except for the memorable debut of Alfredo Griffin.

Griffin, a stylish shortstop, batted .287 and won American League Rookie-of-the-Year honors. He still holds five Blue Jay rookie records: games (153), at-bats (624), hits (179), runs (81), and total bases (227). His .287 average topped AL shortstops.

Griffin did not approach those totals in five succeeding seasons with Toronto. The Blue Jays, urgently needing help in the bullpen, traded Griffin and outfielder Dave Collins to Oakland for Bill Caudill after the 1984 season.

ALL-TIME BLUE JAY SEASON RECORDS

BATTING: Lloyd Moseby, .315, 1983
HRs: Jesse Barfield, 40, 1986
RBIs: George Bell, 108, 1986
Jesse Barfield, 108, 1986
STEALS: Damaso Garcia, 54, 1982
WINS: Doyle Alexander, 17, 1984, 1985
STRIKEOUTS: Dave Stieb, 198, 1984

George Bell shared club lead in RBI with 108.

CALIFORNIA ANGELS

TEAM DIRECTORY: Chairman-Pres.: Gene Autry; VP: Jackie Autry; GM: Mike Port; Dir. Minor League Oper.: Bill Bavasi; Dir. Pub. Rel.: Tim Mead; Trav. Sec.: Frank Sims; Mgr.: Gene Mauch. Home: Anaheim Stadium (65,158). Field distances: 333, l.f. line; 386, l.c.; 404, c.f.; 386, r.c.; 333, r.f. line. Spring training: Palm Springs, Cal.

SCOUTING REPORT

HITTING: Wally Joyner (.290, 22 homers, 100 RBI) is one of the game's best young hitters and the hub of an attack that ranked in the middle of the league in average (.255), home runs (167) and runs (786) in 1986. Doug DeCinces (.256, 26, 96) and Brian Downing (.267, 20, 95) are clutch veterans whom the Angels didn't allow to escape through free agency.

Leadoff hitter Gary Pettis (.258, 5, 58) and Dick Schofield (.249, 13, 57) are developing after sluggish starts as major leaguers. Pettis had 50 stolen bases last season and his ability to reach base is critical because the Angels don't have much speed elsewhere.

The offensive holes created by California's decision to not re-sign free agent Reggie Jackson (.241, 18, 58) and the loss of the retired Bobby Grich (.268, 9, 30) require front-office attention.

PITCHING: Starting pitching, formerly a problem spot for the Angels, is now a strength, as witnessed by the club's 3.84 ERA last season. Few teams can match the combination of right-handers Mike Witt (18-10, 2.84, 14 complete games) and Kirk McCaskill (17-10, 3.36). Don Sutton (15-11, 3.74), a member of the famed 300 Club, still finds a way to get hitters out and John Candelaria (10-2, 2.55) can be a big winner if his elbow troubles are behind him.

The bullpen's success hinges on the performance of ace Donnie Moore (4-5, 2.97, 21 saves). Moore is one of the best closers around when he's healthy, but he was plagued by shoulder problems throughout 1986. Should Moore go down again this season, no replacement is in sight.

FIELDING: The Angels ranked second in the AL with a .983 fielding percentage, making 107 errors. Pettis is a Gold Glove center fielder. The defensive contributions of catcher Bob Boone, whom the Angels were unable to re-sign as a free agent, will be

Wally Joyner made Angels fans forget forget Rod Carew.

missed, despite the addition of ex-Yankee Butch Wynegar. Another potential problem area is at second base, the position vacated by Grich.

OUTLOOK: The Angels finished 92-70 last season and came within one pitch of giving Gene Mauch his first pennant in 25 years as a manager only to lose to Boston in seven games in the AL Championship Series. They won't get that close again this season. Age has to catch up to this team some time and the bullpen looms as a trouble spot. Starting pitching makes California a contender, but nothing more.

CALIFORNIA ANGELS 1987 ROSTER

MANAGER Gene Mauch
Coaches—Bob Clear, Bobby Knoop, Marcel Lachemann, Jimmie Reese, Moose Stubing

PITCHERS

No.	Name	1986 Club	W-L	IP	SO	ERA	B-T	Ht.	Wt.	Born
—	Buice, DeWayne	Edmonton	2-1	12	11	0.73	R-R	6-0	165	8/27/57 Lynwood, CA
		Midland	8-6	78	73	3.45				
45	Candelaria, John	Palm Springs	0-0	7	8	2.57	L-L	6-6	225	11/6/53 Brooklyn, NY
		California	10-2	92	81	2.55				
48	Chadwick, Ray	Edmonton	9-9	124	89	4.72	B-R	6-2	180	12/17/62 Durham, NC
		California	0-5	27	9	7.24				
—	Cliburn, Stew	Edmonton	1-2	23	17	6.94	R-R	6-0	187	12/19/56 Jackson, MS
—	Cook, Mike	Midland	4-6	105	82	3.50	R-R	6-3	200	8/14/63 Charleston, SC
		California	0-2	9	6	9.00				
		Edmonton	4-1	55	35	5.37				
31	Finley, Chuck	Quad City	1-0	12	16	0.00	L-L	6-6	220	11/26/62 Monroe, LA
		California	3-1	46	37	3.30				
52	Fraser, Bill	Palm Springs	9-2	124	99	3.55	R-R	6-3	200	5/26/64 New York, NY
		Edmonton	4-1	40	24	3.12				
		California	0-0	4	2	8.31				
—	Green, Chris	Edmonton	4-5	64	44	4.38	L-L	6-4	210	9/5/60 Los Angeles, CA
36	Lucas, Gary	Palm Springs	0-2	12	9	5.11	L-L	6-5	200	11/8/54 Riverside, CA
		California	4-1	46	31	3.15				
18	Lugo, Urbano	Midland	1-1	11	4	1.64	R-R	6-0	190	8/12/62 Venezuela
		Edmonton	8-6	100	53	4.66				
		California	1-1	21	9	3.80				
—	Martinez, David	Palm Springs	6-4	94	41	5.25	R-R	6-0	190	12/29/65 Austin, TX
15	McCaskill, Kirk	California	17-10	246	202	3.36	R-R	6-1	190	4/9/61 Canada
37	Moore, Donnie	California	4-5	73	53	2.97	R-R	6-0	185	2/13/54 Lubbock, TX
20	Sutton, Don	California	15-11	207	116	3.74	R-R	6-1	190	4/2/45 Clio, AL
39	Witt, Mike	California	18-10	269	208	2.84	R-R	6-7	192	7/20/60 Fullerton, CA

CATCHERS

No.	Name	1986 Club	H	HR	RBI	Pct.	B-T	Ht.	Wt.	Born
—	Fimple, Jack	Albuquerque	85	2	35	.286	R-R	6-2	190	2/10/59 Darby, Pa
		Los Angeles	1	0	2	.077				
32	Miller, Darrell	California	13	0	4	.228	R-R	6-2	200	2/26/59 Washington, DC
		Edmonton	65	8	31	.307				
34	Narron, Jerry	California	21	1	8	.221	L-R	6-3	190	1/15/56 Goldsboro, NC
—	Wynegar, Butch	New York (AL)	40	7	29	.206	B-R	6-1	192	3/14/56 York, PA

INFIELDERS

No.	Name	1986 Club	H	HR	RBI	Pct.	B-T	Ht.	Wt.	Born
11	DeCinces, Doug	California	131	26	96	.256	R-R	6-2	195	8/29/50 Burbank, CA
—	Gerber, Craig	Edmonton	58	0	15	.239	L-R	6-0	175	1/8/59 Chicago, IL
16	Howell, Jack	Edmonton	56	3	28	.359	L-R	6-0	185	8/18/61 Tucson, AZ
		California	41	4	21	.272				
21	Joyner, Wally	California	172	22	100	.290	L-L	6-2	185	6/16/62 Atlanta, GA
28	McLemore, Mark	Midland	75	1	30	.316	B-R	5-11	175	10/4/64 San Diego, CA
		Edmonton	79	0	23	.276				
		California	0	0	0	.000				
—	Merrifield, Billie	Midland	73	8	53	.289	R-R	6-4	195	5/7/62 Waukegan, IL
		Edmonton	53	9	38	.282				
12	Polidor, Gus	Edmonton	143	5	61	.300	R-R	6-0	170	10/26/61 Venezuela
		California	5	0	1	.263				
22	Schofield, Dick	California	114	13	57	.249	R-R	5-10	176	11/21/62 Springfield, IL
9	Wilfong, Rob	California	63	3	33	.219	L-R	6-1	179	9/1/53 Pasadena, CA

OUTFIELDERS

No.	Name	1986 Club	H	HR	RBI	Pct.	B-T	Ht.	Wt.	Born
—	Bichette, Dante	Palm Springs	79	10	73	.276	R-R	6-3	210	11/18/63 W. Palm Beach, FL
		Midland	68	12	36	.280				
5	Downing, Brian	California	137	20	95	.267	R-R	5-10	190	10/9/50 Los Angeles, CA
25	Hendrick, George	California	77	14	47	.272	R-R	6-5	195	10/18/49 Los Angeles, CA
13	Jones, Ruppert	California	90	17	49	.229	L-L	5-10	189	3/12/55 Dallas, TX
—	Montgomery, Reggie	Edmonton	134	18	82	.285	R-R	6-4	235	8/4/62 Los Angeles, CA
24	Pettis, Gary	California	139	5	58	.258	B-R	6-1	160	4/3/58 Oakland, CA
6	Ryal, Mark	Edmonton	163	14	84	.340	L-L	6-0	180	4/28/60 Henrigetta, OK
		California	12	2	5	.375				
30	White, Devon	Edmonton	134	14	60	.291	B-R	6-1	170	12/29/62 Jamaica
		California	12	1	3	.235				

ANGEL PROFILES

WALLY JOYNER 24 6-2 185  **Bats L Throws L**

Eyebrows were raised when Angels handed him first-base job in place of Rod Carew, but this rookie won over the doubters in a hurry . . . Went entire month of April without going hitless in back-to-back games . . . Slugged five home runs in five games from May 12-18 . . . Amassed 20 home runs, 72 RBI by All-Star break . . . Became first rookie to start in All-Star competition since fan voting began in 1970 . . . Established club rookie records in hits (172), at-bats (593), runs (82) and RBI (100) . . . Homered in Game 2 of AL Championship Series, then sat out final four games with a bacterial infection in lower right leg . . . Born June 16, 1962, in Atlanta . . . Selected in third round of June 1983 draft . . . Lettered three years at BYU . . . Convinced Angels he was ready to displace Carew by winning Puerto Rican Winter League triple crown, batting .356 with 14 home runs and 48 RBI in 54 games . . . Runnerup to A's Jose Canseco for AL Rookie-of-the-Year honors.

Year	Club	Pos.	G	AB	R	H	2B	3B	HR	RBI	SB	Avg.
1986	California.	1B	154	593	82	172	27	3	22	100	5	2.90

DOUG DeCINCES 36 6-2 195 **Bats R Throws R**

Third baseman finished strong after a slow start, hinting that he still has some good years left . . . Batted .223 through first 45 games . . . Drove in 40 runs in 45 games between July 23 and Sept. 18 . . . AL Player of the Month in August, when he hit .337 with nine homers and 25 RBI, including five game-winners . . . Compiled .684 slugging percentage and .407 on-base mark that month . . . Set career high with 13 game-winning RBI . . . Compiled .286 average in AL Championship Series with one home run and three RBI . . . Born Aug. 29, 1950, in Burbank, Cal. . . . Acquired from Orioles with Jeff Schneider for Dan Ford on Jan. 28, 1982 . . . Began career with Baltimore after he was selected in the secondary phase of the January 1970 draft . . . Receives daily treatment for chronic back problems.

Year	Club	Pos.	G	AB	R	H	2B	3B	HR	RBI	SB	Avg.
1973	Baltimore.	3B-2B-SS	10	18	2	2	0	0	0	3	0	.111
1974	Baltimore.	3B	1	1	0	0	0	0	0	0	0	.000
1975	Baltimore.	3B-SS-2B-1B	61	167	20	42	6	3	4	23	0	.251
1976	Baltimore.	3B-2B-SS-1B	129	440	36	103	17	2	11	42	8	.234
1977	Baltimore.	3B-2B-1B	150	522	63	135	28	3	19	69	8	.259
1978	Baltimore.	3B-2B	142	511	72	146	37	1	28	80	7	.286
1979	Baltimore.	3B	120	422	67	97	27	1	16	61	5	.230
1980	Baltimore.	3B-1B	145	489	64	122	23	2	16	64	11	.249
1981	Baltimore.	3B-1B-OF	100	346	49	91	23	2	13	55	0	.263
1982	California.	3B-SS	153	575	94	173	42	5	30	97	7	.301
1983	California.	3B	95	370	49	104	19	3	18	65	2	.281
1984	California.	3B	146	547	77	147	23	3	20	82	4	.269
1985	California.	3B	120	427	50	104	22	1	20	78	1	.244
1986	California.	3B	140	512	69	131	20	3	26	96	2	.256
	Totals		1512	5347	712	1397	287	29	221	815	55	.261

BRIAN DOWNING 36 5-10 190 Bats R Throws R

Left fielder's production was never better . . . Posted a career-high 95 RBI last season . . . Ranks first on Angels' all-time RBI list . . . Big swinger who tends to deliver the big blow or nothing at all . . . Of his 137 hits, 51 were for extra bases . . . Performance in AL Championship Series was typical in that he batted only .222 but finished with a team-leading seven RBI . . . His July 17 error against Toronto broke streak of 129 errorless games dating back to July 31, 1985 . . . Holds major-league record for most consecutive errorless games (244) . . . Born Oct. 9, 1950, in Los Angeles . . . Acquired from White Sox with Dave Frost and Chris Knapp for Bobby Bonds, Thad Bosley and Richard Dotson on Dec. 5, 1977 . . . Originally signed as a free agent by White Sox, Aug. 19, 1969 . . . Dubbed "The Incredible Hulk" because he's an avid weightlifter.

Year	Club	Pos.	G	AB	R	H	2B	3B	HR	RBI	SB	Avg.
1973	Chicago (AL)	OF-C-3B	34	73	5	13	1	0	2	4	0	.178
1974	Chicago (AL)	C-OF	108	293	41	66	12	1	10	39	0	.225
1975	Chicago (AL)	C	138	420	58	101	12	1	7	41	13	.240
1976	Chicago (AL)	C	104	317	38	81	14	0	3	30	7	.256
1977	Chicago (AL)	C-OF	69	169	28	48	4	2	4	25	1	.284
1978	California.	C	133	412	42	105	15	0	7	46	3	.255
1979	California.	C	148	509	87	166	27	3	12	75	3	.326
1980	California.	C	30	93	5	27	6	0	2	25	0	.290
1981	California.	OF-C	93	317	47	79	14	0	9	41	1	.249
1982	California.	OF	158	623	109	175	37	2	28	84	2	.281
1983	California.	OF	113	403	68	99	15	1	19	53	1	.246
1984	California.	OF	156	539	65	148	28	2	23	91	0	.275
1985	California.	OF	150	520	80	137	23	1	20	85	5	.263
1986	California.	OF	152	513	90	137	27	4	20	95	4	.267
	Totals		1586	5201	763	1382	235	17	166	734	40	.266

GARY PETTIS 28 6-1 160 **Bats S Throws R**

Sparkled in AL Championship Series, leading Angels to hope he has finally come into his own . . . Batted .346 with one home run, four RBI and four runs scored in postseason . . . Gold Glove winner has no peers in AL as a center fielder . . . First player in club history to record three consecutive 30-plus stolen-base seasons . . . Established career high in runs (93), hits (139), doubles (23) and RBI (58) . . . Succeeded in only nine of first 17 stolen-base attempts, but converted 41 of his last 46 efforts . . . Reached base safely in 115 of 154 regular-season games . . . Born April 3, 1958, in Oakland . . . Chosen in sixth round of June 1979 draft . . . Interested in computers.

Year	Club	Pos.	G	AB	R	H	2B	3B	HR	RBI	SB	Avg.
1982	California	OF	10	5	5	1	0	0	1	1	0	.200
1983	California	OF	22	85	19	25	2	3	3	6	8	.294
1984	California	OF	140	397	63	90	11	6	2	29	48	.227
1985	California	OF	125	443	67	114	10	8	1	32	56	.257
1986	California	OF	154	539	93	139	23	4	5	58	50	.258
	Totals		451	1469	247	369	46	21	12	126	162	.251

DICK SCHOFIELD Jr. 24 5-10 176 **Bats R Throws R**

California's patience paid dividends as this youngster enjoyed a fine season at shortstop . . . Reduced errors from 25 in 1985 to 18 . . . Did not make a miscue until 41st game and committed only seven in first 95 games . . . Established career highs in runs (67), hits (114), home runs (13) and RBI (57) . . . Became first California shortstop to reach double figures in home runs since Jim Fregosi had 22 in 1970 . . . Broke up no-hit bid by Kansas City's Danny Jackson with a ninth-inning single on Oct. 1 . . . Born Nov. 21, 1962, in Springfield, Ill. . . . Selected in first round of June 1981 draft . . . Batted .300 in AL Championship Series with one home run and two RBI . . . Son of former major-league infielder "Ducky" Schofield . . . Spent only two full seasons in minors before making major-league debut at Chicago on Sept. 8, 1983.

Year	Club	Pos.	G	AB	R	H	2B	3B	HR	RBI	SB	Avg.
1983	California	SS	21	54	4	11	2	0	3	4	0	.204
1984	California	SS	140	400	39	77	10	3	4	21	5	.193
1985	California	SS	147	438	50	96	19	3	8	41	11	.219
1986	California	SS	139	458	67	114	17	6	13	57	23	.249
	Totals		447	1350	160	298	48	12	28	123	39	.221

BUTCH WYNEGAR 31 6-1 192 **Bats S Throws R**

Angels sent Ron Romanick to Yankees in December to get this catcher as insurance against the departure of free agent Bob Boone . . . Emotional troubles drove him to leave the Yankees in the middle of last season . . . Departed during road trip on July 31 and was placed on restricted list two days later . . . Distaste for manager Lou Piniella and discomfort with glare of playing in New York contributed to his troubles . . . Happy to be playing for Gene Mauch, who managed him with Twins . . . Irregular duty has hurt his production the last two seasons . . . Born March 14, 1956, in York, Pa. . . . Drafted by Minnesota in second round in June 1974 . . . Became youngest player to appear in a major-league All-Star Game in 1976, a distinction since usurped by Dwight Gooden . . . Suffered from inner-ear problem and sprained lower back during 1985 . . . Came to Yankees from Twins in May 1982 with Roger Erickson for Larry Milbourne, Pete Filson and John Pacella . . . Must prove his problems were function of life as a Yankee.

Year	Club	Pos.	G	AB	R	H	2B	3B	HR	RBI	SB	Avg.
1976	Minnesota	C	149	534	58	139	21	2	10	69	0	.260
1977	Minnesota	C-3B	144	532	76	139	22	3	10	79	2	.261
1978	Minnesota	C-3B	135	454	36	104	22	1	4	45	1	.229
1979	Minnesota	C	149	504	74	136	20	0	7	57	2	.270
1980	Minnesota	C	146	486	61	124	18	3	5	57	3	.255
1981	Minnesota	C	47	150	11	37	5	0	0	10	0	.247
1982	Minn.-NY (AL)	C	87	277	36	74	12	1	4	28	0	.267
1983	New York (AL)	C	94	301	40	89	18	2	6	42	1	.296
1984	New York (AL)	C	129	442	48	118	13	1	6	45	1	.267
1985	New York (AL)	C	102	309	27	69	15	0	5	32	0	.223
1986	New York (AL)	C	61	194	19	40	4	1	7	29	0	.206
	Totals		1243	4183	486	1069	170	14	64	493	10	.255

MIKE WITT 26 6-7 192 **Bats R Throws R**

Soft-spoken right-hander is one of the best pitchers in either league . . . Received Owner's Trophy as team MVP choice of his teammates . . . His 18 regular-season victories were most by an Angels right-hander since Nolan Ryan won 19 games in 1977 . . . His 14 complete games were the most since Ryan's 17 in 1979 . . . Opponents hit only .221 against him . . . AL Player of the Month in August, posting 5-0 record with one earned run in 43 innings . . . Was 1-1 with 2.55 ERA in AL Championship Series . . . Came within an out of giving California its first pennant in Game 5 . . . Pulled by manager Gene Mauch with a 5-4 lead after surrendering two-run home run to Don Baylor a batter before he was removed . . . Pitched into seventh inning or later 32 times . . . Born July 20, 1960, in Fullerton, Cal. . . . Selected in fourth round of June 1978 draft . . . Made jump from El Paso (AA) to majors in 1981.

Year	Club	G	IP	W	L	Pct.	SO	BB	H	ERA
1981	California	22	129	8	9	.471	75	47	123	3.28
1982	California	33	179⅔	8	6	.571	85	47	177	3.51
1983	California	43	154	7	14	.333	77	75	173	4.91
1984	California	34	246⅔	15	11	.577	196	84	227	3.47
1985	California	35	250	15	9	.625	180	98	228	3.56
1986	California	34	269	18	10	.643	208	73	218	2.84
	Totals	201	1228⅓	71	59	.546	821	424	1146	3.52

KIRK McCASKILL 26 6-1 190 Bats R Throws R

Picked baseball over hockey after being an All-American hockey player at University of Vermont . . . Justified decision with an excellent performance in first full major-league season . . . Registered a pair of two-hitters and a one-hitter . . . One-hitter came against Texas June 25 as Steve Buechele led off third inning with a home run . . . Struck out nine or more 10 times . . . Went 4-1 with 1.64 ERA in July . . . Worked into seventh inning or later 28 times . . . Allowed two walks or less in 16 starts . . . Was disappointing in AL Championship Series, going 0-2 with 7.71 ERA . . . Born April 9, 1961, in Kapuskasing, Ontario, Canada . . . Selected in fourth round of June 1982 draft . . . Son of former pro hockey player Ted McCaskill . . . Was first collegian chosen in 1981 NHL draft . . . Signed with Angels and Winnipeg Jets . . . Wasn't getting much playing time in pro hockey, so he turned to baseball.

Year	Club	G	IP	W	L	Pct.	SO	BB	H	ERA
1985	California	30	189⅔	12	12	.500	102	64	189	4.70
1986	California	34	246⅓	17	10	.630	202	92	207	3.36
	Totals	64	436	29	22	.569	304	156	396	3.94

DON SUTTON 41 6-1 190 Bats R Throws R

Long, distinguished career hit milestone on June 18, when he defeated Texas, 5-1, on a three-hitter to become 19th pitcher in history to achieve 300 victories . . . Became fifth-oldest pitcher to join 300 club . . . Has defeated every major-league club . . . Dropped five of first seven decisions and had 7.05 ERA . . . Won six straight from June 3 to July 9 . . . Pitched into seventh inning or later in 19 starts . . . Has had 21 consecutive seasons of more than 100 strikeouts, a major-league record . . . Started 700th game of his career on Sept. 7, second only to Cy Young (818) . . . Pitched well in AL Championship Series, compiling 1.86 ERA in 9⅔ innings, although he didn't earn a decision . . . Born April 2, 1945, in Clio, Ala. . . . Acquired from Oakland on Sept. 10, 1985 for two minor leaguers . . . Originally signed by Dodgers in 1965.

Year	Club	G	IP	W	L	Pct.	SO	BB	H	ERA
1966	Los Angeles	37	226	12	12	.500	209	52	192	2.99
1967	Los Angeles	37	233	11	15	.423	169	57	223	3.94
1968	Los Angeles	35	208	11	15	.423	162	59	179	2.60
1969	Los Angeles	41	293	17	18	.486	217	91	269	3.47
1970	Los Angeles	38	260	15	13	.536	201	78	251	4.08
1971	Los Angeles	38	265	17	12	.586	194	55	231	2.55
1972	Los Angeles	33	273	19	9	.679	207	63	186	2.08
1973	Los Angeles	33	256	18	10	.643	200	56	196	2.43
1974	Los Angeles	40	276	19	9	.679	179	80	241	3.23
1975	Los Angeles	35	254	16	13	.552	175	62	202	2.87
1976	Los Angeles	35	268	21	10	.677	161	82	231	3.06
1977	Los Angeles	33	240	14	8	.636	150	69	207	3.19
1978	Los Angeles	34	238	15	11	.577	154	54	228	3.55
1979	Los Angeles	33	226	12	15	.444	146	61	201	3.82
1980	Los Angeles	32	212	13	5	.722	128	47	163	2.21
1981	Houston	23	159	11	9	.550	104	29	132	2.60
1982	Houston	27	195	13	8	619	139	46	169	3.00
1982	Milwaukee	7	54⅔	4	1	.800	36	18	55	3.29
1983	Milwaukee	31	220⅓	8	13	.381	134	54	209	4.08
1984	Milwaukee	33	212⅔	14	12	.538	143	51	224	3.77
1985	Oak.-Cal.	34	226	15	10	.600	107	59	221	3.86
1986	California	34	207	15	11	.577	116	49	192	3.74
	Totals	723	5002⅔	310	239	.565	3431	1272	4402	3.20

DONNIE MOORE 33 6-0 185 Bats L Throws R

Came within a strike of nailing down Angels' first pennant, then Boston's Dave Henderson slammed his 2-2 forkball for a home run in ninth inning of Game 5 of AL Championship Series . . . After that game, ace reliever admitted that he was less than 100 percent . . . His problems started in spring training, when he had soreness in his right rib cage . . . Suffered from sore shoulder most of the year . . . Disabled from May 28 to June 30 with shoulder stiffness . . . Compiled 4.32 ERA in first 13 appearances compared to 0.89 mark during stellar 1985 campaign . . . Signed three-year, $3-million contract on Jan. 9, 1986 . . . Despite physical problems, he converted 21 of 30 save opportunities . . . Worked five innings in ALCS, going 0-1 with 7.20 ERA . . . Born Feb. 13, 1954, in Lubbock, Tex. . . . Selected after Atlanta exposed him to free-agent compensation pool in January 1985 . . .

Originally drafted by Boston in 12th round in June 1972 . . . First cousin of Montreal shortstop Hubie Brooks.

Year	Club	G	IP	W	L	Pct.	SO	BB	H	ERA
1975	Chicago (NL)	4	9	0	0	.000	8	4	12	4.00
1977	Chicago (NL)	27	49	4	2	.667	34	18	51	4.04
1978	Chicago (NL)	71	103	9	7	.563	50	31	117	4.11
1979	Chicago (NL)	39	73	1	4	.200	43	25	95	5.18
1980	St. Louis	11	22	1	1	.500	10	5	25	6.14
1981	Milwaukee	3	4	0	0	.000	2	4	4	6.75
1982	Atlanta	16	27⅔	3	1	.750	17	7	32	4.23
1983	Atlanta	43	68⅔	2	3	.400	41	10	72	3.67
1984	Atlanta	47	64⅓	4	5	.444	47	18	63	2.94
1985	California	65	103	8	8	.500	72	21	91	1.92
1986	California	49	72⅔	4	5	.444	53	22	60	2.97
	Totals	375	596⅓	36	36	.500	377	165	622	3.64

TOP PROSPECT

DEVON WHITE 24 6-1 170 **Bats S Throws R**

Strong candidate for an outfield position in spring training . . . Played in 112 games for Edmonton (AAA) before Aug. 31 recall . . . Led team in runs (84), triples (10) and stolen bases (42) . . . Has succeeded in first nine stolen-base attempts in majors . . . Appeared at each outfield position after recall . . . Born Dec. 29, 1962, in Kingston, Jamaica . . . Selected in sixth round of June 1981 draft . . . Brought off bench twice in AL Championship Series and scored two runs . . . Hit .235 with one homer and three RBI for Angels down the stretch.

MANAGER GENE MAUCH: "Greatest Manager Who Never Won" tag remains as his Angels bowed to Boston after taking 3-1 lead in AL Championship Series and coming within one strike of their first pennant in Game 5 . . . Some Boston players suggested he was wrong to pull ace Mike Witt with a 5-4 lead in the ninth inning of Game 5, after a two-run home run by Don Baylor . . . Demoralized Angels were outscored, 18-5, in final two ALCS games . . . Has managed 25 years without winning a pennant, a major-league record . . . Still criticized for overworking Jim Bunning and Chris Short when 1964 Phillies blew 6½-game lead in final 12 games . . . His 1982 Angels blew

2-0 edge in best-of-five ALCS against Milwaukee . . . No one is better than this guy, however, at making his teams fundamentally sound . . . Great believer in lost art of sacrifice bunt . . . Started as a shortstop in Brooklyn Dodger organization . . . Played for six major-league teams from 1944-57, batting .239 . . . Took first managerial job at 28, piloting Atlanta Crackers of Southern Association in 1953 . . . Has managed Phillies, Expos, Twins and Angels . . . Born Nov. 18, 1925, in Salina, Kan. . . . Composite major-league record is 1,828-1,950.

GREATEST ALL-TIME ROOKIE

When California bade farewell to Rod Carew to make room for Wally Joyner before the 1986 season, there were the usual skeptics who wondered whether Joyner needed more seasoning.

All doubts were dispelled in the first month of the season as Joyner repeatedly found the home-run range—to the tune of eight homers by May 4. In a five-game stretch later in May, he connected for five homers and he had a total of 20 homers and 72 RBI at the All-Star break.

Fans across the country gave him 917,972 All-Star votes and the first baseman became the first rookie selected to start in the game since fans received the vote.

Joyner finished with club rookie records for hits (172) and RBI (100). He batted .290, had 22 homers and made his claim to the title of Angels' greatest rookie.

ALL-TIME ANGEL SEASON RECORDS

BATTING: Rod Carew, .339, 1983
HRs: Reggie Jackson, 39, 1982
RBIs: Don Baylor, 139, 1979
STEALS: Mickey Rivers, 70, 1975
WINS: Clyde Wright, 22, 1970
Nolan Ryan, 22, 1974
STRIKEOUTS: Nolan Ryan, 383, 1973

CHICAGO WHITE SOX

TEAM DIRECTORY: Chairman: Jerry Reinsdorf; Pres.: Eddie Einhorn; VP-GM: Larry Himes; Exec. VP: Howard Pizer; VP-Baseball Adm.: Jack Gould; Dir. Scouting-Play. Dev.: Al Goldis; Dir. Pub. Rel.: Paul Jensen; Trav. Sec.: Glen Rosenbaum; Mgr.: Jim Fregosi. Home: Comiskey Park (44,087). Field distances: 347, l.f. line; 382, l.c.; 409, c.f.; 382, r.c.; 347, r.f. line. Spring training: Sarasota, Fla.

One of few constants for troubled Sox is Harold Baines.

SCOUTING REPORT

HITTING: Harold Baines (.296, 21 homers, 88 RBI) is one of the few constants in an attack that ranked last in the AL in average (.247) and home runs (121). Greg Walker (.277, 13, 51) is expected to generate more power after a 1986 season that was marred by a broken right wrist.

Carlton Fisk (.221, 14, 63) is nearing the end of the line at age 39 and the effectiveness of Ron Hassey is diminished by bad knees. Ozzie Guillen (.250, 2, 47) is a good contact hitter. Former Oakland infielder Donnie Hill (.283, 4, 29) is a good acquisition, but the White Sox attack needs more help than that.

PITCHING: The White Sox tied Boston for third in the AL with a 3.93 ERA. But starters Floyd Bannister (10-14, 3.54), Joe Cowley (11-11, 3.88) and Rich Dotson (10-17, 5.48) are all ordinary and the status of Neil Allen (7-2, 3.82) is uncertain. He was disabled the second half of last season with torn fibers in his right tricep.

Bob James (5-4, 5.25, 14 saves) also hopes his arm miseries are behind him, but he is a hard thrower who seems destined to break down occasionally. Young right-hander Bobby Thigpen has the makings of a stopper. He was called up in August and went 2-0 with a 1.77 ERA and seven saves in 20 appearances.

FIELDING: The White Sox don't have any Gold Glove winners, but are solid defensively. They were fourth in the AL with a .981 fielding percentage last year, making 117 errors.

Improvement is expected from shortstop Guillen, who was guilty of 22 errors last season—10 more than he committed in 1985, when he was Rookie of the Year. Ron Karkovice, who has displaced Fisk behind the plate, is a good-looking young catcher.

OUTLOOK: The White Sox, 72-90 in 1986, enter their first full season under manager Jim Fregosi with modest expectations. There is a dearth of power and a pitching staff without an ace. Chicago must hope for a big year from Bannister, in his final season before he can become a free agent, or Cowley, who showed his ability with a no-hitter last season but is an erratic performer. This is a mediocre team.

CHICAGO WHITE SOX 1987 ROSTER

MANAGER Jim Fregosi

Coaches—Dick Bosman, Ed Brinkman, Deron Johnson, Art Kusnyer, Dyar Miller, Doug Rader, Glen Rosenbaum

PITCHERS

No.	Name	1986 Club	W-L	IP	SO	ERA	B-T	Ht.	Wt.	Born
33	Allen, Neil	Chicago (AL)	7-2	113	57	3.82	R-R	6-2	190	1/24/58 Kansas City, KS
19	Bannister, Floyd	Chicago (AL)	10-14	165	92	3.54	L-L	6-1	193	6/10/55 Pierre, SD
40	Cowley, Joe	Chicago (AL)	11-11	162	132	3.88	R-R	6-5	210	8/15/58 Lexington, KY
		Buffalo	1-3	36	30	3.96				
52	Davis, Joel	Chicago (AL)	4-5	105	54	4.70	L-R	6-5	205	11/30/65 Jacksonville, FL
		Buffalo	1-4	39	30	4.58				
26	DeLeon, Jose	Pittsburgh	1-3	16	11	8.27	R-R	6-3	215	12/20/60 Dom. Republic
		Hawaii	5-8	106	83	2.46				
		Chicago (AL)	4-5	79	68	2.96				
34	Dotson, Richard	Chicago (AL)	10-17	197	110	5.48	R-R	6-0	204	1/10/59 Cincinnati, OH
43	James, Bob	Chicago (AL)	5-4	58	32	5.25	R-R	6-4	230	8/15/58 Glendale, CA
—	Menendez, Tony	Birmingham	7-8	96	52	5.70	R-R	6-2	189	2/20/65 Cuba
		Peninsula	4-4	63	43	4.57				
50	McKeon, Joel	Buffalo	1-0	8	8	0.00	L-L	6-0	185	2/25/63 Covington, KY
		Chicago (AL)	3-1	33	18	2.45				
—	Nielsen, Scott	Ft. Lauderdale	4-0	34	10	2.10	R-R	6-1	190	12/18/58 Salt Lake City, UT
		Columbus	11-7	117	44	3.47				
		New York (AL)	4-4	56	20	4.02				
24	Schmidt, Dave	Chicago (AL)	3-6	92	67	3.31	R-R	6-1	185	4/22/57 Niles, MI
36	Searage, Ray	Vancouver	2-0	25	20	1.44	L-L	6-1	180	5/1/55 Freeport, NY
		Mil.-Chi. (AL)	1-1	51	36	3.35				
58	Thigpen, Bobby	Birmingham	8-11	160	90	4.68	R-R	6-3	195	7/17/63 Tallahassee, FL
		Chicago (AL)	2-0	36	20	1.77				
—	White, David	Birmingham	11-3	129	70	3.08	R-R	6-4	210	12/18/61 Olympia Fields, IL

CATCHERS

No.	Name	1986 Club	H	HR	RBI	Pct.	B-T	Ht.	Wt.	Born
72	Fisk, Carlton	Chicago (AL)	101	14	63	.221	R-R	6-2	215	12/26/47 Bellows Falls, VT
25	Hassey, Ron	NY (AL)-Chi. (AL)	110	9	49	.323	L-R	6-2	195	2/27/53 Tucson, AZ
53	Karkovice, Ron	Birmingham	90	20	53	.282	R-R	6-1	215	8/8/63 Union, NJ
		Chicago (AL)	24	4	13	.247				

INFIELDERS

No.	Name	1986 Club	H	HR	RBI	Pct.	B-T	Ht.	Wt.	Born
37	Cochrane, Dave	Birmingham	95	27	74	.272	B-R	6-2	180	1/31/63 Riverside, CA
		Buffalo	28	6	16	.226				
		Chicago (AL)	12	1	2	.194				
12	Cruz, Julio	Chicago (AL)	45	0	19	.215	B-R	5-9	180	12/2/54 Brooklyn, NY
18	Giles, Brian	Buffalo	28	3	9	.286	R-R	6-1	175	4/27/60 Manhattan, KS
		Chicago (AL)	3	0	1	.273				
13	Guillen, Ozzie	Chicago (AL)	137	2	47	.250	L-R	5-11	150	1/20/64 Venezuela
—	Hill, Donnie	Oakland	96	4	29	.283	B-R	5-10	160	11/12/60 Pomona, CA
23	Hulett, Tim	Chicago (AL)	120	17	44	.231	R-R	6-0	185	1/12/60 Springfield, IL
—	Manrique, Fred	Louisville	148	9	51	.285	R-R	6-1	175	11/5/61 Venezuela
		St. Louis	3	1	1	.176				
—	Martinez, Carlos	Albany	70	8	39	.277	R-R	6-5	175	8/11/65 Venezuela
		Buffalo	16	2	6	296				
14	Morman, Russ	Buffalo	97	13	57	.266	R-R	6-4	215	4/28/62 Independence, MO
		Chicago AL)	40	4	17	.252				
42	Perconte, Jack	Buffalo	61	0	15	.268	L-R	5-10	165	8/31/54 Joliet, IL
		Chicago (AL)	16	0	4	.219				
5	Salazar, Luis	Appleton	16	2	4	.203	R-R	5-9	180	5/19/56 Venezuela
		Chicago (AL)	1	0	0	.143				
—	Soper, Mike	Albany	28	1	7	.214	R-R	6-1	165	5/23/65 Miami, FL
		Columbus	35	0	12	.196				
29	Walker, Greg	Chicago (AL)	78	13	51	.277	L-R	6-3	198	10/6/59 Douglas, GA

OUTFIELDERS

No.	Name	1986 Club	H	HR	RBI	Pct.	B-T	Ht.	Wt.	Born
3	Baines, Harold	Chicago (AL)	169	21	88	.296	L-L	6-2	189	3/15/59 Easton, MD
8	Boston, Daryl	Buffalo	109	5	41	.303	L-L	6-3	193	1/4/63 Cincinnati, OH
		Chicago (AL)	53	5	22	.266				
22	Calderon, Ivan	Calgary	27	3	18	.333	R-R	6-1	205	3/19/62 Puerto Rico
		Buffalo	23	5	22	.219				
		Sea.-Chi. (AL)	41	2	15	.250				
44	Cangelosi, John	Chicago (AL)	103	2	32	.235	B-L	5-8	150	3/10/63 Brooklyn, NY
17	Hairston, Jerry	Chicago (AL)	61	5	26	.271	B-R	5-10	190	2/16/52 Birmingham, AL
10	Lyons, Steve	Buffalo	22	3	8	.297	L-R	6-3	192	6/3/60 Tacoma, WA
		Bos.-Chi. (AL)	56	1	20	.227				
20	Nichols, Reid	Chicago (AL)	31	1	18	.228	R-R	5-11	172	8/5/58 Ocala, FL
1	Williams, Ken	Birmingham	90	6	40	.331	R-R	6-1	184	4/6/64 Berkeley, CA
		Buffalo	40	4	15	.212				
		Chicago (AL)	4	1	1	.129				

WHITE SOX PROFILES

HAROLD BAINES 28 6-2 189 — Bats L Throws L

Right fielder doesn't say much, but speaks with bat . . . Led club in batting average (.296), home runs (21) and RBI (88) . . . Most prolific left-handed slugger in White Sox history . . . Delivered six of his 21 homers in ninth inning . . . Established club record by hitting 20 or more home runs five consecutive seasons . . . Re-injured right knee in collision with Minnesota pitcher Neal Heaton at first base on Sept. 27 . . . Missed last 10 days of season and had arthroscopic surgery . . . Born March 15, 1959, in Easton, Md. . . . First pick in nation by White Sox in June 1977 draft . . . Late Bill Veeck, former White Sox owner, spotted Baines as a 12-year-old Little Leaguer . . . Spent just three seasons in minors and broke into majors at age 21.

Year	Club	Pos.	G	AB	R	H	2B	3B	HR	RBI	SB	Avg.
1980	Chicago (AL)	OF	141	491	55	125	23	6	13	49	2	.255
1981	Chicago (AL)	OF	82	280	42	80	11	7	10	41	6	.286
1982	Chicago (AL)	OF	161	608	89	165	29	8	25	105	10	.271
1983	Chicago (AL)	OF	156	596	76	167	33	2	20	99	7	.280
1984	Chicago (AL)	OF	147	569	72	173	28	10	29	94	1	.304
1985	Chicago (AL)	OF	160	640	86	198	29	3	22	113	1	.309
1986	Chicago (AL)	OF	145	570	72	169	29	2	21	88	2	.296
	Totals		992	3754	492	1077	182	38	140	589	29	.287

GREG WALKER 27 6-3 198 — Bats L Throws R

First baseman played 163 games in 1985 but did a lot of watching in 1986 due to injury . . . First injured on April 14, when he fell attempting to field bunt on wet grass and suffered a hairline fracture of right wrist . . . Had pounded solo home runs in first two at-bats that night . . . Was disabled until May 14 . . . Batted just .194 in June but production was strong with 23 RBI. . . . Broke a bone in palm of right hand Aug. 2 on checked swing, had surgery and did not play again . . . Born Oct. 6, 1959, in Douglas, Ga. . . . Originally signed by Philadelphia in 1977, Walker was left unprotected in major-league draft in December 1979 and was chosen by White Sox.

Year	Club	Pos.	G	AB	R	H	2B	3B	HR	RBI	SB	Avg.
1982	Chicago (AL)	DH	11	17	3	7	2	1	2	7	0	.412
1983	Chicago (AL)	1B	118	307	32	83	16	3	10	55	2	.270
1984	Chicago (AL)	1B	136	442	62	130	29	2	24	75	8	.294
1985	Chicago (AL)	1B	163	601	77	155	38	4	24	92	5	.258
1986	Chicago (AL)	1B	78	282	37	78	10	6	13	51	1	.277
	Totals		506	1649	211	453	95	16	73	280	16	.275

RON HASSEY 34 6-2 195 **Bats L Throws R**

Excelled at the plate, despite disruptive off-the-field events . . . Was traded by the Yankees to the White Sox on Dec. 12, reacquired by the Yankees on Feb. 13 and traded to the White Sox again on July 29 as part of a six-player swap . . . Usefulness as a catcher is diminished by two bad knees . . . Injury limited him to pinch-hitting and designated-hitting duties in first 13 games in Chicago . . . Started only eight games behind the plate for White Sox . . . Willingly accepts whatever role he is given . . . Learned to pull the ball better after being traded from Cubs to the Yankees on Dec. 4, 1984 . . . Produced 16 multi-hit efforts in 49 games with White Sox . . . Signed with Cleveland after being selected in 18th round of June 1976 draft . . . Born Feb. 27, 1953, in Tucson, Ariz., and still lives there . . . Has degree in public administration from University of Arizona, where he was an All-American on 1976 NCAA champions . . . Father, Bill, was an outfielder in Yankee organization from 1949-52.

Year	Club	Pos.	G	AB	R	H	2B	3B	HR	RBI	SB	Avg.
1978	Cleveland.	C	25	74	5	15	0	0	2	9	2	.203
1979	Cleveland.	C-1B	75	223	20	64	14	0	4	32	1	.287
1980	Cleveland.	C-1B	130	390	43	124	18	4	8	65	0	.318
1981	Cleveland.	C-1B	61	190	8	44	4	0	1	25	0	.232
1982	Cleveland.	C-1B	113	323	33	81	18	0	5	34	3	.251
1983	Cleveland.	C	117	341	48	92	21	0	6	42	2	.270
1984	Cleveland.	C-1B	48	149	11	38	5	1	0	19	1	.255
1984	Chicago (NL)	C-1B	19	33	5	11	0	0	2	5	0	.333
1985	New York (AL)	C-1B	92	267	31	79	16	1	13	42	0	.296
1986	N.Y. (AL)-Chi. (AL)	C	113	341	45	110	25	1	9	49	1	.323
	Totals		793	2331	249	658	121	7	50	322	10	.282

OZZIE GUILLEN 23 5-11 150 **Bats L Throws R**

Shortstop deteriorated in the field from AL Rookie-of-the-Year form of 1985 . . . His 22 errors, mostly throwing, represented increase of 10 from '85 total . . . Had particular trouble making relay throws from outfield . . . Did post streak of 46 errorless games . . . Free-swinging fastball hitter who struck out just 52 times in 547 at-bats . . . Born Jan. 20, 1964, in Ocumare del Tuy, Venezuela . . . Signed by San Diego as free agent

Dec. 17, 1980 . . . Acquired by White Sox after 1984 season with Tim Lollar, Bill Long and Luis Salazar from San Diego for LaMarr Hoyt, Todd Simmons and Kevin Kristan . . . Set club record for fewest errors by a shortstop (12) in 1985 and topped all major-league shortstops with .980 fielding percentage . . . Originally a switch-hitter, Guillen has hit exclusively from left side past three years.

Year	Club	Pos.	G	AB	R	H	2B	3B	HR	RBI	SB	Avg.
1985	Chicago (AL)	SS	150	491	71	134	21	9	1	33	7	.273
1986	Chicago (AL)	SS	159	547	58	137	19	4	2	47	8	.250
	Totals		309	1038	129	271	40	13	3	80	15	.261

CARLTON FISK 39 6-2 215 **Bats R Throws R**

Enters final year of two-year contract . . . Sox aren't sure how to use the veteran catcher . . . Started first 26 games in left field and let his unhappiness affect his hitting . . . Was moved back behind the plate and responded with 12 RBI in first 11 games in which he was primarily a catcher . . . Left wrist bothered him after he was hit by a pitch in spring training . . . Lost 15 pounds while he was out two weeks in July with a virus . . . Born Dec. 26, 1947, in Bellows Falls, Vt. . . . "Pudge," selected by Red Sox as fourth pick in nation in January 1967 free-agent draft, was Boston fixture for 11 seasons before signing with White Sox as free agent in spring of 1981 . . . Ranks second to Yogi Berra in career homers by an AL catcher . . . First catcher in modern history to top century mark in home runs and stolen bases.

Year	Club	Pos.	G	AB	R	H	2B	3B	HR	RBI	SB	Avg.
1969	Boston	C	2	5	0	0	0	0	0	0	0	.000
1971	Boston	C	14	48	7	15	2	1	2	6	0	.313
1972	Boston	C	131	457	74	134	28	9	22	61	4	.293
1973	Boston	C	135	508	65	125	21	0	26	71	7	.246
1974	Boston	C	52	187	36	56	12	1	11	26	5	.299
1975	Boston	C	79	263	47	87	14	4	10	52	4	.331
1976	Boston	C	134	487	76	124	17	5	17	58	12	.255
1977	Boston	C	152	536	106	169	26	3	26	102	7	.315
1978	Boston	C-OF	157	571	94	162	39	5	20	88	7	.284
1979	Boston	C-OF	91	320	49	87	23	2	10	42	3	.272
1980	Boston	C-OF-1B-3B	131	478	73	138	25	3	18	62	11	.289
1981	Chicago (AL) . .	C-1B-3B-OF	96	338	44	89	12	0	7	45	3	.263
1982	Chicago (AL) . .	C-1B	135	476	66	127	17	3	14	65	17	.267
1983	Chicago (AL) . .	C	138	488	85	141	26	4	26	86	9	.289
1984	Chicago (AL) . .	C	102	359	54	83	20	1	21	43	6	.231
1985	Chicago (AL) . .	C	153	543	85	129	23	1	37	107	17	.238
1986	Chicago (AL) . .	OF-C	125	457	42	101	11	0	14	63	2	.221
	Totals		1827	6521	1003	1767	316	42	281	977	115	.271

JOE COWLEY 28 6-5 210 **Bats R Throws R**

Realized every pitcher's dream by firing a 7-1 no-hitter against California on Sept. 19... Walked bases full in sixth inning and probably would have been yanked if he hadn't gotten Reggie Jackson on sacrifice fly... On May 28, he became first major leaguer in this century to strike out first seven batters he faced. Such was his inconsistency, however, that he was relieved after 4⅔ innings... A .500 pitcher with ability of 20-game winner... Has disdain for conditioning and looks it... Born Aug. 15, 1958, in Lexington, Ky.... Obtained from Yankees with Ron Hassey for Britt Burns, Mike Soper and Glen Braxton on Dec. 12, 1985... Led Sox in victories with 11-11 mark and in strikeouts with 132... Optioned to Buffalo (AAA) April 15 after terrible spring... Recalled May 22... Originally signed by Atlanta at tryout camp.

Year	Club	G	IP	W	L	Pct.	SO	BB	H	ERA
1982	Atlanta	17	52⅓	1	2	.333	27	16	53	4.47
1984	New York (AL)	16	83⅓	9	2	.818	71	31	75	3.56
1985	New York (AL)	30	159⅔	12	6	.667	97	85	132	3.95
1986	Chicago (AL)	27	162⅓	11	11	.500	132	83	133	3.88
	Totals	90	457⅔	33	21	.611	327	215	393	3.91

RICHARD DOTSON 28 6-0 204 **Bats R Throws R**

Best aspect of Dotson's season was he remained healthy... Only White Sox starter not to miss a turn... Led club in starts (34) and innings (197) after undergoing chest surgery in 1985 to correct a circulatory problem... Rollercoaster season ended on sour note as he lost last four starts... Born Jan. 10, 1959, in Cincinnati... Selected in first round (seventh pick) of June 1977 draft by California... Acquired with Bobby Bonds and Thad Bosley for Brian Downing, Chris Knapp and Dave Frost on Dec. 5, 1977... Between 1983 and 1984 All-Star Games, he posted 25-6 record with 2.48 ERA.

Year	Club	G	IP	W	L	Pct.	SO	BB	H	ERA
1979	Chicago (AL)	5	24	2	0	1.000	13	6	28	3.75
1980	Chicago (AL)	33	198	12	10	.545	109	87	185	4.27
1981	Chicago (AL)	24	141	9	8	.529	73	49	145	3.77
1982	Chicago (AL)	34	196⅔	11	15	.423	109	73	219	3.84
1983	Chicago (AL)	35	240	22	7	.759	137	106	209	3.23
1984	Chicago (AL)	32	245⅔	14	15	.483	120	103	216	3.59
1985	Chicago (AL)	9	52⅓	3	4	.429	33	17	53	4.47
1986	Chicago (AL)	34	197	10	17	.370	110	69	226	5.48
	Totals	206	1294⅔	83	76	.522	704	510	1281	4.01

FLOYD BANNISTER 31 6-1 193 **Bats L Throws L**

At first glance, it appears Bannister made no progress since 10-14 record was identical to 1985 . . . But he became a pitcher instead of a thrower and lowered ERA from 4.87 to 3.54 . . . Gave up 17 home runs, two inside the park, after surrendering 30 each of past two years . . . Failed to lead Sox in strikeouts for first time in four years with club . . . Suffered injured knee when he slipped on a dugout step in Detroit . . . Made four more starts before he was disabled May 19 and underwent arthroscopic surgery on his left knee . . . Born June 10, 1955, in Pierre, S.D. . . . Nation's No. 1 pick, by Houston, in June 1976 draft after outstanding career at Arizona State . . . Astros traded him to Seattle for Craig Reynolds in December 1978 . . . Sox signed him as free agent in December 1982.

Year	Club	G	IP	W	L	Pct.	SO	BB	H	ERA
1977	Houston	24	143	8	9	.471	112	68	138	4.03
1978	Houston	28	110	3	9	.250	94	63	120	4.83
1979	Seattle	30	182	10	15	.400	115	68	185	4.05
1980	Seattle	32	218	9	13	.409	155	66	200	3.47
1981	Seattle	21	121	9	9	.500	85	39	128	4.46
1982	Seattle	35	247	12	13	.480	209	77	225	3.43
1983	Chicago (AL)	34	217⅓	16	10	.615	193	71	191	3.35
1984	Chicago (AL)	34	218	14	11	.560	152	80	211	4.83
1985	Chicago (AL)	34	210⅔	10	14	.417	198	100	211	4.87
1986	Chicago (AL)	28	165⅓	10	14	.417	92	48	162	3.54
	Totals	300	1832⅓	101	117	.463	1405	680	1771	4.03

NEIL ALLEN 29 6-2 190 **Bats R Throws R**

Most recent of his problems—torn fibers in right tricep—wiped out most of second half of 7-2 season . . . Began year in bullpen, then moved into starting rotation and didn't suffer first loss until July 2 . . . Had scoreless string of 21⅔ innings . . . Obtained on Feb. 13, 1986, from Yankees with Scott Bradley and Glen Braxton in exchange for Ron Hassey, Matt Winters, Eric Schmidt and Chris Alvarez . . . Was one of premier relievers in NL with Mets before being dealt with Rick Ownbey to St. Louis for Keith Hernandez on June 15, 1983 . . . Spent half a season with the Yankees in 1985, when Cardinals traded him for cash and a minor leaguer to be named . . . Possesses excellent breaking ball, but has had trouble controlling it . . . Born Jan. 24, 1958, in Kansas City, Kan.

Year	Club	G	IP	W	L	Pct.	SO	BB	H	ERA
1979	New York (NL)	50	99	6	10	.375	65	47	100	3.55
1980	New York (NL)	59	97	7	10	.412	79	40	87	3.71
1981	New York (NL)	43	67	7	6	.538	50	26	64	2.96
1982	New York (NL)	50	64⅔	3	7	.300	59	30	65	3.06
1983	NY (NL)-St. Louis	46	175⅔	12	13	.480	106	84	179	3.94
1984	St. Louis	57	119	9	6	.600	66	49	105	3.55
1985	St. Louis	23	29	1	4	.200	10	17	32	5.59
1985	New York (AL)	17	29⅓	1	0	1.000	16	13	26	2.76
1986	Chicago (AL)	22	113	7	2	.778	57	38	101	3.82
	Totals	367	793⅔	53	58	.477	508	344	759	3.65

BOB JAMES 28 6-4 230 **Bats R Throws R**

Another case of torn muscle fibers in right tricep . . . Still led club with 14 saves in 24 chances . . . Had 32 saves in 1985, when he set a White Sox record and was second in saves among AL relievers . . . Born Aug. 15, 1958, in Glendale, Cal. . . . Selected by Montreal in first round (ninth pick) of June 1976 draft . . . Acquired from Expos for Vance Law in December 1984 in the hope he'd be the answer to team's bullpen problems . . . Did not pitch regularly until his senior year at California's Verdugo Hills High . . . Previously a catcher . . . Threw two no-hitters as a schoolboy.

Year	Club	G	IP	W	L	Pct.	SO	BB	H	ERA
1978	Montreal	4	4	0	1	.000	3	4	4	9.00
1979	Montreal	2	2	0	0	.000	1	3	2	13.50
1982	Montreal	7	9	0	0	.000	11	8	10	6.00
1982	Detroit	12	19⅔	0	2	.000	20	8	22	5.03
1983	Detroit	4	4	0	0	.000	4	3	5	11.25
1983	Montreal	27	50	1	0	1.000	56	23	37	2.88
1984	Montreal	62	96	6	6	.500	91	45	92	3.66
1985	Chicago (AL)	69	110	8	7	.533	88	23	90	2.13
1986	Chicago (AL)	49	58⅓	5	4	.556	32	23	61	5.25
	Totals	236	353	20	20	.500	306	140	323	3.67

TOP PROSPECT

BOBBY THIGPEN 23 6-3 195 **Bats R Throws R**

Former Mississippi State outfielder made major-league pitching debut against Boston after being called up from Birmingham (AA) on Aug. 6 . . . Gave up five hits and two runs in three innings . . . Wound up appearing in 20 games, with 2-0 mark, 1.77 ERA and seven saves . . . Had one stretch of 28⅓ scoreless innings . . .

Fourth-round pick in June 1985 draft, he went 8-11 with 4.68 ERA in 25 starts at Birmingham . . . Born July 17, 1963, in Tallahasse, Fla.

White Sox count on Ozzie Guillen's return to '85 form.

MANAGER JIM FREGOSI: Replaced Tony LaRussa on June 22 and club responded by winning 11 of Fregosi's first 15 games . . . Finished season with 45-51 mark . . . Retired as player in 1978, after 18 years as infielder for Angels, Mets, Rangers, Pirates . . . Debuted as big-league manager with Angels in summer of 1978, won division title in 1979 and lasted through May 1981 . . . Spent three-and-a-half years as manager of Louisville (AAA) before responding to call from White Sox . . . Experienced the horse-racing world in Kentucky, where "at one time I had 18 quarter-horses, all of them eating, not running." . . . Major-league managing record: 282-299 . . . Born April 4, 1942, in San Francisco.

GREATEST ALL-TIME ROOKIE

Two minor-league seasons. That's all Luis Aparicio needed before embarking on his major-league career with the Chicago White Sox in 1956. That was the year the Venezuelan-born Aparicio showed the qualities that would distinguish him as one of the game's slickest and most durable shortstops.

Aparicio led the American League with 21 stolen bases and topped AL shortstops in putouts and assists. He also tied for the lead in errors, but in some of those cases Aparicio was a victim of his own range. He committed errors on balls other players would not have approached. Aparicio batted .266 as a rookie.

Aparicio's base-running and fielding led to his selection to eight All-Star teams. He twice helped teams into the World Series and enjoyed one of his finest moments in the 1959 World Series, when he batted .308 for the White Sox against the Dodgers.

Aparicio also spent time with Baltimore and Boston. He wound up his 18-year career with the Red Sox in 1973.

ALL-TIME WHITE SOX SEASON RECORDS

BATTING: Luke Appling, .388, 1936
HRs: Dick Allen, 37, 1972
Carlton Fisk, 37, 1985
RBIs: Zeke Bonura, 138, 1936
STEALS: Rudy Law, 77, 1983
WINS: Ed Walsh, 40, 1908
STRIKEOUTS: Ed Walsh, 269, 1908

KANSAS CITY ROYALS

TEAM DIRECTORY: Chairman: Ewing Kauffman; Vice-Chairman: Avron Fogelman; Pres.: Joe Burke; Exec. VP-GM: John Schuerholz; Exec. VP-Adm.: Spencer Robinson; Dir. Scouting: Art Stewart; Dir. Play. Dev.: John Boles; VP-Pub. Rel: Dean Vogelaar; Trav. Sec.: Will Rudd; Mgr.: Dick Howser. Home: Royals Stadium (40,625). Field distances: 330, l.f. line; 385, l.c.; 410, c.f.; 385, r.c.; 330, r.f. line. Spring training: Fort Myers, Fla.

SCOUTING REPORT

HITING: The Royals ended a two-year search for an outfielder with power by obtaining Danny Tartabull (.270, 25 homers, 96 RBI) from Seattle in a December deal that didn't cost them much

Ageless Frank White starts his 16th Royal season.

at all. His presence should greatly help George Brett (.290, 16, 73), who was frustrated by 80 walks last season, and Frank White (.272, 22, 84), who has become more conscious of hitting the long ball in recent seasons.

Even with White's substantial contribution, KC ranked 12th in the AL with 137 home runs and scored the second-fewest runs (654) in the league in 1986. Swift Willie Wilson (.269, 9, 44, 34 stolen bases) and beefy Steve Balboni (.229, 29, 88) are other significant contributors, although Balboni's back could be a big problem. He did not play after Sept. 9 last season. Heisman Trophy winner Bo Jackson (.207, 2, 9), called up last September, remains a raw talent whose time has not yet arrived, and the Royals let Lonnie Smith try his luck as a free agent.

PITCHING: The Royals had some disappointing performances from their pitchers last season and still led the AL with a 3.82 ERA, a sign of this staff's quality. Kansas City can expect better performances from Bret Saberhagen (7-12, 4.15), who crashed after his dream-like Cy Young, World Series MVP season in 1985, and Danny Jackson (11-12, 3.20). Mark Gubicza (12-6, 3.64) is coming into his own and Charlie Leibrandt (14-11, 4.09) is a proven veteran. Scott Bankhead, sent to the Mariners in the Tartabull deal, shouldn't be missed.

The Royals are resorting to a bullpen by committee, with the once-peerless Dan Quisenberry (3-7, 2.77, 12 saves) joined by Bud Black (5-10, 3.20, 9 saves) and Steve Farr (8-4, 3.13, 8 saves).

FIELDING: White returns at second base after adding another Gold Glove to his collection. Veteran Jim Sundberg paced all catchers with a .995 fielding percentage, although base-stealers now take liberties with him. The Royals' shortstop situation is unsettled. Tartabull, who was switched from second base to the outfield with Seattle last season, must improve in right field. He made a total of 18 errors last season, prompting the Mariners to question his work habits and eventually lose patience with him.

OUTLOOK: The Royals finished 76-86 last year, but they have won the AL West seven times in the last 11 years and will knock on the door again. The Royals' pitching in unequalled in the AL and they filled a gaping hole in the lineup by adding Tartabull. But a cloud has been hanging over this team since last July, when it was discovered manager Dick Howser had developed a malignant brain tumor. The Royals have had their share of glory. Now, they're learning about pain and disappointment.

KANSAS CITY ROYALS 1987 ROSTER

MANAGER Dick Howser
Coaches—Gary Blaylock, Billy Gardner, Jose Martinez, Hal McRae, Jim Schaffer

PITCHERS

No.	Name	1986 Club	W-L	IP	SO	ERA	B-T	Ht.	Wt.	Born
40	Black, Bud	Kansas City	5-10	121	68	3.20	L-L	6-2	180	6/30/57 San Mateo, CA
13	Cone, David	Omaha	8-4	71	63	2.79	L-R	6-1	180	1/2/63 Kansas City, MO
		Kansas City	0-0	23	21	5.56				
49	Davis, John	Memphis	6-6	111	69	4.69	R-R	6-7	215	1/5/63 Chicago, IL
		Omaha	0-0	2	1	4.50				
26	Farr, Steve	Kansas City	8-4	109	83	3.13	R-R	5-11	190	12/12/56 Cheverly, MD
39	Gleaton, Jerry	Buffalo	4-3	78	77	3.22	L-L	6-3	210	9/14/57 Brownwood, TX
23	Gubicza, Mark	Kansas City	12-6	181	118	3.64	R-R	6-6	215	8/14/62 Philadelphia, PA
50	Hargesheimer, Al	Omaha	13-6	150	71	3.29	R-R	6-3	200	11/21/56 Chicago, IL
		Kansas City	0-1	13	4	6.23				
25	Jackson, Danny	Kansas City	11-12	186	115	3.20	R-L	6-0	190	1/5/62 San Antonio, TX
37	Leibrandt, Charlie	Kansas City	14-11	231	108	4.09	R-L	6-3	200	10/4/56 Chicago, IL
29	Quisenberry, Dan	Kansas City	3-7	81	36	2.77	R-R	6-2	180	2/7/53 Santa Monica, CA
31	Saberhagen, Bret	Kansas City	7-12	156	112	4.15	R-R	6-1	160	4/11/64 Chicago Heights, IL
57	Sanchez, Israel	Memphis	13-7	184	141	3.47	L-L	5-9	171	8/20/63 Cuba
		Omaha	0-1	3	2	9.00				
48	Shaw, Theo	Omaha	5-9	98	62	3.84	R-R	6-0	185	5/30/62 Cook County, IL

CATCHERS

No.	Name	1986 Club	H	HR	RBI	Pct.	B-T	Ht.	Wt.	Born
34	Bell, Terry	Chattanooga	4	0	3	.333	R-R	6-0	195	10/27/62 Dayton, OH
		Memphis	28	0	12	.226				
		Kansas City	0	0	0	.000				
9	Quirk, Jamie	Kansas City	47	8	26	.215	L-R	6-4	200	10/22/54 Whittier, CA
8	Sundberg, Jim	Kansas City	91	12	42	.212	R-R	6-0	195	5/18/51 Galesburg, IL

INFIELDERS

No.	Name	1986 Club	H	HR	RBI	Pct.	B-T	Ht.	Wt.	Born
45	Balboni, Steve	Kansas City	117	29	88	.229	R-R	6-3	225	1/16/57 Brockton, MA
1	Biancalana, Buddy	Kansas City	46	2	8	.242	B-R	5-11	160	2/2/60 Larkspur, CA
5	Brett, George	Kansas City	128	16	73	.290	L-R	6-0	195	5/15/53 Glendale, WV
51	Delos Santos, Luis	Memphis	159	3	84	.303	R-R	6-5	190	12/29/66 Dom. Republic
36	Johnson, Ron	Omaha	140	1	60	.289	B-R	5-10	160	12/16/58 Bremerton, WA
		Kansas City	8	0	2	.258				
32	Pecota, Bill	Omaha	125	4	54	.264	R-R	6-2	195	2/16/60 Redwood City, CA
		Kansas City	6	0	2	.207				
4	Pryor, Greg	Kansas City	19	0	7	.170	R-R	6-0	185	10/2/49 Marietta, OH
2	Salazar, Angel	Kansas City	73	0	24	.245	R-R	6-0	173	11/4/61 Venezuela
20	White, Frank	Kansas City	154	22	84	.272	R-R	5-11	175	9/4/50 Greenville, MS

OUTFIELDERS

No.	Name	1986 Club	H	HR	RBI	Pct.	B-T	Ht.	Wt.	Born
47	Brewer, Mike	Omaha	99	12	57	.254	R-R	6-5	190	10/24/59 Shreveport, LA
		Kansas City	3	0	0	.167				
16	Jackson, Bo	Memphis	51	7	25	.277	R-R	6-1	222	11/30/62 Bessemer, AL
		Kansas City	17	2	9	.207				
7	Law, Rudy	Kansas City	80	1	36	.261	L-L	6-2	180	10/7/56 Waco, TX
58	Martinez, Chito	Memphis	86	11	44	.304	L-L	5-11	169	12/19/65 Central America
11	McRae, Hal	Kansas City	70	7	37	.252	R-R	5-11	185	7/10/46 Avon Park, FL
3	Orta, Jorge	Kansas City	93	9	46	.277	L-R	5-10	175	11/26/50 Mexico
33	Seitzer, Kevin	Memphis	3	0	1	.273	R-R	5-11	180	3/26/62 Springfield, IL
		Omaha	138	13	74	.319				
		Kansas City	31	2	11	.232				
30	Snider, Van	Memphis	133	26	81	.270	L-R	6-3	180	8/11/63 Birmingham, AL
—	Tartabull, Danny	Seattle	138	25	96	.270	R-R	6-1	185	10/20/62 Puerto Rico
63	Thurman, Gary	Memphis	164	7	62	.312	R-R	5-10	165	11/12/64 Indianapolis, IN
		Omaha	1	0	0	.500				
6	Wilson, Willie	Kansas City	170	9	44	.269	B-R	6-3	195	7/9/55 Montgomery, AL

ROYAL PROFILES

GEORGE BRETT 33 6-0 195 Bats L Throws R

Suffered steep decline in production from 1985 totals . . . His .290 BA still led the Royals . . . Was issued team-high 80 walks, contributing to .401 on-base percentage, third-highest in league . . . Poor lineup surrounding hard-hitting third baseman enabled other clubs to pitch around him . . . Born May 15, 1953, in Glendale, W. Va. . . . Selected by Kansas City in second round of June 1971 draft . . . Royals' all-time leader in hits (2,095) and RBI (1,050) . . . Achieved 2,000th hit May 25 against Chicago . . . Honored with 11th consecutive All-Star selection . . . American League MVP in 1980, when he challenged .400 mark before settling at .390 . . . MVP of 1985 AL Championship Series against Toronto . . . Concern over shoulder problem that troubled him on and off last season.

Year	Club	Pos.	G	AB	R	H	2B	3B	HR	RBI	SB	Avg.
1973	Kansas City	3B	13	40	2	5	2	0	0	0	0	.125
1974	Kansas City	3B-SS	133	457	49	129	21	5	2	47	8	.282
1975	Kansas City	3B-SS	159	634	84	195	35	13	11	89	13	.308
1976	Kansas City	3B-SS	159	645	94	215	34	14	7	67	21	.333
1977	Kansas City	3B-SS	139	564	105	176	32	13	22	88	14	.312
1978	Kansas City	3B-SS	128	510	79	150	45	8	9	62	23	.294
1979	Kansas City	3B-1B	154	645	119	212	42	20	23	107	17	.329
1980	Kansas City	3B-1B	117	449	87	175	33	9	24	118	15	.390
1981	Kansas City	3B	89	347	42	109	27	7	6	43	14	.314
1982	Kansas City	3B-OF	144	552	101	166	32	9	21	82	6	.301
1983	Kansas City	3B-1B-OF	123	464	90	144	38	2	25	93	0	.310
1984	Kansas City	3B	104	377	42	107	21	3	13	69	0	.284
1985	Kansas City	3B	155	550	108	184	38	5	30	112	9	.335
1986	Kansas City	3B	124	441	70	128	28	4	16	73	1	.290
	Totals		1741	6675	1072	2095	428	112	209	1050	141	.314

STEVE BALBONI 30 6-3 225 Bats R Throws R

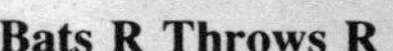

Another all-or-nothing year for the big first baseman . . . Led club with 29 home runs, 88 RBI . . . Those accomplishments were diminished, however, by team-leading 146 strikeouts . . . Set record for consecutive games with at least one strikeout (13) from Aug. 23 to Sept. 5 . . . Has led Royals in homers each of his three years there . . . Became 46th player to hit 100 or more homers in both the majors and the minors . . . Had 153 homers in minors . . . Didn't play after Sept. 9 due to a strange back injury . . . Born Jan. 16, 1957, in Brockton, Mass., birthplace of another slugger, Rocky Marciano . . . Obtained from Yankees with Roger Erickson for Mike Armstrong and Duane

Dewey on Dec. 8, 1983 . . . Led league in home runs and RBI at each minor-league stop . . . Product of Eckerd College.

Year	Club	Pos.	G	AB	R	H	2B	3B	HR	RBI	SB	Avg.
1981	New York (AL)	1B	4	7	2	2	1	1	0	2	0	.286
1982	New York (AL)	1B	33	107	8	20	2	1	2	4	0	.187
1983	New York (AL)	1B	32	86	8	20	2	0	5	17	0	.233
1984	Kansas City	1B	126	438	58	107	23	2	28	77	0	.244
1985	Kansas City	1B	160	600	74	146	28	2	36	88	1	.243
1986	Kansas City	1B	138	512	54	117	25	1	29	88	0	.229
	Totals		493	1750	204	412	81	7	100	276	1	.235

WILLIE WILSON 31 6-3 195 **Bats S Throws R**

Not a typical season for the swift center fielder . . . Average dipped to .269, lowest since he hit .217 in 1978, his first full major-league season . . . Did manage career-high nine home runs, all out of the park . . . Before 1986, 13 of his 21 career homers were inside the park . . . With emphasis on more power, Wilson fanned career-high 97 times . . . Paced Royals in stolen bases for ninth consecutive season with 34 . . . Born July 9, 1955, in Montgomery, Ala. . . . Selected in first round of June 1974 draft . . . Had accepted football scholarship to Maryland before signing with Royals . . . Began switch-hitting at Omaha (AAA) in 1977 . . . Batted .367 in 1985 World Series, second only to teammate George Brett.

Year	Club	Pos.	G	AB	R	H	2B	3B	HR	RBI	SB	Avg.
1976	Kansas City	OF	12	6	0	1	0	0	0	0	2	.167
1977	Kansas City	OF	13	34	10	11	2	0	0	1	6	.324
1978	Kansas City	OF	127	198	43	43	8	2	0	16	46	.217
1979	Kansas City	OF	154	588	113	185	18	13	6	49	83	.315
1980	Kansas City	OF	161	705	133	230	28	15	3	49	79	.326
1981	Kansas City	OF	102	439	54	133	10	7	1	32	34	.303
1982	Kansas City	OF	136	585	87	194	19	15	3	46	37	.332
1983	Kansas City	OF	137	576	90	159	22	8	2	33	59	.276
1984	Kansas City	OF	128	541	81	163	24	9	2	44	47	.301
1985	Kansas City	OF	141	605	87	168	25	21	4	43	43	.278
1986	Kansas City	OF	156	631	77	170	20	7	9	44	34	.269
	Totals		1267	4908	775	1457	176	97	30	357	470	.297

FRANK WHITE 36 5-11 175 **Bats R Throws R**

Kansas City hasn't had to think about second base since the end of 1975 season, thanks to the super-consistent White . . . Always a fine defensive player, he has developed power stroke, too, and he enjoyed his best all-around year offensively in 1986 . . . Equaled career high of 22 home runs set in 1985 and his 154 hits were two shy of his best . . . Set career high in RBI with 84 . . . Named to All-Star squad for fifth time . . . Born Sept. 4, 1950, in Greenville, Miss. . . . Signed as free agent following tryout camp in 1970 . . . Graduate of Royals' Academy . . . Played high-school football and basketball in Kansas City, but school didn't field a baseball team . . . Had career-high seven-RBI game Aug. 19 against Texas, tying club record . . . Led club with 11 game-winning RBI . . . Only second baseman in AL history to win seven Gold Gloves . . . Voted MVP in 1980 AL Championship Series.

Year	Club	Pos.	G	AB	R	H	2B	3B	HR	RBI	SB	Avg.
1973	Kansas City . . .	SS-2B	51	139	20	31	6	1	0	5	3	.223
1974	Kansas City . . .	2B-SS-3B	99	204	19	45	6	3	1	18	3	.221
1975	Kansas City . . .	2B-3B-SS-C	111	304	43	76	10	2	7	36	11	.250
1976	Kansas City . . .	2B-SS	152	446	39	102	17	6	2	46	20	.229
1977	Kansas City . . .	2B-SS	152	474	59	116	21	5	5	50	23	.245
1978	Kansas City . . .	2B	143	461	66	127	24	6	7	50	13	.275
1979	Kansas City . . .	2B	127	467	73	124	26	4	10	48	28	.266
1980	Kansas City . . .	2B	154	560	70	148	23	4	7	60	19	.264
1981	Kansas City . . .	2B	94	364	35	91	17	1	9	38	4	.250
1982	Kansas City . . .	2B	145	524	71	156	45	6	11	56	10	.298
1983	Kansas City . . .	2B	146	549	52	143	35	6	11	77	13	.260
1984	Kansas City . . .	2B	129	479	58	130	22	5	17	56	5	.271
1985	Kansas City . . .	2B	149	563	62	140	25	1	22	69	10	249
1986	Kansas City . . .	2B	151	566	76	154	37	3	22	84	4	.272
	Totals		1803	6100	743	1583	314	53	131	693	166	.260

DANNY TARTABULL 24 6-1 185 Bats R Throws R

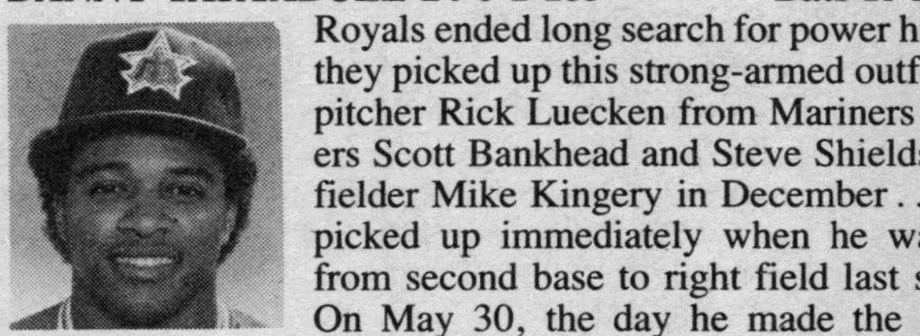

Royals ended long search for power hitter when they picked up this strong-armed outfielder and pitcher Rick Luecken from Mariners for pitchers Scott Bankhead and Steve Shields and outfielder Mike Kingery in December . . . Offense picked up immediately when he was moved from second base to right field last season . . . On May 30, the day he made the move, he went 2-for-4 with a home run . . . Fell two short of tying Alvin Davis' Seattle rookie record of 27 home runs, set in 1984 . . . Disabled in May with vitamin deficiency anemia and complained of fatigue that accounted for his tailing off toward end of year . . . Born Nov. 30, 1962, in San Juan, Puerto Rico . . . Selected by Cincinnati in third round of June 1980 draft . . . Mariners acquired him in 1983 compensation pool after losing free agent Floyd Bannister . . . Father, Jose, was a major-league outfielder with little power . . . Son led all professional baseball with 43 homers at Calgary (AAA) in 1985.

Year	Club	Pos.	G	AB	R	H	2B	3B	HR	RBI	SB	Avg.
1984	Seattle	SS-2B	10	20	3	6	1	0	2	7	0	.300
1985	Seattle	SS-3B	19	61	8	20	7	1	1	7	1	.328
1986	Seattle	OF-SS-2B	137	511	76	138	25	6	25	96	4	.270
	Totals		166	592	87	164	33	7	28	110	5	.277

CHARLIE LEIBRANDT 30 6-3 200 Bats R Throws L

Fell off from 1985 totals but still led Royals in wins (14), starts (34), complete games (eight) and innings pitched (231⅓) . . . Blazing 4-0 April was followed by 0-3 May, setting tone for inconsistent season . . . Workhorse who pitched into seventh inning in 24 of 34 starts . . . Occasional loss of pinpoint control hurt him last season . . . Placed second in AL with 2.69 ERA and compiled career-high 17 victories in 1985 . . . Went from July 12 to Aug. 21 without a win in 1986 . . . Born Oct. 4, 1956, in Chicago . . . Selected by Cincinnati in ninth round of June 1978 draft . . . Acquired from Cincinnati for Bob Tufts on June 7, 1983.

Year	Club	G	IP	W	L	Pct.	SO	BB	H	ERA
1979	Cincinnati	3	4	0	0	.000	1	2	2	0.00
1980	Cincinnati	36	174	10	9	.526	62	54	200	4.24
1981	Cincinnati	7	30	1	1	.500	9	15	28	3.60
1982	Cincinnati	36	107⅔	5	7	.417	34	48	30	5.10
1984	Kansas City	23	143⅔	11	7	.611	53	38	158	3.63
1985	Kansas City	33	237⅔	17	9	.654	108	68	223	2.69
1986	Kansas City	35	231⅓	14	11	.560	108	63	238	4.09
	Totals	173	928⅓	58	44	.569	375	288	979	3.77

BRET SABERHAGEN 22 6-1 160 Bats R Throws R

Dream season of 1985 followed by a nightmare as Cy Young Award winner and World Series MVP went from 20-6 to 7-12 . . . Missed Opening Day assignment with sore right shoulder . . . Made only five starts after July 22 and took mound just once from July 22 to Sept. 20 . . . In that start, Aug. 9 at Yankee Stadium, he was chased by New York after 1⅔ innings . . . Placed on 15-day disabled list next day . . . It's said that Saberhagen's problems resulted from poor offseason preparation . . . Never won consecutive decisions . . . Born April 11, 1964, in Chicago Heights, Ill. . . . Chosen in 19th round of June 1982 draft . . . Within span of 36 hours in 1985, Saberhagen became a father and was named youngest recipient of the World Series MVP Award following his 11-0 five-hitter over St. Louis in Game 7 . . . Was fifth-youngest pitcher to win 20 games . . . Fastball pitcher who can't get by if he's less than 100 percent.

Year	Club	G	IP	W	L	Pct.	SO	BB	H	ERA
1984	Kansas City	38	157⅔	10	11	.476	73	36	138	3.48
1985	Kansas City	32	235⅓	20	6	.769	158	38	211	2.87
1986	Kansas City	30	156	7	12	.368	112	29	165	4.15
	Totals	100	549	37	29	.561	343	103	514	3.41

MARK GUBICZA 24 6-6 215 **Bats R Throws R**

After an 0-4 start, he wound up with great finish . . . Did not lose after Aug. 23 . . . Won nine of last 10 decisions, including final five . . . Has seemingly overcome tendency to overthrow ball . . . Has won in double figures all three major-league seasons . . . Fanned career-high 10 batters in a 5-0 shutout of New York on Aug. 17 . . . Born Aug. 14, 1962, in Philadelphia . . . Selected by Kansas City in second round of June 1981 draft . . . Placed on disabled list on June 6 after being struck in the head by a ball during batting practice . . . First big-league victory was a shutout against Boston on May 12, 1984 . . . Father, Anthony, pitched in White Sox organization.

Year	Club	G	IP	W	L	Pct.	SO	BB	H	ERA
1984	Kansas City	29	189	10	14	.417	111	75	172	4.05
1985	Kansas City	29	177⅓	14	10	583	99	77	160	4.06
1986	Kansas City	35	180⅔	12	6	.667	118	84	155	3.64
	Totals	93	547	36	30	.545	328	236	487	3.92

DANNY JACKSON 25 6-0 190 **Bats R Throws L**

Continues to have mediocre results despite vast potential . . . Was within three outs of no-hitter against California on Oct. 1 before Dick Schofield singled . . . Settled for two-hitter and 2-0 shutout . . . Led KC starters with 3.20 ERA . . . Went 2-3 last seven starts despite 1.60 ERA . . . Hurt his ankle on last day of spring training while shagging fly balls and began year on disabled list . . . Victim of terrible support while losing four straight from May 27 to June 12, as Royals scored total of six runs behind him . . . Born Jan. 5, 1962, in San Antonio, Tex. . . . Selected in first round of January 1982 draft . . . Drafted by Oakland in 1980 but did not sign . . . Attended Oklahoma for one year, posting 6-2 record . . . Started Royals' successful comeback in 1985 World Series, winning Game 5 on five-hitter, 6-1 . . . Was 2-1 with 1.04 ERA in four postseason appearances.

Year	Club	G	IP	W	L	Pct.	SO	BB	H	ERA
1983	Kansas City	4	19	1	1	.500	9	6	26	5.21
1984	Kansas City	15	76	2	6	.250	40	35	84	4.26
1985	Kansas City	32	208	14	12	.538	114	76	209	3.42
1986	Kansas City	32	185⅔	11	12	.478	115	79	177	3.20
	Totals	83	488⅔	28	31	.475	278	196	496	3.54

DAN QUISENBERRY 34 6-2 180 **Bats R Throws R**

Fortunes plunged as he went from being game's premier reliever to career-low 12 saves . . . Royals lost faith in mid-May . . . On May 12, he faced four batters against Detroit and didn't retire any . . . Next outing, May 17, he blew save and Royals lost, 7-2 . . . Had three saves by April 20 but didn't get fourth until June 4 . . . Had outstanding June, allowing one earned run in 14⅔ innings . . . But failed to maintain that form . . . Born Feb. 7, 1953, in Santa Monica, Cal. . . . Signed as free agent on June 7, 1975 . . . Has lifetime contract with Royals . . . Logged 212 saves from 1980 through 1985, highest total in big leagues . . . Established major-league record with 45 saves in 1983 . . . It was tied by Cardinals' Bruce Sutter a year later and broken by Yankees' Dave Righetti with 46 in 1986.

Year	Club	G	IP	W	L	Pct.	SO	BB	H	ERA
1979	Kansas City	32	40	3	2	.600	13	7	42	3.15
1980	Kansas City	75	128	12	7	.632	37	27	129	3.09
1981	Kansas City	40	62	1	4	.200	20	15	59	1.74
1982	Kansas City	72	136⅔	9	7	.563	46	12	126	2.57
1983	Kansas City	69	139	5	3	.625	48	11	118	1.94
1984	Kansas City	72	129⅓	6	3	.667	41	12	121	2.64
1985	Kansas City	84	129	8	9	471	54	16	142	2.37
1986	Kansas City	62	81⅓	3	7	.300	36	24	92	2.77
	Totals	506	845⅓	47	42	.528	295	124	829	2.51

TOP PROSPECT

BO JACKSON 24 6-1 222 **Bats R Throws R**

A coup for the Royals, who gambled by drafting the Heisman Trophy winner from Auburn in the fourth round of the June 1986 draft . . . Jackson was No. 1 player selected in NFL draft, but rejected offer from Tampa Bay Buccaneers for baseball career . . . Called up in September and batted .207 in 25 games with Royals . . . Possesses tremendous power, evident in first major-league homer on Sept. 14, longest in Royals' Stadium history . . . Still a raw talent, he fanned 34 times in 82 at-bats . . . Had same problem when he started at Memphis (AA), striking out 81 times in 184 at-bats . . . Must learn patience at the plate . . . A ragged right fielder at this point . . . Batted .277 with seven homers and 25 RBI in 53 games with Memphis . . . Born Nov. 30, 1962, in Bessemer, Ala.

George Brett needs some support in Royals' lineup.

MANAGER DICK HOWSER: Baseball world was shocked when it learned after the All-Star Game that Howser was suffering from cancerous brain tumor . . . Symptoms were evident at the All-Star Game as Howser, managing the AL squad, became forgetful and confused . . . He was operated on, but did not return to the team he'd led to the World Championship in 1985 . . . Third-base coach Mike Ferraro, who himself had overcome cancer of the kidney, served as interim manager and was released after the season . . . Career record is 507-425 . . . He

was a Yankee coach for 10 years before taking over as rookie manager of the Yankees in 1980 . . . Fired by George Steinbrenner after the Royals swept the Yanks in the AL Championship Series, Howser signed with the Royals late in 1981 and led club to second-half title in split season . . . Took KC to AL West title in 1984 . . . An infielder at Florida State, he played with the A's and the Indians, hitting .248 in 789 major-league games . . . Born May 14, 1936, in Miami.

GREATEST ALL-TIME ROOKIE

Ten major-league starts were all the Royals' Steve Busby needed to pen his name in the record book. Busby hurled a 3-0 no-hitter against Detroit at Tiger Stadium in that 10th start on April 27, 1973.

The no-hitter was Busby's finest moment in a rookie season that more than hinted at future greatness. Busby was named American League Rookie Pitcher of the Year by *The Sporting News* after compiling a 16-15 record with a 4.24 ERA.

Busby would enjoy two more successful seasons, making the All-Star staff in 1974 and 1975 and compiling a 40-16 record in those years. With his 22-14 record in 1974, Busby set a club record for wins that still stands.

One of those victories was Busby's second no-hitter, a 2-0 decision over Milwaukee on June 19, 1974, in which George Scott, who walked, was the only base-runner.

Busby's fame was fleeting, however. The right-hander never was able to come back from surgery midway through the 1976 season to repair a torn rotator cuff. Royals' fans haven't forgotten Busby, though. He joined Amos Otis as the first two inductees in the Royals' Hall of Fame in 1986.

ALL-TIME ROYAL SEASON RECORDS

BATTING: George Brett, .390, 1980
HRs: Steve Balboni, 36, 1985
RBIs: Hal McRae, 133, 1982
STEALS: Willie Wilson, 83, 1979
WINS: Steve Busby, 22, 1974
STRIKEOUTS: Dennis Leonard, 244, 1977

MINNESOTA TWINS

TEAM DIRECTORY: Owner: Carl Pohlad; Pres.: Howard T. Fox, Jr.: Exec. VP-GM: Andy MacPhail; VPs: Dave Moore, Jim McHenry, Don Schiel; Dir. Media Rel.: Tom Mee; Mgr.: Tom Kelly. Home: Hubert H. Humphrey Metrodome (55,244). Field distances: 343, l.f. line; 408, c.f.; 327, r.f. line. Spring training: Orlando, Fla.

SCOUTING REPORT

HITTING: Chunky leadoff hitter Kirby Puckett (.328, 31 homers, 96 RBI) heads an attack that amassed 196 home runs, the second-highest total in the AL. Puckett, an opposite-field hitter when he first came up, doesn't fit that description any longer.

Gary Gaetti (.287, 34, 108) will try to pick up where he left off after turning in the biggest RBI year by a Twin since Larry Hisle knocked in 119 runs in 1977. Kent Hrbek (.267, 29, 91) can be counted on to produce another solid year. However, Tom Brunansky (.256, 23, 75) was the subject of winter trade rumors.

PITCHING: The Twins' pitching can only improve after they surrendered an AL-high 200 home runs and ranked last in the league with a 4.77 ERA last season. It's hard to believe this club passed on a chance to sign Jack Morris as a free agent during the winter.

Bert Blyleven (17-14, 4.01) accounted for one quarter of that gopher-ball total, setting a major-league record he could live without. Mike Smithson (13-14, 4.77) is a .500 pitcher. Left-handers Frank Viola (16-13, 4.51) and Neal Heaton (7-15, 4.08) are long on talent and short on results.

Neither Keith Atherton (6-10, 4.08, 10 saves) nor George Frazier (1-1, 4.39, 6 saves) is a stopper. Middle relief is missing, too, from a bullpen that recorded a major-league-low 24 saves.

FIELDING: The Twins are above average defensively. Puckett, winner of his first Gold Glove, sparkles in center field. Gaetti won his first Gold Glove at third base as his knack for making brilliant stops overcame his 21 errors. Hrbek is well above average at first base, despite his hulking appearance. Greg Gagne must improve after making 26 errors at shortstop. Steve Lombardozzi led all AL second basemen with a .991 fielding percentage.

OUTLOOK: The Twins will benefit from having Tom Kelly as their manager for a full season. He replaced an ineffective Ray Miller Sept. 12. The Twins are better than their 71-91, next-to-last-place finish of 1986 would indicate. But not much better.

AL pitchers couldn't Kirby that Twin terror Puckett.

MINNESOTA TWINS 1987 ROSTER

MANAGER Tom Kelly
Coaches—Tony Oliva, Rick Stelmaszek, Dick Such, Wayne Terwilliger

PITCHERS

No.	Name	1986 Club	W-L	IP	SO	ERA	B-T	Ht.	Wt.	Born
30	Agosto, Juan	Chi. (AL)-Min.	1-4	25	12	8.64	L-L	6-2	187	2/23/58 Puerto Rico
		Toledo	4-3	35	29	2.31				
49	Anderson, Allan	Toledo	2-5	67	37	4.57	L-L	6-0	186	1/7/64 Lancaster, OH
		Minnesota	3-6	84	51	5.55				
22	Atherton, Keith	Oak.-Min.	6-10	97	67	4.08	R-R	6-4	200	2/19/59 Newport News, VA
58	Bianchi, Ben	Visalia	7-2	66	68	2.88	R-R	6-4	200	8/15/61 Ely, NV
		Orlando	5-4	101	58	4.88				
28	Blyleven, Bert	Minnesota	17-14	272	215	4.01	R-R	6-3	205	4/6/51 Holland
32	Clay, Danny	Toledo	8-11	152	105	4.93	R-R	6-1	190	10/24/61 Sun Valley, CA
37	Fontenot, Ray	Chicago (NL)	3-5	56	24	3.86	L-L	6-0	175	8/8/57 Lake Charles, LA
		Minnesota	0-0	16	10	9.92				
39	Frazier, George	Chicago (NL)	2-4	52	41	5.40	R-R	6-5	200	10/13/54 Oklahoma City, OK
		Minnesota	1-1	27	25	4.39				
26	Heaton, Neal	Cle.-Min.	7-15	199	90	4.08	L-L	6-1	205	3/3/60 Jamaica, NY
46	Klink, Joe	Orlando	4-5	68	63	2.51	L-L	5-11	170	2/3/62 Johnstown, PA
31	Perez, Yorkis	Kenosha	4-11	131	144	5.15	L-L	6-0	160	9/30/67 Dominican Republic
36	Portugal, Mark	Toledo	5-1	45	30	2.60	R-R	6-0	200	10/30/62 Los Angeles, CA
		Minnesota	6-10	113	67	4.31				
19	Smith, Roy	Minnesota	0-2	10	8	6.97	R-R	6-3	212	9/6/61 Mt. Vernon, NY
		Toledo	2-1	54	39	1.51				
48	Smithson, Mike	Minnesota	13-14	198	114	4.77	L-R	6-8	215	1/21/55 Centerville, TN
40	Sontag, Alan	Orlando	9-12	171	81	4.84	R-R	6-5	195	10/21/63 Valley Stream, NY
17	Straker, Les	Toledo	6-7	107	50	3.44	R-R	6-1	193	10/10/59 Venezuela
16	Viola, Frank	Minnesota	16-13	246	191	4.51	L-L	6-4	209	4/19/60 Hempstead, NY

CATCHERS

No.	Name	1986 Club	H	HR	RBI	Pct.	B-T	Ht.	Wt.	Born
15	Laudner, Tim	Minnesota	47	10	29	.244	R-R	6-3	214	6/7/58 Mason City, IA
10	Reed, Jeff	Toledo	22	1	14	.310	L-R	6-2	190	11/12/62 Joliet, IL
		Minnesota	39	2	9	.236				
12	Salas, Mark	Minnesota	60	8	33	.233	L-R	6-0	205	3/8/61 Montebello, CA

INFIELDERS

No.	Name	1986 Club	H	HR	RBI	Pct.	B-T	Ht.	Wt.	Born
1	Espinoza, Alvaro	Toledo	71	2	27	.281	R-R	6-0	180	2/19/62 Venezuela
		Minnesota	9	0	1	.214				
8	Gaetti, Gary	Minnesota	171	34	108	.287	R-R	6-0	184	8/19/58 Centralia, IL
7	Gagne, Greg	Minnesota	118	12	54	.250	R-R	5-11	185	11/12/61 Fall River, MA
14	Hrbek, Kent	Minnesota	147	29	91	.267	L-R	6-4	235	5/21/60 Minneapolis, MN
51	Larkin, Gene	Orlando	170	15	104	.321	B-R	6-3	195	10/24/62 Flushing, NY
4	Lombardozzi, Steve	Minnesota	103	8	33	.227	R-R	6-0	175	4/26/60 Malden, MA
18	McDougal, Julius	Winston-Salem	100	1	43	.289	B-R	6-2	185	5/3/63 Jackson, MS
		Orlando	23	1	7	.377				
2	Pittaro, Chris	Minnesota	2	0	0	.095	B-R	5-11	161	9/16/61 Trenton, NJ
		Toledo	107	8	37	.256				
5	Smalley, Roy	Minnesota	113	20	57	.246	B-R	6-1	182	10/25/52 Los Angeles, CA
38	Washington, Ron	Toledo	53	3	19	.268	R-R	5-11	169	4/29/52 New Orleans, LA

OUTFIELDERS

No.	Name	1986 Club	H	HR	RBI	Pct.	B-T	Ht.	Wt.	Born
20	Beane, Billy	Toledo	37	5	17	.294	R-R	6-4	208	3/29/62 Orlando, FL
		Minnesota	39	3	15	.213				
52	Blackwell, Larry	Kenosha	64	5	35	.242	R-R	5-10	165	10/7/64 Petersburg, VA
24	Brunansky, Tom	Minnesota	152	23	75	.256	R-R	6-4	216	8/20/60 Covina, CA
25	Bush, Randy	Minnesota	96	7	45	.269	L-L	6-1	186	10/5/58 Dover, DE
27	Davidson, Mark	Toledo	95	10	38	.268	R-R	6-2	190	2/15/61 Knoxville, TN
		Minnesota	8	0	2	.118				
9	Hatcher, Mickey	Minnesota	88	3	32	.278	R-R	6-2	199	3/15/55 Cleveland, OH
50	Marte, Alex	Toledo	19	1	3	.202	L-L	6-0	168	12/12/62 Dom. Republic
		Orlando	91	1	28	.320				
34	Puckett, Kirby	Minnesota	223	31	96	.328	R-R	5-8	185	3/14/61 Chicago, IL
21	Wilson, Phil	Orlando	154	6	42	.293	R-R	5-8	160	6/1/63 Bamberg, SC

TWIN PROFILES

KIRBY PUCKETT 26 5-8 185 Bats R Throws R

Center fielder blossomed into one of league's dominant players . . . Finished second in AL in runs (119), hits (223) and total bases (365) . . . Was third in batting average (.328) and slugging percentage (.537) . . . Tied for fifth in home runs (31) and doubles (37) . . . Before 1986, he had hit four home runs in two seasons . . . Worked with batting coach Tony Oliva on keeping weight back . . . Concentrated on pulling ball more last season . . . An opposite-field hitter when he came up . . . Now possesses power to all fields . . . AL Player of the Month in April, batting .396 with eight home runs, 16 RBI . . . Voted to first All-Star starting berth . . . Strong case could have been made for him as league MVP if not for Twins' lowly status . . . Contended for batting title until September . . . Tied club record held by Rod Carew with eight four-hit games . . . Born March 14, 1961, in Chicago . . . Minnesota's first-round choice (third pick) in January 1982 draft . . . Became ninth player in history to collect four hits in first big-league nine-inning game on May 8, 1984.

Year	Club	Pos.	G	AB	R	H	2B	3B	HR	RBI	SB	Avg.
1984	Minnesota	OF	128	557	63	165	12	5	0	31	14	.296
1985	Minnesota	OF	161	691	80	199	29	13	4	74	21	.288
1986	Minnesota	OF	161	680	119	223	37	6	31	96	20	.328
	Totals		450	1928	262	587	78	24	35	201	55	.304

KENT HRBEK 26 6-4 235 Bats L Throws R

Big first baseman established a career high with 29 home runs, but otherwise season was disappointing . . . Reported to spring training at 254 pounds . . . Worked himself into better condition, then ballooned to 252 by end of season . . . Extra weight took its toll and his swing lacked snap by season's end . . . AL Player of the Month in June, collecting eight homers and 27 RBI . . . From June 1-22, he batted .451 with eight homers and 24 RBI in 20 games . . . Plunged to .180 in July . . . August not much better at .227 . . . Despite size, he fields position well . . . Born May 21, 1960, in Minneapolis . . . Selected by Twins in 17th round of June 1978 draft . . . Only rookie named to 1982 AL All-Star squad . . . Placed second in Rookie-of-the-Year balloting to Baltimore's

Cal Ripken . . . First major-league homer, on Aug. 24, 1981, defeated Yankees, 3-2, in 12 innings.

Year	Club	Pos.	G	AB	R	H	2B	3B	HR	RBI	SB	Avg.
1981	Minnesota	1B	24	67	5	16	5	0	1	7	0	.239
1982	Minnesota	1B	140	532	82	160	21	4	23	92	3	.301
1983	Minnesota	1B	141	515	75	153	41	5	16	84	4	.297
1984	Minnesota	1B	149	559	80	174	31	3	27	107	1	.311
1985	Minnesota	1B	158	593	78	165	31	2	21	93	1	.278
1986	Minnesota	1B	149	550	85	147	27	1	29	91	2	.267
	Totals		761	2816	405	815	156	15	117	474	11	.289

GARY GAETTI 28 6-0 184 — Bats R Throws R

Third baseman enjoyed a banner season, establishing career highs in average, hits, home runs, runs and RBI . . . With six-RBI game against Kansas City on Sept. 23, he became seventh Twin to attain at least 100 RBI . . . His 108 RBI represented most by a Minnesota player since Larry Hisle's 119 in 1977 . . . Has learned to protect the plate . . . No longer as vulnerable to breaking ball away . . . Much-improved two-strike hitter . . . Born Aug. 19, 1958, in Centralia, Ill. . . . Minnesota's first-round selection in June 1979 draft . . . Previously drafted by St. Louis and Chicago White Sox, but did not sign . . . Became 47th player to homer in first big-league at-bat when he connected off Charlie Hough in Texas on Sept. 20, 1981.

Year	Club	Pos.	G	AB	R	H	2B	3B	HR	RBI	SB	Avg.
1981	Minnesota	3B	9	26	4	5	0	0	2	3	0	.192
1982	Minnesota	3B-SS	145	508	59	117	25	4	25	84	0	.230
1983	Minnesota	3B-SS	157	584	81	143	30	3	21	78	7	.245
1984	Minnesota	3B-OF-SS	162	588	55	154	29	4	5	65	11	.262
1985	Minnesota	3B-OF-1B	160	560	71	138	31	0	20	63	13	.246
1986	Minnesota	3B-OF	157	596	91	171	34	1	34	108	14	.287
	Totals		790	2862	361	728	149	12	107	401	45	.254

GREG GAGNE 25 5-11 185 — Bats R Throws R

Batted .414 with 11 extra-base hits in spring training of 1985 to win shortstop job and has maintained hold on position . . . Batted .302 last May with two homers, eight RBI . . . Otherwise didn't do much with the bat . . . Hit .224 in April, .215 in June, .229 in July . . . Endured 0-for-19 drought in April, longest on club . . . Twins feel he will develop more power and is capable of being a 20-homer man . . . Has good range and an accurate arm . . . Sometimes holds onto the ball too long . . . Born Nov. 12, 1961, in Fall River, Mass. . . . One of nine children . . . All-state baseball and football player in high school . . . Yankees' fourth choice in June 1979 draft . . . Traded to Twins April 10, 1982, with Ron Davis and Paul Boris for Roy Smalley and Gerry Serum . . . Led International League shortstops with 364 assists and 599 total chances for Toledo (AAA) in 1983.

Year	Club	Pos.	G	AB	R	H	2B	3B	HR	RBI	SB	Avg.
1983	Minnesota	SS	10	27	2	3	1	0	0	3	0	.111
1984	Minnesota	PR-PH	2	1	0	0	0	0	0	0	0	.000
1985	Minnesota	SS	114	293	37	66	15	3	2	23	10	.225
1986	Minnesota	SS-2B	156	472	63	118	22	6	12	54	12	.250
	Totals		282	793	102	187	38	9	14	80	22	.236

STEVE LOMBARDOZZI 26 6-0 175 Bats R Throws R

Rookie season was disappointing after Twins had traded Tim Teufel to New York Mets to give Lombardozzi second-base job . . . Wore down as season progressed . . . Did not produce a home run in second half . . . Regarded as having good power and belted seven homers in first 75 games . . . Went 9-for-60 in September and did not drive in any runs . . . Biggest advantage over Teufel is his ability to turn double play . . . Born April 26, 1960, in Malden, Mass. . . . Brother, Chris, is in infielder in Yankees' system . . . Acquired in ninth round of June 1981 draft . . . Led shortstops in fielding percentage in Appalachian League for Elizabethton (A) in 1981 and in California League for Visalia (A) in 1982 . . . Switched to second base in 1984.

Year	Club	Pos.	G	AB	R	H	2B	3B	HR	RBI	SB	Avg.
1985	Minnesota	2B	28	54	10	20	4	1	0	6	3	.370
1986	Minnesota	2B-SS	156	453	53	103	20	5	8	33	3	.227
	Totals		!84	507	63	123	24	6	8	39	6	.243

TOM BRUNANSKY 26 6-4 211 Bats R Throws R

Heard his share of boos during a season in which he never really got going . . . Only strong month was May, when he batted .312 with seven home runs, 18 RBI . . . Month was highlighted by a four-hit game against Toronto on May 27 . . . Suffered through .230 August . . . September was worse at .215 . . . Went from Aug. 2 to Sept. 3, 24 games, without a homer . . . Outfielder used to have an excellent arm, but lost some zip on throws . . . One theory is an extensive weightlifting program created tightness in his shoulder . . . Born Aug. 20, 1960, in Covina, Cal. . . . California's first-round pick in June 1978 . . . Traded to Twins on May 11, 1982, with Mike Walters for Doug Corbett and Rob Wilfong . . . Set club record with 15 game-winning RBI in 1983

. . . Turned down baseball-football scholarship to Stanford . . . Attended Cal-Poly . . . Father, Joseph, was professional football and baseball player and was once an assistant football coach at Duke.

Year	Club	Pos.	G	AB	R	H	2B	3B	HR	RBI	SB	Avg.
1981	California	OF	11	33	7	5	0	0	3	6	1	.152
1982	Minnesota	OF	127	463	77	126	30	1	20	46	1	.272
1983	Minnesota	OF	151	542	70	123	24	5	28	82	2	.227
1984	Minnesota	OF	155	567	75	144	21	0	32	85	4	.254
1985	Minnesota	OF	157	567	71	137	28	4	27	90	5	.242
1986	Minnesota	OF	157	593	69	152	27	1	23	75	12	.256
	Totals		758	2765	369	687	130	11	133	384	25	.248

BERT BLYLEVEN 35 6-3 205 Bats R Throws R

Season was regrettably one for the record books . . . Surrendered 50 home runs, breaking mark set by Robin Roberts in 1956 . . . Roberts allowed 46 . . . No. 47 was hit on Sept. 28 as Cleveland's Jay Bell pounced on first major-league pitch he saw . . . Blyleven has lost a few mph on his fastball . . . Pitching in Metrodome, also known as the Homerdome, doesn't help, either . . . Allowed five home runs, one short of major-league record, in Aug. 13 game against Texas . . . Still fanned 215 batters, giving him AL record of eight seasons with more than 200 strikeouts . . . Led Twins in victories with 17-14 record . . . Born April 6, 1951, in Zeist, Holland . . . Originally selected by Minnesota in third round of June 1969 draft . . . Found his way back there three teams later when obtained on Aug. 1, 1985, from Cleveland for Jay Bell, Jim Weaver, Curt Wardle and Rich Yett . . . AL Rookie Pitcher of the Year in 1970 . . . Hurled 6-0 no-hitter against California on Sept. 22, 1977 . . . Has pitched five one-hitters . . . Possesses one of game's best curveballs.

Year	Club	G	IP	W	L	Pct.	SO	BB	H	ERA
1970	Minnesota	27	164	10	9	.526	135	47	143	3.18
1971	Minnesota	38	278	16	15	.516	224	59	267	2.82
1972	Minnesota	39	287	17	17	.500	228	69	247	2.73
1973	Minnesota	40	325	20	17	.541	258	67	296	2.52
1974	Minnesota	37	281	17	17	.500	249	77	244	2.66
1975	Minnesota	35	276	15	10	.600	233	84	219	3.00
1976	Minn.-Tex.	36	298	13	16	.448	219	81	283	2.87
1977	Texas	30	235	14	12	.538	182	69	181	2.72
1978	Pittsburgh	34	244	14	10	.583	182	66	217	3.02
1979	Pittsburgh	37	237	12	5	.706	172	92	238	3.61
1980	Pittsburgh	34	217	8	13	.381	168	59	219	3.82
1981	Cleveland	20	159	11	7	.611	107	40	145	2.89
1982	Cleveland	4	20⅓	2	2	.500	19	11	16	4.87
1983	Cleveland	24	156⅓	7	10	.412	123	44	160	3.91
1984	Cleveland	33	245	19	7	.731	170	74	204	2.87
1985	Clev.-Minn.	37	293⅔	17	16	.515	206	75	264	3.16
1986	Minnesota	36	271⅔	17	14	.548	215	58	262	4.01
	Totals	541	3988	229	197	.538	3090	1072	3605	3.08

FRANK VIOLA 26 6-4 209 **Bats L Throws L**

Inconsistent pitcher who isn't fulfilling expectations . . . Wins and losses reached double figures for third consecutive year . . . Won four straight, July 21 to Aug. 13 . . . Typically, he followed that with three-game slide . . . In last two games of losing streak, he allowed 14 runs in eight innings against Toronto and Boston . . . Born April 19, 1960, in Hempstead, N.Y. . . . Acquired in second round of June 1981 draft . . . All-American his junior year at St. John's . . . Beat Yale's Ron Darling, 1-0, in 12-inning NCAA regional game in 1981, although Darling held no-hitter through 11 innings . . . Winningest left-hander in majors in 1984 with 18 victories . . . Was 26-2 in three-year college career . . . Blanked Yankees, 2-0, in hometown debut in 1982.

Year	Club	G	IP	W	L	Pct.	SO	BB	H	ERA
1982	Minnesota	22	126	4	10	.286	84	38	152	5.21
1983	Minnesota	35	210	7	15	.318	127	92	242	5.49
1984	Minnesota	35	257⅔	18	12	.600	149	73	225	3.21
1985	Minnesota	36	250⅔	18	14	.563	135	68	262	4.09
1986	Minnesota	37	245⅔	16	13	.552	191	83	257	4.51
	Totals	165	1090	63	64	.496	686	354	1138	4.38

NEAL HEATON 27 6-1 205 **Bats L Throws L**

Twins hoped for better when they acquired him on June 20 from Cleveland for John Butcher . . . Has suffered double figures in losses for three consecutive seasons . . . Lacks consistency to be a major-league winner . . . No question, however, that the material is there . . . Needed eight appearances to get first victory as a Twin . . . Worked 5⅔ innings in 9-5 win over Yankees . . . Did pitch better than his record shows . . . Born March 3, 1960, in Jamaica, N.Y. . . . First player selected in June 1979 draft, by New York Mets, but elected to attend University of Miami . . . Went 41-6 in three seasons at Miami . . . College number (26) was retired . . . Made just 40 appearances as minor leaguer . . . Eleven victories in 1983 represented most by a Cleveland rookie left-hander since Herb Score won 16 in 1955 . . . Fanned 20 batters in a seven-inning game as a high-school senior.

Year	Club	G	IP	W	L	Pct.	SO	BB	H	ERA
1982	Cleveland	8	31	0	2	.000	14	16	32	5.23
1983	Cleveland	39	149⅓	11	7	.611	75	44	157	4.16
1984	Cleveland	38	198⅔	12	15	.444	75	75	231	5.21
1985	Cleveland	36	207⅔	9	17	.346	82	80	244	4.90
1986	Clev.-Minn.	33	198⅔	7	15	.318	90	81	201	4.08
	Totals	154	785⅓	39	56	.411	336	296	865	4.64

MIKE SMITHSON 32 6-8 215 **Bats L Throws R**

Workhorse who provides a lot of innings but mixed results . . . Has made more than 30 starts each of last four years . . . Achieved double figures in wins and losses for fourth consecutive year . . . Rode rollercoaster throughout season . . . Won three straight, April 22 to May 7 . . . Lost three straight, Aug. 8 to 23 . . . Pitched two-hit shutout on Aug. 2 against Oakland . . . Held no-hitter through 6⅓ innings . . . Walked seven before Dwayne Murphy singled to end no-hit bid . . . Made first relief appearance after 144 starts on Sept. 17 due to tender elbow . . . Born Jan. 21, 1955, in Centerville, Tenn. . . . Acquired from Texas on Dec. 7, 1983, with John Butcher and Sam Sorce for Gary Ward . . . Tallest player in majors.

Year	Club	G	IP	W	L	Pct.	SO	BB	H	ERA
1982	Texas	8	46⅔	3	4	.429	24	13	51	5.01
1983	Texas	33	223⅓	10	14	.417	135	71	233	3.91
1984	Minnesota	36	252	15	13	.536	144	54	246	3.68
1985	Minnesota	37	257	15	14	.517	127	78	264	4.34
1986	Minnesota	34	198	13	14	.481	114	57	234	4.77
	Totals	148	977	56	59	.487	544	273	1028	4.19

TOP PROSPECT

STEVE GASSER 19 6-3 190 **Bats R Throws R**

Born in New Philadelphia, Ohio, hometown of Cy Young . . . Has 9-17 career minor-league record only because he has pitched for poor teams . . . Was rated as No. 1 prospect in Midwest League by managers despite 5-10 record and 3.58 ERA at Kenosha (A) in 1986 . . . Club finished 46-92 . . . Struck out 225 batters in 188⅔ innings to set club record and lead league . . . Working on breaking ball to complement 90-mph fastball . . . Born Aug. 5, 1967 . . . Selected by Minnesota in second round of June 1985 draft.

MANAGER TOM KELLY: Named manager in late November after serving as interim manager in place of fired Ray Miller in mid-September . . . Was a minor-league outfielder for 13 years after being the Seattle Pilots' fourth-round pick in June 1968 draft . . . Did get to play in the bigs for 62 games with the Twins in 1975 after he signed as a free agent . . . Most productive years as a player were at Tacoma (AAA) in the Pacific

Coast League, where he wound up managing in the last half of the 1977 season . . . Was Manager of the Year in California League in 1979 and 1980 and in Southern League in 1981 . . . In 1983, he became Twins' third-base coach, first Minnesotan to become member of team's managerial staff . . . Born Aug. 15, 1950, in Graceful, Minn., but has made his home in Sayreville, N.J. . . . Father, Joe, pitched in the New York Giants' chain . . . Kelly grew up in South Amboy, N.J., and played at Mesa (Ariz.) Community College and Monmouth (N.J.) College before launching minor-league career . . . Brings a 12-11 major-league managerial record into his first full season . . .Got his shot after Jim Frey turned down the job in favor of announcing job with the Cubs.

GREATEST ALL-TIME ROOKIE

How determined was Pedro Oliva to leave Pinar del Rio, Cuba for the United States? Determined enough to use his brother's passport and be known as Tony Oliva from then on.

And it was as Tony Oliva that he became one of the great players in Minnesota Twins' history, winning Rookie-of-the-Year honors in 1964. Oliva became the first rookie to win the American League batting title, compiling a .323 mark to go with the league lead in hits (217), doubles (43), and runs (109). Oliva slugged 32 home runs and drove in 94 runs.

Oliva went on to win two more batting titles. He was selected AL Player of the Year by *The Sporting News* in 1965 and 1971 and was selected to the All-Star Game from 1964-71.

Oliva was never the same player, however, after July 29, 1971, when he limped from the field with a severe knee injury after attempting a diving catch in Oakland. Despite four knee operations and rigorous rehabilitation, Oliva could not regain what he had lost.

ALL-TIME TWIN SEASON RECORDS

BATTING: Rod Carew, .388, 1977
HRs: Harmon Killebrew, 49, 1964, 1969
RBIs: Harmon Killebrew, 140, 1969
STEALS: Rod Carew, 49, 1976
WINS: Jim Kaat, 25, 1966
STRIKEOUTS: Bert Blyleven, 258, 1973

OAKLAND A's

TEAM DIRECTORY: Pres.: Roy Eisenhardt; Exec. VP: Wally Haas; VP-Baseball Oper.: Sandy Alderson; Dir. Play. Dev.: Karl Kuehl; Dir. Scouting: Dick Bogard; Dir. Baseball Adm.: Walt Jocketty; Dir. Press Rel.: Ray Fosse; Trav. Sec.: Mickey Morabito; Mgr.: Tony La Russa. Home: Oakland Coliseum (50,219). Field distances: 330, l.f. line; 372, l.c.; 400, c.f.; 372, r.c.; 330, r.f. line. Spring training: Phoenix, Ariz.

SCOUTING REPORT

HITTING: Jose Canseco hopes to avoid the sophomore jinx after fulfilling great expectations and earning designation as Rookie of

It's all or nothing for big-swinging Jose Canseco.

the Year in 1986. He tied for fourth in the AL with 33 home runs and placed second with 117 RBI, although he hit only .240. The A's, eager to improve on a .252 team average that ranked next-to-last in the AL, can live with a certain amount of Canseco strikeouts, but not 175 of them in 600 at-bats.

The A's hope for better results from Mike Davis, who dropped from 82 RBI in 1985 to 55 last year, despite a career-high 19 home runs, and Dwayne Murphy (.252, 9 homers, 39 RBI), who missed 52 games with a ruptured disc in his back. Carney Lansford (.284, 19, 72) and Alfredo Griffin (.285, 4, 51) are good offensive players. Mark McGwire (.189, 3, 9 in 18 games) is a hitter to watch. Oakland hopes DH Reggie Jackson (.241, 18, 58) will pick up the home-run slack left by the departure of free agent Dave Kingman (.210, 35, 94).

PITCHING: Temperamental right-hander Joaquin Andujar (12-7, 3.82) must regain the 20-victory level he achieved in the NL for the A's to seriously contend. Curt Young (13-9, 3.45) and Dave Stewart (9-5, 3.74) were pleasant surprises who will be counted on to continue their success of last season. Moose Haas (7-2, 2.74) can be a big contributor if he sheds injury problems. Jose Rijo (9-11, 4.65) remains a raw, but still promising talent. Gene Nelson (6-6, 3.85), acquired from the White Sox for Donnie Hill in December, might help.

The pivotal figure on the staff, which placed 11th in the AL with a 4.31 ERA, is Jay Howell (3-6, 3.38, 16 saves). Howell is among the AL's premier relievers when healthy. He was plagued by tendinitis in his right elbow in 1986 and the A's had no one to step in when Howell was ailing.

FIELDING: This is the area of greatest concern to Tony LaRussa as he manages the A's for his first full season. The material is there for a better performance. Alfredo Griffin is a solid shortstop. Murphy is a center fielder with Gold Glove ability when healthy. Davis has an extremely strong arm in right.

Canseco, whose 14 errors tied fellow rookie Pete Incaviglia of Texas for the lead among AL outfielders, and McGwire, who made six errors in 18 games, are defensive liabilities.

OUTLOOK: LaRussa inherited a 32-52 last-place club that was disorganized and disheartened at the time of Jackie Moore's dismissal. The resurgent A's wound up tied for third with Kansas City at 76-86. That momentum should carry over, making the A's a factor in the AL West race. But too many pitching uncertainties, particularly in the bullpen, will keep them from the top.

OAKLAND A's 1987 ROSTER

MANAGER Tony LaRussa
COACHES—Dave Duncan, Rene Lachemann, Jim Lefebvre, Dave McKay, Mike Paul, Bob Watson

PITCHERS

No.	Name	1986 Club	W-L	IP	SO	ERA	B-T	Ht.	Wt.	Born
47	Andujar, Joaquin	Oakland	12-7	155	72	3.82	B-R	6-0	190	12/21/52 Dom. Republic
—	Belcher, Tim	Huntsville	2-5	37	25	6.57	R-R	6-3	210	10/19/61 Mt. Gilead, OH
—	Burns, Todd	Huntsville	7-7	125	77	3.75	R-R	6-2	185	7/6/63 Maywood, CA
		Tacoma	0-1	17	14	2.16				
23	Codiroli, Chris	Oakland	5-8	92	43	4.03	R-R	6-1	160	3/26/58 Oxnard, CA
—	Diaz, Carlos	Los Angeles	0-0	25	18	4.26	R-L	6-0	170	1/7/58 Honolulu, HI
		Albuquerque	1-4	22	10	5.64				
59	Dozier, Tom	Tacoma	5-3	75	49	3.35	R-R	6-2	190	9/5/61 Richmond, CA
		Oakland	0-0	6	4	5.68				
30	Haas, Moose	Oakland	7-2	72	40	2.74	R-R	6-0	170	4/22/56 Baltimore, MD
50	Howell, Jay	Modesto	0-0	2	1	13.50	R-R	6-3	205	11/26/55 Miami, FL
		Oakland	3-6	53	42	3.38				
32	Krueger, Bill	Madison	0-0	2	1	0.00	L-L	6-5	205	4/24/58 McMinnville, OR
		Tacoma	3-3	52	41	4.64				
		Oakland	1-2	34	10	6.03				
62	Kyles, Stan	Huntsville	6-1	72	44	2.50	R-R	6-1	165	2/26/61 Chicago, IL
		Tacoma	5-2	52	30	3.27				
35	Mooneyham, Bill	Tacoma	0-1	4	4	12.46	R-R	6-0	175	8/16/60 Los Angeles, CA
		Oakland	4-5	100	75	4.52				
—	Nelson, Gene	Chicago (AL)	6-6	115	70	3.85	R-R	6-0	175	12/3/60 Tampa, FL
53	Ontiveros, Steve	Oakland	2-2	73	54	4.71	R-R	6-0	180	3/5/61 Tularosa, NM
38	Rijo, Jose	Oakland	9-11	194	176	4.65	R-R	6-2	195	5/13/65 Dominican Republic
27	Rodriguez, Rick	Huntsville	0-0	16	14	5.06	R-R	6-3	190	9/21/160 Oakland, CA
		Tacoma	7-8	139	76	3.95				
		Oakland	1-2	16	2	6.61				
34	Stewart, Dave	Philadelphia	0-0	11	9	6.57	R-R	6-2	200	2/19/57 Oakland, CA
		Tacoma	0-0	3	3	0.00				
		Oakland	9-5	149	102	3.74				
57	Von Ohlen, Dave	Miami	6-2	61	32	1.62	L-L	6-2	200	10/25/58 Flushing, NY
		Tacoma	2-1	20	11	1.77				
		Oakland	0-3	15	4	3.52				
29	Young, Curt	Tacoma	4-0	27	28	2.00	R-L	6-1	175	4/16/60 Saginaw, MI
		Oakland	13-9	198	116	3.45				

CATCHERS

No.	Name	1986 Club	H	HR	RBI	Pct.	B-T	Ht.	Wt.	Born
36	Steinbach, Terry	Huntsville	165	24	132	.327	R-R	6-1	195	3/2/62 New Ulm, MN
		Oakland	5	2	4	.333				
6	Tettleton, Mickey	Modesto	10	2	8	.238	B-R	6-2	200	9/16/60 Oklahoma City, OK
		Oakland	42	10	35	.204				

INFIELDERS

No.	Name	1986 Club	H	HR	RBI	Pct.	B-T	Ht.	Wt.	Born
9	Gallego, Mike	Tacoma	122	4	46	.275	R-R	5-8	160	10/31/60 Whittier, CA
		Oakland	10	0	4	.270				
3	Griffin, Alfredo	Oakland	169	4	50	.285	B-R	5-11	165	3/6/57 Dominican Republic
—	Howie, Mark	Madison	144	5	42	.309	R-R	6-0	170	12/27/62 Baton Rouge, LA
4	Lansford, Carney	Oakland	168	19	72	.284	R-R	6-2	195	2/7/57 San Jose, CA
25	McGwire, Mark	Huntsville	59	10	53	.303	R-R	6-5	215	10/1/63 Pomona, CA
		Tacoma	89	13	59	.318				
		Oakland	10	3	9	.189				
49	Nelson, Rob	Tacoma	140	20	108	.276	L-L	6-4	215	5/17/64 Pasadena, CA
		Oakland	2	0	0	.222				
18	Phillips, Tony	Oakland	113	5	52	.256	B-R	5-10	160	11/9/59 Atlanta, GA

OUTFIELDERS

No.	Name	1986 Club	H	HR	RBI	Pct.	B-T	Ht.	Wt.	Born
33	Canseco, Jose	Oakland	144	33	117	.240	R-R	6-3	210	7/2/64 Cuba
16	Davis, Mike	Oakland	131	19	55	.268	L-L	6-3	190	6/11/59 San Diego, CA
44	Jackson, Reggie	California	101	18	58	.241	L-L	6-0	208	5/18/46 Wyncote, PA
—	Johnson, Roy	Huntsville	63	5	27	.344	L-L	6-4	220	6/27/59 Parkin, AR
		Tacoma	85	9	44	.343				
—	Jose, Felix	Modesto	147	14	77	.285	B-R	6-1	190	5/8/65 Dominican Republic
21	Murphy, Dwayne	Madison	0	0	0	.000	L-R	6-1	185	3/18/55 Merced, CA
		Modesto	1	0	0	.200				
		Oakland	83	9	39	.252				
61	Polonia, Luis	Tacoma	165	3	63	.301	B-L	5-8	155	10/12/64 Dom. Republic
—	Tillman, Rusty	Las Vegas	1	0	0	.200	R-R	6-0	190	8/29/60 Jacksonville, FL
		Tacoma	81	3	42	.316				
		Oakland	10	1	6	.256				
24	Wilder, Dave	Huntsville	134	11	85	.301	R-R	6-1	185	10/14/60 Oakland, CA

A's PROFILES

JOSE CANSECO 22 6-3 210 Bats R Throws R

Slugging outfielder met expectations by putting up big numbers and being named AL Rookie of the Year . . . Made bid to become first rookie to lead AL in home runs and RBI since Ted Williams in 1939 . . . Finished tied for fourth with 33 home runs and second to Cleveland's Joe Carter with 117 RBI . . . Led AL rookies in games (157), at-bats (600), runs (85) and total bases (274) . . . Opposing players stop to watch him in batting practice . . . Sometimes lax defensively and generally an unpolished fielder . . . Born July 2, 1964, in Havana, Cuba . . . Reticent with reporters . . .Oakland's 15th-round selection in June 1982 draft . . . Named Minor League Player of the Year in 1985 by *Baseball America*.

Year	Club	Pos.	G	AB	R	H	2B	3B	HR	RBI	SB	Avg.
1985	Oakland.	OF	29	96	16	29	3	0	5	13	1	.302
1986	Oakland.	OF	157	600	85	144	29	1	33	117	15	.240
	Totals		186	696	101	173	32	1	38	130	16	.249

CARNEY LANSFORD 30 6-2 195 Bats R Throws R

Rebounded after missing large portion of 1985 season with broken wrist . . . Matched career high of 19 home runs, set in 1979 with California . . . Homers were well distributed, 10 coming at home and nine on the road . . . A third baseman by trade, Lansford made his major-league debut at second base on Aug. 28 against Baltimore . . . Will probably have to find a position other than third, considering development of Mark McGwire . . . Born Feb. 7, 1957, in San Jose, Cal. . . . Acquired from Boston with Garry Hancock and Jerome King for Tony Armas and Jeff Newman on Dec. 6, 1982 . . . Became California's starting third baseman in 1978 at age 21 . . . Placed third in Rookie-of-the-Year voting . . . Become first right-handed hitter to lead AL in batting since 1970 when he batted .336 in 1981.

Year	Club	Pos.	G	AB	R	H	2B	3B	HR	RBI	SB	Avg.
1978	California.	3B	121	453	63	133	23	2	8	52	20	.294
1979	California.	3B	157	654	114	188	30	5	19	79	20	.287
1980	California.	3B	151	602	87	157	27	3	15	80	14	.261
1981	Boston	3B	102	399	61	134	23	3	4	52	15	.336
1982	Boston	3B	128	482	65	145	28	4	11	63	9	.301
1983	Oakland.	3B-SS	80	299	43	92	16	2	10	45	3	.308
1984	Oakland.	3B	151	597	70	179	31	5	14	74	9	.300
1985	Oakland.	3B	98	401	51	111	18	2	13	46	2	.277
1986	Oakland.	3B-2B	151	591	80	168	16	4	19	72	16	.284
	Totals		1139	4478	634	1307	212	30	113	563	108	.292

ALFREDO GRIFFIN 30 5-11 165 Bats S Throws R

Seems to be getting better with age . . . Led club with .285 average . . . Mark was Griffin's best since he batted a career-high .287 in 1979, when he was Rookie of the Year with Toronto . . . Set career high with 33 steals . . . Extended consecutive-game streak to 334 . . . Eye-catching shortstop with knack for acrobatic play . . . Born March 6, 1957, in Santo Domingo, Dominican Republic . . . Signed as 16-year-old free agent by Cleveland on Aug. 27, 1973 . . . Acquired from Toronto with Dave Collins for Bill Caudill on Dec. 8, 1984 . . . Made major-league debut on Sept. 7, 1975 and began with first-pitch single . . . Awarded Gold Glove at shortstop in 1985 despite 30 errors.

Year	Club	Pos.	G	AB	R	H	2B	3B	HR	RBI	SB	Avg.
1976	Cleveland	SS	12	4	0	1	0	0	0	0	0	.250
1977	Cleveland	SS	14	41	5	6	1	0	0	3	2	.146
1978	Cleveland	SS	5	4	1	2	1	0	0	0	0	.500
1979	Toronto	SS	153	624	81	179	22	10	2	31	21	.287
1980	Toronto	SS	155	653	63	166	26	15	2	41	18	.254
1981	Toronto	SS-3B-2B	101	388	30	81	19	6	0	21	8	.209
1982	Toronto	SS	162	539	57	130	20	8	1	48	10	.241
1983	Toronto	SS-2B	162	528	62	132	22	9	4	47	8	.250
1984	Toronto	SS-2B	140	419	53	101	8	2	4	30	11	.241
1985	Oakland	SS	162	614	75	166	18	7	2	64	24	.270
1986	Oakland	SS	162	594	74	169	23	6	4	50	33	.285
	Totals		1228	4408	501	1133	160	63	19	335	135	.257

MIKE DAVIS 27 6-3 190 Bats L Throws L

Season was somewhat of a disappointment after right fielder's breakthrough year in 1985, when he established career highs in home runs and RBI . . . Slipped to 19 home runs, representing a dropoff of five, and fell 27 short of career-high 82 RBI . . . Belted 12 of his 19 homers at night . . . Ranks sixth on A's all-time list with 102 career steals . . . Possesses one of league's strongest arms . . . Most base-runners don't challenge him . . . Born June 11, 1959, in San Diego . . . Oakland's third-round selection in June 1977 draft . . . Cousin, Dave Grayson, is former star defensive back in NFL . . . Hit .456 in his senior year in high school and was voted San Diego County's MVP . . . Rejected Arizona State scholarship to sign with A's.

Year	Club	Pos.	G	AB	R	H	2B	3B	HR	RBI	SB	Avg.
1980	Oakland	OF-1B	51	95	11	20	2	1	1	8	2	.211
1981	Oakland	OF-1B	17	20	0	1	1	0	0	0	0	.050
1982	Oakland	OF-1B	23	75	12	30	4	0	1	10	3	.400
1983	Oakland	OF	128	443	61	122	24	4	8	62	32	.275
1984	Oakland	OF	134	382	47	88	18	3	9	46	14	.230
1985	Oakland	OF	154	547	92	157	34	1	24	82	24	.287
1986	Oakland	OF	142	489	77	131	28	3	19	55	27	.268
	Totals		649	2051	300	549	111	12	62	263	102	.268

DWAYNE MURPHY 32 6-1 185 Bats L Throws R

Scary time for Gold Glove center fielder as he missed 52 games with a ruptured disk in his back . . . A's aren't sure when injury occurred . . . Problems began in spring training with what he thought were back spasms . . . Sidelined from May 11 to July 5 . . . Was batting only .242 with 14 RBI and two home runs before injury . . . Went 1-for-3 and drove in a run in first game back from DL . . . Finished strong, batting .305 over final 17 games with six multi-hit games . . . Smashed an inside-the-park home run on Sept. 10 against Chicago . . . A near-flawless fielder . . . Chews up ground and possesses good arm . . . Born March 18, 1955, in Merced, Cal. . . . Oakland's 15th-round choice in June 1973 draft . . . Rejected football scholarship to Arizona State and signed with A's.

Year	Club	Pos.	G	AB	R	H	2B	3B	HR	RBI	SB	Avg.
1978	Oakland.	OF	60	52	15	10	2	0	0	5	0	.192
1979	Oakland.	OF	121	388	57	99	10	4	11	40	15	.255
1980	Oakland.	OF	159	573	86	157	18	2	13	68	26	.274
1981	Oakland.	OF	107	390	58	98	10	3	15	60	10	.251
1982	Oakland.	OF-SS	151	543	84	129	15	1	27	94	26	.238
1983	Oakland.	OF	130	471	55	107	17	2	17	75	7	.227
1984	Oakland.	OF	153	559	93	143	18	2	33	88	4	.256
1985	Oakland.	OF	152	523	77	122	21	3	20	59	4	.233
1986	Oakland.	OF	98	329	50	83	10	3	9	39	3	.252
	Totals		1131	3828	575	948	121	20	145	528	95	.248

MOOSE HAAS 30 6-0 170 Bats R Throws R

A winning pitcher when healthy, he has broken down after fast starts in each of last two seasons . . . Hottest pitcher in either league at start of last year, winning first six decisions . . . Didn't suffer first loss until May 11, when Red Sox beat him, 6-5 . . . Won next start but began suffering bursitis in right shoulder after lasting only four innings against Milwaukee on July 19 . . . Didn't pitch again until Oct. 1, when he hurled five scoreless innings against Texas after coming off disabled list . . . A's were encouraged enough to sign him to new one-year contract . . . Born April 22, 1956, in Baltimore . . . Began career as second-round choice of Milwaukee in June 1974 draft . . . Owns black belt in

Tae Kwon Do . . . Also an amateur magician and certified locksmith . . . Started life as Bryan Edmund Haas.

Year	Club	G	IP	W	L	Pct.	SO	BB	H	ERA
1976	Milwaukee	5	16	0	1	.000	9	12	12	3.94
1977	Milwaukee	32	198	10	12	.455	113	84	195	4.32
1978	Milwaukee	7	31	2	3	.400	32	8	33	6.10
1979	Milwaukee	29	185	11	11	.500	95	59	198	4.77
1980	Milwaukee	33	252	16	15	.516	146	56	246	3.11
1981	Milwaukee	24	137	11	7	.611	64	40	145	4.47
1982	Milwaukee	32	193⅓	11	8	.579	104	39	232	4.47
1983	Milwaukee	25	179	13	3	.813	75	42	170	3.27
1984	Milwaukee	31	189⅓	9	11	.450	84	43	205	3.99
1985	Milwaukee	27	161⅔	8	8	.500	78	25	165	3.84
1986	Oakland	12	72⅓	7	2	.778	40	19	58	2.74
	Totals	257	1614⅔	98	81	.547	840	427	1660	3.97

JAY HOWELL 31 6-3 205 — Bats R Throws R

One of the premier relievers when he stays healthy, but has trouble doing that . . . Disabled from May 27 to July 20 with tendinitis in his elbow . . . Had five saves and a 5.89 ERA before he went on DL, so he obviously was not right . . . Still recorded team-high 16 saves in 53⅓ innings . . . Late-season return was marked by eight saves and two victories in final 12 appearances . . . Born Nov. 26, 1955, in Miami . . . Selected by Cincinnati in 31st round of June 1976 draft . . . Acquired from Yankees with Jose Rijo, Tim Birtsas, Eric Plunk and Stan Javier for Rickey Henderson and Bert Bradley on Dec. 8, 1984 . . . Made permanent move to bullpen in 1984 . . . Simply lacked command of enough pitches to succeed as a starter . . . Earned first All-Star berth in 1985, when he saved 29 games, second-highest total in Oakland history.

Year	Club	G	IP	W	L	Pct.	SO	BB	H	ERA
1980	Cincinnati	5	3	0	0	.000	1	0	8	15.00
1981	Chicago(NL)	10	22	2	0	1.000	10	10	23	4.91
1982	New York (AL)	6	28	2	3	.400	21	13	42	7.71
1983	New York(AL)	19	82	1	5	.167	61	35	89	5.38
1984	New York (AL)	61	103⅔	9	4	.692	109	34	86	2.69
1985	Oakland	63	98	9	8	.529	68	31	98	2.85
1986	Oakland	38	53⅓	3	6	.333	42	23	53	3.38
	Totals	202	390	26	26	.500	312	145	399	3.97

CURT YOUNG 26 6-1 175 **Bats R Throws L**

Tendinitis in his left shoulder ruined his 1985 season, but he came back strong . . . Established career high and led club with 13 victories . . . Also set career highs with 116 strikeouts and 198 innings . . . Capped season with a one-hitter against Kansas City on final day, going 6⅔ innings before an infield hit . . . Led A's with 27 starts . . . Much more comfortable at Oakland Coliseum, where he was 8-2, 2.56, compared to 4-7, 5.19 on road . . . Born April 16, 1960, in Saginaw, Mich., and still lives there . . . Oakland's fourth-round selection in June 1981 draft . . . Played baseball, basketball and football in high school and won nine letters.

Year	Club	G	IP	W	L	Pct.	SO	BB	H	ERA
1983	Oakland	8	9	0	1	.000	5	5	17	16.00
1984	Oakland	20	108⅔	9	4	.692	41	31	118	4.06
1985	Oakland	19	46	0	4	.000	19	22	57	7.24
1986	Oakland	29	198	13	9	.591	116	57	176	3.45
	Totals	76	361⅔	22	18	.550	181	115	368	4.43

JOSE RIJO 21 6-2 195 **Bats R Throws R**

Hopes remain high for Rijo, an erratic performer who shows flashes of brilliance . . . Set A's record with 16 strikeouts against Seattle on April 19 . . . Fanned 14 Mariners in his next appearance . . . Led A's in strikeouts (176), but also in walks (108) in 193⅔ innings pitched . . . Surrendered team-high 24 home runs . . . Still a thrower rather than a pitcher . . . Can't always get by with raw power . . . Used as bullpen stopper when Jay Howell was disabled May 10 . . . Resumed as a starter in late June . . . Best suited to that role because of poor control . . . Born May 13, 1965, in San Cristobal, Dominican Republic . . . Signed by Yankees in 1981 as a 16-year-old . . . Acquired from the Yankees with Tim Birtsas, Eric Plunk, Jay Howell and Stan Javier for Rickey Henderson and Bert Bradley on Dec. 8, 1984 . . . Could become dominant pitcher.

Year	Club	G	IP	W	L	Pct.	SO	BB	H	ERA
1984	New York (AL)	24	62⅓	2	8	.200	47	33	74	4.76
1985	Oakland	12	63⅔	6	4	.600	65	28	57	3.53
1986	Oakland	39	193⅔	9	11	.450	176	108	172	4.65
	Totals	75	319⅔	17	23	.425	288	169	303	4.45

JOAQUIN ANDUJAR 34 6-0 190 — Bats S Throws R

String of 20-victory seasons ended at two in a difficult season of adjustment following unexpected trade from St. Louis . . . Obtained Dec. 10, 1985, from Cardinals for Mike Heath and Tim Conroy . . . After being only pitcher in majors to win 20 games in 1984 and 1985, he was upset by the trade . . . Disabled from June 6 to July 18 with pulled hamstring . . . Gave up 23 homers in 26 starts and said AL stadiums resembled softball fields . . . Finished strong to win five of last six starts . . . Born Dec. 21, 1952, in San Pedro de Macoris, Dominican Republic . . . Originally signed by Astros, he developed after June 6, 1981 trade to Cardinals for Tony Scott . . . Pitched poorly in post-season in 1985 and was dragged from the diamond in Game 7 of the World Series after being ejected for arguing balls and strikes . . . Refused to participate in 1985 All-Star Game when NL manager Dick Williams wouldn't name him as starting pitcher.

Year	Club	G	IP	W	L	Pct.	SO	BB	H	ERA
1976	Houston	28	172	9	10	.474	59	75	163	3.61
1977	Houston	26	159	11	8	.579	69	64	149	3.68
1978	Houston	35	111	5	7	.417	55	58	88	3.41
1979	Houston	46	194	12	12	.500	77	88	168	3.43
1980	Houston	35	122	3	8	.273	75	43	132	3.91
1981	Hou.-St.L.	20	79	8	4	.667	37	23	85	4.10
1982	St. Louis	38	265⅔	15	10	.600	137	50	237	2.47
1983	St. Louis	39	225	6	16	.273	125	75	215	4.16
1984	St. Louis	36	261⅓	20	14	.588	147	70	218	3.34
1985	St. Louis	38	269⅔	21	12	.636	112	82	265	3.40
1986	Oakland	28	155⅓	12	7	.632	72	56	139	3.82
	Totals	369	2014	122	108	.530	965	684	1859	3.49

TOP PROSPECT

MARK McGWIRE 23 6-5 215 — Bats R Throws R

"Big Mac" is closing in on A's third-base job . . . Made major-league debut Aug. 22 and went hitless first two games . . . Got first major-league hit off Tommy John of the Yankees on Aug. 24, an RBI double, and went 3-for-5 . . . Split minor-league season between Huntsville (AA) and Tacoma (AAA) . . . Hit above .300 at both stops and excelled at Tacoma with .318 average, 13 homers and 59 RBI in 78 games . . . Batted .189 in 18 games with three homers and nine RBI for Oakland . . . Struck out 18 times in 53 at-bats . . . Appeared slow in the field and made six errors in 18 games . . . Born Oct. 1, 1963, in Pomona, Cal. . . . First-round pick in June 1984 draft.

MANAGER TONY LaRUSSA: Let go in late June by the Chicago White Sox, LaRussa was quickly hired by Oakland and made his July 7 debut with the A's a winning one . . . Inherited 32-52 last-place club . . . Players gave him the credit for bringing a winning attitude as A's rebounded to finish at 76-86, tied for third in AL West with Kansas City . . . Had been White Sox manager since Aug. 2, 1979 . . . Guided White Sox to 99 victories and AL West title in 1983, but they dipped to 74 wins a year later . . . Appears to have been a victim of front-office turmoil in Windy City . . . Had managed parts of two seasons in minors . . . Signed as a shortstop with Kansas City A's in 1962 . . . Spent parts of six years in majors, hitting .199 in career that spanned 1962-77 . . . Holds law degree from Florida State . . . Born Oct. 4, 1944, in Tampa, Fla. . . . Has major-league record of 496-472.

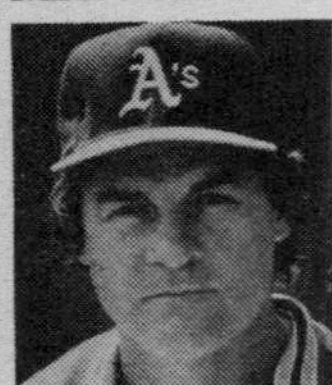

GREATEST ALL-TIME ROOKIE

At Phoenix Stadium, it is 430 feet from home plate to the fence in center field, which is a 45-foot-high wooden backstop.

For most batters, the barrier is imposing. As Jose Canseco prepared for his rookie season at the A's training camp in 1986, it was an irresistible target, one he often struck in batting practice.

Canseco continued his power shows once the season began, amassing 33 home runs and 117 RBI, ranking second in the AL. He outdistanced the Angels' Wally Joyner in the race for AL Rookie-of-the-Year honors and teammate Dave Kingman joined the crowd in raving about the rookie outfielder. "People say I can hit the ball a long way," Kingman said, "but I'll tell you this: I'm not in Jose's league. He's one of a kind."

Canseco had 23 home runs and 78 RBI, earning selection to the All-Star Game, although he did not play. Perhaps the highest honor accorded the Cuban-born, right-handed slugger was unspoken. When he took batting practice, teammates and opposing players stopped to watch.

ALL-TIME A's SEASON RECORDS

BATTING: Napoleon Lajoie, .422, 1901
HRs: Jimmie Foxx, 58, 1932
RBIs: Jimmie Foxx, 169, 1932
STEALS: Rickey Henderson, 130, 1982
WINS: John Coombs, 31, 1910
Lefty Grove, 31, 1931
STRIKEOUTS: Rube Waddell, 349, 1904

SEATTLE MARINERS

TEAM DIRECTORY: Owner: George Argyros; Pres.: Chuck Armstrong; VP-Baseball Oper.: Dick Balderson; Dir. Play. Dev.: Bill Haywood; Dir. Publ.: Bob Porter; Trav. Sec.: Lee Pelekoudas; Mgr.: Dick Williams. Home: Kingdome (59,438). Field distances: 316, l.f. line; 357, l.c.; 410, c.f.; 357, r.c.; 316, r.f. line. Spring training: Tempe, Ariz.

Mark Langston regained form and led AL with 245 Ks.

SCOUTING REPORT

HITTING: Seattle had the dubious distinction of being the victim when Boston's Roger Clemens struck out a major-league-record 20 batters last April 29. And Clemens wasn't the only pitcher who left the Mariners flailing in 1986.

Some of the Mariners' biggest guns misfired most often. Jim Presley (.265, 27 homers, 107 RBI) struck out 172 times. Phil Bradley (.310, 12, 50) had 134 strikeouts. Those hitters must make more frequent contact for Seattle to improve on a .253 team average that ranked 11th in the AL.

Because he is patient at the plate and hits for average and power, Alvin Davis (.271, 18, 72) is a key offensive player. The Mariners traded Danny Tartabull to Kansas City in December and will miss the power he supplied as a rookie.

PITCHING: The Mariners aren't lacking for good, young arms. Mike Moore (11-13, 4.30), Mike Morgan (11-7, 4.53) and Bill Swift (2-9, 5.46) were all first-round draft choices. Mark Langston (12-14, 4.85, league-leading 245 strikeouts) has a terrific arm. During the winter, Seattle added two more promising youngsters—right-hander Scott Bankhead (8-9, 4.61) from Kansas City and left-hander Dennis Powell (2-7, 4.27) from Los Angeles.

The Mariners sent ace reliever Matt Young to the Dodgers and will miss the lefty closer in a thin bullpen. But it is obvious from Seattle's 4.65 ERA last year—only Minnesota's 4.77 was worse—that the deck had to be shuffled.

FIELDING: This was yet another sore spot for the hurting Mariners, who committed 156 errors. Only Cleveland made more errors with 157.

The development of shortstop Rey Quinones (24 errors) is a key to anticipated defensive improvement. Quinones, 23, was an All-Star in each of his three minor-league seasons, but must prove himself in the majors. The Mariners also need to stabilize their catching situation.

OUTLOOK: Demanding manager Dick Williams, known for turning perennial also-rans into contenders, may face his stiffest challenge with the Mariners, who finished at 67-95 last season. Seattle has numerous deficiencies and Williams is still trying to find the speed he needs to instill a more aggressive style. This is a long, painful rebuilding job.

SEATTLE MARINERS 1987 ROSTER

MANAGER Dick Williams

Coaches—Billy Connors, Frank Howard, Phil Roof, Bobby Tolan, Ozzie Virgil

PITCHERS

No.	Name	1986 Club	W-L	IP	SO	ERA	B-T	Ht.	Wt.	Born
—	Bankhead, Scott	Omaha	2-2	48	34	1.49	R-R	5-10	175	7/31/63 Raleigh, NC
		Kansas City	8-9	121	94	4.61				
39	Best, Karl	Seattle	2-3	36	23	4.04	R-R	6-4	208	3/6/59 Aberdeen, WA
		Calgary	0-1	17	20	1.59				
—	Clarke, Stan	Syracuse	8-9	139	64	3.89	L-L	6-0	180	8/9/60 Toledo, OH
		Toronto	0-1	12	9	9.24				
—	Ferreira, Tony	Tidewater	7-5	112	65	3.69	L-L	6-2	160	10/4/62 Riverside, CA
47	Fireovid, Steve	Calgary	6-3	82	29	4.70	B-R	6-2	195	6/6/57 Bryan, OH
		Seattle	2-0	21	10	4.29				
27	Huismann, Mark	KC-Sea.	3-4	97	72	3.79	R-R	6-3	195	5/11/58 Lincoln, NE
46	Ladd, Pete	Seattle	8-6	71	53	3.82	R-R	6-3	240	7/17/56 Portland, ME
12	Langston, Mark	Seattle	12-14	239	245	4.85	R-L	6-2	188	8/20/60 San Diego, CA
34	Monteleone, Rich	Calgary	8-12	158	101	5.31	R-R	6-2	205	3/22/63 Tampa, FL
25	Moore, Mike	Seattle	11-13	266	146	4.30	R-L	6-4	205	11/26/59 Eakly, OK
16	Morgan, Mike	Seattle	11-17	216	116	4.53	R-R	6-2	185	10/8/59 Tulare, CA
30	Nunez, Edwin	Seattle	1-2	22	17	5.82	R-R	6-5	237	5/27/63 Puerto Rico
		Calgary	1-2	14	17	7.07				
—	Powell, Dennis	Los Angeles	2-7	65	31	4.27	L-L	6-3	207	8/13/63 Moultric, GA
		Albuquerque	3-3	42	27	4.10				
31	Reed, Jerry	Calgary	2-1	41	20	4.61	R-R	6-1	190	10/8/55 Bryson City, NC
		Seattle	4-0	35	16	3.12				
—	Shields, Steve	Richmond	9-8	149	124	2.59	R-R	6-5	230	11/30/58 Gadsden, AL
		Atlanta	0-0	13	6	7.11				
		Kansas City	0-0	9	2	2.08				
18	Swift, Bill	Seattle	2-9	115	55	5.46	R-R	6-0	180	10/27/61 S. Portland, ME
		Calgary	4-4	57	29	3.95				
48	Taylor, Terry	Chattanooga	12-8	177	164	4.02	R-R	6-1	180	7/28/64 Crestview, FL
43	Trujillo, Mike	Pawtucket	8-9	84	45	2.66	R-R	6-1	180	1/12/60 Denver, CO
		Bos.-Sea.	3-2	47	23	3.26				
41	Wilkinson, Bill	Calgary	8-8	143	86	4.78	R-L	5-10	160	8/10/64 Greybull, WY

CATCHERS

No.	Name	1986 Club	H	HR	RBI	Pct.	B-T	Ht.	Wt.	Born
7	Bradley, Scott	Buffalo	42	5	20	.333	L-R	5-11	185	3/22/60 Montclair, NJ
		Chi. (AL)-Sea.	66	5	28	.300				
11	Kearney, Bob	Seattle	49	6	25	.240	R-R	6-0	190	10/3/56 San Antonio, TX
5	Valle, David	Calgary	110	21	72	.312	R-R	6-2	200	10/30/60 Bayside, NY
		Seattle	18	5	15	.340				

INFIELDERS

No.	Name	1986 Club	H	HR	RBI	Pct.	B-T	Ht.	Wt.	Born
21	Davis, Alvin	Seattle	130	18	72	.271	L-R	6-1	190	9/19/60 Riverside, CA
2	Jones, Ross	Chattanooga	72	5	42	.313	R-R	6-2	180	1/14/60 Miami, FL
		Calgary	49	4	24	.262				
		Seattle	2	0	0	.095				
44	Phelps, Ken	Seattle	85	24	64	.247	L-L	6-1	200	8/6/54 Seattle, WA
17	Presley, Jim	Seattle	163	27	107	.265	R-R	6-1	190	10/23/61 Pensacola, FL
51	Quinones, Rey	Pawtucket	23	4	18	.264	R-R	5-11	185	11/11/63 Puerto Rico
		Bos.-Sea.	68	2	22	.218				
3	Ramos, Domingo	Seattle	18	0	5	.182	R-R	5-10	170	3/29/58 Dominican Republic
—	Renteria, Rich	Hawaii	122	1	51	.314	R-R	5-9	175	12/25/61 Harbor City, CA
		Pittsburgh	3	0	1	.250				
19	Reynolds, Harold	Calgary	37	1	7	.314	B-R	5-11	165	11/26/60 Eugene, OR
		Seattle	99	1	24	.222				
20	Smith, Brick	Chattanooga	163	23	101	.344	R-R	6-4	225	5/2/59 Charlotte, NC
—	Stapleton, Dave	Boston	5	0	3	.128	R-R	6-1	180	1/16/54 Fairhope, Al

OUTFIELDERS

No.	Name	1986 Club	H	HR	RBI	Pct.	B-T	Ht.	Wt.	Born
29	Bradley, Phil	Seattle	163	12	50	.310	R-R	6-0	185	3/11/59 Bloomington, IN
14	Brantley, Mickey	Calgary	126	30	92	.318	R-R	5-10	180	6/17/61 Catskill, NY
		Seattle	20	3	7	.196				
22	Christensen, John	Pawtucket	41	5	22	.234	R-R	6-0	180	9/5/60 Downey, CA
38	Hengel, Dave	Calgary	116	27	94	.285	R-R	6-0	195	12/18/61 Oakland, CA
		Seattle	12	1	6	.190				
—	Kingery, Mike	Omaha	99	3	47	.332	L-L	6-0	180	3/29/61 St. James, MN
		Kansas City	54	3	14	.258				
26	Moses, John	Calgary	48	3	18	.324	B-L	5-10	170	8/9/57 Los Angeles, CA
		Seattle	102	3	34	.256				

MARINER PROFILES

PHIL BRADLEY 28 6-0 185 **Bats R Throws R**

Left fielder is an accomplished .300 hitter at this point and he did the expected . . . Led club in average (.310) and runs (88) and tied for lead in hits (163) . . . Was hitting .247 when disabled in early June with stress fracture in his left foot . . . Batted .337 from June 12, day he was activated, to end of season . . . Made only one error in 143 games . . . Born March 11, 1959, in Bloomington, Ind. . . . Selected in third round of June 1981 draft . . . Was All-Big Eight quarterback and batted .457 as a senior at Missouri . . . Went his first 398 major-league at-bats without a home run . . . In 1985, he became second Mariner to hit 20 home runs and steal 20 bases in a season.

Year	Club	Pos.	G	AB	R	H	2B	3B	HR	RBI	SB	Avg.
1983	Seattle	OF	23	67	8	18	2	0	0	5	3	.269
1984	Seattle	OF	124	322	49	97	12	4	0	24	21	.301
1985	Seattle	OF	159	641	100	192	33	8	26	88	22	.300
1986	Seattle	OF	143	526	88	163	27	4	12	50	21	.310
	Totals		449	1556	245	470	74	16	38	167	67	.302

Alvin Davis is one reason Mariners have bright future.

ALVIN DAVIS 26 6-1 190 **Bats L Throws R**

Although he hit .271, lowest mark of his three major-league seasons, it was a good year all-around for the first baseman . . . Slugged 18 home runs for second straight year . . . Batted .307 with runners in scoring position . . . Rode 14-game hitting streak May 1-14 . . . Batted .350 in May with four home runs, 22 RBI . . . Established club record with eight RBI against Toronto on May 9 . . . Careful hitter who walked 76 times in 562 plate appearances . . . Has walked 263 times in three years . . . Born Sept. 9, 1960, in Riverside, Cal. . . . Mariners' sixth-round draft choice in June 1982 . . . AL Rookie of the Year in 1984.

Year	Club	Pos.	G	AB	R	H	2B	3B	HR	RBI	SB	Avg.
1984	Seattle	1B	152	567	80	161	34	3	27	116	5	.284
1985	Seattle	1B	155	578	78	166	33	1	18	78	1	.287
1986	Seattle	1B	135	479	66	130	18	1	18	72	0	.271
	Total		442	1624	224	457	85	5	63	266	6	.281

REY QUINONES 23 5-11 185 **Bats R Throws R**

Red Sox dealt him and John Christensen to Mariners for Spike Owen and Dave Henderson on Aug. 19 . . . Quinones, the key to the deal for the Mariners, was an initial disappointment but club is still banking on him as its shortstop . . . Hit only .189 with Mariners . . . Committed nine errors, mostly on throws . . . Born Nov. 11, 1963, in Rio Piedras, Puerto Rico . . . Signed as a free agent in 1982 . . . An All-Star shortstop in each of his three minor-league seasons . . . Has excellent range and Mariners feel he will hit.

Year	Club	Pos.	G	AB	R	H	2B	3B	HR	RBI	SB	Avg.
1986	Bos.-Sea.	SS	98	312	32	68	16	1	2	22	4	.218

JIM PRESLEY 25 6-1 190 **Bats R Throws R**

Underrated third baseman had an excellent season . . . Led club with 33 doubles, 27 home runs, 107 RBI . . . RBI total was second-highest in Seattle history behind teammate Alvin Davis' 116 in 1984 . . . Fourth Mariner to reach 100 RBI . . . Good defensive player who continues to improve . . . Strikeout total jumped alarmingly . . . Fanned club-record 172 times, 72 strikeouts more than in 1985 . . . Opened stance in an effort to see ball better . . . Tied club record with 13 game-winning RBI . . . Born Oct. 23, 1961, in Pensacola, Fla. . . . Seattle's fourth-round choice in June 1979 draft . . . Selected to All-Star squad for first time . . . Led his Pensacola team to 1974 Little League World Series.

Year	Club	Pos.	G	AB	R	H	2B	3B	HR	RBI	SB	Avg.
1984	Seattle	3B	70	251	27	57	12	1	10	36	1	.227
1985	Seattle	3B	155	570	71	157	33	1	28	84	2	.275
1986	Seattle	3B	155	616	83	163	33	4	27	107	0	.265
	Totals		380	1437	181	377	78	6	65	227	3	.262

MIKE MOORE 27 6-4 205 **Bats R Throws R**

Pitcher took some steps backward after promising 17-victory season in 1985 . . . Lost three of first four decisions and six of eight . . . Gained two-hit 1-0 shutout over Minnesota Aug. 15, starting a stretch in which he won four of his next five decisions . . . Pitched a club-record 266 innings to rank fourth in AL . . . Led Mariners with 11 complete games and has 25 in last two seasons . . . Heads Seattle's all-time lists in victories (48) and strikeouts (640) . . . Born Nov. 26, 1959, in Eakly, Okla. . . . Seattle made him first player selected in June 1981 draft . . . Became first right-handed pitcher ever to become nation's No. 1 pick . . . First drafted by St. Louis in third round in June 1978, but did not sign . . . Named to *The Sporting News* All-American team in 1981 after compiling 12-2 record at Oral Roberts University.

Year	Club	G	IP	W	L	Pct.	SO	BB	H	ERA
1982	Seattle	28	144⅓	7	14	.333	73	79	159	5.36
1983	Seattle	22	128	6	8	.429	108	60	130	4.71
1984	Seattle	34	212	7	17	.292	158	85	236	4.97
1985	Seattle	35	247	17	10	.630	155	70	230	3.46
1986	Seattle	38	266	11	13	.458	146	94	279	4.30
	Totals	157	997⅓	48	62	.436	640	388	1034	4.44

MARK LANGSTON 26 6-2 188 **Bats R Throws L**

Led AL with club-record 245 strikeouts in 239⅓ innings pitched . . . Reached double figures in strikeouts in eight games, all coming in last 23 starts . . . Led club in wins with 12-14 record . . . Fanned 15 batters as part of a three-hit 6-1 win over Cleveland on June 25 . . . Struck out 14 batters in a game three times . . . Won five straight June 9-30 but, typical of his inconsistency, a five-game losing streak followed . . . Born Aug. 20, 1960, in San Diego . . . Selected by Mariners in second round of June 1981 draft . . . Became only fourth rookie to lead

AL in strikeouts with 204 in 1984 . . . Finished second to teammate Alvin Davis in Rookie-of-the-Year balloting.

Year	Club	G	IP	W	L	Pct.	SO	BB	H	ERA
1984	Seattle	35	225	17	10	.630	204	118	188	3.40
1985	Seattle	24	126⅔	7	14	.333	72	91	122	5.47
1986	Seattle	37	239⅓	12	14	.462	245	123	234	4.85
	Totals	96	591	36	38	.486	521	332	544	4.43

SCOTT BANKHEAD 23 5-10 175 Bats R Throws R

Former Olympic star became major part of Seattle's pitching plans when Mariners acquired him from Kansas City in December with Mike Kingery and Steve Shields for Danny Tartabull and minor-leaguer Rick Luecken . . . Royals purchased his contract last May from Omaha (AAA) . . . Worked four scoreless innings to gain 17-inning, 2-1 win over White Sox in major-league debut on May 25 . . . Won first three big-league decisions, two in relief . . . Sat out 20 days in September with stiffness in pitching arm . . . Born July 31, 1963, in Raleigh N.C. . . . Selected by Royals in first round of June 1984 draft after 24-3 career at North Carolina . . . Was 1-0 with 0.93 ERA for 1984 silver-medal U.S. Olympic team.

Year	Club	G	IP	W	L	Pct.	SO	BB	H	ERA
1986	Kansas City	24	121	8	9	.471	94	37	121	4.61

BILLY SWIFT 25 6-0 180 Bats R Throws R

Time for Swift to fulfill lofty expectations that have accompanied him to the mound since he became second player chosen overall in June 1984 draft . . . Optioned to Calgary June 24 with 1-4 record and 5.69 ERA . . . Recalled Aug. 4 when pitcher Jerry Reed broke his wrist . . . Was not brought along gradually by Seattle and he's suffering because of that . . . Greatest difficulty appears to be location . . . Ended year with four-game losing streak . . . Brightest moment came on Aug. 30, when he no-hit the Yankees for 7⅔ innings before an infield single by Wayne Tolleson . . . Got last-out help from Matt Young to complete a 1-0 two-hitter . . . Born Oct. 27, 1961, in South Portland, Me. . . . One of 15 children . . . Member of 1984 Olympic team . . . Compiled 26-7 record at University of Maine, where he was an All-American.

Year	Club	G	IP	W	L	Pct.	SO	BB	H	ERA
1985	Seattle	23	120⅔	6	10	.375	55	48	131	4.77
1986	Seattle	29	115⅓	2	9	.182	55	55	148	5.46
	Totals	52	236	8	19	.296	110	103	279	5.11

MIKE MORGAN 27 6-2 185 Bats R Throws R

Year of frustration as he tied Chicago White Sox' Richard Dotson for most losses in AL with 17 . . . Mariners kept sending him out there because they are convinced of his talent . . . Did not win more than two games in a row and was incredibly inconsistent . . . Earned first major-league shutout on Sept. 16, 7-0, on four-hitter over Chicago . . . Was shelled for five runs in 3⅓ innings in next start . . . Born Oct. 8, 1959, in Tulare, Cal. . . . Drafted out of Toronto organization on Dec. 3, 1984 . . . Lost almost all of 1985 season to severe groin pull . . . Made major-league debut on June 11, 1978, one week after signing with Oakland as a No. 1 draft choice (fourth pick).

Year	Club	G	IP	W	L	Pct.	SO	BB	H	ERA
1978	Oakland	3	12	0	3	.000	0	8	19	7.50
1979	Oakland	13	77	2	10	.167	17	50	102	5.96
1982	New York (AL)	30	150⅓	7	11	.389	71	67	167	4.37
1983	Toronto	16	45⅓	0	3	.000	22	21	48	5.16
1985	Seattle	2	6	1	1	.500	2	5	11	12.00
1986	Seattle	37	216⅓	11	17	.393	116	86	243	4.53
	Totals	101	507	21	45	.318	228	237	590	4.92

TOP PROSPECT

MICKEY BRANTLEY 25 5-10 180 Bats R Throws R

Enters spring training in good position to win an outfield job with Mariners . . . Some concern remains after an injury to his right shoulder in 1985 that caused him to lose full range of throwing motion . . . Recalled Aug. 8 after batting .318 for Calgary (AAA) with 30 home runs and 92 RBI in 106 games . . . Used as a leadoff hitter with Mariners . . . Batted only .196 with three homers and seven RBI in brief stint with Mariners . . . Born June 17, 1961, in Catskill, N.Y. . . . Chosen in second round of June 1983 draft.

MANAGER DICK WILLIAMS: Hired May 9 to replace fired Chuck Cottier and begin yet another rebuilding effort with Mariners . . . Posted 58-75 record as he shuffled players constantly . . . Club limped home, dropping its last nine games and 12 of 13 . . . Seattle represents Williams' sixth major-league club in a managerial career that began with Boston in 1967 and took him to Oakland, California, Montreal and San Diego . . . Has

overall managerial mark of 1,470-1,334 . . . Has made four World Series trips, latest coming with San Diego in 1984 . . . Tends to have initial positive impact on a club but wears out his welcome with abrasive personality . . . Likes his teams to run the bases and force mistakes with aggressive play . . . Didn't have the right personnel for that when he arrived at Seattle . . . Resigned from San Diego at start of spring training in bitter exit . . . Signed with Dodgers in 1947 . . . Had .260 career average in 1,023 major-league games as outfielder and infielder . . . Guided Oakland to three straight AL West titles in 1971-73 . . . Born May 7, 1929, in St. Louis.

GREATEST ALL-TIME ROOKIE

Ken Phelps can empathize with Wally Pipp, the Yankee who made way for Lou Gehrig.

Phelps began the 1984 season as Seattle's first baseman, but broke a bone in his hand the first week. Alvin Davis was promoted from Salt Lake City, the Mariners' Triple-A affiliate, after one game there. He has been Seattle's first baseman since.

Davis became the first Mariner to win a major American League award when he was voted Rookie of the Year after batting .284 with 27 home runs and 116 RBI. Davis' RBI total was the highest by a rookie since Al Rosen's 116 in 1950. Davis tied a major-league rookie record set by Philadelphia's Juan Samuel with 13 game-winning RBI and his 16 intentional walks represented another major-league rookie mark.

Davis enjoyed instant success, slamming a game-winning home run in his first start and homering in his second game as well. The Mariners' only representative in the 1984 All-Star Game, he boasted 18 homers at the midseason break.

ALL-TIME MARINER SEASON RECORDS

BATTING: Tom Paciorek, .326, 1981
HRs: Gorman Thomas, 32, 1985
RBIs: Alvin Davis, 116, 1984
STEALS: Julio Cruz, 59, 1978
WINS: Mark Langston, 17, 1984
Mike Moore, 17, 1985
STRIKEOUTS: Mark Langston, 245, 1986

TEXAS RANGERS

TEAM DIRECTORY: Chairman: Eddie Chiles; Pres.: Mike Stone; VP-GM: Tom Grieve; VP-Fin.: Charles Wangner; Asst. GM-Play. Pers./Scouting: Sandy Johnson; Dir. Play. Dev.: Marty Scott; Media Rel. Dir.: John Blake; Trav. Sec.: Dan Schimek; Mgr.: Bobby Valentine. Home: Arlington Stadium (43,508). Field distances: 330, l.f. line; 380, l.c.; 400, c.f.; 380, r.c.; 330, r.f. line. Spring training: Port Charlotte, Fla.

SCOUTING REPORT

HITTING: Pete Incaviglia has made the big difference in the Rangers' suddenly dangerous offense, which produced a .267 average and 184 homers in 1986. Incaviglia, who jumped from Oklahoma State to the majors, lashed 30 home runs, tying the single-season club record, and drove in 88 runs, despite a vision problem that wasn't diagnosed until after the season. The Rangers would be content if he duplicates those numbers in 1987, but would like him to cut down on his major-league-record total of 185 strikeouts.

Oddibe McDowell (.266, 18 homers, 49 RBI, 33 stolen bases) provides speed and power in the leadoff spot. Larry Parrish (.276, 28, 94) and Pete O'Brien (.290, 23, 90) are steady run-producers while Scott Fletcher (.300) has improved dramatically. Free agent Gary Ward (.316, 5, 51), who signed with the Yankees, will be missed.

PITCHING: The Rangers' young pitchers range from brilliant and overpowering one day to wacky and wild the next. Obviously, consistency is missing on a staff that led the AL with 1,059 strikeouts while setting a major-league-record with 94 wild pitches and permitting a major-league-high 736 walks.

Big things are expected from right-hander Bobby Witt (11-9, 5.48), the wildest of this wild bunch, but also the most promising. Witt fanned 174 batters in 157⅔ innings, but he also uncorked an AL-record 22 wild pitches and walked 143 batters. Knuckleballer Charlie Hough (17-10, 3.79) is the old man in the rotation at 39 and the most dependable. Edwin Correa (12-14, 4.23) and Jose Guzman (9-15, 4.54) should improve.

The bullpen is strong with left-hander Mitch Williams, who set a major-league rookie record with 80 appearances, and right-hander Greg Harris, who posted a team-high 20 saves. Williams is expected to displace Harris as the stopper.

Pete Incaviglia's rookie year was a smash—30 of them.

FIELDING: The Rangers have some excellent fielders who go unrecognized. O'Brien finished third among first basemen with a .991 fielding percentage, third baseman Steve Buechele placed second at his position at .968, shortstop Fletcher was fourth at .973.

The Rangers have two major problem areas—catcher and right field. They hope to end a string of three consecutive seasons in which they've led the AL in passed balls. The plodding Incaviglia will wind up a designated hitter if he doesn't improve his defense. He tied for the AL lead with 14 outfield errors.

OUTLOOK: The Rangers enjoyed the greatest improvement of any team in 1986, going from 62-99 in 1985 to 87-75 last year, and further progress can be expected under the careful handling of manager Bobby Valentine. Witt, who won his last seven decisions, is on the verge of becoming a dominant pitcher. This is an intriguing mix of youth and experience that is ready to win the West after challenging throughout last summer.

TEXAS RANGERS 1987 ROSTER

MANAGER Bobby Valentine
Coaches—Joe Ferguson, Tim Foli, Tom House, Art Howe, Tom Robson

PITCHERS

No.	Name	1986 Club	W-L	IP	SO	ERA	B-T	Ht.	Wt.	Born
—	Anderson, Scott	Tulsa	0-0	19	13	1.45	R-R	6-6	185	5/1/62 Corvallis, OR
		Oklahoma City	5-7	82	51	2.96				
43	Brown, Kevin	Sarasota	0-0	6	1	6.00	R-R	6-3½	188	3/14/65 McIntyre, GA
		Tulsa	0-0	10	10	4.50				
		Texas	1-0	5	4	3.60				
21	Correa, Edwin	Texas	12-14	202	189	4.23	R-R	6-2	192	4/29/66 Puerto Rico
23	Guzman, Jose	Texas	9-15	172	87	4.54	R-R	6-3	185	4/9/63 Puerto Rico
27	Harris, Greg	Texas	10-8	111	95	2.83	B-R	6-0	165	11/22/55 Lynwood, CA
45	Henry, Dwayne	Texas	1-0	19	17	4.66	R-R	6-3	205	2/16/62 Elkton, MD
		Oklahoma City	2-1	44	41	5.89				
49	Hough, Charlie	Oklahoma City	0-1	5	3	9.00	R-R	6-2	190	1/5/48 Honolulu, HI
		Texas	17-10	230	146	3.79				
—	Kilgus, Paul	Tulsa	3-7	104	59	3.73	L-L	6-1	175	2/2/62 Bowling Green, KY
46	Loynd, Mike	Tulsa	2-1	29	31	3.68	R-R	6-4	210	3/26/64 St. Louis, MO
		Texas	2-2	42	33	5.36				
16	Mason, Mike	Texas	7-3	135	85	4.33	L-L	6-2	205	11/21/58 Faribault, MN
		Oklahoma City	0-1	3	1	3.00				
38	Meridith, Ron	Iowa-OC	7-7	118	60	4.42	L-L	6-0	174	11/26/56 San Pedro, CA
		Texas	1-0	3	2	3.00				
34	Mohorcic, Dale	Oklahoma City	4-4	38	24	2.39	R-R	6-3	220	1/25/56 Cleveland, OH
		Texas	2-4	79	29	2.39				
—	Rogers, Kenny	Tulsa	0-3	26	13	9.91	L-L	6-1	185	11/10/64 Savannah, GA
		Salem	2-7	66	46	6.27				
40	Russell, Jeff	Oklahoma City	4-1	71	34	3.95	R-R	6-3	210	9/2/61 Cincinnati, OH
		Texas	5-2	82	54	3.40				
—	Taylor, Billy	Tulsa	3-7	68	64	3.95	B-R	6-8	200	10/16/61 Monticello, FL
		Oklahoma City	5-5	102	68	4.60				
28	Williams, Mitch	Texas	8-6	98	90	3.58	L-L	6-4	200	11/17/64 Santa Ana, CA
36	Witt, Bobby	Texas	11-9	158	174	5.48	R-R	6-2	200	5/11/64 Arlington, VA
—	Zaske, Jeff	Hawaii	5-5	114	87	4.12	R-R	6-5	188	10/6/60 Seattle, WA

CATCHERS

No.	Name	1986 Club	H	HR	RBI	Pct.	B-T	Ht.	Wt.	Born
7	Mercado, Orlando	Oklahoma City	47	3	25	.273	R-R	6-0	195	11/7/61 Puerto Rico
		Texas	24	1	7	.235				
12	Petralli, Geno	Texas	35	2	18	.255	B-R	6-1	180	9/25/59 Sacramento, CA
17	Porter, Darrell	Texas	41	12	29	.265	L-R	6-1	202	1/17/52 Joplin, MO
4	Slaught, Don	Oklahoma City	4	0	1	.333	R-R	6-1	190	9/11/58 Long Beach, CA
		Texas	83	13	46	.264				
5	Stanley, Mike	Tulsa	69	6	35	.294	R-R	6-1	185	6/25/63 Ft. Lauderdale, FL
		Texas	10	1	1	.323				
		Oklahoma City	74	5	49	.366				

INFIELDERS

No.	Name	1986 Club	H	HR	RBI	Pct.	B-T	Ht.	Wt.	Born
8	Browne, Jerry	Tulsa	148	2	57	.301	B-R	5-10	165	2/13/66 Virgin Islands
		Texas	10	0	3	.417				
22	Buechele, Steve	Texas	112	18	54	.243	R-R	6-2	190	9/26/61 Lancaster, CA
1	Fletcher, Scott	Texas	159	3	50	.300	R-R	5-11	173	7/30/58 Ft. Walton Beach, FL
11	*Harrah, Toby	Texas	63	7	41	.218	R-R	6-2	180	10/26/48 Sissonville, WV
20	Kunkel, Jeff	Oklahoma City	100	11	51	.244	R-R	6-2	180	3/25/62 West Palm Beach, FL
		Texas	3	1	2	.231				
9	O'Brien, Pete	Texas	160	23	90	.290	L-L	6-1	198	2/9/58 Santa Monica, CA
—	Owen, Dave	Oklahoma City	47	2	22	.250	B-R	6-2	170	4/25/58 Cleburne, TX
44	Paciorek, Tom	Texas	61	4	22	.286	R-R	6-4	205	11/2/46 Detroit, MI
19	Wilkerson, Curtis	Texas	56	0	15	.237	B-R	5-9	158	4/26/61 Petersburg, VA

OUTFIELDERS

No.	Name	1986 Club	H	HR	RBI	Pct.	B-T	Ht.	Wt.	Born
33	Brower, Bob	Oklahoma City	158	13	72	.287	R-R	6-0	190	1/10/60 Queens, NY
		Texas	1	0	0	.111				
—	Espy, Cecil	Hawaii	101	4	38	.263	B-R	6-3	195	1/20/63 San Diego, CA
29	Incaviglia, Pete	Texas	135	30	88	.250	R-R	6-1	220	4/2/64 Pebble Beach, CA
0	McDowell, Oddibe	Texas	152	18	49	.266	L-L	5-9	160	8/25/62 Hollywood, FL
15	Parrish, Larry	Texas	128	28	94	.276	R-R	6-3	215	11/10/65 Winter Haven, FL
3	Sierra, Ruben	Oklahoma City	56	9	41	.296	B-R	6-1	175	10/6/65 Puerto Rico
		Texas	101	16	55	.264				

*Free agent at press time listed with 1986 team

RANGER PROFILES

PETE O'BRIEN 29 6-1 198 Bats L Throws L

First baseman's improvement never seems to end . . . Set career highs in runs (86), hits (160), game-winning RBI (14) and walks (87) . . . Tied for fourth in AL in game-winners . . . Got off to rousing start, batting .410 after first 22 games . . . Led AL in batting at that point . . . Holds club record for home runs by a left-handed hitter with 23 . . . Power hitter who rarely strikes out . . . Fanned just 66 times in 551 at-bats . . . Born Feb. 9, 1958, in Santa Monica, Cal. . . . Selected by Texas in 15th round of June 1979 draft . . . All-Big Eight first baseman for Nebraska in 1979 . . . His first big-league homer was off Seattle's Gaylord Perry in 1982.

Year	Club	Pos.	G	AB	R	H	2B	3B	HR	RBI	SB	Avg.
1982	Texas	OF-1B	20	67	13	16	4	1	4	13	1	.239
1983	Texas	1B-OF	154	524	53	124	24	5	8	53	5	.237
1984	Texas	1B-OF	142	520	57	149	26	2	18	80	3	.287
1985	Texas	1B	159	573	69	153	34	3	22	92	5	.267
1986	Texas	1B	156	551	86	160	23	3	23	90	4	.290
	Totals		631	2235	278	602	111	14	75	328	18	.269

PETE INCAVIGLIA 22 6-1 220 Bats R Throws R

Stocky right fielder became only the third current player to jump from college ball to majors, others being Atlanta's Bob Horner and New York Yankees' Dave Winfield . . . Set club rookie records with 30 homers and 88 RBI . . . The 16th rookie in history to reach 30 homers in a season . . . Slashing hitter set AL record with 185 strikeouts . . . Tied for AL lead in errors by an outfielder with 14 . . . Awkward fielder best suited as a designated hitter . . . Born April 2, 1964, in Pebble Beach, Cal. . . . Father, Tom, was an infielder in Brooklyn Dodger system . . . Selected by San Francisco in 10th round of June 1982 draft but did not sign . . . Was eighth player picked overall, by Montreal, in June 1985 draft . . . Signed by Expos Nov. 2, then traded to Texas for Bob Sebra and Jim Anderson . . . NCAA Player of the Year with Oklahoma State in 1985 . . . Set NCAA single-season records in home runs (48), RBI (143), total bases (285) and slugging percentage (1.140) as he led Oklahoma State to College World Series for third time in his three years there.

Year	Club	Pos.	G	AB	R	H	2B	3B	HR	RBI	SB	Avg.
1986	Texas	OF	153	540	82	135	21	2	30	88	3	.250

SCOTT FLETCHER 28 5-11 173 Bats R Throws R

Sought by several teams in winter of 1985, this shortstop was a great acquisition for Texas . . . Led Rangers with .300 average and set career highs in at-bats (530), runs (82), hits (159), doubles (34), RBI (50), stolen bases (12) and walks (47) . . . AL Player of the Month in July, with .394 average in 26 games . . . Enjoyed career-high 19-game batting streak in July, longest by a Ranger since 1981 . . . Average improved 44 points from career high .256 in 1985 . . . Versatile performer can play second, third or short . . . Born July 30, 1958, in Fort Walton Beach, Fla. . . . Acquired from Chicago White Sox with Ed Correa and Jose Mota on Nov. 22, 1985, for Dave Schmidt and Wayne Tolleson . . . Previously drafted by Los Angeles, Oakland and Houston before signing with Chicago Cubs as first-round pick in June 1979 draft . . . Junior College Player of the Year in 1978 . . . Walloped grand slam in first professional at-bat for Geneva on June 19, 1979.

Year	Club	Pos.	G	AB	R	H	2B	3B	HR	RBI	SB	Avg.
1981	Chicago (NL)	2B-SS-3B	19	46	6	10	4	0	0	1	0	.217
1982	Chicago (NL)	SS	11	24	4	4	0	0	0	1	1	.167
1983	Chicago (AL)	SS-2B-3B	114	262	42	62	16	5	3	31	5	.237
1984	Chicago (AL)	SS-2B-3B	149	456	46	114	13	3	3	35	10	.250
1985	Chicago (AL)	3B-SS-2B	119	301	38	77	8	1	2	31	5	.256
1986	Texas	SS-2B-3B	147	530	82	159	34	5	3	50	12	.300
	Totals		559	1619	218	426	75	14	11	149	33	.263

ODDIBE McDOWELL 24 5-9 160 Bats L Throws L

Center fielder continued to make progress in second season in majors . . . Has unusual power for a leadoff hitter . . . One of four players in AL to hit at least 15 homers and steal at least 30 bases . . . Rangers would like to move him out of leadoff role eventually . . . Set club record with 105 runs, eighth in AL . . . Topped Rangers in at-bats (572) and steals (33) . . . Tied for sixth in AL in steals . . . Worked on improving batting eye . . . Walk total went from 36 as rookie to 65 . . . Average increased 27 points . . . Born Aug. 25, 1962, in Hollywood, Fla. . . . Tabbed in first round of June 1984 draft . . . Wears "O" for Oddibe . . . Started in outfield for 1984 Olympic Team . . . Two-time All-American at Arizona State . . . In 1984, he won Golden Spikes Award, presented to nation's best amateur player.

Year	Club	Pos.	G	AB	R	H	2B	3B	HR	RBI	SB	Avg.
1985	Texas	OF	111	406	63	97	14	5	18	42	25	.239
1986	Texas	OF	154	572	105	152	24	7	18	49	33	.266
	Totals		265	978	168	249	38	12	36	91	58	.255

LARRY PARRISH 33 6-3 215 **Bats R Throws R**

Sidelined from May 22 to June 18 with a pulled rib-cage muscle but still finished with one of his finest seasons . . . Set club records with .509 slugging percentage, ranking seventh in AL, and with 21 homers, 77 RBI as a DH . . . Hit 28 homers in all, best total since 1979 with Montreal . . . Paced Rangers with 94 RBI . . . Appeared in 30 games at third base . . . Exclusively a third baseman in seven-plus seasons with Montreal but has been primarily an outfielder with Texas . . . Born Nov. 10, 1953, in Winter Haven, Fla. . . . Acquired from Montreal with Dave Hostetler on March 31, 1982, for Al Oliver . . . Involved in breeding and developing racehorses . . . With three-homer, six-RBI game against New York on April 29, 1985, he became fifth player to slam three home runs in a game in both leagues.

Year	Club	Pos.	G	AB	R	H	2B	3B	HR	RBI	SB	Avg.
1974	Montreal	3B	25	69	9	14	5	0	0	4	0	.203
1975	Montreal	3B-2B-SS	145	532	50	146	32	5	10	65	4	.274
1976	Montreal	3B	154	543	65	126	28	5	11	61	2	.232
1977	Montreal	3B	123	402	50	99	19	2	11	46	2	.246
1978	Montreal	3B	144	520	68	144	39	4	15	70	2	.277
1979	Montreal	3B	153	544	83	167	39	2	30	82	5	.307
1980	Montreal	3B	126	452	55	115	27	3	15	72	2	.254
1981	Montreal	3B	97	349	41	85	19	3	8	44	0	.244
1982	Texas	OF-3B	128	440	59	116	15	0	17	62	5	.264
1983	Texas	OF	145	555	76	151	26	4	26	88	0	.272
1984	Texas	OF-3B	156	613	72	175	42	1	22	101	2	.285
1985	Texas	OF-3B	94	346	44	86	11	1	17	51	0	.249
1986	Texas	OF-3B	129	464	67	128	22	1	28	94	3	.276
	Totals		1619	5829	739	1552	324	31	210	840	27	.266

CHARLIE HOUGH 39 6-2 190 **Bats R Throws R**

Don't shake knuckleballer's hand to congratulate him on his season . . . Elaborate handshake with a friend caused him to break little finger on right hand and miss first month of season . . . Still finished with career highs in victories (17), starts (33), complete games (seven) and innings pitched (230⅓) . . . Had lowest ERA among Rangers starters at 3.79 . . . Went 5-0 last six starts . . . Became third-oldest pitcher to appear in All-Star Game . . . Allowed two runs in 1⅔ innings as Boston's Rich Gedman couldn't catch dancing knuckleball . . . Pitched 8⅓ no-hit innings against California June 16 before Wally Joyner's clean single . . . Lost game, 2-1, on third-strike passed ball that allowed Joyner to score from second . . . Has learned to accept bizarre life of a knuckleballer . . . Born Jan. 5, 1948, in Honolulu

...Originally drafted by Los Angeles in eighth round in June 1966...Purchased from LA on July 11, 1980...Developed knuckleball in 1969 at Arizona Instructional League after arm injury.

Year	Club	G	IP	W	L	Pct.	SO	BB	H	ERA
1970	Los Angeles..........	8	17	0	0	.000	8	11	18	5.29
1971	Los Angeles..........	4	4	0	0	.000	4	3	3	4.50
1972	Los Angeles..........	2	3	0	0	.000	4	2	2	3.00
1973	Los Angeles..........	37	72	4	2	.667	70	45	52	2.75
1974	Los Angeles..........	49	96	9	4	.692	63	40	65	3.75
1975	Los Angeles..........	38	61	3	7	.300	34	34	43	2.95
1976	Los Angeles..........	77	143	12	8	.600	81	77	102	2.20
1977	Los Angeles..........	70	127	6	12	.333	105	70	98	3.33
1978	Los Angeles..........	55	93	5	5	.500	66	48	69	3.29
1979	Los Angeles..........	42	151	7	5	.583	76	66	152	4.77
1980	Los Angeles..........	19	32	1	3	.250	25	21	37	5.63
1980	Texas..............	16	61	2	2	.500	47	37	54	3.98
1981	Texas..............	21	82	4	1	.800	69	31	61	2.96
1982	Texas..............	34	228	16	13	.552	128	72	217	3.95
1983	Texas..............	34	252	15	13	.536	152	95	219	3.18
1984	Texas..............	36	266	16	14	.533	164	94	260	3.76
1985	Texas..............	34	250⅓	14	16	.467	141	83	198	3.31
1986	Texas..............	33	230⅓	17	10	.630	146	89	188	3.79
	Totals..............	609	2168⅔	131	115	.533	1383	918	1838	3.54

GREG HARRIS 31 6-0 165  **Bats R Throws R**

Doesn't have a big reputation, but he's a durable, effective reliever...Led club with career-high 20 saves, sixth in AL, and set Rangers record with 63 games finished, second in league...Was third in league with 73 appearances...Earned eight saves in 12 appearances May 26 to June 22...Tied for second among AL relievers with 10 wins...Did not lose after July 19...Born Nov. 22, 1955, in Lynwood, Cal....Originally signed by New York Mets as free agent on Sept. 17, 1976...Purchased by Texas from San Diego on Feb. 13, 1985...Opponents batted .186 against Harris in 1985, second-lowest against any AL pitcher with 200 or more batters faced...Led all AL relievers with 111 strikeouts in 1985...Despite success, he's destined to become No. 2 man in pen behind Mitch Williams.

Year	Club	G	IP	W	L	Pct.	SO	BB	H	ERA
1981	New York (NL)........	16	69	3	5	.375	54	28	65	4.43
1982	Cincinnati...........	34	91⅓	2	6	.250	67	37	96	4.83
1983	Cincinnati...........	1	1	0	0	.000	1	3	2	27.00
1984	Mont.-S.D...........	34	54⅓	2	2	.500	45	25	38	2.48
1985	Texas..............	58	113	5	4	.556	111	43	74	2.47
	Totals..............	143	328⅔	12	17	.414	278	136	275	3.61

MITCH WILLIAMS 22 6-4 200 Bats L Throws L

Took major step toward becoming a closer out of the bullpen . . . Topped AL with 80 appearances and established major-league rookie record . . . Brought along carefully by manager Bobby Valentine . . . Used only vs. a left-handed batter or two early in season but time on mound increased gradually . . . Placed second on club with eight saves . . . Went 7-1 after All-Star break . . . Starting pitcher in first four professional seasons . . . Hard thrower was totally unpredictable in 1985, walking 165 in 132 innings in A and AA . . . Walked 79 in 98 innings in rookie season . . . Fanned 90 in 98 innings . . . Born Nov. 17, 1964, in Santa Ana, Cal. . . . Selected by Texas in major-league draft on Dec. 3, 1984, from San Diego system . . . Returned to Padres, then reacquired for Randy Asadoor on April 5, 1985 . . . Prepped for conversion to relief during winter ball in Puerto Rico in 1985 . . . Winningest high-school pitcher in Oregon history as a senior, compiling 17-0 record with 191 strikeouts in 91 innings.

Year	Club	G	IP	W	L	Pct.	SO	BB	H	ERA
1986	Texas	80	98	8	6	.571	90	79	69	3.58

EDWIN CORREA 20 6-2 192 Bats R Throws R

Youngest player in major leagues was also one of most promising . . . Led club and all major-league rookies with 189 strikeouts . . . Marked second-highest total in club history . . . Established club rookie record with 12 wins . . . Placed second on club in wins, starts (32), complete games (four) and innings pitched (202⅓) . . . Went 3-1 with 0.55 ERA in last four starts . . . Hot spell included 25⅓ consecutive scoreless innings . . . Born April 29, 1966, in Hato Rey, Puerto Rico . . . Acquired from White Sox with Scott Fletcher and Jose Mota on Nov. 25, 1985, for Dave Schmidt and Wayne Tolleson . . . Played first professional game in 1982 for Sarasota at age 16 . . . Recorded 436 strikeouts in four minor-league seasons . . . Won first major-league start, 3-2 over Seattle, on last day of 1985 campaign.

Year	Club	G	IP	W	L	Pct.	SO	BB	H	ERA
1985	Chicago (AL)	5	10⅓	1	0	1.000	10	11	11	6.97
1986	Texas	32	202⅓	12	14	.462	189	126	167	4.23
	Totals	37	212⅔	13	14	.481	199	137	178	4.36

BOBBY WITT 22 6-2 200 **Bats R Throws R**

Made club as non-roster player in spring training and had rough moments that might be expected from such a raw talent . . . Became first pitcher to win major-league game with no previous professional victories since David Clyde won major-league debut with Texas in 1973 . . . Witt's came against Toronto on April 22 . . . With 22 wild pitches, he broke by one the record that had been held by Walter Johnson (1910), Earl Wilson (1965) and Nolan Ryan (1977) . . . Told of record wildness, he commented on good company he was keeping . . . Led majors with club-record 143 walks . . . Did not complete any of 31 starts . . . Born May 11, 1964, in Arlington, Va. . . . Chosen in first round of June 1985 draft (third pick) . . . Member of 1984 Olympic team after pitching at Oklahoma . . . Winless in 11 appearances with Tulsa (AA) in 1985.

Year	Club	G	IP	W	L	Pct.	SO	BB	H	ERA
1986	Texas	31	157⅔	11	9	.550	174	143	130	5.48

TOP PROSPECT

JERRY BROWNE 21 5-10 165 **Bats S Throws R**

Should soon become Rangers' regular second baseman . . . Put up impressive totals with Tulsa (AA), compiling .301 average with two home runs, 57 RBI, 39 stolen bases in 128 games . . . Promoted to Texas Sept. 5 and hit .417 in 11 games . . . Started five of club's last six games . . . A potential leadoff hitter . . . Born Feb. 13, 1966, in Christiansted, St. Croix, Virgin Islands . . . Signed March 3, 1983, as free agent.

MANAGER BOBBY VALENTINE: A popular choice for Manager of the Year . . . Gambled on young players and won big . . . Rangers improved 25 games to 87-75, matching second-best record in club history . . . Improvement matched fifth-best leap since division play began in 1969 . . . Was Mets' third-base coach until Rangers hired him in May 1985 . . . Took over 9-23 club and compiled 53-76 record the rest of the way . . . Record as

a manager is 140-151 . . . Was a first-round pick of Los Angeles in 1968 and was mostly an infielder in 10-year career with Dodgers, Angels, Padres, Mets and Mariners . . . A broken leg suffered when he was with California in 1973 prevented him from attaining stardom . . . Hit .260 in 639 games . . . Born May 13, 1950, in Stamford, Conn. . . . Owns restaurants in Connecticut area . . . Wife, Mary, is daughter of former Dodger pitcher Ralph Branca.

GREATEST ALL-TIME ROOKIE

The Rangers faced a difficult decision concerning NCAA Player of the Year Pete Incaviglia as they entered spring training in 1986. They knew there were only two other current major leaguers, Dave Winfield and Bob Horner, who had made the jump from college ball to the majors. They wondered if Oklahoma State's Incaviglia could be the third.

Incaviglia made it easy for the Rangers. The right-handed slugger slammed seven spring-training home runs, a club record, and collected 19 RBI, tying a club record. One screaming line drive ripped off a piece of the wooden fence in left field at old Pompano Stadium.

Except for sturdier fences, it was more of the same in the regular season. Incaviglia set club rookie records with 30 home runs and 88 RBI, including grand slams on Aug. 1 at Milwaukee and Sept. 28 at California.

The only negative note in Incaviglia's rookie season was his strikeout total. He fanned 185 times, an American League record. The Rangers will live with that.

ALL-TIME RANGER SEASON RECORDS

BATTING: Mickey Rivers, .333, 1980
HRs: Jeff Burroughs, 30, 1973
Pete Incaviglia, 30, 1986
RBIs: Jeff Burroughs, 118, 1974
STEALS: Bump Wills, 52, 1978
WINS: Ferguson Jenkins, 25, 1974
STRIKEOUTS: Gaylord Perry, 233, 1975

MAJOR LEAGUE YEAR-BY-YEAR LEADERS

NATIONAL LEAGUE MVP

Year	Player, Club
1931	Frank Frisch, St. Louis Cardinals
1932	Chuck Klein, Philadelphia Phillies
1933	Carl Hubbell, New York Giants
1934	Dizzy Dean, St. Louis Cardinals
1935	Gabby Hartnett, Chicago Cubs
1936	Carl Hubbell, New York Giants
1937	Joe Medwick, St. Louis Cardinals
1938	Ernie Lombardi, Cincinnati Reds
1939	Bucky Walters, Cincinnati Reds
1940	Frank McCormick, Cincinnati Reds
1941	Dolph Camilli, Brooklyn Dodgers
1942	Mort Cooper, St. Louis Cardinals
1943	Stan Musial, St. Louis Cardinals
1944	Marty Marion, St. Louis Cardinals
1945	Phil Cavarretta, Chicago Cubs
1946	Stan Musial, St. Louis Cardinals
1947	Bob Elliott, Boston Braves
1948	Stan Musial, St. Louis Cardinals
1949	Jackie Robinson, Brooklyn Dodgers
1950	Jim Konstanty, Philadelphia Phillies
1951	Roy Campanella, Brooklyn Dodgers
1952	Hank Sauer, Chicago Cubs
1953	Roy Campanella, Brooklyn Dodgers
1954	Willie Mays, New York Giants
1955	Roy Campanella, Brooklyn Dodgers
1956	Don Newcombe, Brooklyn Dodgers
1957	Hank Aaron, Milwaukee Braves
1958	Ernie Banks, Chicago Cubs
1959	Ernie Banks, Chicago Cubs
1960	Dick Groat, Pittsburgh Pirates

Year	Player, Club
1961	Frank Robinson, Cincinnati Reds
1962	Maury Wills, Los Angeles Dodgers
1963	Sandy Koufax, Los Angeles Dodgers
1964	Ken Boyer, St. Louis Cardinals
1965	Willie Mays, San Francisco Giants
1966	Roberto Clemente, Pittsburgh Pirates
1967	Orlando Cepeda, St. Louis Cardinals
1968	Bob Gibson, St. Louis Cardinals
1969	Willie McCovey, San Francisco Giants
1970	Johnny Bench, Cincinnati Reds
1971	Joe Torre, St. Louis Cardinals
1972	Johnny Bench, Cincinnati Reds
1973	Pete Rose, Cincinnati Reds
1974	Steve Garvey, Los Angeles Dodgers
1975	Joe Morgan, Cincinnati Reds
1976	Joe Morgan, Cincinnati Reds
1977	George Foster, Cincinnati Reds
1978	Dave Parker, Pittsburgh Pirates
1979	Keith Hernandez, St. Louis Cardinals
	Willie Stargell, Pittsburgh Pirates
1980	Mike Schmidt, Philadelphia Phillies
1981	Mike Schmidt, Philadelphia Phillies
1982	Dale Murphy, Atlanta Braves
1983	Dale Murphy, Atlanta Braves
1984	Ryne Sandberg, Chicago Cubs
1985	Willie McGee, St. Louis Cardinals
1986	Mike Schmidt, Philadelphia Phillies

AMERICAN LEAGUE MVP

Year	Player, Club
1931	Lefty Grove, Philadelphia Athletics
1932	Jimmy Foxx, Philadelphia Athletics
1933	Jimmy Foxx, Philadelphia Athletics
1934	Mickey Cochrane, Detroit Tigers
1935	Hank Greenberg, Detroit Tigers
1936	Lou Gehrig, New York Yankees
1937	Charley Gehringer, Detroit Tigers
1938	Jimmy Foxx, Boston Red Sox
1939	Joe DiMaggio, New York Yankees
1940	Hank Greenberg, Detroit Tigers
1941	Joe DiMaggio, New York Yankees
1942	Joe Gordon, New York Yankees

Year	Player, Club
1943	Spud Chandler, New York Yankees
1944	Hal Newhouser, Detroit Tigers
1945	Hal Newhouser, Detroit Tigers
1946	Ted Williams, Boston Red Sox
1947	Joe DiMaggio, New York Yankees
1948	Lou Boudreau, Cleveland Indians
1949	Ted Williams, Boston Red Sox
1950	Phil Rizzuto, New York Yankees
1951	Yogi Berra, New York Yankees
1942	Bobby Shantz, Philadelphia Athletics
1953	Al Rosen, Cleveland Indians
1954	Yogi Berra, New York Yankees
1955	Yogi Berra, New York Yankees
1956	Mickey Mantle, New York Yankees
1957	Mickey Mantle, New York Yankees
1958	Jackie Jensen, Boston Red Sox
1959	Nellie Fox, Chicago White Sox
1960	Roger Maris, New York Yankees
1961	Roger Maris, New York Yankees
1962	Mickey Mantle, New York Yankees
1963	Elston Howard, New York Yankees
1964	Brooks Robinson, Baltimore Orioles
1965	Zoilo Versalles, Minnesota Twins
1966	Frank Robinson, Baltimore Orioles
1967	Carl Yastrzemski, Boston Red Sox
1968	Dennis McLain, Detroit Tigers
1969	Harmon Killebrew, Minnesota Twins
1970	Boog Powell, Baltimore Orioles
1971	Vida Blue, Oakland A's
1972	Dick Allen, Chicago White Sox
1973	Reggie Jackson, Oakland A's
1974	Jeff Burroughs, Texas Rangers
1975	Fred Lynn, Boston Red Sox
1976	Thurman Munson, New York Yankees
1977	Rod Carew, Minnesota Twins
1978	Jim Rice, Boston Red Sox
1979	Don Baylor, California Angels
1980	George Brett, Kansas City Royals
1981	Rollie Fingers, Milwaukee Brewers
1982	Robin Yount, Milwaukee Brewers
1983	Cal Ripken Jr., Baltimore Orioles
1984	Willie Hernandez, Detroit Tigers
1985	Don Mattingly, New York Yankees
1986	Roger Clemens, Boston Red Sox

AMERICAN LEAGUE
Batting Champions

Year	Player, Club	Avg.
1901	Napoleon Lajoie, Philadelphia Athletics	.422
1902	Ed Delahanty, Washington Senators	.376
1903	Napoleon Lajoie, Cleveland Indians	.355
1904	Napoleon Lajoie, Cleveland Indians	.381
1905	Elmer Flick, Cleveland Indians	.306
1906	George Stone, St. Louis Browns	.358
1907	Ty Cobb, Detroit Tigers	.350
1908	Ty Cobb, Detroit Tigers	.324
1909	Ty Cobb, Detroit Tigers	.377
1910	Ty Cobb, Detroit Tigers	.385
1911	Ty Cobb, Detroit Tigers	.420
1912	Ty Cobb, Detroit Tigers	.410
1913	Ty Cobb, Detroit Tigers	.390
1914	Ty Cobb, Detroit Tigers	.368
1915	Ty Cobb, Detroit Tigers	.370
1916	Tris Speaker, Cleveland Indians	.386
1917	Ty Cobb, Detroit Tigers	.383
1918	Ty Cobb, Detroit Tigers	.382
1919	Ty Cobb, Detroit Tigers	.384
1920	George Sisler, St. Louis Browns	.407
1921	Harry Heilmann, Detroit Tigers	.393
1922	George Sisler, St. Louis Browns	.420
1923	Harry Heilmann, Detroit Tigers	.398
1924	Babe Ruth, New York Yankees	.378
1925	Harry Heilmann, Detroit Tigers	.393
1926	Heinie Manush, Detroit Tigers	.377
1927	Harry Heilmann, Detroit Tigers	.398
1928	Goose Goslin, Washington Senators	.379
1929	Lew Fonseca, Cleveland Indians	.369
1930	Al Simmons, Philadelphia Athletics	.381
1931	Al Simmons, Philadelphia Athletics	.390
1932	David Alexander, Detroit Tigers-Boston Red Sox	.367
1933	Jimmy Foxx, Philadelphia Athletics	.356
1934	Lou Gehrig, New York Yankees	.365
1935	Buddy Myer, Washington Senators	.349
1936	Luke Appling, Chicago White Sox	.388
1937	Charlie Gehringer, Detroit Tigers	.371
1938	Jimmy Foxx, Boston Red Sox	.349
1939	Joe DiMaggio, New York Yankees	.381
1940	Joe DiMaggio, New York Yankees	.352

Year	Player, Club	Avg.
1941	Ted Williams, Boston Red Sox	.406
1942	Ted Williams, Boston Red Sox	.356
1943	Luke Appling, Chicago White Sox	.328
1944	Lou Boudreau, Cleveland Indians	.327
1945	Snuffy Stirnweiss, New York Yankees	.309
1946	Mickey Vernon, Washington Senators	.353
1947	Ted Williams, Boston Red Sox	.343
1948	Ted Williams, Boston Red Sox	.369
1949	George Kell, Detroit Tigers	.343
1950	Billy Goodman, Boston Red Sox	.354
1951	Ferris Fain, Philadelphia Athletics	.344
1952	Ferris Fain, Philadelphia Athletics	.327
1953	Mickey Vernon, Washington Senators	.337
1954	Bobby Avila, Cleveland Indians	.341
1955	Al Kaline, Detroit Tigers	.340
1956	Mickey Mantle, New York Yankees	.353
1957	Ted Williams, Boston Red Sox	.388
1958	Ted Williams, Boston Red Sox	.328
1959	Harvey Kuenn, Detroit Tigers	.353
1960	Pete Runnels, Boston Red Sox	.320
1961	Norm Cash, Detroit Tigers	.361
1962	Pete Runnels, Boston Red Sox	.326
1963	Carl Yastrzemski, Boston Red Sox	.321
1964	Tony Oliva, Minnesota Twins	.323
1965	Tony Oliva, Minnesota Twins	.321
1966	Frank Robinson, Baltimore Orioles	.316
1967	Carl Yastrzemski, Boston Red Sox	.326
1968	Carl Yastrzemski, Boston Red Sox	.301
1969	Rod Carew, Minnesota Twins	.332
1970	Alex Johnson, California Angels	.329
1971	Tony Oliva, Minnesota Twins	.337
1972	Rod Carew, Minnesota Twins	.318
1973	Rod Carew, Minnesota Twins	.350
1974	Rod Carew, Minnesota Twins	.364
1975	Rod Carew, Minnesota Twins	.359
1976	George Brett, Kansas City Royals	.333
1977	Rod Carew, Minnesota Twins	.388
1978	Rod Carew, Minnesota Twins	.333
1979	Fred Lynn, Boston Red Sox	.333
1980	George Brett, Kansas City Royals	.390
1981	Carney Lansford, Boston Red Sox	.336
1982	Willie Wilson, Kansas City Royals	.332
1983	Wade Boggs, Boston Red Sox	.361
1984	Don Mattingly, New York Yankees	.343

Wade Boggs captured second straight batting title.

Year	Player, Club	Avg.
1985	Wade Boggs, Boston Red Sox	.368
1986	Wade Boggs, Boston Red Sox	.357

NATIONAL LEAGUE
Batting Champions

Year	Player, Club	Avg.
1876	Roscoe Barnes, Chicago	.403
1877	James White, Boston	.385
1878	Abner Dalrymple, Milwaukee	.356
1879	Cap Anson, Chicago	.407
1880	George Gore, Chicago	.365
1881	Cap Anson, Chicago	.399
1882	Dan Brouthers, Buffalo	.367
1883	Dan Brouthers, Buffalo	.371
1884	Jim O'Rourke, Buffalo	.350
1885	Roger Connor, New York	.371
1886	Mike Kelly, Chicago	.388
1887	Cap Anson, Chicago	.421
1888	Cap Anson, Chicago	.343
1889	Dan Brouthers, Boston	.373
1890	Jack Glassock, New York	.336
1891	Billy Hamilton, Philadelphia	.338
1892	Cupid Childs, Cleveland	.335
	Dan Brouthers, Brooklyn	.335
1893	Hugh Duffy, Boston	.378
1894	Hugh Duffy, Boston	.438
1895	Jesse Burkett, Cleveland	.423
1896	Jesse Burkett, Cleveland	.410
1897	Willie Keeler, Baltimore	.432
1898	Willie Keeler, Baltimore	.379
1899	Ed Delahanty, Philadelphia	.408
1900	Honus Wagner, Pittsburgh	.380
1901	Jesse Burkett, St. Louis Cardinals	.382
1902	C.H. Beaumont, Pittsburgh Pirates	.357
1903	Honus Wagner, Pittsburgh Pirates	.355
1904	Honus Wagner, Pittsburgh Pirates	.349
1905	J. Bentley Seymour, Cincinnati Reds	.377
1906	Honus Wagner, Pittsburgh Pirates	.339
1907	Honus Wagner, Pittsburgh Pirates	.350
1908	Honus Wagner, Pittsburgh Pirates	.354
1909	Honus Wagner, Pittsburgh Pirates	.339
1910	Sherwood Magee, Philadelphia Phillies	.331
1911	Honus Wagner, Pittsburgh Pirates	.334
1912	Heinie Zimmerman, Chicago Cubs	.372
1913	Jake Daubert, Brooklyn Dodgers	.350
1914	Jake Daubert, Brooklyn Dodgers	.329

Year	Player, Club	Avg.
1915	Larry Doyle, New York Giants	.320
1916	Hal Chase, Cincinnati Reds	.339
1917	Edd Roush, Cincinnati Reds	.341
1918	Zack Wheat, Brooklyn Dodgers	.335
1919	Edd Roush, Cincinnati Reds	.321
1920	Rogers Hornsby, St. Louis Cardinals	.370
1921	Rogers Hornsby, St. Louis Cardinals	.397
1922	Rogers Hornsby, St. Louis Cardinals	.401
1923	Rogers Hornsby, St. Louis Cardinals	.384
1924	Rogers Hornsby, St. Louis Cardinals	.424
1925	Rogers Hornsby, St. Louis Cardinals	.403
1926	Bubbles Hargrave, Cincinnati Reds	.353
1927	Paul Waner, Pittsburgh Pirates	.380
1928	Rogers Hornsby, Boston Braves	.387
1929	Lefty O'Doul, Philadelphia Phillies	.398
1930	Bill Terry, New York Giants	.401
1931	Chick Hafey, St. Louis Cardinals	.349
1932	Lefty O'Doul, Brooklyn Dodgers	.368
1933	Chuck Klein, Philadelphia Phillies	.368
1934	Paul Waner, Pittsburgh Pirates	.362
1935	Arky Vaughan, Pittsburgh Pirates	.385
1936	Paul Waner, Pittsburgh Pirates	.373
1937	Joe Medwick, St. Louis Cardinals	.374
1938	Ernie Lombardi, Cincinnati Reds	.342
1939	Johnny Mize, St. Louis Cardinals	.349
1940	Debs Garms, Pittsburgh Pirates	.355
1941	Pete Reiser, Brooklyn Dodgers	.343
1942	Ernie Lombardi, Boston Braves	.330
1943	Stan Musial, St. Louis Cardinals	.330
1944	Dixie Walker, Brooklyn Dodgers	.357
1945	Phil Cavarretta, Chicago Cubs	.355
1946	Stan Musial, St. Louis Cardinals	.365
1947	Harry Walker, St. L. Cardinals-Phila. Phillies	.363
1948	Stan Musial, St. Louis Cardinals	.376
1949	Jackie Robinson, Brooklyn Dodgers	.342
1950	Stan Musial, St. Louis Cardinals	.346
1951	Stan Musial, St. Louis Cardinals	.355
1952	Stan Musial, St. Louis Cardinals	.336
1953	Carl Furillo, Brooklyn Dodgers	.344
1954	Willie Mays, New York Giants	.345
1955	Richie Ashburn, Philadelphia Phillies	.338
1956	Hank Aaron, Milwaukee Braves	.328
1957	Stan Musial, St. Louis Cardinals	.351
1958	Richie Ashburn, Philadelphia Phillies	.350

Year	Player, Club	Avg.
1959	Hank Aaron, Milwaukee Braves	.328
1960	Dick Groat, Pittsburgh Pirates	.325
1961	Roberto Clemente, Pittsburgh Pirates	.351
1962	Tommy Davis, Los Angeles Dodgers	.346
1963	Tommy Davis, Los Angeles Dodgers	.326
1964	Roberto Clemente, Pittsburgh Pirates	.339
1965	Roberto Clemente, Pittsburgh Pirates	.329
1966	Matty Alou, Pittsburgh Pirates	.342
1967	Roberto Clemente, Pittsburgh Pirates	.357
1968	Pete Rose, Cincinnati Reds	.335
1969	Pete Rose, Cincinnati Reds	.348
1970	Rico Carty, Atlanta Braves	.366
1971	Joe Torre, St. Louis Cardinals	.363
1972	Billy Williams, Chicago Cubs	.333
1973	Pete Rose, Cincinnati Reds	.338
1974	Ralph Garr, Atlanta Braves	.353
1975	Bill Madlock, Chicago Cubs	.354
1976	Bill Madlock, Chicago Cubs	.339
1977	Dave Parker, Pittsburgh Pirates	.338
1978	Dave Parker, Pittsburgh Pirates	.334
1979	Keith Hernandez, St. Louis Cardinals	.344
1980	Bill Buckner, Chicago Cubs	.324
1981	Bill Madlock, Pittsburgh Pirates	.341
1982	Al Oliver, Montreal Expos	.331
1983	Bill Madlock, Pittsburgh Pirates	.323
1984	Tony Gwynn, San Diego Padres	.351
1985	Willie McGee, St. Louis Cardinals	.353
1986	Tim Raines, Montreal Expos	.334

NATIONAL LEAGUE
Home Run Leaders

Year	Player, Club	HRs
1900	Herman Long, Boston Nationals	12
1901	Sam Crawford, Cincinnati Reds	16
1902	Tom Leach, Pittsburgh Pirates	6
1903	Jim Sheckard, Brooklyn Dodgers	9
1904	Harry Lumley, Brooklyn Dodgers	9
1905	Fred Odwell, Cincinnati Reds	9
1906	Tim Jordan, Brooklyn Dodgers	12
1907	Dave Brian, Boston Nationals	10

Year	Player, Club	HRs
1908	Tim Jordan, Brooklyn Dodgers	12
1909	Jim Murray, New York Giants	7
1910	Fred Beck, Boston Nationals	10
	Frank Schulte, Chicago Cubs	10
1911	Frank Schulte, Chicago Cubs	21
1912	Heinie Zimmerman, Chicago Cubs	14
1913	Gavvy Cravath, Philadelphia Phillies	19
1914	Gavvy Cravath, Philadelphia Phillies	19
1915	Gavvy Cravath, Philadelphia Phillies	24
1916	Dave Robertson, New York Giants	12
	Cy Williams, Chicago Cubs	12
1917	Gavvy Cravath, Philadelphia Phillies	12
	Dave Robertson, New York Giants	12
1918	Gavvy Cravath, Philadelphia Phillies	8
1919	Gavvy Cravath, Philadelphia Phillies	12
1920	Cy Williams, Philadelphia Phillies	15
1921	George Kelly, New York Giants	23
1922	Rogers Hornsby, St. Louis Cardinals	42
1923	Cy Williams, Philadelphia Phillies	41
1924	Jack Fournier, Brooklyn Dodgers	27
1925	Rogers Hornsby, St. Louis Cardinals	39
1926	Hack Wilson, Chicago Cubs	21
1927	Cy Williams, Philadelphia Phillies	30
	Hack Wilson, Chicago Cubs	30
1928	Jim Bottomley, St. Louis Cardinals	31
	Hack Wilson, Chicago Cubs	31
1929	Chuck Klein, Philadelphia Phillies	43
1930	Hack Wilson, Chicago Cubs	56
1931	Chuck Klein, Philadelphia Phillies	31
1932	Chuck Klein, Philadelphia Phillies	38
	Mel Ott, New York Giants	38
1933	Chuck Klein, Philadelphia Phillies	28
1934	Rip Collins, St. Louis Cardinals	35
	Mel Ott, New York Giants	35
1935	Wally Berger, Boston Braves	34
1936	Mel Ott, New York Giants	33
1937	Joe Medwick, St. Louis Cardinals	31
	Mel Ott, New York Giants	31
1938	Mel Ott, New York Giants	36
1939	Johnny Mize, St. Louis Cardinals	28
1940	Johnny Mize, St. Louis Cardinals	43
1941	Dolph Camilli, Brooklyn Dodgers	34
1942	Mel Ott, New York Giants	30
1943	Bill Nicholson, Chicago Cubs	29

Year	Player, Club	HRs
1944	Bill Nicholson, Chicago Cubs	33
1945	Tommy Holmes, Boston Braves	28
1946	Ralph Kiner, Pittsburgh Pirates	23
1947	Ralph Kiner, Pittsburgh Pirates	51
	Johnny Mize, New York Giants	51
1948	Ralph Kiner, Pittsburgh Pirates	40
	Johnny Mize, New York Giants	40
1949	Ralph Kiner, Pittsburgh Pirates	54
1950	Ralph Kiner, Pittsburgh Pirates	47
1951	Ralph Kiner, Pittsburgh Pirates	42
1952	Ralph Kiner, Pittsburgh Pirates	37
	Hank Sauer, Chicago Cubs	37
1953	Eddie Mathews, Milwaukee Braves	47
1954	Ted Kluszewski, Cincinnati Reds	49
1955	Willie Mays, New York Giants	51
1956	Duke Snider, Brooklyn Dodgers	43
1957	Hank Aaron, Milwaukee Braves	44
1958	Ernie Banks, Chicago Cubs	47
1959	Eddie Mathews, Milwaukee Braves	46
1960	Ernie Banks, Chicago Cubs	41
1961	Orlando Cepeda, San Francisco Giants	46
1962	Willie Mays, San Francisco Giants	49
1963	Hank Aaron, Milwaukee Braves	44
	Willie McCovey, San Francisco Giants	44
1964	Willie Mays, San Francisco Giants	47
1965	Willie Mays, San Francisco Giants	52
1966	Hank Aaron, Atlanta Braves	44
1967	Hank Aaron, Atlanta Braves	39
1968	Willie McCovey, San Francisco Giants	36
1969	Willie McCovey, San Francisco Giants	45
1970	Johnny Bench, Cincinnati Reds	45
1971	Willie Stargell, Pittsburgh Pirates	48
1972	Johnny Bench, Cincinnati Reds	40
1973	Willie Stargell, Pittsburgh Pirates	44
1974	Mike Schmidt, Philadelphia Phillies	36
1975	Mike Schmidt, Philadelphia Phillies	38
1976	Mike Schmidt, Philadelphia Phillies	38
1977	George Foster, Cincinnati Reds	52
1978	George Foster, Cincinnati Reds	40
1979	Dave Kingman, Chicago Cubs	48
1980	Mike Schmidt, Philadelphia Phillies	48
1981	Mike Schmidt, Philadelphia Phillies	31
1982	Dave Kingman, New York Mets	37
1983	Mike Schmidt, Philadelphia Phillies	40

Year	Player, Club	HRs
1984	Mike Schmidt, Philadelphia Phillies	36
1984	Dale Murphy, Atlanta Braves	36
1985	Dale Murphy, Atlanta Braves	37
1986	Mike Schmidt, Philadelphia Phillies	37

AMERICAN LEAGUE
Home Run Leaders

Year	Player, Club	HRs
1901	Napoleon Lajoie, Philadelphia Athletics	13
1902	Ralph Seybold, Philadelphia Athletics	16
1903	John Freeman, Boston Pilgrims	13
1904	Harry Davis, Philadelphia Athletics	10
1905	Harry Davis, Philadelphia Athletics	8
1906	Harry Davis, Philadelphia Athletics	12
1907	Harry Davis, Philadelphia Athletics	8
1908	Sam Crawford, Detroit Tigers	7
1909	Ty Cobb, Detroit Tigers	9
1910	Garland Stahl, Boston Red Sox	10
1911	Frank (Home Run) Baker, Philadelphia Athletics	9
1912	Frank (Home Run) Baker, Philadelphia Athletics	10
1913	Frank (Home Run) Baker, Philadelphia Athletics	12
1914	Frank (Home Run) Baker, Philadelphia Athletics	8
	Sam Crawford, Detroit Tigers	8
1915	Bob Roth, Cleveland Indians	7
1916	Wally Pipp, New York Yankees	12
1917	Wally Pipp, New York Yankees	9
1918	Babe Ruth, Boston Red Sox	11
	Clarence Walker, Philadelphia Athletics	11
1919	Babe Ruth, Boston Red Sox	29
1920	Babe Ruth, New York Yankees	54
1921	Babe Ruth, New York Yankees	59
1922	Ken Williams, St. Louis Browns	39
1923	Babe Ruth, New York Yankees	41
1924	Babe Ruth, New York Yankees	46
1925	Bob Meusel, New York Yankees	33
1926	Babe Ruth, New York Yankees	47
1927	Babe Ruth, New York Yankees	60
1928	Babe Ruth, New York Yankees	54
1929	Babe Ruth, New York Yankees	46
1930	Babe Ruth, New York Yankees	49
1931	Babe Ruth, New York Yankees	46
	Lou Gehrig, New York Yankees	46

Year	Player, Club	HRs
1932	Jimmy Foxx, Philadelphia Athletics	58
1933	Jimmy Foxx, Philadelphia Athletics	48
1934	Lou Gehrig, New York Yankees	49
1935	Hank Greenberg, Detroit Tigers	36
	Jimmy Fox, Philadelphia Athletics	36
1936	Lou Gehrig, New York Yankees	49
1937	Joe DiMaggio, New York Yankees	46
1938	Hank Greenberg, Detroit Tigers	58
1939	Jimmy Foxx, Boston Red Sox	35
1940	Hank Greenberg, Detroit Tigers	41
1941	Ted Williams, Boston Red Sox	37
1942	Ted Williams, Boston Red Sox	36
1943	Rudy York, Detroit Tigers	34
1944	Nick Etten, New York Yankees	22
1945	Vern Stephens, St. Louis Browns	24
1946	Hank Greenberg, Detroit Tigers	44
1947	Ted Williams, Boston Red Sox	32
1948	Joe DiMaggio, New York Yankees	39
1949	Ted Williams, Boston Red Sox	43
1950	Al Rosen, Cleveland Indians	37
1951	Gus Zernial, Philadelphia Athletics	33
1952	Larry Doby, Cleveland Indians	32
1953	Al Rosen, Cleveland Indians	43
1954	Larry Doby, Cleveland Indians	32
1955	Mickey Mantle, New York Yankees	37
1956	Mickey Mantle, New York Yankees	52
1957	Roy Sievers, Washington Senators	42
1958	Mickey Mantle, New York Yankees	42
1959	Rocky Colavito, Cleveland Indians	42
	Harmon Killebrew, Washington Senators	42
1960	Mickey Mantle, New York Yankees	40
1961	Roger Maris, New York Yankees	61
1962	Harmon Killebrew, Minnesota Twins	48
1963	Harmon Killebrew, Minnesota Twins	45
1964	Harmon Killebrew, Minnesota Twins	49
1965	Tony Conigliaro, Boston Red Sox	32
1966	Frank Robinson, Baltimore Orioles	49
1967	Carl Yastrzemski, Boston Red Sox	44
	Harmon Killebrew, Minnesota Twins	44
1968	Frank Howard, Washington Senators	44
1969	Harmon Killebrew, Minnesota Twins	49
1970	Frank Howard, Washington Senators	44
1971	Bill Melton, Chicago White Sox	33
1972	Dick Allen, Chicago White Sox	37

Jim Rice has won the AL home-run title three times.

Year	Player, Club	HRs
1973	Reggie Jackson, Oakland A's	32
1974	Dick Allen, Chicago White Sox	32
1975	George Scott, Milwaukee Brewers	36
	Reggie Jackson, Oakland A's	36
1976	Graig Nettles, New York Yankees	32
1977	Jim Rice, Boston Red Sox	39
1978	Jim Rice, Boston Red Sox	46
1979	Gorman Thomas, Milwaukee Brewers	45
1980	Ben Oglivie, Milwaukee Brewers	41
	Reggie Jackson, New York Yankees	41
1981	Bobby Grich, California Angels	22
	Eddie Murray, Baltimore Orioles	22
	Dwight Evans, Boston Red Sox	22
	Tony Armas, Oakland A's	22
1982	Reggie Jackson, California Angels	39
	Gorman Thomas, Milwaukee Braves	39
1983	Jim Rice, Boston Red Sox	39
1984	Tony Armas, Boston Red Sox	43
1985	Darrell Evans, Detroit Tigers	40
1986	Jesse Barfield, Toronto Blue Jays	40

CY YOUNG AWARD WINNERS

(Prior to 1967 there was a single overall major league award.)

Year	Player, Club
1956	Don Newcombe, Brooklyn Dodgers
1957	Warren Spahn, Milwaukee Braves
1958	Bob Turley, New York Yankees
1959	Early Wynn, Chicago White Sox
1960	Vernon Law, Pittsburgh Pirates
1961	Whitey Ford, New York Yankees
1962	Don Drysdale, Los Angeles Dodgers
1963	Sandy Koufax, Los Angeles Dodgers
1964	Dean Chance, Los Angeles Angels
1965	Sandy Koufax, Los Angeles Dodgers
1966	Sandy Koufax, Los Angeles Dodgers

NL CY YOUNG

Year	Player, Club
1967	Mike McCormick, San Francisco Giants
1968	Bob Gibson, St. Louis Cardinals
1969	Tom Seaver, New York Mets
1970	Bob Gibson, St. Louis Cardinals
1971	Ferguson Jenkins, Chicago Cubs
1972	Steve Carlton, Philadelphia Phillies
1973	Tom Seaver, New York Mets
1974	Mike Marshall, Los Angeles Dodgers
1975	Tom Seaver, New York Mets
1976	Randy Jones, San Diego Padres
1977	Steve Carlton, Philadelphia Phillies
1978	Gaylord Perry, San Diego Padres
1979	Bruce Sutter, Chicago Cubs
1980	Steve Carlton, Philadelphia Phillies
1981	Fernando Valenzuela, Los Angeles Dodgers
1982	Steve Carlton, Philadelphia Phillies
1983	John Denny, Philadelphia Phillies
1984	Rick Sutcliffe, Chicago Cubs
1985	Dwight Gooden, New York Mets
1986	Mike Scott, Houston Astros

Dwight Gooden won NL Cy Young Award in 1985.

AL CY YOUNG

Year	Player, Club
1967	Jim Lonborg, Boston Red Sox
1968	Dennis McLain, Detroit Tigers
1969	Mike Cuellar, Baltimore Orioles
	Dennis McLain, Detroit Tigers
1970	Jim Perry, Minnesota Twins
1971	Vida Blue, Oakland A's

AL Cy Young Award went to A's Vida Blue in 1971.

Year	Player, Club
1972	Gaylord Perry, Cleveland Indians
1973	Jim Palmer, Baltimore Orioles
1974	Jim Hunter, Oakland A's
1975	Jim Palmer, Baltimore Orioles
1976	Jim Palmer, Baltimore Orioles
1977	Sparky Lyle, New York Yankees
1978	Ron Guidry, New York Yankees
1979	Mike Flanagan, Baltimore Orioles
1980	Steve Stone, Baltimore Orioles
1981	Rollie Fingers, Milwaukee Brewers
1982	Pete Vuckovich, Milwaukee Brewers
1983	LaMarr Hoyt, Chicago White Sox
1984	Willie Hernandez, Detroit Tigers
1985	Bret Saberhagen, Kansas City
1986	Roger Clemens, Boston Red Sox

AMERICAN LEAGUE
Rookie of Year

Year	Player, Club
1949	Roy Sievers, St. Louis Browns
1950	Walt Dropo, Boston Red Sox
1951	Gil McDougald, New York Yankees
1952	Harry Byrd, Philadelphia Athletics
1953	Harvey Kuenn, Detroit Tigers
1954	Bob Grim, New York Yankees
1955	Herb Score, Cleveland Indians
1956	Luis Aparicio, Chicago White Sox
1957	Tony Kubek, New York Yankees
1958	Albie Pearson, Washington Senators
1959	Bob Allison, Washington Senators
1960	Ron Hansen, Baltimore Orioles
1961	Don Schwall, Boston Red Sox
1962	Tom Tresh, New York Yankees
1963	Gary Peters, Chicago White Sox
1964	Tony Oliva, Minnesota Twins
1965	Curt Blefary, Baltimore Orioles
1966	Tommie Agee, Chicago White Sox
1967	Rod Carew, Minnesota Twins
1968	Stan Bahnsen, New York Yankees
1969	Lou Piniella, Kansas City Royals

Year	Player, Club
1970	Thurman Munson, New York Yankees
1971	Chris Chambliss, Cleveland Indians
1972	Carlton Fisk, Boston Red Sox
1973	Al Bumbry, Baltimore Orioles
1974	Mike Hargrove, Texas Rangers
1975	Fred Lynn, Boston Red Sox
1976	Mark Fidrych, Detroit Tigers
1977	Eddie Murray, Baltimore Orioles
1978	Lou Whitaker, Detroit Tigers
1979	John Castino, Minnesota Twins
	Alfredo Griffin, Toronto Blue Jays
1980	Joe Charboneau, Cleveland Indians
1981	Dave Righetti, New York Yankees
1982	Cal Ripken, Jr., Baltimore Orioles
1983	Ron Kittle, Chicago White Sox
1984	Alvin Davis, Seattle Mariners
1985	Ozzie Guillen, Chicago White Sox
1986	Jose Canseco, Oakland A's

NATIONAL LEAGUE
Rookie of Year

Year	Player, Club
1947	Jackie Robinson, Brooklyn Dodgers
1948	Al Dark, Boston Braves
1949	Don Newcombe, Brooklyn Dodgers
1950	Sam Jethroe, Boston Braves
1951	Willie Mays, New York Giants
1952	Joe Black, Brooklyn Dodgers
1953	Junior Gilliam, Brooklyn Dodgers
1954	Wally Moon, St. Louis Cardinals
1955	Bill Virdon, St. Louis Cardinals
1956	Frank Robinson, Cincinnati Reds
1957	Jack Sanford, Philadelphia Phillies
1958	Orlando Cepeda, San Francisco Giants
1959	Willie McCovey, San Francisco Giants
1960	Frank Howard, Los Angeles Dodgers
1961	Billy Williams, Chicago Cubs
1962	Kenny Hubbs, Chicago Cubs
1963	Pete Rose, Cincinnati Reds

Year	Player, Club
1964	Richie Allen, Philadelphia Phillies
1965	Jim Lefebvre, Los Angeles Dodgers
1966	Tommy Helms, Cincinnati Reds
1967	Tom Seaver, New York Mets
1968	Johnny Bench, Cincinnati Reds
1969	Ted Sizemore, Los Angeles Dodgers
1970	Carl Morton, Montreal Expos
1971	Earl Williams, Atlanta Braves
1972	Jon Matlack, New York Mets
1973	Gary Matthews, San Francisco Giants
1974	Bake McBride, St. Louis Cardinals
1975	John Montefusco, San Francisco Giants
1976	Pat Zachry, Cincinnati Reds
	Butch Metzger, San Diego Padres
1977	Andre Dawson, Montreal Expos
1978	Bob Horner, Atlanta Braves
1979	Rick Sutcliffe, Los Angeles Dodgers
1980	Steve Howe, Los Angeles Dodgers
1981	Fernando Valenzuela, Los Angeles Dodgers
1982	Steve Sax, Los Angeles Dodgers
1983	Darryl Strawberry, New York Mets
1984	Dwight Gooden, New York Mets
1985	Vince Coleman, St. Louis Cardinals
1986	Todd Worrell, St. Louis Cardinals

WORLD SERIES WINNERS

Year	A. L. Champion	N. L. Champion	World Series Winner
1903	Boston Red Sox	Pittsburgh Pirates	Boston, 5-3
1905	Philadelphia Athletics	New York Giants	New York, 4-1
1906	Chicago White Sox	Chicago Cubs	Chicago (AL), 4-2
1907	Detroit Tigers	Chicago Cubs	Chicago, 4-0-1
1908	Detroit Tigers	Chicago Cubs	Chicago, 4-1
1909	Detroit Tigers	Pittsburgh Pirates	Pittsburgh, 4-3
1910	Philadelphia Athletics	Chicago Cubs	Philadelphia, 4-1
1911	Philadelphia Athletics	New York Giants	Philadelphia, 4-2
1912	Boston Red Sox	New York Giants	Boston, 4-3-1
1913	Philadelphia Athletics	Boston Braves	Boston, 4-0
1914	Philadelphia Athletics	New York Giants	Philadelphia, 4-1
1915	Boston Red Sox	Philadelphia Phillies	Boston, 4-1
1916	Boston Red Sox	Philadelphia Phillies	Boston, 4-1
1917	Chicago White Sox	New York Giants	Chicago, 4-2
1918	Boston Red Sox	Chicago Cubs	Boston, 4-2
1919	Chicago White Sox	Cincinnati Reds	Cincinnati, 5-2
1920	Cleveland Indians	Brooklyn Dodgers	Cleveland, 5-2
1921	New York Yankees	New York Giants	New York (NL), 5-3
1922	New York Yankees	New York Giants	New York (NL), 4-0-1
1923	New York Yankees	New York Giants	New York (AL), 4-2
1924	Washington Senators	New York Giants	Washington, 4-2
1925	Washington Senators	Pittsburgh Pirates	Pittsburgh, 4-3
1926	New York Yankees	St. Louis Cardinals	St. Louis, 4-3
1927	New York Yankees	Pittsburgh Pirates	New York, 4-0
1928	New York Yankees	St. Louis Cardinals	New York, 4-0
1929	Philadelphia Athletics	Chicago Cubs	Philadelphia, 4-2
1930	Philadelphia Athletics	St. Louis Cardinals	Philadelphia, 4-2
1931	Philadelphia Athletics	St. Louis Cardinals	St. Louis, 4-3
1932	New York Yankees	Chicago Cubs	New York, 4-0
1933	Washington Senators	New York Giants	New York, 4-1
1934	Detroit Tigers	St. Louis Cardinals	St. Louis, 4-3
1935	Detroit Tigers	Chicago Cubs	Detroit, 4-2
1936	New York Yankees	New York Giants	New York (AL), 4-2
1937	New York Yankees	New York Giants	New York (AL), 4-1
1938	New York Yankees	Chicago Cubs	New York, 4-0
1939	New York Yankees	Cincinnati Reds	New York, 4-0
1940	Detroit Tigers	Cincinnati Reds	Cincinnati, 4-3
1941	New York Yankees	Brooklyn Dodgers	New York, 4-1
1942	New York Yankees	St. Louis Cardinals	St. Louis, 4-1
1943	New York Yankees	St. Louis Cardinals	New York, 4-1
1944	St. Louis Browns	St. Louis Cardinals	St. Louis (NL), 4-2
1945	Detroit Tigers	Chicago Cubs	Detroit, 4-3
1946	Boston Red Sox	St. Louis Cardinals	St. Louis, 4-3
1947	New York Yankees	Brooklyn Dodgers	New York, 4-3
1948	Cleveland Indians	Boston Braves	Cleveland, 4-2
1949	New York Yankees	Brooklyn Dodgers	New York, 4-1
1950	New York Yankees	Philadelphia Phillies	New York, 4-0
1951	New York Yankees	New York Giants	New York (AL), 4-2
1952	New York Yankees	Brooklyn Dodgers	New York, 4-3
1953	New York Yankees	Brooklyn Dodgers	New York, 4-2
1954	Cleveland Indians	New York Giants	New York, 4-0
1955	New York Yankees	Brooklyn Dodgers	Brooklyn, 4-3

Series MVP Ray Knight enjoys Mets' victory parade.

Year	A. L. Champion	N. L. Champion	World Series Winner
1956	New York Yankees	Brooklyn Dodgers	New York, 4-3
1957	New York Yankees	Milwaukee Braves	Milwaukee, 4-3
1958	New York Yankees	Milwaukee Braves	New York, 4-3
1959	Chicago White Sox	Los Angeles Dodgers	Los Angeles, 4-2
1960	New York Yankees	Pittsburgh Pirates	Pittsburgh, 4-3
1961	New York Yankees	Cincinnati Reds	New York, 4-1
1962	New York Yankees	San Francisco Giants	New York, 4-3
1963	New York Yankees	Los Angeles Dodgers	Los Angeles, 4-0
1964	New York Yankees	St. Louis Cardinals	St. Louis, 4-3
1965	Minnesota Twins	Los Angeles Dodgers	Los Angeles, 4-3
1966	Baltimore Orioles	Los Angeles Dodgers	Baltimore, 4-0
1967	Boston Red Sox	St. Louis Cardinals	St. Louis, 4-3
1968	Detroit Tigers	St. Louis Cardinals	Detroit, 4-3
1969	Baltimore Orioles	New York Mets	New York, 4-1
1970	Baltimore Orioles	Cincinnati Reds	Baltimore, 4-1
1971	Baltimore Orioles	Pittsburgh Pirates	Pittsburgh, 4-3
1972	Oakland A's	Cincinnati Reds	Oakland, 4-3
1973	Oakland A's	New York Mets	Oakland, 4-3
1974	Oakland A's	Los Angeles Dodgers	Oakland, 4-1
1975	Boston Red Sox	Cincinnati Reds	Cincinnati, 4-3
1976	New York Yankees	Cincinnati Reds	Cincinnati, 4-0
1977	New York Yankees	Los Angeles Dodgers	New York, 4-2
1978	New York Yankees	Los Angeles Dodgers	New York, 4-2
1979	Baltimore Orioles	Pittsburgh Pirates	Pittsburgh, 4-3
1980	Kansas City Royals	Philadelphia Phillies	Philadelphia, 4-2
1981	New York Yankees	Los Angeles Dodgers	Los Angeles, 4-2
1982	Milwaukee Brewers	St. Louis Cardinals	St. Louis, 4-3
1983	Baltimore Orioles	Philadelphia Phillies	Baltimore, 4-1
1984	Detroit Tigers	San Diego Padres	Detroit, 4-1
1985	Kansas City Royals	St. Louis Cardinals	Kansas City, 4-3
1986	Boston Red Sox	New York Mets	New York, 4-3

(Facing page) 1986 World Champion Mets: Front row (from left)—Trainer Steve Garland, coaches Mel Stottlemyre, Bill Robinson, Bud Harrelson, Vern Hoscheit and Greg Pavlick, assistant trainer Bob Sikes. Second row—Wally Backman, Mookie Wilson, Lee Mazzilli, Keith Hernandez, Dwight Gooden, manager Davey Johnson, Gary Carter, Ron Darling, Darryl Strawberry, Lenny Dykstra. Third row—Assistant to the general manager and travel director Arthur Richman, Rafael Santana, Howard Johnson, Kevin Mitchell, Tim Teufel, Roger McDowell, Doug Sisk, Ray Knight, Sid Fernandez, Randy Myers. Back row—Batboy Paul Greco, equipment manager Charlie Samuels, Rick Anderson, Kevin Elster, Ed Hearn, Randy Niemann, Rick Aguilera, Bob Ojeda, Danny Heep, John Gibbons, assistant equipment manager John Rufino, batboy Mike Rufino. Absent from photo: Jesse Orosco.

1986 WORLD SERIES

BOSTON RED SOX

Batter	AVG	G	AB	R	H	2B	3B	HR	RBI	GW	SH	SF	HB	BB	SO	SB	CS	E
Armas	.000	1	1	0	0	0	0	0	0	0	0	0	0	0	1	0	0	0
Barrett	.433	7	30	1	13	2	0	0	4	0	0	0	0	5	2	0	0	0
Baylor	.182	4	11	1	2	1	0	0	1	0	0	0	1	1	3	0	0	0
Boggs	.290	7	31	3	9	3	0	0	3	1	0	0	0	4	2	0	0	0
Buckner	.188	7	32	2	6	0	0	0	1	0	0	0	1	0	3	0	0	1
Evans	.308	7	26	4	8	2	0	2	9	0	0	0	0	4	3	0	0	1
Gedman	.200	7	30	1	6	1	0	1	1	0	0	0	0	0	10	0	0	2
Greenwell	.000	4	3	0	0	0	0	0	0	0	0	0	0	1	2	0	0	0
Henderson	.400	7	25	6	10	1	1	2	5	0	0	1	1	2	6	0	0	0
Owen	.300	7	20	2	6	0	0	0	2	1	1	1	0	5	6	0	0	0
Rice	.333	7	27	6	9	1	1	0	0	0	0	0	0	6	9	0	0	0
Romero	.000	3	1	0	0	0	0	0	0	0	0	0	0	0	0	0	0	0
Stapleton	.000	3	1	0	0	0	0	0	0	0	0	0	0	0	0	0	0	0
Boyd	—	1	0	0	0	0	0	0	0	0	0	0	0	0	0	0	0	0
Clemens	.000	2	4	1	0	0	0	0	0	0	1	0	0	0	1	0	0	0
Crawford	.000	3	1	0	0	0	0	0	0	0	0	0	0	0	0	0	0	0
Hurst	.000	3	3	0	0	0	0	0	0	0	2	0	0	0	3	0	0	0
Nipper	—	2	0	0	0	0	0	0	0	0	0	0	0	0	0	0	0	0
Sambito	—	2	0	0	0	0	0	0	0	0	0	0	0	0	0	0	0	0
Schiraldi	.000	3	1	0	0	0	0	0	0	0	0	0	0	0	1	0	0	0
Stanley	.000	5	1	0	0	0	0	0	0	0	0	0	0	0	1	0	0	0
TOTALS	.278	7	248	27	69	11	2	5	26	2	4	2	3	28	53	0	0	4

Pitcher		W	L	ERA	G	GS	CG	SHO	SV	IP	H	R	ER	HR	HB	BB	SO	WP
Boyd	R	0	1	7.71	1	1	0	0	0	7.0	9	6	6	1	0	1	3	0
Clemens	R	0	0	3.18	2	2	0	0	0	11.1	9	5	4	0	0	6	11	0
Crawford	R	1	0	6.23	3	0	0	0	0	4.1	5	3	3	2	1	0	4	0
Hurst	L	2	0	1.96	3	3	1	0	0	23.0	18	5	5	1	0	6	17	0
Nipper	R	0	1	7.11	2	1	0	0	0	6.1	10	5	5	2	0	2	2	0
Sambito	L	0	0	27.00	2	0	0	0	0	0.1	2	1	1	0	0	2	0	1
Schiraldi	R	0	2	13.50	3	0	0	0	1	4.0	7	7	6	1	0	3	2	1
Stanley	R	0	0	0.00	5	0	0	0	1	6.1	5	0	0	0	0	1	4	1
TOTALS		3	4	4.31	7	7	1	1	2	62.2	65	32	30	7	1	21	43	3

GAME 1
at NEW YORK
Saturday, October 18
T—2:59; A—55,076

Boston	0	0	0	0	0	0	1	0	0	1	5	0
New York	0	0	0	0	0	0	0	0	0	0	4	1

HURST, Schiraldi (S) (9)
DARLING, McDowell (8)
HR: None

GAME 2
at NEW YORK
Sunday, October 19
T—3:36; A—55,063

Boston	0	0	3	1	2	0	2	0	1	9	18	0
New York	0	0	2	0	1	0	0	0	0	3	8	1

Clemens, CRAWFORD (5), Stanley (S), (7)
GOODEN, Aguilera (6), Orosco (7), Fernandez (9), Sisk (9)
HR: Boston (2)—Henderson, Evans

GAME 3
at BOSTON
Tuesday, October 21
T—2:58; A—33,595

New York	4	0	0	0	0	0	2	1	0	7	13	0
Boston	0	0	1	0	0	0	0	0	0	1	5	0

OJEDA, McDowell (8)
BOYD, Sambito (8), Stanley (8)
HR: New York (1)—Dykstra

GAME 4
at BOSTON
Wednesday, October 22
T—3:22; A—33,920

New York	0	0	0	3	0	0	2	1	0	6	12	0
Boston	0	0	0	0	0	0	0	2	0	2	7	1

DARLING, McDowell (7), Orosco (S) (7)
NIPPER, Crawford (7), Stanley (9)
HR: New York (3)—Dykstra, Carter (2)

NEW YORK METS

Batter	AVG	G	AB	R	H	2B	3B	HR	RBI	GW	SH	SF	HB	BB	SO	SB	CS	E
Backman	.333	6	18	4	6	0	0	0	1	0	1	0	0	3	2	1	1	0
Carter	.276	7	29	4	8	2	0	2	9	1	0	1	0	0	4	0	0	0
Dykstra	.296	7	27	4	8	0	0	2	3	1	2	0	0	2	7	0	0	0
Elster	.000	1	1	0	0	0	0	0	0	0	0	0	0	0	0	0	0	1
Heep	.091	5	11	0	1	0	0	0	2	0	0	0	0	1	1	0	0	0
Hernandez	.231	7	26	1	6	0	0	0	4	0	0	1	0	5	1	0	0	1
Johnson	.000	2	5	0	0	0	0	0	0	0	0	0	0	0	2	0	0	0
Knight	.391	6	23	4	9	1	0	1	5	1	0	0	0	2	2	0	0	1
Mazzilli	.400	4	5	2	2	0	0	0	0	0	0	0	0	0	0	0	0	0
K. Mitchell	.250	5	8	1	2	0	0	0	0	0	0	0	0	0	3	0	0	0
Santana	.250	7	20	3	5	0	0	0	2	0	2	0	0	2	5	0	0	1
Strawberry	.208	7	24	4	5	1	0	1	1	0	0	0	0	4	6	3	1	0
Teufel	.444	3	9	1	4	1	0	1	1	0	0	0	0	1	2	0	0	1
Wilson	.269	7	26	3	7	1	0	0	0	0	0	0	1	1	6	3	0	0
Aguilera	—	2	0	0	0	0	0	0	0	0	0	0	0	0	0	0	0	0
Darling	.000	3	3	0	0	0	0	0	0	0	0	0	0	0	1	0	0	0
Fernandez	.—	3	0	0	0	0	0	0	0	0	0	0	0	0	0	0	0	0
Gooden	.500	2	2	1	1	0	0	0	0	0	0	0	0	0	0	0	0	0
McDowell	—	5	0	0	0	0	0	0	0	0	0	0	0	0	0	0	0	0
Ojeda	.000	2	2	0	0	0	0	0	0	0	0	0	0	0	1	0	0	0
Orosco	1.000	4	1	0	1	0	0	0	1	0	0	0	0	0	0	0	0	0
Sisk	.—	1	0	0	0	0	0	0	0	0	0	0	0	0	0	0	0	0
TOTALS	.271	7	240	32	65	6	0	7	29	3	6	2	1	21	43	7	2	5

PITCHER		W	L	ERA	G	GS	CG	SHO	SV	IP	H	R	ER	HR	HB	BB	SO	WP
Aguilera	R	1	0	12.00	2	0	0	0	0	3.0	8	4	4	1	1	1	4	0
Darling	R	1	1	1.53	3	3	0	0	0	17.2	13	4	3	2	1	10	12	2
Fernandez	L	0	0	1.35	3	0	0	0	0	6.2	6	1	1	0	0	1	10	0
Gooden	R	0	2	8.00	2	2	0	0	0	9.0	17	10	8	2	1	4	9	0
McDowell	R	1	0	4.91	5	0	0	0	0	7.1	10	5	4	0	0	6	2	0
Ojeda	L	1	0	2.08	2	2	0	0	0	13.0	13	3	3	0	0	5	9	1
Orosco	L	0	0	0.00	4	0	0	0	2	5.2	2	0	0	0	0	0	6	0
Sisk	R	0	0	0.00	1	0	0	0	0	0.2	0	0	0	0	0	1	1	0
TOTALS		4	3	3.29	7	7	0	0	2	63.0	69	27	23	5	3	28	53	3

GAME 5
at BOSTON
Thursday, October 23
T—3:09; A—34,010

New York	0	0	0	0	0	0	0	1	1	2	10	1
Boston	0	1	1	0	2	0	0	0	X	4	12	0

GOODEN, Fernandez (5)
HURST
HR: New York (1)—Teufel

GAME 6
at NEW YORK
Saturday, October 25
T—4:02; A—55,078

Boston	1	1	0	0	0	0	1	0	0	2	5	13	3
New York	0	0	0	0	2	0	0	1	0	3	6	8	2

Clemens, SCHIRALDI (8), Stanley (10)
Ojeda, McDowell (7), Orosco (8), AGUILERA (9)
HR: Boston (1)—Henderson

GAME 7
at NEW YORK
Monday, October 27
T—3:11; A—55,032

Boston	0	3	0	0	0	0	0	2	0	5	9	0
New York	0	0	0	0	0	3	3	2	X	8	10	0

Hurst, SCHIRALDI (7), Sambito (7), Stanley (7), Nipper (8), Crawford (8)
Darling, Fernandez (4), MCDOWELL (8), Orosco (S) (9)
HR: Boston (2)—Evans, Gedman; New York (2)—Knight, Strawberry

---

SCORE BY INNINGS

Boston	1	5	5	1	4	0	2	4	1	2	25	69	4
New York	4	0	2	3	6	3	7	6	1	3	33	65	5

Official 1986 National League Records

(Compiled by Elias Sports Bureau, New York)

1986 FINAL STANDINGS

EASTERN DIVISION

	W	L	PCT.	GB
New York	108	54	.667	-
Philadelphia	86	75	.534	21.5
St. Louis	79	82	.491	28.5
Montreal	78	83	.484	29.5
Chicago	70	90	.438	37
Pittsburgh	64	98	.395	44

WESTERN DIVISION

	W	L	PCT.	GB
Houston	96	66	.593	
Cincinnati	86	76	.531	10
San Francisco	83	79	.512	13
San Diego	74	88	.457	22
Los Angeles	73	89	.451	23
Atlanta	72	89	.447	23.5

Championship Series: New York defeated Houston, 4 games to 2

BATTING

INDIVIDUAL BATTING LEADERS

Batting Average	.334	Raines, Mtl.
Games	162	Parker, Cin.
At Bats	642	Gwynn, S.D.
Runs	107	Gwynn, S.D. & Hayes, Phil.
Hits	211	Gwynn, S.D.
Total Bases	304	Parker, Cin.
Singles	157	Gwynn, S.D. & Sax, L.A.
Doubles	46	Hayes, Phil.
Triples	13	Webster, Mtl.
Home Runs	37	Schmidt, Phil.
Runs Batted In	119	Schmidt, Phil.
Game-Winning RBI	16	Carter, N.Y. & Davis, Hou.
Sacrifice Hits	18	Thompson, S.F.
Sacrifice Flies	15	Carter, N.Y.
Hit by Pitch	10	Wallach, Mtl.
Bases on Balls	94	Hernandez, N.Y.
Intentional Bases on Balls	25	Schmidt, Phil.
Strikeouts	142	Samuel, Phil.
Stolen Bases	107	Coleman, St.L.
Caught Stealing	19	Doran, Hou.
Grounded into Double Plays	21	Carter, N.Y., T.Pena, Pitt. & Ray, Pitt.
Slugging Percentage	.547	Schmidt, Phil.
On-Base Percentage	.413	Raines, Mtl.
Longest Batting Streak, Games	25	Sax, L.A. (September 1 - 27)

TOP FIFTEEN QUALIFIERS FOR BATTING CHAMPIONSHIP

(* Left-Handed Batter # Switch-Hitter)

Player, Club	AVG.	G	AB	R	H	TB	2B	3B	HR	RBI	GW RBI	SH	SF	HP	BB	IB	SO	SB	CS	GI DP	SLG	OBP
#Raines, Timothy, Mtl.	.334	151	580	91	194	276	35	10	9	62	8	1	3	2	78	9	60	70	9	6	.476	.413
Sax, Stephen, L.A.	.332	157	633	91	210	279	43	4	6	56	11	6	3	3	59	5	58	40	17	12	.441	.390
*Gwynn, Anthony, S.D.	.329	160	642	107	211	300	33	7	14	59	3	2	2	3	52	11	35	37	9	20	.467	.381
#Bass, Kevin, Hou.	.311	157	591	83	184	287	33	5	20	79	11	1	4	6	38	11	72	22	13	15	.486	.357
*Hernandez, Keith, N.Y.	.310	149	551	94	171	246	34	1	13	83	13	0	3	4	94	9	69	2	1	14	.446	.413
*Hayes, Von, Phil.	.305	158	610	107	186	293	46	2	19	98	14	1	4	1	74	9	77	24	12	14	.480	.379
#Ray, Johnny, Pitt.	.301	155	579	67	174	228	33	0	7	78	7	1	7	3	58	10	47	6	9	21	.394	.363
Knight, C. Ray, N.Y.	.298	137	486	51	145	206	24	2	11	76	13	3	8	4	40	2	63	2	1	19	.424	.351
#Webster, Mitchell, Mtl.	.290	151	576	89	167	248	31	13	8	49	8	3	5	4	57	4	78	36	15	9	.431	.355
Schmidt, Michael, Phil.	.290	160	552	97	160	302	29	1	37	119	13	0	9	7	89	25	84	1	2	8	.547	.390
Pena, Antonio, Pitt.	.288	144	510	56	147	207	26	2	10	52	8	0	1	1	53	6	69	9	10	21	.406	.356
McReynolds, W. Kevin, S.D.	.288	158	560	89	161	282	31	6	26	96	14	5	9	1	66	6	83	8	6	9	.504	.358
Dawson, Andre, Mtl.	.284	130	496	65	141	237	32	2	20	78	7	1	6	6	37	11	79	18	12	13	.478	.338
Sandberg, Ryne, Chi.	.284	154	627	68	178	258	28	5	14	76	5	3	6	0	46	6	79	34	11	11	.411	.330
#Smith, Osborne, St.L.	.280	153	514	67	144	171	19	4	0	54	5	11	3	2	79	13	27	31	7	9	.333	.376

ALL PLAYERS LISTED ALPHABETICALLY

(* Left-Handed Batter # Switch-Hitter)

Player, Club	AVG.	G	AB	R	H	TB	2B	3B	HR	RBI	GW RBI	SH	SF	HP	BB	IB	SO	SB	CS	GI DP	SLG	OBP
Acker, James, Atl.	.107	21	28	1	3	4	1	0	0	0	0	0	0	0	0	0	21	0	0	0	.143	.107
Aguayo, Luis, Phil.	.211	62	133	17	28	48	6	1	4	13	0	0	2	3	8	0	26	1	1	3	.361	.267
Aguilera, Richard, N.Y.	.157	32	51	4	8	14	0	0	2	6	1	3	0	0	3	0	12	0	0	0	.275	.204
*Aldrete, Michael, S.F.	.250	84	216	27	54	84	18	3	2	25	6	4	1	2	33	4	34	1	3	3	.389	.353

Player, Club	AVG.	G	AB	R	H	TB	2B	3B	HR	RBI	GW RBI	SH	SF	HP	BB	IB	SO	SB	CS	GI DP	SLG	OBP
Alexander, Doyle, Atl.	.211	18	38	2	8	9	1	0	0	5	0	6	1	0	0	0	8	0	0	2	.237	.205
Almon, William, Pitt.	.219	102	196	29	43	75	7	2	7	27	3	1	3	0	30	2	38	11	4	5	.383	.319
*Amelung, Edward, L.A.	.091	8	11	0	1	1	0	0	0	0	0	0	0	0	0	0	4	0	0	1	.091	.091
Andersen, Larry, Phil.-Hou.	.000	48	6	0	0	0	0	0	0	0	0	1	0	0	0	0	3	0	0	0	.000	.000
Anderson, David, L.A.	.245	92	216	31	53	65	9	0	1	15	1	2	1	0	22	1	39	5	1	11	.301	.314
Anderson, Richard, N.Y.	.091	15	11	1	1	1	0	0	0	0	0	1	0	0	0	0	4	0	0	0	.091	.091
Asadoor, Randall, S.D.	.364	15	55	9	20	25	5	0	0	7	0	2	0	0	3	1	13	1	2	0	.455	.397
#Ashby, Alan, Hou.	.257	120	315	24	81	117	15	0	7	38	6	1	6	0	39	9	56	1	0	7	.371	.333
*Assenmacher, Paul, Atl.	.000	61	6	0	0	0	0	0	0	0	0	0	0	0	2	0	3	0	0	0	.000	.250
#Backman, Walter, N.Y.	.320	124	387	67	124	149	18	2	1	27	5	14	3	0	36	1	32	13	7	3	.385	.376
#Bailey, J. Mark, Hou.	.176	57	153	9	27	44	5	0	4	15	2	0	1	0	28	6	45	1	1	7	.288	.302
Baller, Jay, Chi.	.000	36	5	0	0	0	0	0	0	0	0	1	0	0	0	0	1	0	0	0	.000	.000
Bargar, Gregory, St.L.	.000	22	2	0	0	0	0	0	0	0	0	0	0	0	0	0	2	0	0	0	.000	.000
#Bass, Kevin, Hou.	.311	157	591	83	184	287	33	5	20	79	11	1	4	6	38	11	72	22	13	15	.486	.357
*Beckwith, T. Joseph, L.A.	—	15	0	0	0	0	0	0	0	0	0	0	0	0	0	0	0	0	0	0	—	—
Bedrosian, Stephen, Phil.	.200	68	5	0	1	1	0	0	0	0	0	0	0	0	1	0	1	0	0	0	.200	.333
Bell, David, Cin.	.278	155	568	89	158	253	29	3	20	75	6	3	6	5	73	4	49	2	8	14	.445	.362
Belliard, Rafael, Pitt.	.233	117	309	33	72	81	5	2	0	31	2	11	1	3	26	6	54	12	2	8	.262	.298
Benedict, Bruce, Atl.	.225	64	160	11	36	48	10	1	0	13	0	4	1	2	15	1	10	1	0	9	.300	.298
Berenguer, Juan, S.F.	.143	46	7	0	1	1	0	0	0	0	0	3	0	0	0	0	1	0	0	0	.143	.143
Berenyi, Bruce, N.Y.	.000	14	11	0	0	0	0	0	0	0	0	1	0	0	0	0	3	0	0	0	.000	.000
Bielecki, Michael, Pitt.	.063	31	48	3	3	3	0	0	0	1	0	4	0	0	2	0	26	0	0	0	.063	.100
Bilardello, Dann, Mtl.	.194	79	191	12	37	54	5	0	4	17	1	7	0	0	14	3	32	1	0	5	.283	.249
Bittiger, Jeffrey, Phil.	.333	3	3	1	1	4	0	0	1	1	1	1	0	0	0	0	1	0	0	0	1.333	.333
#Blue, Vida, S.F.	.093	28	43	3	4	8	1	0	1	3	0	4	0	0	6	0	20	0	0	0	.186	.204
Bochy, Bruce, S.D.	.252	63	127	16	32	65	9	0	8	22	3	1	0	0	14	3	23	1	0	3	.512	.326
*Bockus, Randy, S.F.	.000	6	1	0	0	0	0	0	0	0	0	0	0	0	0	0	1	0	0	0	.000	.000
Boever, Joseph, St.L.	.500	11	2	0	1	1	0	0	0	0	0	0	0	0	0	0	0	0	0	0	.500	.500
*Bonds, Barry, Pitt.	.223	113	413	72	92	172	26	3	16	48	4	2	2	2	65	2	102	36	7	4	.416	.330
#Bonilla, Roberto, Pitt.	.240	63	192	28	46	59	6	2	1	17	1	3	0	1	29	1	39	4	4	5	.307	.342
Booker, Gregory, S.D.	—	9	0	0	0	0	0	0	0	0	0	0	0	0	0	0	0	0	0	0	—	—
*Bosley, Thaddis, Chi.	.275	87	120	15	33	42	4	1	1	9	2	1	0	0	18	3	24	3	0	3	.350	.370
*Bream, Sidney, Pitt.	.268	154	522	73	140	235	37	5	16	77	9	1	7	1	60	5	73	13	7	14	.450	.341
Brenly, Robert, S.F.	.246	149	472	60	116	190	26	0	16	62	4	5	3	3	74	10	97	10	6	4	.403	.350

*Brock, Gregory, L.A.	.234	115	325	33	76	137	13	0	16	52	3	1	4	0	37	5	60	2	5	5	.422	.309
Brooks, Hubert, Mtl.	.340	80	306	50	104	174	18	5	14	58	10	0	5	2	25	3	60	4	2	11	.569	.388
Brown, Curtis, Mtl.	.000	6	1	0	0	0	0	0	0	0	0	0	0	0	0	0	0	0	0	0	.000	.000
Brown, J. Christopher, S.F.	.317	116	416	57	132	175	16	3	7	49	6	0	5	9	33	4	43	13	9	9	.421	.376
Brown, Michael C., Pitt.	.218	87	243	18	53	72	7	0	4	26	3	0	3	0	27	3	32	2	3	9	.296	.293
*Browning, Thomas, Cin.	.163	46	86	9	14	14	0	0	0	3	0	7	0	0	1	0	25	1	0	2	.163	.172
*Bryant, Ralph, L.A.	.253	27	75	15	19	45	4	2	6	13	2	0	1	1	5	0	25	0	1	1	.600	.305
*Bullock, Eric, Hou.	.048	6	21	0	1	1	0	0	0	1	0	0	0	0	0	0	3	2	0	0	.048	.048
Burke, Timothy, Mtl.	.000	68	7	0	0	0	0	0	0	1	0	1	0	0	1	0	2	0	0	0	.000	.125
Burris, B. Ray, St.L.	.148	23	27	0	4	7	3	0	0	7	2	0	0	0	0	0	9	0	0	0	.259	.148
Butera, Salvatore, Cin.	.239	56	113	14	27	41	6	1	2	16	0	2	1	0	21	3	10	0	0	5	.363	.356
Cabell, Enos, L.A.	.256	107	277	27	71	88	11	0	2	29	2	2	3	2	14	2	26	10	4	5	.318	.294
*Calhoun, Jeffrey, Hou.	—	20	0	0	0	0	0	0	0	0	0	0	0	0	0	0	0	0	0	0	—	—
#Candaele, Casey, Mtl.	.231	30	104	9	24	30	4	1	0	6	1	0	1	0	5	0	15	3	5	3	.288	.264
*Carlton, Steven, Phil.-S.F.	.200	22	45	4	9	13	1	0	1	8	0	1	0	0	1	0	7	0	0	3	.289	.217
*Carman, Donald, Phil.	.000	50	31	0	0	0	0	0	0	0	0	2	0	0	0	0	11	0	0	0	.000	.000
Carter, Gary, N.Y.	.255	132	490	81	125	215	14	2	24	105	16	0	15	6	62	9	63	1	0	21	.439	.337
Cedeno, Cesar, L.A.	.231	37	78	5	18	22	2	1	0	6	1	2	0	0	7	0	13	1	1	0	.282	.294
Cey, Ronald, Chi.	.273	97	256	42	70	130	21	0	13	36	1	1	2	3	44	1	66	0	0	5	.508	.384
*Chambliss, C.Christopher, Atl.	.311	97	122	13	38	52	8	0	2	14	1	0	1	0	15	4	24	0	2	2	.426	.384
Childress, Rodney, Phil.	—	2	0	0	0	0	0	0	0	0	0	0	0	0	0	0	0	0	0	0	—	—
*Christmas, Stephen, Chi.	.111	3	9	0	1	2	1	0	0	2	1	0	0	0	0	0	1	0	0	0	.222	.111
Clark, Jack, St.L.	.237	65	232	34	55	98	12	2	9	23	2	0	1	1	45	4	61	1	1	4	.422	.362
*Clark, William, S.F.	.287	111	408	66	117	181	27	2	11	41	8	9	4	3	34	10	76	4	7	3	.444	.343
Clements, Patrick, Pitt.	.000	65	6	0	0	0	0	0	0	0	0	0	0	0	0	0	3	0	0	0	.000	.000
#Coleman, Vincent, St.L.	.232	154	600	94	139	168	13	8	0	29	2	3	5	2	60	0	98	107	14	4	.280	.301
Concepcion, David, Cin.	.260	90	311	42	81	107	13	2	3	30	3	5	4	0	26	1	43	13	2	13	.344	.314
*Conroy, Timothy, St.L.	.138	26	29	2	4	6	2	0	0	6	1	8	0	0	3	0	11	0	0	0	.207	.219
*Corcoran, Timothy, N.Y.	.000	6	7	1	0	0	0	0	0	0	0	0	0	0	2	1	0	0	0	0	.000	.222
Cox, Danny, St.L.	.077	32	65	2	5	7	2	0	0	2	2	16	0	0	2	0	32	0	0	1	.108	.104
*Cruz, Jose, Hou.	.278	141	479	48	133	193	22	4	10	72	12	0	2	0	55	12	86	3	4	9	.403	.351
*Daniels, Kalvoski, Cin.	.320	74	181	34	58	94	10	4	6	23	3	1	1	2	22	1	30	15	2	4	.519	.398
Darling, Ronald, N.Y.	.099	34	81	4	8	10	2	0	0	0	0	10	0	0	3	0	29	0	0	0	.123	.131
Darwin, Danny, Hou.	.063	12	16	0	1	1	0	0	0	0	0	2	0	0	0	0	12	0	0	0	.063	.063
*Daulton, Darren, Phil.	.225	49	138	18	31	59	4	0	8	21	2	2	2	1	38	3	41	2	3	1	.428	.391
#Davis, Charles, S.F.	.278	153	526	71	146	219	28	3	13	70	6	2	5	1	84	23	96	16	13	11	.416	.375
Davis, Eric, Cin.	.277	132	415	97	115	217	15	3	27	71	9	0	3	1	68	5	100	80	11	6	.523	.378

Player, Club	AVG.	G	AB	R	H	TB	2B	3B	HR	RBI	GW RBI	SH	SF	HP	BB	IB	SO	SB	CS	GI DP	SLG	OBP
Davis, Glenn, Hou.	.265	158	574	91	152	283	32	3	34	101	16	0	7	9	64	6	72	3	1	11	.493	.344
Davis, Jody, Chi.	.250	148	528	61	132	226	27	2	21	74	5	4	8	0	41	4	110	0	1	14	.428	.300
*Davis, Mark, S.F.	.125	67	8	0	1	2	1	0	0	0	0	0	0	0	0	0	4	0	0	0	.250	.125
Davis, Ronald, Chi.	.000	17	2	0	0	0	0	0	0	0	0	0	0	0	0	0	2	0	0	0	.000	.000
*Davis, Trench, Pitt.	.130	15	23	2	3	3	0	0	0	1	0	0	1	0	0	0	4	0	0	1	.130	.125
Dawson, Andre, Mtl.	.284	130	496	65	141	237	32	2	20	78	7	1	6	6	37	11	79	18	12	13	.478	.338
Dayett, Brian, Chi.	.269	24	67	7	18	34	4	0	4	11	3	0	3	0	6	0	10	0	1	2	.507	.316
*Dayley, Kenneth, St.L.	.200	32	5	0	1	1	0	0	0	0	0	0	0	0	1	0	2	0	0	0	.200	.333
DeLeon, Jose, Pitt.	.000	9	1	0	0	0	0	0	0	0	0	0	0	1	0	0	1	0	0	0	.000	.500
*Dedmon, Jeffrey, Atl.	.125	57	16	2	2	2	0	0	0	1	0	1	0	0	0	0	7	0	0	0	.125	.125
Denny, John, Cin.	.222	27	54	6	12	12	0	0	0	4	0	5	0	0	3	0	15	2	3	1	.222	.263
Dernier, Robert, Chi.	.225	108	324	32	73	101	14	1	4	18	1	5	0	0	22	1	41	27	2	7	.312	.275
*Deshaies, James, Hou.	.047	26	43	3	2	2	0	0	0	1	0	4	0	0	6	0	31	0	0	0	.047	.163
Diaz, Baudilio, Cin.	.272	134	474	50	129	180	21	0	10	56	8	2	3	0	40	0	52	1	1	11	.380	.327
Diaz, Carlos, L.A.	.000	19	1	0	0	0	0	0	0	0	0	0	0	0	0	0	0	0	0	0	.000	.000
Diaz, Michael, Pitt.	.268	97	209	22	56	101	9	0	12	36	1	0	3	2	19	0	43	0	1	5	.483	.330
*DiPino, Frank, Hou.-Chi.	.167	61	6	0	1	1	0	0	0	0	0	0	0	0	0	0	2	0	0	1	.167	.167
*Distefano, Benito, Pitt.	.179	31	39	3	7	11	1	0	1	5	0	0	2	0	1	0	5	0	0	0	.282	.190
#Doran, William, Hou.	.276	145	550	92	152	205	29	3	6	37	5	4	5	2	81	7	57	42	19	10	.373	.368
Downs, Kelly, S.F.	.172	15	29	1	5	5	0	0	0	0	0	0	0	0	1	0	13	0	1	0	.172	.200
Dravecky, David, S.D.	.140	35	50	3	7	10	0	0	1	7	0	6	0	0	1	0	16	1	0	1	.200	.157
*Driessen, Daniel, S.F.-Hou.	.250	32	40	7	10	16	3	0	1	3	0	0	0	0	9	2	6	0	0	0	.400	.388
#Duncan, Mariano, L.A.	.229	109	407	47	93	124	7	0	8	30	3	5	1	2	30	1	78	48	13	6	.305	.284
Dunston, Shawon, Chi.	.250	150	581	66	145	239	37	3	17	68	8	4	2	3	21	5	114	13	11	5	.411	.278
*Durham, Leon, Chi.	.262	141	484	66	127	219	18	7	20	65	7	0	5	1	67	16	98	8	7	6	.452	.350
*Dykstra, Leonard, N.Y.	.295	147	431	77	127	192	27	7	8	45	7	7	2	0	58	1	55	31	7	4	.445	.377
Earley, William, St.L.	—	3	0	0	0	0	0	0	0	0	0	0	0	0	0	0	0	0	0	0	—	—
Eckersley, Dennis, Chi.	.159	33	69	7	11	20	3	0	2	10	2	2	1	0	1	0	34	0	0	0	.290	.169
Elster, Kevin, N.Y.	.167	19	30	3	5	6	1	0	0	0	0	0	0	0	3	1	8	0	0	0	.200	.242
Esasky, Nicholas, Cin.	.230	102	330	35	76	133	17	2	12	41	5	1	4	1	47	0	97	0	2	8	.403	.325
Fansler, Stanley, Pitt.	.167	5	6	0	1	1	0	0	0	0	0	1	0	0	0	0	2	0	0	0	.167	.167
*Fernandez, C. Sidney, N.Y.	.162	32	68	6	11	14	3	0	0	4	2	6	0	0	3	0	23	1	0	2	.206	.197
Fimple, John, L.A.	.077	13	13	2	1	1	0	0	0	2	0	0	1	0	6	1	6	0	0	0	.077	.350
Fitzgerald, Michael, Mtl.	.282	73	209	20	59	92	13	1	6	37	6	4	2	1	27	6	34	3	2	4	.440	.364

*Flannery, Timothy, S.D.	.280	134	368	48	103	127	11	2	3	28	6	3	2	5	54	4	61	3	6	8	.345	.378
*Foley, Thomas, Phil.-Mtl.	.266	103	263	26	70	94	15	3	1	23	2	2	4	0	30	6	37	10	3	4	.357	.337
*Fontenot, S. Ray, Chi.	.167	42	6	1	1	1	0	0	0	0	0	0	0	0	0	0	5	0	0	0	.167	.167
*Ford, Curtis, St.L.	.248	85	214	30	53	78	15	2	2	29	6	1	2	0	23	2	29	13	5	1	.364	.318
Forsch, Robert, St.L.	.171	34	76	7	13	25	4	1	2	12	1	11	1	0	0	0	24	0	0	1	.329	.169
Foster, George, N.Y.	.227	72	233	28	53	100	6	1	13	38	5	0	2	0	21	1	53	1	1	7	.429	.289
*Franco, John, Cin.	.000	74	4	0	0	0	0	0	0	0	0	0	0	0	0	0	0	0	0	0	.000	.000
*Francona, Terry, Chi.	.250	86	124	13	31	40	3	0	2	8	3	0	2	1	6	0	8	0	1	3	.323	.286
Frazier, George, Chi.	.000	35	4	0	0	0	0	0	0	0	0	0	0	0	0	0	2	0	0	0	.000	.000
Freeman, Marvin, Phil.	.000	3	6	0	0	0	0	0	0	0	0	1	0	0	0	0	3	0	0	0	.000	.000
*Funk, Thomas, Hou.	.000	8	1	0	0	0	0	0	0	0	0	0	0	0	0	0	1	0	0	0	.000	.000
*Gainey, Telmanch, Hou.	.300	26	50	6	15	23	3	1	1	6	1	0	0	0	6	0	19	3	1	0	.460	.375
Galarraga, Andres, Mtl.	.271	105	321	39	87	130	13	0	10	42	4	1	1	3	30	5	79	6	5	8	.405	.338
Galvez, Balvino, L.A.	.000	10	2	0	0	0	0	0	0	0	0	0	0	0	0	0	1	0	0	0	.000	.000
Garber, H. Eugene, Atl.	.167	61	6	0	1	1	0	0	0	0	0	1	0	0	1	0	1	0	0	0	.167	.286
Garner, Philip, Hou.	.265	107	313	43	83	130	14	3	9	41	5	0	3	1	30	2	45	12	6	14	.415	.329
Garrelts, Scott, S.F.	.178	54	45	6	8	12	1	0	1	4	0	7	0	0	1	0	25	1	0	0	.267	.196
Garvey, Steven, S.D.	.255	155	557	58	142	227	22	0	21	81	9	0	3	1	23	5	72	1	2	18	.408	.284
Gibbons, John, N.Y.	.474	8	19	4	9	16	4	0	1	1	0	0	0	0	3	1	5	0	0	1	.842	.545
Gladden, C. Daniel, S.F.	.276	102	351	55	97	127	16	1	4	29	1	7	0	5	39	3	59	27	10	5	.362	.357
Gonzales, Rene, Mtl.	.115	11	26	1	3	3	0	0	0	0	0	0	0	0	2	0	7	0	2	0	.115	.179
Gonzalez, Jose, L.A.	.215	57	93	15	20	33	5	1	2	6	0	2	0	0	7	0	29	4	3	0	.355	.270
Gooden, Dwight, N.Y.	.086	33	81	5	7	9	0	1	0	4	0	13	0	1	2	0	16	0	0	3	.111	.119
*Gorman, Thomas, Phil.	.000	8	1	0	0	0	0	0	0	0	0	0	0	0	0	0	0	0	0	0	.000	.000
Gossage, Richard, S.D.	.000	45	7	0	0	0	0	0	0	0	0	0	0	0	0	0	3	0	0	1	.000	.000
Gott, James, S.F.	.000	9	3	0	0	0	0	0	0	0	0	0	0	1	0	0	1	0	0	0	.000	.250
Grant, Mark, S.F.	.000	4	1	0	0	0	0	0	0	0	0	1	0	0	0	0	1	0	0	0	.000	.000
Green, Gary, S.D.	.212	13	33	2	7	8	1	0	0	2	0	1	0	0	1	0	11	0	0	0	.242	.235
*Griffey, G. Kenneth, Atl.	.308	80	292	36	90	147	15	3	12	32	2	0	1	0	20	4	43	12	7	2	.503	.351
*Gross, Gregory, Phil.	.248	87	101	11	25	30	5	0	0	8	0	1	1	1	21	7	11	1	0	4	.297	.379
Gross, Kevin, Phil.	.188	37	80	6	15	24	4	1	1	5	0	9	0	0	1	0	22	1	0	1	.300	.198
Guante, Cecilio, Pitt.	.000	52	1	0	0	0	0	0	0	0	0	0	0	0	0	0	1	0	0	0	.000	.000
Guerrero, Pedro, L.A.	.246	31	61	7	15	33	3	0	5	10	0	0	0	1	2	0	19	0	0	1	.541	.281
*Gulden, Bradley, S.F.	.091	17	22	2	2	2	0	0	0	1	1	0	0	0	2	2	5	0	0	1	.091	.167
Gullickson, William, Cin.	.076	37	79	3	6	6	0	0	0	2	0	9	0	0	3	0	15	0	0	3	.076	.110
Gumpert, David, Chi.	.000	38	5	0	0	0	0	0	0	0	0	0	0	0	0	0	4	0	0	0	.000	.000
*Gwynn, Anthony, S.D.	.329	160	642	107	211	300	33	7	14	59	3	2	2	3	52	11	35	37	9	20	.467	.381

Player, Club	AVG.	G	AB	R	H	TB	2B	3B	HR	RBI	GW RBI	SH	SF	HP	BB	IB	SO	SB	CS	GI DP	SLG	OBP
#Hall, Albert, Atl.	.240	16	50	6	12	14	2	0	0	1	0	2	0	0	5	0	6	8	3	0	.280	.309
*Hall, Andrew, Chi.	.143	5	7	1	1	1	0	0	0	0	0	0	0	0	1	0	3	0	0	0	.143	.250
Hamilton, Jeffrey, L.A.	.224	71	147	22	33	53	5	0	5	19	3	0	2	0	2	1	43	0	0	3	.361	.232
Harper, Terry, Atl.	.257	106	265	26	68	104	12	0	8	30	6	1	2	1	29	2	39	3	6	13	.392	.330
Hatcher, William, Hou.	.258	127	419	55	108	149	15	4	6	36	5	6	1	5	22	1	52	38	14	3	.356	.302
Hawkins, M. Andrew, S.D.	.149	37	67	2	10	11	1	0	0	2	0	6	0	0	1	0	23	0	0	1	.164	.162
*Hayes, Von, Phil.	.305	158	610	107	186	293	46	2	19	98	14	1	4	1	74	9	77	24	12	14	.480	.379
*Hayward, Raymond, S.D.	.000	4	4	0	0	0	0	0	0	0	0	0	0	0	0	0	0	0	0	1	.000	.000
Hearn, Edward, N.Y.	.265	49	136	16	36	53	5	0	4	10	1	2	1	0	12	0	19	0	1	4	.390	.322
Heath, Michael, St.L.	.205	65	190	19	39	61	8	1	4	25	3	1	1	1	23	4	36	2	3	5	.321	.293
*Heep, Daniel, N.Y.	.282	86	195	24	55	82	8	2	5	33	2	0	1	1	30	5	31	1	4	3	.421	.379
*Hensley, Charles, S.F.	—	11	0	0	0	0	0	0	0	0	0	0	0	0	0	0	0	0	0	0	—	—
*Hernandez, Keith, N.Y.	.310	149	551	94	171	246	34	1	13	83	13	0	3	4	94	9	69	2	1	14	.446	.413
Hernandez, Manuel, Hou.	.000	9	6	0	0	0	0	0	0	1	0	1	0	0	0	0	2	0	0	0	.000	.000
#Herr, Thomas, St.L.	.252	152	559	48	141	185	30	4	2	61	12	6	4	5	73	10	75	22	8	8	.331	.342
Hershiser, Orel, L.A.	.239	37	71	4	17	20	3	0	0	8	0	10	0	0	1	0	17	0	1	1	.282	.250
*Hesketh, Joseph, Mtl.	.000	15	23	0	0	0	0	0	0	0	0	3	0	0	2	0	18	0	0	1	.000	.080
*Hoffman, Guy, Chi.	.067	33	15	2	1	1	0	0	0	1	0	3	0	0	2	0	4	0	0	0	.067	.176
Holton, Brian, L.A.	.000	12	5	0	0	0	0	0	0	0	0	0	0	0	0	0	2	0	0	0	.000	.000
*Honeycutt, Frederick, L.A.	.070	32	43	3	3	4	1	0	0	3	0	6	0	0	8	0	11	0	0	0	.093	.216
Horner, J. Robert, Atl.	.273	141	517	70	141	244	22	0	27	87	11	0	10	2	52	8	72	1	4	16	.472	.336
*Horton, Ricky, St.L.	.056	42	18	0	1	1	0	0	0	0	0	2	0	0	5	0	3	0	0	0	.056	.261
Howell, Kenneth, L.A.	.000	62	5	0	0	0	0	0	0	0	0	0	0	0	0	0	3	0	0	0	.000	.000
Hoyt, D. LaMarr, S.D.	.130	35	46	3	6	7	1	0	0	1	0	3	0	0	1	0	18	0	0	0	.152	.149
Hubbard, Glenn, Atl.	.230	143	408	42	94	124	16	1	4	36	5	6	4	4	66	14	74	3	2	5	.304	.340
Hudson, Charles, Phil.	.047	36	43	2	2	2	0	0	0	0	0	7	0	0	1	0	19	0	0	0	.047	.068
Hume, Thomas, Phil.	.000	48	11	0	0	0	0	0	0	0	0	5	0	0	0	0	6	0	0	0	.000	.000
Hunt, J. Randall, Mtl.	.208	21	48	4	10	16	0	0	2	5	0	0	0	0	5	2	16	0	0	2	.333	.283
*Hurdle, Clinton, St.L.	.195	78	154	18	30	46	5	1	3	15	0	1	2	1	26	0	38	0	0	2	.299	.311
*Iorg, Dane, S.D.	.226	90	106	10	24	34	2	1	2	11	1	0	1	0	2	0	21	0	0	2	.321	.239
Jackson, Michael, Phil.	—	9	0	0	0	0	0	0	0	0	0	0	0	0	0	0	0	0	0	0	—	—
James, D. Christopher, Phil.	.283	16	46	5	13	19	3	0	1	5	1	1	0	0	1	0	13	0	0	1	.413	.298
#Jefferson, Stanley, N.Y.	.208	14	24	6	5	9	1	0	1	3	0	0	0	1	2	0	8	0	0	1	.375	.296
#Jeltz, L. Steven, Phil.	.219	145	439	44	96	115	11	4	0	36	3	3	2	1	65	9	97	6	3	9	.262	.320

#Johnson, Howard, N.Y.	.245	88	220	30	54	98	14	0	10	39	3	1	0	1	31	8	64	8	1	2	.445	.341
Johnson, Joseph, Atl.	.115	17	26	2	3	3	0	0	0	1	0	2	1	0	1	0	12	0	0	0	.115	.143
#Johnson, Wallace, Mtl.	.283	61	127	13	36	44	3	1	1	10	1	0	0	0	7	0	9	6	3	2	.346	.321
Jones, Barry, Pitt.	.200	26	5	0	1	1	0	0	0	1	0	1	0	0	0	0	1	0	0	0	.200	.200
Jones, Christopher, S.F.	.000	3	1	0	0	0	0	0	0	0	0	0	0	0	0	0	0	1	0	0	.000	.000
Jones, James, S.D.	.167	3	6	1	1	1	0	0	0	0	0	0	0	0	0	0	4	0	0	0	.167	.167
Jones, Tracy, Cin.	.349	46	86	16	30	39	3	0	2	10	2	0	1	0	9	1	5	7	1	2	.453	.406
*Kemp, Steven, Pitt.	.188	13	16	1	3	6	0	0	1	1	0	0	0	0	4	0	6	1	0	1	.375	.350
*Kennedy, Terrence, S.D.	.264	141	432	46	114	174	22	1	12	57	10	4	1	2	37	7	74	0	3	10	.403	.324
Keough, Matthew, Chi.-Hou.	.375	29	16	1	6	7	1	0	0	0	0	0	0	0	0	0	4	1	0	0	.438	.375
*Kepshire, Kurt, St.L.	.000	2	1	0	0	0	0	0	0	0	0	1	0	0	0	0	0	0	0	0	.000	.000
Kerfeld, Charles, Hou.	.111	61	9	0	1	1	0	0	0	1	0	0	0	0	1	0	6	0	0	0	.111	.200
Khalifa, Sam, Pitt.	.185	64	151	8	28	34	6	0	0	4	1	3	0	0	19	6	28	0	2	5	.225	.276
Kipper, Robert, Pitt.	.030	21	33	0	1	1	0	0	0	1	1	3	0	0	1	0	11	0	0	0	.030	.059
*Knepper, Robert, Hou.	.099	42	91	2	9	13	2	1	0	1	0	4	0	0	0	0	44	0	0	0	.143	.099
Knicely, Alan, St.L.	.195	34	82	8	16	22	3	0	1	6	1	0	1	0	17	0	21	1	1	1	.268	.330
Knight, C. Ray, N.Y.	.298	137	486	51	145	206	24	2	11	76	13	3	8	4	40	2	63	2	1	19	.424	.351
Knudson, Mark, Hou.	.000	9	10	0	0	0	0	0	0	0	0	3	0	0	1	0	7	0	0	0	.000	.091
Komminsk, Brad, Atl.	.400	5	5	1	2	2	0	0	0	1	0	0	0	0	0	0	1	0	1	0	.400	.400
Krawczyk, Raymond, Pitt.	—	12	0	0	0	0	0	0	0	0	0	0	0	0	0	0	0	0	0	0	—	—
*Krenchicki, Wayne, Mtl.	.240	101	221	21	53	69	6	2	2	23	1	2	2	0	22	3	32	2	4	2	.312	.306
*Kruk, John, S.D.	.309	122	278	33	86	118	16	2	4	38	2	2	2	0	45	0	58	2	4	11	.424	.403
Krukow, Michael, S.F.	.146	35	82	7	12	13	1	0	0	8	1	12	0	0	4	0	25	1	0	1	.159	.186
Kutcher, Randy, S.F.	.237	71	186	28	44	76	9	1	7	16	3	6	0	0	11	0	41	6	5	3	.409	.279
LaCoss, Michael, S.F.	.230	37	61	8	14	22	2	0	2	9	1	5	0	0	3	0	24	0	0	0	.361	.266
*Laga, Michael, St.L.	.217	18	46	7	10	23	4	0	3	8	1	0	0	1	5	1	18	0	0	1	.500	.308
Lahti, Jeffrey, St.L.	—	4	0	0	0	0	0	0	0	0	0	0	0	0	0	0	0	0	0	0	—	—
Lake, Steven, Chi.-St.L.	.294	36	68	8	20	28	2	0	2	14	1	1	0	0	3	1	7	0	0	3	.412	.324
*Lancellotti, Richard, S.F.	.222	15	18	2	4	10	0	0	2	6	0	0	0	0	0	0	7	0	0	0	.556	.222
*Landreaux, Kenneth, L.A.	.261	103	283	34	74	103	13	2	4	29	4	0	4	1	22	3	39	10	5	5	.364	.313
Landrum, T. William, Cin.	.000	10	2	0	0	0	0	0	0	0	0	0	0	0	0	0	0	0	0	0	.000	.000
Landrum, Terry, St.L.	.210	96	205	24	43	58	7	1	2	17	4	1	3	1	20	2	41	3	1	5	.283	.279
*LaPoint, David, S.D.	.000	24	8	0	0	0	0	0	0	0	0	4	0	0	0	0	1	0	0	0	.000	.000
Larkin, Barry, Cin.	.283	41	159	27	45	64	4	3	3	19	2	0	1	0	9	1	21	8	0	2	.403	.320
Laskey, William, S.F.	.000	20	1	0	0	0	0	0	0	0	0	0	0	0	0	0	1	0	0	0	.000	.000
*LaValliere, Michael, St.L.	.234	110	303	18	71	94	10	2	3	30	2	10	0	1	36	5	37	0	1	7	.310	.318
Law, Vance, Mtl.	.225	112	360	37	81	117	17	2	5	44	5	2	2	1	37	1	66	3	5	9	.325	.298

Player, Club	AVG.	G	AB	R	H	TB	2B	3B	HR	RBI	GW RBI	SH	SF	HP	BB	IB	SO	SB	CS	GI DP	SLG	OBP
Lawless, Thomas, St.L.	.282	46	39	5	11	12	1	0	0	3	0	2	1	0	2	0	8	8	1	0	.308	.310
Leach, Terry, N.Y.	—	6	0	0	0	0	0	0	0	0	0	0	0	0	0	0	0	0	0	0	—	—
*Lefebvre, Joseph, Phil.	.111	14	18	0	2	2	0	0	0	0	0	0	0	0	3	0	5	0	0	3	.111	.238
*Lefferts, Craig, S.D.	.125	84	8	1	1	4	0	0	1	1	1	1	0	0	0	0	4	0	0	0	.500	.125
Legg, Gregory, Phil.	.450	11	20	2	9	10	1	0	0	1	0	0	0	0	0	0	3	0	0	0	.500	.450
Leonard, Jeffrey, S.F.	.279	89	341	48	95	130	11	3	6	42	11	1	3	3	20	1	62	16	3	4	.381	.322
*Lerch, Randy, Phil.	.333	4	3	0	1	2	1	0	0	0	0	0	0	0	0	0	1	0	0	0	.667	.333
Lindeman, James, St.L.	.255	19	55	7	14	18	1	0	1	6	0	0	1	0	2	0	10	1	1	2	.327	.276
Lopes, David, Chi.-Hou.	.275	96	255	49	70	107	10	3	7	35	6	2	2	2	43	0	25	25	8	9	.420	.381
Lopez, Aurelio, Hou.	.000	45	9	0	0	0	0	0	0	0	0	1	0	0	0	0	6	0	0	0	.000	.000
Lynch, Edward, N.Y.-Chi.	.033	24	30	0	1	1	0	0	0	0	0	1	0	0	2	0	17	0	0	0	.033	.094
Lyons, Barry, N.Y.	.000	6	9	1	0	0	0	0	0	2	0	0	0	0	1	1	2	0	0	0	.000	.100
*Madden, Michael, Hou.	.000	13	9	0	0	0	0	0	0	0	0	4	0	0	1	0	8	0	0	0	.000	.100
Maddox, Garry, Phil.	.429	6	7	1	3	3	0	0	0	1	0	0	0	0	2	0	1	0	1	0	.429	.556
Maddux, Gregory, Chi.	.333	6	12	0	4	4	0	0	0	0	0	1	0	0	0	0	3	0	0	0	.333	.333
Maddux, Michael; Phil.	.045	16	22	0	1	1	0	0	0	1	1	4	0	0	1	0	7	0	0	0	.045	.087
Madlock, Bill, L.A.	.280	111	379	38	106	153	17	0	10	60	6	1	6	5	30	4	43	3	3	7	.404	.336
*Magadan, David, N.Y.	.444	10	18	3	8	8	0	0	0	3	2	0	0	0	3	0	1	0	0	1	.444	.524
Mahler, Richard, Atl.	.193	40	83	8	16	19	3	0	0	7	0	9	0	0	4	0	14	0	0	2	.229	.230
Maldonado, Candido, S.F.	.252	133	405	49	102	193	31	3	18	85	14	0	4	3	20	4	77	4	4	12	.477	.289
Manrique, R. Fred, St.L.	.176	13	17	2	3	6	0	0	1	1	0	0	0	0	1	0	1	1	0	1	.353	.222
Marshall, Michael A., L.A.	.233	103	330	47	77	145	11	0	19	53	9	0	1	4	27	3	90	4	4	5	.439	.298
*Martin, J. Michael, Chi.	.077	8	13	1	1	2	1	0	0	0	0	0	0	0	2	1	4	0	0	0	.154	.200
Martinez, Carmelo, S.D.	.238	113	244	28	58	95	10	0	9	25	3	1	2	1	35	2	46	1	1	9	.389	.333
*Martinez, David, Chi.	.139	53	108	13	15	21	1	1	1	7	0	0	1	1	6	0	22	4	2	1	.194	.190
Martinez, J. Dennis, Mtl.	.100	19	30	1	3	5	2	0	0	3	0	0	0	0	1	0	14	0	0	0	.167	.129
Mason, Roger, S.F.	.048	11	21	0	1	1	0	0	0	0	0	1	0	0	0	0	13	0	0	0	.048	.048
#Mathews, Gregory, St.L.	.047	23	43	1	2	2	0	0	0	2	0	7	0	2	0	0	19	0	0	1	.047	.089
Matthews, Gary, Chi.	.259	123	370	49	96	177	16	1	21	46	4	0	2	0	60	1	59	3	2	15	.478	.361
*Matuszek, Leonard, L.A.	.261	91	199	26	52	86	7	0	9	28	3	0	1	1	21	1	47	2	2	3	.432	.333
#Mazzilli, Lee, Pitt.-N.Y.	.245	100	151	28	37	53	5	1	3	15	0	0	1	2	38	2	36	4	4	3	.351	.401
McClure, Robert, Mtl.	.250	52	4	0	1	1	0	0	0	0	0	0	0	0	0	0	1	0	0	0	.250	.250
McCullers, Lance, S.D.	.091	76	22	4	2	4	2	0	0	3	0	3	0	0	3	0	11	1	0	0	.182	.200
McDowell, Roger, N.Y.	.278	75	18	1	5	5	0	0	0	3	0	1	0	0	1	0	4	0	0	0	.278	.316

McGaffigan, Andrew, Mtl.	.061	50	33	0	2	2	0	0	0	1	0	4	0	0	1	0	18	0	0	0	.061	.088
#McGee, Willie, St.L.	.256	124	497	65	127	184	22	7	7	48	3	0	4	1	37	7	82	19	16	8	.370	.306
McMurtry, J. Craig, Atl.	.125	40	16	3	2	2	0	0	0	0	0	1	0	0	1	0	9	1	0	0	.125	.176
McReynolds, W. Kevin, S.D.	.288	158	560	89	161	282	31	6	26	96	14	5	9	1	66	6	83	8	6	9	.504	.358
*McWilliams, Larry, Pitt.	.138	50	29	2	4	5	1	0	0	0	0	3	0	0	2	0	11	0	0	0	.172	.194
*Meadows, Michael Ray, Hou.	.333	6	6	1	2	2	0	0	0	0	0	0	0	0	0	0	0	1	0	0	.333	.333
*Melendez, Francisco, Phil.	.250	9	8	0	2	2	0	0	0	0	0	0	0	0	0	0	2	0	0	0	.250	.250
Melvin, Robert, S.F.	.224	89	268	24	60	93	14	2	5	25	2	3	3	0	15	1	69	3	2	7	.347	.262
*Milner, Eddie, Cin.	.259	145	424	70	110	189	22	6	15	47	4	1	1	0	36	2	56	18	11	3	.446	.317
#Minton, Gregory, S.F.	.400	48	5	2	2	3	1	0	0	0	0	0	0	0	2	0	3	0	0	0	.600	.571
Mitchell, John, N.Y.	.000	4	2	0	0	0	0	0	0	0	0	0	0	0	0	0	1	0	0	0	.000	.000
Mitchell, Kevin, N.Y.	.277	108	328	51	91	153	22	2	12	43	7	1	1	1	33	0	61	3	3	6	.466	.344
*Mizerock, John, Hou.	.185	44	81	9	15	21	1	1	1	6	0	0	1	1	24	2	16	0	0	4	.259	.374
Montalvo, Rafael, Hou.	—	1	0	0	0	0	0	0	0	0	0	0	0	0	0	0	0	0	0	0	—	—
Moore, William, Mtl.	.167	6	12	0	2	2	0	0	0	0	0	0	0	0	0	0	4	0	0	0	.167	.167
Moreland, B. Keith, Chi.	.271	156	586	72	159	225	30	0	12	79	6	2	11	0	53	10	48	3	6	15	.384	.326
*Moreno, Omar, Atl.	.234	118	359	46	84	126	18	6	4	27	1	6	0	0	21	2	77	17	16	2	.351	.276
*Morris, John, St.L.	.240	39	100	8	24	29	0	1	1	14	3	0	1	0	7	2	15	6	2	2	.290	.287
Morrison, James, Pitt.	.274	154	537	58	147	259	35	4	23	88	9	0	5	4	47	5	88	9	8	6	.482	.334
Motley, Darryl, Atl.	.200	5	10	1	2	3	1	0	0	0	0	0	0	0	1	1	1	0	0	0	.300	.273
*Moyer, Jamie, Chi.	.091	16	22	3	2	2	0	0	0	0	0	4	0	0	4	0	5	0	0	1	.091	.231
Mulholland, Terence, S.F.	.053	15	19	0	1	1	0	0	0	0	0	1	0	0	0	0	8	0	0	0	.053	.053
#Mumphrey, Jerry, Chi.	.304	111	309	37	94	124	11	2	5	32	5	1	3	0	26	4	45	2	3	3	.401	.355
Murphy, Dale, Atl.	.265	160	614	89	163	293	29	7	29	83	12	0	1	2	75	5	141	7	7	10	.477	.347
*Murphy, Robert, Cin.	.000	34	3	0	0	0	0	0	0	0	0	0	0	0	0	0	1	0	0	0	.000	.000
*Myers, Randall, N.Y.	—	10	0	0	0	0	0	0	0	0	0	0	0	0	0	0	0	0	0	0	—	—
*Nettles, Graig, S.D.	.218	126	354	36	77	134	9	0	16	55	5	0	3	2	41	8	62	0	1	6	.379	.300
#Newman, Albert, Mtl.	.200	95	185	23	37	43	3	0	1	8	2	4	2	0	21	2	20	11	11	4	.232	.279
Niedenfuer, Thomas, L.A.	.500	60	4	1	2	2	0	0	0	2	0	1	0	0	0	0	1	0	0	0	.500	.500
*Niemann, Randy, N.Y.	.333	31	6	1	2	2	0	0	0	0	0	0	0	0	1	0	1	0	0	0	.333	.429
Nieto, Thomas, Mtl.	.200	30	65	5	13	21	3	1	1	7	2	0	0	1	6	1	21	0	1	3	.323	.278
*Oberkfell, Kenneth, Atl.	.270	151	503	62	136	181	24	3	5	48	5	4	4	2	83	6	40	7	4	11	.360	.373
#Oester, Ronald, Cin.	.258	153	523	52	135	186	23	2	8	44	7	7	3	1	52	16	84	9	2	18	.356	.325
*Ojeda, Robert, N.Y.	.113	32	71	3	8	8	0	0	0	0	0	8	0	0	1	0	30	0	0	0	.113	.125
Olwine, Edward, Atl.	.333	37	3	0	1	1	0	0	0	0	0	0	0	0	1	0	1	0	0	0	.333	.500
*O'Neill, Paul, Cin.	.000	3	2	0	0	0	0	0	0	0	0	0	0	0	1	0	1	0	0	0	.000	.333
#Oquendo, Jose, St.L.	.297	76	138	20	41	47	4	1	0	13	2	2	3	0	15	4	20	2	3	3	.341	.359

Player, Club	AVG.	G	AB	R	H	TB	2B	3B	HR	RBI	GW RBI	SH	SF	HP	BB	IB	SO	SB	CS	GI DP	SLG	OBP
Orosco, Jesse, N.Y.	.000	58	3	1	0	0	0	0	0	1	0	0	1	0	2	0	0	0	0	0	.000	.333
*Orsulak, Joseph, Pitt.	.249	138	401	60	100	137	19	6	2	19	1	6	1	1	28	2	38	24	11	4	.342	.299
Ortiz, Adalberto, Pitt.	.336	49	110	11	37	43	6	0	0	14	1	1	2	0	9	0	13	0	1	4	.391	.380
#Ouellette, Philip, S.F.	.174	10	23	1	4	4	0	0	0	0	0	0	0	0	3	0	3	0	0	3	.174	.269
*Owchinko, Robert, Mtl.	.200	3	5	1	1	1	0	0	0	0	0	0	0	0	1	0	3	0	0	0	.200	.333
Ownbey, Richard, St.L.	.000	17	7	0	0	0	0	0	0	0	0	3	0	0	0	0	1	0	0	0	.000	.000
*Palmeiro, Rafael, Chi.	.247	22	73	9	18	31	4	0	3	12	1	0	0	1	4	0	6	1	1	4	.425	.295
Palmer, David, Atl.	.182	35	66	3	12	18	3	0	1	6	1	10	0	0	1	0	17	0	0	1	.273	.194
Pankovits, James, Hou.	.283	70	113	12	32	43	6	1	1	7	1	0	0	0	11	1	25	1	1	4	.381	.347
Parent, Mark, S.D.	.143	8	14	1	2	2	0	0	0	0	0	0	0	0	1	0	3	0	0	1	.143	.200
*Parker, David, Cin.	.273	162	637	89	174	304	31	3	31	116	12	0	6	1	56	16	126	1	6	18	.477	.330
Parrett, Jeffrey, Mtl.	.500	12	2	0	1	1	0	0	0	0	0	0	0	0	0	0	1	0	0	0	.500	.500
Patterson, Bob, Pitt.	.125	11	8	0	1	1	0	0	0	0	0	2	0	0	0	0	6	0	0	0	.125	.125
Pena, Adalberto, Hou.	.207	15	29	3	6	7	1	0	0	2	0	0	0	0	5	2	5	1	0	3	.241	.324
Pena, Alejandro, L.A.	.176	24	17	0	3	3	0	0	0	1	0	3	0	0	0	0	6	0	0	0	.176	.176
Pena, Antonio, Pitt.	.288	144	510	56	147	207	26	2	10	52	8	0	1	1	53	6	69	9	10	21	.406	.356
*Pena, Hipolito, Pitt.	—	10	0	0	0	0	0	0	0	0	0	0	0	0	0	0	0	0	0	0	—	—
#Pendleton, Terry, St.L.	.239	159	578	56	138	177	26	5	1	59	6	6	7	1	34	10	59	24	6	12	.306	.279
Perez, Atanasio, Cin.	.255	77	200	14	51	71	12	1	2	29	5	0	3	0	25	2	25	0	0	6	.355	.333
*Perry, Gerald, Atl.	.271	29	70	6	19	27	2	0	2	11	1	1	1	0	8	1	4	0	1	4	.386	.342
*Perry, W. Patrick, St.L.	.000	46	8	0	0	0	0	0	0	0	0	0	0	0	0	0	4	0	0	0	.000	.000
*Powell, Dennis, L.A.	.214	27	14	1	3	6	3	0	0	0	0	0	0	0	0	0	6	0	0	0	.429	.214
Power, Ted, Cin.	.125	56	24	3	3	4	1	0	0	1	0	3	0	0	3	0	12	1	0	0	.167	.222
Price, Joseph, Cin.	.143	25	7	0	1	1	0	0	0	2	0	0	0	0	1	0	1	0	0	0	.143	.250
*Puhl, Terrance, Hou.	.244	81	172	17	42	61	10	0	3	14	0	4	2	0	15	1	24	3	2	6	.355	.302
Puleo, Charles, Atl.	.333	5	6	0	2	2	0	0	0	3	0	1	0	0	0	0	3	0	0	0	.333	.333
Pyznarski, Timothy, S.D.	.238	15	42	3	10	11	1	0	0	0	0	0	0	1	4	0	11	2	0	2	.262	.319
#Quinones, Luis, S.F.	.179	71	106	13	19	26	1	3	0	11	0	4	1	1	3	1	17	3	1	1	.245	.207
#Raines, Timothy, Mtl.	.334	151	580	91	194	276	35	10	9	62	8	1	3	2	78	9	60	70	9	6	.476	.413
Ramirez, Rafael, Atl.	.240	134	496	57	119	166	21	1	8	33	2	7	3	3	21	1	60	19	8	16	.335	.273
Rawley, Shane, Phil.	.173	23	52	5	9	11	2	0	0	1	0	10	1	0	1	0	18	0	0	2	.212	.185
#Ray, Johnny, Pitt.	.301	155	579	67	174	228	33	0	7	78	7	1	7	3	58	10	47	6	9	21	.394	.363
Ready, Randy, S.D.	.000	1	3	0	0	0	0	0	0	0	0	0	0	0	0	0	1	0	0	0	.000	.000
Reardon, Jeffrey, Mtl.	.125	62	8	0	1	1	0	0	0	0	0	1	0	0	0	0	6	0	0	0	.125	.125
Redus, Gary, Phil.	.247	90	340	62	84	147	22	4	11	33	6	1	1	3	47	4	78	25	7	2	.432	.343

Renteria, Richard, Pitt.	.250	10	12	2	3	4	1	0	0	1	0	0	0	0	0	4	0	0	0	.333	.250
Reuschel, Ricky, Pitt.	.157	43	70	7	11	13	2	0	0	6	0	8	0	0	3	0	19	0	0	0	.186	.192
*Reuss, Jerry, L.A.	.250	19	20	0	5	6	1	0	0	0	0	0	0	0	1	0	6	0	0	0	.300	.286
*Reynolds, G. Craig, Hou.	.249	114	313	32	78	109	7	3	6	41	8	1	3	0	12	5	31	3	1	8	.348	.274
#Reynolds, Robert, Pitt.	.269	118	402	63	108	169	30	2	9	48	4	3	2	1	40	4	78	16	9	10	.420	.335
Reynolds, Ronn, Phil.	.214	43	126	8	27	40	4	0	3	10	1	0	1	0	5	0	30	0	0	4	.317	.242
Rhoden, Richard, Pitt.	.278	41	90	9	25	37	9	0	1	10	1	7	1	0	3	0	13	0	1	5	.411	.298
*Riley, George, Mtl.	—	10	0	0	0	0	0	0	0	0	0	0	0	0	0	0	0	0	0	0	—	—
Rivera, Luis, Mtl.	.205	55	166	20	34	47	11	1	0	13	2	1	1	2	17	0	33	1	1	1	.283	.285
Roberge, Bertrand, Mtl.	.000	21	2	0	0	0	0	0	0	0	0	0	0	0	0	0	0	0	0	0	.000	.000
#Roberts, Leon, S.D.	.253	101	241	34	61	73	5	2	1	12	0	2	1	0	14	1	29	14	12	2	.303	.293
Robinson, Don, Pitt.	.667	50	6	1	4	5	1	0	0	1	0	0	0	0	0	0	1	0	0	0	.833	.667
Robinson, Jeffrey, S.F.	.067	65	15	0	1	1	0	0	0	2	0	1	1	0	0	0	7	0	0	0	.067	.063
Robinson, Ronald, Cin.	.071	70	14	1	1	1	0	0	0	0	0	0	0	0	0	0	3	0	0	1	.071	.071
Rodriguez, Ruben, Pitt.	.000	2	3	0	0	0	0	0	0	0	0	0	0	0	0	0	1	0	0	0	.000	.000
#Roenicke, Ronald, Phil.	.247	102	275	42	68	98	13	1	5	42	7	4	3	0	61	4	52	2	2	4	.356	.381
#Rose, Peter, Cin.	.219	72	237	15	52	64	8	2	0	25	3	0	1	4	30	0	31	3	0	2	.270	.316
Rowdon, Wade, Cin.	.250	38	80	9	20	27	5	1	0	10	1	1	1	1	9	0	17	2	0	0	.338	.330
Royster, Jeron, S.D.	.257	118	257	31	66	93	12	0	5	26	2	6	3	0	32	3	45	3	5	6	.362	.336
*Rucker, David, Phil.	.000	19	1	0	0	0	0	0	0	0	0	0	0	0	0	0	0	0	0	0	.000	.000
Ruffin, Bruce, Phil.	.073	21	55	2	4	5	1	0	0	2	0	1	0	0	0	0	32	0	0	2	.091	.073
Runge, Paul, Atl.	.250	7	8	1	2	2	0	0	0	0	0	0	0	0	2	0	4	0	0	1	.250	.400
#Runnells, Thomas, Cin.	.091	12	11	1	1	2	1	0	0	0	0	0	0	0	0	0	2	0	0	1	.182	.091
Russell, John, Phil.	.241	93	315	35	76	140	21	2	13	60	5	1	4	3	25	2	103	0	1	6	.444	.300
Russell, William, L.A.	.250	105	216	21	54	65	11	0	0	18	2	7	2	2	15	2	23	7	0	6	.301	.302
Ruthven, Richard, Chi.	.000	6	1	0	0	0	0	0	0	0	0	0	0	0	0	0	1	0	0	0	.000	.000
Ryan, L. Nolan, Hou.	.102	30	59	1	6	6	0	0	0	5	1	3	0	0	1	0	22	0	1	2	.102	.117
St. Claire, Randy, Mtl.	.000	11	1	0	0	0	0	0	0	0	0	1	0	0	0	0	1	0	0	0	.000	.000
Sample, William, Atl.	.285	92	200	23	57	86	11	0	6	14	2	2	2	3	14	1	26	4	2	0	.430	.338
Samuel, Juan, Phil.	.266	145	591	90	157	265	36	12	16	78	11	1	7	8	26	3	142	42	14	8	.448	.302
Sandberg, Ryne, Chi.	.284	154	627	68	178	258	28	5	14	76	5	3	6	0	46	6	79	34	11	11	.411	.330
Sanderson, Scott, Chi.	.059	38	51	1	3	4	1	0	0	2	1	6	0	1	0	0	23	0	0	0	.078	.077
Santana, Rafael, N.Y.	.218	139	394	38	86	100	11	0	1	28	2	1	3	2	36	12	43	0	0	15	.254	.285
Santiago, Benito, S.D.	.290	17	62	10	18	29	2	0	3	6	1	0	1	0	2	0	12	0	1	0	.468	.308
*Sauver, Richard, Pitt.	.333	3	3	0	1	1	0	0	0	0	0	1	0	0	0	0	1	0	0	0	.333	.333
Sax, Stephen, L.A.	.332	157	633	91	210	279	43	4	6	56	11	6	3	3	59	5	58	40	17	12	.441	.390
*Schatzeder, Daniel, Mtl.-Phil.	.385	58	26	5	10	17	2	1	1	2	0	0	0	0	5	0	10	0	0	0	.654	.484

Player, Club	AVG.	G	AB	R	H	TB	2B	3B	HR	RBI	GW RBI	SH	SF	HP	BB	IB	SO	SB	CS	GI DP	SLG	OBP
Schmidt, Michael, Phil.	.290	160	552	97	160	302	29	1	37	119	13	0	9	7	89	25	84	1	2	8	.547	.390
Schu, Richard, Phil.	.274	92	208	32	57	93	10	1	8	25	1	3	2	2	18	1	44	2	2	1	.447	.335
*Scioscia, Michael, L.A.	.251	122	374	36	94	129	18	1	5	26	3	6	4	3	62	4	23	3	3	11	.345	.359
Scott, Michael, Hou.	.126	38	95	7	12	14	2	0	0	3	0	10	0	0	2	0	48	0	0	0	.147	.144
Sebra, Robert, Mtl.	.207	18	29	2	6	7	1	0	0	0	0	0	0	0	1	0	5	0	0	1	.241	.233
See, R. Lawrence, L.A.	.250	13	20	1	5	7	2	0	0	2	0	0	0	0	2	0	7	0	0	0	.350	.318
Shields, Stephen, Atl.	.000	6	1	0	0	0	0	0	0	0	0	0	0	0	0	0	1	0	0	0	.000	.000
Shipley, Craig, L.A.	.111	12	27	3	3	4	1	0	0	4	0	1	0	1	2	1	5	0	0	1	.148	.200
Show, Eric, S.D.	.163	24	43	2	7	9	2	0	0	1	0	3	0	0	1	0	14	0	0	0	.209	.182
#Simmons, Ted, Atl.	.252	76	127	14	32	49	5	0	4	25	5	0	4	1	12	5	14	1	0	1	.386	.313
Sisk, Douglas, N.Y.	.000	41	4	0	0	0	0	0	0	0	0	0	0	0	0	0	2	0	0	0	.000	.000
*Smiley, John, Pitt.	—	12	0	0	0	0	0	0	0	0	0	0	0	0	0	0	0	0	0	0	—	—
Smith, Bryn, Mtl.	.138	30	58	3	8	12	1	0	1	7	0	5	0	0	4	0	17	0	0	0	.207	.194
Smith, David, Hou.	.000	54	2	0	0	0	0	0	0	0	0	0	0	0	0	0	0	0	0	0	.000	.000
Smith, Lee, Chi.	.000	66	5	0	0	0	0	0	0	0	0	0	0	0	0	0	5	0	0	0	.000	.000
Smith, Michael, Cin.	—	2	0	0	0	0	0	0	0	0	0	0	0	0	0	0	0	0	0	0	—	—
#Smith, Osborne, St.L.	.280	153	514	67	144	171	19	4	0	54	5	11	3	2	79	13	27	31	7	9	.333	.376
*Smith, Zane, Atl.	.085	43	59	2	5	5	0	0	0	3	1	9	0	0	2	0	19	0	0	0	.085	.115
Soff, Raymond, St.L.	.000	30	2	0	0	0	0	0	0	0	0	1	0	0	0	0	2	0	0	0	.000	.000
Solano, Julio, Hou.	.000	16	6	0	0	0	0	0	0	0	0	1	0	0	0	0	5	0	0	0	.000	.000
Soto, Mario, Cin.	.111	20	27	2	3	4	1	0	0	1	0	6	0	0	0	0	6	0	0	0	.148	.111
Speck, R. Clifford, Atl.	.000	13	3	0	0	0	0	0	0	0	0	1	0	0	1	0	3	0	0	0	.000	.250
Speier, Chris, Chi.	.284	95	155	21	44	70	8	0	6	23	0	4	1	1	15	3	32	2	2	4	.452	.349
*Spilman, W. Harry, S.F.	.287	58	94	12	27	40	7	0	2	22	4	0	0	0	12	3	13	0	0	0	.426	.368
Stewart, David, Phil.	—	8	0	0	0	0	0	0	0	0	0	0	0	0	0	0	0	0	0	0	—	—
#Stillwell, Kurt, Cin.	.229	104	279	31	64	72	6	1	0	26	8	4	0	2	30	1	47	6	2	5	.258	.309
Stoddard, Robert, S.D.	.000	18	1	0	0	0	0	0	0	0	0	0	0	0	0	0	1	0	0	0	.000	.000
Stoddard, Timothy, S.D.	.250	30	4	1	1	4	0	0	1	1	0	0	0	0	0	0	2	0	0	0	1.000	.250
*Stone, Jeffery, Phil.	.277	82	249	32	69	101	6	4	6	19	3	2	0	4	20	0	52	19	6	3	.406	.341
*Strawberry, Darryl, N.Y.	.259	136	475	76	123	241	27	5	27	93	15	0	9	6	72	9	141	28	12	4	.507	.358
*Stubbs, Franklin, L.A.	.226	132	420	55	95	177	11	1	23	58	9	4	2	2	37	11	107	7	1	9	.421	.291
*Sutcliffe, Richard, Chi.	.208	29	53	3	11	16	2	0	1	4	0	4	0	1	2	0	13	0	0	1	.302	.250
Sutter, H. Bruce, Atl.	.000	16	1	0	0	0	0	0	0	0	0	0	0	0	0	0	1	0	0	0	.000	.000
Tejada, Wilfredo, Mtl.	.240	10	25	1	6	7	1	0	0	2	0	0	0	0	2	1	8	0	0	1	.280	.296
Tekulve, Kenton, Phil.	.000	73	5	1	0	0	0	0	0	0	0	0	0	0	1	0	1	0	0	0	.000	.167

#Templeton, Garry, S.D.	.247	147	510	42	126	157	21	2	2	44	4	1	2	1	35	21	86	10	5	12	.308	.296
Terry, Scott, Cin.	.250	30	4	3	1	1	0	0	0	0	0	1	0	0	1	0	1	0	0	0	.250	.400
Teufel, Timothy, N.Y.	.247	93	279	35	69	103	20	1	4	31	3	3	3	1	32	1	42	1	2	6	.369	.324
Thomas, Andres, Atl.	.251	102	323	26	81	120	17	2	6	32	3	2	2	0	8	2	49	4	6	14	.372	.267
*Thompson, Jason, Mtl.	.196	30	51	6	10	14	4	0	0	4	1	0	0	0	18	2	12	0	1	0	.275	.406
*Thompson, Milton, Phil.	.251	96	299	38	75	102	7	1	6	23	4	4	2	1	26	1	62	19	4	4	.341	.311
Thompson, Robert, S.F.	.271	149	549	73	149	203	27	3	7	47	4	18	1	5	42	0	112	12	15	11	.370	.328
Thon, Richard, Hou.	.248	106	278	24	69	93	13	1	3	21	3	1	1	0	29	5	49	6	5	8	.335	.318
*Thurmond, Mark, S.D.	.250	18	24	0	6	7	1	0	0	6	1	2	0	0	0	0	3	0	0	1	.292	.250
Tibbs, Jay, Mtl.	.130	36	54	2	7	8	1	0	0	0	0	4	0	0	4	0	31	0	0	0	.148	.190
Toliver, Freddie, Phil.	.000	5	6	0	0	0	0	0	0	0	0	0	0	1	1	0	1	1	0	0	.000	.250
*Tomlin, David, Mtl.	—	7	0	0	0	0	0	0	0	0	0	0	0	0	0	0	0	0	0	0	—	—
Trevino, Alejandro, L.A.	.262	89	202	31	53	78	13	0	4	26	3	2	1	1	27	2	35	0	0	6	.386	.351
Trillo, J. Manuel, Chi.	.296	81	152	22	45	58	10	0	1	19	2	2	2	0	16	0	21	0	2	2	.382	.359
*Trout, Steven, Chi.	.209	37	43	5	9	10	1	0	0	3	2	4	0	0	1	0	15	0	0	1	.233	.227
*Tudor, John, St.L.	.153	30	72	6	11	12	1	0	0	6	1	13	1	0	1	0	22	0	0	0	.167	.162
#Uribe, Jose, S.F.	.223	157	453	46	101	127	15	1	3	43	2	3	0	0	61	19	76	22	11	2	.280	.315
Valdez, Sergio, Mtl.	.125	5	8	0	1	1	0	0	0	0	0	0	0	0	0	0	3	0	0	0	.125	.125
*Valenzuela, Fernando, L.A.	.220	39	109	5	24	28	4	0	0	7	0	6	1	0	0	0	11	0	0	1	.257	.218
Vande Berg, Edward, L.A.	.000	60	1	0	0	0	0	0	0	0	0	0	0	0	0	0	1	0	0	0	.000	.000
Van Gorder, David, Cin.	.000	9	10	0	0	0	0	0	0	0	0	0	0	0	1	0	2	0	0	1	.000	.091
*Van Slyke, Andrew, St.L.	.270	137	418	48	113	189	23	7	13	61	9	1	3	1	47	5	85	21	8	2	.452	.343
*Venable, W. McKinley, Cin.	.211	108	147	17	31	46	7	1	2	15	1	2	2	0	17	2	24	7	2	0	.313	.289
Virgil, Osvaldo, Atl.	.223	114	359	45	80	134	9	0	15	48	6	2	3	4	63	5	73	1	0	9	.373	.343
*Vosberg, Edward, S.D.	.000	5	2	0	0	0	0	0	0	0	0	0	0	0	0	0	1	0	0	0	.000	.000
Walk, Robert, Pitt.	.154	44	39	2	6	9	3	0	0	7	0	1	1	0	1	0	11	0	2	0	.231	.171
Walker, Anthony, Hou.	.222	84	90	19	20	33	7	0	2	10	1	0	0	0	11	2	15	11	3	3	.367	.307
#Walker, Cleotha, Chi.	.277	28	101	21	28	38	3	2	1	7	1	0	1	0	10	0	20	15	4	3	.376	.339
Wallach, Timothy, Mtl.	.233	134	480	50	112	190	22	1	18	71	9	0	5	10	44	8	72	8	4	16	.396	.308
*Walling, Dennis, Hou.	.312	130	382	54	119	183	23	1	13	58	10	0	4	0	36	5	31	1	1	8	.479	.367
*Walter, Gene, S.D.	.200	57	10	0	2	3	1	0	0	0	0	2	0	0	1	0	4	0	0	0	.300	.273
Ward, R. Duane, Atl.	.000	10	1	0	0	0	0	0	0	0	0	0	0	0	0	0	0	0	0	0	.000	.000
*Washington, Claudell, Atl.	.270	40	137	17	37	63	11	0	5	14	2	1	1	0	14	0	26	4	7	4	.460	.336
#Washington, U.L., Pitt.	.200	72	135	14	27	35	0	4	0	10	3	4	1	0	15	2	27	6	0	1	.259	.278
Wasinger, Mark, S.D.	.000	3	8	0	0	0	0	0	0	1	0	1	0	0	0	0	2	0	0	0	.000	.000
#Webster, Mitchell, Mtl.	.290	151	576	89	167	248	31	13	8	49	8	3	5	4	57	4	78	36	15	9	.431	.355
Welch, Robert, L.A.	.105	35	76	2	8	11	0	0	1	4	0	5	0	1	4	0	23	0	0	0	.145	.160
Wellman, Brad, S.F.	.154	12	13	0	2	2	0	0	0	1	0	0	0	0	1	0	2	0	0	0	.154	.214

Player, Club	AVG.	G	AB	R	H	TB	2B	3B	HR	RBI	GW RBI	SH	SF	HP	BB	IB	SO	SB	CS	GI DP	SLG	OBP
*Welsh, Christopher, Cin.	.119	24	42	3	5	10	2	0	1	4	0	4	0	0	2	0	19	1	0	0	.238	.159
#White, Jerry, St.L.	.125	25	24	1	3	6	0	0	1	3	1	1	2	0	2	0	3	0	0	1	.250	.179
*Whitfield, Terry, L.A.	.071	19	14	0	1	1	0	0	0	0	0	0	0	0	5	2	2	0	0	1	.071	.316
Whitson, Eddie, S.D.	.167	17	18	1	3	3	0	0	0	0	0	2	0	0	0	0	8	0	0	0	.167	.167
Williams, Frank, S.F.	.500	36	2	0	1	1	0	0	0	0	0	1	0	0	0	0	1	0	0	0	.500	.500
Williams, Reginald, L.A.	.277	128	303	35	84	114	14	2	4	32	3	9	1	2	23	9	57	9	3	8	.376	.331
*Willis, Carl, Cin.	.333	29	3	0	1	1	0	0	0	0	0	1	0	0	0	0	0	0	0	1	.333	.333
Wilson, Glenn, Phil.	.271	155	584	70	158	241	30	4	15	84	8	0	9	4	42	1	91	5	1	15	.413	.319
#Wilson, William, N.Y.	.289	123	381	61	110	164	17	5	9	45	5	0	1	1	32	5	72	25	7	5	.430	.345
Wine, Robert, Hou.	.250	9	12	2	3	4	1	0	0	0	0	0	0	0	1	0	4	0	0	0	.333	.308
Winn, James, Pitt.	.063	50	16	1	1	2	1	0	0	0	0	1	0	0	1	0	8	0	0	1	.125	.118
*Winningham, Herman; Mtl.	.216	90	185	23	40	64	6	3	4	11	2	1	0	0	18	3	51	12	7	4	.346	.286
Wohlford, James, Mtl.	.266	70	94	10	25	36	4	2	1	11	2	2	1	0	9	3	17	0	2	2	.383	.327
Wojna, Edward, S.D.	.143	7	14	1	2	2	0	0	0	0	0	2	0	0	0	0	11	0	0	1	.143	.143
*Woodard, Michael, S.F.	.253	48	79	14	20	27	2	1	1	5	1	1	0	0	10	0	9	7	2	0	.342	.337
Worrell, Todd, St.L.	.143	74	7	0	1	3	0	1	0	0	0	0	0	0	0	0	5	0	0	0	.429	.143
#Wright, George, Mtl.	.188	56	117	12	22	31	5	2	0	5	0	1	3	1	11	0	28	1	1	3	.265	.258
*Wynne, Marvell, S.D.	.264	137	288	34	76	120	19	2	7	37	7	1	3	1	15	2	45	11	11	5	.417	.300
Youmans, Floyd, Mtl.	.160	33	75	4	12	15	0	0	1	7	0	2	0	0	5	0	29	0	0	0	.200	.213
Youngblood, Joel, S.F.	.255	97	184	20	47	74	12	0	5	28	2	2	3	1	18	0	34	1	1	2	.402	.320

CLUB BATTING

Club	AVG.	G	AB	R	H	TB	2B	3B	HR	RBI	GW RBI	SH	SF	HP	BB	IB	SO	SB	CS	GI DP	LOB	SHO	SLG	OBP
New York	.263	162	5558	783	1462	2229	261	31	148	730	102	75	53	31	631	68	968	118	48	122	1192	4	.401	.339
San Diego	.261	162	5515	656	1442	2139	239	25	136	629	72	66	35	18	484	74	917	96	68	130	1099	9	.388	.321
Chicago	.256	160	5499	680	1409	2186	258	27	155	638	64	54	51	15	508	56	966	132	62	113	1087	10	.398	.318
Houston	.255	162	5441	654	1388	2071	244	32	125	613	90	53	41	24	536	78	916	163	75	126	1113	6	.381	.322
Montreal	.254	161	5508	637	1401	2086	255	50	110	602	73	53	42	33	537	72	1016	193	95	113	1137	11	.379	.322
Cincinnati	.254	162	5536	732	1404	2143	237	35	144	670	79	65	41	18	586	55	920	177	53	127	1129	7	.387	.325
San Francisco	.253	162	5501	698	1394	2063	269	29	114	637	77	101	34	37	536	86	1087	148	93	83	1132	12	.375	.322
Philadelphia	.253	161	5483	739	1386	2192	266	39	154	696	82	66	51	40	589	70	1154	153	59	98	1151	7	.400	.327
Los Angeles	.251	162	5471	638	1373	2023	232	14	130	599	68	81	39	32	478	58	966	155	67	109	1083	14	.370	.313
Atlanta	.250	161	5384	615	1348	2051	241	24	138	575	66	79	42	24	538	62	904	93	76	124	1145	10	.381	.319
Pittsburgh	.250	162	5456	663	1366	2038	273	33	111	618	59	68	44	20	569	55	929	152	84	132	1100	10	.374	.321
St. Louis	.236	161	5378	601	1270	1756	216	48	58	550	69	108	46	20	568	69	905	262	78	83	1129	13	.327	.309
TOTALS	.253	969	65730	8096	16643	24977	2991	387	1523	7557	901	869	519	312	6560	803	11648	1842	858	1360	13497	113	.380	.322

PITCHING

INDIVIDUAL PITCHING LEADERS

Games Won	21	Valenzuela, L.A.
Games Lost	18	Mahler, Atl.
Won-Lost Percentage	.783	Ojeda, N.Y.
Earned Run Average	2.22	Scott, Hou.
Games	83	Lefferts, S.D.
Games Started	39	Browning, Cin. & Mahler, Atl.
Complete Games	20	Valenzuela, L.A.
Games Finished	60	Worrell, St.L.
Shutouts	5	Knepper, Hou. & Scott, Hou.
Saves	36	Worrell, St.L.
Innings	275.1	Scott, Hou.
Hits	283	Mahler, Atl.
Batsmen Faced	1102	Valenzuela, L.A.
Runs	139	Mahler, Atl.
Earned Runs	129	Mahler, Atl.
Home Runs	28	K.Gross, Phil.
Sacrifice Hits	22	Knepper, Hou.
Sacrifice Flies	13	Gullickson, Cin.
Hit Batsmen	8	K.Gross, Phil. & Reuschel, Pitt.
Bases on Balls	118	Youmans, Mtl.
Intentional Bases on Balls	16	Worrell, St.L.
Strikeouts	306	Scott, Hou.
Wild Pitches	15	Ryan, Hou.
Balks	7	Deshaies, Hou.
Games Won, Consecutive	7	Fernandez, N.Y. (June 8 - July 11), McDowell, N.Y. (April 21 - June 28), Rawley, Phil. (May 23 - July 7) & Robinson, Cin. (April 12 - July 7)
Games Lost, Consecutive	8	LaCoss, S.F. (July 18 - Sept. 4) & Sutcliffe, Chi. (June 7 - Sept. 16)

TOP FIFTEEN QUALIFIERS FOR EARNED RUN AVERAGE CHAMPIONSHIP
(* Left-Handed Pitcher)

Pitcher, Club	W	L	PCT.	ERA	G	GS	CG	GF	SHO	SV	IP	H	TBF	R	ER	HR	SH	SF	HB	BB	IB	SO	WP	BK
Scott, Michael, Hou.	18	10	.643	2.22	37	37	7	0	5	0	275.1	182	1065	73	68	17	8	6	2	72	6	306	3	0
*Ojeda, Robert, N.Y.	18	5	.783	2.57	32	30	7	1	2	0	217.1	185	871	72	62	15	10	3	2	52	3	148	2	1
Darling, Ronald, N.Y.	15	6	.714	2.81	34	34	4	0	2	0	237.0	203	967	84	74	21	10	6	3	81	2	184	7	3
Rhoden, Richard, Pitt.	15	12	.556	2.84	34	34	12	0	1	0	253.2	211	1015	82	80	17	6	5	2	76	8	159	6	4
Gooden, Dwight, N.Y.	17	6	.739	2.84	33	33	12	0	2	0	250.0	197	1020	92	79	17	10	8	4	80	3	200	4	4
Cox, Danny, St.L.	12	13	.480	2.90	32	32	8	0	0	0	220.0	189	881	85	71	14	8	3	2	60	6	108	3	4
*Tudor, John, St.L.	13	7	.650	2.92	30	30	3	0	0	0	219.0	197	879	81	71	22	9	8	1	53	5	107	2	1
Krukow, Michael, S.F.	20	9	.690	3.05	34	34	10	0	2	0	245.0	204	987	90	83	24	10	5	4	55	4	178	4	0
Garrelts, Scott, S.F.	13	9	.591	3.11	53	18	2	27	0	10	173.2	144	717	65	60	17	10	7	2	74	11	125	9	1
*Knepper, Robert, Hou.	17	12	.586	3.14	40	38	8	1	5	0	258.0	232	1053	100	90	19	22	5	4	62	13	143	5	0
*Valenzuela, Fernando, L.A.	21	11	.656	3.14	34	34	20	0	3	0	269.1	226	1102	104	94	18	15	3	1	85	5	242	13	0
Forsch, Robert, St.L.	14	10	.583	3.25	33	33	3	0	0	0	230.0	211	939	91	83	19	5	9	2	68	11	104	7	0
Welch, Robert, L.A.	7	13	.350	3.28	33	33	7	0	3	0	235.2	227	981	95	86	14	7	8	7	55	6	183	2	1
*Honeycutt, Frederick, L.A.	11	9	.550	3.32	32	28	0	2	0	0	171.0	164	713	71	63	9	6	1	3	45	4	100	4	1
Ryan, L. Nolan, Hou.	12	8	.600	3.34	30	30	1	0	0	0	178.0	119	729	72	66	14	5	4	4	82	5	194	15	0

ALL PITCHERS LISTED ALPHABETICALLY
(* Left-Handed Pitcher)

Pitcher, Club	W	L	PCT.	ERA	G	GS	CG	GF	SHO	SV	IP	H	TBF	R	ER	HR	SH	SF	HB	BB	IB	SO	WP	BK
Acker, James, Atl.	3	8	.273	3.79	21	14	0	3	0	0	95.0	100	402	47	40	7	6	4	1	26	3	37	2	0
Aguilera, Richard, N.Y.	10	7	.588	3.88	28	20	2	2	0	0	141.2	145	605	70	61	15	6	5	7	36	1	104	5	3
Alexander, Doyle, Atl.	6	6	.500	3.84	17	17	2	0	0	0	117.1	135	496	58	50	9	8	1	0	17	1	74	1	0
Andersen, Larry, Phil.-Hou.	2	1	.667	3.03	48	0	0	8	0	1	77.1	83	323	30	26	2	10	5	1	26	10	42	1	0
Anderson, Richard, N.Y.	2	1	.667	2.72	15	5	0	4	0	1	49.2	45	201	17	15	3	2	4	0	11	3	21	1	1

*Assenmacher, Paul, Atl.	7	3	.700	2.50	61	0	0	27	0	7	68.1	61	287	23	19	5	7	1	0	26	4	56	2	3
Baller, Jay, Chi.	2	4	.333	5.37	36	0	0	16	0	5	53.2	58	248	37	32	7	4	3	2	28	4	42	2	4
Bargar, Gregory, St.L.	0	2	.000	5.60	22	0	0	10	0	0	27.1	36	126	19	17	3	2	2	3	10	1	12	2	0
Beckwith, T. Joseph, L.A.	0	0	—	6.87	15	0	0	4	0	0	18.1	28	86	16	14	5	0	0	0	6	0	13	0	0
Bedrosian, Stephen, Phil.	8	6	.571	3.39	68	0	0	56	0	29	90.1	79	381	39	34	12	3	3	0	34	10	82	5	2
Berenguer, Juan, S.F.	2	3	.400	2.70	46	4	0	17	0	4	73.1	64	314	23	22	4	2	1	2	44	3	72	4	2
Berenyi, Bruce, N.Y.	2	2	.500	6.35	14	7	0	2	0	0	39.2	47	184	30	28	5	1	3	1	22	0	30	4	0
Bielecki, Michael, Pitt.	6	11	.353	4.66	31	27	0	0	0	0	148.2	149	667	87	77	10	7	6	2	83	3	83	7	5
Bittiger, Jeffrey, Phil.	1	1	.500	5.52	3	3	0	0	0	0	14.2	16	68	10	9	2	1	0	1	7	1	8	2	2
*Blue, Vida, S.F.	10	10	.500	3.27	28	28	0	0	0	0	156.2	137	663	65	57	19	7	6	0	77	3	100	5	1
Bockus, Randy, S.F.	0	0	—	2.57	5	0	0	1	0	0	7.0	7	36	5	2	1	1	0	0	6	1	4	0	0
Boever, Joseph, St.L.	0	1	.000	1.66	11	0	0	4	0	0	21.2	19	93	5	4	2	0	0	0	11	0	8	1	0
Booker, Gregory, S.D.	1	0	1.000	1.64	9	0	0	4	0	0	11.0	10	47	5	2	0	0	0	0	4	2	7	0	0
Brown, Curtis, Mtl.	0	1	.000	3.00	6	0	0	2	0	0	12.0	15	53	6	4	0	3	1	0	2	2	4	0	0
*Browning, Thomas, Cin.	14	13	.519	3.81	39	39	4	0	2	0	243.1	225	1016	123	103	26	14	12	1	70	6	147	3	0
Burke, Timothy, Mtl.	9	7	.563	2.93	68	2	0	25	0	4	101.1	103	451	37	33	7	6	2	4	46	13	82	4	0
Burris, B. Ray, St.L.	4	5	.444	5.60	23	10	0	5	0	0	82.0	92	361	52	51	13	4	0	4	32	4	34	0	0
Butera, Salvatore, Cin.	0	0	—	0.00	1	0	0	1	0	0	1.0	0	4	0	0	0	0	0	0	1	0	1	0	0
*Calhoun, Jeffrey, Hou.	1	0	1.000	3.71	20	0	0	7	0	0	26.2	28	119	16	11	3	1	0	0	12	1	14	2	0
*Carlton, Steven, Phil.-S.F.	5	11	.313	5.89	22	22	0	0	0	0	113.0	138	533	90	74	19	6	3	1	61	4	80	5	1
*Carman, Donald, Phil.	10	5	.667	3.22	50	14	2	13	1	1	134.1	113	545	50	48	11	5	3	3	52	11	98	6	2
Childress, Rodney, Phil.	0	0	—	6.75	2	0	0	0	0	0	2.2	4	12	3	2	0	0	0	0	1	0	1	0	0
*Clements, Patrick, Pitt.	0	4	.000	2.80	65	0	0	19	0	2	61.0	53	256	20	19	1	7	4	2	32	6	31	2	0
*Conroy, Timothy, St.L.	5	11	.313	5.23	25	21	1	2	0	0	115.1	122	513	72	67	15	0	10	3	56	7	79	7	0
Cox, Danny, St.L.	12	13	.480	2.90	32	32	8	0	0	0	220.0	189	881	85	71	14	8	3	2	60	6	108	3	4
Darling, Ronald, N.Y.	15	6	.714	2.81	34	34	4	0	2	0	237.0	203	967	84	74	21	10	6	3	81	2	184	7	3
Darwin, Danny, Hou.	5	2	.714	2.32	12	8	1	2	0	0	54.1	50	222	19	14	3	1	3	0	9	0	40	2	1
*Davis, Mark, S.F.	5	7	.417	2.99	67	2	0	20	0	4	84.1	63	342	33	28	6	5	5	1	34	7	90	3	0
Davis, Ronald, Chi.	0	2	.000	7.65	17	0	0	5	0	0	20.0	31	91	18	17	3	0	1	0	3	0	10	0	1
*Dayley, Kenneth, St.L.	0	3	.000	3.26	31	0	0	13	0	5	38.2	42	170	19	14	1	4	1	1	11	3	33	0	0
DeLeon, Jose, Pitt.	1	3	.250	8.27	9	1	0	5	0	1	16.1	17	83	16	15	2	1	0	1	17	3	11	1	0
Dedmon, Jeffrey, Atl.	6	6	.500	2.98	57	0	0	22	0	3	99.2	90	424	43	33	8	7	2	4	39	5	58	3	2
Denny, John, Cin.	11	10	.524	4.20	27	27	2	0	1	0	171.1	179	731	89	80	15	9	4	4	56	9	115	2	1

Pitcher, Club	W	L	PCT.	ERA	G	GS	CG	GF	SHO	SV	IP	H	TBF	R	ER	HR	SH	SF	HB	BB	IB	SO	WP	BK
*Deshaies, James, Hou.	12	5	.706	3.25	26	26	1	0	1	0	144.0	124	599	58	52	16	4	3	2	59	2	128	0	7
*Diaz, Carlos, L.A.	0	0	—	4.26	19	0	0	9	0	0	25.1	33	113	14	12	2	1	1	0	7	2	18	2	0
*DiPino, Frank, Hou.-Chi.	3	7	.300	4.37	61	0	0	26	0	3	80.1	74	345	45	39	11	9	3	2	30	6	70	3	0
Downs, Kelly, S.F.	4	4	.500	2.75	14	14	1	0	0	0	88.1	78	372	29	27	5	4	4	3	30	7	64	3	2
*Dravecky, David, S.D.	9	11	.450	3.07	26	26	3	0	1	0	161.1	149	677	68	55	17	12	5	1	54	7	87	0	1
*Earley, William, St.L.	0	0	—	0.00	3	0	0	2	0	0	3.0	0	11	0	0	0	0	0	0	2	0	2	0	0
Eckersley, Dennis, Chi.	6	11	.353	4.57	33	32	1	0	0	0	201.0	226	862	109	102	21	13	10	3	43	3	137	2	5
Fansler, Stanley, Pitt.	0	3	.000	3.75	5	5	0	0	0	0	24.0	20	99	12	10	2	2	1	0	15	0	13	0	0
*Fernandez, C. Sidney, N.Y.	16	6	.727	3.52	32	31	2	1	1	1	204.1	161	855	82	80	13	9	7	2	91	1	200	6	0
*Fontenot, S. Ray, Chi.	3	5	.375	3.86	42	0	0	11	0	2	56.0	57	241	30	24	5	6	0	0	21	3	24	4	1
Forsch, Robert, St.L.	14	10	.583	3.25	33	33	3	0	0	0	230.0	211	939	91	83	19	5	9	2	68	11	104	7	0
*Franco, John, Cin.	6	6	.500	2.94	74	0	0	52	0	29	101.0	90	429	40	33	7	8	3	2	44	12	84	4	2
Frazier, George, Chi.	2	4	.333	5.40	35	0	0	12	0	0	51.2	63	243	36	31	5	2	3	1	34	4	41	3	0
Freeman, Marvin, Phil.	2	0	1.000	2.25	3	3	0	0	0	0	16.0	6	61	4	4	0	0	1	0	10	0	8	1	0
*Funk, Thomas, Hou.	0	0	—	6.48	8	0	0	2	0	0	8.1	10	41	6	6	1	0	0	0	6	0	2	0	0
Galvez, Balvino, L.A.	0	1	.000	3.92	10	0	0	2	0	0	20.2	19	91	10	9	3	0	0	0	12	2	11	0	2
Garber, H. Eugene, Atl.	5	5	.500	2.54	61	0	0	48	0	24	78.0	76	319	23	22	3	5	1	1	20	7	56	4	0
Garrelts, Scott, S.F.	13	9	.591	3.11	53	18	2	27	0	10	173.2	144	717	65	60	17	10	7	2	74	11	125	9	1
Gooden, Dwight, N.Y.	17	6	.739	2.84	33	33	12	0	2	0	250.0	197	1020	92	79	17	10	8	4	80	3	200	4	4
*Gorman, Thomas, Phil.	0	1	.000	7.71	8	0	0	1	0	0	11.2	21	61	10	10	0	0	1	0	5	1	8	4	0
Gossage, Richard, S.D.	5	7	.417	4.45	45	0	0	38	0	21	64.2	69	281	36	32	8	2	4	2	20	0	63	4	0
Gott, James, S.F.	0	0	—	7.62	9	2	0	3	0	1	13.0	16	66	12	11	0	1	1	0	13	2	9	1	1
Grant, Mark, S.F.	0	1	.000	3.60	4	1	0	3	0	0	10.0	6	39	4	4	0	0	0	0	5	0	5	0	1
*Gross, Gregory, Phil.	0	0	—	0.00	1	0	0	1	0	0	0.2	1	4	0	0	0	0	0	0	1	0	2	0	0
Gross, Kevin, Phil.	12	12	.500	4.02	37	36	7	0	2	0	241.2	240	1040	115	108	28	8	5	8	94	2	154	2	1
Guante, Cecilio, Pitt.	5	2	.714	3.35	52	0	0	24	0	4	78.0	.65	326	32	29	11	3	2	3	29	3	63	2	1
Gullickson, William, Cin.	15	12	.556	3.38	37	37	6	0	2	0	244.2	245	1014	103	92	24	12	13	2	60	10	121	3	0
Gumpert, David, Chi.	2	0	1.000	4.37	38	0	0	12	0	2	59.2	60	259	32	29	4	4	1	1	28	7	45	3	0
*Hall, Andrew, Chi.	1	2	.333	4.56	5	4	1	1	0	1	23.2	24	101	12	12	3	1	0	0	10	0	21	0	0
Hawkins, M. Andrew, S.D.	10	8	.556	4.30	37	35	3	0	1	0	209.1	218	905	111	100	24	7	6	5	75	7	117	6	2
*Hayward, Raymond, S.D.	0	2	.000	9.00	3	3	0	0	0	0	10.0	16	51	12	10	1	0	0	0	4	0	6	5	1

*Hensley, Charles, S.F.	0	0	—	2.45	11	0	0	2	0	1	7.1	5	30	2	2	2	0	0	0	2	0	6	0	1
Hernandez, Manuel, Hou.	2	3	.400	3.90	9	4	0	1	0	0	27.2	33	125	15	12	2	4	1	0	12	3	9	1	0
Hershiser, Orel, L.A.	14	14	.500	3.85	35	35	8	0	1	0	231.1	213	988	112	99	13	14	6	5	86	11	153	12	3
*Hesketh, Joseph, Mtl.	6	5	.545	5.01	15	15	0	0	0	0	82.2	92	362	46	46	11	2	2	2	31	4	67	4	3
*Hoffman, Guy, Chi.	6	2	.750	3.86	32	8	1	6	0	0	84.0	92	357	37	36	6	4	3	2	29	7	47	5	1
Holton, Brian, L.A.	2	3	.400	4.44	12	3	0	4	0	0	24.1	28	106	13	12	1	2	1	1	6	2	24	1	0
*Honeycutt, Frederick, L.A.	11	9	.550	3.32	32	28	0	2	0	0	171.0	164	713	71	63	9	6	1	3	45	4	100	4	1
*Horton, Ricky, St.L.	4	3	.571	2.24	42	9	1	12	0	3	100.1	77	387	25	25	7	3	3	1	26	7	49	1	0
Howell, Kenneth, L.A.	6	12	.333	3.87	62	0	0	36	0	12	97.2	86	437	48	42	7	8	3	3	63	9	104	4	0
Hoyt, D. LaMarr, S.D.	8	11	.421	5.15	35	25	1	2	0	0	159.0	170	699	100	91	27	10	3	3	68	8	85	2	2
Hudson, Charles, Phil.	7	10	.412	4.94	33	23	0	2	0	0	144.0	165	638	87	79	20	10	3	0	58	1	82	2	2
Hume, Thomas, Phil.	4	1	.800	2.77	48	1	0	9	0	4	94.1	89	402	37	29	5	5	7	3	34	5	51	6	0
Iorg, Dane, S.D.	0	0	—	12.00	2	0	0	2	0	0	3.0	5	15	4	4	2	0	0	0	1	0	2	0	0
Jackson, Michael, Phil.	0	0	—	3.38	9	0	0	4	0	0	13.1	12	54	5	5	2	0	0	2	4	1	3	0	0
Johnson, Joseph, Atl.	6	7	.462	4.97	17	15	2	1	0	0	87.0	101	390	58	48	8	3	1	2	35	4	49	1	1
Jones, Barry, Pitt.	3	4	.429	2.89	26	0	0	10	0	3	37.1	29	159	16	12	3	2	1	0	21	2	29	2	0
Jones, James, S.D.	2	0	1.000	2.50	3	3	1	0	1	0	18.0	10	65	6	5	1	1	0	0	3	0	15	0	0
Keough, Matthew, Chi.-Hou.	5	4	.556	3.94	29	7	0	5	0	0	64.0	58	272	31	28	9	3	1	2	30	4	44	6	2
Kepshire, Kurt, St.L.	0	1	.000	4.50	2	1	0	1	0	0	8.0	8	35	4	4	2	0	0	0	4	0	6	0	1
Kerfeld, Charles, Hou.	11	2	.846	2.59	61	0	0	29	0	7	93.2	71	390	32	27	5	6	7	2	42	3	77	7	2
*Kipper, Robert, Pitt.	6	8	.429	4.03	20	19	0	1	0	0	114.0	123	496	60	51	17	3	3	2	34	3	81	3	3
*Knepper, Robert, Hou.	17	12	.586	3.14	40	38	8	1	5	0	258.0	232	1053	100	90	19	22	5	4	62	13	143	5	0
Knudson, Mark, Hou.	1	5	.167	4.22	9	7	0	1	0	0	42.2	48	191	23	20	5	3	0	1	15	5	20	1	0
Krawczyk, Raymond, Pitt.	0	1	.000	7.30	12	0	0	2	0	0	12.1	17	65	13	10	3	1	1	0	10	0	7	0	0
Krukow, Michael, S.F.	20	9	.690	3.05	34	34	10	0	2	0	245.0	204	987	90	83	24	10	5	4	55	4	178	4	0
LaCoss, Michael, S.F.	10	13	.435	3.57	37	31	4	1	1	0	204.1	179	842	99	81	14	16	3	6	70	8	86	5	5
Lahti, Jeffrey, St.L.	0	0	—	0.00	4	0	0	1	0	0	2.1	3	10	0	0	0	0	0	0	1	0	3	0	0
Landrum, T. William, Cin.	0	0	—	6.75	10	0	0	4	0	0	13.1	23	65	11	10	0	1	1	0	4	0	14	0	0
*LaPoint, David, S.D.	1	4	.200	4.26	24	4	0	4	0	0	61.1	67	274	37	29	8	5	1	1	24	4	41	1	4
Laskey, William, S.F.	1	1	.500	4.28	20	0	0	7	0	1	27.1	28	117	14	13	5	1	1	0	13	1	8	0	0
Law, Vance, Mtl.	0	0	—	2.25	3	0	0	3	0	0	4.0	3	16	2	1	0	0	0	0	2	0	0	1	0
Leach, Terry, N.Y.	0	0	—	2.70	6	0	0	1	0	0	6.2	6	30	3	2	0	0	0	0	3	0	4	0	0
*Lefferts, Craig, S.D.	9	8	.529	3.09	83	0	0	36	0	4	107.2	98	446	41	37	7	9	5	1	44	11	72	1	1

Pitcher, Club	W	L	PCT.	ERA	G	GS	CG	GF	SHO	SV	IP	H	TBF	R	ER	HR	SH	SF	HB	BB	IB	SO	WP	BK
*Lerch, Randy, Phil.	1	1	.500	7.88	4	0	0	1	0	0	8.0	10	42	8	7	0	0	0	0	7	1	5	1	0
Lopez, Aurelio, Hou.	3	3	.500	3.46	45	0	0	22	0	7	78.0	64	321	32	30	6	3	4	0	25	1	44	0	0
Lynch, Edward, N.Y.-Chi.	7	5	.583	3.73	24	13	1	3	1	0	101.1	107	416	48	42	10	5	3	1	23	6	58	0	0
*Madden, Michael, Hou.	1	2	.333	4.08	13	6	0	1	0	0	39.2	47	185	20	18	3	4	1	0	22	3	30	5	0
Maddux, Gregory, Chi.	2	4	.333	5.52	6	5	1	1	0	0	31.0	44	144	20	19	3	1	0	1	11	2	20	2	0
Maddux, Michael, Phil.	3	7	.300	5.42	16	16	0	0	0	0	78.0	88	351	56	47	6	3	3	3	34	4	44	4	2
Mahler, Richard, Atl.	14	18	.438	4.88	39	39	7	0	1	0	237.2	283	1056	139	129	25	10	8	3	95	10	137	5	1
Martinez, J. Dennis, Mtl.	3	6	.333	4.59	19	15	1	1	1	0	98.0	103	416	52	50	11	8	1	3	28	4	63	2	2
Mason, Roger, S.F.	3	4	.429	4.80	11	11	1	0	0	0	60.0	56	262	35	32	5	2	3	3	30	3	43	1	0
*Mathews, Gregory, St.L.	11	8	.579	3.65	23	22	1	1	0	0	145.1	139	591	61	59	15	7	1	2	44	3	67	5	6
*McClure, Robert, Mtl.	2	5	.286	3.02	52	0	0	15	0	6	62.2	53	257	22	21	2	3	2	1	23	2	42	1	1
McCullers, Lance, S.D.	10	10	.500	2.78	70	7	0	29	0	5	136.0	103	550	46	42	12	8	3	4	58	9	92	5	3
McDowell, Roger, N.Y.	14	9	.609	3.02	75	0	0	52	0	22	128.0	107	524	48	43	4	7	3	3	42	5	65	3	3
McGaffigan, Andrew, Mtl.	10	5	.667	2.65	48	14	1	8	1	2	142.2	114	583	49	42	9	10	5	2	55	8	104	5	4
McMurtry, J. Craig, Atl.	1	6	.143	4.74	37	5	0	5	0	0	79.2	82	356	46	42	7	0	2	2	43	5	50	2	0
*McWilliams, Larry, Pitt.	3	11	.214	5.15	49	15	0	11	0	0	122.1	129	545	75	70	16	8	0	7	49	5	80	5	0
Minton, Gregory, S.F.	4	4	.500	3.93	48	0	0	28	0	5	68.2	63	296	35	30	4	7	3	1	34	15	34	3	0
Mitchell, John, N.Y.	0	1	.000	3.60	4	1	0	1	0	0	10.0	10	40	4	4	1	0	0	0	4	0	2	2	0
Montalvo, Rafael, Hou.	0	0	—	9.00	1	0	0	0	0	0	1.0	1	6	1	1	0	0	0	0	2	0	0	0	0
*Moyer, Jamie, Chi.	7	4	.636	5.05	16	16	1	0	1	0	87.1	107	395	52	49	10	3	3	3	42	1	45	3	3
*Mulholland, Terence, S.F.	1	7	.125	4.94	15	10	0	1	0	0	54.2	51	245	33	30	3	5	1	1	35	2	27	6	0
*Murphy, Robert, Cin.	6	0	1.000	0.72	34	0	0	12	0	1	50.1	26	195	4	4	0	3	3	0	21	2	36	5	0
*Myers, Randall, N.Y.	0	0	—	4.22	10	0	0	5	0	0	10.2	11	53	5	5	1	0	0	1	9	1	13	0	0
Niedenfuer, Thomas, L.A.	6	6	.500	3.71	60	0	0	27	0	11	80.0	86	345	35	33	11	5	3	1	29	15	55	2	0
*Niemann, Randy, N.Y.	2	3	.400	3.79	31	1	0	11	0	0	35.2	44	158	17	15	2	2	1	0	12	2	18	2	0
*Ojeda, Robert, N.Y.	18	5	.783	2.57	32	30	7	1	2	0	217.1	185	871	72	62	15	10	3	2	52	3	148	2	1
*Olwine, Edward, Atl.	0	0	—	3.40	37	0	0	12	0	1	47.2	35	189	20	18	5	1	1	1	17	7	37	5	2
*Orosco, Jesse, N.Y.	8	6	.571	2.33	58	0	0	40	0	21	81.0	64	338	23	21	6	2	3	3	35	3	62	2	0
*Owchinko, Robert, Mtl.	1	0	1.000	3.60	3	3	0	0	0	0	15.0	17	62	6	6	1	0	0	0	3	0	6	1	0
Ownbey, Richard, St.L.	1	3	.250	3.80	17	3	0	4	0	0	42.2	47	185	20	18	4	2	2	2	19	0	25	2	0
Palmer, David, Atl.	11	10	.524	3.65	35	35	2	0	0	0	209.2	181	889	98	85	17	4	5	5	102	8	170	9	0

Parrett, Jeffrey, Mtl.	0	1	.000	4.87	12	0	0	6	0	0	20.1	19	91	11	11	3	0	1	0	13	0	21	2	0
*Patterson, Bob, Pitt.	2	3	.400	4.95	11	5	0	2	0	0	36.1	49	159	20	20	0	1	1	0	5	2	20	0	1
Pena, Alejandro, L.A.	1	2	.333	4.89	24	10	0	6	0	1	70.0	74	309	40	38	6	3	1	1	30	5	46	1	1
*Pena, Hipolito, Pitt.	0	3	.000	8.64	10	1	0	3	0	1	8.1	7	38	10	8	3	0	0	1	3	1	6	0	0
*Perry, W. Patrick, St.L.	2	3	.400	3.80	46	0	0	20	0	2	68.2	59	288	31	29	5	0	7	0	34	9	29	5	0
*Powell, Dennis, L.A.	2	7	.222	4.27	27	6	0	5	0	0	65.1	65	272	32	31	5	5	2	1	25	7	31	7	2
Power, Ted, Cin.	10	6	.625	3.70	56	10	0	30	0	1	129.0	115	537	59	53	13	9	6	1	52	10	95	5	1
*Price, Joseph, Cin.	1	2	.333	5.40	25	2	0	2	0	0	41.2	49	194	30	25	5	0	5	0	22	2	30	1	0
Puleo, Charles, Atl.	1	2	.333	2.96	5	3	1	2	0	0	24.1	13	97	10	8	4	2	1	1	12	1	18	0	0
*Rawley, Shane, Phil.	11	7	.611	3.54	23	23	7	0	1	0	157.2	166	673	67	62	13	5	2	1	50	4	73	1	1
Reardon, Jeffrey, Mtl.	7	9	.438	3.94	62	0	0	48	0	35	89.0	83	368	42	39	12	9	1	1	26	2	67	0	0
Reuschel, Ricky, Pitt.	9	16	.360	3.96	35	34	4	0	2	0	215.2	232	930	106	95	20	9	10	8	57	2	125	6	1
*Reuss, Jerry, L.A.	2	6	.250	5.84	19	13	0	3	0	1	74.0	96	331	57	48	13	5	0	2	17	4	29	2	0
Reynolds, G. Craig, Hou.	0	0	—	27.00	1	0	0	1	0	0	1.0	3	8	3	3	0	0	0	0	2	0	1	1	0
Rhoden, Richard, Pitt.	15	12	.556	2.84	34	34	12	0	1	0	253.2	211	1015	82	80	17	6	5	2	76	8	159	6	4
*Riley, George, Mtl.	0	0	—	4.15	10	0	0	4	0	0	8.2	7	43	4	4	0	0	1	1	8	3	5	0	0
Roberge, Bertrand, Mtl.	0	4	.000	6.28	21	0	0	10	0	1	28.2	33	128	20	20	2	3	2	1	10	3	20	1	2
Robinson, Don, Pitt.	3	4	.429	3.38	50	0	0	41	0	14	69.1	61	295	27	26	5	5	4	2	27	3	53	4	1
Robinson, Jeffrey, S.F.	6	3	.667	3.36	64	1	0	22	0	8	104.1	92	431	46	39	8	1	3	1	32	7	90	11	0
Robinson, Ronald, Cin.	10	3	.769	3.24	70	0	0	32	0	14	116.2	110	487	44	42	10	4	3	2	43	8	117	3	0
*Rucker, David, Phil.	0	2	.000	5.76	19	0	0	5	0	0	25.0	34	119	19	16	4	2	3	0	14	3	14	2	0
*Ruffin, Bruce, Phil.	9	4	.692	2.46	21	21	6	0	0	0	146.1	138	600	53	40	6	2	4	1	44	6	70	0	1
Ruthven, Richard, Chi.	0	0	—	5.06	6	0	0	3	0	0	10.2	12	47	9	6	4	0	0	0	6	0	3	0	0
Ryan, L. Nolan, Hou.	12	8	.600	3.34	30	30	1	0	0	0	178.0	119	729	72	66	14	5	4	4	82	5	194	15	0
St. Claire, Randy, Mtl.	2	0	1.000	2.37	11	0	0	2	0	1	19.0	13	76	5	5	2	0	0	0	6	1	21	1	0
Sanderson, Scott, Chi.	9	11	.450	4.19	37	28	1	2	1	1	169.2	165	697	85	79	21	6	5	2	37	2	124	3	1
*Sauver, Richard, Pitt.	0	0	—	6.00	3	3	0	0	0	0	12.0	17	57	8	8	3	1	0	2	6	0	6	0	2
*Schatzeder, Daniel, Mtl.-Phil.	6	5	.545	3.26	55	1	0	19	0	2	88.1	81	375	43	32	9	5	3	0	35	9	47	1	0
Scott, Michael, Hou.	18	10	.643	2.22	37	37	7	0	5	0	275.1	182	1065	73	68	17	8	6	2	72	6	306	3	0
Sebra, Robert, Mtl.	5	5	.500	3.55	17	13	3	4	1	0	91.1	82	377	39	36	9	3	3	3	25	2	66	2	3
Shields, Stephen, Atl.	0	0	—	7.11	6	0	0	2	0	0	12.2	13	55	10	10	4	0	0	0	7	0	6	0	0
Show, Eric, S.D.	9	5	.643	2.97	24	22	2	1	0	0	136.1	109	569	47	45	11	10	1	4	69	4	94	3	2
Sisk, Douglas, N.Y.	4	2	.667	3.06	41	0	0	15	0	1	70.2	77	312	31	24	0	3	0	5	31	5	31	2	1

Pitcher, Club	W	L	PCT.	ERA	G	GS	CG	GF	SHO	SV	IP	H	TBF	R	ER	HR	SH	SF	HB	BB	IB	SO	WP	BK
*Smiley, John, Pitt.	1	0	1.000	3.86	12	0	0	2	0	0	11.2	4	42	6	5	2	0	0	0	4	0	9	0	0
Smith, Bryn, Mtl.	10	8	.556	3.94	30	30	1	0	0	0	187.1	182	807	101	82	15	10	3	6	63	6	105	4	2
Smith, David, Hou.	4	7	.364	2.73	54	0	0	51	0	33	56.0	39	223	17	17	5	4	1	1	22	3	46	2	0
Smith, Lee, Chi.	9	9	.500	3.09	66	0	0	59	0	31	90.1	69	372	32	31	7	6	3	0	42	11	93	2	0
Smith, Michael, Cin.	0	0	—	13.50	2	1	0	1	0	0	3.1	7	18	5	5	0	0	0	0	1	0	1	0	0
*Smith, Zane, Atl.	8	16	.333	4.05	38	32	3	2	1	1	204.2	209	889	109	92	8	13	6	5	105	6	139	8	0
Soff, Raymond, St.L.	4	2	.667	3.29	30	0	0	9	0	0	38.1	37	162	17	14	4	2	2	0	13	1	22	2	1
Solano, Julio, Hou.	3	1	.750	7.59	16	1	0	3	0	0	32.0	39	155	28	27	5	3	1	3	22	2	21	3	1
Soto, Mario, Cin.	5	10	.333	4.71	19	19	1	0	1	0	105.0	113	461	61	55	15	6	4	1	46	6	67	3	0
Speck, R. Clifford, Atl.	2	1	.667	4.13	13	1	0	3	0	0	28.1	25	123	13	13	2	1	1	1	15	0	21	2	1
Stewart, David, Phil.	0	0	—	6.57	8	0	0	2	0	0	12.1	15	56	9	9	1	0	3	0	4	0	9	1	3
Stoddard, Robert, S.D.	1	0	1.000	2.31	18	0	0	5	0	1	23.1	20	102	7	6	1	1	1	1	11	1	17	2	0
Stoddard, Timothy, S.D.	1	3	.250	3.77	30	0	0	9	0	0	45.1	33	203	20	19	6	4	0	0	34	6	47	2	0
Sutcliffe, Richard, Chi.	5	14	.263	4.64	28	27	4	0	1	0	176.2	166	764	92	91	18	6	2	1	96	8	122	13	1
Sutter, H. Bruce, Atl.	2	0	1.000	4.34	16	0	0	11	0	3	18.2	17	80	9	9	3	1	0	0	9	2	16	0	0
Tekulve, Kenton, Phil.	11	5	.688	2.54	73	0	0	34	0	4	110.0	99	446	35	31	2	4	4	0	25	10	57	3	1
Terry, Scott, Cin.	1	2	.333	6.14	28	3	0	7	0	0	55.2	66	258	40	38	8	5	1	0	32	3	32	2	0
*Thurmond, Mark, S.D.	3	7	.300	6.50	17	15	2	0	1	0	70.2	96	328	58	51	7	4	2	0	27	5	32	0	1
Tibbs, Jay, Mtl.	7	9	.438	3.97	35	31	3	2	2	0	190.1	181	797	96	84	12	13	4	3	70	3	117	7	2
Toliver, Freddie, Phil.	0	2	.000	3.51	5	5	0	0	0	0	25.2	28	112	14	10	0	3	0	0	11	0	20	2	0
*Tomlin, David, Mtl.	0	0	—	5.23	7	0	0	6	0	0	10.1	13	52	8	6	1	2	1	1	7	2	6	1	0
*Trout, Steven, Chi.	5	7	.417	4.75	37	25	0	3	0	0	161.0	184	711	88	85	6	9	6	1	78	13	69	6	1
*Tudor, John, St.L.	13	7	.650	2.92	30	30	3	0	0	0	219.0	197	879	81	71	22	9	8	1	53	5	107	2	1
Valdez, Sergio, Mtl.	0	4	.000	6.84	5	5	0	0	0	0	25.0	39	120	20	19	2	0	0	1	11	0	20	2	0
*Valenzuela, Fernando, L.A.	21	11	.656	3.14	34	34	20	0	3	0	269.1	226	1102	104	94	18	15	3	1	85	5	242	13	0
*Vande Berg, Edward, L.A.	1	5	.167	3.41	60	0	0	29	0	0	71.1	83	325	32	27	8	4	1	1	33	7	42	1	0
*Vosberg, Edward, S.D.	0	1	.000	6.59	5	3	0	0	0	0	13.2	17	65	11	10	1	0	0	0	9	1	8	0	1
Walk, Robert, Pitt.	7	8	.467	3.75	44	15	1	7	1	2	141.2	129	592	66	59	14	6	5	3	64	7	78	12	1
*Walter, Gene, S.D.	2	2	.500	3.86	57	0	0	19	0	1	98.0	89	422	47	42	7	5	3	4	49	7	84	6	0
Ward, R. Duane, Atl.	0	1	.000	7.31	10	0	0	6	0	0	16.0	22	73	13	13	2	2	0	0	8	0	8	0	1
Welch, Robert, L.A.	7	13	.350	3.28	33	33	7	0	3	0	235.2	227	981	95	86	14	7	8	7	55	6	183	2	1

*Welsh, Christopher, Cin.	6	9	.400	4.78	24	24	1	0	0	0	139.1	163	598	79	74	9	10	4	3	40	4	40	5	0
Whitson, Eddie, S.D.	1	7	.125	5.59	17	12	0	0	0	0	75.2	85	337	48	47	8	2	2	0	37	0	46	1	0
Williams, Frank, S.F.	3	1	.750	1.20	36	0	0	12	0	1	52.1	35	194	8	7	0	3	1	4	21	4	33	1	0
Willis, Carl, Cin.	1	3	.250	4.47	29	0	0	7	0	0	52.1	54	233	29	26	4	5	1	1	32	9	24	3	1
Winn, James, Pitt.	3	5	.375	3.58	50	3	0	18	0	3	88.0	85	377	44	35	9	4	3	2	38	7	70	9	1
Wojna, Edward, S.D.	2	2	.500	3.23	7	7	1	0	0	0	39.0	42	176	19	14	2	2	0	1	16	3	19	0	0
Worrell, Todd, St.L.	9	10	.474	2.08	74	0	0	60	0	36	103.2	86	430	29	24	9	7	6	1	41	16	73	1	0
Youmans, Floyd, Mtl.	13	12	.520	3.53	33	32	6	1	2	0	219.0	145	905	93	86	14	6	7	4	118	4	202	10	1

CLUB PITCHING

Club	W	L	ERA	G	CG	SHO	SV	IP	H	TBF	R	ER	HR	SH	SF	HB	BB	IB	SO	WP	BK
New York	108	54	3.11	162	27	11	46	1484.0	1304	6165	578	513	103	62	43	31	509	29	1083	40	16
Houston	96	66	3.15	162	18	19	51	1456.1	1203	6010	569	509	116	82	42	23	523	60	1160	50	11
San Francisco	83	79	3.33	162	18	10	35	1460.1	1264	6093	618	541	121	79	44	29	591	78	992	58	15
St. Louis	79	82	3.37	161	17	4	46	1466.1	1364	6061	611	549	135	53	54	22	485	73	761	38	13
Los Angeles	73	89	3.76	162	35	14	25	1454.1	1428	6199	679	608	115	75	30	26	499	79	1051	51	10
Montreal	78	83	3.78	161	15	9	50	1466.1	1350	6208	688	616	119	80	38	33	566	61	1051	49	20
Philadelphia	86	75	3.85	161	22	11	39	1451.2	1473	6244	713	621	130	58	47	22	553	71	874	45	17
Pittsburgh	64	98	3.90	162	17	9	30	1450.2	1397	6201	700	629	138	66	46	37	570	55	924	59	20
Cincinnati	86	76	3.91	162	14	8	45	1468.0	1465	6240	717	638	136	86	60	17	524	81	924	39	5
Atlanta	72	89	3.97	161	17	5	39	1424.2	1443	6125	719	629	117	70	34	26	576	63	932	44	11
San Diego	74	88	3.99	162	13	7	32	1443.1	1406	6212	723	640	150	82	36	27	607	75	934	38	18
Chicago	70	90	4.49	160	11	6	42	1445.0	1546	6248	781	721	143	76	45	19	557	78	962	55	20
TOTALS	969	969	3.72	969	224	113	480	17471.0	16643	74006	8096	7214	1523	869	519	312	6560	803	11648	566	176

OFFICIAL 1986 AMERICAN LEAGUE RECORDS

compiled by

SPORTS INFORMATION CENTER

FINAL STANDINGS OF CLUBS AT CLOSE OF 1986 SEASON

American League West

	Won	Lost	Pct.	Games Behind
California	92	70	.568	
Texas	87	75	.537	5
Kansas City	76	86	.469	16
Oakland	76	86	.469	16
Chicago	72	90	.444	20
Minnesota	71	91	.438	21
Seattle	67	95	.414	25

American League East

	Won	Lost	Pct.	Games Behind
Boston	95	66	.590	
New York	90	72	.556	5½
Detroit	87	75	.537	8½
Toronto	86	76	.531	9½
Cleveland	84	78	.519	11½
Milwaukee	77	84	.478	18
Baltimore	73	89	.451	22½

Championship Series: Boston defeated California, 4 games to 3

TOP FIFTEEN QUALIFIERS FOR BATTING CHAMPIONSHIP
(502 OR MORE PLATE APPEARANCES)

* BATS LEFTHANDED †SWITCH HITTER

BATTER AND CLUB	AVG	G	AB	R	H	TB	2B	3B	HR	RBI	GW RBI	SH	SF	HB	BB	IBB	SO	SB	CS	GI DP	SLG	OBP
BOGGS, WADE, BOS.*	.357	149	580	107	207	282	47	2	8	71	10	4	4	0	105	14	44	0	4	11	.486	.453
MATTINGLY, DON, N.Y.*	.352	162	677	117	238	388	53	2	31	113	15	1	10	1	53	11	35	0	0	17	.573	.394
PUCKETT, KIRBY, MINN.	.328	161	680	119	223	365	37	6	31	96	5	2	0	7	34	4	99	20	12	14	.537	.366
TABLER, PAT, CLEV	.326	130	473	61	154	205	29	2	6	48	8	2	1	3	29	3	75	3	1	11	.433	.368
RICE, JIM, BOS	.324	157	618	98	200	303	39	2	20	110	12	0	9	4	62	5	78	0	1	19	.490	.384
YOUNT, ROBIN, MILW	.312	140	522	82	163	235	31	7	9	46	8	5	2	4	62	7	73	14	5	9	.450	.388
FERNANDEZ, TONY, TOR.†	.310	163	687	91	213	294	33	9	10	65	8	5	4	4	27	0	52	25	12	8	.428	.338
BRADLEY, PHIL, SEA	.310	143	526	88	163	234	27	4	12	50	5	1	2	8	77	1	134	21	12	9	.445	.405
BELL, GEORGE, TOR	.309	159	641	101	198	341	38	6	31	108	15	0	6	2	41	3	62	7	8	15	.532	.349
FRANCO, JULIO, CLEV.	.306	149	599	80	183	253	30	5	10	74	9	0	5	0	32	1	66	10	7	28	.422	.338
MURRAY, EDDIE, BALT.†	.305	137	495	61	151	229	25	1	17	84	4	0	5	0	78	7	49	3	0	17	.463	.396
EASLER, MIKE, N.Y.*	.302	146	490	64	148	220	26	2	14	78	7	2	5	0	49	13	87	3	2	17	.449	.362
CARTER, JOE, CLEV	.302	162	663	108	200	341	36	9	29	121	11	1	8	5	32	3	95	29	7	8	.514	.335
BERNAZARD, TONY, CLEV.†	.301	146	562	88	169	256	28	4	17	73	11	7	8	6	53	5	77	17	8	6	.456	.362
FLETCHER, SCOTT, TEX.	.300	147	530	82	159	212	34	5	3	50	6	10	3	4	47	0	59	12	11	10	.400	.360

INDIVIDUAL BATTING
(ALL PLAYERS LISTED ALPHABETICALLY)

* BATS LEFTHANDED †SWITCH HITTER

BATTER AND CLUB	AVG	G	AB	R	H	TB	2B	3B	HR	RBI	GW RBI	SH	SF	HB	BB	IBB	SO	SB	CS	GI DP	SLG	OBP
ADDUCI, JIM, MILW.*	.091	3	11	2	1	2	1	0	0	0	0	1	0	0	1	0	2	0	0	0	.182	.167
ALLANSON, ANDY, CLEV	.225	101	293	30	66	82	7	3	1	29	1	11	4	1	14	0	36	10	1	7	.280	.260

* BATS LEFTHANDED †SWITCH HITTER

BATTER AND CLUB	AVG	G	AB	R	H	TB	2B	3B	HR	RBI	GW RBI	SH	SF	HB	BB	IBB	SO	SB	CS	GI DP	SLG	OBP
ANDERSON, ALLEN, MINN.*	—	22	0	0	0	0	0	0	0	0	0	0	0	0	0	0	0	0	0	0	—	—
ARMAS, TONY, BOS.	.264	121	425	40	112	174	21	4	11	58	6	0	2	2	24	1	77	0	3	12	.409	.305
BAINES, HAROLD, CHI.*	.296	145	570	72	169	265	29	2	21	88	10	0	8	2	38	9	89	2	1	14	.465	.338
BAKER, DOUG, DET.†	.125	13	24	1	3	4	1	0	0	0	0	4	0	0	2	0	7	0	0	0	.167	.192
BAKER, DUSTY, OAK	.240	83	242	25	58	78	8	0	4	19	1	0	2	0	27	1	37	0	1	8	.322	.314
BALBONI, STEVE, K.C	.229	138	512	54	117	231	25	1	29	88	9	0	6	1	43	2	146	0	0	8	.451	.286
BANDO, CHRIS, CLEV.†	.268	92	254	28	68	83	9	0	2	26	3	10	3	1	22	0	49	0	1	8	.327	.325
BARFIELD, JESSE, TOR.	.289	158	589	107	170	329	35	2	40	108	13	0	5	8	69	5	146	8	8	9	.559	.368
BARRETT, MARTY, BOS	.286	158	625	94	179	238	39	4	4	60	9	18	4	1	65	0	31	15	7	13	.381	.353
BATHE, BILL, OAK	.184	39	103	9	19	37	3	0	5	11	1	6	0	1	2	0	20	0	0	2	.359	.208
BAYLOR, DON, BOS.	.238	160	585	93	139	257	23	1	31	94	13	0	5	35	62	8	111	3	5	12	.439	.344
BEANE, BILLY, MINN	.213	80	183	20	39	54	6	0	3	15	2	0	0	0	11	0	54	2	3	6	.295	.258
BELL, GEORGE, TOR	.309	159	641	101	198	341	38	6	31	108	15	0	6	2	41	3	62	7	8	15	.532	.349
BELL, JAY, CLEV	.357	5	14	3	5	10	2	0	1	4	0	0	0	0	2	0	3	0	0	0	.714	.438
BELL, TERRY, K.C	.000	8	3	0	0	0	0	0	0	0	0	0	0	0	2	0	1	0	0	0	.000	.400
BENIQUEZ, JUAN, BALT	.300	113	343	48	103	136	15	0	6	36	1	2	6	3	40	1	49	2	3	12	.397	.372
BERGMAN, DAVE, DET.*	.231	65	130	14	30	41	6	1	1	9	3	0	0	0	21	0	16	0	0	3	.315	.338
BERNAZARD, TONY, CLEV.†	.301	146	562	88	169	256	28	4	17	73	11	7	8	6	53	5	77	17	8	6	.456	.362
BERRA, DALE, N.Y	.231	42	108	10	25	38	7	0	2	13	2	2	1	1	9	0	14	0	0	0	.352	.294
BIANCALANA, BUDDY, K.C.†	.242	100	190	24	46	64	4	4	2	8	0	4	0	0	15	0	50	5	1	3	.337	.298
BOCHTE, BRUCE, OAK.*	.256	125	407	57	104	137	13	1	6	43	5	0	1	0	65	3	68	3	2	9	.337	.357
BOGGS, WADE, BOS.*	.357	149	580	107	207	282	47	2	8	71	10	4	4	0	105	14	44	0	4	11	.486	.453
BONILLA, BOBBY, CHI.†	.269	75	234	27	63	83	10	2	2	26	1	2	1	1	33	2	49	4	1	4	.355	.361
BONILLA, JUAN, BALT	.243	102	284	33	69	84	10	1	1	18	1	4	0	3	25	0	21	0	0	14	.296	.311
BONNELL, BARRY, SEA	.196	17	51	4	10	12	2	0	0	4	0	0	1	0	1	0	13	0	1	2	.235	.208
BOONE, BOB, CAL	.222	144	442	48	98	135	12	2	7	49	4	12	6	0	43	1	30	1	0	15	.305	.287
BOSTON, DARYL, CHI.*	.266	56	199	29	53	85	11	3	5	22	3	3	1	0	21	3	33	9	5	4	.427	.335
BRADLEY, PHIL, SEA	.310	143	526	88	163	234	27	4	12	50	5	1	2	8	77	1	134	21	12	9	.445	.405
BRADLEY, SCOTT, CHI.-SEA.*	.300	77	220	20	66	95	8	3	5	28	1	2	2	4	13	4	7	1	2	13	.432	.347
BRAGGS, GLENN, MILW	.237	58	215	19	51	75	8	2	4	18	1	2	3	1	11	0	47	1	1	6	.349	.274

BRANTLEY, MICKEY, SEA.	.196	27	102	12	20	36	3	2	3	7	1	1	0	0	10	0	21	1	1	3	.353	.268
BRETT, GEORGE, K.C.*	.290	124	441	70	128	212	28	4	16	73	10	0	4	4	80	18	45	1	2	6	.481	.401
BREWER, MIKE, K.C	.167	12	18	0	3	4	1	0	0	0	0	0	0	0	2	0	6	0	1	0	.222	.250
BROOKENS, TOM, DET	.270	98	281	42	76	100	11	2	3	25	1	6	2	1	20	0	42	11	8	4	.356	.319
BROWER, BOB, TEX	.111	21	9	3	1	2	1	0	0	0	0	0	0	0	0	0	3	1	2	0	.222	.111
BROWNE, JERRY, TEX.†	.417	12	24	6	10	12	2	0	0	3	0	0	0	0	1	0	4	0	2	0	.500	.440
BRUNANSKY, TOM, MINN	.256	157	593	69	152	251	28	1	23	75	6	1	7	1	53	4	98	12	4	15	.423	.315
BUCKNER, BILL, BOS.*	.267	153	629	73	168	265	39	2	18	102	12	0	8	4	40	9	25	6	4	25	.421	.311
BUECHELE, STEVE, TEX	.243	153	461	54	112	189	19	2	18	54	7	9	3	5	35	1	98	5	8	10	.410	.302
BURLESON, RICK, CAL	.284	93	271	35	77	106	14	0	5	29	1	6	1	1	33	1	32	1	3	2	.391	.363
BUSH, RANDY, MINN.*	.269	130	357	50	96	150	19	7	7	45	3	1	1	4	39	2	63	5	3	7	.420	.347
BUTLER, BRETT, CLEV.*	.278	161	587	92	163	220	17	14	4	51	6	17	5	4	70	1	65	32	15	8	.375	.356
CALDERON, IVAN, SEA.-CHI	.250	50	164	16	41	56	7	1	2	15	3	0	0	1	9	1	39	3	1	1	.341	.293
CANGELOSI, JOHN, CHI.†	.235	137	438	65	103	131	16	3	2	32	3	6	3	7	71	0	61	50	17	5	.299	.349
CANSECO, JOSE, OAK	.240	157	600	85	144	274	29	1	33	117	14	0	9	8	65	1	175	15	7	12	.457	.318
CARTER, JOE, CLEV	.302	162	663	108	200	341	36	9	29	121	11	1	8	5	32	3	95	29	7	8	.514	.335
CASTILLO, CARMEN, CLEV	.278	85	205	34	57	90	9	0	8	32	1	1	1	1	9	0	48	2	1	9	.439	.310
CASTILLO, JUAN, MILW.†	.167	26	54	6	9	11	0	1	0	5	0	2	0	1	5	0	12	1	1	2	.204	.250
CERONE, RICK, MILW	.259	68	216	22	56	82	14	0	4	18	2	5	5	1	15	0	28	1	1	5	.380	.304
CLARK, DAVE, CLEV.*	.276	18	58	10	16	26	1	0	3	9	0	2	1	0	7	0	11	1	0	1	.448	.348
COCHRANE, DAVE, CHI.†	.194	19	62	4	12	17	2	0	1	2	0	1	0	0	5	1	22	0	0	2	.274	.254
COLES, DARNELL, DET	.273	142	521	67	142	236	30	2	20	86	7	7	8	6	45	3	84	6	2	8	.453	.333
COLLINS, DAVE, DET.†	.270	124	419	44	113	138	18	2	1	27	2	9	2	2	44	0	49	27	12	9	.329	.340
COOPER, CECIL, MILW.*	.258	134	542	46	140	202	24	1	12	75	6	1	4	1	41	2	87	1	2	15	.373	.310
COTTO, HENRY, N.Y.	.213	35	80	11	17	23	3	0	1	6	0	0	1	0	2	0	17	3	0	3	.288	.229
COWENS, AL, SEA.	.183	28	82	5	15	19	4	0	0	6	1	1	1	0	3	0	18	1	0	3	.232	.209
COWLEY, JOE, CHI.*	—	28	0	0	0	0	0	0	0	0	0	0	0	0	0	0	0	0	0	0	—	—
CRAIG, RODNEY, CHI.†	.200	10	10	3	2	2	0	0	0	0	0	0	0	0	2	0	2	0	0	0	.200	.333
CRUZ, JULIO, CHI.†	.215	81	209	38	45	47	2	0	0	19	2	2	3	0	42	0	28	7	2	4	.225	.343
DAVID, ANDRE, MINN.*	.200	5	5	0	1	1	0	0	0	0	0	0	0	1	0	0	2	0	0	0	.200	.333
DAVIDSON, MARK, MINN	.118	36	68	5	8	11	3	0	0	2	0	3	0	0	6	0	22	2	3	1	.162	.189
DAVIS, ALVIN, SEA.*	.271	135	479	66	130	204	18	1	18	72	8	2	2	3	76	10	68	0	3	11	.426	.373
DAVIS, MIKE, OAK.*	.268	142	489	77	131	222	28	3	19	55	5	4	5	1	34	2	91	27	4	7	.454	.314
DAWLEY, BILL, CHI	.000	46	2	0	0	0	0	0	0	0	0	0	0	0	0	0	0	0	0	0	.000	.000

* BATS LEFTHANDED †SWITCH HITTER

BATTER AND CLUB	AVG	G	AB	R	H	TB	2B	3B	HR	RBI	GW RBI	SH	SF	HB	BB	IBB	SO	SB	CS	GI DP	SLG	OBP
DECINCES, DOUG, CAL	.256	140	512	69	131	235	20	3	26	96	13	2	4	2	52	4	74	2	2	19	.459	.325
DEER, BOB, MILW	.232	134	466	75	108	230	17	3	33	86	5	2	3	3	72	3	179	5	2	4	.494	.336
DEJESUS, IVAN, N.Y	.000	7	4	1	0	0	0	0	0	0	0	0	0	0	1	0	1	0	0	0	.000	.200
DEMPSEY, RICK, BALT	.208	122	327	42	68	124	15	1	13	29	5	7	0	3	45	0	78	1	0	5	.379	.309
DIAZ, EDGAR, MILW	.231	5	13	0	3	3	0	0	0	0	0	0	0	0	1	0	3	0	0	0	.231	.286
DODD, TOM, BALT	.231	8	13	1	3	6	0	0	1	2	0	0	0	1	2	0	2	0	0	1	.462	.375
DODSON, PAT, BOS.*	.417	9	12	3	5	10	2	0	1	3	0	0	0	0	3	0	3	0	0	0	.833	.533
DOWNING, BRIAN, CAL	.267	152	513	90	137	232	27	4	20	95	13	3	8	17	90	2	84	4	4	14	.452	.389
DWYER, JIM, BALT.*	.244	94	160	18	39	78	13	1	8	31	3	0	4	2	23	1	31	0	2	2	.488	.339
EASLER, MIKE, N.Y.*	.302	146	490	64	148	220	26	2	14	78	7	2	5	0	49	13	87	3	2	17	.449	.362
ENGLE, DAVE, DET	.256	35	86	6	22	29	7	0	0	4	1	0	0	0	7	0	13	0	0	2	.337	.312
ESPINO, JUAN, N.Y	.162	27	37	1	6	8	2	0	0	5	1	0	1	0	2	0	9	0	0	0	.216	.200
ESPINOZA, ALVARO, MINN	.214	37	42	4	9	10	1	0	0	1	0	2	0	0	1	0	10	0	1	0	.238	.233
EVANS, DARRELL, DET.*	.241	151	507	78	122	224	15	0	29	85	10	0	2	1	91	5	105	3	2	6	.442	.356
EVANS, DWIGHT, BOS	.259	152	529	86	137	252	33	2	26	97	8	2	6	6	97	4	117	3	3	11	.476	.376
FELDER, MIKE, MILW.†	.239	44	155	24	37	50	2	4	1	13	2	1	5	0	13	1	16	16	2	2	.323	.289
FERNANDEZ, TONY, TOR.†	.310	163	687	91	213	294	33	9	10	65	8	5	4	4	27	0	52	25	12	8	.428	.338
FIELDER, CECIL, TOR	.157	34	83	7	13	27	2	0	4	13	1	0	0	1	6	0	27	0	0	3	.325	.222
FIELDS, BRUCE, DET	.279	16	43	4	12	15	1	1	0	6	1	1	2	0	1	0	6	1	1	0	.349	.283
FISCHLIN, MIKE, N.Y	.206	71	102	9	21	23	2	0	0	3	0	5	1	0	8	0	29	0	1	3	.225	.261
FISK, CARLTON, CHI	.221	125	457	42	101	154	11	0	14	63	7	0	6	6	22	2	92	2	4	10	.337	.263
FLETCHER, SCOTT, TEX	.300	147	530	82	159	212	34	5	3	50	6	10	3	4	47	0	59	12	11	10	.400	.360
FONTENOT, RAY, MINN.*	.000	15	1	0	0	0	0	0	0	0	0	0	0	0	0	0	1	0	0	0	.000	.000
FOSTER, GEORGE, CHI	.216	15	51	2	11	18	0	2	1	4	0	0	0	0	3	0	8	0	0	2	.353	.259
FRANCO, JULIO, CLEV	.306	149	599	80	183	253	30	5	10	74	9	0	5	0	32	1	66	10	7	28	.422	.338
GAETTI, GARY, MINN	.287	157	596	91	171	309	34	1	34	108	12	1	6	6	52	4	108	14	15	18	.518	.347
GAGNE, GREG, MINN	.250	156	472	63	118	188	22	6	12	54	10	13	3	6	30	0	108	12	10	4	.398	.301
GALLEGO, MIKE, OAK	.270	20	37	2	10	12	2	0	0	4	0	2	0	0	1	0	6	0	2	0	.324	.289
GANTNER, JIM, MILW.*	.274	139	497	58	136	184	25	1	7	38	4	6	7	6	26	2	50	13	7	13	.370	.313
GARCIA, DAMASO, TOR	.281	122	424	57	119	159	22	0	6	46	7	2	3	4	13	0	32	9	6	14	.375	.306

GEDMAN, RICH, BOS.*	.258	135	462	49	119	196	29	0	16	65	6	1	5	4	37	13	61	1	0	15	.424	.315
GERHART, KEN, BALT	.232	20	69	4	16	21	2	0	1	7	0	0	2	0	4	0	18	0	1	1	.304	.267
GIBSON, KIRK, DET.*	.268	119	441	84	118	217	11	2	28	86	12	1	4	7	68	4	107	34	6	8	.492	.371
GILES, BRIAN, CHI	.273	9	11	0	3	3	0	0	0	1	0	0	0	0	0	0	2	0	0	1	.273	.273
GREENWELL, MIKE, BOS.*	.314	31	35	4	11	13	2	0	0	4	0	0	0	0	5	0	7	0	0	1	.371	.400
GRICH, BOBBY, CAL	.268	98	313	42	84	129	18	0	9	30	4	10	1	3	39	1	54	1	3	9	.412	.354
GRIFFEY, KEN, N.Y.*	.303	59	198	33	60	94	7	0	9	26	2	1	4	1	15	0	24	2	2	7	.475	.349
GRIFFIN, ALFREDO, OAK.†	.285	162	594	74	169	216	23	6	4	51	8	12	6	2	35	6	52	33	16	5	.364	.323
GROSS, WAYNE, OAK.*	.000	3	2	0	0	0	0	0	0	0	0	0	0	0	1	0	0	0	0	0	.000	.333
GRUBB, JOHN, DET.*	.333	81	210	32	70	124	13	1	13	51	6	0	3	2	28	0	28	0	1	0	.590	.412
GRUBER, KELLY, TOR	.196	87	143	20	28	49	4	1	5	15	0	2	2	0	5	0	27	2	5	4	.343	.220
GUILLEN, OZZIE, CHI.*	.250	159	547	58	137	170	19	4	2	47	8	12	5	1	12	1	52	8	4	14	.311	.265
GUTIERREZ, JACKIE, BALT	.186	61	145	8	27	30	3	0	0	4	0	2	1	1	3	0	27	3	1	3	.207	.207
HAIRSTON, JERRY, CHI.†	.271	101	225	32	61	91	15	0	5	26	4	0	1	1	26	3	26	0	0	9	.404	.348
HALL, MEL, CLEV.*	.296	140	442	68	131	218	29	2	18	77	3	0	3	2	33	8	65	6	2	8	.493	.346
HARPER, BRIAN, DET	.139	19	36	2	5	6	1	0	0	3	0	1	1	0	3	0	3	0	0	1	.167	.200
HARRAH, TOBY, TEX	.218	95	289	36	63	106	18	2	7	41	0	3	3	2	44	0	53	2	5	7	.367	.322
HASSEY, RON, N.Y.-CHI.*	.323	113	341	45	110	164	25	1	9	49	4	1	2	3	46	3	27	1	1	15	.481	.406
HATCHER, MICKEY, MINN	.278	115	317	40	88	116	13	3	3	32	0	0	4	0	19	2	26	2	1	8	.366	.315
HEARRON, JEFF, TOR	.217	12	23	2	5	6	1	0	0	4	0	0	0	0	3	0	7	0	0	1	.261	.308
HEATH, MIKE, DET	.265	30	98	11	26	41	3	0	4	11	2	0	1	0	4	0	17	4	1	1	.418	.291
HENDERSON, DAVE, SEA.-BOS	.265	139	388	59	103	178	22	4	15	47	4	2	1	2	39	4	110	2	3	6	.459	.335
HENDERSON, RICKEY, N.Y	.263	153	608	130	160	285	31	5	28	74	9	0	2	2	89	2	81	87	18	12	.469	.358
HENDERSON, STEVE, OAK	.077	11	26	2	2	3	1	0	0	3	0	0	1	0	0	0	5	0	0	3	.115	.074
HENDRICK, GEORGE, CAL	.272	102	283	45	77	134	13	1	14	47	2	4	3	1	26	5	41	1	1	11	.473	.332
HENGEL, DAVE, SEA	.190	21	63	3	12	16	1	0	1	6	1	1	0	1	1	0	13	0	0	1	.254	.215
HERNANDEZ, LEO, N.Y	.227	7	22	2	5	10	2	0	1	4	1	0	0	0	1	0	8	0	0	0	.455	.261
HERNDON, LARRY, DET	.247	106	283	33	70	109	13	1	8	37	5	0	5	1	27	2	40	2	1	3	.385	.310
HILL, DONNIE, OAK.†	.283	108	339	37	96	128	16	2	4	29	4	4	0	0	23	1	38	5	2	9	.378	.329
HILL, MARC, CHI.	.158	22	19	2	3	3	0	0	0	0	0	0	0	1	1	0	3	0	0	0	.158	.238
HOFFMAN, GLENN, BOS	.217	12	23	1	5	7	2	0	0	1	0	0	1	0	2	0	3	0	0	1	.304	.269
HOUSEHOLDER, PAUL, MILW.†	.218	26	78	4	17	25	3	1	1	16	0	2	2	1	7	0	16	1	2	1	.321	.284
HOWELL, JACK, CAL.*	.272	63	151	26	41	71	14	2	4	21	3	3	2	0	19	0	28	2	0	1	.470	.349
HRBEK, KENT, MINN.*	.267	149	550	85	147	263	27	1	29	91	11	0	7	6	71	9	81	2	2	15	.478	.353

* BATS LEFTHANDED †SWITCH HITTER

BATTER AND CLUB	AVG	G	AB	R	H	TB	2B	3B	HR	RBI	GW RBI	SH	SF	HB	BB	IBB	SO	SB	CS	GI DP	SLG	OBP
HUDLER, REX, BALT	.000	14	1	1	0	0	0	0	0	0	0	0	0	0	0	0	0	1	0	0	.000	.000
HULETT, TIM, CHI	.231	150	520	53	120	197	16	5	17	44	4	6	4	1	21	0	91	4	1	11	.379	.260
INCAVIGLIA, PETE, TEX	.250	153	540	82	135	250	21	2	30	88	11	0	7	4	55	2	185	3	2	9	.463	.320
IORG, GARTH, TOR	.260	137	327	30	85	115	19	1	3	44	2	1	2	1	20	0	47	3	0	7	.352	.303
JACKSON, BO, K.C	.207	25	82	9	17	27	2	1	2	9	1	0	0	2	7	0	34	3	1	1	.329	.286
JACKSON, REGGIE, CAL.*	.241	132	419	65	101	171	12	2	18	58	9	0	3	3	92	11	115	1	1	14	.408	.379
JACOBY, BROOK, CLEV	.288	158	583	83	168	257	30	4	17	80	9	1	1	0	56	5	137	2	1	15	.441	.350
JAVIER, STAN, OAK.†	.202	59	114	13	23	31	8	0	0	8	1	0	0	1	16	0	27	8	0	2	.272	.305
JOHNSON, CLIFF, TOR	.250	107	336	48	84	143	12	1	15	55	4	0	2	4	52	1	57	0	1	9	.426	.355
JOHNSON, RONDIN, K.C.†	.258	11	31	1	8	10	0	1	0	2	0	0	0	0	0	0	3	0	0	0	.323	.258
JONES, BOBBY, TEX.*	.095	13	21	1	2	2	0	0	0	3	1	0	0	0	2	0	5	0	0	0	.095	.174
JONES, LYNN, K.C.	.128	67	47	1	6	8	2	0	0	1	0	1	0	0	6	0	5	0	0	2	.170	.226
JONES, RICKIE, BALT	.182	16	33	2	6	8	2	0	0	4	0	0	0	0	6	0	8	0	0	0	.242	.308
JONES, ROSS, SEA	.095	11	21	0	2	2	0	0	0	0	0	0	0	0	0	0	4	0	1	0	.095	.095
JONES, RUPPERT, CAL.*	.229	126	393	73	90	168	21	3	17	49	3	7	3	3	64	5	87	10	3	8	.427	.339
JOYNER, WALLY, CAL.*	.290	154	593	82	172	271	27	3	22	100	14	10	12	2	57	8	58	5	2	11	.457	.348
KARKOVICE, RON, CHI	.247	37	97	13	24	43	7	0	4	13	1	1	1	1	9	0	37	1	0	3	.443	.315
KEARNEY, BOB, SEA	.240	81	204	23	49	77	10	0	6	25	2	9	1	0	12	1	35	0	2	6	.377	.281
KIEFER, STEVE, MILW	.000	2	6	0	0	0	0	0	0	0	0	0	0	0	0	0	4	0	0	0	.000	.000
KINGERY, MIKE, K.C.*	.258	62	209	25	54	81	8	5	3	14	1	0	2	0	12	2	30	7	3	4	.388	.296
KINGMAN, DAVE, OAK	.210	144	561	70	118	242	19	0	35	94	10	0	7	3	33	3	126	3	3	16	.431	.255
KITTLE, RON, CHI.-N.Y	.218	116	376	42	82	158	13	0	21	60	4	0	8	3	35	1	110	4	1	10	.420	.284
KUNKEL, JEFF, TEX	.231	8	13	3	3	6	0	0	1	2	0	0	0	0	0	0	2	0	0	0	.462	.231
LACY, LEE, BALT	.287	130	491	77	141	192	18	0	11	47	6	4	5	0	37	2	71	4	6	12	.391	.334
LAGA, MIKE, DET.*	.200	15	45	6	9	19	1	0	3	8	1	0	0	0	5	1	13	0	0	0	.422	.280
LANGFORD, RICK, OAK	—	17	0	0	0	0	0	0	0	0	0	0	0	0	0	0	0	0	0	0	—	—
LANSFORD, CARNEY, OAK	.284	151	591	80	168	249	16	4	19	72	10	1	4	5	39	2	51	16	7	16	.421	.332
LAUDNER, TIM, MINN	.244	76	193	21	47	87	10	0	10	29	5	1	2	3	24	0	56	1	0	5	.451	.333
LAW, RUDI, K.C.*	.261	87	307	42	80	119	26	5	1	36	4	2	1	2	29	0	22	14	6	5	.388	.327
LEACH, RICK, TOR.*	.309	110	246	35	76	107	14	1	5	39	2	0	7	0	13	3	24	0	0	6	.435	.335

LEE, MANNY, TOR.†	.205	35	78	8	16	21	0	1	1	7	2	2	1	0	4	0	10	0	1	5	.269	.241
LEMON, CHET, DET	.251	126	403	45	101	164	21	3	12	53	5	3	4	8	39	3	53	2	1	15	.407	.326
LITTLE, BRYAN, CHI.-N.Y.†	.184	34	76	6	14	16	2	0	0	2	0	0	0	0	6	0	11	0	0	3	.211	.244
LOLLAR, TIM, BOS.*	1.000	33	1	0	1	1	0	0	0	0	0	0	0	0	0	0	0	0	0	0	1.000	1.000
LOMBARDI, PHIL, N.Y	.278	20	36	6	10	19	3	0	2	6	1	0	0	1	4	0	7	0	0	2	.528	.366
LOMBARDOZZI, STEVE, MINN	.227	156	453	53	103	157	20	5	8	33	1	9	0	1	52	2	76	3	1	8	.347	.308
LOWRY, DWIGHT, DET.*	.307	56	150	21	46	59	4	0	3	18	2	3	0	4	17	0	19	0	0	4	.393	.392
LYNN, FRED, BALT.*	.287	112	397	67	114	198	13	1	23	67	11	0	4	2	53	1	59	2	2	20	.499	.371
LYONS, STEVE, BOS.-CHI.*	.227	101	247	30	56	74	9	3	1	20	2	4	4	1	19	2	47	4	6	4	.300	.280
MADISON, SCOTTI, DET.†	.000	2	7	0	0	0	0	0	0	1	0	0	1	0	0	0	3	0	0	0	.000	.000
MANNING, RICK, MILW.*	.254	89	205	31	52	89	7	3	8	27	2	1	3	1	17	2	20	5	3	5	.434	.310
MARTINEZ, BUCK, TOR	.181	81	160	13	29	43	8	0	2	12	3	4	1	0	20	0	25	0	0	5	.269	.271
MATTINGLY, DON, N.Y.*	.352	162	677	117	238	388	53	2	31	113	15	1	10	1	53	11	35	0	0	17	.573	.394
MCDOWELL, ODDIBE, TEX.*	.266	154	572	105	152	244	24	7	18	49	5	3	2	1	65	5	112	33	15	12	.427	.341
MCGRIFF, FRED, TOR.*	.200	3	5	1	1	1	0	0	0	0	0	0	0	0	0	0	2	0	0	0	.200	.200
MCGWIRE, MARK, OAK	.189	18	53	10	10	20	1	0	3	9	0	0	0	1	4	0	18	0	1	0	.377	.259
MCLEMORE, MARK, CAL.†	.000	5	4	0	0	0	0	0	0	0	0	1	0	0	1	0	2	0	1	0	.000	.200
MCRAE, HAL, K.C	.252	112	278	22	70	105	14	0	7	37	6	0	2	1	18	4	39	0	0	9	.378	.298
MEACHAM, BOBBY, N.Y.†	.224	56	161	19	36	45	7	1	0	10	1	4	0	3	17	0	39	3	6	6	.280	.309
MERCADO, ORLANDO, TEX	.235	46	102	7	24	30	1	1	1	7	0	1	2	1	6	0	13	0	1	5	.294	.279
MILLER, DARRELL, CAL	.228	33	57	6	13	17	2	1	0	4	1	0	1	0	4	0	8	0	0	3	.298	.274
MOLITOR, PAUL, MILW	.281	105	437	62	123	186	24	6	9	55	6	2	3	0	40	0	81	20	5	9	.426	.340
MOORE, CHARLIE, MILW	.260	80	235	24	61	88	12	3	3	39	3	4	3	0	21	1	38	5	5	6	.374	.317
MORMAN, RUSS, CHI	.252	49	159	18	40	57	5	0	4	17	3	1	2	2	16	0	36	1	0	5	.358	.324
MOSEBY, LLOYD, TOR.*	.253	152	589	89	149	246	24	5	21	86	10	2	7	6	64	3	122	32	11	7	.418	.329
MOSES, JOHN, SEA.†	.256	103	399	56	102	133	16	3	3	34	4	5	4	0	34	3	65	25	18	7	.333	.311
MOTLEY, DARRYL, K.C	.203	72	217	22	44	76	9	1	7	20	2	1	0	0	11	1	31	0	2	8	.350	.241
MULLINIKS, RANCE, TOR.*	.259	117	348	50	90	145	22	0	11	45	1	1	2	1	43	1	60	1	1	12	.417	.340
MULLINS, FRAN, CLEV	.175	28	40	3	7	11	4	0	0	5	0	1	1	0	2	0	11	0	0	0	.275	.209
MURPHY, DWAYNE, OAK.*	.252	98	329	50	83	127	11	3	9	39	6	7	4	4	56	4	80	3	1	4	.386	.364
MURRAY, EDDIE, BALT.†	.305	137	495	61	151	229	25	1	17	84	4	0	5	0	78	7	49	3	0	17	.463	.396
NARRON, JERRY, CAL.*	.221	57	95	5	21	29	3	1	1	8	0	1	1	1	9	0	14	0	0	5	.305	.292
NELSON, RICKEY, SEA.*	.167	10	12	2	2	2	0	0	0	1	1	0	0	0	0	0	4	1	0	0	.167	.167
NELSON, ROBERT, OAK.*	.222	5	9	1	2	3	1	0	0	0	0	0	0	0	1	0	4	0	0	0	.333	.300

* BATS LEFTHANDED †SWITCH HITTER

BATTER AND CLUB	AVG	G	AB	R	H	TB	2B	3B	HR	RBI	GW RBI	SH	SF	HB	BB	IBB	SO	SB	CS	GI DP	SLG	OBP
NICHOLS, CARL, BALT	.000	5	5	0	0	0	0	0	0	0	0	0	0	0	1	1	4	0	0	0	.000	.167
NICHOLS, REID, CHI	.228	74	136	9	31	41	4	0	2	18	5	1	2	0	11	0	23	5	4	2	.301	.282
NIXON, OTIS, CLEV.†	.263	105	95	33	25	31	4	1	0	8	0	2	0	0	13	0	12	23	6	1	.326	.352
NOKES, MAT, DET.*	.333	7	24	2	8	12	1	0	1	2	1	0	0	0	1	1	1	0	0	1	.500	.360
O'BRIEN, PETE, TEX.*	.290	156	551	86	160	258	23	3	23	90	14	0	3	0	87	11	66	4	4	19	.468	.385
OGLIVIE, BEN, MILW.*	.283	103	346	31	98	135	20	1	5	53	8	1	7	0	30	6	33	1	2	7	.390	.334
O'MALLEY, TOM, BALT.*	.254	56	181	19	46	58	9	0	1	18	1	1	1	0	17	1	21	0	1	4	.320	.317
ONTIVEROS, STEVE, OAK	—	47	0	0	0	0	0	0	0	0	0	0	0	0	0	0	0	0	0	0	—	—
ORTA, JORGE, K.C.*	.277	106	336	35	93	138	14	2	9	46	7	0	2	0	23	3	34	0	3	9	.411	.321
OWEN, SPIKE, SEA.-BOS.†	.231	154	528	67	122	163	24	7	1	45	7	9	3	2	51	1	51	4	4	13	.309	.300
PACIOREK, TOM, TEX	.286	88	213	17	61	80	7	0	4	22	1	0	1	3	3	0	41	1	3	5	.376	.305
PAGLIARULO, MIKE, N.Y.*	.238	149	504	71	120	234	24	3	28	71	8	1	2	4	54	10	120	4	1	10	.464	.316
PARDO, AL, BALT.†	.137	16	51	3	7	11	1	0	1	3	0	0	0	0	0	0	14	0	0	2	.216	.137
PARIS, KELLY, BALT	.200	5	10	0	2	2	0	0	0	0	0	0	0	0	0	0	3	0	1	1	.200	.200
PARRISH, LANCE, DET	.257	91	327	53	84	158	6	1	22	62	8	1	3	5	38	3	83	0	0	3	.483	.340
PARRISH, LARRY, TEX	.276	129	464	67	128	236	22	1	28	94	12	0	6	2	52	7	114	3	1	16	.509	.347
PASQUA, DAN, N.Y.*	.293	102	280	44	82	147	17	0	16	45	7	1	1	3	47	3	78	2	0	4	.525	.399
PECOTA, BILL, K.C	.207	12	29	3	6	8	2	0	0	2	0	0	1	1	3	0	3	0	2	1	.276	.294
PERCONTE, JACK, CHI.*	.219	24	73	6	16	17	1	0	0	4	0	1	0	0	11	1	10	2	0	2	.233	.321
PETERS, RICKY, OAK.†	.184	44	38	7	7	8	1	0	0	1	0	0	0	0	7	1	7	2	2	2	.211	.311
PETRALLI, GENO, TEX.†	.255	69	137	17	35	56	9	3	2	18	1	0	0	0	5	0	14	3	0	7	.409	.282
PETTIS, GARY, CAL.†	.258	154	539	93	139	185	23	4	5	58	6	15	5	0	69	2	132	50	13	7	.343	.339
PHELPS, KEN, SEA.*	.247	125	344	69	85	181	16	4	24	64	6	0	3	6	88	6	96	2	3	4	.526	.406
PHILLIPS, TONY, OAK.†	.256	118	441	76	113	152	14	5	5	52	3	9	3	3	76	0	82	15	10	2	.345	.367
PITTARO, CHRIS, MINN.†	.095	11	21	0	2	2	0	0	0	0	0	0	0	0	0	0	8	0	0	0	.095	.095
POLIDOR, GUS, CAL	.263	6	19	1	5	6	1	0	0	1	0	0	0	0	1	0	0	0	0	2	.316	.300
PORTER, DARRELL, TEX.*	.265	68	155	21	41	83	6	0	12	29	3	0	0	1	22	0	51	1	1	3	.535	.360
PRESLEY, JIM, SEA	.265	155	616	83	163	285	33	4	27	107	13	3	5	4	32	3	172	0	4	18	.463	.303
PRYOR, GREG, K.C	.170	63	112	7	19	23	4	0	0	7	0	2	0	0	3	0	14	1	1	5	.205	.191
PUCKETT, KIRBY, MINN	.328	161	680	119	223	365	37	6	31	96	5	2	0	7	34	4	99	20	12	14	.537	.366

QUINONES, REY, BOS.-SEA.	.218	98	312	32	68	92	16	1	2	22	1	5	2	3	24	0	57	4	3	7	.295	.279
QUIRK, JAMIE, K.C.*	.215	80	219	24	47	81	10	0	8	26	3	0	1	1	17	3	41	0	1	4	.370	.273
RAMOS, DOMINGO, SEA	.182	49	99	8	18	20	2	0	0	5	0	2	0	1	8	0	13	0	1	7	.202	.250
RANDOLPH, WILLIE, N.Y	.276	141	492	76	136	170	15	2	5	50	9	8	4	3	94	0	49	15	2	11	.346	.393
RAYFORD, FLOYD, BALT	.176	81	210	15	37	65	4	0	8	19	2	3	0	0	15	0	50	0	0	7	.310	.231
READY, RANDY, MILW	.190	23	79	8	15	22	4	0	1	4	1	1	0	0	9	0	9	2	0	3	.278	.273
REED, JEFF, MINN.*	.236	68	165	13	39	53	6	1	2	9	0	3	0	1	16	0	19	1	0	2	.321	.308
REYNOLDS, HAROLD, SEA.†	.222	126	445	46	99	129	19	4	1	24	2	9	0	3	29	0	42	30	12	6	.290	.275
RICE, JIM, BOS	.324	157	618	98	200	303	39	2	20	110	12	0	9	4	62	5	78	0	1	19	.490	.384
RILES, ERNEST, MILW.*	.252	145	524	69	132	187	24	2	9	47	12	6	3	1	54	0	80	7	7	14	.357	.321
RIPKEN, CAL, BALT	.282	162	627	98	177	289	35	1	25	81	15	0	6	4	70	5	60	4	2	19	.461	.355
ROBIDOUX, BILLY JOE, MILW.*	.227	56	181	15	41	52	8	0	1	21	3	0	1	0	33	1	36	0	0	8	.287	.344
ROENICKE, GARY, N.Y	.265	69	136	11	36	50	5	0	3	18	0	0	1	1	27	0	30	1	1	1	.368	.388
ROHN, DAN, CLEV.*	.200	6	10	1	2	2	0	0	0	2	1	0	0	0	1	0	1	0	0	0	.200	.273
ROMERO, ED, BOS	.210	100	233	41	49	66	11	0	2	23	1	7	3	2	18	0	16	2	0	5	.283	.270
ROMINE, KEVIN, BOS	.257	35	35	6	9	11	2	0	0	2	0	1	0	0	3	0	9	2	0	1	.314	.316
RYAL, MARK, CAL.*	.375	13	32	6	12	18	0	0	2	5	1	0	0	0	2	1	4	1	0	1	.563	.412
SAKATA, LENN, OAK	.353	17	34	4	12	14	2	0	0	5	0	0	1	0	3	0	6	0	1	1	.412	.395
SALAS, MARK, MINN.*	.233	91	258	28	60	99	7	4	8	33	2	5	3	1	18	2	32	3	1	8	.384	.282
SALAZAR, ANGEL, K.C	.245	117	298	24	73	97	20	2	0	24	1	5	1	2	7	0	47	1	1	3	.326	.266
SALAZAR, LUIS, CHI	.143	4	7	1	1	1	0	0	0	0	0	0	0	0	1	0	3	0	0	0	.143	.250
SANCHEZ, ALEX, MINN	.125	8	16	1	2	2	0	0	0	1	0	0	0	0	1	0	8	0	0	2	.125	.176
SAX, DAVE, BOS	.455	4	11	1	5	9	1	0	1	1	1	0	0	0	0	0	1	0	0	0	.818	.455
SCHOFIELD, DICK, CAL	.249	139	458	67	114	182	17	6	13	57	5	9	9	5	48	2	55	23	5	8	.397	.321
SCHROEDER, BILL, MILW	.212	64	217	32	46	81	14	0	7	19	1	4	1	6	9	0	59	1	0	3	.373	.262
SEITZER, KEVIN, K.C	.323	28	96	16	31	43	4	1	2	11	2	0	0	1	19	0	14	0	0	0	.448	.440
SHEETS, LARRY, BALT.*	.272	112	338	42	92	165	17	1	18	60	8	1	2	2	21	3	56	2	0	16	.488	.317
SHELBY, JOHN, BALT.†	.228	135	404	54	92	147	14	4	11	49	5	2	2	2	18	0	75	18	6	3	.364	.263
SHEPHERD, RON, TOR	.203	65	69	16	14	24	4	0	2	4	0	1	0	0	3	0	22	0	0	1	.348	.236
SHERIDAN, PAT, DET.*	.237	98	236	41	56	85	9	1	6	19	1	2	2	1	21	4	57	9	2	3	.360	.300
SIERRA, RUBEN, TEX.†	.264	113	382	50	101	182	13	10	16	55	8	1	5	1	22	3	65	7	8	8	.476	.302
SKINNER, JOEL, CHI.-N.Y	.232	114	315	23	73	99	9	1	5	37	1	2	2	1	16	0	83	1	4	6	.314	.269
SLAUGHT, DON, TEX	.264	95	314	39	83	141	17	1	13	46	4	3	3	5	16	0	59	3	1	8	.449	.308
SMALLEY, ROY, MINN.†	.246	143	459	59	113	201	20	4	20	57	6	1	2	0	68	4	80	1	3	10	.438	.342

* BATS LEFTHANDED †SWITCH HITTER

BATTER AND CLUB	AVG	G	AB	R	H	TB	2B	3B	HR	RBI	GW RBI	SH	SF	HB	BB	IBB	SO	SB	CS	GI DP	SLG	OBP
SMITH, LONNIE, K.C.	.287	134	508	80	146	209	25	7	8	44	6	2	2	10	46	0	78	26	9	10	.411	.357
SNYDER, CORY, CLEV	.272	103	416	58	113	208	21	1	24	69	8	1	0	0	16	0	123	2	3	8	.500	.299
SPILMAN, HARRY, DET.*	.245	24	49	6	12	23	2	0	3	8	1	1	0	0	3	0	8	0	0	1	.469	.288
STANLEY, MIKE, TEX	.333	15	30	4	10	16	3	0	1	1	0	0	0	0	3	0	7	1	0	0	.533	.394
STAPLETON, DAVE, BOS	.128	39	39	4	5	6	1	0	0	3	0	1	0	0	2	0	10	0	0	1	.154	.171
STEFERO, JOHN, BALT.*	.233	52	120	14	28	36	2	0	2	13	0	0	1	0	16	0	25	0	1	1	.300	.321
STEINBACH, TERRY, OAK	.333	6	15	3	5	11	0	0	2	4	1	0	0	0	1	0	0	0	0	0	.733	.375
STENHOUSE, MIKE, BOS.*	.095	21	21	1	2	3	1	0	0	1	1	1	0	0	12	0	5	0	0	1	.143	.424
STIEB, DAVE, TOR	—	38	0	1	0	0	0	0	0	0	0	0	0	0	0	0	0	0	0	0	—	—
SULLIVAN, MARC, BOS	.193	41	119	15	23	30	4	0	1	14	1	3	1	4	7	0	32	0	0	1	.252	.260
SUNDBERG, JIM, K.C	.212	140	429	41	91	138	9	1	12	42	5	2	3	0	57	1	91	1	1	7	.322	.303
SVEUM, DALE, MILW.†	.246	91	317	35	78	116	13	2	7	35	5	5	1	1	32	0	63	4	3	7	.366	.316
TABLER, PAT, CLEV	.326	130	473	61	154	205	29	2	6	48	8	2	1	3	29	3	75	3	1	11	.433	.368
TARTABULL, DANNY, SEA	.270	137	511	76	138	250	25	6	25	96	6	2	3	1	61	2	157	4	8	10	.489	.347
TARVER, LASCHELLE, BOS.*	.120	13	25	3	3	3	0	0	0	1	0	0	0	0	1	0	4	0	1	0	.120	.154
TAYLOR, DWIGHT, K.C.*	.000	4	2	1	0	0	0	0	0	0	0	0	0	0	0	0	0	0	0	0	.000	.000
TETTLETON, MICKEY, OAK.†	.204	90	211	26	43	82	9	0	10	35	0	7	4	1	39	0	51	7	1	3	.389	.325
THOMAS, GORMAN, SEA.-MILW	.187	101	315	45	59	117	8	1	16	36	5	3	0	1	58	4	105	3	4	5	.371	.316
THORNTON, ANDRE, CLEV	.229	120	401	49	92	157	14	0	17	66	9	0	8	1	65	0	67	4	1	11	.392	.333
TILLMAN, RUSTY, OAK	.256	22	39	6	10	14	1	0	1	6	1	0	0	0	3	0	11	2	0	0	.359	.310
TOLLESON, WAYNE, CHI.-N.Y.†	.265	141	475	61	126	161	16	5	3	43	4	13	4	2	52	0	76	17	10	6	.339	.338
TOLMAN, TIM, DET	.176	16	34	4	6	7	1	0	0	2	0	2	1	0	6	0	4	1	1	0	.206	.293
TRABER, JIM, BALT.*	.255	65	212	28	54	100	7	0	13	44	3	0	5	5	18	2	31	0	0	6	.472	.321
TRAMMELL, ALAN, DET	.277	151	574	107	159	269	33	7	21	75	8	11	4	5	59	4	57	25	12	7	.469	.347
UPSHAW, WILLIE, TOR.*	.251	155	573	85	144	211	28	6	9	60	8	4	4	2	78	4	87	23	5	5	.368	.341
VALLE, DAVID, SEA	.340	22	53	10	18	36	3	0	5	15	0	0	0	0	7	0	7	0	0	2	.679	.417
WALKER, GREG, CHI.*	.277	78	282	37	78	139	10	6	13	51	5	0	3	2	29	4	44	1	2	4	.493	.345
WARD, GARY, TEX	.316	105	380	54	120	154	15	2	5	51	5	1	2	4	31	3	72	12	8	10	.405	.372
WASHINGTON, CLAUDELL, N.Y.*	.237	54	135	19	32	55	5	0	6	16	3	0	0	2	7	0	33	6	1	3	.407	.285
WASHINGTON, RON, MINN	.257	48	74	15	19	34	3	0	4	11	0	2	2	0	3	0	21	1	2	0	.459	.278

WEGMAN, BILL, MILW	—	37	0	1	0	0	0	0	0	0	0	0	0	0	0	0	0	0	0	0	—	—
WHITAKER, LOU, DET.*	.269	144	584	95	157	255	26	6	20	73	8	0	4	0	63	5	70	13	8	20	.437	.338
WHITE, DEVON, CAL.†	.235	29	51	8	12	18	1	1	1	3	0	0	0	0	6	0	8	6	0	0	.353	.316
WHITE, FRANK, K.C	.272	151	566	76	154	263	37	3	22	84	11	2	7	2	43	5	88	4	4	10	.465	.322
WHITT, ERNIE, TOR.*	.268	131	395	48	106	177	19	2	16	56	6	0	3	0	35	3	39	0	1	11	.448	.326
WIGGINS, ALAN, BALT.†	.251	71	239	30	60	65	3	1	0	11	1	5	4	0	22	0	20	21	7	0	.272	.309
WILFONG, ROB, CAL.*	.219	92	288	25	63	89	11	3	3	33	4	8	2	2	16	2	34	1	4	4	.309	.263
WILKERSON, CURTIS, TEX.†	.237	110	236	27	56	72	10	3	0	15	1	0	1	1	11	0	42	9	7	2	.305	.273
WILLARD, JERRY, OAK.*	.267	75	161	17	43	62	7	0	4	26	0	4	4	2	22	0	28	0	1	4	.385	.354
WILLIAMS, ED, CLEV	.143	5	7	2	1	1	0	0	0	1	0	0	0	0	0	0	3	0	0	0	.143	.143
WILLIAMS, KENNY, CHI	.129	15	31	2	4	7	0	0	1	1	0	0	0	1	1	0	11	1	1	1	.226	.182
WILSON, WILLIE, K.C.†	.269	156	631	77	170	231	20	7	9	44	5	3	1	9	31	1	97	34	8	6	.366	.313
WINFIELD, DAVE, N.Y	.262	154	565	90	148	261	31	5	24	104	6	2	6	2	77	9	106	6	5	20	.462	.349
WOODS, AL, MINN.*	.321	23	28	5	9	16	1	0	2	8	1	0	1	0	3	0	5	0	0	0	.571	.375
WRIGHT, GEORGE, TEX.†	.217	49	106	10	23	34	3	1	2	7	1	0	1	1	4	1	23	3	5	2	.321	.250
WRIGHT, RICKY, TEX.*	—	23	0	0	0	0	0	0	0	0	0	0	0	0	0	0	0	0	0	0	—	—
WYNEGAR, BUTCH, N.Y.†	.206	61	194	19	40	67	4	1	7	29	6	0	2	0	30	2	21	0	0	9	.345	.310
YEAGER, STEVE, SEA	.208	50	130	10	27	35	2	0	2	12	0	2	1	0	12	0	23	0	0	5	.269	.273
YOUNG, MIKE, BALT.†	.252	117	369	43	93	137	15	1	9	42	3	2	3	3	49	2	90	3	1	13	.371	.342
YOUNT, ROBIN, MILW	.312	140	522	82	163	235	31	7	9	46	8	5	2	4	62	7	73	14	5	9	.450	.388
ZUVELLA, PAUL, N.Y.	.083	21	48	2	4	5	1	0	0	2	0	4	0	0	5	0	4	0	0	1	.104	.170

CLUB BATTING

CLUB	AVG	G	AB	R	OR	H	TB	2B	3B	HR	GS	RBI	GW	SH	SF	HB	BB	IBB	SO	SB	CS	GIDP	LOB	SHO	SLG	OBP
CLEVELAND	.284	163	5702	831	841	1620	2451	270	45	157	3	775	80	56	49	24	456	26	944	141	54	129	1122	4	.430	.337
NEW YORK	.271	162	5570	797	738	1512	2397	275	23	188	1	745	82	36	46	28	645	52	911	139	48	142	1217	9	.430	.347
BOSTOI	.271	161	5498	794	696	1488	2282	320	21	144	7	752	84	44	52	66	595	56	707	41	34	142	1213	11	.415	.346
TORON'O	.269	163	5716	809	733	1540	2438	285	35	181	3	767	82	24	49	33	496	23	848	110	59	122	1099	6	.427	.329
TEXAS	.267	162	5529	771	743	1479	2365	248	43	184	4	725	80	31	42	35	511	33	1088	103	85	133	1038	4	.428	.331
DETRUIT	.263	162	5512	798	714	1447	2335	234	30	198	6	751	85	52	49	43	613	35	885	138	58	99	1164	5	.424	.338

CLUB	AVG	G	AB	R	OR	H	TB	2B	3B	HR	GS	RBI	GW	SH	SF	HB	BB	IBB	SO	SB	CS	GIDP	LOB	SHO	SLG	OBP
MINNESOTA	.261	162	5531	741	839	1446	2369	257	39	196	2	700	64	44	38	37	501	33	977	81	61	123	1087	11	.428	.325
BALTIMORE	.258	162	5524	708	760	1425	2181	223	13	169	7	669	69	33	51	31	563	26	862	64	34	159	1159	13	.395	.327
CALIFORNIA	.255	162	5433	786	684	1387	2196	236	36	167	7	743	83	91	61	40	671	45	860	109	42	134	1182	10	.404	.338
MILWAUKEE	.255	161	5461	667	734	1393	2105	255	38	127	0	625	71	53	53	27	530	26	986	100	50	122	1143	6	.385	.321
SEATTLE	.253	162	5498	718	835	1392	2191	243	41	158	5	681	65	52	29	34	572	38	1148	93	76	125	1104	13	.399	.326
KANSAS CITY	.252	162	5561	654	673	1403	2168	264	45	137	3	618	73	24	33	36	474	40	919	97	46	101	1142	12	.390	.313
OAKLAND	.252	162	5435	731	760	1370	2122	213	25	163	1	683	70	56	51	32	553	24	983	139	61	105	1087	6	.390	.322
CHICAGO	.247	162	5406	644	699	1335	1963	197	34	121	1	605	67	50	53	34	487	29	940	115	54	123	1036	13	.363	.310
TOTALS	.262	1134	77376	10449	10449	20237	31563	3520	468	2290	50	9839	1055	646	656	500	7667	486	13058	1470	762	1759	15793	123	.408	.330

TOP FIFTEEN DESIGNATED HITTERS
(BASED ON TIMES AT BAT)

BATTER	BATS	CLUB	AVG	G	AB	R	H	TB	2B	3B	HR	RBI	GW RBI	SH	SF	HB	BB	IBB	SO	SB	CS	GI DP	SLG	OBP
KINGMAN	R	OAK	.214	140	552	70	118	242	19	0	35	94	10	0	7	3	33	3	125	3	3	16	.438	.259
BAYLOR	R	BOS	.245	143	527	84	129	242	21	1	30	92	13	0	5	34	54	7	95	3	5	9	.459	.350
EASLER	L	N.Y.	.302	129	450	58	136	199	26	2	11	70	6	2	5	0	42	12	81	2	1	16	.442	.358
JACKSON	L	CAL	.236	121	403	63	95	164	11	2	18	54	8	0	3	3	89	11	113	1	1	14	.407	.376
SMALLEY	S	MINN	.253	114	396	51	100	184	16	4	20	51	6	1	2	0	56	4	67	0	3	9	.465	.344
THORNTON	R	CLEV	.223	110	391	48	87	147	12	0	16	60	8	0	8	1	65	0	66	4	1	11	.376	.329
PARRISH	R	TEX	.284	99	359	54	102	188	21	1	21	77	9	0	6	2	36	3	89	2	1	11	.524	.347
JOHNSON	R	TOR	.248	95	326	48	81	140	12	1	15	51	3	0	1	4	49	0	56	0	1	9	.429	.353
ORTA	L	K.C.	.277	87	318	33	88	130	13	1	9	42	6	0	2	0	22	3	33	0	3	9	.409	.322
KITTLE	R	CHI 62																						
		N.Y. 24	.217	86	299	35	65	128	9	0	18	52	4	0	8	2	24	1	86	3	0	7	.428	.273
THOMAS G.	R	SEA 52																						
		MILW 36	.192	88	291	40	56	111	8	1	15	35	5	3	0	1	51	4	9&5	2	4	5	.381	.315
MCRAE	R	K.C.	.238	75	244	21	58	89	13	0	6	32	5	0	2	1	15	3	37	0	0	7	.365	.282
SHEETS	L	BALT	.302	58	205	30	62	105	11	1	10	41	4	1	0	1	13	3	32	1	0	11	.512	.347
COOPER	L	MILW	.254	44	177	18	45	68	6	1	5	28	0	0	1	1	15	0	40	1	1	6	.384	.314
OGLIVIE	L	MILW	.226	42	159	9	36	44	5	0	1	19	2	0	4	0	15	1	18	0	2	4	.277	.287

PITCHING

TOP FIFTEEN QUALIFIERS FOR EARNED-RUN LEADERSHIP

(162 OR MORE INNINGS)

*THROWS LEFTHANDED

PITCHER AND CLUB	W	L	PCT	ERA	G	GS	CG	SHO	GF	SV	IP	H	TBF	R	ER	HR	SH	SF	HB	TBB	IBB	SO	WP	BK
CLEMENS, ROGER, BOS	24	4	.857	2.48	33	33	10	1	0	0	254.0	179	997	77	70	21	4	6	4	67	0	238	11	3
HIGUERA, TED, MILW.*	20	11	.645	2.79	34	34	15	4	0	0	248.1	226	1031	84	77	26	7	11	3	74	5	207	3	0
WITT, MIKE, CAL	18	10	.643	2.84	34	34	14	3	0	0	269.0	218	1071	95	85	22	3	5	3	73	2	208	6	0
HURST, BRUCE, BOS.*	13	8	.619	2.99	25	25	11	4	0	0	174.1	169	721	63	58	18	5	3	3	50	2	167	6	0
JACKSON, DANNY, K.C.*	11	12	.478	3.20	32	27	4	1	3	1	185.2	177	789	83	66	13	10	4	4	79	1	115	7	0
MORRIS, JACK, DET	21	8	.724	3.27	35	35	15	6	0	0	267.0	229	1092	105	97	40	7	3	0	82	7	223	12	0
MCCASKILL, KIRK, CAL	17	10	.630	3.36	34	33	10	2	1	0	246.1	207	1013	98	92	19	6	5	5	92	1	202	10	2
YOUNG, CURT, OAK.*	13	9	.591	3.45	29	27	5	2	0	0	198.0	176	826	88	76	19	8	9	7	57	1	116	7	2
BANNISTER, FLOYD, CHI.*	10	14	.417	3.54	28	27	6	1	0	0	165.1	162	688	81	65	17	7	5	2	48	0	92	5	0
CANDIOTTI, TOM, CLEV	16	12	.571	3.57	36	34	17	3	1	0	252.1	234	1078	112	100	18	3	9	8	106	0	167	12	4
KEY, JIMMY, TOR.*	14	11	.560	3.57	36	35	4	2	0	0	232.0	222	959	98	92	24	10	6	3	74	1	141	3	0
GUBICZA, MARK, K.C	12	6	.667	3.64	35	24	3	2	2	0	180.2	155	765	77	73	8	4	8	5	84	2	118	15	0
SUTTON, DON, CAL	15	11	.577	3.74	34	34	3	1	0	0	207.0	192	853	93	86	31	3	3	3	49	2	116	4	1
BOYD, DENNIS, BOS	16	10	.615	3.78	30	30	10	0	0	0	214.1	222	893	99	90	32	3	6	2	45	1	129	3	0
HOUGH, CHARLIE, TEX	17	10	.630	3.79	33	33	7	2	0	0	230.1	188	958	115	97	32	9	1	9	89	2	146	16	0

INDIVIDUAL PITCHING

(ALL PLAYERS LISTED ALPHABETICALLY)

*THROWS LEFTHANDED

PITCHER AND CLUB	W	L	PCT	ERA	G	GS	CG	SHO	GF	SV	IP	H	TBF	R	ER	HR	SH	SF	HB	TBB	IBB	SO	WP	BK
AASE, DON, BALT	6	7	.462	2.98	66	0	0	0	58	34	81.2	71	337	29	27	6	3	2	0	28	2	67	4	0
ACKER, JIM, TOR	2	4	.333	4.35	23	5	0	0	6	0	60.0	63	259	34	29	6	6	5	2	22	3	32	3	1
AGOSTO, JUAN, CHI.-MINN.*	1	4	.200	8.64	26	1	0	0	4	1	25.0	49	139	30	24	1	2	0	2	18	0	12	1	0
AKERFELDS, DARREL, OAK	0	0	—	6.75	2	0	0	0	2	0	5.1	7	26	5	4	2	0	0	0	3	1	5	2	0
ALEXANDER, DOYLE, TOR	5	4	.556	4.46	17	17	3	0	0	0	111.0	120	470	56	55	18	3	3	4	20	1	65	1	0
ALLEN, NEIL, CHI	7	2	.778	3.82	22	17	2	2	1	0	113.0	101	466	50	48	8	5	7	2	38	1	57	4	0
ANDERSON, ALLEN, MINN.*	3	6	.333	5.55	21	10	1	0	3	0	84.1	106	371	54	52	11	2	3	1	30	3	51	2	2

*THROWS LEFTHANDED

PITCHER AND CLUB	W	L	PCT	ERA	G	GS	CG	SHO	GF	SV	IP	H	TBF	R	ER	HR	SH	SF	HB	TBB	IBB	SO	WP	BK
ANDUJAR, JOAQUIN, OAK	12	7	.632	3.82	28	26	7	1	2	1	155.1	139	647	70	66	23	1	4	4	56	1	72	2	4
AQUINO, LUIS, TOR	1	1	.500	6.35	7	0	0	0	3	0	11.1	14	50	8	8	2	0	1	0	3	1	5	1	0
ARMSTRONG, MIKE, N.Y	0	1	.000	9.35	7	1	0	0	4	0	8.2	13	42	9	9	4	0	0	0	5	1	8	0	0
ARNOLD, TONY, BALT	0	2	.000	3.55	11	0	0	0	3	0	25.1	25	104	15	10	0	3	0	0	11	3	7	0	0
ARNSBERG, BRAD, N.Y	0	0	—	3.38	2	1	0	0	1	0	8.0	13	39	3	3	1	0	0	0	1	0	3	0	0
ARROYO, FERNANDO, OAK	0	0	—	—	1	0	0	0	0	0	0.0	0	3	0	0	0	0	0	0	3	0	0	0	0
ATHERTON, KEITH, OAK.-MINN	6	10	.375	4.08	60	0	0	0	36	10	97.0	100	431	47	44	11	6	6	1	46	4	67	2	0
BAILES, SCOTT, CLEV.*	10	10	.500	4.95	62	10	0	0	22	7	112.2	123	500	70	62	12	7	4	1	43	5	60	4	2
BAIR, DOUG, OAK	2	3	.400	3.00	31	0	0	0	17	4	45.0	37	189	15	15	5	3	3	0	18	0	40	2	0
BANKHEAD, SCOTT, K.C	8	9	.471	4.61	24	17	0	0	2	0	121.0	121	517	66	62	14	5	5	3	37	7	94	1	0
BANNISTER, FLOYD, CHI.*	10	14	.417	3.54	28	27	6	1	0	0	165.1	162	688	81	65	17	7	5	2	48	0	92	5	0
BEATTIE, JIM, SEA	0	6	.000	6.02	9	7	0	0	0	0	40.1	57	188	28	27	7	2	2	3	14	2	24	1	0
BELL, ERIC, BALT.*	1	2	.333	5.01	4	4	0	0	0	0	23.1	23	105	14	13	4	1	1	0	14	0	18	0	0
BEST, KARL, SEA	2	3	.400	4.04	26	0	0	0	15	1	35.2	35	163	19	16	3	2	2	1	21	2	23	2	1
BIRKBECK, MIKE, MILW	1	1	.500	4.50	7	4	0	0	2	0	22.0	24	97	12	11	0	0	0	0	12	0	13	1	0
BIRTSAS, TIM, OAK.*	0	0	—	22.50	2	0	0	0	2	0	2.0	2	12	5	5	1	1	0	0	4	1	1	0	0
BLACK, BUD, K.C.*	5	10	.333	3.20	56	4	0	0	26	9	121.0	100	503	49	43	14	4	4	7	43	5	68	2	2
BLYLEVEN, BERT, MINN	17	14	.548	4.01	36	36	16	3	0	0	271.2	262	1126	134	121	50	5	4	10	58	4	215	4	0
BODDICKER, MIKE, BALT	14	12	.538	4.70	33	33	7	0	0	0	218.1	214	934	125	114	30	3	6	11	74	4	175	7	0
BORDI, RICH, BALT	6	4	.600	4.46	52	1	0	0	22	3	107.0	105	464	56	53	13	2	3	4	41	5	83	1	0
BOSIO, CHRIS, MILW	0	4	.000	7.01	10	4	0	0	3	0	34.2	41	154	27	27	9	1	0	0	13	0	29	2	1
BOYD, DENNIS, BOS	16	10	.615	3.78	30	30	10	0	0	0	214.1	222	893	99	90	32	3	6	2	45	1	129	3	0
BROWN, KEVIN, TEX	1	0	1.000	3.60	1	1	0	0	0	0	5.0	6	19	2	2	0	0	0	0	0	0	4	0	0
BROWN, MIKE, BOS.-SEA	4	6	.400	5.79	21	12	0	0	2	0	73.0	91	334	49	47	14	3	3	1	36	1	41	4	1
BRYDEN, T.R., CAL	2	1	.667	6.55	16	0	0	0	7	0	34.1	38	159	25	25	4	1	4	2	21	0	25	2	0
BURTT, DENNIS, MINN	0	0	—	31.50	3	0	0	0	1	0	2.0	7	16	7	7	1	0	0	0	3	1	1	0	0
BUTCHER, JOHN, MINN.-CLEV	1	8	.111	6.56	29	18	2	1	5	0	120.2	168	554	93	88	17	2	6	4	37	1	45	6	0
CAMACHO, ERNIE, CLEV	2	4	.333	4.08	51	0	0	0	37	20	57.1	60	267	26	26	1	5	6	2	31	6	36	3	1
CAMPBELL, BILL, DET	3	6	.333	3.88	34	0	0	0	19	3	55.2	46	229	26	24	5	4	3	1	21	5	37	1	0
CANDELARIA, JOHN, CAL.*	10	2	.833	2.55	16	16	1	1	0	0	91.2	68	365	30	26	4	3	3	3	26	2	81	2	1
CANDIOTTI, TOM, CLEV	16	12	.571	3.57	36	34	17	3	1	0	252.1	234	1078	112	100	18	3	9	8	106	0	167	12	4
CARLTON, STEVE, CHI.*	4	3	.571	3.69	10	10	0	0	0	0	63.1	58	259	30	26	6	2	2	0	25	0	40	2	1
CARY, CHUCK, DET.*	1	2	.333	3.41	22	0	0	0	6	0	31.2	33	140	18	12	3	2	2	0	15	4	21	1	1
CAUDILL, BILL, TOR	2	4	.333	6.19	40	0	0	0	20	2	36.1	36	163	25	25	6	2	0	2	17	1	32	0	1

CERUTTI, JOHN, TOR.*	9	4	.692	4.15	34	20	2	1	3	1	145.1	150	616	73	67	25	4	5	1	47	2	89	8	0
CHADWICK, RAY, CAL	0	5	.000	7.24	7	7	0	0	0	0	27.1	39	133	26	22	5	1	0	1	15	0	9	1	0
CLANCY, JIM, TOR	14	14	.500	3.94	34	34	6	3	0	0	219.1	202	913	100	96	24	5	9	4	63	0	126	4	0
CLARK, BRYAN, CHI.*	0	0	—	4.50	5	0	0	0	2	0	8.0	8	31	4	4	0	0	0	0	2	0	5	0	0
CLARKE, STAN, TOR.*	0	1	.000	9.24	10	0	0	0	6	0	12.2	18	62	13	13	4	3	1	0	10	1	9	0	2
CLEAR, MARK, MILW	5	5	.500	2.20	59	0	0	0	52	16	73.2	53	306	23	18	4	1	4	1	36	2	85	8	2
CLEMENS, ROGER, BOS	24	4	.857	2.48	33	33	10	1	0	0	254.0	179	997	77	70	21	4	6	4	67	0	238	11	3
CLUTTERBUCK, BRYAN, MILW	0	1	.000	4.29	20	0	0	0	7	0	56.2	68	250	32	27	8	1	1	2	16	2	38	2	0
COCANOWER, JAIME, MILW	0	1	.000	4.43	17	2	0	0	2	0	44.2	40	205	29	22	1	3	1	2	38	0	22	5	0
CODIROLI, CHRIS, OAK	5	8	.385	4.03	16	16	1	0	0	0	91.2	91	406	54	41	15	1	1	2	38	2	43	4	0
CONE, DAVID, K.C.	0	0	—	5.56	11	0	0	0	5	0	22.2	29	108	14	14	2	0	0	1	13	1	21	3	0
COOK, MIKE, CAL	0	2	.000	9.00	5	1	0	0	1	0	9.0	13	46	12	9	3	0	0	0	7	1	6	0	0
CORBETT, DOUG, CAL	4	2	.667	3.66	46	0	0	0	32	10	78.2	66	312	36	32	11	1	2	1	22	2	36	2	0
CORREA, ED, TEX	12	14	.462	4.23	32	32	4	2	0	0	202.1	167	886	102	95	15	4	3	3	126	2	189	19	2
COWLEY, JOE, CHI	11	11	.500	3.88	27	27	4	0	0	0	162.1	133	692	81	70	20	6	4	3	83	1	132	4	0
CRAWFORD, STEVE, BOS	0	2	.000	3.92	40	0	0	0	15	4	57.1	69	248	29	25	5	3	2	0	19	7	32	2	0
DARWIN, DANNY, MILW	6	8	.429	3.52	27	14	5	1	4	0	130.1	120	537	62	51	13	5	6	3	35	1	80	5	0
DAVIS, JOEL, CHI	4	5	.444	4.70	19	19	1	0	0	0	105.1	115	468	64	55	9	3	2	1	51	0	54	4	1
DAVIS, RON, MINN	2	6	.250	9.08	36	0	0	0	28	2	38.2	55	198	42	39	7	2	1	4	29	8	30	4	0
DAVIS, STEVE, TOR.*	0	0	—	17.18	3	0	0	0	0	0	3.2	8	22	7	7	2	0	0	0	5	1	5	1	0
DAVIS, STORM, BALT	9	12	.429	3.62	25	25	2	0	0	0	154.0	166	657	70	62	16	3	2	0	49	2	96	5	0
DAWLEY, BILL, CHI	0	7	.000	3.32	46	0	0	0	23	2	97.2	91	405	38	36	10	5	3	1	28	3	66	5	0
DELEON, JOSE, CHI	4	5	.444	2.96	13	13	1	0	0	0	79.0	49	325	30	26	7	4	1	4	42	0	68	6	0
DIXON, KEN, BALT	11	13	.458	4.58	35	33	2	0	1	0	202.1	194	874	111	103	33	5	6	1	83	6	170	7	3
DOTSON, RICHARD, CHI	10	17	.370	5.48	34	34	3	1	0	0	197.0	226	861	125	120	24	4	4	2	69	2	110	10	0
DOZIER, TOM, OAK	0	0	—	5.68	4	0	0	0	4	0	6.1	6	30	6	4	1	0	2	0	5	1	4	1	1
DRABEK, DOUG, N.Y.	7	8	.467	4.10	27	21	0	0	2	0	131.2	126	561	64	60	13	5	2	3	50	1	76	2	0
EASTERLY, JAMIE, CLEV.*	0	2	.000	7.64	13	0	0	0	4	0	17.2	27	89	16	15	3	1	2	0	12	0	9	2	0
EICHHORN, MARK, TOR	14	6	.700	1.72	69	0	0	0	38	10	157.0	105	612	32	30	8	9	2	7	45	14	166	2	1
FARR, STEVE, K.C.	8	4	.667	3.13	56	0	0	0	33	8	109.1	90	443	39	38	10	3	2	4	39	8	83	4	1
FILSON, PETE, MINN.-CHI.*	0	1	.000	6.00	7	1	0	0	4	0	18.0	27	89	13	12	5	0	0	1	7	0	8	1	0
FINLEY, CHUCK, CAL.*	3	1	.750	3.30	25	0	0	0	7	0	46.1	40	198	17	17	2	4	0	1	23	1	37	2	0
FIREOVID, STEVE, SEA	2	0	1.000	4.29	10	1	0	0	2	0	21.0	28	89	11	10	1	0	0	1	4	0	10	1	0
FISCHER, TODD, CAL	0	0	—	4.24	9	0	0	0	5	0	17.0	18	73	8	8	4	1	1	0	8	2	7	0	1
FISHER, BRIAN, N.Y.	9	5	.643	4.93	62	0	0	0	26	6	96.2	105	424	61	53	14	5	2	1	37	2	67	2	0
FLANAGAN, MIKE, BALT.*	7	11	.389	4.24	29	28	2	0	0	0	172.0	179	747	95	81	15	10	6	1	66	4	96	8	1
FONTENOT, RAY, MINN.*	0	0	—	9.92	15	0	0	0	7	0	16.1	27	81	19	18	3	0	0	2	4	0	10	2	0

*THROWS LEFTHANDED

PITCHER AND CLUB	W	L	PCT	ERA	G	GS	CG	SHO	GF	SV	IP	H	TBF	R	ER	HR	SH	SF	HB	TBB	IBB	SO	WP	BK
FORSCH, KEN, CAL	0	1	.000	9.53	10	0	0	0	4	1	17.0	24	85	21	18	4	1	2	2	10	0	13	0	0
FORSTER, TERRY, CAL.*	4	1	.800	3.51	41	0	0	0	17	5	41.0	47	182	18	16	2	3	1	3	17	1	28	0	0
FRASER, WILLIE, CAL	0	0	—	8.31	1	1	0	0	0	0	4.1	6	20	4	4	0	1	1	0	1	0	2	0	0
FRAZIER, GEORGE, MINN	1	1	.500	4.39	15	0	0	0	10	6	26.2	23	119	13	13	2	1	3	0	16	1	25	1	0
GARDNER, WES, BOS	0	0	—	9.00	1	0	0	0	0	0	1.0	1	4	1	1	0	0	1	0	0	0	1	0	0
GIBSON, BOB, MILW	1	2	.333	4.73	11	1	0	0	5	0	26.2	23	123	18	14	3	0	1	0	23	1	11	3	0
GORDON, DON, TOR	0	1	.000	7.06	14	0	0	0	6	1	21.2	28	102	20	17	1	1	2	1	8	1	13	0	0
GUBICZA, MARK, K.C	12	6	.667	3.64	35	24	3	2	2	0	180.2	155	765	77	73	8	4	8	5	84	2	118	15	0
GUETTERMAN, LEE, SEA.*	0	4	.000	7.34	41	4	1	0	8	0	76.0	108	353	67	62	7	3	5	4	30	3	38	2	0
GUIDRY, RON, N.Y.*	9	12	.429	3.98	30	30	5	0	0	0	192.1	202	809	94	85	28	5	4	1	38	2	140	3	0
GUZMAN, JOSE, TEX	9	15	.375	4.54	29	29	2	0	0	0	172.1	199	757	101	87	23	7	4	6	60	2	87	3	0
HAAS, MOOSE, OAK	7	2	.778	2.74	12	12	1	0	0	0	72.1	58	290	23	22	4	2	2	1	19	1	40	0	0
HABYAN, JOHN, BALT	1	3	.250	4.44	6	5	0	0	1	0	26.1	24	117	17	13	3	2	1	0	18	2	14	1	0
HARGESHEIMER, ALAN, K.C	0	1	.000	6.23	5	1	0	0	2	0	13.0	18	61	9	9	1	0	0	1	7	2	4	0	0
HARRIS, GREG, TEX	10	8	.556	2.83	73	0	0	0	63	20	111.1	103	462	40	35	12	3	6	1	42	6	95	2	1
HAVENS, BRAD, BALT.*	3	3	.500	4.56	46	0	0	0	19	1	71.0	64	294	37	36	7	6	1	0	29	1	57	6	0
HEATON, NEAL, CLEV.-MINN.*	7	15	.318	4.08	33	29	5	0	2	1	198.2	201	850	102	90	26	6	5	2	81	8	90	4	0
HENKE, TOM, TOR	9	5	.643	3.35	63	0	0	0	51	27	91.1	63	370	39	34	6	2	6	1	32	4	118	3	1
HENRY, DWAYNE, TEX	1	0	1.000	4.66	19	0	0	0	4	0	19.1	14	93	11	10	1	1	2	1	22	0	17	7	1
HERNANDEZ, WILLIE, DET.*	8	7	.533	3.55	64	0	0	0	53	24	88.2	87	376	35	35	13	1	3	5	21	1	77	2	1
HIGUERA, TED, MILW.*	20	11	.645	2.79	34	34	15	4	0	0	248.1	226	1031	84	77	26	7	11	3	74	5	207	3	0
HOLLAND, AL, N.Y.*	1	0	1.000	5.09	25	1	0	0	10	0	40.2	44	177	29	23	5	1	3	0	9	2	37	0	0
HOUGH, CHARLIE, TEX	17	10	.630	3.79	33	33	7	2	0	0	230.1	188	958	115	97	32	9	1	9	89	2	146	16	0
HOWELL, JAY, OAK	3	6	.333	3.38	38	0	0	0	33	16	53.1	53	230	23	20	3	3	1	1	23	4	42	4	0
HUISMANN, MARK, K.C.-SEA	3	4	.429	3.79	46	1	0	0	19	5	97.1	98	408	47	41	19	0	3	1	25	0	72	5	0
HURST, BRUCE, BOS.*	13	8	.619	2.99	25	25	11	4	0	0	174.1	169	721	63	58	18	5	3	3	50	2	167	6	0
JACKSON, DANNY, K.C.*	11	12	.478	3.20	32	27	4	1	3	1	185.2	177	789	83	66	13	10	4	4	79	1	115	7	0
JACKSON, ROY, MINN	0	1	.000	3.86	28	0	0	0	8	1	58.1	57	249	29	25	7	2	5	3	16	0	32	3	2
JAMES, BOB, CHI	5	4	.556	5.25	49	0	0	0	40	14	58.1	61	263	36	34	8	4	4	4	23	3	32	5	1
JOHN, TOMMY, N.Y.*	5	3	.625	2.93	13	10	1	0	2	0	70.2	73	290	27	23	8	5	3	2	15	1	28	2	0
JOHNSON, JOE, TOR	7	2	.778	3.89	16	15	0	0	0	0	88.0	94	368	39	38	3	4	4	3	22	1	39	2	0
JOHNSON, JOHN HENRY, MILW.*	2	1	.667	2.66	19	0	0	0	5	1	44.0	43	184	15	13	2	3	0	0	10	1	42	5	0
JONES, DOUG, CLEV	1	0	1.000	2.50	11	0	0	0	5	1	18.0	18	79	5	5	0	1	1	1	6	1	12	0	0
JONES, ODELL, BALT	2	2	.500	3.83	21	0	0	0	12	0	49.1	58	219	22	21	4	2	4	0	23	6	32	2	0

KELLY, BRYAN, DET	1	2	.333	4.50	6	4	0	0	1	0	20.0	21	88	11	10	4	0	0	0	10	1	18	0	0
KERN, JIM, CLEV	1	1	.500	7.90	16	0	0	0	4	0	27.1	34	142	28	24	1	2	0	3	23	0	11	3	0
KEY, JIMMY, TOR.*	14	11	.560	3.57	36	35	4	2	0	0	232.0	222	959	98	92	24	10	6	3	74	1	141	3	0
KING, ERIC, DET	11	4	.733	3.51	33	16	3	1	9	3	138.1	108	579	54	54	11	6	1	8	63	3	79	4	3
KINNUNEN, MIKE, BALT.*	0	0	—	6.43	9	0	0	0	4	0	7.0	8	31	6	5	1	0	0	0	5	0	1	1	0
KNUDSON, MARK, MILW	0	1	.000	7.64	4	1	0	0	1	0	17.2	22	82	15	15	7	0	0	0	5	1	9	1	0
KRUEGER, BILL, OAK.*	1	2	.333	6.03	11	3	0	0	4	1	34.1	40	149	25	23	4	1	2	0	13	0	10	3	1
LADD, PETE, SEA	8	6	.571	3.82	52	0	0	0	33	6	70.2	69	294	33	30	10	0	6	3	18	3	53	2	0
LAMP, DENNIS, TOR	2	6	.250	5.05	40	2	0	0	11	2	73.0	93	329	50	41	5	4	1	0	23	6	30	2	0
LANGFORD, RICK, OAK	1	10	.091	7.36	16	11	0	0	1	0	55.0	69	251	49	45	13	0	2	1	18	0	30	2	0
LANGSTON, MARK, SEA.*	12	14	.462	4.85	37	36	9	0	1	0	239.1	234	1057	142	129	30	5	8	4	123	1	245	10	3
LAPOINT, DAVE, DET.*	3	6	.333	5.72	16	8	0	0	2	0	67.2	85	314	49	43	11	4	1	0	32	3	36	2	1
LATHAM, BILL, MINN.*	0	1	.000	7.31	7	2	0	0	2	0	16.0	24	77	14	13	1	1	2	1	6	0	8	0	0
LAZORKO, JACK, DET	0	0	—	4.05	3	0	0	0	2	0	6.2	8	31	3	3	0	0	0	0	4	1	3	0	0
LEARY, TIM, MILW	12	12	.500	4.21	33	30	3	2	2	0	188.1	216	817	97	88	20	4	6	7	53	4	110	7	0
LEIBRANDT, CHARLIE, K.C.*	14	11	.560	4.09	35	34	8	1	0	0	231.1	238	975	112	105	18	14	5	4	63	0	108	2	1
LEIPER, DAVE, OAK.*	2	2	.500	4.83	33	0	0	0	9	1	31.2	28	136	17	17	3	2	3	2	18	4	15	2	0
LEONARD, DENNIS, K.C	8	13	.381	4.44	33	30	5	2	0	0	192.2	207	821	106	95	22	4	9	4	51	6	114	6	1
LOLLAR, TIM, BOS.*	2	0	1.000	6.91	32	1	0	0	4	0	43.0	51	211	35	33	7	2	4	3	34	3	28	5	1
LOYND, MIKE, TEX	2	2	.500	5.36	9	8	0	0	1	1	42.0	49	193	30	25	4	1	2	2	19	1	33	2	0
LUCAS, GARY, CAL.*	4	1	.800	3.15	27	0	0	0	11	2	45.2	45	185	19	16	1	0	1	0	6	0	31	5	0
LUGO, URBANO, CAL	1	1	.500	3.80	6	3	0	0	0	0	21.1	21	86	9	9	4	1	0	0	6	0	9	0	0
MAHLER, MICKEY, TEX.-TOR.*	0	2	.000	4.08	31	5	0	0	8	3	64.0	72	284	31	29	3	1	4	4	29	2	28	5	0
MARTINEZ, DENNIS, BALT	0	0	—	6.75	4	0	0	0	1	0	6.2	11	33	5	5	0	0	1	0	2	0	2	1	0
MARTINEZ, TIPPY, BALT.*	0	2	.000	5.63	14	0	0	0	5	1	16.0	18	74	10	10	1	0	1	0	12	1	11	1	0
MASON, MIKE, TEX.*	7	3	.700	4.33	27	22	2	1	2	0	135.0	135	587	71	65	11	3	3	0	56	3	85	5	1
MCCASKILL, KIRK, CAL	17	10	.630	3.36	34	33	10	2	1	0	246.1	207	1013	98	92	19	6	5	5	92	1	202	10	2
MCCLURE, BOB, MILW.*	2	1	.667	3.86	13	0	0	0	7	0	16.1	18	75	7	7	2	1	1	0	10	1	11	0	0
MCGREGOR, SCOTT, BALT.*	11	15	.423	4.52	34	33	4	2	1	0	203.0	216	868	110	102	35	3	6	3	57	0	95	5	0
MCKEON, JOEL, CHI.*	3	1	.750	2.45	30	0	0	0	5	1	33.0	18	129	10	9	2	1	2	0	17	2	18	0	0
MERIDITH, RON, TEX.*	1	0	1.000	3.00	5	0	0	0	0	0	3.0	2	10	1	1	0	1	1	0	1	1	2	0	0
MIRABELLA, PAUL, SEA.*	0	0	—	8.53	8	0	0	0	2	0	6.1	13	34	7	6	1	0	0	0	3	0	6	1	0
MOHORCIC, DALE, TEX	2	4	.333	2.51	58	0	0	0	20	7	79.0	86	325	25	22	5	1	0	1	15	6	29	1	0
MONTEFUSCO, JOHN, N.Y	0	0	—	2.19	4	0	0	0	1	0	12.1	9	50	3	3	2	0	0	0	5	0	3	0	0
MOONEYHAM, BILL, OAK	4	5	.444	4.52	45	6	0	0	18	2	99.2	103	456	53	50	4	3	2	3	67	4	75	2	0
MOORE, DONNIE, CAL	4	5	.444	2.97	49	0	0	0	42	21	72.2	60	295	28	24	10	7	3	0	22	4	53	4	1
MOORE, MIKE, SEA	11	13	.458	4.30	38	37	11	1	1	1	266.0	279	1145	141	127	28	10	6	12	94	6	146	4	1

*THROWS LEFTHANDED

PITCHER AND CLUB	W	L	PCT	ERA	G	GS	CG	SHO	GF	SV	IP	H	TBF	R	ER	HR	SH	SF	HB	TBB	IBB	SO	WP	BK
MORGAN, MIKE, SEA	11	17	.393	4.53	37	33	9	1	2	1	216.1	243	951	122	109	24	7	3	4	86	3	116	8	1
MORRIS, JACK, DET	21	8	.724	3.27	35	35	15	6	0	0	267.0	229	1092	105	97	40	7	3	0	82	7	223	12	0
MUSSELMAN, JEFF, TOR.*	0	0	—	10.13	6	0	0	0	0	0	5.1	8	29	7	6	1	0	0	0	5	1	4	0	0
NELSON, GENE, CHI	6	6	.500	3.85	54	1	0	0	26	6	114.2	118	488	52	49	7	7	1	3	41	5	70	3	0
NIEKRO, JOE, N.Y	9	10	.474	4.87	25	25	0	0	0	0	125.2	139	571	84	68	15	1	0	1	63	3	59	10	1
NIEKRO, PHIL, CLEV	11	11	.500	4.32	34	32	5	0	1	0	210.1	241	951	126	101	24	7	2	6	95	1	81	9	2
NIELSEN, SCOTT, N.Y	4	4	.500	4.02	10	9	2	2	1	0	56.0	66	235	29	25	12	0	0	2	12	0	20	0	0
NIEVES, JUAN, MILW.*	11	12	.478	4.92	35	33	4	3	0	0	184.2	224	834	124	101	17	3	5	1	77	0	116	3	1
NIPPER, AL, BOS	10	12	.455	5.38	26	26	3	0	0	0	159.0	186	702	108	95	24	4	5	4	47	2	79	1	1
NOLES, DICKIE, CLEV	3	2	.600	5.10	32	0	0	0	9	0	54.2	56	251	33	31	9	3	5	5	30	4	32	1	1
NUNEZ, EDWIN, SEA	1	2	.333	5.82	14	1	0	0	6	0	21.2	25	93	15	14	5	0	0	0	5	1	17	0	0
OELKERS, BRYAN, CLEV.*	3	3	.500	4.70	35	4	0	0	8	1	69.0	70	318	38	36	13	3	2	6	40	2	33	4	0
O'NEAL, RANDY, DET	3	7	.300	4.33	37	11	1	0	9	2	122.2	121	522	69	59	13	3	6	3	44	9	68	8	0
ONTIVEROS, STEVE, OAK	2	2	.500	4.71	46	0	0	0	27	10	72.2	72	305	40	38	10	1	6	1	25	3	54	4	0
PACELLA, JOHN, DET	0	0	—	4.09	5	0	0	0	1	1	11.0	10	51	5	5	0	2	2	0	13	1	5	0	1
PASTORE, FRANK, MINN	3	1	.750	4.01	33	1	0	0	15	2	49.1	54	223	28	22	4	4	4	0	24	6	18	1	0
PETRY, DAN, DET	5	10	.333	4.66	20	20	2	0	0	0	116.0	122	520	78	60	15	3	3	5	53	3	56	5	0
PLESAC, DAN, MILW.*	10	7	.588	2.97	51	0	0	0	33	14	91.0	81	377	34	30	5	6	5	0	29	1	75	4	0
PLUNK, ERIC, OAK	4	7	.364	5.31	26	15	0	0	2	0	120.1	91	537	75	71	14	2	3	5	102	2	98	9	6
PORTUGAL, MARK, MINN	6	10	.375	4.31	27	15	3	0	7	1	112.2	112	481	56	54	10	5	3	1	50	1	67	5	0
PULIDO, ALFONSO, N.Y.*	1	1	.500	4.70	10	3	0	0	3	1	30.2	38	135	17	16	8	1	1	0	9	0	13	1	0
QUISENBERRY, DAN, K.C	3	7	.300	2.77	62	0	0	0	54	12	81.1	92	352	30	25	2	4	5	3	24	12	36	0	0
RASMUSSEN, DENNIS, N.Y.*	18	6	.750	3.88	31	31	3	1	0	0	202.0	160	819	91	87	28	1	5	2	74	0	131	5	0
REED, JERRY, SEA	4	0	1.000	3.12	11	4	0	0	4	0	34.2	38	152	13	12	3	0	0	0	13	0	16	1	0
RIGHETTI, DAVE, N.Y.*	8	8	.500	2.45	74	0	0	0	68	46	106.2	88	435	31	29	4	5	4	2	35	7	83	1	0
RIJO, JOSE, OAK	9	11	.450	4.65	39	26	4	0	9	1	193.2	172	856	116	100	24	10	9	4	108	7	176	6	4
RITTER, REGGIE, CLEV	0	0	—	6.30	5	0	0	0	2	0	10.0	14	48	10	7	1	0	2	1	4	0	6	0	0
RODRIGUEZ, RICK, OAK	1	2	.333	6.61	3	3	0	0	0	0	16.1	17	72	12	12	4	0	0	0	7	0	2	2	1
ROMAN, JOSE, CLEV	1	2	.333	6.55	6	5	0	0	0	0	22.0	23	105	20	16	3	1	4	1	17	0	9	0	0
ROMANICK, RON, CAL	5	8	.385	5.50	18	18	1	1	0	0	106.1	124	470	68	65	13	3	5	0	44	0	38	4	0
ROZEMA, DAVE, TEX	0	0	—	5.91	6	0	0	0	0	0	10.2	19	52	9	7	1	0	2	0	3	0	3	0	0
RUHLE, VERN, CAL	1	3	.250	4.15	16	3	0	0	5	1	47.2	46	197	25	22	5	1	2	1	7	0	23	1	0
RUSSELL, JEFF, TEX	5	2	.714	3.40	37	0	0	0	9	2	82.0	74	338	40	31	11	1	2	1	31	2	54	5	0
SABERHAGEN, BRET, K.C	7	12	.368	4.15	30	25	4	2	4	0	156.0	165	652	77	72	15	3	3	2	29	1	112	1	1

SAMBITO, JOE, BOS.*	2	0	1.000	4.84	53	0	0	0	27	12	44.2	54	200	26	24	4	1	0	2	16	3	30	4	0
SCHERRER, BILL, DET.*	0	1	.000	7.29	13	0	0	0	8	0	21.0	19	103	19	17	3	2	0	1	22	4	16	1	0
SCHIRALDI, CALVIN, BOS	4	2	.667	1.41	25	0	0	0	21	9	51.0	36	198	8	8	5	2	1	1	15	2	55	1	0
SCHMIDT, DAVE, CHI.	3	6	.333	3.31	49	1	0	0	21	8	92.1	94	394	37	34	10	3	3	5	27	7	67	5	0
SCHROM, KEN, CLEV	14	7	.667	4.54	34	33	3	1	1	0	206.0	217	883	118	104	34	8	12	12	49	3	87	2	1
SCHULZE, DON, CLEV	4	4	.500	5.00	19	13	1	0	1	0	84.2	88	371	48	47	9	0	1	5	34	0	33	6	0
SCURRY, ROD, N.Y.*	1	2	.333	3.66	31	0	0	0	10	2	39.1	38	177	18	16	1	2	0	2	22	1	36	5	0
SEARAGE, RAY, MILW.-CHI.*	1	1	.500	3.35	46	0	0	0	17	1	51.0	44	220	20	19	7	1	2	1	28	4	36	1	1
SEAVER, TOM, CHI.-BOS	7	13	.350	4.03	28	28	2	0	0	0	176.1	180	759	83	79	17	7	6	7	56	2	103	4	0
SELLERS, JEFF, BOS	3	7	.300	4.94	14	13	1	0	0	0	82.0	90	366	56	45	13	2	2	3	40	1	51	4	1
SHIELDS, STEVE, K.C	0	0	—	2.08	3	0	0	0	2	0	8.2	3	33	3	2	1	0	2	0	4	1	2	1	0
SHIRLEY, BOB, N.Y.*	0	4	.000	5.04	39	6	0	0	9	3	105.1	108	454	60	59	13	5	8	3	40	1	64	1	0
SLATON, JIM, CAL.-DET	4	6	.400	5.08	36	12	0	0	13	2	113.1	130	497	70	64	14	1	8	3	40	4	43	2	0
SMITH, ROY, MINN	0	2	.000	6.97	5	0	0	0	2	0	10.1	13	50	8	8	1	0	0	1	5	1	8	0	0
SMITHSON, MIKE, MINN	13	14	.481	4.77	34	33	8	1	1	0	198.0	234	880	123	105	26	5	8	14	57	4	114	15	1
SNELL, NATE, BALT	2	1	.667	3.86	34	0	0	0	18	0	72.1	69	297	36	31	9	3	3	1	22	4	29	2	0
STANLEY, BOB, BOS	6	6	.500	4.37	66	1	0	0	50	16	82.1	109	366	48	40	9	2	4	0	22	8	54	1	0
STEWART, DAVE, OAK	9	5	.643	3.74	29	17	4	1	2	0	149.1	137	644	67	62	15	4	4	3	65	0	102	9	0
STEWART, SAMMY, BOS	4	1	.800	4.38	27	0	0	0	5	0	63.2	64	295	33	31	7	1	5	0	48	2	47	5	1
STIEB, DAVE, TOR	7	12	.368	4.74	37	34	1	1	2	1	205.0	239	919	128	108	29	6	6	15	87	1	127	7	0
STODDARD, TIM, N.Y	4	1	.800	3.83	24	0	0	0	6	0	49.1	41	208	23	21	6	6	2	0	23	3	34	3	0
SUTTON, DON, CAL	15	11	.577	3.74	34	34	3	1	0	0	207.0	192	853	93	86	31	3	3	3	49	2	116	4	1
SWAGGERTY, BILL, BALT	0	0	—	18.00	1	0	0	0	0	0	1.0	6	9	2	2	0	0	0	0	1	1	1	1	0
SWIFT, BILL, SEA	2	9	.182	5.46	29	17	1	0	3	0	115.1	148	534	85	70	5	5	3	7	55	2	55	2	1
SWINDELL, GREG, CLEV.*	5	2	.714	4.23	9	9	1	0	0	0	61.2	57	255	35	29	9	3	1	1	15	0	46	3	2
TANANA, FRANK, DET.*	12	9	.571	4.16	32	31	3	1	1	0	188.1	196	812	95	87	23	8	5	3	65	9	119	7	1
TERRELL, WALT, DET	15	12	.556	4.56	34	33	9	2	1	0	217.1	199	918	116	110	30	2	3	3	98	5	93	5	0
TEWKSBURY, BOB, N.Y	9	5	.643	3.31	23	20	2	0	0	0	130.1	144	558	58	48	8	4	7	5	31	0	49	3	2
THIGPEN, BOB, CHI	2	0	1.000	1.77	20	0	0	0	14	7	35.2	26	142	7	7	1	1	1	1	12	0	20	0	0
THURMOND, MARK, DET.*	4	1	.800	1.92	25	4	0	0	5	3	51.2	44	209	13	11	7	3	1	0	17	2	17	1	0
TRUJILLO, MIKE, BOS.-SEA	3	2	.600	3.26	14	4	1	1	5	1	47.0	39	197	17	17	5	3	1	0	21	3	23	1	0
VIOLA, FRANK, MINN.*	16	13	.552	4.51	37	37	7	1	0	0	245.2	257	1053	136	123	37	4	5	3	83	0	191	12	0
VON OHLEN, DAVE, OAK.*	0	3	.000	3.52	24	0	0	0	3	1	15.1	18	68	7	6	0	1	0	0	7	2	4	1	0
VUCKOVICH, PETE, MILW	2	4	.333	3.06	6	6	0	0	0	0	32.1	33	139	18	11	3	2	3	2	11	0	12	2	2
WARD, DUANE, TOR	0	1	.000	13.50	2	1	0	0	1	0	2.0	3	15	4	3	0	0	0	1	4	0	1	1	0
WEGMAN, BILL, MILW	5	12	.294	5.13	35	32	2	0	1	0	198.1	217	836	120	113	32	4	5	7	43	2	82	5	2
WHITSON, ED, N.Y	5	2	.714	7.54	14	4	0	0	6	0	37.0	54	189	37	31	5	2	3	0	23	1	27	2	0

*THROWS LEFTHANDED

PITCHER AND CLUB	W	L	PCT	ERA	G	GS	CG	SHO	GF	SV	IP	H	TBF	R	ER	HR	SH	SF	HB	TBB	IBB	SO	WP	BK
WILCOX, MILT, SEA	0	8	.000	5.50	13	10	0	0	2	0	55.2	74	259	38	34	11	1	3	1	28	1	26	0	1
WILLIAMS MI, MITCH, TEX.*	8	6	.571	3.58	80	0	0	0	38	8	98.0	69	435	39	39	8	1	3	11	79	8	90	5	5
WILLS, FRANK, CLEV	4	4	.500	4.91	26	0	0	0	16	4	40.1	43	182	23	22	6	6	2	0	16	4	32	2	0
WITT, BOBBY, TEX	11	9	.550	5.48	31	31	0	0	0	0	157.2	130	741	104	96	18	3	9	3	143	2	174	22	3
WITT, MIKE, CAL	18	10	.643	2.84	34	34	14	3	0	0	269.0	218	1071	95	85	22	3	5	3	73	2	208	6	0
WOODWARD, ROB, BOS	2	3	.400	5.30	9	6	0	0	0	0	35.2	46	161	26	21	4	0	2	1	11	0	14	5	1
WRIGHT, RICKY, TEX.*	1	0	1.000	5.03	21	1	0	0	2	0	39.1	44	177	22	22	1	1	0	0	21	0	23	2	0
YETT, RICH, CLEV	5	3	.625	5.15	39	3	1	1	17	1	78.2	84	350	48	45	10	2	4	1	37	4	50	8	0
YOUNG, CURT, OAK.*	13	9	.591	3.45	29	27	5	2	0	0	198.0	176	826	88	76	19	8	9	7	57	1	116	7	2
YOUNG, MATT, SEA.*	8	6	.571	3.82	65	5	1	0	32	13	103.2	108	458	50	44	9	4	3	8	46	2	82	7	1

CLUB PITCHING

CLUB	W	L	ERA	G	CG	SHO	REL	SV	IP	H	TBF	R	ER	HR	SH	SF	HB	TBB	IBB	SO	WP	BK
KANSAS CITY	76	86	3.82	162	24	13	230	31	1440.2	1413	6093	673	612	121	51	48	38	479	46	888	43	6
CALIFORNIA	92	70	3.84	162	29	12	246	40	1456.0	1356	6066	684	621	153	41	44	27	478	19	955	44	6
CHICAGO	72	90	3.93	162	18	8	297	38	1442.1	1361	6115	699	630	143	54	43	33	561	28	895	55	3
BOSTON	95	66	3.93	161	36	6	254	41	1429.2	1469	6102	696	625	167	38	48	26	474	35	1033	55	8
MILWAUKEE	77	84	4.01	161	29	12	237	32	1431.2	1478	6150	734	638	158	42	49	29	494	22	952	57	9
DETROIT	87	75	4.02	162	33	12	239	38	1443.2	1374	6158	714	645	183	47	35	30	571	61	880	50	8
TORONTO	86	76	4.08	163	16	12	290	44	1476.0	1467	6264	733	669	164	59	51	45	487	39	1002	38	6
TEXAS	87	75	4.11	162	15	8	328	41	1450.1	1356	6311	743	662	145	37	42	41	736	37	1059	94	13
NEW YORK	90	72	4.11	162	13	8	289	58	1443.1	1461	6173	738	659	175	48	44	24	492	25	878	40	3
BALTIMORE	73	89	4.30	162	17	6	262	39	1436.2	1451	6164	760	687	177	46	43	21	535	41	954	52	4
OAKLAND	76	86	4.31	162	22	8	286	37	1433.0	1334	6208	760	686	166	44	55	34	667	35	937	62	19
CLEVELAND	84	78	4.58	163	31	7	290	34	1447.2	1548	6439	841	736	167	55	60	57	605	34	744	63	13
SEATTLE	67	95	4.65	162	33	5	281	27	1439.2	1590	6345	835	744	171	41	44	49	585	27	944	46	10
MINNESOTA	71	91	4.77	162	39	6	240	24	1432.2	1579	6264	839	759	200	43	50	46	503	37	937	58	5
TOTALS	1133	1133	4.18	1134	355	123	3769	524	20203.1	20237	86852	10449	9373	2290	646	656	500	7667	486	13058	757	113

TV/RADIO ROUNDUP

NETWORK COVERAGE

NBC-TV: This is NBC's year for the All-Star Game, the American and National League Championship Series, plus Saturday Game of the Week and assorted prime-time regular-season games. Vin Scully, Joe Garagiola, Bob Costas and Tony Kubek are the talent.

ABC-TV: Monday Night Baseball and some likely late-season Sunday afternoon games will lead up to coverage of the 1987 World Series. Al Michaels, Jim Palmer and Tim McCarver are likely members of the network's two announcing teams.

NATIONAL LEAGUE

ATLANTA BRAVES: WSB Radio (750) and WTBS-TV (Channel 17) are the anchor stations for the Braves' network. Ernie Johnson, Pete Van Wieren, John Stirling and Skip Caray do the honors.

CHICAGO CUBS: Harry Caray, Steve Stone and Dewayne Staats describe the action for WGN-TV (Channel 9), while Lou Boudreau, Jim Frey, Carey and Staats do it for WGN radio (720).

CINCINNATI REDS: Marty Brennaman, Joe Nuxhall and Steve Physioc are on WLWT-TV (Channel 5). Brennaman and Nuxhall team up on WLW radio (700).

HOUSTON ASTROS: Milo Hamilton, Larry Dierker and Jerry Tripiano are in the starting lineup for the corps that mans the microphones on KTRH radio (740) and KTXH-TV (Channel 20).

LOS ANGELES DODGERS: Vin Scully, Ross Porter and Jerry Doggett broadcast over KABC radio (790) and KTTV-TV (Channel 11). Spanish coverage is provided by Jaime Jarrin and Rene Cardenas on KTNQ radio (1020).

MONTREAL EXPOS: Dave Van Horne works the games for the English-speaking audience on CFCF radio (600) and the CBC-TV network. Jacques Doucet and Rodger Brulotte say it in French for radio CKAC (730), while Raymond Lebrun and Claude Raymond are the French play-by-play announcers for CBC-TV. There will also be coverage by Tommy Hutton and Ken Singleton on TSN Cable TV.

NEW YORK METS: Ralph Kiner, Tim McCarver and Steve Zabriskie handle television on WOR (Channel 9) and will be joined by Fran Healy on Sports Channel. Bob Murphy and Gary Thorne have radio duties for WHN (1050).

PHILADELPHIA PHILLIES: Harry Kalas, Andy Musser, Chris Wheeler and Richie Ashburn describe the action on WCAU radio (1210) and WTAF-TV (Channel 29).

PITTSBURGH PIRATES: Larry Frattare and Jim Rooker work the games for KDAK radio (1020) and doing the honors for KDAK-TV (Channel 2) are John Sanders, Steve Blass and Alan Cutler. Steve Blass, Mike Lange and Greg Brown are on the Pirate Cable Network.

ST. LOUIS CARDINALS: Jack Buck, Mike Shannon and Ken Wilson are on KMOX radio (1120) and are joined by Jay Randolph on KSDK-TV (Channel 5).

SAN DIEGO PADRES: Jerry Coleman and Dave Campbell handle the play-by-play for KFMB radio (760) and KUSI-TV (Channel 51). Gustavo Lopez and Gustavo Lopez Jr. will work games in Spanish for XEXX radio (1420).

SAN FRANCISCO GIANTS: Plans were uncertain at press time.

AMERICAN LEAGUE

BALTIMORE ORIOLES: Jon Miller describes the action for WCBM radio (680), while Chuck Thompson and Brooks Robinson perform the chores for WMAR-TV (Channel 2). Mel Proctor, Rex Barney and John Lowenstein work the games for Home Team Sports cable network.

BOSTON RED SOX: Ken Coleman and Joe Castiglione broadcast over the Campbell Sports Network, including WRKO (680), while Ned Martin and Bob Montgomery handle television on WSBK-TV (Channel 38) and New England Sports Network cable.

CALIFORNIA ANGELS: Al Conin and Ron Fairly describe the action on KMPC radio (710). Telecasts will be carried by KTLA-TV (Channel 5), with Bob Starr and Joe Torre expected to man the mikes.

CHICAGO WHITE SOX: Don Drysdale and Frank Messer are the crew for WFLD-TV (Channel 32) and Sports Vision cable. Lorn Brown and Del Crandall call the action on WMAQ radio (670).

CLEVELAND INDIANS: Herb Score and Steve LaMar will be behind the mike for WWWE (1100), the flagship station for a multi-state radio network. WUAB-TV (Channel 43) will carry games, but announcers were not determined at press time.

DETROIT TIGERS: Ernie Harwell and Paul Carey broadcast on a radio network originating with WJR (760). George Kell and Al Kaline handle the chores for WDIV-TV (Channel 4).

KANSAS CITY ROYALS: Denny Trease, Denny Matthews and Fred White call the shots for WDAF-TV (Channel 4), while White and Matthews share radio time on a network headed by KMBZ (980) and WIBW (580).

MILWAUKEE BREWERS: Jim Paschke and Mike Hegan describe the action for WVTV-TV (Channel 18). Bob Uecker and Pat Hughes work the radio for WTMJ (620).

MINNESOTA TWINS: Games will be carried by KMSP-TV (Channel 9), but announcers had not been determined at press time. Herb Carneal and a partner unnamed at press time will call the plays for a radio network headed by WCCO (830).

NEW YORK YANKEES: Phil Rizzuto and Bill White are the heart of the team that will call it for WPIX-TV (Channel 11). Mickey Mantle and Mel Allen work the games for Sports Channel cable and voices were unconfirmed for radio coverage on a network originating with WABC (770).

OAKLAND A's: Bill King and Lon Simmons do the play-by-play on KFSO radio (560) and are joined by Ted Robinson on KPIX-TV (Channel 5).

SEATTLE MARINERS: Dave Niehaus and Rick Rizzs play it again for radio station KIRO (710) and KIRO-TV (Channel 7).

TORONTO BLUE JAYS: Tom Cheek and Jerry Howarth do the radio play-by-play on a network that originates with CJCL (1430). Don Chevrier, Tony Kubek and Fergie Olver are behind the mike for CTV Network. Olver, Kubek and Ken Singleton handle TSN Pay TV.

TEXAS RANGERS: Eric Nadel and Mark Holtz work the games for WBAP radio (820). Bob Carpenter will do the honors for KTVT-TV (Channel 11).

OFFICIAL 1987

EAST

	AT CHICAGO	AT MONTREAL	AT NEW YORK
Chicago		April 24,25,26 June 29*,30 July 1* Oct. 2*,3,4	June 23*,24*,25 August 6*,7*,8*,9 Sept. 14*,15*
Montreal	April 17,18,19 July 28,29,30 Sept. 11,12,13		April 30*, May 1*,2,3 August 10*,11*,12 Sept. 23*,24*
New York	June 8,9,10 August 13,14,15,16 Sept. 21,22	June 15*,16*,17*,18* July 31*, August 1*,2 Sept. 16*,17*	
Philadelphia	June 15,16,17,18 July 31, August 1,2 Sept. 23,24	April 20,22,23 June 12*,13*,14 Sept. 18*,19*,20	June 19*,20*,21 August 3*,4*,5* Sept. 7*,8*,9*
Pittsburgh	April 15,16 June 19,20,21,22 Sept. 7,8,9	June 8*,9*,10* August 13*,14*,15*,16 Sept. 21*,22*	April 7,9 June 5*,6,7 (dh) Sept. 25*,26,27
St. Louis	April 7,9 June 4,5,6,7 Sept. 25,26,27	June 26*,27*,28 August 3*,4*,5* Sept. 7,8*,9*	April 24*,25,26 June 29*,30*, July 1* Sept. 11*,12,13
Atlanta	May 22,23,24 August 25,26,27	May 11*,12* July 16*,17*,18*,19	April 10*,11,12 July 20*,21*,22
Cincinnati	May 19,20,21 Sept. 4,5,6	May 13*,14* July 23*,24*,25*,26	May 5*,6* July 16*,17*,18*,19
Houston.........	June 1,2,3 August 21,22,23	May 8*,9,10 July 20*,21*,22*	April 27*,28*,29* July 24*,25,26
Los Angeles	May 4,5 July 9,10,11,12	May 15*,16*,17 August 18*,19*,20*	May 22*,23,24 August 24*,25*,26*
San Diego	May 1,2,3 July 6,7,8	June 2*,3*,4* July 3*,4*,5	May 18*,19*,20* August 21*,22*,23
San Francisco....	April 28,29,30 July 3,4,5	May 18*,19*,20* August 21*,22*,23	May 15*,16*,17 August 18*,19*,20

* NIGHT GAME
HEAVY BLACK FIGURES DENOTE SUNDAYS
NIGHT GAMES: ANY GAME STARTING AFTER 5:00 p.m.

NATIONAL LEAGUE SCHEDULE

EAST

	AT PHILADELPHIA	AT PITTSBURGH	AT ST. LOUIS
Chicago	April 10*,11*,12,13* August 10*,11*,12 Sept. 16*,17	June 26*,27*,28 August 3*,4*,5* Sept. 29*,30*, Oct. 1*	April 21*,22*,23 June 12*,13,14 Sept. 18*,19*,20
Montreal	April 27*,28*,29* June 5*,6*,7 Sept. 25*,26*,27	June 23*,24*,25* August 6*,7*,8*,9 Sept. 14*,15*	April 14*,16 June 19*,20*,21,22* Sept. 29*,30*, Oct. 1*
New York	April 14*,15*,16* June 26*,27,28 Sept. 28*,29*,30*	April 20*,21*,22* June 12*,13*,14 Sept. 18*,19*,20	April 17*,18*,19 July 28*,29*,30* Oct. 2*,3,4
Philadelphia		April 17*,18,19 July 28*,29*,30* Oct. 2*,3*,4	June 23*,24*,25* August 13*,14*,15*,16 Sept. 21*,22*
Pittsburgh	April 24*,25*,26 June 29*,30*, July 1* Sept. 11*,12*,13		June 15*,16*,17*,18* July 31*, August 1*,2 Sept. 23*,24*
St. Louis	June 8*,9*,10* August 6*,7*,8*,9 Sept. 14*,15*	April 10*,11,12,13 August 10*,11*,12* Sept. 16*,17*	
Atlanta	May 13*,14* July 23*,24*,25*,26	May 15*,16*,17 August 31*, Sept. 1*,2*	May 25*,26*,28 August 28*,29,30
Cincinnati	May 1*,2*,3 July 20*,21*,22*	May 29*,30*,31 August 24*,25*,26*	May 15*,16*,17 August 31*, Sept. 1*,2*
Houston	May 5*,6* July 2*,3*,4,5	May 18*,19*,20* August 28*,29*,30	May 29*,30*,31 August 24*,25*,26
Los Angeles	May 18*,19*,20* August 21*,22,23	April 28*,29*,30* July 3*,4,5	May 1*,2*,3 July 6*,7*,8*
San Diego	May 15*,16*,17 August 18*,19*,20*	May 12*,13*,14* July 10*,11*,12	April 28*,29*,30 Sept. 4*,5*,6
San Francisco	May 22*,23*,24 August 24*,25*,26*	May 1*,2*,3 July 6*,7*,8*	May 4*,5 July 9*,10*,11*,12

JULY 14 — ALL STAR GAME AT OAKLAND

OFFICIAL 1987

WEST

	AT ATLANTA	AT CINCINNATI	AT HOUSTON
Chicago	May 29*,30*,31 August 18*,19*,20*	May 25,26*,27* August 28*,29*,30	May 15*,16,17 August 31*, Sept. 1*,2*
Montreal	May 4*,5*,6* Sept. 4*,5*,6	April 6,8 July 9*,10*,11*,12	April 10*,11,12 July 6*,7*,8*
New York	May 8*,9,10 July 6*,7*,8*	May 11*,12* July 2*,3*,4*,5	May 13*,14* July 9*,10*,11,12
Philadelphia	April 7*,9* July 9*,10,11*,12	May 8*,9,10 July 6*,7*,8*	May 11*,12* July 16*,17*,18*,19
Pittsburgh	June 2*,3*,4* August 21*,22*,23	May 22*,23*,24 August 18*,19*,20*	May 25*,26*,27* Sept. 4*,5*,6
St. Louis	May 19*,20*,21* July 3*,4,5	June 1*,2*,3* August 21*,22*,23	May 22*,23*,24 August 18*,19*,20
Atlanta		April 28*,29*,30 June 11*,12*,13*,14 Sept. 28*,29	April 21*,22*,23* August 14*,15*,16,17* Sept. 30* Oct. 1*
Cincinnati	April 13*,14*,15* June 18*,19*,20,21 Sept. 14*,15*		April 24*,25*,26 June 15*,16*,17* Oct. 2*,3,4
Houston	May 1*,2*,3 July 28*,29*,30* Sept. 22*,23*,24*	April 17*,18,19 (dh) June 30*, July 1* Sept. 25*,26,27	
Los Angeles	June 8*,9*,10* July 31*, August 1*,2 Sept. 11*,12,13	June 5*,6*,7 August 3*,4*,5* Sept. 7,8*,9*	April 6*,7*,8 June 18*,19*,20,21 Sept. 28*,29*
San Diego	June 5*,6*,7 August 4*,5*,6* Sept. 7,8*,9*	April 10*,11,12 July 28*,29*,30* Sept. 22*,23*,24	June 8*,9*,10* July 31*, August 1*,2 Sept. 18*,19*,20
San Francisco	April 24*,25,26,27* June 16*,17* Sept. 25*,26*,27	June 8*,9*,10 July 31*, August 1,2 Sept. 11*,12*,13	June 5*,6*,7 August 3*,4*,5* Sept. 7*,8*,9*

* NIGHT GAME
HEAVY BLACK FIGURES DENOTE SUNDAYS
NIGHT GAMES: ANY GAME STARTING AFTER 5:00 p.m.

NATIONAL LEAGUE SCHEDULE

WEST

	AT LOS ANGELES	AT SAN DIEGO	AT SAN FRANCISCO
Chicago	May 11*,12*,13* July 24*,25,**26**	May 8*,9*,**10** July 20*,21*,22*	May 6*,7* July 16*,17*,18,**19**
Montreal	May 25*,26*,27* August 28*,29*,**30**	May 22*,23*,**24** August 25*,26*,27*	May 29*,30,**31** August 31*, Sept. 1*,2
New York	June 1*,2*,3* Sept. 4*,5*,**6**	May 29*,30*,**31** August 31*, Sept. 1*,2*	May 25,26*,27 August 28*,29,**30**
Philadelphia	May 29*,30,**31** August 31*, Sept. 1*,2*	May 25*,26*,27* August 28*,29*,**30**	June 1*,2*,3 Sept. 4*,5,**6**
Pittsburgh	May 6*,7* July 16*,17*,18*,**19**	May 4*,5* July 23,24*,25*,**26**	May 8*,9,**10** July 20*,21*,22
St. Louis	May 8*,9*,**10** July 21*,22*,23*	May 6*,7 July 16*,17*,18,**19**	May 12*,13 July 24*,25,**26 (dh)**
Atlanta	June 23*,24*,25* August 7*,8,**9** Sept. 18*,19*,**20**	June 26*,27*,**28** August 10*,11*,12*,13 Sept. 16*,17	April 17*,18,**19** June 29*,30*, July 1 Oct. 2*,3,**4**
Cincinnati	June 26*,27*,**28** August 10*,11*,12*,13 Sept. 17 (dh)	April 20*,21*,22*,23 August 14* (tn),**16** Sept. 30*, Oct. 1	June 23*,24,25* August 7*,8,**9 (dh)** Sept. 19,**20**
Houston	April 13*,14*,15* June 11*,12*,13*,**14** Sept. 14*,15*	June 23*,24*,25 August 7*,8*,**9** Sept. 10*,11*,**13**	June 26*,27,**28** August 10*,11*,12,13 Sept. 16,17
Los Angeles		April 16,17*,18,**19** June 16*,17 Oct. 2*,3*,**4**	April 20*,21*,22* August 14*,15,**16** Sept. 21*,22*,23*
San Diego	April 24*,25*,**26** June 29*,30*, July 1* Sept. 25*,26,**27**		April 6,7*,8 June 11*,12*,13,**14** Sept. 14*,15*
San Francisco	April 9,10*,11*,**12** July 27*,28*,29* Sept. 30*, Oct. 1*	April 13*,14*,15* June 18*,19*,20*,**21** Sept. 28*,29*	

JULY 14 — ALL STAR GAME AT OAKLAND

OFFICIAL 1987 AMERICAN LEAGUE SCHEDULE

BOLD = SUNDAY ( ) = HOLIDAY * = NIGHT GAME TN = TWI-NIGHT [DH] = DOUBLEHEADER

	AT SEATTLE	AT OAKLAND	AT CALIFORNIA	AT TEXAS	AT KANSAS CITY	AT MINNESOTA	AT CHICAGO
SEATTLE		April 24*,25,**26** Aug. 3*,4,5	April 7,8*,9* July 31* Aug. 1*,**2**	June 29*,30* July 1* Oct. 1*,2*,3*,**4**	June 26*,27*,**28** Sept. 28*,29*,30*	April 20*,21*,22 Aug. 14*,15*,**16**,17*	June 22*,23*,24* Sept. 17*,18*,19*,**20**
OAKLAND	April 16*,17*,18*,**19** Aug. 10*,11*,12		April 20*,21*,22 Aug. 14*,15*,**16**,17*	June 12*,13*,**14*** Sept. 14*,15*,16*	June 15*,16*,17* Sept. 18*,19*,**20**	April 7*,8*,9 Aug. 6*,7*,8*,**9**	June 29*,30* July 1* Oct. 2*,3*,**4**
CALIFORNIA	April 13*,14*,15 Aug. 6*,7*,8*,**9**	April 10*,11,**12** July 27*,28*,29		June 22*,23*,24* Sept. 18*,19*,**20**	June 12*,13*,**14** Sept. 14*,15*,16*,17*	April 23*,24*,25*,**26** Aug. 11*,12*,13	June 26*,27,**28** Sept. 29*,30* Oct. 1*
TEXAS	June 8*,9*,10* Sept. 25*,26*,**27**	June 19*,20,**21**[DH] Sept. (7*),8*,9	June 15*,16*,17* Sept. 10*,11*,12*,**13**		May 29*,30*,**31** Aug. 24*,25*,26*,27*	June 5*,6*,**7** Sept. 22*,23*,24*	May 15*,16*,**17** Sept. 1*,2*,3*
KANSAS CITY	June 4*,5*,6*,**7** Sept. 21*,22*,23*	June 22*,23*,24 Sept. 10,11*,12,**13**	June 18*,19*,20*,**21** Sept. (7),8*	May 22*,23*,**24** Aug. 17*,18*,19*		June 8*,9*,10* Sept. 25*,26,**27**	May (25*),26*,27* Aug. 28*,29*,**30**,31*
MINNESOTA	April 10*,11*,**12** July 27*,28*,29	April 13*,14*,15 July 31* Aug. 1,**2**	April 17*,18*,**19** Aug. 3*,4*,5	June 26*,27TN,**28*** Sept. 28*,29*,30*	June 29*,30* July 1*,2* Oct. 2*,3*,**4**		June 11*,12*,13*,**14** Sept. 14*,15*,16*
CHICAGO	June 15*,16*,17 Sept. 11*,12*,**13**	June 8*,9*,10 Sept. 24*,25*,26,**27**	June 4*,5*,6,**7** Sept. 21*,22*,23*	June 1*,2*,3* Aug. 20*,21*,22,**23***	April 6,8*,9* Sept. 4*,5*,**6**	June 19*,20*,**21** Sept. (7),8*,9*	

MILWAUKEE	May 1*,2*,**3** July 6*,7*,8*	April 29*,30 July 9*,10*,11,**12**	April 27*,28* July 2*,3*,(4*),**5**	April 10*,11*,**12** July 27*,28*,29*	May 15*,16*,**17** Sept. 1*,2*,3*	May 26*,27*,28* Sept. 4*,5*,**6**	April 20*,21*,22* Aug 7*,8*,**9**
DETROIT	April 27*, 28* July 2*,3*,(4),**5**	May 1*,2,**3** July 6*,7*,8	April 29*,30* July 9*,10,11*,**12**	May 18*,19*,20* Sept. 4*,5*,**6***	April 14*,15* Aug. 13*,14*,15*,**16**	May 22*,23*,**24** Aug. 24*,25*,26*	April 10,11*,**12** Aug. 10*,11*,12
CLEVELAND	June 12*,13*,**14** Sept. 14*,15*,16	June 5*,6,**7** Sept. 29*,30* Oct. 1	June 8,9*,10* Oct.2*,3,**4**	May 5*,6* July 9*,10*,11*,**12***	May 1*,2*,**3** July 20*,21*,22*	June 23*,24*,25 Sept. 18*,19,**20**	May 13*,14* July 16,17*,18*,**19**
TORONTO	May 22*,23*,**24,**(25) Aug. 24*,25*	May 15*,16,**17** Aug. 18*,19,20	May 18*,19*,20* Aug. 21*,22*,**23**	May 8*,9*,**10** July 20*,21*,22*	May 4*,5*,6* July 3*,(4*),**5**	May 13*,14* July 16,17*,18*,**19**	April 24*,25*,**26** Aug. 3*,4*,5*
BALTIMORE	May 18*,19*,20 Aug. 21*,22*,**23**	May 22*,23,**24,**(25*) Aug. 24*,25	May 15*,16,**17** Aug. 18*,19*,20*	April 21*,22*,23* July 31* Aug. 1*,**2***	April 28*,29* July 16*,17*,18,**19**	May 5*,6*,7 July 3*,(4*),**5**	May 8*,9*,**10** July 20*,21*,22*
NEW YORK	May 15*,16*,**17** Aug. 18*,19*,20*	May 18*,19*,20* Aug. 21*,22,**23**	May 22*,23*,**24,**(25) Aug. 24*,25*	April 28*,29* July 16*,17*,18*,**19***	April 10*,11,**12** Aug. 10*,11*,12*	May 1*,2*,**3** July 20*,21*,22*	May 4*,5*,6* July 24*,25,**26**
BOSTON	April 29*,30* July 9*,10*,11*,**12**	April 27*,28* July 2*,3*,(4),**5**	May 1*,2*,**3** July 6,7*,8*	April 24*,25*,**26** Aug. 3*,4*,5*	May 18*,19*,20* July 31* Aug. 1*,**2**	May 15*,16*,**17** Sept. 1*,2*,3	May 29*,30,**31** Aug. 17*,18*,19*

ALL-STAR GAME AT THE OAKLAND COLISEUM, IN OAKLAND, JULY 14

OFFICIAL 1987 AMERICAN LEAGUE SCHEDULE

BOLD = SUNDAY ( ) = HOLIDAY * = NIGHT GAME TN = TWI-NIGHT [DH] = DOUBLEHEADER

	AT MILWAUKEE	AT DETROIT	AT CLEVELAND	AT TORONTO	AT BALTIMORE	AT NEW YORK	AT BOSTON
SEATTLE	May 8*,9,**10** July 20*,21*,22	May 5*,6 July 16*,17*,18*,**19**	June 19*,20,**21** Sept. (7),8*,9*	June 1*,2*,3 Sept. 4*,5,**6**	May 29*,30*,**31** Aug. 31* Sept. 1*,2*	May 27*,28* Aug. 27,28*,29*,**30**	May 11*,12*,13* July 24*,25,**26**
OAKLAND	May 12*,13 July 23*,24*,25*,**26**	May 8*,9*,**10** July 20*,21*,22*	June 26*,27,**28** Sept. 21*,22*,23*	May 27*,28* Aug. 27*,28*,29,**30**	June 1*,2*,3* Sept. 4*,5*,**6**	May 29*,30*,**31** Aug. 31* Sept. 1*,2*	May 5*,6* July 16*,17*,18,**19**
CALIFORNIA	May 5*,6 July 16, 17*,18*,**19**	May 11*,12*,13* July 24*,25,**26**	June 29*,30* July 1* Sept. 25*,26,**27**	May 29*,30,**31** Aug. 31* Sept. 1*,2	May 27*,28* Aug. 27*,28*,29*,**30**	June 1*,2*,3* Sept. 4*,5,**6**	May 8*,9,**10** July 20*,21*,22*
TEXAS	April 17*,18,**19** Aug. 10*,11*,12	May (25*),26*,27* Aug. 28*,29*,**30**	May 11*,12* July 23*,24*,25,**26**	May 1*,2,**3** July 6*,7*,8*	April 6,8,9* Aug. 7*,8*,**9**	May 13*,14 July 2*,3*,(4),**5**	April 13,14,15 Aug. 14*,15,**16**
KANSAS CITY	June 1*,2*,3 Aug. 21*,22*,**23**	April 24*,25,**26** Aug. 3*,4*,5*	May 8*,9,**10** July 6*,7*,8*	May 11*,12* July 9*,10*,11,**12**	May 13*,14* July 23*,24*,25*,**26**	April 17*,18,**19** July 28*,29,30*	April 20,21*,22* Aug. 7*,8,**9**
MINNESOTA	June 15*,16*,17 Aug. 28*,29*,**30**	May 29*,30*,**31** Aug. 18*,19*,20	May 19*,20*,21* Sept. 11*,12,**13**	April 28*,29* July 23*,24*,25,**26**	May 11*,12* July 9*,10*,11*,**12**	May 8*,9*,**10** July 6*,7*,8	June 1*,2*,3* Aug. 21*,22,**23**
CHICAGO	May 19*,20 July 30*,31* Aug. 1*,**2**	April 17*,18,**19** July 27*,28*,29*	April 28*,29* July 2*,3*,(4),**5**	April 14*,15* Aug. 13*,14*,15,**16**	May 1*,2*,**3** July 6*,7*,8*	May 11*,12* July 9*,10*,11,**12**	May 22*,23,**24** Aug. 24*,25*,26*

MILWAUKEE		June 9*,10*,11 Sept. 18*,19,**20**	May 29*,30,**31** Aug. 17*,18*,19*,20*	June 18*,19*,20,**21** Sept. 28*,29*,30*	April 13*,14*,15* Aug. 13*,14*,15*,**16**	June 12*,13*,**14** Sept. 14*,15*,16*	June 22*,23*,24* Oct. 2*,3,**4**
DETROIT	June 29*,30* July 1 Sept. 10*,11*,12*,**13**		June 1*,2*,3* Aug. 21*,22,**23**	June 15*,16*,17 Sept. 24*,25*,26,**27**	June 19*,20*,**21** Sept. (7*),8*,9*	April 20*,21*,22* July 31* Aug. 1,**2**	June 4*,5*,6,**7** Sept. 21*,22*,23*
CLEVELAND	May 22*, 23*,**24** Aug. 25*,26*,27	May 15*,16*,**17** Aug. 31* Sept. 1*,2*,3*		April 6,8,9 July 31* Aug. 1,**2**	April 16*,17*,18*,**19** Aug. 10*,11*,12*	April 13,14*,15* Aug. 14*,15*,**16**	May (25*),26*,27*,28* Sept. 4*,5,**6**
TORONTO	June 26*,27*,**28** Sept. (7),8*,9*	June 22*,23*,24* Oct. 2*,3,**4**	April 20*,21*,22* Aug. 6*,7*,8,**9**		June 11*,12*,13*,**14** Sept. 21*,22*,23*	June 8*,9*,10* Sept. 17*,18*,19,**20**	April 10,11,**12** Aug. 10*,11*,12*
BALTIMORE	April 24*,25,**26** Aug. 4*,5*,6	June 26*,27*,**28** Sept. 28*,29*,30* Oct. 1*	April 10,11,**12** July 28*,29*,30*	June 5*,6,**7** Sept. 14*,15*,16*		June 15*,16*,17*,18* Oct. 2*,3*,**4**	June 29*,30* July 1* Sept. 10*,11*,12,**13**
NEW YORK	June 4*,5*,6*,**7** Sept. 21*,22*,23*	April 6,8,9 Aug. 6*,7*,8,**9**	April 23*,24*,25,**26** Aug. 3*,4*,5*	June 29*,30* July 1 Sept. 11*,12,**13**	June 22*,23*,24* Sept. 25*,26TBA,**27**		June 19*,20,**21** Sept. (7*),8*,9*
BOSTON	April 6,8*,9 Sept. 24*,25*,26,**27**	June 12*,13,**14** Sept. 14*,15*,16*	June 16*,17*,18* Aug. 28*,29,**30**	April 16*,17,18,**19** July 27*,28*,29*	June 8*,9*,10* Sept. 18*,19*,**20**	June 26*,27*,**28** Sept. 28*,29*,30* Oct. 1*	

ALL-STAR GAME AT THE OAKLAND COLISEUM, IN OAKLAND, JULY 14